D1498093

The Voting Rights Act

Landmark Events in
U.S. History Series

The Declaration of Independence: Origins and Impact
Scott Douglas Gerber, Editor

The Louisiana Purchase: Emergence of an American Nation
Peter J. Kastor, Editor

Marbury Versus Madison: Documents and Commentary
Mark A. Graber and Michael Perhac, Editors

The Voting Rights Act: Securing the Ballot
Richard M. Valelly, Editor

Watergate and the Resignation of Richard Nixon: Impact of a Constitutional Crisis
Harry P. Jeffrey and Thomas Maxwell-Long, Editors

The Voting Rights Act
Securing the Ballot

Richard M. Valelly, Editor

CQ PRESS

A Division of Congressional Quarterly Inc.
Washington, D.C.

CQ Press
1255 22nd Street, NW, Suite 400
Washington, DC 20037

Phone: 202-729-1900; toll-free, 1-866-427-7737 (1-866-4CQ-PRESS)

Web: www.cqpress.com

Cover design: Naylor Design Inc.

Cover photo: UPI/Corbis. Text on image: From President Lyndon B. Johnson's remarks at the signing of the Voting Rights Act, August 6, 1965.

∞ The paper used in this publication exceeds the requirements of the American National Standard for Information Sciences—Permanence of Paper for Printed Library Materials, ANSI Z39.48-1992.

Printed and bound in the United States of America

09   08   07   06   05   1   2   3   4   5

Library of Congress Cataloging-in-Publication Data

The Voting Rights Act : securing the ballot / Richard M. Valelly, editor.
    p. cm.
  Includes bibliographical references and index.
  ISBN 1-56802-989-6 (alk. paper)
  1. United States. Voting Rights Act of 1965.   2. African Americans—Suffrage—History.   3. Minorities—Suffrage—United States—History.
  I. Valelly, Richard M.

JK1924.V68   2006
324.6'208996073—dc22

2005033371

Contents

List of Documents

IV. Expanding National Protection and Oversight of Minority Rights

Preface

The struggle for African American voting rights has been a unique element of the historical battle in the United States for political democracy. Indeed, the United States is the only democracy that has enfranchised a very large part of its adult population and then disenfranchised it through democratic means, such as constitutional conventions, statutes passed by elected legislatures, and majority votes on ballot questions, thereby forcing the excluded group to somehow find its way back into the political process. The passage in 1965 of the Voting Rights Act thus represented a fundamental turning point in American democracy, one recognized and thoroughly examined by this volume, the fifth in CQ Press's Landmark Events in U.S. History reference series.

The 1965 Voting Rights Act sought to reestablish voting rights that had been established in the late 1860s and then dismantled by the 1890s. That restoration was an urgent task. Millions of American citizens faced injustice. Racial discrimination in the electoral process deprived them of their birthright. The Declaration of Independence and the Constitution nowhere state that democratic citizenship belongs to white people alone because of their skin color or that full citizenship does not belong to people of color because of theirs. Yet the actual operation of American politics overtly reflected and perpetuated such racist tenets.

For a nation priding itself on the rule of law, it was an embarrassment to many of its citizens that the Fifteenth Amendment, a provision that forbids racial discrimination in the electoral process, was regularly violated in large parts of the country—and had been for several decades. It was also appalling that publicly elected and appointed officials were parties to such violations of the Constitution. Then there was the extralegal violence directed against citizens seeking to exercise their right to vote. In some states and localities, public officials tolerated the white-on-black mayhem. In Alabama and Mississippi, some (though by no means all) officials and law enforcement officers actually encouraged intimidation or engaged in it themselves. Official lawlessness rose to a level that offended political democracy.

To paraphrase Abraham Lincoln, the country suffered from the crisis of a house divided. The Republic was half-democratic, half-white supremacist and authoritarian. Such a crisis could not continue. To resolve this intolerable contradiction, the Eighty-ninth Congress passed and President Lyndon B. Johnson signed the Voting Rights Act. Nothing less was at stake than every American's fundamental interest in belonging to a democracy whose institutions and practices accorded with its own widely venerated principles. The Voting Rights Act was, in effect, politically redemptive legislation.

In that respect, the Voting Rights Act partly resembles two other new beginnings in American political development: the 1865 passage and ratification of the Thirteenth Amendment to the Constitution abolishing slavery, and the Supreme Court's unanimous 1954 decision in *Brown v. Board of Education* striking down de jure segregation of public schools. These other new beginnings were not, of course, self-executing, nor was the Voting Rights Act.

Soon after ratification of the Thirteenth Amendment, southern states legislated the reenslavement of the freedmen and freed-women. Had Congress not enacted Reconstruction over President Andrew Johnson's opposition, the southern legislatures would have succeeded with their plan. Similarly, school desegregation really did not begin until the mid-1960s, when Congress conditioned federal aid to public schools on compliance with *Brown*. It stumbled along in many instances and has faltered badly in the past decade.

Making the Voting Rights Act work has been difficult and has required several extensions. Both Congress and the Supreme Court have strengthened the act in important ways. But this time around, happily, the work has paid off in contrast with how the first great national effort to establish African American voting rights during the nineteenth century ended. The 1965 Voting Rights Act has played a central role in helping Americans move toward the realization of full minority enfranchisement.

As this volume goes to press, Congress has begun considering the 2007 reauthorization of the Voting Rights Act (see Appendix, Reauthorization of the 1965 Voting Rights Act: What Expires and What Does Not, p. 353). Because the president and members of Congress envisioned in 1965 an end someday to the incentives for minority disenfranchisement, the act's enforcement provisions were temporary. These include the attorney general's authority to send federal examiners and election observers to areas of the country forced to comply with the act (known as the "covered jurisdictions"). If massive resistance to minority voting somehow reemerged, the United States could step in on an emergency basis and ensure registration of and balloting by minority voters. Another vital temporary enforcement measure is the requirement that new election laws enacted by the covered jurisdictions not go into effect until the Department of Justice or the U.S. District Court for the District of Columbia review them in a timely manner. In this way, subtle strategies for resisting minority enfranchisement could not slip quietly into law, rolling back the clock.

These powerful elements of the statute were made subject to removal if and when it becomes clear to Congress that they are no longer needed. Congress therefore reconsidered the operation and impact of the temporary enforcement measures in 1970, 1975, and 1982—and it is doing so again today.

The success of the Voting Rights Act and the passage of time inevitably raise a controversial and delicate issue: How does the country know when the act is no longer necessary to achieve its goals? The great sociologist W. E. B. DuBois put his finger on why this is a hard question. Writing in 1906, he said, "We have a way in America of wanting to be 'rid' of problems. It is not so much a desire to reach the best and largest solution as it is to clean the board and start a new game. For instance, most Americans are simply tired and impatient over our . . . social problem, the Negro. They do not want to solve it, they do not want to understand it, they want simply to be done with it and hear the last of it. Of all possible attitudes, this is the most dangerous."[1]

The issues are all the more complicated because the Voting Rights Act has broadened well beyond its original concern with the disenfranchisement of African American voters in the South. The act protects Latino voters in Arizona, California, Texas, and New York, particularly New York City. The act also protects Native American voters in Alaska and South Dakota, among other places, and it mandates language assistance on election day in several dozen local jurisdictions around the country. Finally, because of the Voting Rights Act, national elections bring hundreds of federal observers to the polls in many parts of the country. In significant measure, the Voting Rights Act no longer regulates elections in a region of the country; rather, it regulates much of the electoral process across the United States.

Any assessment of whether the Voting Rights Act has, or someday will, become unnecessary requires broad and deep knowledge of American law and history. This volume seeks to help readers grasp the intricacies of the issues that surround the contemporary discussion of the Voting Rights Act.

The particular strengths of this volume in meeting that challenge are the historical perspective that informs the essays and selection of documents, the volume's descriptive and analytical precision, and its scholarship, which is at once scrupulous and meticulous. The volume's ten essays, all by first-rate scholars, and the primary documents illuminating the topics covered in the essays illustrate how the struggle for minority enfranchisement has been a salient, often defining element of American politics for a very long time.

Broadly speaking, the volume's essays and documents are organized, first, to allow recognition and a grasp of the dynamics of the two periods during which the struggle for minority enfranchisement captured the attention of all Americans. Chapters 1, 4, and 5 cover these highly dramatic eras. The book's elements also frame the disenfranchisement of African Americans as a pivotal process. It had striking implications for constitutional law and enormous ramifications for national policy over several decades (see chapters 2 and 3). Finally, the volume examines the operation of the Voting Rights Act and its political and legal impact from several different points of view (chapters 6–10).

Chapter 1 by historian Xi Wang tells the story of how the struggle for black enfranchisement became a dominant aspect of American politics in the mid-1860s. It reveals that several decades before the Civil War—that is, no sooner than the country's founding period was over— black suffrage became an issue in many northern states, prefiguring the issue's dominance over several decades of the nineteenth century.

In chapter 2, Robert C. Lieberman, an authority on the connections between race relations and social policy, traces the consequences for the development of social rights during and after the New Deal of the black disenfranchisement that occurred several decades earlier. Lieberman shows that disenfranchisement perversely paved the way for the federal government to use federal social policy to disproportionately help whites—white affirmative action, as it were—putting them even further ahead in reaping the rewards of the American dream.

Michael J. Klarman, a legal historian, describes in chapter 3 how the Supreme Court handled the crisis in constitutional law represented by black disenfranchisement. Among the strengths of his chapter is his refusal to simply condemn the Court but to focus instead on how it actually wrestled with disenfranchisement. The result is an accessible and lucid treatment of the Court's role and decisions.

Chapter 4 by political scientist Paula D. McClain and her students Michael C. Brady, Niambi M. Carter, Efrén O. Pérez, and Victoria M. DeFrancesco Soto takes readers deep into the rarely examined social networks, associations, churches, and businesses of black southerners, who leveraged these institutions to mount a constant struggle against the denial of their full citizenship. The result was a widening gyre of citizen activity that brought America to the brink of sweeping democratic change. One lesson of this chapter is that a group that must re-create democratic institutions effectively acts on behalf of the whole when and as it acts in its own behalf. That group is in a vital sense the custodian and agent of a democratic nation's core values.

Chapter 5, by a British historian of American history, Stephen Tuck, captures the con-

tingencies and drama of the ten-month period in which the Voting Rights Act was written, debated, and enacted. It provides insight into the planning and behavior of the Johnson administration that cannot be found elsewhere. Also, Tuck's retelling of the Selma campaign is thorough, vivid, and lucid.

In chapter 6, political scientist Colin D. Moore carefully narrates and compares the several extensions of the Voting Rights Act. His discussion sheds new light on the roles of Congress and the president in these extensions, and he very ably traces the contours of the evolution of the Voting Rights Act as a statute. Of particular importance is the emphasis that Moore places on the amendment of Section 2 of the act during its 1982 extension. Amended Section 2 explicitly safeguards the rights of minorities to vote on candidates of their choosing. Just two years earlier, in 1980, a Supreme Court opinion had caused widespread concern about the prospect of continued progress in minority officeholding. The opinion for the Court interpreted the Fifteenth Amendment, which as of 1870, the year of its ratification, forbade racial discrimination in the electoral process. The amendment says nothing explicitly about the right to hold office. Thus in 1980 the Court held, for the first time, that the Fifteenth Amendment did not confer on minorities a right to public elective office. Yet there was considerable evidence before Congress of resistance to minority officeholding in the jurisdictions covered by the Voting Rights Act. Thus the amended Section 2 states that minority voters must be given ample fair opportunities to elect candidates of their choice. The result is that the interaction of Section 2, as amended, with the act's enforcement provisions has gradually ground down resistance to minority officeholding.

Chapter 7, by David A. Bositis, an expert on parties, voting, elections, and minority office-holding, outlines the rise and limitations of black political influence in southern politics by tracing the simultaneous impact of the Voting Rights Act on white conservatism. His lively essay reveals that, ironically, the act has been a trigger for the rise in political strength of southern white conservatives. Bositis rightly forces readers to grasp that the massive changes in electoral regulation, and their consequences for African American voting and of-ficeholding, have had equally massive second-order effects on parties and ideology. These effects have created, again ironically, new structural limits to the political influence of African Americans. As he says, "The changes experienced by African Americans have a certain bittersweet quality."

Pei-te Lien, a political scientist who has pioneered the scientific analysis of Asian American political behavior at a time when the Asian American population has grown very rapidly, charts in chapter 8 the implications of the Voting Rights Act for nonblack minority voters. Bositis covers the impact of the "core" Voting Rights Act in chapter 7, whereas Lien describes the impact and significance of the "extended" Voting Rights Act for Latinos, Asian Americans, and Native Americans.

Lien's meticulously substantiated chapter underscores something exceptionally important about the Voting Rights Act: it is no longer just a black and white issue. The act has now effectively created a broad, cross-ethnic coalition of stakeholders in its continuation, and its operations are essential for the enfranchisement of Native Americans—the "first Americans." The act is also affecting the political incorporation of immigrant populations who are building on the impact of Latinos and Asian Americans, some of the earliest nonblack and nonwhite settlers in the United States. Lien's chapter thus broadens the conversation about the Voting Rights Act in an unusual—and for many Americans completely new—way.

Because the Voting Rights Act sets up a regulatory system, its operation has received much scrutiny from those who worry about regulatory excess. Neoconservative critics have often looked for—and found—unintended or perverse consequences of government action. As a prime example of strong governmental intervention, the Voting Rights Act was bound to be subjected to close scrutiny by political scientists with such concerns.

In chapter 9, Mark Rush, a scholar of voting rights law and politics, surveys the political science that finds fault with the remedies imposed by the act and how such academic discontent, in a rare instance of political science having an effect outside colleges and universities, has affected the Supreme Court over the past decade and a half. Among the strengths of Rush's contribution is the graceful way in which he calmly guides readers through two decades of scholarly research and debate that have been fierce and often impenetrable to lay readers.

The last chapter, by one of America's leading voting rights lawyers, Laughlin McDonald, recapitulates the overall legal and constitutional history of the struggle for minority voting rights and connects it to developments in other areas of election law since Congress passed the Voting Rights Act. The act, he shows, has prompted a trend toward increased federal electoral regulation. Also, McDonald examines the connections between partisan realignment in the South and the impact of the act, a vital theme covered by Bositis, but he adds fresh and very vivid detail about the cultural symbols involved in that process.

The scholarly contributions are followed by a documents section that is a mix of the formal and the relatively intimate—that is, it ranges from legal text and statutes to recorded voice transcripts, urgent reportage, and letters and memos. The last document is the complaint issued by a coalition of civil rights groups seeking to stop the voter ID provision enacted by Georgia in 2005—a kind of Jim Crow poll tax (as Garry Trudeau dubbed it in his "Doonesbury" strip of November 6, 2005). When read by themselves or in conjunction with the scholarly essays, the documents make the struggle for minority enfranchisement come alive in such venues as Congress, the inaugural podium of a president just sworn into office, the Supreme Court chambers, and on the ground in Mississippi. The superb selection of photographs that complement the scholarly essays also convey a visceral sense of all the many places where the struggle—and the political and legal responses to it—occurred.

Whatever readers of this volume conclude about the Voting Rights Act, they are certain to see the country's once and future national discussion of it as part of a very long historical process. The American novelist William Faulkner once said, "The past is never dead. It's not even past." The act and the debates about it are not just historical artifacts in the vast hall of American political evolution. They are also the mutual learning and engagement

that have occurred as Americans with very different experiences of voting and officeholding have collaborated in building democracy. The costs have sometimes been frightful. As poet and statesman James Weldon Johnson put it in these verses from "Lift Every Voice and Sing," a poem often called the African American national anthem,

> We have come over a way
> That with tears hath been watered.
> We have come treading our paths
> Through the blood of the slaughtered.

But, the anthem adds, "Now we stand at last / Where the white gleam / Of our bright star is cast." These lines rightly suggest that whatever the precise outcome of its evolution, the Voting Rights Act is and always will be a symbol and record of Americans' deepest aspirations as a political people.

Acknowledgments

In this undertaking, Freddie LaFemina, Ayana Maurice, and Jacob Savage, undergraduates at Princeton University, provided invaluable and highly competent research assistance. I also thank the Center for the Study of Democratic Politics at Princeton University, its staff, Diane Price and Helene Wood, and its director, Larry Bartels, the Donald E. Stokes Professor of Public and International Affairs, for providing a truly congenial environment for my work on this volume while I was a visiting research fellow for the academic year 2004–2005.

Peyton McCrary and Michael J. Klarman helped me find documents, and I thank them for their assistance. Peyton has taught me much of what I know about the Voting Rights Act, and in an important sense this book represents one of the fruits of his patient instruction over the past decade.

The contributors and the people of CQ Press were all a great pleasure to work with, in particular, Doug Goldenberg-Hart, January Layman-Wood, Sabra Ledent, Sally Ryman, and Joan Gossett. Nanette Tobin, my wife, was exceptionally understanding of the pressures that came with trying to get this book out; she is as certain as I am of the volume's importance.

Richard M. Valelly
Swarthmore, Pennsylvania

Notes

1. W. E. B. DuBois, "The Color Line Belts the World," in *W. E. B. DuBois—A Reader,* ed. David Levering Lewis (New York: Holt, 1995), 42–43.

Contributors

About the Editor

Richard M. Valelly is professor of political science at Swarthmore College. He is the author of *The Two Reconstructions: The Struggle for Black Enfranchisement* (2004) and *Radicalism in the States: The American Political Economy and the Minnesota Farmer-Labor Party* (1989). *The Two Reconstructions* received the 2005 J. David Greenstone Prize for the best book in the field of Politics and History, which is awarded by the Politics and History Section of the American Political Science Association (APSA). The text also won the 2005 Ralph J. Bunche Prize of the APSA, which honors excellence in scholarship on racial, ethnic, and cultural pluralism.

About the Contributors

David A. Bositis is a senior political analyst at the Joint Center for Political and Economic Studies. A widely published voting rights and redistricting expert, he has appeared as an expert witness in both state and federal courts. Bositis is the author of the annual Joint Center series Black Elected Officials: A Statistical Analysis, as well as *Redistricting and Minority Representation* (1998) and the forthcoming *Voting Rights and Minority Representation*.

Michael C. Brady is a doctoral student in political science at Duke University. His primary teaching and research interests are congressional politics and bargaining, campaigns and elections, methodology, and racial and ethnic politics.

Niambi M. Carter is a doctoral student in political science at Duke University and is currently in residence as a predoctoral fellow at the Center for the Study of African-American Politics at the University of Rochester. Her dissertation, "The Black/White Paradigm Revisited," examines how southern blacks are responding to the changing socio-racial landscape precipitated by Latino immigration.

Michael J. Klarman is James Monroe Distinguished Professor of Law and professor of history at the University of Virginia. His book *From Jim Crow to Civil Rights: The Supreme Court and the Struggle for Racial Equality* (2004) won the 2005 Bancroft Prize from Columbia University.

Robert C. Lieberman is associate professor of political science and public affairs at Columbia University. His most recent book is, *Shaping Race Policy: The United States in Comparative Perspective* (2005). Lieberman is also the author of the prize-winning *Shifting the Color Line: Race and the American Welfare State* (1998).

Paula D. McClain is professor of political science and codirector of the Center for the Study of Race, Ethnicity and Gender in the Social Sciences at Duke University. In addition, she is the author, with Joseph Stewart Jr., of *Can We All Get Along? Racial and Ethnic Minorities in American Politics* (4th ed., 2005). She is currently working on the effects on the black-white dynamic of Latino immigration into the southern United States.

Laughlin McDonald has been director of the Voting Rights Project of the American Civil Liberties Union in Atlanta since 1972. He has represented minorities in numerous discrimination cases, specializing in the area of voting rights. He has testified frequently before Congress and written for scholarly and popular publications on civil liberties issues. His most recent book is *A Voting Rights Odyssey: Black Enfranchisement in Georgia* (2003).

Colin D. Moore is a doctoral student in government at Harvard University. He is currently researching a dissertation examining the ties between Christian evangelical groups and the expansion of American administrative capacity.

Pei-te Lien is associate professor of political science and ethnic studies at the University of Utah. She is the author of *The Politics of Asian Americans: Diversity and Community* (2004), with Margaret M. Conway and Janelle Wong, and the award-winning *The Making of Asian America through Political Participation* (2001).

Efrén O. Pérez is a doctoral student in political science at Duke University and a National Science Foundation graduate fellow. His current research examines the dynamics of anti-immigrant opinion in the United States.

Mark Rush is Robert G. Brown Professor of Politics and Law, head of the department of politics, and director of the Williams School program in international commerce at Washington and Lee University. He has published numerous articles, books, and papers on election reform, redistricting, and voters' rights. He is currently working on *The Judicial Struggle with Democracy,* an analysis of American and Canadian voting rights jurisprudence.

Victoria M. DeFrancesco Soto is a doctoral student in political science at Duke University. Her dissertation is entitled "Identity Fluidity in the Voting Booth: The Influence of Latino Group Identity on the Evaluation of Latino Candidates." Her research focuses on interminority relations and immigration.

Stephen Tuck is university lecturer in American history at Oxford University, England. He is the author of *Beyond Atlanta: The Struggle for Racial Equality in Georgia, 1940–1980* (2001) and is currently working on a broader study of the struggle for civil rights from emancipation to the present.

Xi Wang is professor of history at Indiana University of Pennsylvania and holds a Changjiang chair professorship at Beijing University, China. He is the author of *Principles and Compromises: The Spirit and Practice of the American Constitution* (expanded ed., 2005) (in Chinese) and *The Trial of Democracy: Black Suffrage and Northern Republicans, 1860–1910* (1997). He is the translator of the Chinese edition of Eric Foner's *The Story of American Freedom* (2002).

The Voting Rights Act

1

Building African American Voting Rights in the Nineteenth Century

Xi Wang

On March 15, 1965, President Lyndon B. Johnson addressed a joint session of Congress on the proposed Voting Rights Act, which promised firm national action to eliminate every voting barrier against African Americans and to guarantee them what the president called "the most basic right of all." A former schoolteacher of history, Johnson knew well how to use history to strengthen his argument. In the speech, he linked the nation's current struggle for black voting rights to the Civil War. African Americans had been promised freedom over a century earlier, and yet they were still "not fully free." The United States as a nation "founded with a purpose," Johnson said, "cannot, must not refuse to protect the right of every American to vote in every election that he may desire to participate in." Urging lawmakers to pass the proposed law, Johnson proclaimed, "We have already waited a hundred years and more, and the time for waiting is gone" (Johnson 1966, 1:281–287).

Powerful and memorable, Johnson's speech accurately captured the spirit and momentum of the civil rights movement. But the president left out some important and relevant historical references, such as the story of Reconstruction (1865–1877), which is a story about how

African American voting rights were established and enforced as a central piece of the nation's new constitutional and political order after the Civil War. The president also could have reminded lawmakers that the proposed Voting Rights Act was actually a renewed national commitment to completing the nation's revolution of building an interracial democracy that had begun during the Civil War but had been left unfinished.

This chapter is about the missing story of Reconstruction. It reviews the history of how African Americans and their allies in the Republican Party struggled to establish the constitutional principle and practice of black suffrage after the Civil War; how the national government enforced the Fifteenth Amendment, which epitomized political equality between blacks and whites; and how and why federal enforcement eventually failed. The story begins with a brief review of African American voting rights before the Civil War.

Black Suffrage before the Civil War

Suffrage, or the right to vote on public issues, is now regarded as an essential right accorded to every adult citizen of the United States. But this was not always the case. For much of the nation's history, suffrage was a privilege limited to only select groups of citizens. Although the Declaration of Independence pronounced popular sovereignty to be the nation's founding principle and that principle was recognized by the Constitution, which attributed its power to "We the People," the right to vote was never granted or exercised as a universal entitlement from the beginning of the nation. Under the unamended Constitution, it was the state governments, not the federal government, that prescribed the qualifications for voters in each state. The states' power to control suffrage was a feature of the antebellum constitutional order and remained unchallenged until Reconstruction.

None of the original thirteen states granted universal suffrage in the constitutions drafted during the Revolutionary era. Rather, they adopted a wide range of qualifications to exclude undesirable inhabitants from political participation. All states required property holding for voting, although the requirement varied from possessing fifty acres of land in Virginia to being able to pay taxes in Pennsylvania. Six states expressly limited suffrage to men, but women were generally barred from voting in all states, except in New Jersey where widows who met the state's property requirement could vote.

Race was another major disqualifier. Three slaveholding states in the South—Georgia, South Carolina, and Virginia—specifically limited suffrage to "whites," and three other states—Maryland, North Carolina, and Pennsylvania—allowed only "freemen" to vote (Keyssar 2000, Table A1). The elusive wording in the latter case might have allowed free blacks who met other qualifications to vote,

even in slaveholding North Carolina. But the property-holding requirement and other requisites such as literacy, freeman status, and citizenship, together with the deep-seated racial prejudice exhibited by the citizenry, effectively prevented the majority of the free black population from voting.

In the first half of the nineteenth century, states revised their voting requirements, in part to respond to the rising popular demands for greater democracy, which were in turn generated by the rapid economic development, westward territorial expansion, and emergence of mass party politics in the era of "Jacksonian democracy." Property and religious qualifications gradually disappeared. Of the thirty-one states in the Union before the Civil War, South Carolina was the only state that continued to require white male voters to possess freehold property (unmovable property such as land), although some states retained the taxpaying requirement. Most of the eighteen states admitted into the Union between 1791 and 1850 had no property-holding requirements whatsoever for voting.

During the same period, race was added as a voting qualification. Starting with Delaware in 1792 and Maryland in 1801, six of the original states added the word *white* to their constitutions or passed statutory laws to restrict suffrage to whites. New Jersey, by oversight, had originally allowed free blacks and women to vote, but it barred both in 1807. Connecticut, in 1818, allowed only those blacks to vote who had been freemen prior to 1804. In 1821 New York removed property requirements for whites, but required a black voter to own a freehold valued at $250 or more. This discriminatory requirement effectively denied voting rights to the majority of black citizens, especially those living in New York City. North Carolina and Pennsylvania disenfranchised their black voters in 1835 and 1838, respectively. That said, by 1804 all of the original northern states (except for Delaware) had abolished slavery, although slaves continued to reside in those states.

Elsewhere, in contrast to their seemingly "liberal" practice of imposing no property qualification for voting, most of the new states imposed racial qualifications and limited suffrage to whites. Even in states such as California, Illinois, Iowa, Michigan, Minnesota, Nevada, Ohio, and Oregon that declared themselves free of slavery, blacks were barred from voting (some of these states also barred the immigration of free blacks). On the eve of the Civil War, free blacks could vote only in five New England states—Maine, Massachusetts, New Hampshire, Rhode Island, and Vermont—where less than 7 percent of the small northern black population lived. Meanwhile, all states barred women from voting. Clearly, then, the expansion of white male suffrage in the first half of the nineteenth century—a much admired development of democracy noted by the French observer Alexis de Tocqueville—was in fact accompanied by the extensive exclusion of free blacks and women from the electorate.

Free blacks and their white allies did challenge state-imposed political discriminations, but, except in Rhode Island where blacks had secured equal voting rights as a result of Dorr's Rebellion in 1841–1842, most such efforts did not succeed. In the second half of the 1850s, the newly organized Republican Party tried in several northern and midwestern states to push for black suffrage as part of its antislavery program, but voters rejected such a linkage. In New York, for example, voters gave the Republican presidential candidate, Abraham Lincoln, a resounding victory in 1860, but they defeated the party's proposal of removing the discriminatory property requirement for black voters. The Republican Party's platform in 1860 vowed to stop the expansion of slavery, but it was silent on the issue of black rights, fearing that any pro-black rights language would alienate its supporters.

The Civil War and the Origins of Black Suffrage

Thus on the eve of the Civil War few Republicans or Northerners anticipated the abolition of slavery, much less the enfranchisement of former slaves. Many, including Lincoln, perceived the war as a fight to preserve the original constitutional order that would confine, not eliminate, slavery.

But African Americans, free or in bondage, had a different expectation. From the outbreak of the war at Fort Sumter, South Carolina, on April 12, 1861, slaves saw the war as a millennial event that would offer them the opportunity for emancipation, and they wasted no time in taking action to free themselves from slavery. The first group of fugitive slaves (later known as "contrabands") entered the Union army line in Virginia only a few weeks after the war started. Slaves' voluntary acts of self-emancipation, entirely unexpected by Lincoln and the Republican Party, compelled both to reconsider the original objectives of the war and to face the issue of emancipation.

After the Union army took in many contrabands, Congress passed two confiscation acts, one in August 1861 and one in July 1862, to declare freedom for those slaves who had been used by the Confederacy for military purposes and to employ them as a labor force for the Union army. These laws marked the first legislative steps toward the abolition of slavery. Lincoln acted even more cautiously. To secure the loyalty of the slaveholding border states, he had earlier nullified emancipation orders issued by Union generals. But on September 22, 1862, a week after the Union army had scored a costly victory at Antietam, he issued a preliminary Emancipation Proclamation, by which he would free all the slaves who lived in the Confederate-controlled areas if the South refused to lay down arms in one hundred days. On January 1, 1863, the Emancipation Proclamation took effect.

At the time of its issuance, the Emancipation Proclamation may have, in reality, freed no slaves, but its impact was profound in terms of changing the objective of the Civil War and laying the groundwork for Reconstruction. By declaring freedom for slaves, Lincoln asserted national authority over slavery, thereby dealing with an issue sidestepped by the framers of the Constitution in 1787. By justifying emancipation as "an act of justice," Lincoln gave the war a higher moral objective, thereby redefining the meaning of American freedom and constitutionalism. But the policy most vitally relevant to the postwar establishment of black enfranchisement was Lincoln's invitation to former slaves to join the Union army. By this invitation, Lincoln conferred on former slaves the responsibilities of citizen-soldiers in the time of national crisis. In other words, African Americans were asked to defend and serve the nation *before* the nation constitutionally rec-

ognized them as citizens and granted them any rights citizens were entitled to enjoy.

African Americans did not hesitate to assume their first civic obligation, and they responded to Lincoln's call by joining the Union army. Between late 1862 and the end of the war, nearly 200,000 African American men served in the Union army and navy, and another 300,000 African Americans served as laborers. Black participation contributed much needed manpower to the Union army, and, as noted by the famed Union general William Tecumseh Sherman, laid the foundation for their demand for suffrage. "When the fight is over," Sherman remarked, "the hand that drops the musket cannot be denied the ballot" (quoted in Keyssar 2000, 88). Some Republican leaders, such as Lincoln's secretary of the Treasury Salmon P. Chase, quickly saw other implications of black participation for the postwar settlements. Because the war had consolidated the hostility of southern whites toward the Union, Chase predicted that former slaves would probably be "the only loyal population worth counting" for establishing a new political order in the South after the war (quoted in Wang 1997, 10).

African Americans were, of course, among those who foresaw the possibility of redefining their civil and political status after the war. Shortly after Lincoln issued the Emancipation Proclamation, Frederick Douglass, the leading black abolitionist, urged blacks to seize the opportunity to embrace "the great national family of America" by joining the Union army. In return, he argued, the Union should reward black soldiers with "all the rights, privileges and immunities enjoyed by any other members of the body politic." When Lincoln announced on November 19, 1863, in his Gettysburg Address that the United States would have "a new birth of freedom" after the war, Douglass quickly responded that the new American freedom should make "every slave free, and every freeman a voter." A black convention held in Kansas in December 1863 also declared that blacks' right to vote was "natural and inherent" and that "the restoration of the Union" and "the elevation of the black man" must go hand in hand (all quotes from Wang 1997, 11–12). At the first national black convention, held in Syracuse, New York, in October 1864, equal suffrage for blacks and whites was the first and most important right demanded by the convention's speakers.

But Lincoln's wartime reconstruction policy did not respond to blacks' demands for suffrage. The policy, issued in December 1863 and known as the "Ten Percent Plan," offered pardons and restoration of property, "except as to slaves," for those who had engaged in rebellion but would take an oath of allegiance to the Union. When the oath-taking voters in a state reached 10 percent of its registered voting population as of 1860, the voters could reestablish a new state government that Lincoln promised to recognize. This policy excluded former slaves and free blacks in the South from the process of reconstructing new state governments. Nor did Lincoln set black enfranchisement as a precondition for the states' readmission to the Union.

African Americans protested against the whites-only reconstruction plan when it was implemented in Union army–occupied areas such as Louisiana. African Americans in New Orleans organized themselves to demand participation in the state's constitutional convention. As part of their efforts, they sent two representatives—New Orleans businessmen Jean-Baptiste Roudanez and E. Arnold Bertonneau—to Washington, D.C., in early 1864 to lobby Congress and President Lincoln for making black suffrage a national requirement for reestablishing the "republican form of government" in the former Confederate states. Lincoln did not change his policy immediately, but he privately suggested to Louisiana's military governor on the day after he received the two black representatives in the White House that the state might consider giving voting rights to those blacks who had "fought gallantly" for the Union and who were "intelligent," because these people could help "to keep the jewel of liberty within the family of freedom" (quoted in Wang 1997, 19).

Congress, dominated by a Republican majority, refused to move beyond the traditional constitutional framework to overtake the states' control of suffrage at this time. The reform-minded Radical Republicans, who were not numerous, had made several attempts to tie black enfranchisement to emancipation, but they could not galvanize enough support from the party. The most important congressional reconstruction plan during the wartime, the so-called Wade-Davis bill, offered terms to the South identical to those in Lincoln's plan except that it increased the number of oath-taking voters from 10 to 50 percent. The bill, eventually pocket-vetoed by Lincoln, made no mention of black voting rights at all. When Congress debated the proposed Thirteenth Amendment in late 1864, Radical Republicans tried once again to insert in it rights for the freedmen, including voting rights and emancipation, but the majority of their colleagues refused to cooperate. The amendment, ratified in December 1865, abolished slavery in the United States, but it offered no rights to those it freed.

The Making of Black Suffrage Laws during Reconstruction

Both the constitutional hindrances and the political barriers contributed to the inaction of President Lincoln and the Republican Congress on the issue of black suffrage during the wartime phase of Reconstruction. The Constitution requires every state to have a "republican form of government," but, as noted earlier, it also left the power to control suffrage to individual states. To extend voting rights to freedmen, the federal government would have to break new constitutional ground, a step that neither Lincoln nor Congress was willing to take despite their abolition of slavery. This early conservatism on black suffrage was related in part to the concern that, once freedmen in the South were enfranchised, the federal government would be pressed to enfranchise women as well, a goal of the women's suffrage movement, which had existed since 1848. The federal government might also be dragged into interfering with the disenfranchisement of free blacks in most northern states—a situation described earlier. For many Republican politicians, such interference would amount to political suicide. Finally, the Constitution offered no ready guidance as to who—Congress or the president—should lead the reconstruction of the South, something the framers had, after all, never expected. The interinstitutional rivalry in American national politics made development of a clear, uniform policy difficult.

The political difficulties stemmed largely from the Republican Party's divided vision of black suffrage and its relationship to Reconstruction. Conservative Republicans saw Reconstruction as no more than the restoration of the traditional constitutional framework minus slavery. They did not want to interfere with the states' reserved power to control suffrage and hoped that a conciliatory policy would win back the loyalty of the defeated South. The moderates, who made up a majority of the party, had no plan to reduce the Confederate states to "conquered territories" and strip them of all their rights as guaranteed by the Constitution. They did, however, want to see slavery abolished and the rebels who had betrayed the Union punished. They were also willing to offer limited national protection to the newly freed slaves who might be subject to the control of their former masters. By contrast, Radical Republicans shared part of African American leaders' views and envisioned Reconstruction as an opportunity for conducting democratic and egalitarian reform. Their program included black suffrage, the redistribution of land to freedmen, and the political demise of former rebels. For them, black suffrage was especially crucial, not only to securing the outcomes of the Civil War, but also to creating a new political people out of the freedmen, whose votes would, in turn, effectively help the party to implement its ideology of free labor republicanism and to develop an industrial-capitalist market economy in the South. They wanted to make universal manhood suffrage a prerequisite for the readmission of the former Confederate states to the Union.

The Radicals, a minority within the party, would never have had the opportunity to convince the moderates to accept their stance on black suffrage had it not been for the arrogance of President Andrew Johnson and the resistance of the southern states to black suffrage. After he succeeded to the presidency in April 1865 upon Lincoln's assassination, Johnson promised the Radicals that he would consider the possibility of including black suffrage in his reconstruction plan. But when his plan was announced in May 1865, the Radicals felt betrayed. Johnson's program included generous amnesties and restitution of property, except slaves, for former rebels who would take an oath of allegiance (the bigger property owners also would receive presidential pardons), with the exception of high-ranking Confederate officials. Those who received amnesties and pardons could conduct the work of reestablishing government and could elect delegates to frame a new state constitution. Like Lincoln, then, Johnson limited suffrage to whites.

While undergoing reconstruction under Johnson's plan, the southern states refused to grant suffrage to freedmen. Instead, they adopted what became known as the "Black Codes," a series of state laws that regulated and restrained the rights and freedoms of freedmen in the name of maintaining social order. To counter the Black Codes, moderate Republicans in Congress moved in early 1866 to enact two laws: the second Freedmen's Bureau Act and the Civil Rights Act. The Freedmen's Bureau Act extended the tenure of the wartime federal agency that had been invested with a wide range of power to help freedmen adjust to their freedom and to enforce federal laws in the South. The Civil Rights Act conferred national citizenship on all freedmen and guaranteed them some essential civil and eco-

nomic rights, including the right to own property, make contracts, and sue. Although none of the bills touched on political rights, they represented moderate Republicans' efforts to supplement what had been left out by Andrew Johnson's reconstruction plan and to stop southern states from further infringing on freedmen's rights and freedoms. Moderate Republicans hoped Johnson would sign the bills.

Instead, Johnson vetoed both bills; he believed they violated the original constitutional order. Enraged and frustrated, moderate Republicans joined the Radicals in early 1866 to repass both bills over Johnson's vetoes. To secure the national protection of freedmen's civil rights on a more permanent basis, the united Republicans proposed what would become the Fourteenth Amendment *(see Document 2).* The second section of the amendment dealt indirectly with the voting rights of African Americans in the South. Instead of declaring explicitly that all freedmen should have the right to vote, the section stipulated that if a state denied its adult male citizens the right to vote, its number of representatives to the House of Representatives would be reduced in proportion. It is not clear how the reduction was to be measured or implemented, because the section was never enforced. But the arrangement was the product of careful compromises among Republicans. Ninety percent of the nation's four million blacks lived in the South, and so the section punished the South for withholding the suffrage of freedmen. However, it allowed northern states to continue to disenfranchise blacks with great impunity, because the black population in those states was too small to make any real difference in representation. By not mentioning

Map 1.1 Presidential Reconstruction

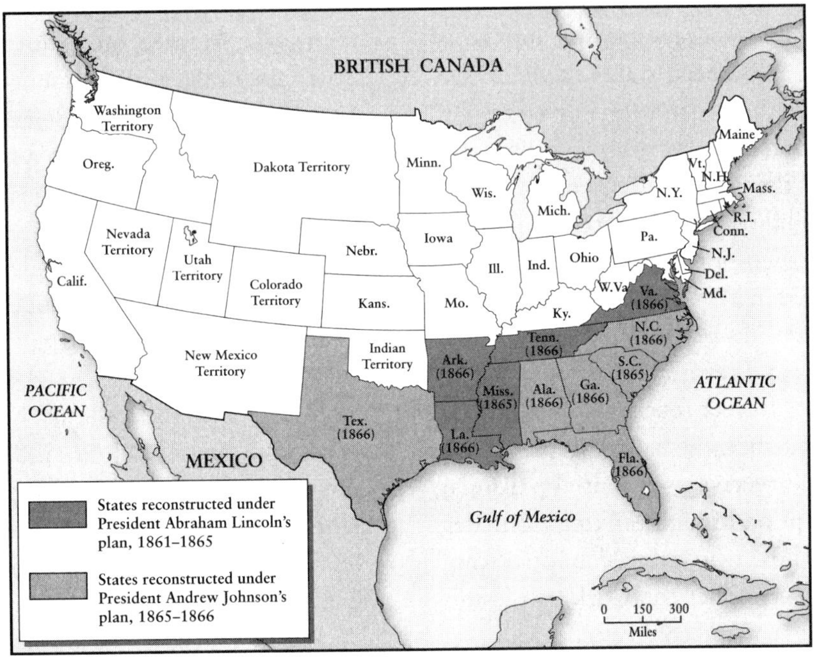

Source: Adapted from Arwin D. Smallwood (with Jeffrey M. Elliott), *The Atlas of African American History and Politics: From the Slave Trade to Modern Times* (New York: McGraw-Hill, 1998), Map 77.

black suffrage, the section avoided conferring on freedmen the right to vote and continued to allow states to exercise other restrictions such as gender.

The rationale behind Section 2 of the Fourteenth Amendment appeared similar to that of presidential reconstruction plans: let states take the initiative to grant suffrage to freedmen. There was, however, a crucial difference. The presidential reconstruction plans never penalized the South for withholding voting rights from freedmen, but the Fourteenth Amendment did—at least on paper. The greater significance of this section (and to an extent Section 3, which excluded high-ranking Confederate officials from the process of reconstruction) lay in its implied new power for the national government—the power that the national government could enlist to punish states for denying voting rights to U.S. citizens as recognized by Section 1 of the amendment. Constitutionally, this was an important stepping-stone for the federal government toward regulating suffrage in the areas under its direct jurisdiction. Seizing the momentum, Radical Republicans began to push for black enfranchisement in the District of Columbia, the nation's capital, and in other areas directly under the control of the national government.

By February 1867, Congress had succeeded in enfranchising African American men in the District of Columbia and the unorganized federal territories. It also made impartial suffrage—equal voting rights for adult male citizens regardless of color—a precondition for the admission of Nebraska and Colorado to the Union. President Johnson vetoed all the bills, but the united Radical Republicans and moderate Republicans succeeded in overriding Johnson's vetoes. Emerging from the heated debates of these measures was the new rationale that, when a state deprived its citizens of the right to vote purely for racial reasons, Congress was empowered by the Constitution to impose impartial suffrage as a condition for the reorganization of the state so that it could have a "republican form of government" as required by the Constitution. Such a rationale profoundly changed the meaning of the original American federalism and tactically paved the way for Congress to regulate suffrage in the former Confederate states if they continued to deny voting rights to freedmen or to refuse to approve the Fourteenth Amendment.

Indeed, with President Johnson's encouragement, all southern states rejected the Fourteenth Amendment. To become law, the amendment had to be ratified by at least four southern states, plus all of the Republican-controlled states in the rest of the country. Facing Johnson's opposition and the southern states' refusal to cooperate, Radical Republicans and the moderate Republicans once again united to create a congressional reconstruction plan. The victorious return of a two-thirds majority in both houses of Congress in the 1866 elections was interpreted by the Republicans in Congress as a national mandate for supporting a more radical reconstruction policy.

Overriding Johnson's veto, Congress enacted the first Reconstruction Act on March 2, 1867 (see Document 1). The act, which ushered in the period of congressional reconstruction or "Radical Reconstruction," divided ten of the eleven former Confederate states—Alabama, Arkansas, Florida, Georgia, Louisi-ana, Mississippi, North Carolina, South Carolina, Virginia, and Texas (Tennessee was exempted)—into five military districts subject to the control of the federal military forces occupying the districts (see map, page 10). The act called for each state to hold a constitutional convention, whose delegates would be elected by manhood suffrage. The new state constitutions drafted by the conventions were required to include black suffrage, and the new state legislatures were obligated to ratify the Fourteenth Amendment. Those persons disqualified by Section 3 of the Fourteenth Amendment were prohibited from taking part in the making of the new state constitutions. With the adoption of the Reconstruction Act, the moderates finally accepted the Radicals' argument that the enfranchisement of former slaves was the only viable way to secure ratification of the Fourteenth Amendment and to defeat Johnson's reconstruction plan.

The impact of black enfranchisement in the South was profound. About 735,000 blacks and 635,000 whites were registered in the ten unreconstructed states. In five of those states—Alabama, Florida, Louisiana, Mississippi, and South Carolina—blacks constituted a majority of voters (McPherson 2003, 577). Black and white Republicans made up a majority of the delegates in the state conventions, but in only two states, Louisiana and South Carolina, were blacks a majority of delegates to the conventions. These conventions produced the most democratic and progressive constitutions in the nation during this period. They adopted universal manhood suffrage, statewide systems of public schools for both races, and new government responsibilities in creating and maintaining social services for the poor and disabled.

Map 1.2 Congressional Reconstruction and the Rise of Black Elected Officials in the South

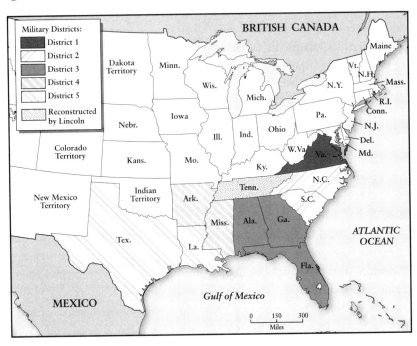

Source: Adapted from Arwin D. Smallwood (with Jeffrey M. Elliott), *The Atlas of African American History and Politics: From the Slave Trade to Modern Times* (New York: McGraw-Hill, 1998), Map 78.

With the aid of another Reconstruction Act enacted on March 11, 1868, and which accepted ratification of a new state constitution by only a majority of those actually voting, six states ratified their constitutions, and their new state legislatures ratified the Fourteenth Amendment. In June 1868, seven states—Alabama, Arkansas, Florida, Georgia, Louisiana, North Carolina, and South Carolina—were readmitted to the Union with the "fundamental condition" that the states must never amend their constitutions to deny African Americans the right to vote. In 1869 and 1870, Mississippi, Texas, and Virginia were readmitted to the Union after completing the required ratifications. Also in 1870, Hiram Revels of Mississippi was seated in the Senate

as the nation's first black senator. Over the next thirty years, altogether twenty-two African American men would be elected to Congress from the South. Another 1,400 would hold public office at the state and local levels during the same period (Foner 1993, xiv–xv).

The successful implementation of black suffrage in the South encouraged Radical Republicans to push for nationwide enfranchisement of blacks. Meanwhile, advocates of suffrage for blacks and women urged the Republican Party at large to support such a step. But the defeat of black suffrage proposals in Kansas, Michigan, Minnesota, and Ohio in 1867 and 1868 prevented the party from subscribing to nationwide black suffrage. Its 1868 platform celebrated black suffrage in the South as a pol-

Hiram R. Revels, from Mississippi, was the first African American U.S. Senator. In 1870 he was elected to serve the remainder of the term vacated by confederate president Jefferson Davis. George H. White, from North Carolina, was the last African American member of the U.S. House of Representatives after Reconstruction. In his farewell address to Congress in 1901 (see Document 8) White predicted: "This is perhaps the Negroes' temporary farewell to the American Congress; but let me say, Phoenix-like he will rise up some day and come again." It was not until 1928 that another African American was elected to Congress. *Source: Ohio Historical Society.*

The Late Rev. Hiram R. Revels,
Of Mississippi, First Negro U. S. Senator.

Hon. George H. White,
Of North Carolina, Last Negro
Member U. S. Congress.

icy demanded "by every consideration of public safety, of gratitude, and of justice," but it left black suffrage in "all the loyal States" to "the people of those States" (quoted in McPherson 2003, 584). Although the party's candidate, Ulysses S. Grant, won the presidency in 1868, Grant's modest victory, a plurality of 300,000 out of 5.7 million votes cast, as well as his Democratic opponent's victories in three northern states (New Jersey, New York, and Oregon) and three border states (Delaware, Kentucky, and Maryland) alarmed many Republicans. The Radical Republican leader

Charles Sumner of Massachusetts argued that had blacks in northern and border states been given the right to vote, they would have supported Republicans.

Political calculations aside, the ideological discrepancy embodied in the party's double standard toward black suffrage in the South and North bothered many Republicans. More important, the party was concerned about permanently guaranteeing black voting rights in the South, because the former Confederate states were quickly returning to Congress. Bowing to these concerns, during the short session between Grant's election in late 1868 and his inauguration in early 1869 Republicans in Congress—who maintained majorities of two-thirds in the House and four-fifths in the Senate—began the work of drafting a new constitutional amendment to secure black suffrage on a more permanent basis.

Out of a host of proposals three versions of the would-be Fifteenth Amendment emerged *(see Document 3)*. The first simply forbade states to deny citizens the right to vote on the grounds of race, color, or previous condition of servitude. The second further forbade states to impose literacy, property, or nativity qualifications for voting in addition to racial qualification. The third simply declared that all adult male citizens were entitled to vote. Fearing that a more stringent version would lead to the defeat of the amendment, moderates adopted on February 26, 1869, the first and most conservative version, an action that outraged Radical Republicans who had preferred the third version. Ratification of the amendment went rather quickly. The seventeen Republican-controlled state legislatures then in session ratified the amendment. Four

southern states—Georgia, Mississippi, Texas, and Virginia—were required to ratify the amendment to fulfill the additional prerequisite for readmission. By March 30, 1870, the Fifteenth Amendment had become part of the Constitution.

Like the Thirteenth and Fourteenth Amendments, the Fifteenth Amendment was largely the work of moderate Republicans. It did not affirmatively confer voting rights on African Americans; it simply prohibited states from denying voting rights for racial reasons. It did not grant voting rights to women, still a taboo subject, even for many Radical Republicans. But it did give the states wide latitude to continue to disenfranchise citizens by means of literacy, residence, and nativity qualifications. Overall, the amendment recognized the political equality of blacks and whites as a fundamental constitutional principle. It also gave Congress the power to enforce this principle in the years to come.

Enforcing the Fifteenth Amendment in the 1870s and 1880s

Upon ratification of the Fifteenth Amendment, President Grant, in his special message to Congress in 1870, optimistically predicted that black suffrage would be "out of politics and reconstructions completed" (quoted in Wang 1997, 53). But black suffrage was not out of politics, and Reconstruction continued after the Fifteenth Amendment became law.

The rising and widespread violence perpetrated by the Ku Klux Klan and similar organizations in the South was the foremost challenge. The Klan became active in late 1866, but its terrorization of blacks intensified after freedmen began to exercise the right to vote. White supremacists and former Confederates resorted to terrorism to win elections and to remove newly enfranchised freedmen from the political process. Southern states passed anti-Klan laws, but they had no resources to enforce them. In the meantime, unchecked election fraud strengthened the influence of the Democratic Party in the major cities in the North where noncitizen immigrants frequently cast fraudulent votes. To guarantee the rights of southern blacks to vote and to establish a uniform federal mechanism for supervising elections, the Republican Congress moved to put teeth in the Fifteenth Amendment immediately after its ratification. According to Sen. John Sherman, R-Ohio, without federal enforcement the amendment would be interpreted as dead letters in those state courts "where there is a strong prejudice against negro voting" (quoted in Wang 1997, 56).

Between May 1870 and April 1871, Congress enacted three laws to enforce the Fifteenth Amendment. These laws were later referred to as the Enforcement Acts or, derogatorily, as the "Force Acts," because they involved the use of government forces. The first of these laws, the Enforcement Act of May 31, 1870, had twenty-three sections and was the most important *(see Document 4)*. It placed the exercise of voting rights "at any elections by the people" under the protection of the federal government. It called for fining and imprisoning any state officials and private citizens who used force, bribery, threats, or intimidation to prevent citizens from registering or voting. The act also established the mechanisms for enforcement. It gave federal district courts the authority to hear enforcement cases, federal district attorneys and marshals the

authority to investigate violations of the Fifteenth Amendment and to make arrests, and the president the authority to use military force to keep order at the polls if needed. The law also banned fraudulent practices in elections. Enacted ninety-five years before the Voting Rights Act of 1965, this law launched the federal government's use of its power to protect African American voters.

The second Enforcement Act, enacted on February 28, 1871, strengthened the first law by adding sections that meticulously spelled out the guidelines for enforcement procedures and the responsibilities of enforcement officers.

The third law, known as Ku Klux Klan Act, was enacted on April 20, 1871. It enlarged the president's power to use military force to suppress domestic disturbances and to suspend the writ of habeas corpus when needed, and it banned Klan members from serving on juries and punished those who aided the Klansmen. The law also spelled out more than twenty kinds of practices that were, under the law, illegal, including the use of intimidation to interfere with any citizen's exercise of voting rights in federal elections. The swift enactment of these laws effectively helped to transform the Fifteenth Amendment into a concrete and enforceable federal policy. It also represented an unprecedented effort to build a centralized state power to protect freedmen's civil and political rights.

Federal enforcement in the early 1870s was characterized by firmness, effectiveness, and relatively smooth cooperation between Congress and the president. Grant played an active role in the early phases of enforcement, although he was rather cautious and selective in using military force to aid the Republican state governments in the South. In 1870 alone, federal troops were dispatched more than two hundred times at the request of state and federal civil authorities. In October 1871, Grant suspended the writ of habeas corpus in the Klan-ridden areas of South Carolina and ordered federal troops to give prompt aid to enforcement officers. The military escorted federal enforcement officials to make arrests. Their presence was crucial to the early success of enforcement.

Federal courts and the newly created Department of Justice (founded in 1870) shouldered the bulk of the enforcement work. Led by Grant's second attorney general, Amos T. Akerman, the Department of Justice prosecuted large numbers of Klansmen. But Democrats mounted fights against the federal prosecutors during the trials. One of the tensest exchanges and contests between federal enforcement officers and southern Democrats over enforcement was displayed in the so-called Great South Carolina Ku Klux Klan Trials, conducted in Columbia in the winter of 1871–1872. At those trials, two of the nation's ablest constitutional lawyers, hired by Democrats, defended the Klan members who had used to violence against black voters.

The outcome of enforcement was impressive. Before the end of 1870, the attorney general reported that forty-five cases had been prosecuted under the Enforcement Act, of which thirty-four resulted in convictions; 271 cases were pending in federal courts. In 1871, 314 cases were pursued under the Enforcement Acts, and 128 of the 206 cases from the South that year ended in convictions. The number of enforcement cases tripled in 1872, and 456 of the 603 cases from the South ended

in convictions. The effective enforcement demonstrated the enormous power of the national government in enforcing the Reconstruction amendments and also brought peace to the polls nationwide. The presidential election of 1872, at which Grant was reelected in a landslide, was the most peaceful one of the nineteenth century.

The vigor of enforcement began to decline, however, after the 1872 elections. Administratively, enforcement, conducted as an experiment instead of a long-term mission, constantly suffered from a lack of adequate resources and manpower. Attorney General Akerman's dismissal in 1872 deprived the mission of able leadership. The economic panic of 1873 shifted national attention to the financial crisis and the rising labor strife. The freedmen's political radicalism and demands for land distribution raised doubts in the minds of northerners, and their support for black rights began to wane. The decline of northern support resulted in no small measure from the strenuous opposition to enforcement voiced by liberal Republicans, a group of self-claimed independents, reformers, and publicists who began to advocate a "let-alone" policy toward the South. Disgusted by and resentful of the Grant administration, which was marred by corruption and cronyism, the liberals believed further enforcement would lead to more widespread manipulation of ignorant black voters in the South by Republican power seekers.

But the most destructive blow came from the Supreme Court. In its 1873 ruling in the *Slaughterhouse Cases* the Court offered a very narrow and conservative interpretation of the Fourteenth Amendment, which, in the Court's view, did not allow the federal government to protect most of the basic civil rights traditionally controlled by the state governments. Following this rationale, the Court limited the federal government's power to enforce the Fifteenth Amendment as well. Three years later in *United States v. Reese* (1876), which involved a state official's refusal of the registration of a black voter in Kentucky, the Court declared Sections 3 and 4 of the Enforcement Act of May 31, 1870, "insufficient," because they failed to specifically link the crimes stipulated for punishment under the sections to the racially related motives. The same year, in *United States v. Cruikshank,* the Court deemed Section 6 of the same enforcement law defective for failing to specify the exact rights to be protected under the Fourteenth and Fifteenth Amendments *(see Document 6).* The Court did not declare the enforcement law unconstitutional, but it did suggest that Congress make new laws to enforce voting rights. In the midterm elections of 1874, the Democrats regained the House and vowed to block any further enforcement legislation. In the lame-duck session of the Forty-third Congress, which met from December 7, 1874, to March 3, 1875, Republicans managed to pass the Civil Rights Act of 1875—which prohibited racial segregation in public facilities—but it failed to pass a new enforcement law.

All these developments affected the course of federal enforcement. In 1873, 36 percent of the 1,304 enforcement cases ended in convictions, but in 1874 the conviction rate dropped to 10 percent—only 102 of the 966 reported enforcement cases ended in convictions. In 1876 the number of enforcement cases dropped to 149, of which only three resulted in convictions.

Black Disenfranchisement in the 1880s and 1890s

The final blow to black suffrage was dealt by the 1876 presidential election, perhaps the most bitterly fought presidential contest of the nineteenth century. Problems arose from the disputed election returns from the three former Confederate states that were still under the control of Republican Party—Florida, Louisiana, and South Carolina—along with those from Oregon. As part of the "bargain" struck by the Democrats and Republicans behind the scenes, Rutherford B. Hayes, the Republican presidential candidate, received the disputed electoral votes and was therefore elected, but in return Hayes promised to restore "home rule" in the South and withdraw federal troops guarding the statehouses in South Carolina and Louisiana. As soon as the federal troops withdrew in April 1877, the Republican governments in those two states collapsed, completing the Democrats' recapture of all southern states from the Republican Party, or the "Redemption."

A new wave of black disenfranchisement had in fact begun before the Compromise of 1877, the term applied to Hayes's presidential "bargain." The most notorious and violent was the so-called Mississippi Plan, which was implemented in 1875 by the state's Democrats to win back the state government. "Redeemers" resorted to violence, intimidation, and the threat of unemployment to stop African Americans from voting. After 1877 even more illegal tactics were adopted by various states such as stuffing ballot boxes, which was one of most common methods of fraud in the South in the late 1870s. Other irregularities included stealing and destroying votes. In 1882 the South Carolina legislature adopted various disenfranchisement measures, including the so-called Eight Box Law, which called for different ballot boxes for national, state, and local offices to confuse illiterate black voters; secret ballots, which constituted an attempt to prevent the parties from giving instructions to black supporters; and a complex registration system intended to confuse and intimidate black and illiterate voters.

At the national level, after regaining both houses of Congress in 1878 Democrats launched seven attempts between 1879 and 1880 to repeal the enforcement laws enacted by Republicans between 1870 and 1871. Hayes, regretting his misguided reconciliation policy, vetoed all bills that sought to repeal enforcement. Although the total number of federal prosecutions under the enforcement laws rose slightly in the early 1880s, the conviction rates for the period remained low. In 1885 Grover Cleveland, the first Democratic president since the Civil War, entered office, and during two years of his term there were no convictions under the enforcement laws from the South. Yet the Supreme Court did reverse its earlier positions and provide a more supportive interpretation of the Fifteenth Amendment and of the power of the federal government to enforce the amendment. In its rulings on *Ex parte Siebold* (1880), *Ex parte Clarke* (1880), and *Ex parte Yarbrough* (1884), the Court affirmed the power of Congress to enforce the Fifteenth Amendment, and it announced that the prohibition of state denial of voting rights on basis of race should be understood as conferring upon freedmen the right to vote *(see Document 7 for the opinion in* Ex parte Yar-

brough). But these decisions came too late for federal enforcement to regain its vigor and vitality. In the late 1870s, the annual average number of federal prosecutions for southern states under the enforcement acts consistently fell below one hundred, and convictions never exceeded twenty. Because neither Democrats nor Republicans were able to control both Congress and the presidency between 1875 and 1888, the enforcement laws could not be repealed or revitalized. The period, as noted by Alexander Keyssar (2000, 108), was one "of limbo and contestation, of participation coexisting with efforts at exclusion."

Not until after Republicans regained control of Congress and sent Benjamin Harrison to the White House in 1889 did they began to launch a new and final attempt to revive federal enforcement of the Fifteenth Amendment. The Federal Elections Bill, better known as the Lodge Elections Bill, was introduced in 1890 by Henry Cabot Lodge, R-Mass., in the House and George Frisbie Hoar, R-Mass., in the Senate. The bill, an updated version of the existing enforcement laws, was primarily intended to carry out two objectives: protecting black voters in the South and halting election fraud in the North and South. The real purpose of the bill, according to Lodge, was to establish a uniform national system of election supervision to secure the "free ballot and fair count." It therefore called for the creation of a board of canvassers who would be appointed by the appropriate federal circuit court when petitioned by citizens from any congressional district. Such a board would monitor elections, inspect registration lists, challenge doubtful voters, and, most important, certify the final count. The board was also given the power to overturn election results as declared by state officials.

The elections bill passed the House, but it became stalled in the Senate when higher priority was given to discussion of a tariff bill that Republicans had hoped to use to help the party win the 1890 midterm elections. When the elections bill was brought up again for debate in early 1891, eight Republican senators from western mining states who were angry about the tariff and currency policies of the party's eastern wing joined the Democratic minority in the Senate to set aside the bill after a prolonged Democratic filibuster failed to defeat it. The close vote of 35–34, with nineteen abstentions, ended not only the debate on the federal elections bill, but also the Republican Party's thirty-year struggle to establish and enforce black suffrage.

The black disenfranchisement movement already under way before defeat of the Lodge bill was ostensibly being conducted to reform the ballot and break the fusion of the Republican and Populist votes in various southern states. One of the mechanisms produced by the movement was the poll tax, which was adopted first by Florida and Tennessee in 1889 and then by other states between 1890 and 1908. The secret ballot was introduced to keep black voters away from polling places. The 1890 Mississippi constitutional convention also adopted a literacy test and increased the residency requirement. So that the literacy test would not disqualify large numbers of white voters, state officials received discretion in the state constitution to determine whether an applicant demonstrated the desirable level of "understanding" of the required literacy test. The longer residency requirement was intended to deny voting rights to transient and mobile

black laborers. In 1895 South Carolina also adopted a literacy test and an "understanding" clause, a provision that required a voter to demonstrate adequate and correct understanding of a paragraph or section of state constitution read to him by state registration officials (of course, the state registration officials were the persons to perform the test and judge the quality of understanding), as well as the practice of gerrymandering, which prevented the state's black voters from electing more than one black representative in the 1880s and early 1890s. In 1898 Louisiana adopted the "grandfather clause," which allowed those who had been eligible or whose father or grandfather had been eligible to vote before 1867 (the year the Reconstruction Act was implemented) to qualify to vote without taking the literacy test.

These elaborate voting restrictions substantively disenfranchised African Americans in the South at the turn of the twentieth century. For those blacks who managed to register to vote, their attempt to exercise the right of suffrage was further curtailed by the white primary, a mechanism that restricted participation in the Democratic Party primary elections to whites. As a result, after 1890 fewer than 9,000 out of 147,000 voting-age blacks were registered to vote in Louisiana. By the early twentieth century, in the South as a whole voter turnout had dropped from 85 percent to 50 percent for whites and black voter turnout had dropped to a single digit.

At the national level, after Democrats regained control of both houses of Congress and the presidency in 1894, they quickly repealed the existing federal enforcement laws in spite of the strenuous resistance of the Republicans in both houses. However, several Republicans, including Sen. William Stewart of Nevada, who had drafted the Fifteenth Amendment and led the debate of the first enforcement law in 1870, voted with Democrats to repeal the Enforcement Acts. The Republican Party regained control of the national government between 1897 and 1910, but it made no effort to revive black suffrage enforcement.

Black disenfranchisement was challenged by African Americans, but the Supreme Court refused to intervene. In 1898 the Court ruled in *Williams v. Mississippi* that the "understanding clause" in the second "Mississippi Plan" was permissible under the Constitution *(see Document 11)*. This ruling, together with the Court's earlier ruling in the landmark *Plessy v. Ferguson* (1896), which upheld legally mandated racial segregation and served as the basis for the "separate but equal" doctrine, marked what African American historian Rayford W. Logan called the "nadir" of African American experience in the postemancipation period.

Yet at the same time a movement directed at regaining voting rights was emerging under the leadership of a new generation of African American leaders at both the national and grassroots levels. The Niagara Movement of 1905, led by sociologist W. E. B. DuBois and others, followed in the footsteps of the first black national convention forty years earlier and announced that enforcement of the Fourteenth and Fifteenth Amendments was its foremost goal. Shortly after its establishment in 1909, the National Association for the Advancement of Colored People (NAACP) filed an amicus curiae (friend-of-the-court) brief in *Guinn v. United States* (1915). In this case, the Court invalidated the grandfather clause, finding it to be a violation of the Fifteenth Amendment *(see Document 13)*. Although full reenfranchisement of African Americans would have to wait another fifty years, or until implementation of the Voting Rights Act of 1965, the legacy of the first Reconstruction served as a powerful memory and a source of inspiration for new generations of black and white builders of America's new interracial democracy.

References

Belz, Herman. 1978. "Origins of Negro Suffrage during the Civil War." *Southern Studies* 17 (summer): 115–130.

Benedict, Michael Les. 1978. "Preserving Federalism: The Waite Court and Reconstruction." *Supreme Court Review* 39–79.

Finkelman, Paul, ed. 1992. *African Americans and the Right to Vote*. New York: Garland.

Foner, Eric. 1988. *Reconstruction: America's Unfinished Revolution, 1863–1877*. New York: Knopf.

———. 1993. "Introduction." In *Freedmen's Lawmakers: A Directory of Black Office-holders during Reconstruction*. New York: Oxford University Press.

Gillette, William. 1965. *The Right to Vote: Politics and the Passage of the Fifteenth Amendment*. Baltimore: Johns Hopkins University Press.

———. 1979. *Retreat from Reconstruction, 1869–1979*. Baton Rouge: Louisiana State University Press.

Goldman, Robert M. 2001. *"A Free Ballot and a Fair Count": The Department of Justice and the Enforcement of Voting Rights in the South, 1877–1893*. New York: Fordham University Press.

———. 2001. *Reconstruction and Black Suffrage: Losing the Vote in Reese and Cruikshank*. Lawrence: University Press of Kansas.

Grossman, Lawrence. *1976. The Democratic Party and the Negro: Northern and National Politics, 1868–92*. Urbana: University of Illinois Press.

Holt, Thomas. 1977. *Black over White: Negro Political Leadership in South Carolina during Reconstruction*. Urbana: University of Illinois Press.

Johnson, Lyndon B. 1966. *Public Papers of the Presidents of the United States: Lyndon B. Johnson, 1965*. Vol. 1, entry 107, 281–287. Washington, D.C.: Government Printing Office.

Kaczorowski, Robert J. 2005. *The Politics of Judicial Interpretation: The Federal Courts, Department of Justice, and Civil Rights, 1866–1876.* New York: Fordham University Press (originally published in 1985).

Keyssar, Alexander. 2000. *The Right to Vote: The Contested History of Democracy in the United States.* New York: Basic Books.

Kousser, J. Morgan. 1974. *The Shaping of Southern Politics: Suffrage Restriction and the Establishment of the One-Party South, 1880–1910.* New Haven, Conn.: Yale University Press.

———. 1999. *Colorblind Injustice: Minority Voting Rights and the Undoing of the Second Reconstruction.* Chapel Hill: University of North Carolina Press.

Litwack, Leon F. 1998. *Trouble in Mind: Black Southerners in the Age of Jim Crow.* New York: Knopf. See especially Chapter 5.

McPherson, James M. 2003. *Ordeal by Fire: The Civil War and Reconstruction.* Boston: McGraw-Hill.

Nieman, Donald G. 1992. *Promises to Keep: African Americans and the Constitutional Order: 1776 to the Present.* New York: Oxford University Press. See especially Chapters 3–5.

Perman, Michael. 2001. *Struggle for Mastery: Disfranchisement in the South, 1888–1908.* Chapel Hill: University of North Carolina Press.

Rogers, Donald W., ed. 1992. *Voting and the Spirit of American Democracy: Essays on the History of Voting and Voting Rights in America.* Urbana: University of Illinois Press.

Swinney, Everette. 1987. *Suppressing the Ku Klux Klan: The Enforcement of the Reconstruction Amendments: 1870–1877.* New York: Garland.

Tergorg-Penn, Rosalyn. 1998. *African American Women in the Struggle for the Vote, 1850–1920.* Bloomington: Indiana University Press.

Upchurch, Thomas Adams. 2004. *Legislating Racism: The Billion Dollar Congress and the Birth of Jim Crow.* Lawrence: University Press of Kentucky. See especially Chapters 4–7.

Wang, Xi. 1997. *The Trial of Democracy: Black Suffrage and Northern Republicans, 1860–1910.* Athens and London: University of Georgia Press.

Williams, Lou Falkner. 1996. *The Great South Carolina Ku Klux Klan Trials, 1871–1872.* Athens: University of Georgia Press.

Woodward, C. Vann. 1974. *The Strange Career of Jim Crow.* 3d rev. ed. New York: Oxford University Press.

2

Disenfranchisement and Its Impact on the Political System

ROBERT C. LIEBERMAN

On February 9, 1935, Charles Hamilton Houston testified before the Finance Committee of the U.S. Senate. Houston was not unused to such occasions. A graduate of Harvard Law School where he was the first African American editor of the *Harvard Law Review,* he was at age thirty-nine already an accomplished lawyer—and one who had served as vice dean of Howard University Law School in his native Washington, D.C. As counsel to the National Association for the Advancement of Colored People (NAACP), he was preparing to argue his first case before the U.S. Supreme Court.

Nor was the scene in the committee room by itself terribly unusual—an American speaking on behalf of millions of his fellow citizens, presenting to their elected representatives their views and perspectives on an important matter of public policy being considered by Congress. Except that, for most of the twelve million African Americans in the United States, the senators sitting on the committee were *not* their elected representatives, even though the committee was chaired by Democrat Pat Harrison of Mississippi, a state with a black population larger than that of any other state but one. Because they could not vote, black Americans had, in effect, no elected representatives

in the national government, and the men sitting before them on the committee dais (and they were all men—there was only one woman in the Senate at the time, Hattie Caraway of Arkansas, but she was not a member of the Finance Committee) had little reason to regard Houston's testimony as anything more than a distraction.

The topic of Houston's testimony was the Social Security bill, which was to lay the foundation for the modern American welfare state by creating old-age pensions (Social Security), Unemployment Insurance, and public assistance programs for the poor and disabled. Houston voiced the anxieties of his fellow African Americans when he told the committee, "From a Negro's point of view, [the bill] looks like a sieve with the holes just big enough for the majority of Negroes to fall through" (U.S. Congress 1935, 641). Social Security, he explained, did not cover occupations such as farm labor and domestic service, and thereby would exclude most African Americans from the program's benefits.

The bill also left too much power in the hands of state and local authorities, which meant that southern blacks would continue to be subjected to the discriminatory practices of southern society. "There are," Houston acknowledged, "plenty of decent people down South, but we also know from experience . . . that it is the same as political suicide to take an advanced stand on racial issues in many cases" (pp. 641–42). Leaving the social and economic welfare of southern blacks to the care of state and local public policy, he explained, was tantamount to leaving them without protection at all, or worse. "We have had the most disgusting experiences in the matter of public health," he told the senators. "If you want to know how much handicap the Negro citizen suffers, the only thing you have got to do is to try to get a job, travel, or else get sick" (p. 646). He implored the senators to write into the bill an explicit guarantee that its programs could not discriminate on the basis of race. And he reminded the senators that what he was asking on behalf of African Americans was no more and no less than equal treatment on the basis of common citizenship. "We simply want to have all citizens share in the benefits under the law. . . . We Negroes are United States citizens who have never failed to shoulder our full share of the national burden; if we have not paid you more money in taxes, it is because you have denied us equal opportunity to work" (p. 647). Yet not only were his pleas ignored, but the committee, along with its counterpart (the House Ways and Means Committee), actually expanded the scope of the exclusions and other provisions that Houston objected to before it passed the bill that President Franklin D. Roosevelt would sign into law that August.

Houston's appearance before the committee, and its outcome, were emblematic of the consequences of black disenfranchisement dur-

ing the first two-thirds of the twentieth century. Stripped of the capacity to commit the essential act of democratic citizenship—voting—African Americans were located outside the normal democratic channels of policy making. Democratic politics depends on the ability of citizens to have a voice in governing their own affairs by expressing their dissatisfaction with present realities and their expectations for the future to an audience of policy makers whose continuing power depends on the votes of those citizens. An even stronger claim for the importance of voting rights is that political (as well as civil) rights are a necessary prelude to the granting of social rights—"from the right to a modicum of economic welfare and security to the right to share to the full in the social heritage and to live the life of a civilized being according to the standards prevailing in the society," as defined by the English sociologist T. H. Marshall (1964, 72). Without political rights, individuals and groups cannot make legitimate claims for the benefits and protections that come with membership in society. As those benefits and protections expand for some citizens, the lack of political rights for others can widen inequity by leaving those deprived of rights even further behind. Thus the absence of political rights may have real and far-reaching consequences for the opportunities and life chances of those systematically excluded from the democratic process.

Houston's testimony also highlighted the extent of the consequences of black disenfranchisement for both African Americans and U.S. public policy more generally. The effects of disenfranchisement reached well beyond the South, where segregation and white supremacy seemed firmly entrenched in the 1930s. Indeed, it hardly seems possible that public policy could have made the political, economic, and social repression of black Americans appreciably worse than it was under the states' discriminatory "Jim Crow" laws and practices. Yet the effects of disenfranchisement extended to a wide range of public policy arenas, many of which were not explicitly race policies. These effects included both actions—the frequent adoption and implementation of racially imbalanced policies—and nonactions—the failure to pursue other policies that might have advanced the cause of racial equality. The overall consequence, by the time the Voting Rights Act of 1965 reversed disenfranchisement, was a policy landscape very different from what might have evolved under conditions of political equality, and one that sharply differentiated between the benefits and protections available to white Americans and black Americans.

Disenfranchisement and the American Political System

Disenfranchisement by itself is a serious handicap in a democratic political system. The ability of citizens to choose officeholders and then to punish them by withholding votes is perhaps the most important mechanism underlying democratic policy making. It provides the incentive for elected officials to listen to the voices and attend to the interests of citizens. Without this tool of electoral influence—that is, the threat that an elected official might lose his or her job—groups who seek benefits or protection in the policy process must fall back on the good will of policy makers, which is hardly a reliable means of ensuring policy responsiveness and, in any event, was in very

short supply for African Americans in the mid-twentieth century.

But even beyond this fairly straightforward political relationship, the situation for African Americans before passage of the Voting Rights Act was even more limiting and debilitating because of the particular structural characteristics and institutional patterns of the American political system during the first two-thirds of the twentieth century. The structure of American politics intensified and magnified the consequences of southern disenfranchisement in such a way that the nondemocratic practices of the South often held the rest of the nation in thrall to the imperatives of segregation and white supremacy. To paraphrase the historian Edmund S. Morgan (1975, 387), twentieth-century America was, in many respects, the South writ large.

Concentration of Blacks in the South

Several factors contributed to this state of affairs. The first was simply the concentration of African Americans in the South. At the beginning of the twentieth century, nearly 90 percent of black Americans lived in the South. Many African Americans moved north during and after World War I, but in the 1930s and 1940s three-fourths remained in the South. Another, larger wave of northward migration followed World War II, but in 1960 almost 60 percent of American blacks still lived in the South (Grossman 1989; Lemann 1991). Even though African Americans outside the South were typically able to vote, they tended to be too few and too powerless to have a strong voice in shaping public policy.

The political economy of the South depended heavily on agriculture, particularly on the cultivation of cotton, which required a large amount of unskilled, low-wage labor. Although many poor whites also toiled at the low end of the southern economy, black labor was the backbone of this economic system. Before the Civil War, slave labor was the basis of the southern economy. After emancipation, slavery was replaced not by the redistribution of land to former slaves that Reconstruction seemed to promise but by a system of share-cropping, tenant farming, debt peonage, and wage labor that kept many black families nearly as tied to the land and subordinate to white landowners as before (Wright 1986; Cooper, Holt, and Scott 2000). Many African American women worked not only in the fields but also as servants in white households.

The social class structure of the South complemented this economic structure. Its fundamental principle was the subordination of blacks to whites, regardless of income, occupation, or level of education—the conventional markers of socioeconomic status. All whites—rich and poor, planter and dirt farmer, industrialist and laborer—were united across the social and economic lines that might otherwise have divided them. Their common ground was the social superiority they derived from not being black. Even W. E. B. DuBois (1903)—the great theorist and exemplar of the African American elite—felt the weight of this social hierarchy, writing famously of the "double consciousness" of the African American, caught between the universal aspirations of the American ideal and the realities of segregation. This social hierarchy was enforced by an elaborate system of law and custom, backed by violent repression, that kept southern African Americans firmly in their place.

The chief political ramification of this social and economic system was southern whites' use of white supremacy as the dominant political tactic. It was by no means the only racial current in southern politics—many southern whites regarded segregation and white supremacy as backward-looking relics that were holding back southern progress, and many of these people occupied prominent positions in politics, journalism, business, and the professions from which they could advance the cause of racial equality. But the central tendency in southern politics in the first part of the twentieth century was white supremacy. As political scientist V. O. Key (1949) argued, the white elites of the cotton-growing regions of the South, where African Americans were the most heavily concentrated, dominated southern political life, and it was these elites who had the most at stake in preserving the racial hierarchy in place at the end of Reconstruction. Racial moderates such as Governors Ellis Arnall of Georgia and "Big Jim" Folsom of Alabama were not entirely unsuccessful in southern politics. But their victories were often short-lived, and successful racial moderates were often replaced by more strident segregationists, such as Eugene Talmadge, who succeeded Arnall, and George C. Wallace, who defeated Folsom in his bid for a third term. At times, politicians reinvented themselves as segregationists when the softer racial appeals of their earlier careers led them to defeat—Populist-turned-white-supremacist Tom Watson of Georgia, for example, or Wallace himself, who, after losing his first bid for governor to a more orthodox segregationist, vowed that he would not be "out-niggered" again (Carter 1995, 96). Despite whatever other differences southern politicians may have had, white supremacy consistently proved a strong unifying force.

The White South and the Party System

The second major factor responsible for the extraordinary impact of black disenfranchisement was the connection between the white South and the Democratic Party. The Democratic Party's dominance of southern politics was near total from about the turn of the century into the 1960s. Since the Civil War, the Democratic Party had been aligned with the interests of the white South, while the Republican Party had been associated with Abraham Lincoln (the first Republican president), emancipation, Reconstruction—and, through the late nineteenth century, black voting rights (Valelly 2004). The last third of the nineteenth century was a period of extremely close and competitive national elections in which control of the presidency and Congress shuttled frequently back and forth between the parties.

To remain competitive during this period, the Republican Party actively contested elections and sought voters in the South and thus supported the protection of voting rights for African Americans, who were reliable Republican voters. Within the South, a variety of political movements—from the Readjusters to the Populists—attempted to forge class-based biracial alliances (Dailey 2000; Hahn 2003). But after the collapse of the Populist insurgency in the 1890s, Republicans found themselves able to win national elections without the South, and their interest in promoting the franchise withered. Southern Democrats capitalized on this Republican disengagement. They recaptured control of southern state governments and gradually imposed the legal and extralegal

Jim Crow system of segregation, including disenfranchising African Americans (Kousser 1974). Even the Republican Party moved away from its stance of supporting African American rights and toward the "lily white" approach that prevailed within the party organization beginning in the second half of the Theodore Roosevelt administration. For most of the twentieth century, in fact, there was little difference between the parties on issues of civil rights (Carmines and Stimson 1989).

Thus was born the "Solid South." From the turn of the century until 1960, the eleven former Confederate states elected not a single Republican to the U.S. Senate and only a handful to the House of Representatives (typically from districts in eastern Tennessee or western Virginia or North Carolina sympathetic to the Union during the Civil War, thereby revealing the deep roots of southern partisan attachments). Although southern Democrats of this era are commonly portrayed as monolithically conservative, they were in fact a more politically and ideologically diverse lot than commonly believed. But southern Democrats in Congress did reliably coalesce on two issues: race and labor. On these issues, southern Democrats regularly joined with Republicans to form a voting bloc (commonly known as the Conservative Coalition) in opposition to the policy goals of the more liberal northern Democrats (Katznelson, Geiger, and Kryder 1993).

During the first third of the twentieth century, a period of Republican dominance of national politics, the South was the most stalwart Democratic region of the country, and southerners generally constituted a majority of the Democratic minority in Congress. Thus when Democrats achieved a majority in Congress in the 1930s, southern members had been around longer than other Democrats and so were immediately able to step into the congressional leadership. Democrats maintained their majorities in Congress almost uninterrupted until 1994 (Republicans controlled both houses from 1946 to 1948 and from 1952 to 1954 and the Senate from 1980 to 1986), and southerners retained their disproportionate seniority into the 1970s. During this period, southern Democrats were perceived as extremely unlikely presidential candidates, largely because of long northern memories of secession and civil war (Black and Black 1992, 83–87). Consequently, they were more likely to see a congressional career as a professional goal rather than as a stepping-stone to higher aspirations. Moreover, before 1936 the Democratic Party required a two-thirds vote at its national convention to nominate a presidential candidate, a rule that effectively gave the South veto power over the party's presidential nominations, but also made it very unlikely that a southern candidate (or one too closely linked to southern interests) would be nominated. An example of the dilemmas posed by this situation was the 1924 Democratic National Convention, which was deadlocked for more than two weeks in choosing between former Treasury secretary William Gibbs McAdoo, a Californian who was supported by the Ku Klux Klan, and New York governor Alfred E. Smith, a Catholic opponent of Prohibition with very little southern support. (The convention eventually settled on a compromise candidate, John W. Davis, a West Virginia lawyer who went on to defend public school segregation before the Supreme Court in *Brown v. Board of Education* [1954]. Smith

won the nomination in 1928, but uncharacteristically for a Democrat lost several southern states.)

The South and National Political Institutions

The third factor underlying the impact of disenfranchisement was the institutional structure of American politics and policy making, which gave the white South and its interests a disproportionate influence over national affairs for much of the twentieth century. In particular, the organizational structure of Congress further enhanced the influence of white southern Democrats during this period (Bensel 1984; Shepsle 1989; Schickler 2001). Several structural characteristics of Congress were particularly significant. The first was seniority as the most important means to power within Congress. Although formally each member of Congress has a single vote in the legislative process, some members of the House and Senate are more powerful and influential than others. Beginning in the early twentieth century, important positions within the House and Senate—particularly seats on powerful committees and committee chairmanships—were almost universally granted to the most senior members—that is, those who had the longest terms of continuous service in Congress. Seniority was figured by party, so that the chairman of a congressional committee, for example, was typically the committee member from the majority party who had been in the House or Senate the longest. Thus the principal pathway to legislative influence within Congress was reelection. In the mid-twentieth century, the Solid South generated tremendous seniority advantages for southern Democrats, who were more likely than any other Democratic members of Congress to be reelected regularly.

Seniority was important for policy making because committees played such a big role in the legislative process during this period. Like today, the committees in Congress with jurisdiction over legislation in particular subject areas—agriculture, commerce, foreign affairs, defense, and the like—had to approve any legislative initiative falling into their respective areas before that legislation could be considered by the entire House or Senate and then, if approved, forwarded to the other house for approval or to the president for signature or veto. Committees thus acted as gatekeepers of legislation; without committee action, legislative proposals would languish and die on committee dockets. Committee chairs were especially important in orchestrating the legislative process and controlling committee action. Chairs set committee agendas—that is, they decided which proposals their committees would consider, when, and under what procedures.

Because for most of the twentieth century committee chairs were allocated strictly by seniority, chairs had little to fear from colleagues if they bottled up bills that were not to their liking or modified bills to suit their own policy preferences. The most powerful congressional committees were especially prone to southern control. To take two examples, the House Ways and Means Committee and the Senate Finance Committee, which control tax and social welfare policy, were led by southern Democrats from the 1930s to the 1970s, except for the two brief episodes of Republican control. Also during this era, the Democratic members of the House Ways and Means Committee served as the House Democrats'

"committee on committees," which allocated their party's committee seats. The chair of the House Ways and Means was therefore one of the most influential members of Congress. Southerners used their dominant position on the House Rules Committee, which regulates the flow of legislative business in the House, to slow and often to block civil rights and other legislation that might otherwise have gained wide support. By occupying these and other key parts of the congressional hierarchy, white southerners were able to wield a disproportionately large influence on U.S. policy for a long stretch of the twentieth century.

One peculiarity of the Senate's rules gave southerners yet another powerful legislative lever—the filibuster. Under Senate rules, debate on any measure is unlimited unless the Senate itself agrees to limit it. In the absence of such an agreement, any senator who has the floor may speak for as long as he or she likes, and during that time no other business can be conducted. This procedural rule gives small but determined groups of senators the means to hold up indefinitely legislation they oppose by, in effect, talking it to death, a tactic known as a filibuster. From 1917 to 1975, a two-thirds vote of the entire Senate was required to end a filibuster (before 1917 there was no way to end a filibuster; in 1975 the vote needed to end a filibuster was lowered to three-fifths).

In principle, any group of senators can mount a filibuster, but over the course of the twentieth century southern Democrats were the most effective wielders of the filibuster, which they used frequently to lock, delay, or modify civil rights legislation (Binder and Smith 1997; Caro 2002; Wawro and Schickler forthcoming). Among the most famous filibusterers was

Sen. Strom Thurmond of South Carolina, who spoke for more than twenty-four hours straight in opposition to the Civil Rights Act of 1957. (Then a Democrat, Thurmond switched parties and became a Republican in 1964, just weeks after the Civil Rights Act of that year became law.) Southern Democrats combined efforts to mount a three-month-long filibuster against the Civil Rights Act of 1964, which ended only when northern Democrats and Republicans agreed on a compromise that narrowed the scope of the legislation.

Disenfranchisement and Public Policy

Under these institutional conditions, the effects of disenfranchisement on public policy were dramatic and widespread. The first effect was actually a series of nonevents—that is, the policy-making system, Congress in particular, failed to take serious action on civil rights or racial equality. In the Civil Rights Act of 1875, Congress prohibited racial discrimination in public accommodations such as railroads and other public transportation, restaurants and hotels, and theatres. The act also protected the right of African Americans to serve on juries. In 1883 the Supreme Court ruled in the *Civil Rights Cases* that the 1875 act was unconstitutional. This opinion was followed in 1896 by the Court's declaration in *Plessy v. Ferguson* that states could mandate segregated facilities by race as long as they were "equal." Between 1875 and 1957, Congress passed no federal civil rights legislation.

Opposition to lynching, which became a nationwide crusade and one of the central policy objectives of the civil rights community in the early twentieth century, was the most visible ex-

ample of nonaction on civil rights. In the late nineteenth and early twentieth centuries, lynchings of African Americans became commonplace in the South, but because criminal law was a state matter, few perpetrators were caught or punished. In 1918 Republican representative Leonidas Dyer of Missouri introduced a bill to make lynching a federal crime. The Dyer bill quickly gained the support of the NAACP. The bill passed the House of Representatives in 1922, but it was killed in the Senate by a southern filibuster. In the 1930s, antilynching legislation was introduced once again in Congress, this time by Democratic senators Edward Costigan of Colorado and Robert Wagner of New York. Proponents, including the NAACP, had high hopes that President Franklin Roosevelt, who was being egged on by his wife, Eleanor, would throw his support behind the bill. But he did not, explaining that although he sympathized with its aims he could ill afford to alienate the South, whose support he needed both for the success of his program in Congress and for his own reelection.

The second principal policy effect of disenfranchisement was not inaction but rather policy action that resulted in differential treatment of white and black Americans. As Charles Houston observed in his Senate testimony in 1935, many of the major policy developments of the first part of the twentieth century effectively, if not explicitly, excluded African Americans from the social and economic protections of the Progressive Era and the New Deal. This description certainly applied to Social Security and Unemployment Insurance, which were the subjects of Houston's testimony. By excluding farmers, farm laborers, and household servants from coverage, these programs left more than half of the country's black workers unprotected (Lieberman 1998). The dominant southern members of Congress, worried about the possibility that the emerging national welfare state might undermine the racial hierarchy of the southern political economy, insisted on these exclusions (Quadagno 1988; Poole forthcoming). The Fair Labor Standards Act of 1938, which established the minimum wage and regulated working conditions, also excluded farm and domestic labor (Farhang and Katznelson 2005).

Another racially imbalanced policy instrument often found in Progressive Era and New Deal social and economic legislation was decentralization—the tilt toward state and local discretion in ostensibly national programs. For example, the public assistance provisions of the Social Security Act—most significantly Aid to Dependent Children (later Aid to Families with Dependent Children), the program mostly commonly identified with "welfare"—allowed states to set eligibility requirements and benefit levels, with discriminatory results. The result was continuation of a pattern of dramatic racial imbalances in spending on whites and blacks in existing federal assistance programs, such as vocational education under the Smith-Hughes Act (1917) and agricultural extension work under the Smith-Lever Act (1914). (The principal exception to this pattern was land-grant colleges; federal funding for black and white institutions was basically proportional to the population balance throughout the South. Unlike other federal grant legislation, however, the Morrill Act, which governed land-grant colleges, had been amended in 1890—before disenfranchisement, by a Republican president and Congress—

explicitly to prohibit discrimination in the allocation of federal funds.) Federal legislation also failed to prevent discrimination by private organizations such as labor unions. The original draft of the National Labor Relations Act of 1935 (also known as the Wagner Act), which guaranteed the right of labor to organize and bargain collectively, contained a clause prohibiting discrimination by unions. The clause did not survive the legislative process.

Legislation was not the only vehicle for discriminatory public policy under disenfranchisement. The administrative state also made policy decisions that systematically disadvantaged African Americans. The Home Owners' Loan Corporation, established by the federal government during the depression to help beleaguered homeowners refinance mortgages and prevent mass foreclosures, developed a system of rating neighborhoods to assess the creditworthiness of property by location. It published a series of detailed city maps with neighborhoods color-coded to show levels of credit risk: green shading indicated low risk, blue and yellow moderate risk, and red high risk. Black neighborhoods were almost invariably colored red, making mortgages less available and more expensive for African Americans—and giving rise to the term *redlining* to describe a variety of housing discrimination practices that have maintained residential segregation in American cities (Jackson 1985; Massey and Denton 1993).

But federal housing policy was far from unique. The Tennessee Valley Authority, one of the most far-reaching and transformative of the New Deal's economic development and recovery programs, perpetuated and deepened locally entrenched racial hierarchies in the region where it operated. More broadly, the federal government itself was segregated for much of the twentieth century, and African Americans were restricted to low-status, poorly paid positions in the civil service (King 1995).

Yet the policy landscape for African Americans was not altogether as bleak as this litany suggests. Some programs moved toward color-blind fairness despite disenfranchisement. Within two decades of its creation, for example, Social Security had expanded to include farm workers, domestic employees, and other previously excluded workers and was well on its way toward providing broad social protection across racial lines (Lieberman 1998). In some instances, federal program administrators used their leverage to enforce racial fairness in the operation of their programs, particularly in some (although by no means all) of the work relief agencies of the early New Deal such as the Works Progress Administration, the Public Works Administration, and the National Youth Administration (Sullivan 1996; Amenta 1998).

The executive branch also took other steps to challenge racial discrimination, such as the creation of a Fair Employment Practices Committee (FEPC) during World War II to investigate and challenge discrimination in defense industries; the establishment of a civil rights section in the Justice Department; and the integration of the armed forces (Riley 1999, 145–155). The federal courts invalidated such practices as segregation in public primary, secondary, and higher education; whites-only primary elections; and restrictive racial covenants in the buying and selling of real estate (Klarman 2004). Although these were important accomplishments, they proved in some cases to

be Pyrrhic victories. The FEPC, for example, proved to be short-lived (and its re-creation would be one of the civil rights movement's chief legislative goals in the 1960s), and the Supreme Court's ruling against public school segregation in *Brown v. Board of Education* was followed by uneven enforcement and massive resistance among white southerners. The positive developments resulted largely from political pressure applied through means other than voting, such as litigation and protest. The rarity of these moments when federal authorities forced the issue of racial equality, often at considerable cost, underscores the critical point that integration in national policy was the hard-won exception under disenfranchisement rather than the rule. Nevertheless, these cases demonstrated some potential pathways for national action on race policy and foreshadowed both the accomplishments and conflicts of the civil rights era.

Disenfranchisement, then, affected the cumulative shape of American public policy as it evolved over the course of the twentieth century. Between the turn of the century and the 1960s, the modern American welfare state, administrative state, and regulatory state all took shape, and it made an important difference that they did so in a context not only of racial heterogeneity but also of hierarchy and political exclusion. Overall, the political inequality produced by disenfranchisement has had the effect of inhibiting the construction of social solidarity across lines of race and class, an essential political component of welfare state development in many industrial societies. Consequently, the United States has a less expansive and robust welfare state than it might otherwise have, in part because of the racial divide in American politics (Alesina, Glaeser, and Sacerdote 2001; Lieberman 2005). For example, the politics of race inhibited national education policy in the years after World War II. In the 1950s and early 1960s, Rep. Adam Clayton Powell Jr., an African American Democrat from Harlem, regularly offered nondiscrimination amendments to federal education legislation. The clause, known as the Powell Amendment, would have allowed federal aid to go only to integrated schools, and it became a poison pill that for many years prevented the passage of federal school funding legislation. Republicans would join with northern Democrats in supporting the Powell Amendment, which would pass the House and thus become part of the bill. But the presence of the amendment would turn southern Democrats, who generally favored federal school aid, against the bill, and they would then join with Republicans to defeat the legislation.

Seeds of Change

Despite these obstacles, some events and trends of the disenfranchisement era did prepare the ground for a more forthright political challenge to racial inequality. This challenge ultimately prevented the New Deal's racial limitations from simply reinforcing historical patterns of racial inequality, further limiting the possibilities for racially balanced policies, and ultimately becoming self-fulfilling. The first was the rise of black political support for the New Deal and the Democratic Party. Through the late nineteenth and early twentieth centuries, black voters (almost exclusively northern) strongly supported the Republican Party—the "party of Lincoln"—but in the

1930s this allegiance began to shift toward Franklin Roosevelt and the Democrats. By the time of Roosevelt's first reelection campaign in 1936, African American voters were by and large solidly Democratic, and they have remained so since (Weiss 1983).

There were several reasons for this shift in political allegiance. First, despite its limitations the public policies of the New Deal greatly benefited African Americans. Because they were disproportionately poor and economically vulnerable, African Americans were among the hardest-hit victims of the Great Depression, and even though the New Deal's relief and economic reconstruction policies often systematically relegated African Americans to secondary status, they certainly provided assistance to black Americans to a greater extent than any previous federal government policy. Many African Americans also came to feel a personal allegiance to Roosevelt himself, and especially to his wife, Eleanor, who was a vigorous and vocal advocate for civil rights and racial equality both during her husband's administration and afterward. Roosevelt's presidency also oversaw a general expansion of the size and scope of the federal government and the deployment of this expanded national state in behalf of economic protections for working- and lower-class Americans. Although African Americans were often denied the full benefit of these protections, they saw much potential in the development of a national government committed to caring for the less fortunate members of American society, among whom they certainly numbered. Finally, toward the end of his presidency Roosevelt began to articulate a broad vision of universal economic rights—a "second bill of rights" that included the rights to a job and a livelihood, education, health care, and cradle-to-grave economic protection—and it resonated deeply with the aspirations of African Americans (Hamilton and Hamilton 1997). This vision was consistent with the general drift of American liberalism, which was abandoning its emphasis on economic restructuring in favor of a doctrine centered on protecting the rights of both individuals and what Supreme Court Justice Harlan Fiske Stone, in *United States v. Carolene Products* (1938), called "discrete and insular minorities" (Brinkley 1995).

The puzzle that the rise of black allegiance to the Democratic Party posed is that it put African Americans into an uncomfortable political embrace with white southern Democrats. The resulting coalition brought together partners committed, on the one hand, to an expansive vision of universal economic protection and, on the other, to the preservation of a brutal system of regional apartheid—a marriage of Sweden and South Africa, as some commentators have described it. Entering into this coalition certainly entailed a compromise for African Americans, for it ensured that large-scale progress on civil rights and racial equality was kept off the national agenda in favor of economic and other policies that could gain broad support within the Democratic Party.

Participation in the New Deal coalition did, however, bring political benefits that helped to construct a basis for future political achievements. The New Deal provided at least symbolic opportunities for high-ranking black officials in the federal government, highlighted by the "black cabinet," an informal group of African Americans who worked in New Deal agencies and federal departments and whom

Roosevelt consulted on minority affairs. Among the black cabinet's most prominent members were Mary McLeod Bethune, Ralph Bunche, William Henry Hastie (who later became the first African American federal judge), and Robert C. Weaver (who in 1966 became the first African American cabinet secretary). Blacks' participation in the New Deal coalition also created a platform for access to national policy makers, particularly in the executive branch, that long outlasted the mostly symbolic activity of the black cabinet. African American leaders were increasingly able to gain insider status in policy deliberations, and they deftly used their access to influence policy decisions. The creation of the FEPC, for example, was the result of a deal struck between Roosevelt and A. Philip Randolph, a black labor leader who had proposed holding a march on Washington to protest discrimination. Later contacts proved equally influential in shaping the direction of both the civil rights movement and national policy.

The effects of the black alliance with the Democratic Party were amplified by the mass migration of African Americans from south to north—migration that began to transform the country's political geography in fundamental ways. African Americans moved primarily to take advantage of the new economic opportunities that became available to them in the great industrial cities of the Northeast and Midwest, although they began increasingly to encounter job discrimination, housing segregation, and violence in the North as well (Sugrue 1996). In the North, however, blacks could vote. In the wake of the New Deal relief efforts, African American electoral loyalties had gradually shifted to the Democrats, and black voters in northern cities became crucial to the Democratic Party's electoral prospects in the years following World War II. At the same time, the war itself, which the United States had fought against a racist regime on behalf of the principles of democracy and human freedom, highlighted the incongruities of American race relations (Myrdal 1944; Klinkner 1999; Kryder 2000). Later, in the emerging cold war with the Soviet Union, this gap between the American professions of democratic equality and the realities of racial inequality would become an important force pushing civil rights onto the national agenda (Dudziak 2000).

In this new political landscape, President Harry S. Truman chose to take steps toward a federal commitment to civil rights (Riley 1999, 155–164). In 1946 he appointed a Presidential Commission on Civil Rights whose report, *To Secure These Rights,* called for federal action against segregation and discrimination, including such measures as ending poll taxes and other restrictions on voting rights (see Document 17). Some of the commission's recommendations, such as integrating the military, Truman undertook through executive action. But in doing so he alienated the party's southern wing, and when the 1948 Democratic National Convention, which nominated Truman for reelection, adopted a mild pro–civil rights platform plank, a group of southern delegates walked out of the convention. These "Dixiecrats" held their own convention and chose Strom Thurmond, then governor of South Carolina, as their presidential candidate. Although Thurmond won four southern states (capturing thirty-nine electoral votes), Truman was reelected.

The Dixiecrat revolt did not last, but the events of 1948 signaled an impending shift in the Democratic Party and the politics of civil rights. The tight embrace between the Democratic Party and the white South was beginning to weaken (Black and Black 2002; Lublin 2004). Nowhere was this change more apparent than in the career of Lyndon B. Johnson, who was elected to the Senate from Texas in 1948. The ambitious Johnson rose quickly to become Senate majority leader in 1955, but he realized that his hopes for the Democratic presidential nomination rested on his ability to appeal to northern voters as something more than a civil rights obstructionist (Dallek 1991; Caro 2002). It was Johnson—a southerner—who engineered the passage of the substantively limited but symbolically important Civil Rights Act of 1957, just as it was to be Johnson—the first southerner to occupy the White House in nearly one hundred years—who would seal the civil rights revolution by signing the Civil Rights Act and Voting Rights Act.

The end of the disenfranchisement era was thus a product of many of the very same factors that had, nearly a century before, been instrumental in producing disenfranchisement and shaping its consequences in the intervening decades. Disenfranchisement itself was a product of a configuration of national political institutions—the party system, federalism, and national electoral and governing structures—that at a decisive moment in the course of American political history gave voice and power to the racist white elites of the South. Disenfranchisement itself predictably robbed African Americans of the political rights of citizenship and the ability to advance claims for equal treatment and a fair share of the benefits and protections of the regulatory and welfare state that emerged in full flower—perhaps not coincidentally—during the disenfranchisement era. The particular patterns of racial exclusion, however, were similarly produced by many of the very same institutional factors that were behind the establishment of disenfranchisement in the first place. Among these were the party system and the Solid South, federalism and the role of the states in constraining and shaping national policy initiatives, and the separation of powers—particularly the structure of Congress and the nature of presidential-congressional relations. These factors, then, were responsible for the distinctive pattern of racial divisions, exclusions, and silences of New Deal era policy, which cumulatively amounted to the development of a racially bifurcated policy regime that relegated African Americans to second-class social citizenship.

Yet ironically, as political conditions changed over the course of the twentieth century, many of these same factors provided openings to African Americans and their allies who sought to challenge disenfranchisement and the other forms of racial inequality. These factors were the party system and the growing importance of northern blacks to the Democratic Party; federalism and its associated electoral geography, which gave locally concentrated African Americans enhanced electoral importance; and the shape of national policy-making institutions, which, despite continuing disenfranchisement, gave African Americans access to policy-making processes, particularly through the courts and the executive branch. These institutional opportunities were not, of course, self-executing. Progress toward civil and voting rights required concerted and courageous action by thousands of Americans, black and white alike, who organized to challenge

segregation and disenfranchisement and did so by exploiting the limited but nevertheless powerful possibilities that were open to them. Their actions, set in context and animated by the distinctive shape of the American political system, brought an end to disenfranchisement and set the stage for African Americans and other minorities, so long excluded from the possibilities of American politics, to claim the full equality and promise of American citizenship.

References

Alesina, Alberto, Edward Glaeser, and Bruce Sacerdote. 2001. "Why Doesn't the United States Have a European-Style Welfare State?" *Brookings Papers on Economic Activity* 2:187–254.

Amenta, Edwin. 1998. *Bold Relief: Institutional Politics and the Origins of Modern American Social Policy.* Princeton, N.J.: Princeton University Press.

Bensel, Richard Franklin. 1984. *Sectionalism and American Political Development: 1880–1980.* Madison: University of Wisconsin Press.

Binder, Sarah A., and Steven S. Smith. 1997. *Politics or Principle? Filibustering in the United States Senate.* Washington, D.C.: Brookings.

Black, Earl, and Merle Black. 1992. *The Vital South: How Presidents Are Elected.* Cambridge, Mass.: Harvard University Press.

———. 2002. *The Rise of Southern Republicans.* Cambridge, Mass.: Harvard University Press.

Brinkley, Alan. 1995. *The End of Reform: New Deal Liberalism in Recession and War.* New York: Knopf.

Carmines, Edward G., and James A. Stimson. 1989. *Issue Evolution: Race and the Transformation of American Politics.* Princeton, N.J.: Princeton University Press.

Caro, Robert A. 2002. *Master of the Senate.* New York: Knopf.

Carter, Dan T. 1995. *The Politics of Rage: George Wallace, the Origins of the New Conservatism, and the Transformation of American Politics.* New York: Simon and Schuster.

Cooper, Frederick, Thomas C. Holt, and Rebecca J. Scott. 2000. *Beyond Slavery: Explorations of Race, Labor, and Citizenship in Postemancipation*

Societies. Chapel Hill: University of North Carolina Press.

Dailey, Jane. 2000. *Beyond Jim Crow: The Politics of Race in Postemancipation Virginia.* Chapel Hill: University of North Carolina Press.

Dallek, Robert. 1991. *Lone Star Rising: Lyndon Johnson and His Times, 1908–1960.* New York: Oxford University Press.

DuBois, W. E. B. 1903. *The Souls of Black Folk.* Chicago: A. McClurg.

Dudziak, Mary L. 2000. *Cold War Civil Rights: Race and the Image of American Democracy.* Princeton, N.J.: Princeton University Press.

Farhang, Sean, and Ira Katznelson. 2005. "The Southern Imposition: Congress and Labor in the New Deal and Fair Deal." *Studies in American Political Development.* 19:1–30.

Grossman, James R. 1989. *Land of Hope: Chicago, Black Southerners, and the Great Migration.* Chicago: University of Chicago Press.

Hahn, Steven. 2003. *A Nation under Our Feet: Black Political Struggles in the Rural South, from Slavery to the Great Migration.* Cambridge, Mass.: Harvard University Press.

Hamilton, Dona Cooper, and Charles V. Hamilton. 1997. *The Dual Agenda: The African-American Struggle for Civil Rights and Economic Equality.* New York: Columbia University Press.

Jackson, Kenneth T. 1985. *Crabgrass Frontier: The Suburbanization of the United States.* New York: Oxford University Press.

Katznelson, Ira, Kim Geiger, and Daniel Kryder. 1993. "Limiting Liberalism: The Southern Veto in Congress, 1933–1950." *Political Science Quarterly* 108 (summer): 283–306.

Key, V. O., Jr. 1949. *Southern Politics in State and Nation.* New York: Knopf.

King, Desmond. 1995. *Separate and Unequal: Black Americans and the US Federal Government.* Oxford: Oxford University Press.

Klarman, Michael J. 2004. *From Jim Crow to Civil Rights: The Supreme Court and the Struggle for Racial Equality.* Oxford: Oxford University Press.

Klinkner, Philip A, with Rogers M. Smith. 1999. *The Unsteady March: The Rise and Decline of Racial Equality in America.* Chicago: University of Chicago Press.

Kousser, J. Morgan. 1974. *The Shaping of Southern Politics: Suffrage Restriction and the Establish-ment of the One-Party South, 1880–1910.* New Haven, Conn.: Yale University Press.

Kryder, Daniel. 2000. *Divided Arsenal: Race and the American State During World War II.* Cambridge: Cambridge University Press.

Lemann, Nicholas. 1991. *The Promised Land: The Great Migration and How It Changed America.* New York: Knopf.

Lieberman, Robert C. 1998. *Shifting the Color Line: Race and the American Welfare State.* Cambridge, Mass.: Harvard University Press.

————. 2005. *Shaping Race Policy: The United States in Comparative Perspective.* Princeton, N.J.: Princeton University Press.

Lublin, David. 2004. *The Republican South: Democratization and Political Change.* Princeton, N.J.: Princeton University Press.

Marshall, T. H. 1964. *Class, Citizenship, and Social Development.* Garden City, N.Y.: Doubleday.

Massey, Douglas S., and Nancy A. Denton. 1993. *American Apartheid: Segregation and the Making of the Underclass.* Cambridge, Mass.: Harvard University Press.

Morgan, Edmund S. 1975. *American Slavery, American Freedom: The Ordeal of Colonial Virginia.* New York: Norton.

Myrdal, Gunnar. 1944. *An American Dilemma: The Negro Problem and Modern Democracy.* New York: Harper and Brothers.

Poole, Mary. Forthcoming. *The Segregated Origins of Social Security: African Americans and the Welfare State.* Chapel Hill: University of North Carolina Press.

Quadagno, Jill. 1988. *The Transformation of Old Age Security: Class and Politics in the American Welfare State.* Chicago: University of Chicago Press.

Riley, Russell L. 1999. *The Presidency and the Politics of Racial Inequality: Nation-Keeping from 1831 to 1965.* New York: Columbia University Press.

Schickler, Eric. 2001. *Disjointed Pluralism: Institutional Innovation and the Development of the U.S. Congress.* Princeton, N.J.: Princeton University Press.

Shepsle, Kenneth A. 1989. "The Changing Textbook Congress." In *Can the Government Govern?* edited by John E. Chubb and Paul E. Peterson. Washington, D.C.: Brookings.

Sugrue, Thomas J. 1996. *The Origins of the Urban Crisis: Race and Inequality in Postwar Detroit.* Princeton, N.J.: Princeton University Press.

Sullivan, Patricia. 1996. *Days of Hope: Race and Democracy in the New Deal Era.* Chapel Hill: University of North Carolina Press.

U.S. Congress. Senate. Committee on Finance. 1935. *Economic Security Act.* 74th Cong., 1st sess., February 9.

Valelly, Richard M. 2004. *The Two Reconstructions: The Struggle for Black Enfranchisement.* Chicago: University of Chicago Press.

Wawro, Gregory J., and Eric Schickler. Forthcoming. *Filibuster: Obstruction and Lawmaking in the U.S. Senate.* Princeton, N.J.: Princeton University Press.

Weiss, Nancy J. 1983. *Farewell to the Party of Lincoln: Black Politics in the Age of FDR.* Princeton, N.J.: Princeton University Press.

Wright, Gavin. 1986. *Old South, New South: Revolutions in the Southern Economy since the Civil War.* New York: Basic Books.

3

The Supreme Court and Black Disenfranchisement

Michael J. Klarman

The Fifteenth Amendment, adopted in 1870, barred the disenfranchisement of voters because of race *(see Document 3)*. With their suffrage rights secured, huge numbers of southern blacks turned out to vote, overwhelmingly for Republicans. Because all southern states had large black populations and five had black majorities, Republican candidates won resounding victories everywhere, and many blacks were elected to office. At times during Reconstruction, blacks made up nearly half of the lower-house delegates in Mississippi and Louisiana and a majority in South Carolina. Sixteen blacks served in Congress, and thousands of blacks held local offices such as sheriff or county magistrate.

The political power of southern blacks was short-lived, however. Southern whites, even where in the minority, wielded preponderant economic, social, and physical power. Through fraud, intimidation, and violence, whites eventually succeeded in suppressing black voting, which, in turn, enabled Democrats to "redeem" the South from Republican rule. Republican president Ulysses S. Grant sporadically used military intervention to suppress electoral violence until the fall of 1875, when the administration calculated that further such interventions would alienate too many northern voters, who had grown weary of military coercion. Freed from external constraint, southern whites did whatever they thought necessary to regain political control.

Black voting in the South, though reduced, did not end with the demise of Reconstruction in 1877. A majority of blacks still voted in most southern states in 1880, and many blacks continued to sit in state legislatures and hold local offices. Not until about 1890 did the political participation of southern blacks decline precipitously.

Formal disenfranchisement took many forms. Complex registration requirements conferred broad discretion on (white) registrars and disadvantaged illiterates and itinerants—groups assumed to be disproportionately black. Residency requirements also penalized itinerants. Secret-ballot laws functioned as literacy tests, requiring voters to read and mark ballots themselves. Disenfranchisement for crimes was gerrymandered to reflect white perceptions of black criminal propensities.

Most southern states adopted literacy tests, which would have disproportionately disqualified blacks even if applied fairly because of blacks' higher rates of illiteracy. But nobody expected registrars appointed by white supremacist Democrats to impartially administer the tests. Moreover, most literacy tests were qualified by "understanding clauses," which permitted registrars to enroll (white) illiterates who could understand a constitutional provision read to them. Grandfather clauses likewise exempted from literacy tests those eligible to vote before 1867, when southern blacks were first enfranchised, and their descendants; occasionally former soldiers and their descendants were grandfathered as well. In addition, every southern state adopted a poll tax as a voting restriction—a measure that disparately affected poorer blacks and disenfranchised many farm workers, most of whom lived on credit. Most states also adopted white primaries, excluding blacks from the only southern elections that mattered after the 1890s: Democratic primaries.

As a result of formal and informal disenfranchisement, black voter registration and turnout were virtually eliminated by the early twentieth century. In Louisiana, black voter registration fell from 95.6 percent before an 1896 registration law, to 9.5 percent immediately thereafter, to 1.1 percent in 1904. Black voter registration in Alabama plummeted from 180,000 in 1900 to 3,000 in 1903. Registration figures undoubtedly overstated turnout. In Mississippi, black voter turnout was estimated at 29 percent in 1888, 2 percent in 1892, and 0 percent in 1895.

Disenfranchisement had calamitous consequences for southern blacks. When blacks could not vote, neither could they be elected to office. No blacks sat in the Mississippi legislature after 1895, down from a high of sixty-four in 1873. In South Carolina's lower house, which had a black majority during Reconstruction, a single black remained in 1896. The last southern black congressman (until the 1970s) relinquished his seat in 1901.

More important, disenfranchisement meant that almost no blacks held local offices. Sheriffs, justices of the peace, county commissioners, and school board members were the most important governmental actors at this time. The preferred method of whites to deny constitutional rights to blacks was to vest broad discretion in local officials and trust them to preserve white supremacy. Disenfranchisement was essential to this strategy, and it led to the exclusion of blacks from juries, the diversion of blacks' share of public school funds, and a dramatic rise in the number of (unpunished) lynchings of blacks.

The Supreme Court Confronts Disenfranchisement

The legal question confronting the Supreme Court during this period was whether disenfranchisement measures violated the Fifteenth Amendment, which provides that the right of citizens to vote "shall not be denied or abridged by the United States or by any State on account of race, color, or previous condition of servitude." In general, southern whites avoided imposing express racial conditions on suffrage, because they assumed that flagrant contravention of the amendment would prompt federal intervention.

Yet most white southerners thought the Fifteenth Amendment was illegitimate. A leading Louisiana disenfranchiser stated a view prevalent at the time when he called the amendment "the greatest crime of the Nineteenth Century" (Eaton 1899, 289). Crazed Republicans bent on partisan gain had forcibly imposed ignorant

"Negro domination" on the South. Deterred from explicitly nullifying the amendment, white southerners generally felt morally justified in evading it, and they were not subtle about their objectives. At the Virginia disenfranchisement convention of 1901–1902, one delegate acknowledged that his mission was "to discriminate to the very extremity of permissible action under the limitations of the Federal Constitution" (Buck 1937, 287).

The original understanding of the Fifteenth Amendment seemed to permit suffrage restrictions that disparately affected blacks. Many Republicans in 1869–1870 had favored a broader amendment forbidding suffrage qualifications based on property and education, but they had failed in their objectives, in part because New England Republicans intent on disenfranchising illiterate Irish immigrants and California Republicans intent on disenfranchising Chinese aliens opposed the broader measures. To the extent that Supreme Court justices around the turn of the century felt constrained by original intent, they could not have invalidated literacy tests or poll taxes based simply on disparate racial impact. With black illiteracy rates remaining at roughly 50 percent and most southern blacks still impecunious tenant farmers and sharecroppers, such voting qualifications, even if fairly administered, would have disenfranchised most blacks.

To be sure, other grounds for challenging disenfranchisement did exist. First, the grandfather clause could be attacked as a surrogate racial classification. The criterion determining voter eligibility—whether a person or his ancestors had voted before 1867—was simply a stand-in for race. Second, one could challenge voter qualifications based on the discrimina-

tory motive animating them. Third, one could argue that the vast discretion conferred by literacy tests on voter registrars to determine the "good character" and "understanding" of prospective voters violated the Constitution. And, fourth, one could challenge actual—as opposed to merely potential—discrimination in the administration of voter qualifications.

In *Williams v. Mississippi* (1898), the Court considered and rejected two challenges to black disenfranchisement—that the new literacy tests and poll taxes had been adopted for discriminatory purposes and that the literacy tests conferred unbridled discretion on registrars (see Document 11). In response to the first objection, the Court invoked the traditional judicial aversion to examining legislative motive. As for the second, the justices distinguished an earlier decision, *Yick Wo v. Hopkins* (1886), which had invalidated a local ordinance requiring persons establishing laundries in wooden buildings, but not in stone or brick ones, to secure permits from the board of supervisors. In *Yick Wo*, the Court had struck down the laundry ordinance because it gave administrators unfettered discretion, thus inviting discrimination. In *Williams*, the justices ruled that "good character" and "understanding" clauses provided administrators with sufficient guidance to withstand a constitutional challenge for vagueness.

Broad administrative discretion can also be challenged as applied, which was another basis on which the Court had invalidated the laundry ordinance in *Yick Wo*. In *Williams*, the Court rejected the "as applied" claim, because the actual administration of Mississippi's voter requirements had not been shown to be discriminatory. That issue returned to the Court in *Giles v. Harris* (1903), in which the plaintiff sought to enjoin race discrimination in the administration of a state constitutional provision requiring that voters be of "good character and understanding." Writing for the majority, Justice Oliver Wendell Holmes ruled that even if the allegations were proved, the plaintiff was not entitled to the requested relief. First, if the allegation of fraudulent administration were true, the Court, by ordering registration, would then be party to the sham. Second, such an order would be "an empty form" if Alabama whites really had conspired to disenfranchise blacks. In such a case, the Court would be powerless to enforce its order, and thus the plaintiff's remedy must come from the political branches of government.

Holmes did not rule out a suit for money damages, but when the same plaintiff brought such a claim, the Court in *Giles v. Teasley* (1904) rejected it on similar grounds. First, if the registration board acted in a patently unconstitutional fashion, then it could do the plaintiff no harm. Second, the Court could provide no effective relief against this sort of state political action.

One other disenfranchisement decision issued by the Court during this period was notable as well. Since the 1870s, the question had arisen whether Congress, under its power to enforce the Fifteenth Amendment, could criminalize racially motivated acts of interference with the franchise by *private* individuals. The constitutional text seems to say that Congress cannot do such a thing, because it forbids abridgement of the right to vote on account of race by *the United States or by any state*. Yet several federal court decisions in the early 1870s had rejected constitutional challenges to federal prosecutions of private individuals for interfering with the rights of blacks, and dicta from the Supreme Court decision in *United States v. Cruikshank* (1876) had intimated a similar view *(see Document 6)*. In *James v. Bowman* (1903), however, the Court squarely rejected the notion that Congress could constitutionally criminalize private interferences with the voting rights of blacks.

Indeed, during this era the Court rejected all constitutional challenges to black disenfranchisement. (Several other suits seeking to enjoin registration and vote tabulations because of black disenfranchisement were dismissed as moot because elections had already occurred.) The extraordinary *Giles* rulings suggest that one reason was the justices' recognition of their own limited power. Another reason was that the justices were probably no more committed to protecting black suffrage than were most white Americans at the time.

By 1900 most white southerners were determined to eliminate black suffrage by any means necessary. In 1898 whites in Wilmington, North Carolina, concluded a political campaign fought under the banner of white supremacy by killing roughly a dozen blacks and driving fourteen hundred more out of the city. As a result of this and other similar displays of violence, many southern blacks abandoned politics. Many political Progressives, both in the North and in the South, came to regard the disenfranchisement of blacks as an enlightened response to election violence and fraud. On June 23, 1915, the *New York Times*, noting "the determination of the white man to rule the land wherein he lives," preferred the "more peaceful methods" of disenfranchisement to "terrorism."

The commitment of northern whites to black suffrage had greatly eroded since Reconstruction. The ideal of universal manhood suffrage was undermined by concerns about enfranchising millions of southern and eastern

European immigrants and by the nation's imperialist adventures of the 1890s. The *Nation* on May 26, 1898, noted the coincidence of *Williams v. Mississippi* with the country's efforts to deal with the "varied assortment of inferior races in different parts of the world, which must be governed somehow, and which, of course, could not be allowed to vote." As the Civil War receded in memory, northern whites, desiring sectional reconciliation, became even less inclined to contest the disenfranchisement of southern blacks. Finally, the electoral realignment of the mid-1890s, which left Republicans securely in control of national politics, reduced that party's incentive to protect the voting rights of southern blacks.

This decline in support for black suffrage was reflected in congressional action. In 1893–1894 Democrats took advantage of their simultaneous control of Congress and the presidency for the first time since the 1850s to repeal most of the Reconstruction-era voting rights legislation. When Republicans regained national control from 1897 to 1910, they made no effort to reenact these measures. Moreover, Congress failed to remedy patent violations of Section 2 of the Fourteenth Amendment, which *requires* reduction of a state's congressional representation if its adult male citizens are disenfranchised for any reason other than crime. The Court, like Congress, broadly reflects public opinion. If Congress was unwilling to enforce the Fourteenth Amendment, then the reluctance of the justices to order remedies for violations of the Fifteenth Amendment is unsurprising.

The Grandfather Clause

The first victory for black voting rights in the Supreme Court was achieved during the Pro-

gressive Era. Ironically, racial attitudes and practices had become even more regressive by then. Significant numbers of blacks still voted in many southern states in the mid-1890s, but not by 1910. The last blacks were evicted from local offices in the first decade of the twentieth century. With black political power completely nullified in the South, radical racists swept to power. In 1911 Cole Blease bragged that he would resign as governor of South Carolina and "lead the mob" rather than use his office to protect a "nigger brute" from lynching.[1] Sen. James Vardaman of Mississippi promised that "every Negro in the state will be lynched" if necessary to maintain white supremacy (Litwack 1998, 295). In his inaugural address in 1909, President William Howard Taft endorsed the efforts of white southerners to avoid domination by an "ignorant, irresponsible electorate" and conceded that public opinion probably no longer supported the Fifteenth Amendment *(see Document 12)*.

This was the political context within which the Supreme Court considered the constitutionality of the grandfather clause. Southern disenfranchisement of blacks through literacy tests was politically feasible only because illiterate whites were insulated either through "understanding clauses," which permitted the registration of those who could demonstrate satisfactory understanding of a state constitutional provision read to them, or through grandfather clauses. Those southern whites fearful of conferring broad discretion on officials who might use it to favor particular factions preferred the latter method of limiting the disenfranchising effect of literacy tests. Half a dozen southern states adopted such provisions, which exempted from literacy tests those who qualified to vote before 1867, the year that most southern blacks were first enfranchised, and their lineal descendants.

Many southern whites had warned that courts were unlikely to tolerate such blatant circumventions of the Fifteenth Amendment. In 1898 some delegates to Louisiana's constitutional convention, which was the first to adopt a grandfather clause, predicted that courts would invalidate the measure as a "weak and transparent subterfuge." The convention conferred with the state's two U.S. senators, who agreed that the provision was "grossly unconstitutional" (Mabry 1936, 304, 306). Every state but Oklahoma that adopted a grandfather clause limited its duration, hoping to accomplish its purpose before legal challenges commenced.

In 1915 in *Guinn v. United States,* the Supreme Court invalidated the one permanent grandfather clause *(see Document 13).* The issue was probably not difficult for the justices, because, as the *Washington Post* observed on June 23, 1915, the grandfather clause "was so obvious an evasion that the Supreme Court could not have failed to declare it unconstitutional." A commentator in the *Harvard Law Review* similarly queried, "Is it not a trespass on the dignity of a court to expect it to refuse to brush aside so thin a gauze of words?" (Monnet 1912, 57). Of the more than 55,000 blacks residing in Oklahoma in 1900, only fifty-seven came from states that permitted blacks to vote in 1866.

Even those northern whites most sympathetic to the disenfranchisement of blacks in the South did not necessarily countenance nullification of the Constitution. President Taft, who endorsed white political supremacy, decried the grandfather clause as a repudiation of the Constitution. On June 23, 1915, the *New York Times*, which saw the Fifteenth Amendment as "a blunder in statesmanship [that] left terrible consequences," declared that "no other decision was possible" in *Guinn,* because the grandfather clause "had no reason for being unless it was for the purpose of nullifying the Fifteenth Amendment, and the court is not there to nullify the Constitution."

Guinn's implications for black suffrage were trivial. As a newspaper in Richmond, Virginia, accurately observed, because other states had limited the duration of their grandfather clauses, these measures had already "served their purpose" by 1915 and were "no longer vital to the South's protection" (Schmidt 1982, 879). Moreover, *Guinn* explicitly approved of literacy tests uncorrupted by grandfather clauses. Disenfranchisement pioneers such as Mississippi and South Carolina had already demonstrated that a literacy test without a grandfather clause could effectively nullify black suffrage. So long as registrars committed to white supremacy exercised broad discretion in administering literacy tests, illiterate whites could generally register, while literate blacks could not. As late as the 1950s, Alabama registrars were finding blacks with doctorates from Tuskegee Institute illiterate.

Guinn also had no effect on other disenfranchisement techniques, such as poll taxes, white primaries, complex registration requirements, fraud, and violence. For these reasons, a New Orleans newspaper confidently concluded that the ruling was "not of the slightest political importance in the South" (Schmidt 1982, 879–880). The August 1915 issue of the *Crisis* reproduced the observations of a New York newspaper that observed that blacks would likely discover that "getting the right to vote from the Supreme Court in Washington is not exactly the same thing as getting the right from the election board in their own voting district." Earlier, on June 22, 1915, the *New York Times* had assured readers that, *Guinn* notwithstanding, "the white man will rule his land. The only question left by the Supreme Court's decision is how he will rule it."

In Oklahoma itself, the legislature immediately responded to *Guinn* by "grandfathering" the grandfather clause. Under the new statute, voters in the 1914 congressional election, when the grandfather clause was in effect, were automatically registered. All other eligible voters (including essentially all blacks) had to register within a twelve-day period in the spring of 1916 or be forever disenfranchised. The federal government failed to challenge this patent evasion, and the justices had no opportunity to invalidate it until 1939. In the absence of subsequent enforcement litigation, *Guinn* was easily circumvented. Follow-up litigation was hard to come by at a time when the annual legal budget of the National Association for the Advancement of Colored People (NAACP) was roughly $5,000 and it had fewer than fifteen local branches, almost all of them in the North.

The White Primary

The white primary was another principal mechanism for disenfranchising southern blacks. Because Democrats completely dominated southern politics after the 1890s, excluding blacks from party primaries effectively nullified their political influence. In the 1890s, state parties in the South adopted the first rules barring blacks from primaries. In 1923 Texas became the first state to bar blacks from primaries by law. By 1930 blacks were excluded from Democratic primaries in almost all southern states by custom or party rule, though by law only in Texas.

In *Nixon v. Herndon* (1927), the Supreme Court invalidated the Texas statute. Steps taken by a political party to exclude blacks raised complicated questions about the scope of the state-action requirement of the Fourteenth and Fifteenth Amendments, but in *Herndon* black participation was barred by statute, not party rule. Justice Oliver Wendell Holmes, writing for a unanimous Court, thought the issue was easy. His two-page opinion declined to reach the Fifteenth Amendment question, because "it seems to us hard to imagine a more direct and obvious infringement of the 14th."

Herndon was a quintessential example of the proclivity of constitutional law toward suppressing outliers: Texas's white primary law was the only one of its kind in the nation. Moreover, the Texas statute illustrated the tendency of "Jim Crow" laws (laws enacted to enforce racial hierarchy) to reflect, rather than to create, norms of white supremacy. Prior to enactment of the statute, most Texas counties already excluded blacks from Democratic primaries. The law at issue in *Herndon* was enacted at the behest of a politician from one of the few Texas counties that permitted black participation in Democratic primaries after an election in which black suffrage was a prominent issue. Thus *Herndon* invalidated an outlier statute that itself suppressed an outlier practice.

After *Herndon*, the Texas legislature immediately passed a law empowering the parties' executive committees to prescribe membership qualifications. As anticipated and intended, the Texas Democratic executive committee quickly passed a resolution excluding blacks. In *Nixon v. Condon* (1932), a narrowly divided Court found discriminatory state action on the ground that the Texas legislature, not the state Democratic Party, had empowered the executive committee to prescribe membership qualifications.

The only effect of the *Condon* decision was to defer for three years the more fundamental question of whether a political party's exclusion of blacks was state action (even in the absence of a statute specifying which entity within the party determined membership qualifications). Three weeks after *Condon,* the annual convention of the Texas Democratic Party resolved to exclude blacks. In *Grovey v. Townsend* (1935), the Court unanimously upheld the exclusion.

Grovey was a confusing opinion. Justice Owen Roberts conceded the ways in which Texas regulated primaries—for example, requiring that they be held, that voter qualifications be the same as in general elections, and that absentee voting be permitted. Roberts found two differences between primary and general elections determinative on the issue of state action: Texas did not cover the expenses for primary elections, nor did it furnish or count the ballots. But Roberts failed to explain why certain forms of state involvement in primaries, but not others, constituted state action.

Overall, *Grovey* was probably an accurate reflection of national public opinion on whether southern blacks should participate in politics. Through the 1920s, prominent Republicans had continued to lament the Fifteenth Amendment "as one of the greatest mis-

takes ever made in this country" (Sen. William Borah as quoted in the *Crisis,* August 1926), and an occasional appeal by Republican congressmen to enforce Section 2 of the Fourteenth Amendment had fallen on deaf ears. The *Washington Post* observed on March 8, 1927, that the nation was "tacitly" consenting to an "arrangement" in which southern whites maintained political supremacy by disenfranchising blacks. In the mid-1930s, the national Democratic Party and President Franklin D. Roosevelt's Justice Department declined to challenge the legality of the white primary. Only World War II would fundamentally transform the views of the nation, and of the justices, on black suffrage.

The Poll Tax

Most southern states adopted poll taxes around the turn of the century. The tax was usually due several months before an election—timing that increased the likelihood that the voter would misplace the receipt, which had to be produced to vote. The principal purpose of the tax was to disenfranchise blacks, though poor whites were a subsidiary target. Unlike literacy tests, poll taxes did not contain built-in immunities for whites.

Constitutional challenges to the poll tax faced daunting legal hurdles. The Constitution explicitly authorizes states to set voter qualifications, including those for national elections. The Fifteenth Amendment qualifies this grant of power, forbidding denial of the vote to U.S. citizens on account of race. But that amendment does not clearly prohibit nonracial voter qualifications simply because they have the purpose or effect of disenfranchising disproportionate numbers of blacks. The Congress that approved the amendment contemplated forbidding property and education qualifications but lacked the votes to do so.

After the *Williams* ruling rejected the relevance of legislative motive in a challenge to black disenfranchisement, it would have been difficult for the Court to invalidate poll taxes because they were intended to disenfranchise blacks. Poll taxes could also be challenged because they disadvantaged poor people, but as of the 1930s the Court had never suggested that legislation disproportionately burdening the poor raised serious constitutional questions.

Breedlove v. Suttles, the poll tax challenge that reached the Court in 1937, did not even raise the race issue. Breedlove was an indigent white male from Georgia, who challenged the poll tax as arbitrary under the equal protection clause of the Fourteenth Amendment because it applied only to those aged twenty-one to sixty. The Court did not take such challenges to age discrimination seriously until the 1970s, and even then it rejected them. *Breedlove* said nothing about the racial motivation or racial impact of the poll tax. Only after another thirty years of New Deal policies and a presidentially declared War on Poverty would the Court in 1966 invalidate the poll tax as unfair to the poor.

Only three southern states had abolished the poll tax on their own before *Breedlove*: North Carolina (1920), Louisiana (1934), and Florida (1937). In those states, proponents of repeal had emphasized class and downplayed race, and the number of black voters did not increase appreciably after the tax was abolished. The national crusade against the poll tax, led by New Dealers seeking to enfranchise their natural political allies, did not commence

until a year or two after *Breedlove*. President Roosevelt criticized the tax as outmoded in September 1938, and the liberal Southern Conference for Human Welfare called for its repeal at its inaugural conference two months later. The House of Representatives did not pass the first of its five anti–poll tax bills until 1942. For the justices to have invalidated the tax in 1937 would have placed them in the vanguard of a movement for social reform—a position they have rarely occupied.

The Grandfather Clause—Again

In 1934 I. W. Lane tried to register to vote in Wagoner County, Oklahoma, where only a few of the seven thousand black residents were registered. Lane was rejected because he had missed the twelve-day registration window established in 1916 under the law adopted after *Guinn* to grandfather the grandfather clause. In 1939 the Supreme Court in *Lane v. Wilson* invalidated this transparent evasion of its earlier ruling.

On the merits, *Lane* was easy. If the grandfather clause was unconstitutional, then Oklahoma had no legitimate interest in grandfathering its effects. The only debatable legal issue in *Lane* was whether litigants were required to exhaust state court challenges before suing in federal court. Lower federal courts had rejected Lane's lawsuit partly on this ground, and an important Fifth Circuit ruling in 1933 had imposed a similar exhaustion requirement. The *Lane* decision rejected this approach, ruling that federal litigants need exhaust only their state *administrative* remedies, not *judicial* ones. Noting that times had changed, the NAACP observed in its July 1939 issue of *Crisis* that the Supreme Court now resolved cases involving the rights of blacks "without hairsplitting technicalities."

Lane had little effect on black voting. Despite the 1916 statute, blacks had been permitted to register and vote in most Oklahoma counties. Whites in Oklahoma had a more tolerant view of black suffrage than did whites in most of the South. Oklahoma had a thriving two-party political system, and blacks made up only 7 percent of the population. Moreover, because Oklahoma's grandfathering statute was unique, *Lane* had no direct consequences elsewhere. All it did was invalidate an outlier statute that was already generally ignored.

The Demise of the White Primary

World War II was a watershed event in the history of American race relations. The ideology of the war was antifascist and pro-democratic, and yet the United States fought with a racially segregated army. The NAACP pointed out in the April 1938 issue of the *Crisis* that "our government, raising its hands in horror over persecution on the other side of the world, might take a moment to glance at its own back yard," where it would see "Hitlerism . . . directed against citizens who happen not to be white." President Roosevelt urged Americans to "refut[e] at home the very theories which we are fighting abroad" (Wynn 1976, 45), and Justice Frank Murphy told his colleagues in his concurring opinion in *Hirabayashi v. United States* (1943) that statutory racial distinctions are "at variance with the principles for which we are now waging war."

During the war, blacks began to demand their citizenship rights more forcefully. One

white southerner observed with a sense of wonder that "it is as if some universal message had reached the great mass of Negroes, urging them to dream new dreams and to protest against the old order" (Odum 1948, 247). Southern blacks registered to vote in record numbers and demanded admission to Democratic primaries. One NAACP branch told a recalcitrant voter registrar that "you do not seem to realize that the social order [has] changed [now that] over ten thousand Negro men and women died in World War II for world democracy." [2] Weary of Jim Crow indignities, many southern blacks refused to be segregated any longer on streetcars and buses, stood their ground when challenged, and thus provoked almost daily racial altercations. Hundreds of thousands of blacks channeled their militancy into NAACP membership, which increased ninefold during the war.

Heightened black militancy occurred in a context of growing black political power. In the 1940s, over 1.5 million southern blacks, pushed by changes in southern agriculture and pulled by wartime industrial demand, migrated to northern cities. As blacks relocated from a region of nearly universal disenfranchisement to one without significant suffrage restrictions, their political power grew. The war gave blacks unprecedented political opportunities to leverage concessions from the Roosevelt administration, which was determined to avoid divisive racial protest during wartime. The prospect of a march on Washington, D.C., by 100,000 angry blacks protesting racial segregation in the military induced President Roosevelt to issue an executive order banning employment discrimination in defense industries. In 1948 the political influence of northern blacks helped to convince President Harry S. Truman to issue executive orders desegregating the military and the federal civil service.

In 1944 the Supreme Court in *Smith v. Allwright* overruled *Grovey* and invalidated the white primary when adopted by party rule *(see Document 16)*. Noting that "the party takes its character as a state agency from the duties imposed upon it by state statutes," *Smith* emphasized the many ways in which Texas regulated parties and primaries. But the Court also emphasized an apparently distinct point—that Texas could not escape responsibility by "casting its electoral processes in a form which permits a private organization to practice racial discrimination in the election." This latter language suggested that the justices might deem primaries to be state action, regardless of how state law regulated them.

The vote in *Smith* was 8–1. This shift, within the short span of nine years, from a unanimous decision sustaining white primaries to a near-unanimous ruling invalidating them is unprecedented in American constitutional history. One might attribute the turnabout to Roosevelt's nearly complete reconstitution of the Court. Only Chief Justice Harlan Fiske Stone changed his mind in the intervening years. The other justice remaining from the Court that decided *Grovey* was the author of that ruling, Justice Owen Roberts, who bitterly dissented in *Smith*.

However, to focus on judicial turnover as the explanation for *Smith* is to overlook the fundamental importance of World War II. The justices cannot have missed the contradiction between a war purportedly being fought for democratic ends and the pervasive disenfranchisement of southern blacks. With black soldiers dying on battlefields around the world, the justices must have been tempted, as the *New York Times* observed on April 5, 1944, to help put America "a little nearer to a more perfect democracy, in which there will be but one class of citizens."

Moreover, the outcome in *Smith* probably reflected national public opinion. A Gallup poll conducted in the 1940s revealed that nearly 70 percent of Americans favored repealing the poll tax. Northerners had little reason to feel differently about white primaries and poll taxes, both of which restricted suffrage in only seven or eight southern states by the mid-1940s. Indeed, these polls showed that a clear majority of *southern* whites favored abolishing the poll tax.

Smith did not definitively resolve the white primary issue. To the extent that the decision turned on the extensive regulation of parties and primaries by the state of Texas, deregulation was a natural response. Within two weeks, the governor of South Carolina, Olin T. Johnston, had convened a special legislative session to repeal all 150 state statutes regulating parties. Other Deep South states watched and waited to see how the courts would respond.

In *Elmore v. Rice* (1947), Federal District Judge J. Waties Waring invalidated the exclusion of blacks from Democratic primaries in South Carolina, notwithstanding the legislature's efforts at political deregulation. Waring emphasized the determinative nature of Democratic primaries in South Carolina—in seven of the last eight presidential elections Republican candidates had won less than 5 percent of the vote—and the extent to which state law had previously regulated political parties. He called "pure sophistry" the notion that legislative deregulation had altered political realities. Waring also denied that "the skies [would] fall," as predicted, if Democrats permitted blacks to participate in their primaries. The Fourth Circuit Court of Appeals affirmed Waring in a less flamboyant opinion. Probably delighted to have southern judges running interference on a sensitive racial issue, the justices denied review.

One last iteration of the white primary remained for the Court's consideration, *Terry v. Adams* (1953). In Fort Bend County, Texas, the Jaybird Democratic Association had been excluding blacks from its pre-primary selection of candidates since 1889. The association, whose membership consisted of all whites residing in the county, selected candidates who invariably became the Democratic nominees and then were elected to office. Though the Jaybirds were not created to circumvent *Smith* and *Elmore*, it is easy to imagine much of the South following suit had the Court sustained this scheme. At the conference on *Terry,* Justice Harold Burton warned, "If this is approved it will be seized upon." [3]

The difficulty for the justices, though, was that finding state action in the Jaybirds' scheme risked eliminating protection for private political association, which many justices believed the First Amendment guaranteed. In *Terry,* they were being asked to forbid discrimination by a political club that state law did not regulate. Would they next be asked to prohibit individuals from mobilizing their friends in support of candidates who espoused white supremacy? At the conference, Justice Robert Jackson expressed concern that the "people have some rights" to political affiliation.[4]

The conflict felt by the justices is apparent in *Terry*'s seesaw history and its poorly reasoned opinions. The initial conference vote was 5–4 to *reject* the constitutional challenge on the ground that state action was absent. A second vote was 4–4, with Justice Felix Frankfurter passing. He then changed his vote without explanation, thereby creating a 5–4 majority to invalidate the Jaybirds' scheme. But four justices—Fred Vinson, Stanley Reed, Sherman Minton, and Robert Jackson—remained slated to dissent, and Jackson actually drafted an opinion that lambasted his colleagues for sacrificing "sound principle[s] of interpretation" in their haste to enter the "hateful little local scheme." [5] Yet, when *Terry* was announced, only Minton dissented.

None of the three opinions for the majority in *Terry* is convincing. Justice Hugo Black's plurality opinion and Justice Tom Clark's concurrence emphasize two points. First, Texas was responsible for establishing an electoral system in which private discriminatory groups could control the results. Second, the Jaybirds had won every election in Fort Bend County for the past half-century. Yet under these criteria, virtually any political result disfavoring blacks could have been ruled unconstitutional. For example, a legislature's choice to apportion seats on a geographic rather than a proportional basis often disadvantages minority groups. There is little chance that this Court would have invalidated geographic districting, yet using the analyses of Black and Clark it is not clear why: the state chose the method of apportionment, and its consistent effect was to reduce the political influence of blacks.

Frankfurter's concurring opinion in *Terry* is even less persuasive. He insisted that the participation of county officials, albeit as private citizens, in the selection of Jaybird candidates constituted state action. This reasoning is hard to follow. Did Frankfurter mean that the attendance of a public official at a private dinner excluding blacks was unconstitutional? His rationale in *Terry* would suggest so, but this result seems inconceivable.

No one in the *Terry* majority convincingly responded to Minton's dissent. The Jaybirds' scheme may have been "unworthy," Minton noted, but to condemn it required expanding state action to include private behavior that, one could argue, was entitled to First Amendment protection. Minton acidly observed in a note to Jackson, "When the Jaybird opinion comes down, there may be some question as to which election returns the Court follows! It will be damn clear they aren't following any law" (Tushnet 1994, 112).

The Consequences

In 1940 just 3 percent of southern black adults were registered to vote, but by 1952, 20 percent were registered *(see Document 21 for data on black voter registration in the South for this period)*. The most rapid transformation occurred in Georgia, where black voter registration increased from roughly 20,000 in 1940 to 125,000 in 1947. The number of registered black voters in Louisiana increased from 8,000 to 43,000 within an eight-month period in 1948 and then rose to 107,000 by 1952. In Florida, roughly 20,000 black voters were registered in 1944, 49,000 in 1947, and 116,000 in 1950. Even in Mississippi, where white resistance to black suffrage remained intense,

black voter registration increased from 2,500 in 1946 to 20,000 in 1950.

Southern blacks put to good use their newly secured suffrage rights, extracting concessions from increasingly responsive local governments. Protection against police brutality was a top priority for many blacks, and after the war dozens of southern cities hired their first black police officers since Reconstruction. Southern cities also began to provide black communities with better public services and recreational facilities, and some counties began to appoint black voter registrars for black precincts. By 1950 black candidates were running for office in cities of the peripheral South and occasionally winning.

That *Smith* had such a dramatic effect on black voter registration while lower-court decisions invalidating white primaries in Virginia and Florida in the early 1930s did not suggests the importance of changing social and political conditions. One significant factor was the greater acceptance of black voting by southern whites. A white Democrat in South Carolina wrote to Thurgood Marshall to distance himself from his party's efforts to exclude blacks, which "profane[d] the Bill of Rights." [6] A white Democrat in Alabama criticized her party's proscription of blacks as a "cruel and shameful thing." [7] Progressive white southerners appreciated that black enfranchisement would probably benefit economically populist and racially moderate politicians, such as Democratic governors Earl Long of Louisiana and James "Big Jim" Folsom of Alabama, both of whom actively encouraged the surge in black voter registration that followed *Smith*.

Another change in circumstance that enhanced *Smith*'s efficacy was the greater capacity of southern blacks to capitalize on it. The Court's ruling encouraged southern blacks to register to vote and to demand access to Democratic Party primaries. Thousands of returning black veterans took their military service release papers, which entitled them to exemption from the poll tax, and went directly to city hall to demand registration. Southern blacks established progressive voters' leagues, which organized registration campaigns and conducted voter education classes.

The greater militancy of southern blacks was apparent in the proliferation of lawsuits that challenged the continuing exclusion of blacks from Democratic primaries in recalcitrant locales. The NAACP favored deferring civil suits until the Justice Department had decided whether to criminally prosecute violations of *Smith*. Yet before the association's national office could communicate its preferences, the branch in Columbus, Georgia, had already gone too far down the litigation path to change course; the branch president explained that "the people demanded that we continue the case." [8] The branch in Jackson, Mississippi, was also reluctant to postpone litigation, because many members "are becoming impatient . . . and we are anxious to try to do something." [9]

The proliferation of NAACP branches in the South and the rising economic status of southern blacks—further consequences of the war—facilitated an increase in litigation. NAACP membership grew from roughly 50,000 in 1940 to 450,000 in 1946, and the number of branches rose from 355 to 1,073. More branches meant more communities able to support litigation. Increased membership also translated into larger budgets for the na-

tional office, which was finally able to hire several lawyers to supplement Thurgood Marshall's herculean efforts.

Threats of litigation supplied government and party officials with direct incentives to comply with the Constitution. Although most of them probably opposed black suffrage, they were not willing to incur personal liability by illegally obstructing it. After Judge Waring invalidated efforts by South Carolina Democrats to evade *Smith* and threatened them with contempt, 35,000 blacks were quickly registered. In Washington Parish, Louisiana, blacks were denied registration until they formed an NAACP branch and filed suit before a sympathetic judge, J. Skelly Wright, who enjoined the registrar from further discrimination. As a result, Washington Parish registered its first black voter in 1950, and blacks in several other parishes filed suits that induced registrars to enroll them.

By the mid-1940s, recalcitrant officials also had to worry about the prospect of criminal prosecution. One important consequence of the growing political power of northern blacks was that the Justice Department became more solicitous of the voting rights of southern blacks. NAACP lawyers bombarded the Justice Department with affidavits from southern blacks that attested to persistent voting rights violations and demanded federal prosecutions. An NAACP officer in Birmingham bragged that he was sending "a bag of evidence almost daily" to the department.[10]

Even if the department failed to prosecute, it launched investigations and dispatched agents of the Federal Bureau of Investigation (FBI) to southern communities to gather evidence. Such tactics gave southern officials who might be contemplating interference with blacks' voting rights food for thought. Birmingham lawyer Arthur Shores reported that the U.S. attorney's visit to the board of registrars "had a very wholesome effect on helping us get . . . a large number [of black voters] registered." [11] Harry T. Moore, founder of the Florida Progressive Voters' League, believed that a federal investigation of the incident in Greensboro, Florida, in which two black brothers were attacked and then run out of town in retaliation for their registration activities would have "a healthy effect in all of those counties, where Negroes have been kept from the polls through intimidation." [12] One of the brothers reported that the appearance of the FBI in Greensboro had the "crackers . . . looking very sick." [13]

Even apart from this greater federal presence, the South was safer for blacks by the mid-1940s than it had been a decade earlier— a change that contributed to the greater aggressiveness with which blacks pursued enforcement of their constitutional rights. Election riots in Ocoee, Florida, in 1920 had led to the death of as many as thirty blacks, and witnesses to the slaughter were afraid to testify before an investigating committee in Washington, D.C. By contrast, hundreds of blacks flocked to Senate committee hearings that investigated Sen. Theodore Bilbo's incitement of Mississippi whites to violence in the 1946 Senate primary—hearings that took place not in the relative safety of Washington, D.C., but in Jackson, Mississippi. By the mid-1940s, the Ku Klux Klan, which was defending itself from state efforts to revoke its charter and from federal efforts to prosecute its leaders for tax evasion, was no longer in a position to intimidate many black voters. Though the Deep

South remained dangerous for blacks intent on exercising their rights, the degree of danger had decreased somewhat, thereby enabling blacks generally to exercise their rights without endangering their lives.

Another important factor in the increased black voter registration of the 1940s was the generous interpretations of *Smith* and the Fifteenth Amendment offered by lower-court judges. In the 1930s, southern judges rejected voting rights claims on technicalities and were willfully blind to the racially discriminatory administration of racially neutral voter qualifications. Postwar judges proved much more supportive of blacks' voting rights.

Smith did not necessarily invalidate all white primaries, because the decision relied on the way that Texas law treated parties, and primaries, and other states regulated differently. For example, Texas required parties to conduct primaries, but Georgia did not. More important, to the extent that *Smith* turned on the fact that Texas regulated political parties, it might be possible to avoid the ruling by repealing all such regulations, which is precisely what South Carolina did after *Smith*.

Lower courts generally invalidated such evasions. The Fifth Circuit Court of Appeals affirmed a district court ruling that rejected proffered distinctions between the white primaries of Georgia and Texas, and the Florida Supreme Court issued a similar decision. Meanwhile, as noted earlier, Judge Waring sternly rejected South Carolina's effort to evade *Smith* by deregulating the Democratic Party, and the Fourth Circuit Court of Appeals affirmed that decision. These and other lower-court decisions required expansive interpretations of *Smith*.

In the wake of *Smith,* some southern states continued to try to obstruct black voter registration. For example, in 1946 Alabama voters adopted the Boswell amendment, which required registrants to "understand and explain" a constitutional provision, not just to read it, and also required them to "understand the duties and obligations of good citizenship." Amendment supporters did not disguise their intention to confer broad discretion on registrars with which to preserve white political supremacy.

Voter registrars often devised their own stratagems for obstructing black suffrage. Some registration boards closed to prevent black enrollment, and others registered voters at undisclosed times in secret locations, contrary to statutory requirements. Whites discovered through word of mouth where and when to show up to register, while blacks were kept in the dark. Registrars required blacks to fill out their own forms and flunked them for trivial errors, while filling out whites' forms for them. Blacks but not whites were asked to recite from memory the entire U.S. Constitution. Some registrars did not even make a pretense of legality. They simply informed blacks that they could not register regardless of their qualifications.

For the first time ever, southern judges ruled such behavior unconstitutional. A three-judge federal court invalidated the Boswell amendment. Other southern judges also enjoined registrars from discriminating, suspending the customary presumption that public officials had fulfilled their duties in good faith. When registrars in roughly thirty Georgia counties began purging black voters at the behest of a former governor, a federal judge quickly enjoined them.

As one astute commentator observed, the judges in these decisions adopted "broad and discerning" rather than "narrow and literal" interpretations of the law as they rejected repeated efforts of white southerners "to find the magic combination of ambiguous wording, legalisms and technicalities which will allow them to make possible the impossible" (*New South* 1949, 1, 4). Moreover, not all of these judges shared the relatively progressive racial views of a Judge Waring; by the late 1940s even some less egalitarian jurists were willing to interpret the law to protect black suffrage.

None of the conditions that enabled *Smith* to be efficacious—greater white acceptance of black voting, heightened black militancy in demanding rights, the greater physical security of southern blacks, the NAACP's broader presence, the increased threat of federal prosecution of rights violators, and the expansiveness of lower-court interpretations of black suffrage rights—was itself a product simply of *Smith.* Thus, although *Smith* may have been critical to mobilizing black voter registration in the South, it probably would have been inefficacious in the absence of supportive social and political conditions.

Limitations

The *Smith* decision did inspire blacks to register and to vote, but it also mobilized opposition among southern whites, many of whom warned that elimination of the white primary would jeopardize segregation and racial purity. The most virulent political backlash against *Smith* came in Georgia, Mississippi, and South Carolina—the states with the highest percentages of blacks. In Georgia, Eugene Talmadge ran for governor in 1946 on a platform of reinstating the white primary and keeping blacks "in their place." He and his supporters raged against "Negro lovers" in the Supreme Court (Brooks 2000, 585, 586), and Talmadge himself warned that if blacks were permitted to vote in Democratic primaries, politicians would have to "kiss their babies if [they] want to be elected," and "our pretty white children will be going to school with Negroes" (Sullivan 1996, 211).

In South Carolina, a few days after the *Smith* ruling Democratic senator Burnet Maybank warned that white southerners "will not accept these interferences" and that "we of the South will maintain our political and social institutions as we believe to be in the best interest of our people" (quoted in the *New York Times,* April 14, 1944). Gov. Olin Johnston called the legislature into special session a few days later. Proclaiming that "history has taught us that we must keep our white democratic primaries pure and unadulterated," he urged the repeal of all state laws that regulated parties in the hope that such a step would remove judicial objections to the white primary. Should such deregulation prove unavailing, though, Johnston warned that "we South Carolinians will use the necessary methods to retain white supremacy in all primaries and to safeguard the homes and happiness of our people." He concluded by declaring that "white supremacy will be maintained in our primaries. Let the chips fall where they may." [14]

In Mississippi, Democratic senator Theodore Bilbo ran for reelection in 1946 invoking the specter of "Negro domination" in a state that had just ceased having a black majority. In a widely reported speech, Bilbo exhorted every "red blooded white man to use any means to keep the Niggers away from the polls." Declining to explicitly advocate violence, he slyly observed that "you and I know what's the best way to keep the Nigger from voting. You do it the night before the election. I don't have to tell you any more than that. Red blooded men know what I mean" (Dittmer 1994, 2).

Throughout Mississippi, enthusiastic supporters took the senator at his word. They burned crosses in Jackson. In Biloxi, a street sign warned blacks to "vote at your own risk." In Pucket, four whites beat and threatened to kill a black man for attempting to register. Whites brandishing pistols repulsed several black veterans from the polls, including Medgar Evers, who later became the NAACP's chief organizer in the state.

The backlash against *Smith* generated a counterbacklash. Mississippi Democrats could threaten and beat black voters without serious consequences in 1875 or even 1935, but that was no longer true by 1945. Bilbo's thinly veiled exhortations to violence left the U.S. Senate with little choice but to conduct investigative hearings that educated northerners and motivated Mississippi blacks. The *Washington Post* declared on December 6, 1946, that it was impossible to read the committee report without "a sense of sickness" at the brutality. Roughly 150 Mississippi blacks—many of them war veterans and some displaying their good-conduct medals—volunteered to testify at committee hearings in Jackson about the violence they had endured while attempting to vote. The year after the hearings, black voter registration in Mississippi rose by 50 percent.

Not only did *Smith* generate a political backlash in the Deep South, but it was also far less effective at increasing black voter registration in rural areas than in cities. Although an estimated 22,000 blacks had registered to vote in Atlanta by 1946, in dozens of Deep South counties, many of them with black majorities, not a single black person was registered. Black voter registration in Louisiana rose from 8,000 to 43,000 in 1948, but roughly 50 percent of registered blacks lived in New Orleans, and in half of the state's sixty-four parishes not a single black person voted. By 1948 well over 100,000 blacks were registered in Georgia and 150,000–200,000 in Texas, whereas black voter registration in Mississippi and Alabama was limited to a paltry 3,000 and 8,000, respectively.

The threat and reality of physical violence remained a formidable obstacle to black voting in rural areas. Although the South was less dangerous for blacks than it had been even a decade earlier, it was still violent. Blacks seeking to register in rural parts of Florida faced intimidation from the Ku Klux Klan, letters warning those who dared to vote that they would "be floating up and down the river." [15] When war veteran Etoy Fletcher tried to register in rural Mississippi in 1946, the registrar informed him that "niggers are not allowed to vote in Rankin County, and if you don't want to get into serious trouble, get out of this building." [16] While waiting for a bus out of town, Fletcher was assaulted by four whites who drove him several miles into the woods, beat him severely, and warned him that he would be killed if he ever again attempted to vote.

In 1946 in Montgomery County, Georgia, D. V. Carter organized an NAACP branch that consisted mainly of farmers and sharecroppers and was principally devoted to voter registra-

tion. Several hundred blacks registered as a result. After ignoring repeated Klan warnings to desist, Carter was severely beaten in 1948. Isaac Nixon, whom Carter had persuaded to vote, was murdered. An all-white jury acquitted the two whites who killed him.

Although the Justice Department was more attentive to NAACP concerns by the late 1940s, it remained reluctant to prosecute officials who obstructed black voting. Democratic administrations in Washington had political incentives not to prosecute southern Democrats. Federal prosecutors in the South, especially those who were ambitious for elective office, were also unenthusiastic about pursuing such cases. Even for those who were willing, these were difficult cases to win. Witnesses were hard to locate, and white jurors generally would not convict officials for adhering to traditional mores rejecting black suffrage. Thus NAACP pressure on the Justice Department to prosecute proved unavailing, and empty threats of federal prosecution proved inadequate to deter those southern whites who were most committed to obstructing black suffrage through force and fraud.

Blacks would not vote in large numbers in rural parts of the Deep South until after further interventions by the Court and, more important, by Congress and the president—developments that mainly did not take place until the 1960s. Only the federal executive could secure the physical safety of southern black voters. Only Congress could shift the burden of litigating suffrage cases from individual blacks to the federal government, empowering the attorney general to seek injunctions against registrars who practiced race discrimination—a remedy that also had the advantage of avoiding southern (white) juries. More important, only Congress could replace local registrars with federal officials where necessary to secure black voter registration. In 1966 the Supreme Court finally invalidated poll taxes in the few southern states that continued to use them as a restriction on the suffrage. Yet because the Court as late as 1959 continued to reject constitutional challenges to literacy tests, further congressional intervention was necessary to eliminate that substantial barrier to black suffrage.

Notes

1. Reported in the December 1911 issue of the *Crisis,* the journal of the National Association for the Advancement of Colored People.
2. G. M. Johnson to Nora Windon, August 18, 1948, NAACP Papers, microfilm collection, part 4, reel 8, frame 592.
3. Burton conference notes, *Terry v. Adams,* January 17, 1953, Box 244, Burton Papers, Library of Congress.
4. Ibid.
5. Jackson draft dissent, *Terry v. Adams,* pp. 1, 9, Box 179, Jackson Papers, Library of Congress.
6. John M. Lofton Jr. to Thurgood Marshall, undated, NAACP Papers, part 4, reel 9, frame 957.
7. Dorothy Q. Rainey to J. Lon Duckworth, June 20, 1944, NAACP Papers, part 4, reel 7, frames 592–593.
8. W. M. Thomas to Thurgood Marshall, August 28, 1944, NAACP Papers, part 4, reel 8, frame 90.
9. J. Wesley Dixon to Thurgood Marshall, NAACP Papers, August 28, 1944, part 4, reel 7, frame 420.
10. Emory O. Jackson to Thurgood Marshall, February 16, 1945, NAACP Papers, part 4, reel 6, frame 131.
11. Arthur Shores to Thurgood Marshall, September 16, 1939, NAACP Papers, part 4, reel 3, frame 182.
12. Harry T. Moore to Thurgood Marshall, July 12, 1948, NAACP Papers, part 4, reel 6, frame 791.

13. J. T. Smith to NAACP, August 20, 1948, NAACP Papers, part 4, reel 6, frame 798.
14. Olin T. Johnston, speech to Joint Assembly and General Assembly of South Carolina, April 14, 1944, NAACP Papers, part 4, reel 10, frames 481–482.
15. Anonymous letter from Milton, Florida, to NAACP, April 14, 1948, NAACP Papers, part 4, reel 6, frame 936.
16. Etoy Fletcher, affidavit, June 15, 1946, NAACP Papers, part 4, reel 8, frame 894.

References

Brooks, Jennifer E. 2000. "Winning the Peace: Georgia Veterans and the Struggle to Define the Political Legacy of World War II." *Journal of Southern History* 66 (August): 563–604.

Buck, Paul H. 1937. *The Road to Reunion, 1865–1900.* Boston: Little, Brown.

Dittmer, John. 1994. *Local People: The Struggle for Civil Rights in Mississippi.* Urbana: University of Illinois Press.

Eaton, Amasa M. 1899. "The Suffrage Clause in the New Constitution of Louisiana." *Harvard Law Review* 13 (December): 278–293.

Gillette, William. 1965. *Right to Vote: Politics and the Passage of the Fifteenth Amendment.* Baltimore: Johns Hopkins University Press.

Hine, Darlene Clark. 1979. *Black Victory: The Rise and Fall of the White Primary in Texas.* Millwood, N.Y.: KTO Press.

Keyssar, Alexander. 2000. *The Right to Vote: The Contested History of Democracy in the United States.* New York: Basic Books.

Klarman, Michael J. 2004. *From Jim Crow to Civil Rights: The Supreme Court and the Struggle for Racial Equality.* New York: Oxford University Press.

Kousser, J. Morgan. 1974. *The Shaping of Southern Politics: Suffrage Restriction and the Establishment of the One-Party South, 1880–1910.* New Haven, Conn.: Yale University Press.

Lewinson, Paul. 1932. *Race, Class, and Party: A History of Negro Suffrage and White Politics in the South.* London: Oxford University Press.

Litwack, Leon. 1998. *Trouble in Mind: Black Southerners in the Age of Jim Crow.* New York: Vintage Books.

Mabry, William Alexander. 1936. "Louisiana Politics and the 'Grandfather Clause.' " *North Carolina Historical Review* 13 (October): 290–310.

Monnet, Julian C. 1912. "The Latest Phase of Negro Disfranchisement." *Harvard Law Review* 26 (November): 42–63.

New South. 1949. "The Right to Vote." 4 (February).

Odum, Howard W. 1948. "Social Change in the South." In *The Southern Political Scene, 1938–1948*, edited by Taylor Cole and John H. Hallowell. Gainesville, Fla.: Journal of Politics.

Perman, Michael. 2001. *Struggle for Mastery: Disfranchisement in the South, 1888–1908*. Chapel Hill: University of North Carolina Press.

Schmidt, Benno C., Jr. 1982. "Principle and Prejudice: The Supreme Court and Race in the Progressive Era. Part 3: Black Disfranchisement from the KKK to the Grandfather Clause." *Columbia Law Review* 82 (June): 835–905.

Sullivan, Patricia. 1996. *Days of Hope: Race and Democracy in the New Deal Era*. Chapel Hill: University of North Carolina Press.

Tushnet, Mark V. 1994. *Making Civil Rights Law: Thurgood Marshall and the Supreme Court, 1936–1961*. New York: Oxford University Press.

Wang, Xi. 1997. *The Trial of Democracy: Black Suffrage and Northern Republicans, 1860–1910*. Athens: University of Georgia Press.

Wynn, Neil A. 1976. *The Afro-American and the Second World War*. New York: Holmes and Meier Publishers.

4

Rebuilding Black Voting Rights before the Voting Rights Act

Paula D. McClain,
Michael C. Brady, Niambi M.
Carter, Efrén O. Pérez, and
Victoria M. DeFrancesco Soto

The eminent historian Rayford W. Logan in his 1954 book, *The Negro in American Life and Thought: The Nadir, 1877–1901*, refers to the last decade of the nineteenth century and beginning of the twentieth century as the *nadir* (lowest point) of African American political life in the United States (Logan 1954, 52). Even before Reconstruction was officially ended with the Compromise of 1877, which allowed the South to regain its independence with the removal of federal troops and freed the region to handle the "Negro problem" as it saw fit, many southern states were acting to prevent the full participation of the newly freed blacks. By the end of the nineteenth century white rule had been reestablished in the entire South (Logan 1954, 21).

In his book, Logan laments that many blacks, particularly Booker T. Washington in his 1895 "Atlanta Exposition Speech," were willing to participate in the effort to keep blacks second-class citizens by abdicating the fight for equal and full rights as American citizens. Recalling the Supreme Court's declaration in *Plessy v. Ferguson* in 1896 that "separate but equal" treatment of whites and blacks was constitutional, Logan offers a poignant summary of the situation for black Americans

at that time: "At the beginning of the twentieth century, what is now called second-class citizenship for Negroes was accepted by Presidents, the Supreme Court, Congress, organized labor, the majority of Americans, North and South, and by the 'leader' of the Negro race [Booker T. Washington]. One is tempted to refer to this quarter of a century as 'The Dark Ages of Recent American History' " (Logan 1954, ix).

The symbolic end of black representation in the American political system came in January 1901, when the last black member of the U.S. House of Representatives, George H. White of North Carolina, left office. North Carolina, like all other southern states, had passed a constitutional amendment disqualifying virtually all blacks from voting. In his farewell speech to Congress *(Document 8)*, White summed up the political situation for blacks: "This, Mr. Chairman, is perhaps the Negroes' temporary farewell to the American Congress; but let me say, Phoenix-like he will rise up some day and come again. These parting words are in behalf of an outraged, heart-broken, bruised and bleeding, but God-fearing people, faithful, industrious, loyal, rising-people—full of potential force" (Logan 1954, 92).

Historians of African American history have not reached a consensus on when blacks began to emerge from the *nadir*. For W. E. B. DuBois, the first meeting of the Niagara Movement in 1905 in Niagara Falls, Canada, was the beginning of the emergence, yet for John Hope Franklin what he calls "The Long Dark Night" continued into the 1920s (Logan 1965, 11). Others have associated the emergence with the founding of the National Association for the Advancement of Colored People (NAACP) in 1909 and the National Urban League in 1911. For still others, it was the death of Booker T. Washington in 1915 (Logan 1965, 11). Whatever the exact date, the early years of the twentieth century, particularly the years leading up to World War I, saw a flurry of increased political activity among black Americans, despite the legal barriers put in place to keep them from becoming full citizens of the United States and participating in politics.

This chapter highlights some of the activities aimed at regaining black voting rights, from the early years of the twentieth century to the passage of the Voting Rights Act of 1965. The chapter first examines the elements that provided the wherewithal for blacks to fight for voting rights in the face of almost total legal disenfranchisement—that is, it looks at the black social networks that led to the development of black social capital. It then examines the role of the NAACP, which went to the courts during this period to challenge blacks' legal disenfranchisement. World War II provided an opening, albeit a small one, for moving black voting rights forward, and the role of returning black World War II veterans is highlighted in the next section. Finally, the chapter looks at the role of citizenship schools in the

struggle to gain voting rights. The organized activities, such as Freedom Vote and Freedom Summer, that grew out of these schools are discussed in the section that follows.

Black Social Networks and Social Capital

One principal resource that was central to African Americans' struggle to regain the vote was the black social networks that led, in turn, to the development of black social capital. Social capital consists of social structures that facilitate collective action. Robert D. Putnam (1993, 167) has described social capital as the "features of social organizations, such as trust, norms, and networks that can improve the efficiency of society by facilitating coordinated actions." At its core, the capital garnered through networks, at either the individual or the collective level, allows people to work toward resolving the dilemmas of collective action. Social capital increases the availability of information, while lowering the costs of gathering the information needed to act collectively. It requires favorable circumstances and individuals willing to invest in the structure of relationships, if a social network is not in place to fill that function.

Social capital exists at several levels—micro, meso, and macro. At the micro level, horizontal networks, such as racially homogeneous organizations, serve a "bonding" function. At the meso level, horizontal and vertical relations exist among groups, such as regional associations, that serve a "bridging" function. National institutions come into play at the macro level (Grootaert and van Bastelaer 2002). In the pre–civil rights era, bonding social capital was crucial. Because blacks were unable to rely on white institutions, they had to form their own organizations, businesses, and other institutions to meet their most basic needs.

Among the first elements of the development of black social capital was the establishment of mutual aid or mutual benefit societies to address the needs of the various black communities (Fay 1999, 1373). After the Civil War, mutual benefit societies flourished, particularly in the South. They provided social welfare services, ranging from health care to burial to scholarships. These societies represented significant bonding of social capital in many black communities. For example, in 1910 the total membership of various mutual benefit societies in Mississippi was more than eight thousand.

Another element of black social capital was the founding of black educational institutions. Among the earliest was an academy for girls in Washington, D.C.; the Miner's School, also known as the School for Colored Girls, opened its doors in 1851.[1] The first colleges established for blacks were the Institute for Colored Youth (now Cheney University in Pennsylvania) in 1837, Ashmum Institute (now Lincoln University in Pennsylvania) in 1854, and Wilberforce University in Ohio in 1855 (Franklin 1967, 231).

Black fraternal organizations, starting with freemasonry, were significant players in the quest for black equality in American society and central to the development of black social capital. Fraternal organizations are "self-selecting brotherhoods and associated female groups—and sometimes gender integrated brotherhoods and sisterhoods" (Skocpol and Oser 2004, 370). These organizations were devised in the late eighteenth century and continued to flourish into the twentieth century.

Although they often seemed to mirror the white fraternal organizations that barred their membership, that resemblance was generally in name only, because black fraternal organizations were self-consciously concerned with the uplift and survival of their community (Beito 2000; Trotter 2004). These organizations offered blacks a space for organizing free of white surveillance. In fact, fraternal organizations remained a prominent feature of black life "not only in the transition from slavery to freedom, but also from farm to factory and from the South to the urban North and West" (Trotter 2004, 362).

Black churches also played an important role in the development of black social capital (see Calhoun-Brown 2000 for a good summary and introduction to the classic references). Their contributions took several forms. First, black churches were natural venues for gatherings of local black residents to discuss issues. Local and national leaders as well as larger organizations could rely on these churches as a means of gaining access to black residents. Consequently, black churches served as focal points for grassroots mobilization and for passing on information about the movement to regain voting rights. They also provided blacks with the space and opportunity to develop skills, especially political mobilization, that could then be transferred to the political arena (Verba, Schlozman, and Brady 1995).

Second, black churches were active voices in civil rights protests and decision making, especially in the earliest parts of the campaign against the "Jim Crow" laws enacted to enforce racial discrimination—that is, during that period before secular groups and spokesmen gained a foothold. Because black ministers and clergy were not economically dependent on the white community, they were especially fitted to take leadership roles in voting reform movements both locally and nationally. This independence gave church leaders more freedom to discuss controversial topics.

Finally, black churches have been credited with providing the moral basis for the nonviolent approach to the civil rights movement. During this period, many of the clerical leaders of the movement were able to weave theology into their approaches, contributing to a more peaceful protest methodology (Findlay 1990; Calhoun-Brown 2000).

Although the centrality of the black church as a great galvanizing force in the black community is unquestioned (Dawson 1994; Raboteau 1999), fraternal organizations were pivotal to blacks' quest for greater equality in the American sociopolitical system. In fact, black fraternal orders offered some of the earliest successful resistance to the Jim Crow laws. Through one Supreme Court case in 1912, *Creswill v. Grand Lodge,* and one in 1929, *Ancient Egyptian Arabic Order of Nobles of Mystic Shrine v. Michaux,* black fraternal orders were able to give the larger community both real and symbolic victories over white supremacy (Liazos and Ganz 2004). These early cases on behalf of black fraternal orders allowed their attorneys, some of whom went on to work for the NAACP, to hone the skills that would be pivotal to the legal attack the NAACP would later launch against the Jim Crow laws (Liazos and Ganz 2004).

An integral player in the struggle for voting rights was the black business community, whose role went far beyond monetary support. Through their work in service to black people,

its members were able to carry the message of voting rights to a broad swath of the black community (Gill 2004). In doing so, they became attractive and necessary allies of the early voting rights movement. For example, beauty industry professionals, who by virtue of their trade were able to relate the message of civil rights to the masses of black people, were often pursued by those working for this cause (Gill 2004).[2] Moreover, because the services industry was segregated, black entrepreneurs generally served a racially homogeneous clientele, which gave them relative financial independence from the white community (Weare 1973; Weems 1996; Walker 1998; Willett 2000) and left them free to organize in service to the race with few, if any, financial repercussions from the white community (Gill 2004).

Many of these entrepreneurs also had the ability to organize, which was integral to their profession (Whitaker 2003, 166). In fact, the "organizing efforts and fund-raising capabilities" that many black women learned from their employment served as the foundation for many of the activities of the civil rights movement (Whitaker 2003; Gill 2004). Despite its much nuanced history, then, the black business community was an extraordinary partner in the struggle for black voting rights (Silverman 1998; Walker 1998). Its members felt they had an obligation to their community that superseded their profit margin. The irony is that the segregation that they were trying to dismantle was the very thing that enabled them to achieve greater political incorporation.

As for the role of women in efforts to build black social capital, it was not just limited to that of black women entrepreneurs. As early as the eighteenth century, black women began forming their own organizations to work in their behalf. They also began to work on the issue of black suffrage. Moving into the twentieth century, black women quickly realized that despite white women's use of the universal term *women,* white women's organizations were not interested in working in behalf of the needs of black women. This dynamic was particularly present in the push for voting rights for women.

Black women had been involved in the suffrage movement from its earliest days, beginning with the Seneca Falls meeting of 1848. Black women and men, such as Sojourner Truth and Frederick Douglass, were active participants in the movement, and their presence grew as the movement progressed (Collier-Thomas 1997; Terborg-Penn 1998). Blacks' involvement in the women's rights movement, however, was more about universal suffrage than about enfranchising women. Ratification of the Fourteenth and Fifteenth Amendments *(Documents 2 and 3)* in 1868 and 1870, respectively, created problems for black women's involvement in the suffrage movement. The Fifteenth Amendment extended the franchise to black men, and leaders of the women's suffrage movement, particularly Susan B. Anthony and Elizabeth Cady Stanton, were offended that former black male slaves were given the right to vote before white women (DuBois 1978). As a result, Anthony and Stanton tolerated antiblack rhetoric and permitted alliances with those actively seeking to disenfranchise black people (Collier-Thomas 1997).

Black women also formed clubs and voluntary associations in order to address other issues, such as education. Largely headed by middle-class, educated women, these organizations proliferated rapidly, so that by the late 1890s their large number allowed them to come together and form, under the leadership of Mary Church Terrell, the National Association of Colored Women (NACW), the first national body of black women (Nelson 1979; Harley 1988; Williams 1990; Green 1997; Hunter 1997; Goodstein 1998; Terborg-Penn 1998; Schechter 2001; White 2001; Wolcott 2001).

Another type of organization developed by black women was the training school that focused exclusively on the betterment of black girls. These institutions cropped up all over the United States. One prominent example was the National Training School for Women and Girls in Washington, D.C., founded in 1909 by Nannie Helen Burroughs (in 1964 it was renamed the Nannie Helen Burroughs School). Burroughs recognized that black girls needed to be skilled in trades if they were going to contribute effectively to the progress of the broader black community. To this end, Burroughs concentrated her efforts not only on domestic trades, but also on various professional occupations, such as bookkeeping. Clearly, the formation of local and national organizations and educational institutions played a significant role in providing blacks with the social capital needed to fight for the right to vote during the *nadir.*

Securing the Ballot:
The NAACP Defeats the White Primary and Increases Voter Registration

In 1909 W. E. B. DuBois and other members of the Niagara Movement were invited to a conference organized by several whites interested in the problems of black Americans. The organizers were Mary White Ovington, a New York social worker; William English Walling, a prominent writer who had written about the Springfield, Illinois, race riots in 1908; and Oswald Garrison Villard, the grandson of the abolitionist William Lloyd Garrison. At the conference, which was held on Abraham Lincoln's birthday, participants made plans for the establishment of a permanent organization eventually called the National Association for the Advancement of Colored People. Those attending the conference agreed that the organization would pledge itself to working "for the abolition of all forced segregation, equal education for Negro and white children, the complete enfranchisement of the Negro, and the enforcement of the Fourteenth and Fifteenth Amendments" (Franklin 1967, 447). The formal organization was launched in May 1910.

Litigation became the primary means of formally attacking political discrimination. The leaders of the organization shared the view that the Supreme Court was capable of delivering decisions without prejudice based on the merits of the Fourteenth and Fifteenth Amendments. Consequently, the legal strategy of the NAACP in its early years was geared toward attacking the constitutionality of various discriminatory practices, such as poll taxes, literacy tests, and the white primary (Hine 1979).

The NAACP had some early success with cases such as *Guinn v. United States (see Document 13)*. In this 1915 case, the Supreme Court struck down Oklahoma's grandfather clause, which required literacy tests of anyone who could not vote prior to 1866 or was not a descendent of such a person. With passage of

the Texas white primary law in 1923, the national organization geared up to fight in collaboration with local NAACP chapters (Hine 1979; Lawson, 1999).

From the beginning, the white primary cases were linked to local efforts. During the NAACP's 1923 national meeting, the president of the El Paso, Texas, chapter raised the issue of challenging the new white primary statute, and he was told to find a plaintiff. A forty-one-year-old practicing doctor and businessman, Lawrence A. Nixon, seemed to be the perfect candidate. When he tried to vote in a primary in July 1924 but was turned away by election officials, the first white primary case, *Nixon v. Herndon,* was born. Ultimately, the Supreme Court heard the case and decided unanimously in 1927 that the 1923 Texas white primary law violated the Fourteenth Amendment, because the actions of the state denied equal protection under the law to blacks (Marshall 1957; Hine 1979; Lawson 1999).

Though the *Nixon v. Herndon* ruling was decisive, the Texas legislature attempted to circumvent it by repealing the 1923 statute and then passing in 1928 a law that empowered the executive committees of political parties to make policy on voter eligibility. Almost immediately, local NAACP chapters began challenging the new policy and searching for a good legal test case. Yet the El Paso chapter beat them to the punch by convincing the national NAACP to back another suit with Nixon as plaintiff. As before, Mr. Nixon attempted to vote in the mid-July 1928 primary and was turned away by election officials. As expected, the case *Nixon v. Condon* was eventually heard and decided by the Supreme Court. On May 2, 1932, the Court decided 5–4 in Nixon's favor. It held that a party's state executive committee was an agent of the state, as implied by the need to pass the law empowering the committee. As such, the action of the committee banning blacks from voting violated the Fourteenth Amendment (Marshall 1957; Hine 1979; Lawson 1999).

Unfortunately, the Court's decision left the door open for the continuation of white primaries by implying that the true power to set primary policy lay with a party's state convention. Three weeks after the *Nixon v. Condon* ruling, the Texas Democratic Party called a convention to ban blacks from participating in primaries. Once again, local NAACP chapters helped to file legal challenges, but they lost in the lower courts. In 1935 one case, *Grovey v. Townsend,* was heard by the Supreme Court. This time the case originated in Houston, and the plaintiff, Richard Randolph Grovey, was the prominent leader of the Third Ward Civic Club, a grassroots political organization. When the Court unanimously decided the case on April 1, 1935, it ruled against Grovey, holding that state conventions and parties were not vestiges of the state and possessed the power to decide their own membership (Marshall 1957; Hine 1979; Lawson 1999).

Although *Grovey v. Townsend* was clearly a setback, it did not last long. After the elections of 1940, more suits were filed to challenge the white primary, but few were appealed and the one that was slated to go to the Supreme Court was withdrawn. In 1943 the NAACP filed a new case, *Smith v. Allwright,* that did go before the Court *(see Document 16)*. In 1944 in an 8–1 decision, the Court held in favor of Smith and ruled, in effect, that primaries were in fact agents of the state because the state determined

the candidates on the general election ballot. Thus, by permitting policies that banned party members from participating in primaries because of their race, the parties and the state were violating the Fourteenth and Fifteenth Amendments. Although the southern parties in Texas and elsewhere did make several attempts to work around the decision, the precedent set by *Smith v. Allwright* was clear, and the white primary was defeated (Marshall 1957; Hine 1979; Lawson 1999).

The defeat of the white primary in *Smith v. Allwright* removed one of the major barriers to the franchise for blacks across the South. Yet to really make the decision count, the NAACP and other local groups had to convince blacks to register and attempt to vote as a means of pushing the issue, organizing against intimidation, and confronting the remaining vestiges of Jim Crow. While the NAACP Legal Defense and Education Fund continued to push for statutory and Justice Department intervention, the national association worked to encourage local groups to take the lead on voter registration drives and education. In the next election cycle (1946), blacks in the South sought to exert their new right to vote in primaries.

World War II Black Veterans and Voting Rights

By the end of World War II, more that one million African Americans had served in the U.S. armed forces. Yet black participation in the war effort was not limited to military service. Blacks were integral components of the various wartime industries. The prospect and ultimate entry of the United States into World War II brought about major institutional

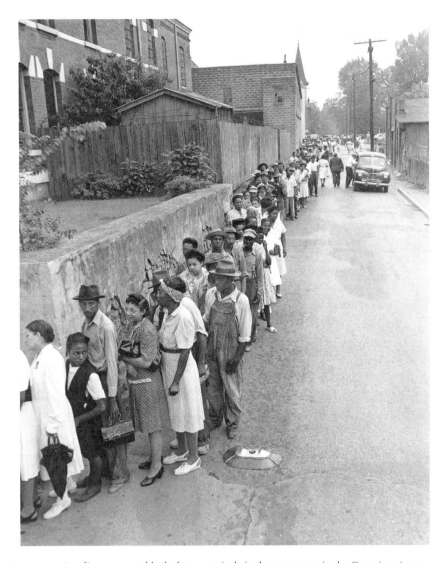

African American voters, in a line over two blocks long, await their chance to vote in the Georgia primary in 1946. The defeat of the white primary in the 1944 Supreme Court decision *Smith v. Allwright* removed one of the major barriers to black voter participation in the South. *Source: AP/Wide World Photos.*

reorganizations of both the armed services and the economy. These changes provided black Americans with openings to confront existing racially oppressive institutions. The war effort in general provided an economic and political climate conducive to seeking out racial justice. Within that climate, black World War II veterans and their organizations and associations played an essential role in widening the political openings brought about by the war.

At the conclusion of the war, black Americans were still segregated in the armed forces and American society in general. The preconditions for a break with existing racial institutions were, however, in place. Antiracism and antifascism campaigns and the threats of mass demonstrations contributed to the foundation that would later serve to propel the civil rights movement of the 1960s.

Black World War II veterans entered into and returned from the war with a less idealistic view of what postwar racial conditions would be like. They were not as naïve in 1945, but hoped that the war not only would make the world safe for democracy, but also would bring democracy to Mississippi and other southern states as well (Dittmer 1994, 17). These veterans were equipped with more technical and mechanical skills as a result of the diminished restrictions on blacks within the military. And, like all veterans, they returned stateside with a heightened sense of civic duty. For the black veteran, this sense translated into a desire to continue the fight on the home front for democratic ideals and fulfill the second V of the "Double V" campaign—victory at home and abroad (Brooks 2004, 19). This desire created an effective and organized impetus for change, which would culminate in the events of the 1960s.

Upon returning home, black veterans became active politically and pushed for full inclusion as first-class citizens in the American political arena. An example of black veteran activism and the subsequent white backlash it triggered was the 1946 reelection of Theodore Bilbo, a Democrat from Mississippi, to his third term in the U.S. Senate. This victory was achieved amidst massive voter intimidation

aimed at keeping black voters from registering and voting. Black veterans, together with black community leaders, filed a complaint with the U.S. Senate Committee to Investigate Campaign Expenditures, "claiming that Bilbo had subjected blacks to a 'reign of terror' during the campaign and urging the full Senate to impeach Bilbo and remove him from office" (Dittmer 1994, 3). But the proceedings were biased toward Bilbo, and the Senate was divided on sanctions against him. The senator then stepped aside temporarily and died shortly thereafter. The events surrounding the Bilbo election did not constitute an outright victory for blacks, but it significantly contributed to the process of destabilizing the system of white supremacy and strengthening the voting rights of black Americans.

During the same election year in Georgia, various black civic and veterans associations came together to expand black registration and voting and to campaign for the more racially moderate candidates. The umbrella organization for these efforts was the All Citizens Registration Committee, or ACRC (Brooks 2004, 29). The ACRC was composed of the Georgia Veterans League (GVL), a black veterans association very active in registration and canvassing efforts; the Progressive Citizens League (PCL), which attracted large numbers of black veterans; and the WWII Veterans Association. The civic action committee of the WWII Veterans Association held mass meetings, rallies, and house-to-house canvassing to encourage registration and voting. The WWII Veterans Association's goal of registering twenty thousand blacks was almost met. However, this victory must be viewed against a background of more negative outcomes—none of the racially progressive candidates was elected, and these efforts sparked a white backlash.

Seen in isolation, the efforts by World War II black veterans to confront racial injustices were not momentous. Organizations such as the GVL had few if any outright victories. However, black veterans and their organizations were able to chip away at the cracks in the foundation of the southern racial structure, and, together with the larger black society, keep up the momentum of societal restructuring that was advanced during the war. Perhaps most important, black veterans, together with other civil rights leaders, were able to organize and coordinate the movement directed toward realizing the voting rights afforded to blacks by *Smith v. Allwright.*

Citizenship Schools and Voter Registration

Like the activities of the black World War II veterans, many of the activities surrounding the push for the right to vote grew out of grassroots activism and organization. Yet grassroots activism does not always happen spontaneously; many times it is nurtured and developed. One manifestation of grassroots activism was the "citizenship schools" that developed throughout the southern United States in the early 1950s. These schools played a critical role in producing dramatic increases in black voter registration during the 1950s and early 1960s, and they provided local communities with the political skills, strategies, and manpower needed to help mount a national movement for black civil rights.

Although citizenship schools were established in the early 1950s, the concept dated

back to the years of the Great Depression. National crises place citizens under daunting pressures. Yet these same stresses lead some people, such as Rayford Logan, to identify opportunities for growth and survival. As a leading black intellectual during the depression era, Logan sensed that the political fortunes of African Americans were more than ever inextricably linked to their participation in civic affairs. Because African Americans were embedded in an electoral system in which majorities determined outcomes, Logan believed that the path to black political power lay in an informed and politically active black citizenry. To that end, Logan launched an "Education for Citizenship" campaign to increase black voter registration and participation by educating black adults about their voting rights, which were constantly violated through legal and extralegal means across the South. As a member of one of the leading black college fraternities at the time, Alpha Phi Alpha (AΦA), Logan relied on his network of fraternity brothers to implement his vision of "Education for Citizenship."

This vision became reality when the first citizenship school opened at the Butler Street YMCA in Atlanta in April 1933. The primary objective of this educational center was to increase black voter registration by running students through rigorous mock voter registrations. Students were intensely interrogated and taught to deal effectively with the verbal subterfuges employed by election officials to bar blacks from the voting rolls. The school was so successful that new centers were founded by AΦA members in cities across the South. Five years after the founding of the first school in Atlanta, Logan claimed to have reached nearly 100,000 African Americans through his network of citizenship schools. The explicit political purpose of these educational centers, however, ignited internecine conflicts within AΦA, because some fraternity members believed AΦA was a social, not a political, organization. AΦA's social faction eventually outmaneuvered its more politically inclined fraternity brothers, and the initial energy behind the idea of citizenships schools died out. The idea of citizenship schools eventually rose again, however—this time under new leadership and a more firmly committed cadre of operatives (Janken 1993, 99–106).

While Logan was fielding his "Education for Citizenship" schools, Myles Horton was establishing the Highlander Folk School in Grundy County, Tennessee, in the Appalachian Mountains (Glen 1996, 23). The purpose of the school, which opened its doors on November 1, 1932, was to develop an educational program that would lead to the political and economic empowerment of workers in Grundy County. Highlander's contribution to the struggle for black political and economic equality emerged in 1953 in anticipation of the Supreme Court's decision in *Brown v. Board of Education.* Myles Horton and the Highlander staff believed the high court would render a decision against the desegregation of public schools. Thus if the issue of desegregation were to remain alive after such a decision, the campaign to desegregate would have to be conducted at the local level. Highlander then proceeded to organize the first in a series of yearly workshops that would prepare residents from communities across the South to participate in the transition from segregated to desegregated schools.

The overall aim of these workshops was to train black and white citizens from all social segments—teachers, farmers, trade unionists, college students, and civic leaders—to become stakeholders in the process of desegregation. To that end, the workshops taught participants how to design and implement strategies to enlist the support of local leaders and civic organizations in the crusade for desegregated schools. By the time the Supreme Court ruled in *Brown v. Board of Education,* participants from the previous Highlander workshops were prepared to spearhead local drives for desegregation in communities in Alabama, Georgia, Tennessee, and South Carolina (Glen 1996, 154–161).

This broadening of the focus of the Highlander workshops served as the foundation for the new citizenship schools. Septima Clark, director of the Highlander workshops in 1956, was at its center. Clark was a woman of strong convictions about the meaning of leadership. Leadership, in her view, was not an activity confined to a select few. Nor, for that matter, were leaders to function as shepherds of the masses. The main objective of a leader was to unlock that leadership potential in others, so that communities could depend on themselves rather than on outsiders (Payne 1995, 75–76). Such was the governing spirit of the new citizenship schools.

The idea for a citizenship school took root in a conversation between Septima Clark and her former student Essau Jenkins. Jenkins was a respected black citizen of Johns Island, South Carolina, who had lost a recent bid for the Sea Islands school board. Although he received 203 black votes, that number represented only 18 percent of blacks eligible to vote. The major obstacles to the registration of black voters on the Sea Islands and across other parts of the

South were the strict and racist literacy requirements for voter registration.

Essau discussed with Clark opening up a school to prepare blacks to register to vote, and, with her backing, he received a $1,500 loan from Highlander to establish a school for adults on Johns Island. Essau and his associates—known as the Progressive Club—purchased a dilapidated building. To disguise their efforts from local whites and to earn money to repay the loan, they converted the front of the building into a grocery store; the back functioned as the classroom (Payne 1995). The political effects of the citizenship school were dramatic. In 1956, before establishment of the school, there were only two hundred registered black voters on the Sea Islands. By 1960—three years after the school opened—black voter registration had reached seven hundred, with turnout usually at 100 percent (Glen 1996, 199).

The pattern set by this citizenship school served as the model for subsequent and similar ventures in other areas of the South. Through a series of workshops for men and women interested in launching a citizenship school in their own community, Highlander taught participants to take a bottom-up approach to teaching poor blacks how to read and write and, more important, about the significance and importance of voting and taking ownership of their local political system. In 1961, in an effort to promote the growth of citizenship schools across the South, Highlander hosted a series of teacher training workshops attended by eighty-eight teachers. Those individuals, in turn, went back to more than forty communities to establish citizenship schools. Together, they enrolled approximately fifteen hundred

students, more than seven hundred of whom registered to vote by September 1961 (Glen 1996, 201).

Removing the Remaining Barriers to Voting

Next to physical intimidation, the poll tax remained perhaps the biggest barrier to the franchise. Yet if a person could pay the tax, there was little way to keep someone from voting. Thus the NAACP and other organizations ran a "pay your poll tax" campaign to increase the number of eligible voters. In 1946 the Atlanta All Citizens Registration Committee formed and registered eighteen thousand blacks in its first four months. In other towns, churches took up this role and used the pulpit to encourage congregations to go and register (Lawson 1999).

Placing a black candidate on the ballot proved to be an effective way to energize voters to get involved and register to vote. In Winston-Salem, North Carolina, the American Federation of Labor–Congress of Industrial Organizations (AFL-CIO) ran a large "pay your poll tax" campaign aimed at both white and black citizens. It helped to register three thousand black voters. The result was the election in 1947 of the first black alderman since Reconstruction (Hine 1979; Lawson 1999).

Although the defeat of the white primary in *Smith v. Allwright* allowed local groups to make serious inroads into voter registration and win a few local political battles, the gains fell far short of reaching the goals of the NAACP and other black groups. The poll tax, literacy tests, and especially voter intimidation were still exacting a high price from registration and turnout. In Georgia, members of the Ku Klux Klan, in a rally before an election, threatened potential voters, screaming "blood would flow" if blacks went to the polls (Lawson 1999). With the threat of violence looming over many blacks who wanted to vote, the point of registering seemed futile. By 1955 it seemed as if local groups had done all they could on the coattails of *Smith v. Allwright*— it was time for federal involvement once more (Lawson 1999).

The first attempt at a solution came in the form of the Civil Rights Act of 1957.[3] Essentially, the 1957 act established the Commission on Civil Rights, intended to investigate the state of civil rights across the country. It also created a civil rights division in the Justice Department, so that the federal government could prosecute people involved in voter intimidation, and it provided for the appointment of federal referees to investigate alleged abuses at polling places. Unfortunately, because of political machinations during the drafting of the bill, the 1957 act required a local jury trial for anyone charged with a crime under the act. Consequently, the legal punishments were relatively toothless in the South, because juries were composed primarily of white males.

Despite the act's failings, the opportunity to levy charges against those involved in voter intimidation was a welcome one. It also served as another way to energize potential voters and stress the need for further legal reform because of the flaws in the 1957 act. In 1957 the NAACP held a major conference dedicated to registration and voting. The broad accomplishments of the conference were, first, emphasizing the need for more of the association's resources to be dedicated to local chapters and

other groups involved in the registration and voting project and, second, setting a goal to register three million blacks by 1960 (*Papers of the NAACP* 1995). In this new initiative, the NAACP made extra efforts to utilize and coordinate grassroots efforts. In 1958 the NAACP held a conference with ministers of primarily black churches to brainstorm on ways in which the churches could mobilize blacks to register.

By the end of 1959, numerous local voter registration drives had been held across the South, but Jim Crow was resilient, and the NAACP goal of three million registered blacks was still far away. In Memphis, Tennessee, local efforts added fifteen thousand names to the registration rolls and helped to organize the campaign of a black man for public works commissioner. The efforts of assorted NAACP local chapters led to a flurry of blacks elected to city councils in North Carolina, helped to launch the campaign of a black candidate for the Virginia Senate, and led to the electoral defeat of a public official who swore out arrest warrants against Medgar Evers, the head of the NAACP in Mississippi. Yet despite all of these local efforts, the number of blacks registered to vote in 1960 was only about 1.4 million in the South.

There were many reasons for the failure of the 1957 Civil Rights Act, but one of them was the slow start by the division of the Justice Department devoted to civil rights. The department received few formal complaints, perhaps because blacks were uncertain about the statute's possible uses. Furthermore, the division was slow to act on complaints out of fear that cases would inherently bring up the question of the constitutionality of the 1957 act, which could lead to devastating results. In 1959, in what many division lawyers considered the best-prepared case, the lower court hearing the case actually declared the 1957 act unconstitutional, despite strong evidence of race-coded registration cards to allow for easy "disposal" of legitimate registrants, inconsistent registration procedures for blacks, and the blatant discriminatory application of literacy tests. The Supreme Court ultimately reversed the ruling, but the fact that these discriminatory practices occurred without efficient legal recourse or executive branch intervention points to the shortcomings of the 1957 Civil Rights Act. Its weaknesses set the stage for the passage of the Civil Rights Act of 1960 (Lawson 1999).

After the 1960 Civil Rights Act: Freedom Vote and Freedom Summer

The 1960 Act incorporated a key lesson from the 1957 legislation. It allowed court-appointed referees to register eligible voters who had been denied registration at the hands of local election officials. Unfortunately, the process was cumbersome, and the enforcement of penalties was sporadic. Furthermore, the bill did little to give the executive branch the power to intervene; it did not affect the "legal" use of poll taxes or literacy tests, nor did it effectively preempt the threat of violence or voter intimidation. Still, for many blacks and local groups the 1960 act suggested that the federal government was still willing to address civil rights issues.

The NAACP continued its coordination and support of local registration efforts across the country and primarily in the South. In 1961

over seventy-eight grassroots voter registration programs, poll tax drives, and get-out-the-vote efforts were under way in southern states (*Papers of the NAACP* 1995). In 1963 the local Student Nonviolent Coordinating Committee (SNCC) in Selma, Alabama, declared a "Freedom Day" in response to repeated efforts by the local sheriff to intimidate and arrest potential registrants and protesters. On this day, three hundred blacks went peacefully to the courthouse to attempt to register. As expected, the sheriff harassed the group, but arrested only two people because representatives of the Justice Department were there to document the obvious discrimination.

Mississippi was another source of frustration for the NAACP and other groups because of the persistent use of violence and intimidation of anti–civil rights groups. Many successful registration campaigns were under way under the local leadership of Medgar Evers, but results were difficult to achieve. In 1961 only 6.9 percent of eligible blacks were registered to vote in Mississippi. Violence against activists, protesters, and those who tried to register was rampant, and on June 12, 1963, Medgar Evers was assassinated. Because of the difficulty and dangers in running programs throughout Mississippi, the SNCC–Voter Education Project (VEP) coalition created a bold plan for what would be one of the most dramatic voter registration projects leading to the passage of the Civil Rights Act of 1964 and Voting Rights Act of 1965 (Lawson 1999).

In 1963 local leaders across the state decided to hold a "Freedom Vote"—that is, a mock election paralleling the 1963 Mississippi governor's race. The plan was to demonstrate that blacks cared about politics, wanted to vote, and would exercise their right to vote if given the opportunity. Although the election was coordinated by the SNCC's Bob Moses, it required the effort of all organizations and built heavily on the earlier work of the NAACP's Medgar Evers. The organizers also encouraged blacks to attempt to vote in the actual primaries as well. In the mock primary, over 27,000 blacks cast their protest votes. In preparation for the Freedom Vote, which was scheduled around the general election, local leaders selected their own multiracial ticket of candidates and developed an issue platform. By doing so, the Freedom Vote helped to bridge gaps that had formed between the various organizations in the state, making their grassroots efforts even more effective.

The Freedom Vote candidates began their campaign in October and volunteers from around the country flocked to Mississippi to help with the education and registration efforts. Freedom Vote, however, was not without opposition. Local police forces created fictitious reasons to arrest or fine volunteers; some municipalities banned information leaflets; and volunteers faced repeated threats of violence. Yet volunteers kept coming, and organizations around the country raised funds for the Mississippi campaign. The mock election was scheduled for November 2–4 so that it would not interfere with the actual election. It was estimated that volunteers had a network able to reach over 400,000 blacks statewide, but white backlash severely hampered the ability of the volunteers to turn out black voters. For example, in the town of Canton twenty-five additional police officers were added to stop people from participating in the Freedom Vote. Nevertheless, by the end of the mock election

an estimated 72,000 people had turned out. Perhaps even more important than the turnout and local mobilization was the national attention that the Freedom Vote brought to the problems blacks faced in voting in Mississippi and other southern locations. The exercise demonstrated that once registration was equitable and polling places were safely accessible, blacks were eager and ready to go to the polls (Lawson 1999; Sinsheimer 1989).

After the Freedom Vote, civil rights leaders began planning an even larger project for the summer of 1964 in Mississippi. In the spring of 1964, the Council of Federated Organizations (COFO), made up of nearly all the civil rights–related groups in the state, launched their own political party in protest of the state Democratic Party's insistence on excluding blacks. The Mississippi Freedom Democratic Party (MFDP) created a duplicate party structure with the goal of giving black Democrats an organization through which to organize politically and recruit delegates. Later that year, the MFDP sent an all-black delegation, led by Fannie Lou Hamer, to the Democratic National Convention in Atlantic City to challenge the state party's slate of delegates. Building off of the MFDP, the COFO developed a summer-long series of voter registration and education programs known as the "Freedom Summer." Intended to be not only a grassroots campaign but also another vehicle for bringing national attention to voting rights issues in Mississippi and the South, Freedom Summer attracted about one thousand white student volunteers from around the country. As in 1963, the volunteers faced violence, which only served to create national concern about the students working with the project. Three volunteers—

Andrew Goodman, James Chaney, and Michael Schwerner—were murdered by a group of whites, including law enforcement officials, in Philadelphia, Mississippi. Against the backdrop of this tragedy, the grassroots organizations and outside volunteers had mobilized over seventeen thousand people by the end of the summer of 1964 to attempt to register and had held twenty-eight "Freedom Schools" geared toward civic education (McMillen 1977; Lawson 1999; Bond 2000)

While the Freedom Summer was in full swing, President Lyndon B. Johnson signed another Civil Rights Act into law on July 2, 1964. The new law brought sweeping changes to the segregation permeating public life, education, and employment, and made a few changes to voting rights by making it harder for election officials to deny the franchise on the basis of literacy tests and other "technicalities." The success of the Freedom Vote, the MFDP, and Freedom Summer helped to bring the issue of discrimination in voting rights to the forefront for the 1964 election and contributed to moving forward legislation aimed at fixing the voting rights problems not corrected by the acts of 1957, 1960, and 1964. With passage of the Voting Rights Act of 1965, the courts and the Department of Justice would finally have the legal tools they needed to allow programs such as Freedom Summer to register larger numbers of voters and give those citizens a safer environment in which to vote.

Conclusion

In the face of their almost complete legal exclusion from the political process, black Americans used their organizational abilities to create institutions that provided the social capital necessary to fight their exclusion. Through national, regional, and local social, political, fraternal, community, legal, and business organizations, blacks put together broad successful strategies to gain their voting rights. From Logan's *nadir*, blacks did what Rep. George White of North Carolina predicted in 1901—they rose up "Phoenix-like" and fought for the right to vote.

Notes

1. This eventually evolved into Miner's Teachers College, which in 1955 merged with the Wilson Teachers College, for white teachers, to become D.C. Teachers College, which, in turn, was absorbed into the University of the District of Columbia in 1977.
2. This was especially true for black women in the beauty culture industry. Although they were engaged in work that seemed quite peripheral to the cause, as aestheticians they were in a position to be powerful advocates for change in America because they controlled their own capital, their own space (the beauty salon), and their network of clients. For a more detailed discussion of these issues, see Gill (2004).
3. For more detail on the politics and national protests leading to its passage, see Chapters 6 and 7 in Lawson (1999).

References

Adams, Frank. 1972. "Highlander Folk School: Getting Information, Going Back and Teaching It." *Harvard Educational Review* 38 (winter): 497–520.

Beito, David T. 2000. *From Mutual Aid to the Welfare State: Fraternal Societies and Social Services, 1890–1967.* Chapel Hill: University of North Carolina Press.

Bond, Julian. 2000. "SNCC: What We Did— Student Nonviolent Coordinating Committee." *Monthly Review* 52 (October): 14–39.

Brehm, John, and Wendy Rahn. 1997. "Individual-Level Evidence for the Causes and Consequences of Social Capital." *American Journal of Political Science* 41 (3): 999–1023.

Brooks, Jennifer E. 2004. *Defining the Peace: World War II Veterans, Race, and the Remaking of Southern Political Tradition.* Chapel Hill: University of North Carolina Press.

Brooks, Joanna. 2005. "The Early American Public Sphere and the Emergence of a Black Print Counterpublic." *William and Mary Quarterly* 62 (1): 67–92.

Brown, Elsa Barkley. 1994. "Negotiating and Transforming the Public Sphere: African American Political Life in the Transition from Slavery to Freedom." *Public Culture* 7 (1): 107–146.

Calhoun-Brown, Allison. 2000. "Upon this Rock: The Black Church, Nonviolence, and the Civil Rights Movement." *PS: Political Science and Politics* 33 (2): 168–174.

Clark, Septima P. 1990. *Ready from Within: Septima Clark and the Civil Rights Movement.* Trenton, N.J.: Africa World Press.

Collier-Thomas, Bettye. 1997. "Frances Ellen Watkins Harper: Abolitionist and Feminist Reformer, 1825–1911." In *African-American Women and the Vote, 1837–1965*, edited by Ann D. Gordon. Amherst: University of Massachusetts Press.

Dawson, Michael. 1994. "The Black Counterpublic? Economic Earthquakes, Racial Agenda(s), and Black Politics." *Public Culture* 7 (1): 195–223.

Dittmer, John. 1994. *Local People: The Struggle for Civil Rights in Mississippi.* Urbana: University of Illinois Press.

DuBois, Ellen Carol. 1978. *Feminism and Suffrage: The Emergence of an Independent Women's Movement in America, 1848–1869.* Ithaca, N.Y.: Cornell University Press.

Fay, Robert. 1999. "Mutual Benefit Societies." In *Africana: The Encyclopedia of the African and African American Experience*, edited by Kwame Anthony Appiah and Henry Louis Gates Jr. New York: Basic Books.

Findlay, James F. 1990. "Religion and Politics in the Sixties: The Churches and the Civil Rights Act of 1964." *Journal of American History* 77 (1): 66–92.

Franklin, John Hope. 1967. *From Slavery to Freedom: A History of Negro Americans.* 3d ed. New York: Vintage Books.

Gill, Tiffany M. 2004. "Civic Beauty: Beauty Culturalists and the Politics of African American Female Entrepreneurship." *Enterprise and Society* 5 (4): 583–593.

Glen, John M. 1996. *Highlander: No Ordinary School.* Knoxville: University of Tennessee Press.

Goodstein, Anita Shafer. 1998. "A Rare Alliance: African-American and White Women in the Tennessee Elections of 1919 and 1920." *Journal of Southern History* 64:219–246.

Grootaert, Christian, and Thierry van Bastelaer, eds. 2002. *Understanding and Measuring Social Capital: A Multidisciplinary Tool for Practitioners.* Washington, D.C.: World Bank.

Green, Elna C. 1997. *Southern Strategies: Southern Women and the Woman Suffrage Question.* Chapel Hill: University of North Carolina Press.

Harley, Sharon. 1988. "Mary Church Terrell: Genteel Militant." In *Black Leaders of the Nineteenth Century*, edited by Leon Litwack and August Meier. Urbana: University of Illinois Press.

Hine, Darlene Clark. 1979. *Black Victory: The Rise and Fall of the White Primary in Texas.* Millwood, N.Y.: KTO Press.

———. 1984. *When the Truth Is Told: A History of Black Women's Culture and Community in Indiana, 1875–1950.* Bloomington: Indiana University Press.

Hunter, Tera W. 1997. *To "Joy My Freedom": Southern Black Women's Lives and Labors after the Civil War.* Cambridge, Mass.: Harvard University Press.

Janken, Kenneth Robert. 1993. *Rayford W. Logan and the Dilemma of the African-American Intellectual.* Amherst: University of Massachusetts Press.

Jordan, William. 1995. " 'The Damnable Dilemma': African-American Accommodation and Protest during WWI." *Journal of American History* 81 (4): 1562–1583.

Lawson, Steven F. 1999. *Black Ballots: Voting Rights in the South, 1944–1969.* Lanham, Md.: Lexington Books.

Liazos, Ariane, and Marshall Ganz. 2004. "Duty to the Race: African American Fraternal Orders and the Legal Defense of the Right to Organize." *Social Science History* 28 (3): 485–534.

Logan, Rayford W. 1954. *The Negro in American Life and Thought: The Nadir, 1877–1901.* New York: Dial Press.

———. 1965. *The Betrayal of the Negro: From Rutherford B. Hayes to Woodrow Wilson.* New York: Collier Books.

Marshall, Thurgood. 1957. "The Rise and Collapse of the 'White Democratic Primary.' " *Journal of Negro Education, The Negro Voter in the South* 26 (summer): 249–254.

McMillen, Neil R. 1977. "Black Enfranchisement in Mississippi: Federal Enforcement and Black Protest in the 1960s." *Journal of Southern History* 43 (August): 351–372.

Morris, Aldon D. 1984. *The Origins of the Civil Rights Movement: Black Communities Organizing for Change.* New York: Free Press.

Nelson, Marjory. 1979. "Women, Suffrage, and Race." *Off Our Backs: A Women's Newsjournal.* 9 (10): 6–12.

Onkst, David. H. 1998. " 'First a Negro . . . Incidentally a Veteran': Black World War Two Veterans and the G.I. Bill of Rights in the Deep South, 1944–1948." *Journal of Social History* 31 (3): 517–539.

Orr, Marion. 1999. *Black Social Capital: The Politics of School Reform in Baltimore, 1986–1998.* Lawrence: University Press of Kansas.

Papers of the NAACP: Supplement to Part 4, Voting Rights, General Office Files, 1956–1965. 1995. Bethesda, Md.: University Publications of America. Microform, reel 1.

Payne, Charles M. 1995. *I've Got the Light of Freedom: The Organizing Tradition and the Mississippi Freedom Struggle.* Berkeley: University of California Press.

Putnam, Robert D. 1993. *Making Democracy Work: Civic Traditions in Modern Italy.* Princeton, N.J.: Princeton University Press.

Raboteau, Albert J. 1999. *African-American Religion.* New York: Oxford University Press.

Schechter, Patricia. 2001. *Ida B. Wells-Barnett and American Reform, 1880–1930.* Chapel Hill: University of North Carolina Press.

Scott, Anne Frior. 1990. "Most Invisible of All: Black Women's Voluntary Associations." *Journal of Southern History* 56 (1): 3–22.

Silverman, Robert Mark. 1998. "The Effects of Racism and Racial Discrimination on Minority Business Development: The Case of Black Manufacturers in Chicago's Ethnic Beauty Aids Industry." *Journal of Social History* 31 (spring): 571–597.

Sinsheimer, Joseph A. 1989. "The Freedom Vote of 1963: New Strategies of Racial Protest in Mississippi." *Journal of Southern History* 55 (May): 217–244.

Skocpol, Theda, and Jennifer Lynn Oser. 2004. "Organization Despite Adversity: The Origins and Development of African American Fraternal Associations." *Social Science History* 28 (3): 367–437.

Stauffer, John. 2004. *The Black Hearts of Men: Radical Abolitionists and the Transformation of Race.* Cambridge, Mass.: Harvard University Press.

Terborg-Penn, Rosalyn. 1998. *African American Women in the Struggle for the Vote, 1850–1920.* Bloomington: Indiana University Press.

Trotter, Joe W. 2004. "African American Fraternal Associations in American History: An Introduction." *Social Science History* 28 (3): 355–366.

Verba, Sidney, Kay Lehman Schlozman, and Henry E. Brady. 1995. *Voice and Equality: Civic Voluntarism in American Politics.* Cambridge, Mass.: Harvard University Press.

Walker, Juliet E. K. 1998. *The History of Black Business in America: Capitalism, Race, Entrepreneurship.* New York: Twayne.

Weare, Walter B. 1973. *Black Business in the New South: A Social History of the North Carolina Mutual Life Insurance Company.* Urbana: University of Illinois Press.

Weems, Robert E., Jr. 1996. *Black Business in the Black Metropolis: The Chicago Metropolitan Assurance Company, 1925–1985.* Bloomington: Indiana University Press.

Whitaker, Matthew C. 2003. " 'Creative Conflict': Lincoln and Eleanor Ragsdale, Collaboration and Community Activism in Phoenix, 1953–1965." *Western Historical Quarterly* 34 (summer): 165–190.

White, E. Francis. 2001. *Dark Continent of Our Bodies: Black Feminism and the Politics of Respectability.* Philadelphia: Temple University Press.

Willett, Julie. 2000. *Permanent Waves: The Making of the American Beauty Shop.* New York: New York University Press.

Williams, Lillian S. 1990. "And Still I Rise: Black Women and Reform, Buffalo, New York,

1900–1940." *Afro-Americans in New York Life and History* 14 (2): 7–33.

Wolcott, Victoria W. 1997. " 'Bible, Bath, and Broom': Nannie Helen Burroughs's National Training School and African-American Racial Uplift." *Journal of Women's History* 9 (1): 88–110.

———. 2001. *Remaking Respectability: African American Women in Interwar Detroit.* Chapel Hill: University of North Carolina Press.

Wynn, Neil A. 1993. *The Afro-American and the Second World War.* 2d ed. New York: Holmes and Meier.

5

Making the Voting Rights Act

STEPHEN TUCK

On August 6, 1965, President Lyndon B. Johnson signed the Voting Rights Act. Flanked by Rev. Martin Luther King and other civil rights leaders, Johnson described the act as "one of the most monumental laws in the entire history of American freedom . . . a victory for the freedom of the American Nation" (Johnson various years, 2:843). Three years later, at his final news conference, Johnson called passage of the act his "greatest accomplishment as President." He went on to point out: "To me it was like Lincoln's Emancipation Proclamation . . . it is really going to make democracy real" (Johnson various years, 2:1354). Civil rights leaders concurred. John Lewis, leader of the Student Nonviolent Coordinating Committee (SNCC), described the act as a "milestone and every bit as momentous and significant . . . as the Emancipation Proclamation or the 1954 Supreme Court decision" (Lawson 1976, 321).

If people agreed on the importance of the act, there was little consensus as to who should get the credit for its passage. Johnson himself argued that voting rights legislation had always been a key part of his domestic reform program (Johnson, various years, 2:841). After signing the Civil Rights Act on July 2, 1964, Johnson apparently told his attorney general,

Nicholas Katzenbach, "What are we going to do next year in civil rights? . . . Let's get a voting rights bill" (Firestone and Vogt 1989, 172). Johnson later explained in his memoirs, "In many ways I believed this act would be even more critical than the previous one" (Johnson 1971, 161).

In the summer of 1965, Martin Luther King also praised Johnson's efforts. In a personal letter King wrote, "I am convinced that you will go down in history as the president who issued the second and final Emancipation Proclamation" (Stern 1992, 228). However, at the end of 1964 voting rights did not seem to be on the legislative horizon. Neither King nor his colleagues in the Southern Christian Leadership Conference (SCLC) believed that the administration intended to introduce a bill in 1965 (Young 1996, 342). Passage of the Civil Rights Act had led to one of the bitterest conflicts in Congress for many years. King reckoned that Johnson would not risk another political battle for the sake of voting rights. In private, Johnson told King that there was no chance of forcing voting rights legislation through Congress in 1965. In public, Johnson called for an end to "barriers to the right to vote" by "Negro Americans" in his State of the Union address on January 4, 1965. But it hardly appeared to be a priority—he devoted only two sentences to the topic, and he placed it toward the end of a long list of domestic goals (Johnson various years, 1:5–6). In his inaugural address on January 20, 1965, Johnson did not mention voting rights at all.

Thus King and his associates decided that they had to take the initiative on black voting rights. On November 4, 1964, the day after Johnson's election, King told a *New York Times* reporter, "We will probably have demonstrations in the very near future in Alabama and Mississippi based around the right to vote" (Stern 1992, 216). Two months later, the SCLC led demonstrations in Selma, Alabama, with the sole intention of forcing the government to act. As Andrew Young, a colleague of King's, explained to a reporter, "Just as the 1964 civil rights bill was written in Birmingham [the scene of mass demonstrations] . . . we hope that new federal voting legislation will be written here" (Garrow 1986, 390). The ensuing crisis in Selma, where police repeatedly assaulted nonviolent demonstrators, kept the issue of voting rights in the public eye.

Many observers ascribed the passage of the Voting Rights Act to the crisis in Selma. Julian Bond, a leader of the student movement, concluded that "the SCLC approach really resulted in the 1965 Voting Rights Act. If it hadn't been for their ability to really capitalise on what happened in Selma . . . you wouldn't have had that Act" (Joseph 1973, 70). Yet Katzenbach, reflecting on his time as attorney general, downplayed the significance of Selma. According to Katzenbach, the authority and outlook of the president at the start of 1965, and the compliant nature of Congress, meant that "civil rights groups were not so badly needed for this bill and thus had little effect on its outcome" (Harvey 1973, 33).

In fact, the Voting Rights Act owed its passage to demonstrations on Selma's streets and to discussions in Washington's corridors of power. The outlook of the president and Congress made a Voting Rights Act possible, but it was protests on the ground that made a potent act necessary. Civil rights activists did not compel Johnson to act, but they certainly rushed him. In Selma, the SCLC conducted its campaign to take full advantage of the opportunities presented by a responsive executive and legislature. In Washington, the president and a decisive liberal majority in Congress took advantage of the opportunities presented by the Selma crisis to drive through legislation to end voter disenfranchisement once and for all. Although he was sometimes loath to admit it publicly, Johnson was in regular communication with Martin Luther King. They were far from allies, but both Johnson and King were dependent on each other, and the power that each man represented.

Limited Changes, 1957–1964

Debates over voting rights hit the headlines in 1965. But the momentum to pass voting rights legislation had been building for at least a generation. As Chapter 4 describes, civil rights demonstrators had long campaigned for the vote, with increasing success and publicity from the World War II era onward. Simultaneously, parts of the federal government began to consider civil rights for the first time since the 1890 Federal Elections Bill. Step by step, the Justice Department realized the need to pursue voting rights, and step by step the department began to develop the machinery to do so. In no sense should these developments in successive administrations be interpreted as a series of milestones leading inexorably to voting rights legislation—they were far too tentative and limited for that. But the Justice Department's increasing interest and expertise in voting rights help to explain the swift passage of a comprehensive act when the issue came to prominence.

In 1939 Attorney General Frank Murphy created a civil rights section within the Justice Department's Criminal Division, and it began to investigate civil rights violations. In 1948 President Harry S. Truman's Committee on Civil Rights proposed the creation of a civil rights division in its own right within the Justice Department to "give the federal civil rights enforcement program prestige, power, and efficiency that it now lacks" (Landsberg 1997, 9). But, in fact, the proposal for a civil rights division was only taken up almost a decade later with passage of the 1957 Civil Rights Act. The act also created a Civil Rights Commission to investigate and report on civil rights issues. In practice, the creation of the division and commission did little to improve the prestige or efficiency of the enforcement program, and it gave the federal government very little power to challenge the disenfranchisement of black voters. (Lyndon Johnson, then Senate majority leader, played a leading role in watering down the bill.) Nevertheless, the act was a significant piece of legislation. It was the first civil rights act of any kind for almost a century. Both the division and the commission would later become important institutions in support of voting rights.

A second Civil Rights Act in 1960 increased the Justice Department's ability to investigate civil rights abuses and to introduce litigation. But again this act left the Civil Rights Division without real power to press for sweeping change. The act left the attorney general with few options for challenging disenfranchisement—primarily he brought civil litigation against local election officials in federal district courts on a case-by-case basis (Valelly 2004, 187). Such a process was time-consuming at best, beyond the resources of the division. And often it was fruitless, because many federal district judges opposed any federal interference in local elections. In the Deep South, some judges openly supported disenfranchisement.

Still, the two acts meant that white supremacist registrars in the South were now being challenged, albeit not forced to change. With the onset of the modern civil rights movement, the challenges increased. All the major protest organizations called for fair access to the ballot. Since the start of the century, the National Association for the Advancement of Colored People (NAACP) had filed countless suits, with some successes, leading to the enfranchisement of thousands of black voters in southern cities. Since its founding after the Montgomery bus boycott, Martin Luther King's SCLC had campaigned for black voter registration. Most notable of all, beginning in 1963 the Student Nonviolent Coordinating Committee (SNCC) sent teams to try and register black voters in Mississippi and southwestern Georgia, two of the most repressive areas in the South.

President John F. Kennedy's administration actively encouraged these efforts to increase black voter registration. With his attention fixed on cold war politics, Kennedy hoped that a voting campaign would provoke less trouble (and thus fewer negative headlines in the world's press) than civil rights demonstrations. Kennedy could hardly have been more wrong. During the first two years of the Southwest Georgia Project, every single student activist was attacked at some stage. In Mississippi, hundreds of students from northern schools joined the Freedom Summer of 1964. In the White House, President Johnson, who acceded to the presidency when Kennedy was assassinated in November 1963, watched the well-publicized course of events in Mississippi with "concern and dread." Dozens of civil rights campaigners were attacked; four were murdered. Meanwhile, mass demonstrations against segregation continued throughout the South, most famously in Birmingham, Alabama, during 1963 (see Dittmer 1995; Payne 1996; Tuck 2003).

With the eyes of the nation fixed on southern white supremacy, Congress passed the Civil Rights Act of 1964 that outlawed segregation and gave the attorney general the power to sue any state government that maintained segregated schools. But the act did not address the problem of disenfranchisement. (At an early stage in the drafting of the bill Kennedy had proposed that federal registrars be sent to areas in which less than 15 percent of potential black voters were registered, but the provision never made it into the act). By the end of 1964, less than half of black southerners who were old enough to vote were registered. In Alabama, it was less than one in five; in Mississippi, it was less than one in ten. Within the administration, a Task Force on Civil Rights remained concerned about "whether the pending bill provides the gains expected by Negroes in the area

of voting" (Stern 1992, 215). It went on to say that it was "doubtful that the enactment of the pending civil rights bill will stave off the pressure for further formal and binding action for more than a brief period" (Graham 1990, 154).

Selma

The period before renewed "pressure for further formal and binding action" was indeed brief. By the beginning of 1965, King had joined a local voter registration campaign in Selma, Alabama, with the intention of provoking a crisis that would force the issue of disenfranchisement to the top of the legislative agenda. Within weeks, the demonstrations hit the national headlines. Situated in Dallas County, Selma was the capital of Alabama's "black belt." It also seemed to be the capital of Alabama's system of white supremacy. Andrew Young remembered that "Selma was symbolic of race relations in any small Southern town trapped in a time warp; we could have chosen any of a hundred similar towns, but we could not have found a more exemplary case of social polarity, or a more abused and oppressed black community" (Young 1996, 341). The local White Citizens' Council was the largest chapter in the state. One council spokesman explained its purpose, "If we let them [blacks] have one inch, they would want to go all the way" (Watters and Cleghorn 1967, 250). To make sure they did not get an inch, in the summer of 1964 a local judge had banned any meeting of more than three people convened to discuss civil rights.

Selma epitomized the problem of disenfranchisement. As the White Citizens' Council recognized early on, "the integration fight is going to be won or lost at the ballot box" (Watters and Cleghorn 1967, 249). In Dallas County, black residents formed the majority of the voting-age population, but barely 1 percent of the registered voters (U.S. Commission on Civil Rights 1968, 10). Selma also exposed the limits of federal power. In April 1961, Attorney General Robert F. Kennedy filed a voting rights suit against Dallas County—but it took the government two years to gain access to the county registrar's files. In 1963 the local federal district court prohibited the county registrar from rejecting black applicants for making mistakes when filling in a registration questionnaire. But the prohibition made almost no impact on registration. The county registrar simply introduced a more stringent registration test. Between May 1962 and August 1964, seven out of every eight black applicants in the county were rejected by the local board of registrars. Moreover, Dallas County's Board of Registrars only opened twice a month, and it registered a maximum of thirty new voters at each session. Campaigners calculated that even if the board accepted every black applicant, it would take at least ten years to bring black registration up to the level of white registration. Martin Luther King pointed out that, judging on past performance, it would more likely take 103 years (Watters and Cleghorn 1967, 249).

Such flagrant abuses made Selma an ideal place for King to bring the issue of disenfranchisement to national attention. So, too, did the presence of Dallas County Sheriff Jim Clark. Wearing a "Never" button on his lapel and dressed in the style of a wartime general, Clark seemed to be a stereotype drawn directly from central casting. His racism, red-hot temper, and desire to prove himself to local white voters meant that Clark was never far from losing control. Time and again the SCLC goaded Clark, and time and again Clark reacted. At various points during the campaign, Clark ordered police to attack a crowd that included journalists, used electric cattle prods to round up a group of teenagers, fired tear gas to halt a nonviolent march, clubbed (in the presence of a newspaper photographer) a woman waiting to register, and appeared to punch one of King's colleagues in the face right in front of a television camera (in fact, Clark's deputy landed the blow, but Clark took the credit). After one such incident, Ralph Abernathy, one of the founders of the SCLC, "propose[d] for honorary membership the name of Sheriff Jim Clark, who did more for our organization this day than anyone else in the city of Selma" (Abernathy 1989, 317). Wilson Baker, Selma's director of public safety, believed the SCLC manipulated Clark "just like an expert playing a violin" (Fairclough 1987, 210). When Clark checked into a hospital for exhaustion, the SCLC sent him flowers and directed two thousand children to the courthouse to pray for him.

The SCLC also came to Selma because it was impressed by the commitment of local campaigners. SNCC activists had arrived in Selma in 1963, and they worked closely with the local Dallas County Voters League. Mass meetings in the local churches were attended by up to a thousand people. Amelia Boynton, a founder of the Dallas County league, appealed to SCLC leaders in 1964 to join the league's campaign. Although progress may have seemed excruciatingly slow to outsiders, local activists believed there were grounds for optimism. In 1964 Selma's black voters, though few in number, had been significant in James Smitherman's victory in the election for mayor. Although Smitherman supported segregation, he was more restrained than his predecessor, Chris Heinz, whose racial attitudes had been hardened after a black man molested his daughter. This split between moderates and hardliners was most apparent in the rivalry between Wilson Baker and Sheriff Jim Clark (Thornton 2002, 434). Baker was hardly a liberal. As Selma's director of public safety, he reckoned, "If we can only get the bastards out of town without getting them arrested, we'll have 'em whipped" (Lawson 1997, 107). But Baker ordered Clark's police to stay away from protests in Selma. The problem for Baker, though, was that once applicants for the vote reached the county courthouse, they came under Clark's jurisdiction. To the amazement of protesters, Clark and Baker rowed publicly. Abernathy concluded that they "clearly hated one another more than they hated us" (Abernathy 1989, 318).

Thus the Selma campaign was rooted in the politics of the county courthouse, the local churches, and the town square. But from the outset, the SCLC's focus was on national opinion, Congress, and the White House. When King announced the resumption of demonstrations on January 2, 1965, he told the audience of seven hundred people, "We are not asking, we are demanding the ballot" (Fairclough 1987, 229). At every turn, the SCLC used the local crisis to illustrate the wider problem, and King was in regular contact with Washington to drive home the point.

The campaign proper began on January 18, when King and John Lewis led four hundred applicants to the main entrance of the Dallas County Courthouse. Sheriff Clark insisted they line up at a side door. Despite the tension—American Nazi leader George Rockwell had joined the hecklers—there were no arrests. The next day, applicants refused to move from the main entrance. Their defiance incensed Clark. During the next two days, Clark arrested over two hundred applicants. But Clark's strong-arm tactics were counterproductive. On January 23, Judge Daniel Thomas of the federal district court issued a temporary restraining order against Clark and four other officials. Thomas had previously sided with segregationists, delaying federal suits against Dallas County registrars for months on end. But Thomas was clearly frustrated with Clark's behavior and "a senseless discussion of which was the front door of the courthouse" (Thornton 2002, 481) However, Thomas's order failed to reduce the tension. By February 5, more than 2,400 people had been arrested. Crucially, one of those arrested was Martin Luther King.

With King behind bars, Selma became a front-page story. The *New York Times* published a letter from King in which he pointed out that there were more black people in Selma's jail than were registered to vote. But King wanted to convert media coverage into political action. While still in jail, he sent a message to President Johnson asking for assistance. Upon his release from jail on Friday, February 5, King met with a delegation of fifteen members of Congress, who had come to Selma to see the problem for themselves. All but one of the delegates telegraphed the president: "Local authorities will not act in good faith to protect the right of franchise. Further legislation is necessary to insure the right to vote." Upon their return to Washington, five of the members filed voting rights bills (Stern 1992, 221–222).

King also announced upon his release from jail that he would be going to Washington to meet the president. Some White House staffers were annoyed by King's presumptuousness, and Johnson refused to agree to a meeting. But King's tactics had the desired effect. On February 6, George Reedy, the White House press secretary, when questioned about King's request for a meeting, announced that the government would make a "strong recommendation" to Congress about voting rights. On February 9, Johnson did meet with King, though he insisted beforehand that King's visit to the White House be billed as a meeting with Vice President Hubert H. Humphrey. King outlined the nature of problem and asked for legislation to outlaw literacy tests. Afterward, King praised the president's "deep commitment to obtaining the right to vote for all Americans," and he made sure Johnson's private assurances went on record: "The president made it very clear to me that he was determined during his administration to see all remaining obstacles removed to the right of Negroes to vote" (Garrow 1986, 386–387; Fairclough 1987, 236).

Back in Selma, the conflict escalated. On February 10, Clark arrested 120 black students and used electric cattle prods to force them to run into the countryside. After two outraged mass meetings that evening, King and his staffers asked themselves, "How far can Selma take us on the right to vote?" (Garrow 1986, 388). The SCLC then decided to broaden the campaign to the surrounding counties, where there were virtually no registered black voters. On February 18, after an evening mass meet-

ing in Marion, Perry County, protesters marched to the county courthouse. Almost immediately the street lights dimmed and state troopers and county police attacked the crowd. Jimmie Lee Jackson, trying to protect his family, was mortally wounded (Lawson 1997, 107). At Jackson's March 2 funeral, King announced to some two thousand mourners that there would be a march to Montgomery on Sunday, March 7, to demand the vote. It would be the set-piece confrontation the SCLC had been hoping for.

The Selma to Montgomery march proved to be the defining moment of the campaign, and in some ways the defining moment of the civil rights movement as a whole. Fearing violence, Baker sought to arrest the marchers before they left Selma, but he was overruled by Mayor Smitherman. Baker's fears were more than justified. As the six hundred marchers crossed Selma's Edmund Pettus Bridge on the road to Montgomery, county police and state troopers stopped them with tear gas. Wearing gas masks, the police attacked, and continued their assault even as the marchers fled. Fifty-six marchers were taken to hospital; eighteen stayed overnight. Amelia Boynton was knocked unconscious; John Lewis suffered a fractured skull.

Bloody Sunday shook the nation. Some fifty million viewers watched fifteen minutes of footage of the violence on ABC (Valelly 2004, 193). One of those viewers, President Johnson, recalled later, "I felt a deep outrage" (Johnson 1971, 162). Ironically, ABC broke into a movie called *Judgement at Nuremberg*. Plenty of commentators proceeded to make the connection between Adolf Hitler's troops and southern police. In response to Bloody Sunday, ten thousand people marched in Detroit, fifteen

John Lewis, leader of the Student Nonviolent Coordinating Committee (SNCC), led a march of about 600 people from Selma to Montgomery, Alabama, on March 7, 1965, to dramatize the African American struggle for voting rights. On what became known as Bloody Sunday, the marchers crossed the Edmund Pettus Bridge in Selma and were charged and beaten by police officers. Lewis suffered a fractured skull. *Source: AP/Wide World Photos.*

thousand in Harlem, and fifteen thousand in Washington, D.C. Even the *Birmingham News* declared support for King. Moreover, at least 450 white clergy from across America responded to King's call to come to Selma (Fairclough 1987, 247). After arresting a group of white northerners outside the mayor's house, Wilson Baker admitted to reporters that "this has ceased to be a Negro movement." Listening to their attempts to sing "We Shall Overcome," Baker reflected on a movement that was now beyond his control, "At least we had good music when the Negroes were demonstrating" (Watters and Cleghorn 1967, 248).

Bloody Sunday placed voting rights at the top of the political agenda. According to Democratic senator Walter F. Mondale of Minnesota, Selma made "passage of legislation to guarantee Southern Negroes the right to vote an absolute imperative for Congress this year" (Garrow 1986, 399). Congress pressed Johnson for more decisive action. King sought to make the pressure irresistible; he called on supporters to deluge the White House with telegrams. King rescheduled the march to Montgomery for Tuesday, March 9, even though a federal judge had issued a decree postponing it until formal hearings later in the week. Fearing a potential Bloodier Tuesday, Johnson sent an emissary to try to negotiate a compromise, and he made a public statement on Tuesday morning calling on all sides to obey the law. Determined not to defy the law, King accepted a compromise. He led the marchers across the bridge, knelt to pray, and then turned the march around. Some SNCC activists were livid (Lewis 1998, 334). But that was not the story that reached the media. Later that evening, three white clergymen who had traveled to support the movement were attacked. One of them, Rev. James Reeb, died two days later.

The march was rescheduled for March 21. In the interim, President Johnson addressed a joint session of Congress on March 15 to urge the passage of a voting rights proposal *(see Document 22)*. In front of a televised audience of seventy million, Johnson told Congress that he wanted "no delay, no hesitation, no compromise." Johnson had invited King to be present, but King declined because it clashed with Reeb's funeral. As they together watched Johnson's speech on television, King's colleagues saw him weep publicly for the first time since the movement began. Johnson presented his proposals to Congress two days later. When the march finally began on March 21, it was no longer an appeal but a celebration. On arrival in Montgomery on March 25, King declared, "We have overcome

After the violence of Bloody Sunday on March 7, 1965, participants in a rescheduled voting rights march from Selma to Montgomery, Alabama, finally stream across the Alabama river on March 21, 1965. *Source: AP/Wide World Photos.*

today." At a massive rally, King repeated the question and answer "How long? Not long" *(see Document 23)*. Soon afterward, news filtered through that Viola Liuzzo, the mother of five who was helping to transport the marchers, had been shot dead (Garrow 1986, 413).

The President and Congress

It would be easy to ascribe the Voting Rights Act to the Selma campaign alone. In 1968 the first report of the U.S. Commission on Civil Rights after the act did exactly that. "In 1965, the American public witnessed on television the beating of demonstrators in Selma. . . . Congress thereupon adopted a more direct approach to dealing with these problems" (U.S. Commission on Civil Rights 1968, 10). In his final press conference before leaving office, Johnson recalled that the act "finally came to pass after a tragedy at Selma" (Johnson various years, 2:843). In early 1965, leading politicians certainly seemed to be reacting to Selma. Johnson's first public commitment to introducing voting legislation followed King's release from jail and call to meet the president. Johnson's announcement of a specific date for the legislation followed the events of Bloody Sunday. In the first months after his election victory in 1964, Johnson's public comments in support of voting rights legislation had been brief at best, and most of them had been in off-the-record briefings. But in the wake of Bloody Sunday, he firmly identified himself with the cause. In the climax to his speech in Congress on March 15, 1965, Johnson borrowed the movement's rallying cry, "We Shall Overcome." It was the most passionate and effective speech of his presidency.

The Eighty-Ninth Congress (1965–1967), like its predecessors, initially showed little inclination to tackle the question of voting rights. For example, the Senate minority leader, Republican Everett Dirksen of Illinois, a supporter of civil rights, had hoped that the 1964 act would satisfy activists for the time being. During 1965 he admitted, "We felt we had made some real honest-to-God progress last year. We felt everything would fall into its slot. We thought we were out of the civil rights woods" (MacNeil 1970, 252). But after watching the vicious behavior of the Alabama police, Dirksen told Katzenbach that he was prepared to support a "revolutionary" bill if need be (Lawson 1976, 309). As events in Selma progressed, some 122 U.S. senators and representatives gave 199 speeches in support of voting rights. Only sixty speeches criticized the voting rights campaign, and more than half of those were by Alabama politicians. (By comparison, only ten senators and representatives had spoken out in support of the 1963 campaign in Birmingham.) On March 9 alone, forty-three representatives and seven senators called for voting rights legislation (Garrow 1978, 145).

A closer look at the formulation and passage of the legislation, however, reveals that the relationship between Selma and the Voting Rights Act was not quite as neat a cause and effect as the public outcry might suggest. Under Katzenbach's guidance, the Justice Department had prepared options for the president to consider before the Selma campaign had even been announced. The final draft of the bill was prepared two days before Bloody Sunday. One of King's advisers, Stanley Levison, recognized that Selma alone could not provide the full explanation. "We would be at fault if we believed our own propaganda that Selma was a terrible expression of brutality and terrorism. . . . The bombings in Birmingham and the deliberate and continuous violence . . . there were far worse. Yet Selma provoked a far greater indignation and resolution to halt the injustice" (Garrow 1986, 419).

For one thing, Johnson had already proved himself to be a supporter of civil rights. He had used his first speech after Kennedy's assassination in 1963 to urge passage of the Civil Rights Act, and he had worked tirelessly to push it through. For another, unlike Kennedy Johnson was prepared to confront southern politicians who defended white supremacy. After Bloody Sunday, Johnson summoned Alabama's governor, the notorious segregationist George C. Wallace, to the White House to give him a dressing-down. Johnson sat Wallace on a squishy sofa and gave him a long lecture littered with expletives. Three hours later, Wallace emerged and told reporters, "Hell, if I'd stayed in there much longer, he'd have had me coming out for civil rights" (Dallek 1998, 217). Soon afterward, Wallace asked Johnson to take over the Alabama National Guard to protect the march to Montgomery. King's deputy, Ralph Abernathy, reflected later that "it may be unpopular to say so, but I don't believe under President Kennedy we would have gotten either [the Civil Rights Act of 1964 or the Voting Rights Act]" (Abernathy 1989, 322).

This is not to say that Johnson was a pioneer in civil rights. He had, after all, opposed much of the 1957 Civil Rights Act. During the debate over the voting rights bill, House minority leader Gerald R. Ford accused him of being a "Johnny-come-lately" to the issue. Nor

did Johnson meekly follow the agenda of the civil rights movement. For example, he outraged many civil rights activists when he refused to seat delegates from the Mississippi Freedom Democratic Party at the Democratic National Convention in 1964. (The party had been organized by civil rights organizations during the Freedom Summer). Anxious not to lose the support of the southern wing of the Democratic Party, Johnson had recognized the regular, all-white, Mississippi Democratic delegation instead.

Nevertheless, Johnson genuinely believed the black vote was central to unraveling the system of white supremacy. As he told Vice President Hubert Humphrey well before the Selma campaign began, when blacks get the vote "they'll have every politician, north and south, east and west, kissing their ass, begging for support." Johnson also recognized that it would be a popular move, at least outside the South. He had an almost obsessive interest in public opinion. As one biographer put it, "Television and radio were his constant companions" (Goodwin 1987, vii–viii). He would have known, then, that polls consistently found that the voting rights campaign had more legitimacy than any other civil rights campaign. In one Gallup poll taken shortly after Bloody Sunday, 76 percent of respondents (and even a majority of white southerners) said they would support a law that empowered federal officials to ensure that black voters could register and vote (Garrow 1978, 157).

Johnson was also acutely aware that more black voters would benefit his reelection prospects. In the 1964 election, Johnson lost the majority of the white vote in every southern state except his home state of Texas, and consequently he trailed in the South 49 to 48.5 percent overall. In a memo to Johnson entitled the "Negro Vote in the South," presidential aide Lawrence O'Brien pointed out that black voters had provided Johnson with his margin of victory in four southern states (Stern 1992, 211). What this meant in practice was that Johnson had failed to carry only those southern states with less than 45 percent of voting-age blacks registered. Of course, pushing for civil rights legislation was not without risk of alienating southern white voters further. But, unlike the Civil Rights Act of 1964, enfranchising black voters in the South also promised a handsome political tradeoff.

The swift passage of the legislation also depended on the willingness of Congress to support the president. The 1964 election left the Democrats in firm control of the House and the Senate. The 295–140 majority in the House was the largest since 1936. Meanwhile, in the presidential race Johnson's overwhelming victory against Republican senator Barry Goldwater of Arizona, who had vehemently opposed the civil rights bill, gave him a personal mandate for further reform. With Johnson at the head of the ticket, Democrats had gained thirty-eight seats in the House and two in the Senate. All in all, it added up to a rare opportunity for Johnson—one that led him to launch the ambitious Great Society program. After the election of 1964, Johnson told Lawrence O'Brien, "We can pass it all now" (Stern 1992, 211). *Congressional Quarterly* calculated that 68.4 percent of proposals submitted by Johnson in 1965 were approved by Congress, the highest since the *Quarterly* began keeping records in 1954 (Evans and Novak 1967, 497). In the Senate, both the ma-

jority and minority leaders supported Johnson's voting rights bill.

In terms of Democratic strength in Congress and his own personal mandate, Johnson was in the most powerful position of any president since Franklin D. Roosevelt during the New Deal. Unlike in Roosevelt's time, however, southern Democrats now had less control over their party and thus Congress as a whole. The weakness of southern Democrats was crucial to the course of voting rights legislation. The election of 1948, which brought an influential group of northern liberal Democrats to Congress, had begun the swing away from conservative domination of the party (Zelizer 2004). The 1964 election completed the turnaround. The balance of votes ensured a comfortable liberal majority, based on northern Democrats, for any bill. In the House, thirty-five new representatives who supported civil rights legislation won elections against incumbents who had opposed it. Indeed, some of the new intake of southern Democratic senators and representatives, especially those representing urban areas with black voters, supported civil rights legislation. Meanwhile, the seemingly clear mandate from the electorate led a further twenty-five representatives (including ten southern Democrats) who had opposed civil rights legislation to support the bill (Brady and Sinclair 1984, 1054). Considering that southern Democrats had ultimately been unable to derail the controversial civil rights bill in 1964, they were hardly likely to stop a bill calling for the most basic of American rights in 1965.

Moreover, southern Democrats had lost some of their key positions of power in the Senate. Lyndon Johnson had been replaced as majority leader by Mike Mansfield of Montana. Known as a straight shooter, Mansfield felt no obligation to cut deals with southern Democrats (Valeo 1999). Prior to 1965, Democratic senator James Eastland of Mississippi, a staunch segregationist, had used his position as chair of the Judiciary Committee to kill off over a hundred civil rights bills. But after the 1964 election, the Judiciary Committee had a clear liberal majority, leaving Eastland powerless to obstruct voting rights legislation. Meanwhile the de facto leader of southern resistance, Georgia senator Richard Russell, was ill. He was defeatist, too. As he explained to one colleague, "If there is anything I could do, I would do it, but I assume the die is cast" (Lawson 1976, 309). Overall in the Senate after the 1964 elections, southern Democrats willing and able to oppose voting rights dropped from 31 percent to 23 percent of all senators (Valelly 2004, 197). In 1964 they had led the longest filibuster in congressional history in an attempt to derail the civil rights bill. In 1965 their filibuster was little more than a whimper.

Meanwhile, there was increasing support for voting rights legislation from within the federal bureaucracy. In June 1964, the administration's Task Force on Civil Rights pointed out that "strong moves to assure the speediest possible accession of Negroes to voting rolls . . . are essential." Justice Department officials recognized that the voting rights aspect of the civil rights bill had achieved virtually nothing, as the resistance to registration during the Mississippi Freedom Summer made clear. Attorney General Katzenbach was a stickler for not interfering with states' rights, but even he conceded the need to go far beyond the "torturous, often ineffective pace of litigation" (Graham 1990, 163). As he explained later in an interview, "We brought the voting case by

case. It was just an impossible system of law enforcement . . . [that] just took forever."

Making the Act

Clearly, then, voting rights campaigners were presented with an opportunity unprecedented since Reconstruction. But details of the passage of the act reveal that both the timing and, especially, the form of the legislation were dependent on the pressure the Selma campaign brought to bear. On December 18, 1964, Katzenbach sent Johnson a memo suggesting three possible ways to tackle disenfranchisement. Katzenbach's preferred option was a constitutional amendment that would prohibit any voter qualifications apart from age, a short period of residency, and conviction for a felony or confinement in a mental institution. However, Katzenbach conceded that the process of passing an amendment would be slow and risky, and that an amendment might arouse opposition from those with genuine concerns about extending federal influence. Katzenbach's second suggestion was legislation to create a new federal commission that would appoint federal registrars to oversee federal elections. Finally, in line with previous recommendations from the U.S. Civil Rights Commission and President Kennedy, Katzenbach proposed legislation granting an existing federal agency "power to assume direct control of registration for voting in both federal and state elections in any area where the percentage of potential Negro registrants actually registered is low" (Graham 1990, 164).

At first, Johnson was in no hurry to make a public decision. Even after he had committed himself to introducing legislation, he refused to give details of the timing or content of the bill, not even in private conversations with King. He may have just been guarded, but apparently the administration did not decide to abandon the idea of an amendment and push for voting rights legislation before early February. From then on, the administration seemed rushed. In his memoirs, Johnson admits that his March 15 speech to Congress was not finished until the very last minute, and that he had to deliver the first half using notes, because it was not set up on the TelePrompTer in time.

With the timetable accelerated by Selma, Johnson called on the Justice Department to act. Assistant Attorney General Ramsey Clark remembered that in early 1965 Johnson "was the one who was prodding us to get a voting rights act out, and he was angry that we had been unable to develop the formulas we needed" (Stern 1992, 223). The problem was to find a formula, ostensibly race-neutral, that would apply only to those parts of the South that restricted black voting. Justice Department lawyers settled on a formula based on a "trigger" provision. Literacy tests or similar ballot access tests would be automatically suspended in those areas where less than 50 percent of the voting-age population had registered or cast votes in the 1964 elections. In addition, the attorney general would be empowered to send federal examiners to these areas to ensure that qualified applicants could register. Solicitor General Archibald Cox sent Katzenbach a first draft of the legislation on February 23. But Cox realized the formula was far from precise. As it stood, the act would not cover Arkansas, Florida, Tennessee, or Texas in the South, but it would trigger Alaska, Arizona, Idaho, and Maine. Cox also feared it was

vulnerable to a legal challenge on the grounds of federal interference in state control over elections.

Nevertheless, this formula was the substance of the bill submitted to both houses of Congress on March 17. In the Senate, the Judiciary Committee—now with a liberal majority—strengthened the bill by banning the poll tax as a suffrage requirement and adding a further trigger to send federal voting examiners to districts in which less than 25 percent of eligible voters from racial minorities were registered. Fearing that a poll tax ban might arouse opposition and scupper the passage of the bill, Dirksen and Mansfield introduced a substitute version that omitted the ban on the poll tax. The substitute, which was backed by President Johnson, passed narrowly, 49–45. Meanwhile, in the House William McCulloch, the Republican ranking member on the Judiciary Committee, and Gerald Ford proposed a substitute bill that would have replaced the automatic trigger to suspend literacy tests with one authorizing the appointment of voting examiners in any political subdivision in which the attorney general received twenty-five meritorious complaints. McCulloch and Ford argued that their formula would diminish federal interference and cover more territory. But twenty-five Republicans ignored the party leadership, concerned about the implications of lining up alongside southern Democrats who planned to use the substitute as a way to force a stalemate. In the end, the House approved a strengthened bill, which included a poll tax ban.

As the bill made its way through Congress, civil rights groups kept up the pressure. For example, in a mock election held in Mississippi in the fall of 1964 three black activists were "elected" to the House of Representatives. During the summer of 1965, they protested that they had the right to be seated in place of the white representatives from Mississippi. Meanwhile, the two versions of the bill were being debated in the House-Senate Conference Committee. Members from the House argued strongly in favor of a ban on the poll tax. But under pressure from the administration (which feared that such a ban would be ruled unconstitutional) and from civil rights supporters, including Martin Luther King (who feared the bill would stall over the argument), they agreed to drop the anti–poll tax provision. In turn, the Senate members of the committee dropped the additional triggering formula. In effect, then, the House and Senate members canceled each other out. The only significant change to the original bill was a provision for federal examiners to monitor elections in districts that had been triggered by the bill.

The final version, as it turned out, was almost exactly what the administration had first sought. Section 2 outlawed any voting test or qualification that would "deny or abridge the right of any citizen of the United States to vote on account of race or color" *(see Document 25)*. Section 4 introduced the triggering formula to suspend tests, but it included a "bailout" option that allowed districts outside the South to appeal to the district court in Washington. Section 5 froze voting laws in areas covered by the act, pending federal approval of any changes proposed after November 1, 1964. Any changes to local registration practices had to be approved by the Justice Department or the district court in Washington, and approval would be forthcoming only if the practices did "not have the purpose and . . .

[would] not have the effect of denying or abridging the right to vote on account of race or color." Sections 4 and 5 were temporary provisions intended to remain in place for five years. Sections 6–8 enabled the attorney general to send in federal voting "examiners" and "poll watchers" to ensure that legally qualified persons could register and then vote in all elections. Section 10 instructed the attorney general "forthwith" to challenge the constitutionality of poll taxes as voting prerequisites in state and local elections.

Thus the final version of the bill allowed direct enforcement of voting rights by the executive branch of the government. Rather than the Justice Department having to litigate on a case-by-case basis, local registrars now had to prove that their procedures were nondiscriminatory if they wanted to avoid federal supervision. Rep. Emanuel Celler of New York, chair of the House Judiciary Committee, believed the act would eliminate "legal dodges and subterfuges" and be "impervious to all legal trickery and evasion" (Davidson and Grofman 1992, 17). On August 3, the House adopted the report 328–74. The next day, the Senate adopted it 79–18. Some thirty-seven southern Democratic representatives and six southern Democratic senators voted to support the bill. On August 6, Johnson signed the act into law on Capitol Hill. Meanwhile, a substantial majority in the House dismissed the challenge to the white Mississippi delegation, trusting that the Voting Rights Act would ensure fair representation in due course.

Not surprisingly, six states challenged the core provisions of the act, claiming that they exceeded the powers of Congress and encroached on an area reserved to the states by

After signing the Voting Rights Act on August 6, 1965, President Lyndon Johnson reaches to shake hands with Dr. Martin Luther King Jr., as other civil rights leaders look on. *Source: Lyndon Baines Johnson Library and Museum/Yoichi R. Okamoto.*

the Constitution. But in 1966 the Supreme Court ruled in *South Carolina v. Katzenbach* that the act was "a valid means for carrying out the commands of the 15th Amendment. . . . Hopefully, millions of non-white Americans will now be able to participate for the first time on an equal basis in the government under which they live" *(Document 27)*. In turn, Attorney General Katzenbach challenged the poll tax, and in 1966 federal courts struck down the requirement that voters pay a poll tax in order to register in Alabama, Mississippi, Texas, and Virginia. Thus the Court upheld the principle that racial barriers of any kind to registering were illegal, and the Court confirmed that Congress had the authority to dismantle any such barriers (Keyssar 2000, 267).

As the next chapters will show, the Voting Rights Act was far from the end of the voting rights story. Southern defiance and civil rights protests did not end with act. The temporary nature of some sections of the act ensured that debate would be rejoined. Moreover, although the act ruled on the question of registration and voting, it did not address the question of equal representation. Still, the act changed the South. Nowhere was this clearer than in Dallas County, Mississippi. On May 3, 1964, only 320 black voters were registered, or a mere 2.1 percent of potential voters. By October 31, 1967, 10,644 blacks were registered, or over 70 percent of the total number eligible to vote. In what turned out to be a close 1966 primary election for sheriff of Dallas County, the local executive committee tried to reject votes from black wards. The Justice Department brought suit, and the votes were counted. Sheriff Jim Clark, having unintentionally helped the cause of black voting rights, was voted out of office (Landsberg 1997, 8).

References

Abernathy, Ralph. 1989. *And the Walls Came Tumbling Down.* New York: Harper and Row.

Brady, David, and Barbara Sinclair. 1984. "Building Majorities for Policy Changes in the House of Representatives." *Journal of Politics* 46 (November): 1033–1060.

Dallek, Robert. 1998. *Flawed Giant: Lyndon Johnson and His Times, 1961–73.* New York: Oxford University Press.

Davidson, Chandler, and Bernard Grofman, eds. 1992. *Controversies in Minority Voting: The Voting Rights Act in Perspective.* Washington, D.C.: Brookings.

Dittmer, John. 1995. *Local People: The Struggle for Civil Rights in Mississippi.* Urbana: University of Illinois Press.

Evans, Rowland, and Robert Novak. 1967. *Lyndon B. Johnson: The Exercise of Power.* London: George Allen.

Fairclough, Adam. 1987. *To Redeem the Soul of America: The Southern Christian Leadership Conference and Martin Luther King, Jr.* Athens: University of Georgia Press.

Firestone, Bernard, and Robert Vogt, eds. 1989. *Lyndon Baines Johnson and the Uses of Power.* Westport, Conn.: Greenwood Press.

Garrow, David J. 1978. *Protest at Selma: Martin Luther King, Jr., and the Voting Rights Act of 1965.* New Haven, Conn.: Yale University Press.

———. 1986. *Bearing the Cross: Martin Luther King, Jr., and the Southern Christian Leadership Conference.* New York: Morrow.

Goodwin, Doris Kearns. 1987. *Lyndon Johnson and the American Dream.* New York: St. Martin's Press.

Graham, Hugh Davis. 1990. *The Civil Rights Era: Origins and Development of National Policy 1960–1972.* New York: Oxford University Press.

Harvey, James C. 1973. *Black Civil Rights during the Johnson Administration.* Jackson: University and College Press of Mississippi.

Hulsey, Byron. 2000. *Everett Dirksen and His Presidents: How a Senate Giant Shaped American Politics.* Lawrence: University of Kansas Press.

Johnson, Lyndon Baines. 1971. *The Vantage Point: Perspectives of the Presidency, 1963–1969.* London: Weidenfeld and Nicolson.

Johnson, Lyndon B. Various years. *Public Papers of the Presidents of the United States: Lyndon B. Johnson, 1964–1969.* Washington, D.C.: Government Printing Office.

Joseph, Peter, ed. 1973. *Good Times: An Oral History of America in the Nineteen Sixties.* New York: Charterhouse.

Keyssar, Alexander. 2000. *The Right to Vote: The Contested History of Democracy in the United States.* New York: Basic Books.

Landsberg, Brian K. 1997. *Enforcing Civil Rights: Race Discrimination and the Department of Justice.* Lawrence: University Press of Kansas.

Lawson, Steven F. 1976. *Black Ballots, Voting Rights in the South.* New York: Columbia University Press.

———. 1997. *Running for Freedom: Civil Rights and Black Politics in American since 1941.* New York: McGraw-Hill.

Lewis, John. 1998. *Walking with the Wind: A Memoir of the Movement.* New York: Simon and Schuster.

MacNeil, Neil. 1970. *Dirksen: Portrait of a Public Man*. New York: World Publishing Company.

Payne, Charles. 1996. *I've Got the Light of Freedom: The Organizing Tradition and the Mississippi Freedom Struggle*. Berkeley: University of California Press.

Stern, Mark. 1992. *Calculating Visions: Kennedy, Johnson and Civil Rights*. New Brunswick, N.J.: Rutgers University Press.

Thornton, J. Mills. 2002. *Dividing Lines: Municipal Politics and the Struggle for Civil Rights in Montgomery, Birmingham, and Selma*. Tuscaloosa: University of Alabama Press.

Tuck, Stephen. 2003. *Beyond Atlanta: The Struggle for Racial Equality in Georgia, 1940–1980*. Athens: University of Georgia Press.

U.S. Commission on Civil Rights. 1968. *Political Participation*. Washington, D.C.

Unger, Irwin, and Debi Unger. 1999. *LBJ: A Life*. New York: Wiley.

Valelly, Richard. 2004. *The Two Reconstructions: The Struggle for Black Enfranchisement*. Chicago: University of Chicago Press.

Valeo, Francis. 1999. *Mike Mansfield, Majority Leader: A Different Kind of Senate, 1961–1976*. New York: M. E. Sharpe.

Watters, Pat, and Reese Cleghorn. 1967. *Climbing Jacob's Ladder: The Arrival of Negroes in Southern Politics* New York: Harcourt, Brace, and World.

Young, Andrew. 1996. *An Easy Burden: The Civil Rights Movement and the Transformation of America*. New York: Harper Collins.

Zelizer, Julian. 2004. *On Capitol Hill: The Struggle to Reform Congress and Its Consequences, 1948–2000*. New York: Cambridge University Press.

Extensions of the Voting Rights Act

COLIN D. MOORE

In 1969 at his final press conference, President Lyndon B. Johnson declared the Voting Rights Act (VRA) of 1965 to be his proudest achievement (Lawson 1985, 4). Borrowing the legendary words of Abraham Lincoln, Johnson expressed his confidence that this monumental piece of legislation would "make it possible for this government to endure, not half slave and half free, but united." The White House press corps warmly received Johnson's optimism that afternoon, but most probably realized that this lovely sentiment glossed over an important stipulation in the VRA, a fact that Johnson, one of the great masters of Washington politics and the author of so many pieces of legislation, knew all too well: the crucial enforcement provisions of the VRA were *temporary*. Unlike nearly every other piece of civil rights legislation, from the Emancipation Proclamation to the Civil Rights Act of 1964, crucial sections of the VRA would have to be extended again and again, and this extension requirement was potentially the Achilles' heel of Johnson's "goddamnedest toughest" voting rights bill.

The Voting Rights Act of 1965 *(Document 25)* was designed to provide effective enforcement of the Fifteenth Amendment *(Document 3)*. It upheld African American voting rights in

the South with federal power, and, unlike several previous federal voting rights statutes, it reversed the burden of proof, requiring southern jurisdictions to demonstrate to the Justice Department that blacks were being given fair and equal access to the ballot.[1] As one scholar of voting rights has observed, "The legislation dramatically shifted the burden from the victim of racially discriminatory voting practices to the perpetrator of these practices and brought the discussion of these issues to the Washington, D.C., environment rather than leave these legal issues to be resolved in local, parochial federal district courts in the South" (Ball, Krane, and Lauth 1982, 49–50). Section 2, a permanent feature of the act, echoed the language of the Fifteenth Amendment and mandated that "[n]o voting qualification or prerequisite to voting, or standard, practice, or procedure shall be imposed or applied by any State or political subdivision to deny or abridge the right of any citizen of the United States to vote on account of race or color." Sections 4–9 of the VRA, better known as the "special provisions," were its teeth, but they were also only temporary features of the law and would have to be extended as early as 1970. Section 4 described the conditions that would bring a jurisdiction under the protection of the act. This "triggering formula," as it is sometimes known, applied to states that required voters to take a test to prove their competence or moral fitness to participate in the November 1, 1964, elections *and* had a voting registration or turnout of less than 50 percent of voting-age residents in the 1964 presidential elections (Davidson 1992, 18). Finally, Section 5, which would soon become one of the most important of the act's temporary provisions, required any change in the voting laws of covered jurisdictions to be approved by the attorney general or the U.S. District Court of the District of Columbia, a requirement that would become known as "preclearance."

Some of most expansive authorizations of the VRA were in Sections 6, 7, and 8, which gave the attorney general the power to send election observers and examiners[2] to supervise elections in the jurisdictions covered. The Department of Justice, however, conscious of the possible southern reaction to its sending an army of federal election examiners to the South, used its powers rather sparingly. In the first two years of the act's existence, federal examiners worked in only sixty counties, and the Justice Department studiously avoided the home counties of powerful southern Democrats, such as Sunflower County, Mississippi, the home of Sen. James O. Eastland. Indeed, although examiners did register over 150,000 black voters in the first two and a half years of the VRA, most of the registration was carried out by civil rights groups such as the National Association for the Advancement of Colored People (NAACP) and the Student Nonviolent Coordinating Committee (Ball, Krane, and Lauth 1982, 56). Still, the very threat of federal examiners may have mo-

tivated southern registrars to open up ballot access (for many southern elites nothing could be worse than the indignity of having their cities invaded by federal elections examiners). As one black politician noted to members of the U.S. Commission on Civil Rights, "Birmingham would be appalled and embarrassed if examiners were sent back here" (U.S. Commission on Civil Rights 1975, 34).

The use of election observers was far more common. During the first decade of the VRA, more than 6,500 observers were sent to monitor elections, and nearly half of them were sent to Mississippi (U.S. Commission on Civil Rights 1975, 36). As both civil rights activists and their southern opponents realized, these temporary enforcement features of the VRA—preclearance, federal examiners, election observers—were essential to the fulfillment of the act. Without them, the Voting Rights Act would quickly become a mere paper tiger, no more effective than the Fifteenth Amendment in the wake of Reconstruction's collapse.

Over the past four decades, the VRA has become immensely more popular with politicians of all stripes. At the same time, the act itself has become substantially more permanent and extensive. This chapter compares the politics surrounding each extension of the VRA by examining the similarities, evolutionary trends, and one significant expansion of the VRA between 1965 and today. As for similarities, the VRA extension periods are characterized by three broad ones: (1) divided government; (2) presidential diffidence, bungling, or opposition, which is in marked contrast to most theories of presidential leadership; and (3) bipartisan congressional leadership, particularly in the Senate. These similarities are accompanied by evolutionary trends, the most important of which are (1) the growing awareness of the black vote; (2) the decline in the Dixiecratic argument of racial segregation, but the persistence of sectional resentment ("the South has been punished enough, the Civil War is over"); and (3) the growing debate about whether voting equality has been achieved and the act can be retired—a factor that will likely be important when the special provisions (Sections 4–9) of the Voting Rights Act expire in August 2007 (*see Appendix*). Finally, the act has expanded significantly beyond its original 1965 scope. Today, it covers jurisdictions far beyond the South and is also a more potent piece of legislation—a result of express authorizations by Congress and some landmark Supreme Court decisions. These broad trends and themes will guide this brief story of the battles to reauthorize the Voting Rights Act. The story begins with a review of the southern reaction to the VRA and of its effectiveness in stemming the tide of minority vote dilution.

Southern Responses to the 1965 Act: Minority Vote Dilution

The Supreme Court affirmed the constitutionality of the Voting Rights Act in the 1966 landmark cases of *South Carolina v. Katzenbach (Document 27)* and *Morgan v. Katzenbach* and so, for the first time since 1898, African Americans began to elect their own candidates to public office. Yet a newer form of discrimination was beginning to take hold, one that was designed to work within the confines of the VRA. Because they could no longer forbid blacks to vote through law or intimidation—practices explicitly forbidden by the VRA—some southern

communities introduced policies designed to dilute minority voting strength and maintain political power for whites by passing laws that restricted minority voting without appearing discriminatory. Many cities, for example, began to change the way they elected members of their town council—from multimember districts to at-large elections. In Alabama, twenty-five counties switched from single-member districts to at-large elections (Davidson 1992, 25). Although such laws did not *prevent* black candidates from running for or winning office, they substantially reduced the likelihood that a single black candidate would win. According to political scientist Gerald Rosenberg (1993, 81), "When blacks attempted to run as candidates, discriminatory administration of neutral laws resulted in the following: abolition of office, extension of the term of the white incumbent; substitution of appointment for election; increase in filing fees; raising of requirements for independent candidates; increase in property qualifications; withholding nominating petitions. And finally, of course, there are the time-honored practices of gerrymandering, county consolidation, switching to at-large elections, and the like, which all can act to continue to deprive blacks of any political representation."

The Supreme Court, however, found that many of these laws did indeed violate the VRA, and in *Allen v. State Board of Elections* (1969), the Court articulated the first strong use of Section 5 *(see Document 28)*. Writing for the Court, Chief Justice Earl Warren held that "[t]he Voting Rights Act was aimed at the subtle, as well as the obvious, state regulations which have the effect of denying citizens their right to vote because of their race." Any effort to reduce the effectiveness of minority voting, even laws that were racially neutral, was now a violation of the VRA; the shape of electoral districts, registration requirements, and voter qualifications all had to be approved prior to their implementation. Justice Warren's expansive interpretation of Section 5 thus solved the problem of minority vote dilution and effectively forbade southern efforts to dilute minority voting power. Not surprisingly, southern politicians were not at all pleased by this decision, and many were eager for their chance to end VRA coverage of the South or to subject the rest of the country to the same indignity. They would get their chance in 1970.

The Struggle for Extension in 1970

The special provisions of the VRA were due to expire on August 6, 1970. At that time, a covered jurisdiction would be allowed to "bail out" by proving to the U.S. District Court for the District of Columbia that no discriminatory tests or devices had been employed for the past five years (Grofman, Handley, and Niemi 1992). By 1970 even opponents of the VRA generally acknowledged how successful it had been, and some of them began to argue that an extension would be unnecessary.

By contrast, many proponents on the left expected a long struggle to reauthorize the special provisions of the VRA. When Republican Richard Nixon was elected to the presidency in 1968, civil rights activists became especially worried. Much of Nixon's support in the 1968 election had come from the South, and liberals feared that he would be less concerned about the plight of southern blacks than the generally sympathetic LBJ. The Leadership Conference on Civil Rights, for example, was worried that

Nixon was "ready to sabotage the [civil rights] program—through indifference, through insufficient effort, through ignorance of what terrible consequences can follow relaxation of enforcement" (quoted in Lawson 1985, 124). Their fears were well placed. As Howard "Bo" Calloway, a member of the Republican national committee from Georgia, declared, "I believe most southerners would feel that the Nixon Administration broke a strong commitment to the South if it allowed an extension of the present Bill. We expect [the president] to have a straight forward Bill that says what it means and means what it says and applies to all sections of the county equally" (quoted in Lawson 1985, 131).

In the beginning of this struggle to reauthorize the VRA, however, the Nixon administration surprised both its supporters and its critics by steering a middle path. The first reports from Attorney General George Mitchell's Justice Department indicated the administration would likely support extension of the VRA. Eventually, Assistant Attorney General Jerris Leonard recommended that the act be extended for three years and include a ban on all literacy tests throughout the country (Lawson 1985, 131). Civil rights activists worried about proposals to extend the VRA to nonsouthern states or ban literacy tests nationwide, because such changes would spread federal enforcement too thin when it was needed so badly in the South. According to historian Steven F. Lawson (1985, 134), "While the department drafted its measure, the civil rights forces moved to obtain a simple extension of the original statute. As a practical matter, they frowned upon any design to amend the law by abolishing literacy tests nationwide."

The Nixon administration remained relatively silent as Congress began its deliberations on May 14, 1969. On June 26, however, the attorney general announced the administration's plans to place a nationwide ban on literacy tests until January 1, 1974, to remove most state residency requirements for presidential elections, and to allow the Justice Department to send election examiners anywhere in the county. The administration reasoned that if southerners were faced with the indignity of submitting their election practices to Washington bureaucrats for approval, then the entire country should face the same indignity—there was no reason why Minnesota should be treated differently than the Mississippi Delta. The most important change, however, dealt with the crucial preclearance guidelines under Section 5. Mitchell proposed that the Justice Department use litigation to challenge new election rules that it believed were discriminatory. Thus the Justice Department would have to prove that southern election rules were *illegal* rather than the current practice of requiring the supervised jurisdiction to prove that they were *legal*, thereby critically shifting the burden of proof.

Civil rights activists were not at all happy with the Nixon administration's proposal. As noted earlier, they believed that if the Justice Department were responsible for enforcing the VRA in Idaho as well as Alabama, the department's resources would be spread far too thin to enforce the provisions of the act where they were most needed—in the Deep South. As one prominent civil rights activist wrote, "This is a sophisticated, a calculated, incredible effort on the part of the chief lawyer of the Government of the United States to make it impossible for us to continue on the constitutional course that we have followed in exercising the tools . . . that we have had in protecting the right to vote" (quoted in Lawson 1985, 137–138). Nevertheless, the objections from civil rights activists were not enough to stop the growing support for the administration's amended bill, and on December 11, 1969, the House approved the Nixon administration's amended version of the bill 234–179 with the support of "every lawmaker representing districts in the jurisdictions covered under the 1965 statute" (Lawson 1985, 144).

Civil rights leaders were plainly shocked at this outcome, and they worked to develop a new strategy in the Senate, where they would face the powerful chair of the Senate Judiciary Committee, Democrat Samuel J. Ervin Jr. of North Carolina, an outspoken critic of the VRA. Ervin's initial proposal was to apply the VRA nationally and to substitute the 1968 presidential election for the 1964 election. To understand the significance of this change it is important to recall that the original bill triggered coverage based on voting turnout for the 1964 presidential election. If the 1968 election were used instead—an election in which voting examiners were present to ensure black voting—many southern states would no longer be under the thumb of the VRA's special provisions. As one civil rights attorney argued, "The 1968 situation is to a high degree an artificial situation created by a law under which examiners went in and other methods such as abolishing test were used to get registration" (quoted in Lawson 1985, 140). Most civil rights activists justifiably believed that the minute southern jurisdictions were no longer under the watchful eye of the Department of

Justice, they would return to their old discriminatory practices. By this time, most southern politicians had changed their rhetoric from exuding overt racism to wallowing in wounded southern pride. Why, they asked, is only the *South* subject to the provisions of the VRA? If Congress was so interested in extending voting rights, then why not apply the act to the entire country? Despite a great deal of suspicion about the motives of these politicians who only a few years before had vehemently opposed any extension of voting rights, the question seemed reasonable.

In the face of this opposition, two liberal members of the Senate Judiciary Committee, Philip A. Hart, D-Mich., and Hugh D. Scott Jr., R-Pa., began to develop a compromise bill to offer in place of the House bill. The Scott-Hart compromise, as it came to be known, extended the VRA for five years, but it also incorporated the ban on literacy tests found in the House bill. The Senate bill, however, did not authorize the nationwide appointment of election observers—a power that civil rights activists feared would dilute the power of the VRA and spread the resources of the Justice Department too thin.

On March 1, 1970, the Senate began to consider the House bill and the Hart-Scott substitute. Just nine days later, however, Sen. John Sherman Cooper, a Republican from Kentucky, offered an amendment that was to become part of the final Senate bill. Cooper's amendment replaced the 1964 presidential election with the 1968 election as the standard for coverage—a move that meant that, for the first time, northern counties would fall under the VRA's strict provisions. Cooper's amendment passed, but the liberals countered with a second amend-

ment that proposed reducing the voting age to eighteen. The amendment was quickly approved 64–17. After adopting the Cooper and voting-age amendments, the Senate approved the final bill 64–12 and the House followed suit with a 272–132 final vote.

Although eleven of the twelve senators voting against the bill were from the South, it is more telling that six southern senators, including four southern Democrats, joined the majority and that they did not attempt to mount a filibuster (see Table 6-1, which shows the shifting votes on VRA extensions over a roughly thirty-year span). The electoral logic of the VRA, it seems, was beginning to work, and for the first time in anyone's memory southern senators began to fret about what their black constituents might be thinking. In probably the most telling statement to emerge from the debate, Democratic senator Ernest F. Hollings of South Carolina privately declared, "Don't ask me to go out and filibuster. I'm not going back to my state and explain a filibuster against black voters" (quoted in Lawson 1985, 152). Faced with the politically unpalatable prospect of vetoing the VRA, which was supported by a hundred Republican congressmen and thirty-three Republican senators, Nixon signed the VRA extension into law on June 22, 1970 *(see Document 30).*

In the end, the 1970 extension maintained the special provisions of the act for five more years (until August 6, 1975), kept the original preclearance requirements intact, instituted a more minor provision that formalized residency requirements for presidential elections, and, finally, lowered the voting age for federal elections to eighteen. The literacy test was also outlawed nationwide for five years. Finally, be-

Table 6-1 Roll Call Votes on Voting Rights Act Extensions: 1965, 1970, 1975, 1982, 1992

	Members Voting	Yea	Nay		Members Voting	Yea	Nay
House Roll Call, 1965				Republicans	33	27	6
Democrats	272	218	54	Independents	2	1	1
Northern Democrats	180	180	0	Total		77	12
Southern Democrats	92	38	54	**House Roll Call, 1982**			
Republicans	130	110	20	Democrats	234	227	7
Total		328	74	Northern Democrats	157	156	1
Senate Roll Call, 1965				Southern Democrats	77	71	6
Democrats	66	49	17	Republicans	178	161	17
Northern Democrats	44	43	1	Independents	1	1	0
Southern Democrats	22	6	16	Total		389	24
Republicans	31	30	1	**Senate Roll Call, 1982**			
Total		79	18	Democrats	42	42	0
House Roll Call, 1970				Northern Democrats	28	28	0
Democrats	228	172	56	Southern Democrats	14	14	0
Northern Democrats	144	138	6	Republicans	50	43	7
Southern Democrats	84	34	50	Independents	1	0	1
Republicans	176	100	76	Total		85	8
Total		272	132	**House Roll Call, 1992 (bilingual ballot provisions)**			
Senate Roll Call, 1970				Democrats	219	191	28
Democrats	42	31	11	Northern Democrats	155	146	9
Northern Democrats	28	27	1	Southern Democrats	64	45	19
Southern Democrats	14	4	10	Republicans	142	45	97
Republicans	34	33	1	Independents	1	1	0
Total		64	12	Total		237	125
House Roll Call, 1975				**Senate Roll Call, 1992 (bilingual ballot provisions)**			
Democrats	269	249	20	Democrats	54	50	4
Northern Democrats	187	186	1	Northern Democrats	38	36	2
Southern Democrats	82	63	19	Southern Democrats	16	14	2
Republicans	132	96	36	Republicans	41	25	16
Total		345	56	Total		75	20
Senate Roll Call, 1975							
Democrats	54	49	5				
Northern Democrats	38	38	0				
Southern Democrats	16	11	5				

Source: Keith T. Poole and Howard Rosenthal, "Roll Call Displays of the U.S. Congress, 1789–2000," *Voteview for Windows* v. 3.0.1, 2002.

cause the triggering mechanism was now based on turnout for the 1968 presidential election, for the first time areas outside the South fell under the VRA's jurisdiction. They were three boroughs of New York City—Manhattan, Brooklyn, and the Bronx.

The 1975 Extension: Expanding Protection to Language Minorities

In the years following the 1970 extension of the Voting Rights Act, the Supreme Court ruled in two landmark cases that were to have far-reaching implications for the act's preclearance provisions. In *White v. Regester* (1973), the Court held that multimember districts in Dallas County and Bexar County, Texas, improperly diluted black and Latino votes, and thus left these voters with "less opportunity than . . . other residents in the district to participate in the political process and to elect legislators of their choice." The problem with this case, however, is that the Court's reasoning was rather ambiguous. As one prominent scholar of the VRA has written, "It left practically unanswered the question of what were the criteria by which judges could determine if a voting system diluted minority votes" (Davidson 1992, 32–33). That same year, the Fifth Circuit Court of Appeals clarified this question and ruled in *Zimmer v. McKeithen* that electoral laws could be invalidated if they had the *effect* of racial bias. Up to this point, litigants had been required to demonstrate that electoral laws were created with the intention of discriminating against minority votes. Now, litigants were required merely to prove that these laws harmed the chances of minority participation or, more common, the chance to

elect a minority candidate to public office. These court cases, as well as the political fallout after Richard Nixon's resignation from the presidency in 1974, colored the terms of the 1975 extension process.

But even with this political upheaval, the logic of extension in 1975 was not terribly different from that in 1970. Once again civil rights activists were unsure of the level of support they could expect from the president— now Gerald R. Ford. As a Republican congressman from Michigan, Ford had supported the original VRA and the 1970 extension, but he had also expressed strong reservations about the act's exclusive application to the South. Predictably, in 1975 most southerners called for expanding the act nationwide, just as they had in 1970. On the other side, the civil rights coalition argued for extending it for ten more years, a position that was supported by the U.S. Commission on Civil Rights. In defending its position, the commission noted, "No black holds statewide office in the South and no black candidate for statewide office has ever come close to election" (quoted in Davidson 1992, 34). Furthermore, the commission reasoned that it was especially important to extend the preclearance requirements until after the 1980 census, when there would be numerous opportunities for legislative redistricting. However, Ford's attorney general, William B. Saxbe, recommended a more moderate course and advocated a simple five-year extension of the law. Despite these disagreements in the length of the extension, few politicians by 1975 believed that the special provisions would not be renewed.

On February 25, 1975, Peter W. Rodino Jr., D-N.J., and Don Edwards, D-Calif., two members of the House Judiciary Subcommittee, introduced a bill to extend the act for ten more years. J. Edward Hutchinson, R-Mich., countered with the administration's proposal for a five-year extension. Time was crucial to the strategy of both sides. Republicans wanted to pass a bill quickly, so that there would be plenty of time for President Ford to veto a ten-year extension plan and for Congress to approve the five-year plan he preferred. Congressional liberals, banking on their belief that Ford would not let the VRA lapse, wanted to pass the final bill as close as they possibly could to the August 6 deadline (Lawson 1985).

The Ford administration and its conservative allies were principally concerned about the bailout provisions. By this point, the covered jurisdictions had been under the control of the act for ten years, and conservatives believed it was high time to allow the more responsible districts to exit from the act's preclearance requirements. After all, they reasoned, if the covered jurisdictions are never allowed to bail out, then where was the incentive to improve? Republican M. Caldwell Butler of Virginia proposed an amendment that would allow covered jurisdictions to bail out of the act, but, in a concession to congressional liberals, he also made the requirements more stringent. The Butler amendment would have allowed jurisdictions to exit from VRA special coverage if at least 60 percent of citizens were registered to vote, if the jurisdiction had submitted to the Justice Department for approval all changes in its electoral law, and, finally, if it had introduced a program to actively encourage minority political involvement. On May 3, however, Butler's careful compromise failed to pass, largely because of fears about its effects on the

redistricting that would follow the 1980 census (Lawson 1985, 242). On May 14, the ten-year plan favored by Rodino and Edwards was sent to the floor of the House.

In the midst of these negotiations between civil rights liberals and their opponents, Rep. Barbara Jordan sponsored an amendment that greatly complicated the negotiations. Jordan, an African American from Texas, proposed that voting rights protection be expanded to language minorities. If Jordan's amendment passed, some states in the Southwest, as well as Alaska with its large American Indian population, would come under the provisions of the act. The new formula developed by Jordan would have triggered coverage if more than 5 percent of the voting-age population belonged to an Asian American, American Indian, Alaska Native, or Latino language group, if fewer than 50 percent of a jurisdiction's voting-age citizens had voted in the 1972 presidential election, and if ballots in that election were provided only in English. The amendment created, for all intents and purposes, a VRA for the Southwest. Jordan also added a bilingual ballot amendment to Section 203(c) of the VRA that further required the use of bilingual ballot materials if at least 5 percent of the jurisdiction's citizens belonged to a language minority and if that group had an English illiteracy rate higher than the national rate (Grofman, Handley, and Niemi 1992).

Although Jordan's amendment was controversial, voting rights protection for Hispanic voters in the Southwest was greatly needed. In Arizona, for example, a 1971 "purge law" that required all voters to reregister, along with the general indifference of state officials to registering voters in heavily Latino areas, had resulted in the state having the lowest rate of voter registration of any northern or western state (Bridges 1997, 188). And Arizona was not alone in these discriminatory practices; the situation was strikingly similar in Texas and southern California. From the outset, however, the Jordan amendment was opposed by powerful interests, including the governor of Texas, who responded to Jordan's proposal by quickly introducing legislation for compulsory bilingual ballots in a last-minute attempt to block Texas's inclusion under VRA jurisdiction. As Jordan later recalled in her autobiography, "Every elected official in the state opposed the idea of including Texas. . . . State officials were aghast. *Federales* would be intruding into local elections" (Jordan and Hearon 1979, 210). Even many civil rights liberals, such as Clarence Mitchell of the NAACP, were worried about how introducing this new proposal would affect the VRA's chances for extension (Lawson 1985, 229). Yet despite this opposition, Jordan's proposal was added to the bill.

Despite the addition of the Jordan amendment to expand coverage to the Southwest, there were few strong congressional opponents of the bill. After living under the VRA for a decade, most southern conservatives were now unwilling to engage in their usual subterfuge, and only three weeks after the bill was sent to the House floor from the Rules Committee the House renewed the VRA for ten more years in a lopsided 341–70 vote on June 4, 1975.

The bill may have sailed through the House, but civil rights activists knew Senate passage would be more difficult, especially because they had to face Democratic senator James Eastland of Mississippi, the conservative chair of the Senate Judiciary Committee. With only two months remaining until the special provisions expired, an obstructionist conservative could do a great deal of damage to the VRA's prospects for extension. As the Senate waited for the Judiciary Committee to release its final report, however, Majority Leader Mike Mansfield, D-Mont., moved to consider the recently passed House bill on July 21. To avoid the possibility that southern conservatives would attempt to filibuster this proposal, Mansfield called for two cloture motions, both of which passed with relative ease (Lawson 1985, 246).

The Ford administration finally broke its silence in early July. Ford recognized that extension of the VRA was inevitable, but he also supported the southern position of expanding the act to the rest of the nation. Furthermore, the 1976 presidential election was approaching quickly, and he needed to somehow find a middle ground between these two extremes. If the president did not give southern conservatives some support, they would be furious. At the same time, if he appeared to give too many concessions to white southerners, he would be pilloried by civil rights leaders. On July 17, just as the extension debate was heating up in the Senate, Ford announced that he was considering the possibility of expanding the act nationwide. Ford's final decision, however, did little to mollify either side.

Ford's clumsy intervention wreaked havoc in the Senate (Lawson 1985, 248). Bolstered by the president's support, southern conservatives once again introduced amendments to expand VRA coverage to the entire nation. As Republicans moved to support the president's position, the bipartisan coalition that had held off these amendments in the past began to atrophy.

On July 23, however, Ford finally realized that his attempt to expand VRA coverage was endangering the act's extension, and he modified his position to support a simple reauthorization. In the end, however, the Republicans did get a substantial concession: the act was renewed for seven years instead of ten and would therefore have to be reauthorized in 1982. With Ford's support and the slight reduction in the length of the extension, the House version of the bill passed the Senate 77–12; eleven Democrats and two Republicans from the South voted with the majority. What is more remarkable than the bill's approval, however, was the support it received from southern Democrats. As Table 6-1 shows, sixty-three southern Democrats in the House, a strong majority, supported the VRA in 1975, a vast improvement from 1970. As Rep. John H. Buchanan Jr. of Alabama explained, "The increased participation of black Americans in the political process through the protections afforded in this act, notwithstanding the fears and dire predications concerning its effects on States like mine which were voiced in 1965, has hurt our State approximately as much as black participation has hurt . . . the University of Alabama's basketball team" (quoted in Lawson 1985, 244).

The 1975 extension, then, demonstrated the strong support the act had gained. Not only was it renewed for seven years, but it also permanently eliminated literacy tests, expanded protection to language minorities, and required local governments to provide bilingual voting registration materials and ballots *(see Document 32)*. The most important of these achievements, however, was the expansion of VRA protection beyond the original southern core. With the stroke of the president's pen, the VRA was no longer a southern bill; it now covered all of Alaska, Arizona, and Texas, and parts of California, Florida, New York, and South Dakota.

1982 Extension under Reagan

Two important events structured the VRA extension battle in 1982. First, former California governor Ronald Reagan, a conservative Republican, defeated Jimmy Carter, the liberal Democratic president, in the 1980 presidential election. Thus once again the VRA would come up for extension under a Republican president. Much like Nixon and Ford before him, Reagan remained uncommitted until very late in the extension debate. Second, the Supreme Court's ruling in *City of Mobile v. Bolden* (1980) dramatically shifted the test for discrimination in election laws. The Court held that any state electoral rule "that is racially neutral on its face violates the Fifteenth Amendment only if motivated by discriminatory purpose." In *Mobile*, then, the Court abolished the White-Zimmer test, which required only that the litigants prove that electoral laws had the effect of racial discrimination, and returned to the older test of racial intent. Despite these setbacks, civil rights activists went into the battle for extension of the VRA well prepared, but their struggle would be nowhere near as fierce as it had been in the past. By the 1980s, there was very little direct opposition to voting rights, and, unlike when the act was first approved in the 1965, the civil rights liberals clearly had more support and resources than the opposing forces.

On April 7, 1982, Peter Rodino, now chair of the House Judiciary Committee, introduced a bill that proposed extending the VRA and the bilingual ballot amendments for ten more years, until August 6, 1992. Rodino also inserted some new language into the act that was designed to force the Court to return to the old White-Zimmer test in Section 5 preclearance cases. The revised text read (Rodino's changes are in italics), "No voting qualification or prerequisite to voting or standard, practice, or procedure shall be imposed or applied by any State or political subdivision *in a manner which results in a denial or abridgement of* the right of any citizen of the United States to vote on account of race or color." Although Rodino added only eleven words to Section 2, it radically changed the scope of the act. Now, for the first time, the statute began to provide some protection for minority office holding.

Rodino's bill was referred to the House Judiciary Subcommittee on Civil and Constitutional Rights, chaired by Democratic representative Don Edwards of California. Although Edwards favored Rodino's amendments, they were greeted with some skepticism by Illinois Republican Henry Hyde, a fellow member of the subcommittee (Boyd and Markman 1983, 1357). Although Hyde had voted for the 1975 act, he remained uncomfortable with some of its provisions and so decided to propose his own bill. Rather than require all covered jurisdictions to submit their electoral changes to the Justice Department, the Hyde bill reversed the burden of proof and required the Justice Department to sue the jurisdictions that were in violation of the act.

As the extension debate dragged on, the committee went on the road and held meetings in Austin, Texas, and Montgomery, Alabama, where committee members heard testimony

from both sides. Some of the most important testimony came from ordinary African Americans who testified that polling places were often located in white-owned stores or were only open during the middle of the day to prevent working blacks from registering (Boyd and Markman 1983, 1361). In response, Representative Hyde, well known for his judicious style, began to moderate his message somewhat, especially after hearing testimony from African Americans in Alabama about the difficulties in registering to vote. Upon hearing a series of especially disturbing stories about the bizarre and plainly discriminatory obstacles to voting registration in the South, even Hyde, a veteran of the rough and tumble world of Chicago-area politics, cried, "That is outrageous, absolutely outrageous." Still, Hyde continued to support a more liberal bailout policy. At the same hearings, Hyde declared, "I think we must, in fairness, recognize progress and compliance with the letter and the spirit of the law where it has occurred and provide an incentive for jurisdictions to comply, while retaining administrative preclearance for those areas as yet recalcitrant" (U.S. Congress 1981).

Despite his qualms about the bailout procedures, Hyde was, on the whole, supportive of reauthorizing the VRA, and he also saw it as an opportunity to broaden the appeal of the Republican Party to blacks. In a private memo to Reagan, he wrote, "If you move quickly, you may be able to broaden your constituency by eliminating a fear which plagues the black community most: that the time will soon return when they [are] literally unable to vote, or in the alternative, made to feel that they have no meaningful impact whatsoever on their destiny" (quoted in Boyd and Markman 1983,

1369n106). As the full Judiciary Committee took up consideration of the bill on July 21, both Rodino and Edwards worked to develop a compromise. They eventually settled on an amendment that tightened somewhat the bailout requirements designed by Hyde and also modified Rodino's language in Section 2 to read: "[the] fact that members of minority group have not been elected in numbers equal to the group's proportion of the population shall not, *in and of itself,* constitute a violation of this section."

During the House's August recess, civil rights forces sprang into action. The NAACP launched its "Operation Network," which organized supporters in congressional districts throughout the country (Boyd and Markman 1983, 1387). Evidently the pressure was effective, because in September 1982 the VRA extension bill was reported to the floor, and, despite a brief attempt to eliminate the bilingual ballot amendments, it passed easily, 389–24. More remarkable, however, was the coalition that voted in support of the extension. Along with northern Democrats—the traditional supporters of voting rights—seventy-one southerners voted aye, apparently in response to the growing political power of blacks in their districts. For some of these representatives, reelection rested in the hands of black voters. But it is also likely that some southern politicians recognized that the VRA was a positive statute, one that had actually been immensely good for the South.

On the Senate side, Democrat Edward M. Kennedy of Massachusetts proposed a bill that was identical to the original Rodino House bill. The Kennedy bill "proposed to extend the preclearance requirement for covered jurisdic-

tions an additional ten years, conform the expiration date of the bilingual provisions to the preclearance requirements, and establish a results test in Section 2 of the Voting Rights Act" (quoted in Boyd and Markman 1983, 1380). Before Kennedy's bill could be reported to the floor, however, Kennedy and his allies had to face Republican senator Orrin Hatch of Utah and the powerful chair of the Judiciary Committee, Sen. Strom Thurmond, a Republican from South Carolina who was a notorious opponent of civil rights and the VRA. When the Subcommittee on the Constitution began deliberations on January 27, 1982, it quickly became clear that both Hatch and Thurmond had some serious problems. Predictably, Thurmond echoed the traditional southern concerns about Section 5's focus on the South. Hatch, however, as a western conservative, was mainly concerned with the change in Section 2 standards. Much like Hyde, Hatch favored the intent standard articulated by the Court in *Mobile,* and he was loath to accept Rodino's new language (Boyd and Markman 1983, 1382). The main problem for Hatch and Thurmond, however, was that they simply could not get enough support to defeat Kennedy and the other liberal senators.

The impasse was finally broken by Republican senator Robert J. Dole of Kansas, who, in statesmanlike fashion, proposed a compromise that he developed with leaders of the civil rights community. The Dole compromise extended Section 5 coverage for twenty-five years rather than making it permanent and authorized bilingual ballots in Section 203 until 1992.[3] After President Reagan announced his support, the Judiciary Committee approved the bill, and, despite some weak threats to filibuster "until the cows come home" by Sen. Jesse Helms, a Republican from North Carolina, the Senate approved the extension by a vote of 85–8 on June 15, with every southern Democrat in the Senate voting in the affirmative. The bill was signed by President Reagan on June 29, 1982 *(see Document 34).*

Dynamics of Extension and Expansion

One of the most remarkable things about the extension and expansion of the Voting Rights Act is that it was reauthorized each time under divided government and with very little presidential leadership, two rather surprising similarities that cut across the grain of some prominent theories in political science. Political scientists have long held that divided government slows down the democratic process and that significant episodes of lawmaking will decline during these periods (Cutler 1988, Sundquist 1988–1989, but see Mayhew 1991 for an alternative view). Yet for extensions of the VRA, the pattern was often more sectional than partisan. During each extension process, northern Republicans sided with northern Democrats to defeat the objections of Democrats and Republicans from the South. The battles for extension, however, have become less fierce over the years, and, at least during the extensions in 1975 and 1982, no legislators stooped to defend electoral systems that keep blacks from voting.

Weak or bungling presidential leadership is another pattern that runs through past extensions. Nixon, Ford, and Reagan remained noncommittal until the very end, and none of these presidents marshaled the prestige of his office to defeat or promote extension of the VRA.

This is an unexpected finding as well. Indeed, most scholarly theories of presidential action find modern presidents, beginning with Franklin D. Roosevelt, to be intimately involved in the legislative process, some going so far as to call the president "Chief Legislator" (Sundquist 1981).

The extension episodes have also been characterized by several positive evolutionary trends, the most important of which are (1) the increasing importance of the black vote—particularly for southern politicians; (2) the expansion of the VRA beyond its original core jurisdiction of the South; and (3) the decline of strong racist opposition to black voting rights among southern whites. The fourth trend is the evolution of the basic question of whether the VRA has equalized voting rights to such an extent that it is no longer necessary.

At the most basic level, the increasing support for the VRA—even among white southern politicians—demonstrates the happy logic of democracy: as blacks were extended voting rights, southern politicians became much warier about going on the record against such popular policies. This sequence of events does, of course, make perfect sense. If it is assumed that the primary goal of all politicians is reelection, then they will be highly responsive to changes in their constituency (Downs 1957; Mayhew 1975).

In more recent years, the sectional flavor of VRA battles has become less prominent, and in that respect the battle for VRA extension demonstrates the shift in party coalitions that has occurred over the past forty years as the Republican Party has become the conservative party in the South. Indeed, following the logic of party competition, the Republicans had a chance to capture conservative southern voters in the formerly "Solid South"—and they did. The voices of opposition to VRA extension in 1975 and 1982 were almost entirely Republican ones (as the old southern Democrats were defeated or died, their seats were increasingly filled by Republicans). Furthermore, once African Americans were enfranchised under the VRA, the Democratic Party had to finally confront its longtime schism with its southern half (Carmines and Stimson 1989).

It is very likely that the VRA will be renewed in 2007, but it may not be renewed without a fight. The 2007 extension could be different in several important respects. No matter which party is in power, the electoral costs to both parties would probably be far too great to oppose reauthorization. Democrats have long counted on African Americans and Latino voters, and Republicans are working to attract more minority voters to their party, especially Latino voters in the Southwest.

Any additional requirements that might be recommended, however, will likely be controversial. One issue likely to arise is a debate over felony disenfranchisement laws. In recent years, the number of black males disenfranchised because of felony convictions has skyrocketed, and today nearly 13 percent of black males cannot vote in federal elections, a fact that was highlighted in the 2000 Florida election debacle (Human Rights Watch 1998). Many civil rights leaders see this issue as a top priority, and they will likely push hard during the extension debates to attack this practice.

Notwithstanding these potential problems, it is likely that the basic provisions of the VRA will be renewed yet again in 2007. The act continues to be popular with the vast majority of Americans, it imposes relatively few costs, and strong and vocal organizations will work to see it pass. Although traditional African American civil rights groups such as the NAACP will be at the forefront of these lobbies, Latino organizations that have become vastly more powerful since the last extension in 1982 will also play a central role. Today, the Latino vote is heavily courted by both Democrats and Republicans, and the political strength of Latinos stems in no small part from their unwillingness to become exclusively associated with either of the two major parties. Indeed, Latinos have achieved political prominence in both major political parties, such as Republican senator Mel Martinez of Florida and Democratic governor Bill Richardson of New Mexico. In this new political climate, the potential cost to either of the parties of opposing VRA extension is far greater than any possible benefits.

Conclusion

One of the most persistent Internet rumors in recent memory claims that African Americans will lose their right to vote when the special provisions of the Voting Rights Act expire in August 2007 (*see Appendix*). Although this rumor, like so many spread through cyberspace, is false, it has caused enough concern that both the Department of Justice and the NAACP have released press bulletins to reassure African Americans that their sacred right to vote is guaranteed forever by the Fifteenth Amendment and will never disappear. That idle rumors could elicit such a powerful response illustrate how the VRA has become an important symbol of political equality in the modern era, but they also demonstrate the great fear among minorities that, at any moment, their hard-won voting rights could be snatched back. This palpable sense of fear, expressed so well by Henry Hyde in his memo to Ronald Reagan during the 1982 extension, may be rooted in the temporary nature of the enforcement provisions. The dark legacy of America's first Reconstruction demonstrates all too clearly how mere parchment barriers, to borrow a phrase from the *The Federalist Papers*, do little to combat injustices without effective enforcement.

Notes

1. The original areas of VRA jurisdiction were Alabama, Georgia, Louisiana, Mississippi, South Carolina, Virginia, and much of North Carolina.
2. Examiners registered voters by first creating a list of all eligible voters and issuing each a certificate proving his or her eligibility to vote in federal, state, and local elections, and then sending this list to local registrars, who were required to include the names of these citizens on the official registration rolls. The role of election observers was slightly less invasive. They were required to simply watch the polls and ensure that all eligible citizens were allowed to vote and that all ballots were counted accurately (U.S. Commission on Civil Rights 1975, 32–35).
3. The bilingual ballot amendments (Section 203) were extended to 2007 in 1992.

References

Ball, Howard, Dale Krane, and Thomas P. Lauth. 1982. *Compromised Compliance: Implementation of the 1965 Voting Rights Act*. Westport, Conn.: Greenwood Press.

Boyd, Thomas M., and Stephen J. Markman. 1983. "The 1982 Amendments to the Voting Rights Act: A Legislative History." *Washington and Lee Law Review* 40:1347–1380.

Bridges, Amy. 1997. *Morning Glories: Municipal Reform in the Southwest*. Princeton, N.J.: Princeton University Press.

Carmines, Edward, and James Stimson. 1989. *Issue Evolution*. Princeton, N.J.: Princeton University Press.

Cutler, Loyd N. 1988. "Some Reflections about Divided Government." *Presidential Studies Quarterly* 18:485–92.

Davidson, Chandler. 1992. "The Voting Rights Act: A Brief History." In *Controversies in Minority Voting: The Voting Rights Act in Perspective*, edited by Bernard Grofman and Chandler Davidson. Washington, D.C.: Bookings.

Davidson, Chandler, and Bernard Grofman, eds. 1994. *Quiet Revolution in the South: The Impact of the Voting Rights Act, 1965–1990*. Princeton, N.J.: Princeton University Press.

Derfner, Armand. 1989. "Vote Dilution and the Voting Rights Act Amendments of 1982." In *Minority Vote Dilution*, edited by Chandler Davidson. Washington, D.C.: Howard University Press.

Downs, Anthony. 1957. *An Economic Theory of Democracy*. New York: Harper and Row.

Grofman, Bernard, Lisa Handley, and Richard G. Niemi. 1992. *Minority Representation and the Quest for Voting Equality*. Cambridge: Cambridge University Press.

Human Rights Watch. 1998. *Losing the Vote: The Impact of Felony Disenfranchisement Laws in the United States*. http://www.hwr.org/reports98/vote/ (accessed May 2, 2005).

Jordan, Barbara, and Shelby Hearon. 1979. *Barbara Jordan: A Self-Portrait*. Garden City, N.Y.: Doubleday.

Key, V. O. 1950. *Southern Politics in State and Nation*. New York: Knopf.

Lawson, Steven F. 1985. *In Pursuit of Power: Southern Blacks and Electoral Politics, 1965–1982*. New York: Columbia University Press.

Mayhew, David. 1975. *Congress: The Electoral Connection*. New Haven, Conn.: Yale University Press.

———. 1991. *Divided We Govern: Party Control, Lawmaking, and Investigations, 1946–1990*. New Haven, Conn.: Yale University Press.

Rosenberg, Gerald. 1993. *The Hollow Hope: Can Courts Bring About Social Change?* Chicago: University of Chicago Press.

Schattschneider, E. E. 1942. *Party Government*. New York: Rinehart.

Shefter, Martin. 1994. *Political Parties and the*

State: American Historical Perspectives. Princeton, N.J.: Princeton University Press.

Sundquist, James L. 1981. *The Decline and Resurgence of Congress.* Washington, D.C.: Brookings.

———. 1988–1989. "Needed: A Political Theory for the New Era of Coalition Government in the United States." *Political Science Quarterly* 103: 613–635.

U.S. Commission on Civil Rights. 1975. *The Voting Rights Act: Ten Years After.* Washington, D.C.: Government Printing Office.

U.S. Congress. House. 1981. *Hearings before the Subcommittee on Civil and Constitutional Rights of the House Committee of the Judiciary.* 97th Cong., 1st sess., part I.

Valelly, Richard M. 2004. *The Two Reconstructions: The Struggle for Black Enfranchisement.* Chicago: University of Chicago Press.

7

Impact of the 'Core' Voting Rights Act on Voting and Officeholding

David A. Bositis

In the forty years since its passage in 1965, the Voting Rights Act has fundamentally transformed southern—and American—politics. The South is and was the focus of the black voting rights movement, because a majority of black people live in the South and it was in the southern states that their right to vote was largely denied. Many of the changes are astonishing when viewed through the lens of pre-1965 southern states. A majority of African Americans are now registered to vote and comprise a significant share of actual voters in many of these states.[1] The number of black elected officials has grown more than tenfold since 1965,[2] and over the same period the number of African Americans in Congress has increased from six U.S. House members to forty-three members of Congress: one U.S. senator, forty U.S. House members, and two nonvoting delegates (one from the District of Columbia and the other from the Virgin Islands). This advancement in the fortunes of African Americans in politics has been accompanied by an even greater advancement in the views and interests of a group of people who were most opposed to the passage of the Voting Rights Act—conservative southern whites.

Since the passage of the Voting Rights Act and the Civil Rights Act—both supported by Democratic president Lyndon B. Johnson and his party—the Democratic and Republican parties have been transformed by the Democrats' acceptance of the goals of the civil rights movement and the subsequent movement of southern whites away from their traditional Democratic attachments. In 1965 thirty-two Republicans sat in the U.S. Senate, but only two of them were from the group of eleven states that had made up the Confederacy. Sen. John Tower of Texas, elected in 1961, was the first Republican U.S. senator from the South since Reconstruction. The other southern Republican senator at that time, Strom Thurmond, was elected as a Democrat in 1960 and switched parties in 1964. The House had only a handful of Republican members from the South. In fact, Republicans were a small minority in every southern state legislative body. Forty years later, the southern states represent the GOP's most important base of support, and southern Republicans dominate leadership positions in the federal government.

Voting: Then and Now

The Voting Rights Act gave most southern blacks the opportunity to vote for the first time. In 1960, the year Democrat John F. Kennedy was elected president and five years before the Voting Rights Act was passed, only 5.2 percent of African Americans in Mississippi were registered to vote; in Alabama and South Carolina only 13.7 percent were registered to vote (U.S. Commission on Civil Rights 1968, 12–13). At that time, Tennessee was the only southern state in which a majority of blacks were registered, 59.1 percent; in the remaining southern states black registration rates were between 20 and 40 percent. By 1968, the year of the first presidential election after passage of the Voting Rights Act, a majority of African Americans were registered to vote in every southern state.

Since 1968 African Americans have generally registered and voted at lower rates than whites, both nationally and in the South. In the first eight federal elections after passage of the Voting Rights Act, black registration and turnout rates were usually about ten percentage points (plus or minus two points) below those of whites nationally, with the gap slightly smaller in the southern states (Bositis 2004, 17). In 1984, when Rev. Jesse Jackson ran for the Democratic presidential nomination, the gap between black and white registration and turnout rates began to narrow because of the Jackson campaign's grassroots mobilization effort. The success of Jackson's efforts in 1984 manifested itself in the 1986 midterm elections, when black registration and turnout rates in the South matched those of whites. Democrats picked up U.S. Senate seats in Alabama, Florida, Georgia, and North Carolina that year, which helped them to take control of that body. In 2004 turnout among African Americans reached 60 percent nation-

wide, just five percentage points below that of whites.

The gap between black and white registration and turnout rates continues to exist for several reasons. For one thing, a majority of African Americans live in the South, and southern states tend to have electoral laws that do not encourage voting. Among the practices found in these states are limiting the number of places to register (apart from "motor voter" locations), restricting who may register people, closing the registration process early, purging voter lists frequently, and imposing expensive identification requirements. These practices tend to most affect poor and black people, and the states that impose them generally rank in the bottom half of states in voter turnout rates.

The states with the highest registration and turnout rates—all in the North—are those that have large majorities of white citizens and that strongly encourage participation by voters by allowing, for example, mail-in ballots and same-day registration and voting. In the 2004 presidential election, the top states in voter turnout were Minnesota (which has same-day registration), 76.2 percent; Wisconsin, 73.7 percent; New Hampshire, 71.6 percent; and South Dakota, 68.2 percent (Committee for the Study of the American Electorate 2004, 4). Age is a significant correlate of voter turnout. Older persons are more likely to vote, but the black population (median age 30 years) is significantly younger than the (non-Hispanic) white population (39.7 years). Furthermore, African American men are substantially over-represented among classes of adults that are ineligible to vote—for example, of the 2.1 million inmates in federal and state prisons and local jails, 44 percent are black.

Realignment in the South

When Gov. Adlai E. Stevenson II of Illinois, the leader of the liberal wing of the Democratic Party, ran for the presidency against Gen. Dwight D. Eisenhower in 1952, seven of the nine states he carried were in the old Confederacy, including all five states in the "Deep South" (Key 1950).[3] In 1956, when Stevenson challenged Eisenhower's bid for reelection, five of the seven states Stevenson carried were in the South. That same year the Democratic National Convention had only twenty-four black delegates, 1.7 percent of the total, and the Republican National Convention had thirty-six black delegates, 2.7 percent of the total (Bositis 2004, 18, 24). That southern white voters would support Adlai Stevenson was certainly indicative of their attachment to the Democratic Party, whereas, even though most blacks could not vote at that time, a significant proportion of those that could remained loyal to their historic Republican ties—39 percent supported Eisenhower (Bositis 2004, 9).

In 1964 Sen. Barry Goldwater, the leader of the conservative wing of the Republican Party, ran against President Lyndon Johnson, the Texan responsible for passage of the Civil Rights Act that year. Five of the six states carried by Goldwater were in the Deep South (the sixth was his home state of Arizona). At the Republican National Convention in 1964, there were only fourteen black delegates, 1 percent of the total. The Democratic National Convention drew sixty-five black delegates, 2.8 percent of the total. More important, in a compromise reached by all Democratic delegates, Fannie Lou Hamer and the Mississippi Freedom Democratic Party were awarded two del-

egate seats—and a resolution was passed outlawing racial discrimination in the delegate selection process (Baer and Bositis 1988, 63). However, the most conservative southern whites would not support a party or candidate who advocated black rights. Johnson received only 12.9 percent of the vote in Mississippi in 1964, and he was not even on the ballot in Alabama that year. Even though many blacks still could not vote, a historically low 6 percent voted for the Republican nominee, Goldwater.

After the 1964 election, the partisanship of white southerners began to change. In 1966, the first federal election after the Voting Rights Act was passed, Sen. Strom Thurmond of South Carolina was elected for the first time as a Republican after switching parties two years earlier. He was joined in the Senate by Republican Howard H. Baker Jr. of Tennessee. That same year, Republicans won the governorships of Arkansas and Florida.

In the eventful year of 1968, the changes taking place in the parties and in the South became more apparent. The Democrats nominated Vice President Hubert H. Humphrey, a longtime champion of African Americans, as their presidential nominee. Of the Democratic delegates at the convention that year, 6.7 percent were black, more than twice the proportion at any previous convention. Republicans nominated former vice president Richard Nixon to head their ticket. Nixon's goal was to increase his party's share of the white southern vote by employing a "southern strategy"—that is, he would appeal to southern whites through wedge issues that usually had an unspoken racial dimension, such as being tough on crime or against school busing (see Murphy 1971). However, Nixon carried only five southern states because Alabama governor George C. Wallace, a segregationist who ran on the American Independent Party ticket, also carried five states—four in the Deep South and Arkansas. Vice President Humphrey carried only a single southern state—President Johnson's home state of Texas. More ominously, Humphrey finished third to Nixon and Wallace in five southern states. Also in 1968 the Republicans elected another southern U.S. senator, this time from Florida. The next year, a Republican was elected governor of Virginia, and in 1970 yet another was elected to the U.S. Senate from Tennessee.

At their 1972 convention, which was something of a debacle, Democrats nominated their most liberal candidate, Sen. George S. McGovern of South Dakota, to the presidency. The convention played an important role in the party's relationship to African Americans because it adopted the McGovern-Fraser report, which, among other things, called for the proportional representation of minorities in the selection of delegates to the national convention (Baer and Bositis 1988, 64). (At that convention, 14.6 percent of the delegates were black.) This development launched a phase of Democratic politics in which Democrats increasingly integrated African American leaders and activists into their party and its leadership. In the election, President Nixon carried every southern state easily. Republicans also elected two new southern U.S. senators, Jesse Helms in North Carolina and William L. Scott in Virginia, and North Carolina elected a Republican governor as well. Yet, despite the Democrats' debacle and Nixon's landslide, the 1972 presidential election turned out to be only a temporary plateau for Republicans in the

South because of two things on the horizon: the Watergate scandal and Democrat Jimmy Carter.

The Watergate scandal, which ended in Nixon's resignation from presidency, greatly weakened the Republican Party and President Gerald R. Ford's campaign in 1976. Ford's fight with former California governor Ronald Reagan for the nomination further added to the damage. On the Democratic side, in nominating Jimmy Carter, a moderate from Georgia, to the presidency, Democrats picked an ideal candidate to compete in the South. Carter was a "born-again" Christian and a former naval officer, two attributes that resonated with conservative white southerners. In the election, Carter carried all of the southern states except Virginia, which was becoming reliably Republican in presidential elections. It was the best performance by a Democratic candidate in the South since Franklin D. Roosevelt swept the southern states in 1944. Also in the 1976 election, Democrats captured a Republican Senate seat in Tennessee and the governor's office in North Carolina. This was the only presidential election in which blacks and a significant portion of southern whites, including majorities in Arkansas and Georgia, voted alike. And, in fact, over the second half of the twentieth century this election represented Democrats' high point in the South—a high point from which they would soon precipitously fall.

If 1976 was a bad year for Republicans, 1980 was far worse for the Democrats. The 1980 presidential election was a disaster for the Democratic Party in the South and elsewhere. Inflation and the Iran hostage crisis dominated the campaign, and Carter's contentious primary challenge from Sen. Edward M. Kennedy further damaged his standing. Ronald Reagan was nominated to great acclaim at that year's Republican convention and went on to win forty-four states in the general election, including Massachusetts. President Carter carried his home state of Georgia, and lost all of the other southern states. Republicans, after capturing U.S. Senate seats in Alabama, Florida, Georgia, and North Carolina, took control of the U.S. Senate.

In 1984 and 1988, neither Democratic presidential nominee carried a southern state. However, Democrats—who controlled the state legislatures and thus congressional redistricting—were able to maintain their dominance in the U.S. House. Indeed, as late as 1990 Republicans held only 39 of 116 congressional seats in the southern states. Democrats also returned to dominance in the U.S. Senate, when they recaptured the four U.S. Senate seats lost in the 1980 Reagan landslide. Jesse Jackson's 1984 presidential race, which mobilized millions of black voters in the South, and a strong black turnout and support for the Democrats in 1986 contributed to this reversal in fortunes. Democrats also held nine of eleven southern governors' offices.

The 1992 presidential election was a good one for Democrats across the board, but it masked the seismic shifts that were to occur shortly in the South. In winning the presidency, former Arkansas governor Bill Clinton carried four southern states, including two in the Deep South. However, unlike Carter's victories in 1976, Clinton's victories in Georgia and Louisiana were largely the result of large black turnouts; President George Bush received about 60 percent of the white vote. More sig-

nificant for the Democrats, 1992 was the first year in which large numbers of black-majority U.S. House and state legislative districts were created in response to the 1982 amendments to the Voting Rights Act as interpreted by the U.S. Supreme Court. After the 1992 election, the number of black southern U.S. House members increased from five to seventeen, and the number of white southern Democratic members declined from seventy-two to sixty. Most noteworthy but less noticed, the number of Republican U.S. House members from the South increased from thirty-nine to forty-eight—a gain that matched exactly the number of House seats the southern states added from the 1990 reapportionment. Meanwhile, similar shifts were occurring in the southern state legislatures (this development is discussed later in this chapter).

The Republican landslide in the 1994 midterm election changed the region's politics. Even though white voters continued their shift toward the GOP during the 1970s and 1980s, the South had a two-party system that still leaned toward the Democrats in nonpresidential races. After 1994 the South had a two-party system that leaned Republican at all levels. In 1994 Republicans picked up three U.S. Senate seats, two in Tennessee and one in Texas, and after the election Sen. Richard Shelby of Alabama switched parties, for a net gain of four. In U.S. House elections in the South, sixteen white Democratic members were replaced by white Republicans. For the first time, then, a majority of southern U.S. House members were Republicans. In the Senate, the thirteen (of twenty-two) Republican U.S. senators from the South represented a majority of southern senators. Overall, in the

104th Congress 64 of 125 members from southern states were Republicans.

Although the Democrats were occasionally successful, such as in gubernatorial elections in 1998–1999 in Alabama, Georgia, Mississippi, and South Carolina, the 1994 elections marked the beginning of Republican dominance across the South. Bill Clinton was able to once again win Arkansas, Louisiana, and Tennessee when he ran for reelection in 1996—and he added Florida to his column—but Georgia voted Republican that year. By 2000 the Democrats were clearly on the defensive. In 2000 George W. Bush carried all of the South, including Democratic nominee Al Gore's home state of Tennessee, although the Florida vote was disputed. In 2004 he carried all of the southern states by even larger margins. In 2002 and 2004, Democrats lost additional U.S. House and Senate seats, so that by 2005, 82 percent of the region's U.S. senators (18 of 22) and 64 percent of its U.S. representatives (83 of 129) were Republican. Seven of eleven southern governors were Republicans as well.

The Birth of Racially Polarized Voting in the South

The partisan changes in the South stemmed from shifts by white voters. Before passage of the Voting Rights Act of 1965, racially polarized voting was virtually nonexistent in the South; because African Americans accounted for such a small portion of voters, their votes effectively did not count. But by the 1970s, even though some old-style Democrats such as Gov. George Wallace of Alabama and Sen. John Stennis of Mississippi were still receiving significant support from conservative southern

whites, a new southern politics was emerging. Black voters were registering and voting in larger numbers, and new-style southern Democrats, such as Jimmy Carter, were appealing for black support as the large—and solidly Democratic—bloc of black voters became an important force in Democratic Party primaries. These new Democrats adopted moderate (or moderately conservative) positions to appeal to southern whites. The percentage of the white vote these Democrats needed depended on the size and turnout of the state's black voting population. In states such as Louisiana and Georgia a Democrat could win with only 35 percent of the white vote, because that candidate could regularly count on 95 percent or more of the black vote.

Today, although the new southern Republicans occasionally appeal to southern whites with racial messages, more often they appeal to them by embracing traditional white southern values and icons (such as the Confederate flag) and political policy stances. Thus speeches may be larded with references to low taxes and pro-gun, pro-privatization, pro-military, pro–capital punishment, antiunion, fundamentalist rhetoric. For example, in 2000, after President George W. Bush lost the New Hampshire primary to Arizona senator John McCain, his first campaign stop for the upcoming South Carolina Republican primary was at Bob Jones University, a fundamentalist religious institution that banned interracial dating. While there, Bush defended flying the Confederate flag over the state capitol building. Republicans also recognize that unions are not popular in the South. Of the twenty-two states in the United States that have right-to-work laws (that is, workers cannot be required to join a union), the eleven states of the South represent half the total. As for capital punishment, of the eleven states with the highest numbers of executions, nine are in the South and two occupy the first and second places. Few blacks in the South support Republicans even when they do not use overt racial appeals in their campaigns, because blacks view traditional southern culture as racist, and their political views are generally opposed to those of conservative southern whites.

The new southern Democrats have fared poorly, despite the fact that they can often win elections by capturing only a comparatively modest share of the southern white vote—even as small as one in three white voters in Louisiana. Thus the racial coalitional politics of southern Democrats certainly looks endangered—at least for the near future.

Indeed, the degree of racially polarized voting in the South is increasing, not decreasing. For example, in the 2004 presidential election 80 percent of whites in Alabama voted for President Bush, compared with only 6 percent of African Americans—a gap of seventy-four percentage points.[4] In Mississippi, 85 percent of whites supported Bush, but only 10 percent of African Americans did so. The gaps between black and white voters ranged from 42 percent in Florida, the only southern state where Democrat John Kerry received more than 40 percent of the white vote, to 75 percent in Mississippi, where Kerry carried 15 percent of the white vote (in both cases, not including Hispanics).

The fact that a Massachusetts Democrat did poorly among southern white voters is hardly a new story. White southern antipathy to the northeastern liberal establishment or Yankee politicians is not a new phenomenon. However, a closer look at the U.S. Senate seats lost by Democrats in the South shows the extent of the racial divide. In Louisiana, Democratic representative Chris John (in a multicandidate field) received only 21 percent of the white vote. President Bill Clinton's former chief of staff, Erskine Bowles, received only 30 percent of the white vote in North Carolina. In South Carolina, State Education Superintendent Inez Tenenbaum, who had twice won statewide office, managed to win only 28 percent of the white vote in her U.S. Senate race. All of these contests were for open seats held by retiring Democrats.

The racially polarized voting that defines much of southern politics at this time is in certain ways re-creating the segregated system of the old South, albeit a de facto system with minimal violence rather than the de jure system of late. If, again, the political parties in the South are a substitute for racial labels, then black aspirations there will continue to be limited. Unfortunately, a racially polarized party system will inevitably affect African Americans in other ways, including their voting rights.

Efforts to Keep Blacks from Voting in the South

The Voting Rights Act of 1965 effectively ended the disenfranchisement of African Americans in the South. However, southern resistance to the new system has never entirely ended, and, as the great southern writer William Faulkner noted, the past is not forgotten. With the passage of time, the Republican Party has become dominated by southern whites and the Democratic Party by blacks. Thus Republican campaigns and political operatives have strategized to diminish the black vote in the South. Many of tactics that have been employed are subtle, and often legal, rather than blunt. Among the tactics reported in the press are moving polling places in black precincts after each election, including primary elections; stationing state police cars near black polling places; and locating polling places in venues where some African Americans are nervous about venturing—including near reputed hangouts of Ku Klux Klan members in the 1970s. Other tactics include giving black polling stations inadequate supplies so that they run out of ballots in the event of a large turnout of blacks, or giving them an inadequate number of voting machines (or defective voting machines) so that black voters will have to wait in long lines before they cast their ballots. These tactics are not meant to keep all African Americans from voting. However, if in close elections they can discourage 2 or even 5 percent of the blacks who show up at the polling place from casting their ballots, then they will have achieved their goals.

Another method, and one of questionable legality, used by southern Republicans to reduce the black vote is "ballot security" programs. Laughlin McDonald of the American Civil Liberties Union refers to them as "the new poll tax" (McDonald 2005; also see Chapter 10 in this volume). Ballot security programs are inherently partisan and racially prejudiced, because they are aimed invariably only at minority populations—and they are used only in elections in which the outcomes are believed to be very close. The 1986 U.S. Senate election in Louisiana between Democrat John Breaux and Republican Henson Moore is a good example of a ballot security program in action. The Moore campaign arranged to have letters sent to all registered voters in parishes in which Democrat Walter F. Mondale received more votes than Republican Ronald Reagan in the 1984 presidential election. Of course, all of those parishes were black because Reagan had overwhelmingly won the white vote in Louisiana that year. Using intimidating language, the letters suggested that if the recipients attempted to vote but all of the information on their registration forms was not completely accurate, they would be prosecuted for committing a serious crime. The registrations of those living at addresses where the letters were returned to the sender were challenged. Before the runoff between Breaux and Moore, documents came to light revealing that a Republican National Committee official said the program would eliminate 60,000–80,000 names from the rolls and could keep the black vote down considerably. In the civil case that followed, GOP officials entered into a consent decree in which they said they did nothing wrong, but promised not to do it again.

Probably a more important method used by southern Republicans to diminish the voting rights of African Americans is felony disenfranchisement—that is, barring ex-felons from voting. This practice predates the transformation of southern party politics after the Voting Rights Act, but it has played a role in shaping that transformation's impact. In some states with such felony disenfranchisement laws, the ban is in effect only until the end of parole or probation, but in others—including several southern states—it is permanent. These laws, both in the South and elsewhere in the country, are not new. However, changes in the criminal justice system and the changing politics of the South have made them a major issue for the supporters of voting rights.

In the last two decades of the twentieth century, the U.S. prison population more than doubled because of tougher drug laws and mandatory minimum sentences advocated largely by Republicans. Black men accounted for about half of that growth. The growth in the prison population, and thus in the number of ex-felons, parolees, and probationers, has translated into an increase in the number of disenfranchised persons. The racial impact of disenfranchisement laws is substantial. As Jamie Fellner and Marc Mauer (1998, 8) note: "Thirteen percent of all adult black men—1.4 million—are disenfranchised, representing one-third of the total disenfranchised population and reflecting a rate of disenfranchisement that is seven times the national average. Election voting statistics offer an approximation of the political importance of black disenfranchisement: 1.4 million black men are disenfranchised compared to 4.6 million black men who voted in 1996."

The effects of these laws are evident in several southern states. In Alabama and Florida, 31 percent of all black men are permanently disenfranchised; in Mississippi one in four black men is permanently disenfranchised; and in Texas one in five is currently disenfranchised (Fellner and Mauer 1998, 8). If southern politics were not so racially polarized, felony disenfranchisement would perhaps be a less partisan matter. But southern politics is racially polarized, and in southern state legislatures Republicans have effectively blocked changes to these laws, because they would increase the number of black, and presumably Democratic, voters. The organized campaigns to keep

African Americans from voting will continue to cast a shadow over the legacy of the Voting Rights Act and raise legitimate doubts about whether a majority of southern whites have ever genuinely accepted the 1965 legislation.

Blacks in Elected Offices

Newly enfranchised black voters were soon followed by black candidates for elected office. By 1970 the number of black elected officials in the South, and throughout the country, had begun to grow significantly. Nationwide, 1,469 blacks held elected office in 1970, 565 of them in the states of the old Confederacy (Joint Center for Political and Economic Studies 2002, 26). African Americans were still greatly underrepresented at that time—holding less than seven-tenths of 1 percent of all elected offices in the southern states. Furthermore, then as now, most blacks in office represented black constituencies. The number of black elected officials increased steadily throughout the 1970s and 1980s, and then fairly dramatically after the Voting Rights Act was amended in 1982 to prohibit dilution of the black vote and the U.S. Supreme Court handed down an important voting rights decision in 1986, *Thornburgh v. Gingles*. The Court's decision virtually mandated that black-majority districts be created where there was a large and concentrated enough black population to constitute a majority.

From 1970 to 2000, the number of blacks in office in the South grew tenfold—from 565 to 5,579. Between those years, the number of blacks holding elected office at all levels increased in Mississippi from 81 to 897, in Alabama from 86 to 731, in Georgia from 40 to 582, and in South Carolina from 38 to 540

(Joint Center for Political and Economic Studies 2002, 26). The number of black elected officials also rose in other parts of the country. In Illinois, for example, the number of black elected officials increased from 74 to 621 over this period. But the South was the most important region, because approximately 62 percent of all African Americans holding office are from the southern states.

Most of the African Americans elected to public office in the South are in localities where black voters are in the majority; in fact, three out of four local offices are held by blacks. But these higher numbers of black local elected officials do not necessarily mean that black representation and influence in government have increased commensurately. There are, however, two types of offices that are emblematic of black political influence in the South—state legislative office and statewide elected office. An examination of these offices gives a fair assessment of the political fortunes of African Americans in the South since passage of the Voting Rights Act.

State Legislatures

In 1965 African Americans were not represented in southern state legislatures. But by 1970 that situation was slowly changing. In 1970 six black state senators (out of the 457 total state senators in the South) were serving in four states—two each in Georgia and Tennessee and one each in Texas (Barbara Jordan) and Virginia (future governor Douglas Wilder). The seven other southern states had no blacks in their state senates. Also at that time, 34 of the 1,325 state representatives were black. However, Georgia with thirteen and Tennessee with six accounted for more than half that number, and thus the other southern states averaged one or two black representatives in legislative bodies that had between 100 and 150 members.

Between 1970 and 1980, the number of black state legislators increased modestly. By 1980 several southern state houses were seeing significant increases in black membership, with Alabama (with a total of thirteen), Georgia (twenty-one), Louisiana (ten), Mississippi (fifteen), South Carolina (fifteen), and Texas (thirteen) experiencing the most growth. Despite

Barbara Jordan smiles and waves a victory sign as she talks on the phone after winning the Democratic nomination to the Texas State Senate in 1966. Jordan was the first African American Texas state senator since Reconstruction. She went on to serve in the U.S. House of Representatives from 1973 to 1977.
Source: Bettmann/CORBIS.

the increases, the number of black members in the lower houses of southern legislatures remained substantially below the proportion of the black voting-age population in these states (see Table 7-1). The number of black members in the southern state senates also remained small—there were now sixteen—and three states—Florida, South Carolina, and Texas—had no black members in their state senates.

Through the decade of the 1980s, the number of southern black state legislators grew steadily, albeit more in the lower chambers than the upper chambers. However, early in the decade (1982), the Voting Rights Act was amended to discourage dilution of the black vote. After black voters won the effective right to vote in 1965, southern legislatures had regularly drawn state house and senate districts—

Table 7-1 Black Representation, Southern State Legislatures: Selected Years, 1970–2004 (percent)

	Upper House					Lower House				
	1970	1980	1990 (Old District Lines)	1992 (New District Lines)	2004	1970	1980	1990 (Old District Lines)	1992 (New District Lines)	2004
Ala.	0.0 (0.0)	8.6 (37.6)	14.3 (63.0)	20.0 (88.1)	22.9 (95.4)	1.9 (8.3)	12.4 (54.1)	18.1 (79.7)	25.7 (113.2)	25.7 (107.1)
Ark.	0.0 (0.0)	2.9 (21.3)	8.6 (62.8)	8.6 (62.8)	8.6 (61.9)	0.0 (0.0)	4.0 (29.4)	9.0 (65.7)	10.0 (73.0)	13.0 (93.5)
Fla.	0.0 (0.0)	0.0 (0.0)	5.0 (43.9)	12.5 (109.6)	15.0 (118.1)	1.7 (13.6)	3.3 (30.6)	10.0 (87.7)	12.5 (109.6)	15.0 (118.1)
Ga.	3.6 (15.7)	3.6 (14.5)	14.3 (58.1)	17.9 (72.8)	17.9 (67.3)	7.2 (31.4)	11.7 (47.0)	15.0 (61.0)	17.8 (72.3)	21.7 (82.2)
La.	0.0 (0.0)	5.1 (19.2)	10.3 (36.9)	20.5 (73.5)	23.1 (77.8)	1.0 (3.8)	9.5 (35.7)	14.3 (51.3)	21.0 (75.1)	21.9 (73.7)
Miss.	0.0 (0.0)	3.8 (12.3)	3.8 (12.0)	19.2 (60.8)	19.2 (58.0)	0.8 (2.5)	12.3 (39.9)	15.6 (49.4)	25.4 (80.4)	29.5 (89.1)
N.C.	0.0 (0.0)	2.0 (9.7)	10.0 (49.8)	14.0 (67.6)	12.0 (60.0)	1.7 (8.8)	1.7 (8.2)	11.7 (56.5)	14.2 (70.5)	15.0 (75.0)
S.C.	0.0 (0.0)	0.0 (0.0)	13.0 (48.3)	15.2 (56.5)	17.4 (64.0)	2.4 (9.1)	12.1 (43.7)	11.3 (42.0)	19.4 (72.0)	19.4 (71.3)
Tenn.	6.1 (43.9)	12.2 (84.7)	9.1 (63.2)	9.1 (63.2)	9.1 (61.5)	6.1 (43.9)	9.1 (63.2)	10.1 (70.1)	14.6 (101.4)	15.2 (102.7)
Texas	3.2 (7.8)	0.0 (0.0)	6.5 (58.0)	6.5 (58.0)	6.5 (59.1)	1.3 (11.5)	8.7 (79.1)	8.7 (77.7)	9.3 (83.3)	9.3 (84.5)
Va.	2.5 (15.1)	2.5 (14.0)	7.5 (42.6)	12.5 (71.0)	12.5 (67.9)	2.0 (12.0)	4.0 (22.3)	7.0 (39.8)	8.0 (45.5)	11.0 (59.8)
Total	1.3 (7.1)	3.5 (19.0)	9.4 (51.1)	14.7 (80.0)	15.3 (83.2)	2.6 (14.1)	8.4 (45.7)	13.0 (70.7)	16.3 (81.5)	18.2 (87.0)

Source: Joint Center for Political and Economic Studies, Washington, D.C.

Note: Table shows black membership as a percentage of total membership and, in parentheses, black membership as a percentage of each state's black voting-age population (parity).

and U.S. House districts—in such a way that black populations were split between multiple districts and constituted a majority in comparatively few districts. The 1982 amendments, effectively operationalized by the U.S. Supreme Court in the 1986 *Gingles* decision, reduced this practice. But because the anti–vote dilution provisions were passed after the 1980s redistricting, its effects were limited during the 1980s, and those districts that were redrawn were generally in response to successful litigation.

After the 1990s redistricting, however, the number of state legislative districts likely to elect black members increased significantly, to the point that the proportion of black members in the southern state legislatures began to approximate the black voting-age populations of those states. In 1980 black membership in the southern state senates reflected only 19 percent of the black voting-age populations. After the 1992 elections, the sixty-one African Americans serving in the southern state senates reflected 80 percent of the black voting-age populations in those states. The (proportional) representation of African Americans in the southern state houses improved from 45.7 percent in 1980 to 81.5 percent after the 1992 elections.

The period after the 1992 elections probably represented the high point in black influence and effective representation in southern state legislatures. The number of black state senators and representatives had increased substantially and was about proportional to the various state black populations. In the North Carolina house, an African American representative, Dan Blue, presided as Speaker, and black members chaired committees in most of the southern legislative bodies. But then black influence began to decline, because all but two of the black southern state legislators were Democrats and partisan control of many of those legislative bodies was about to change.

Between 1970 and 1990, the South voted increasingly Republican in presidential and U.S. Senate races. Only in state legislatures, and to the lesser degree in the U.S. House, did the GOP lag. Because the state legislatures drew the U.S. House districts, Democrats continued to dominate—the GOP increased its number of southern U.S. House seats only from 35 (of 116) in 1982 to 39 in 1990 (Bositis 1995, 72–80).

Before the 1990s, the Republicans never controlled any southern state legislative body except the Tennessee house, which they briefly controlled after the 1968 election. But throughout the 1980s, Republicans in several southern states began to narrow that gap, and the 1992 elections were important to achieving their goals. They achieved dominance after the 1990 redistricting, and black-majority districts had to be created.

When southern Democrats first engaged in diluting black votes, their goal was to diminish black influence. However, as southern whites began to vote more Republican, Democrats had to rely on black votes to remain in office. Meanwhile, more and more southern Democrats accepted the goals of the civil rights movement and became "national" Democrats. Dilution of the black vote then evolved from thwarting black political aspirations to protecting white Democrats and Democratic majorities. Republicans encouraged the creation of black districts because they believed the bleaching process that occurred in districts surrounding black majority districts would open up opportunities for them. Thus they supported black districts not to increase black influence but to win legislative majorities for themselves.

The Republicans' first victories in state legislatures came with their landslide in 1994, when they gained majorities in the Florida state senate and lower houses in North Carolina and South Carolina (but Democrats eventually regained control in North Carolina). In 1996 Republicans gained control of the Florida house and for the first time controlled a southern state legislature. In 1999 the GOP won control of the Virginia legislature, and between 2000 and 2002 Republicans gained control of the state legislatures in South Carolina and Texas. The GOP took control of the Georgia state senate in 2002 and the state house in 2004. Tennessee's state senate went Republican for the first time in 2004.

Even at the peak of their influence in 1993–1994, black state legislators, while a major bloc within the various Democratic majorities in southern state legislatures, were a distinct minority within those legislatures. However, once Republicans began achieving majority status, blacks state legislators were truly weakened; they became a "minority within a minority." From the early 1970s, when the number of black state senators and representatives began to rise, until 1994, all but a handful of them served in the majority, and many eventually achieved positions of some influence, including house Speaker, majority leader, and committee chair. But that political environment has now changed throughout much of the South: almost half of black state legislators—48.6 percent of all black state senators and 44.5 percent of black state representatives—are now members of the minority party.

Much of what has happened to black state legislators in the South has also happened to black members of the U.S. House of Representatives. The post–1992 election period was a high point in numbers and influence for the Congressional Black Caucus, but since the Republican takeover of the U.S. House in 1994, its influence has been greatly diminished.

In summary, the Voting Rights Act has led to fewer (but still some) barriers to voting. Likewise, prohibitions against black vote dilution have given rise to greater black representation in southern legislatures, but the partisan change that has occurred alongside the growth in the numbers of blacks in state elected offices has diminished their political influence.

Statewide Elected Offices

The election of black candidates to statewide constitutional offices differs from election to the state legislature, because in statewide elections the state is the district, and whites are the majority in all southern states. Among all states, Mississippi has the proportionally largest black voting-age population—about one-third. Thus black candidates seeking a statewide office must receive the votes of a large percentage of white voters. Another important difference between the two types of office is the generally small number of statewide constitutional offices. Apart from their two U.S. senators, the southern states have between three (Virginia) and ten (North Carolina) statewide constitutional offices. The number of slots is therefore small, and naturally the competition for the positions is great.

Very few African Americans have been elected to statewide constitutional office in the South. For one thing, no African American has been elected to the U.S. Senate in a southern state.[5] Of the six black major-party nominees for the U.S. Senate—Maurice Dawkins, a Virginia Republican, in 1988; Harvey Gantt, a North Carolina Democrat, in 1990 and 1996; Troy Brown, a Mississippi Democrat, in 2000; Ron Kirk, a Texas Democrat, in 2002; and Denise Majette, a Georgia Democrat, in 2004—all lost badly except for Harvey Gantt in 1990.

One African American has been elected governor (and lieutenant governor) in the South, Virginia Democrat Douglas Wilder, who won election in 1989. Of the three other black major-party nominees for governor, all Democrats—Theo Mitchell from South Carolina and Cleo Fields and William Jefferson from Louisiana—none received more than 37 percent in the general election.

Apart from Douglas Wilder, only four black candidates have been elected to statewide constitutional office in the southern states. Democrat Ralph Campbell Jr. was elected state auditor in North Carolina in 1992 and reelected twice. In Georgia, Democrat Thurbert Baker was elected state attorney general in 1998 and reelected in 2002. The same years, Democrat Michael Thurmond was elected and reelected Georgia state labor commissioner. Finally, Republican Michael Williams was elected to the Texas Railroad Commission (which regulates the important oil and gas industries there) in 2000 and reelected in 2004.

A handful of black justices (including chief justices on the state supreme courts) do sit in the high courts of Alabama, Florida, Georgia, Mississippi, North Carolina, Tennessee, and Texas. Most of these justices were originally appointed to these nonpartisan positions and

then faced statewide retention elections in which they had no opponent. Arkansas, Louisiana, and South Carolina have never elected (or retained) a black candidate running in a statewide election.

Voting Rights, 1965–2005

The Voting Rights Act of 1965 brought momentous changes to the South and the country as a whole. However, viewed from the perspective of forty years the changes experienced by African Americans have a certain bittersweet quality. Although it is true that most African Americans can vote, systematic efforts are still being made to diminish their political influence. Moreover, even though many blacks have been elected to positions of significant leadership, much of the policy making and legislation of the twenty-first century seems to be an expression of those white southern cultural and political values that the civil rights movement sought to overturn.

Notes

1. According to the 2000 U.S. Census, the black voting-age populations of the states of the old Confederacy are (in descending order) 33.1 percent, Mississippi; 29.7 percent, Louisiana; 27.2 percent, South Carolina; 26.6 percent Georgia; 24 percent, Alabama; 20 percent, North Carolina; 18.4 percent, Virginia; 14.8 percent, Tennessee; 13.9 percent, Arkansas; 12.7 percent, Florida; and 11.0 percent, Texas.

2. All information about black elected officials was provided by the Joint Center for Political and Economic Studies. From 1970 until 1993, the Joint Center published a series titled "Black Elected Officials: A National Roster." Each edition in the series listed the names, locations, and offices of all black elected officials in the United States. Since 1993, the Joint Center has

maintained the same information in the form of an electronic roster of black elected officials.

3. In V. O. Key's parlance, the "Deep South" refers to the parts of the South where the black population is proportionally largest. The five states that stretch from Louisiana in the west to South Carolina in the east have the proportionally largest black populations.

4. The 2004 election results by race are from the Edison/Mitofsky exit polls.

5. The two black U.S. senators who served during Reconstruction were chosen by the state legislature.

References

Baer, Denise L., and David A. Bositis. 1988. *Elite Cadres and Party Coalitions: Representing the Public in Party Politics.* Westport, Conn.: Greenwood Press.

Bositis, David A. 1995. *Redistricting and Representation: The Creation of Majority-Minority Districts and the Evolving Party System in the South.* Washington, D.C.: Joint Center for Political and Economic Studies.

———. 2004. *Blacks and the 2004 Democratic National Convention.* Washington, D.C.: Joint Center for Political and Economic Studies.

Committee for the Study of the American Electorate. 2004. "President Bush, Mobilization Drives Propel Turnout to Post-1968 High." Washington, D.C., November 4.

Fellner, Jamie, and Marc Mauer. 1998. *Losing the Vote: The Impact of Felony Disenfranchisement Laws in the United States.* Washington, D.C.: Human Rights Watch and the Sentencing Project.

Joint Center for Political and Economic Studies. 2002. *Black Elected Officials: A Statistical Summary 2000.* Washington, D.C.: Joint Center for Political and Economic Studies.

Key, V. O. 1950. *Southern Politics in State and Nation.* New York: Knopf.

McDonald, Laughlin. 2005. "The New Poll Tax," American Prospect Online, December 30, 2002. http://www.prospect.org (accessed September 16, 2005).

Murphy, Reg. 1971. *The Southern Strategy.* New York: Scribner.

U.S. Commission on Civil Rights. 1968. *Political Participation: A Report of the United States Commission on Civil Rights.* Washington, D.C.: Government Printing Office.

8

The Voting Rights Act and Its Implications for Three Nonblack Minorities

Pei-te Lien

The Voting Rights Act (VRA) has been called the single most effective piece of civil rights legislation ever passed by Congress. However, judgments of its success have been based primarily on the higher levels of voting and officeholding evident among black southerners. The impact of the 1965 Voting Rights Act and its amendments on the voting and officeholding of American Indians, Latinos, and Asian Americans has been less clear. This chapter empirically assesses the political participation and integration of these nonblack minorities and their relationships to the VRA extensions by taking into consideration the distinct legal, historical, and community structure factors that affect the participation of these groups.

To illuminate to what extent and in what ways American Indians, Latinos, and Asian Americans have responded to the VRA extensions, the chapter begins with a brief account of the evolution of these three nonwhite communities in terms of citizenship and immigration policies. This account is followed by a description of the actual provisions of the VRA that apply to these groups. That description includes when the provisions were enacted and extended, the geographic areas of coverage, and the issues related to implementation and

enforcement. The chapter then introduces facts and figures that help to contextualize the significance of the VRA extensions to these multiethnic communities such as the size and growth rate of the U.S. population in 2000, residential concentration and settlement patterns, the shares of foreign-born and those of limited English proficiency, and indicators of economic well-being. It then closely examines and summarizes the patterns and trends of voting and officeholding for each of the nonwhite communities. The concluding section provides insight into whether and how the VRA has had an impact on the voting rights of the three minority populations.

American Indians, Latinos, and Asian Americans: Immigration and Citizenship

The United States has been called a nation of immigrants. However, in 1790 the first national census revealed that approximately 13 percent of the population was of indigenous descent. These first Americans, along with the 16 percent of the U.S. population, almost all of African descent, who were enslaved, were excluded from the concept of U.S. citizenship, defined in the Nationality Act of 1790 as a status reserved for "free, white persons." Although the Fourteenth Amendment of 1868 guaranteed citizenship to all *(see Document 2)*, only blacks were incorporated through this means. The citizenship of other nonwhite racial and ethnic groups would come in piecemeal fashion. Because citizenship is a prerequisite for voting registration, which, in turn, is a prerequisite for voting, participation in voting and elections by these minorities has been deferred by their belated incorporation into the American citizenry.

American Indians

Between the mid-1850s and the early 1900s, thousands of American Indians (also called Native Americans) were rewarded with citizenship when they accepted an allotment (a parcel of land) and left behind the tribal way of life. Unconditional federal citizenship arrived with the American Indian Citizenship Act of 1924, but many states continued to deny these Americans voting rights as late as 1956. Utah was the last state to grant American Indians voting rights. In *Allen v. Merrell* (1956), the state supreme court upheld the attorney general's finding that American Indians residing on reservations were not state residents and thus had no rights to vote in state and local elections. The state legislature overturned the ruling in 1957 under threat of reversal by the U.S. Supreme Court.

The concept of citizenship and voting rights for American Indians has been complicated by their triple citizenship—tribal, state, and federal—as well as by the tribal nations' unique sovereign governmental status and land-owning rights. Despite the potential conflicts between participation in tribal and nontribal elections, American Indians have registered, voted, and campaigned in nontribal elections in unprecedented numbers in recent years in order to preserve or protect their sovereignty, lands, treaty rights, and gaming interests.

Latinos

Latino and *Hispanic* are terms usually applied to people of Latin American origin (for example, Mexicans, Puerto Ricans, and Cubans) who are either indigenous to or immigrated to United States. Like American Indians, Mexicans were indigenous to the ten-state region known today as the American Southwest and West. Those living in this region gained U.S. citizenship at the end of the Mexican-American War (1846–1848) by means of the Treaty of Guadalupe Hidalgo of 1848.

Residents of the island of Puerto Rico received quasi-citizenship as U.S. nationals through the Jones Act of 1917. Puerto Rico is officially a commonwealth associated with the United States. Puerto Ricans may not vote in U.S. national elections, but they may carry U.S. passports for foreign travel and migrate to the U.S. mainland without immigration restrictions.

Mostly admitted as political refugees after the Cuban Revolution in 1959, Cuban immigrants were eligible to seek U.S. citizenship under expedited conditions. Generally, immigrants who have been lawfully admitted to reside in the United States on a permanent basis and who have lived in this country for at least five years, including a period of thirty or more months of continuous stay, are eligible to petition for naturalization. The probation time may be reduced by one or two years if the petitioner has refugee status or is married to a U.S. citizen.

Mexican nationals as well as other legal Latino immigrants from South and Central America and the Caribbean who came in increasingly larger numbers in recent decades may become citizens through naturalization. However, except for the Cuban-born, Latino immigrants have been among the lowest-ranked groups in terms of naturalization rates.

Asian Americans

Contemporary Asian American immigrants are also able to acquire U.S. citizenship through naturalization. Among all immigrant groups, Asians in general are the most likely to acquire citizenship. Yet it was not until 1952, after the racial restrictions set forth in the Nationality Act of 1790 were rescinded, that all Asian American groups were able to petition for naturalization. Until passage of the Immigration Act of 1965, the immigration of Asians was either completely blocked (for example, the Chinese could not immigrate between 1882 and 1943, and Japanese and Korean immigration was forbidden between 1924 and 1952) or maintained at a token number (such as an annual quota of one hundred for Filipinos between 1934 and 1965 and for Asian Indians between 1947 and 1965). Because the Immigration Act abolished national origin quotas and allocated an equal number of visas (twenty thousand per year) to each country, Asians, for the first time, had an equal opportunity to immigrate.

Since 1965, both the Asian American and Latino communities have experienced exponential growth. These nonwhite immigrants began to arrive in greater numbers at the same time that the federal government was vowing to take proactive actions to protect minority voting rights. As shown in the following sections, the ability of these communities to benefit from the expanding protections of the franchise may depend largely on their ability to overcome demographic barriers and to meet the eligibility requirements for citizenship and voting. Among the eligible voters, enforcement problems may hinder their chances to vote and elect their own representatives.

Extending Voting Rights Protections

A right to immigrate and to apply for U.S. citizenship does not automatically translate into qualification to vote. Although in 1870 the Fifteenth Amendment established national voting standards (see Document 3), for women of all colors and racial minorities of both sexes suffrage was not a citizenship right to be assumed but to be earned. Even if white women earned the right to vote through passage of the Nineteenth Amendment in 1920, the federal government's commitment to outlawing group-based discrimination was not clearly articulated until the Civil Rights Act of 1964. Only after that landmark legislation could the federal government make another commitment to sweeping away the remaining legal barriers to voting—first, for blacks in the South and, second, for language minorities of American Indian, Alaska Native, Latino, or Asian descent.

The Voting Rights Act of 1965

The Voting Rights Act of 1965 (Document 25) was complex legislation (see Chapter 6 for a more detailed description of the VRA and its extensions). It included an interlocking set of permanent provisions that applied nationwide—for example, Section 2 prohibited the use of any voting procedure or practice that might result in denial or abridgement of the right to vote on account of race or color. And it contained special provisions that applied only in jurisdictions that had used a "test or device" for voting and in which voting and registration were depressed. For example, the preclearance provision of Section 5 required the covered jurisdictions to obtain advance approval from federal authorities for any proposed changes in their voting laws or procedures. The act's initial goal was to protect blacks—specifically those residing in the six southern states of Alabama, Georgia, Louisiana, Mississippi, South Carolina, Virginia, and part of North Carolina. Over the years, the act has been amended four times to generally expand the definition of the protected populations and the scope of the geographic coverage.

The 1970 Extension

In 1970, prompted by concerns about manipulation of the electorate through gerrymandering, annexation, adoption of at-large elections, and other structural changes to prevent newly registered black voters from effectively using the ballot, Congress extended the preclearance and other provisions of the act for five years and expanded its coverage to include any state or political subdivision that maintained a test or device on November 1, 1968, and had less than a 50 percent turnout or registration rate in the 1968 presidential election *(see Document 30)*. The act also established a five-year nationwide ban on the use of literacy tests or other devices, prohibited the use of durational residency requirements for presidential elections, and reduced the voting age to eighteen. With these changes, the act's cover-

age was extended to four counties with significant Latino populations—Apache County in Arizona, Imperial County in California, and Kings and New York Counties in New York.

The 1975 Extension

In 1975 Congress extended the act for another seven years *(see Document 32)*. In doing so, it made permanent the nationwide ban on the use of literacy tests and other devices for registering or voting in any federal, state, or local election, and it broadened the scope of voting rights protection to language minorities of American Indian or Alaska Native, Latino, or Asian American descent. Under Section 203, members of these communities were eligible to receive bilingual voting assistance if (1) they resided in a jurisdiction (an entire state or its political subdivisions) where at least 5 percent of the voting-age citizens belonged to the same single-language minority community, and (2) the illiteracy rate (the percentage of the citizen population eighteen years and over completing less than five years of school) of citizens in the language minority was higher than the national average. Because of the expansive definition of the protected populations in the act, the geographic boundaries of the VRA were significantly extended to areas in which the three nonblack minorities congregated. Jurisdictions covered by the bilingual election requirement included the entire states of California and Texas and several hundred counties and townships in twenty-six other states. Because of the inclusion of English-only election materials as part of the tests or devices that require preclearance, the geographic coverage of the act under Section 5 also expanded to counties in California, Florida, Michigan, New Hampshire, New York, and South Dakota, and to the states of Arizona and Texas.

The 1982 Extension

The 1982 extension came with an amendment to Section 2, in response to the decision of the U.S. Supreme Court in 1980 in *City of Mobile v. Bolden,* that soon helped with the creation of voting districts that included a majority of black, Latino, or American Indian voters and a concentration of Asian American voters in the next rounds of redistricting *(see Document 34).* Its dramatic result was evident after the 1992 elections, when the number of blacks in Congress jumped from twenty-five to thirty-eight and the number of Latinos from ten to seventeen. Nevertheless, in three separate cases filed in Georgia, North Carolina, and Texas in the mid-1990s the Supreme Court outlawed some of these congressional districts in which over half of the population was nonwhite. The Court pointed out that the process of redrawing these districts was dominated by concerns about race, which made it constitutionally suspect. After the 2002 elections, Latinos gained four new seats in Congress, but blacks gained none. Although no American Indian or Asian American has been elected to Congress as a result of Section 2, more than a few state and local victories have been attributed to it. Many more Latinos were able to win office at the state and local levels because of litigation pursued under Section 5 to combat the illegal adoption of at-large elections, annexations, and gerrymandering.

The 1992 Extension

In 1982 Congress extended the preclearance provision for twenty years and the bilingual provision for ten years. Because the 5 percent threshold to qualify for bilingual voting assistance was too high for any Asian American language community, only Hawaii and the city of San Francisco could receive coverage under Section 203. In 1992 lobbying efforts spearheaded by the Asian American community, with assistance from a broad coalition of community advocacy groups and other civil rights organizations, paid off. Section 203 was extended fifteen years and its coverage was expanded to language-minority communities that either met the 5 percent threshold or had at least ten thousand voting-age citizens in a jurisdiction populated by a single-language minority community with limited English abilities *(see Document 36).* This change added several major cities such as Los Angeles, New York, and Philadelphia to the sixty-eight counties already covered under the 5 percent threshold.

Despite the federal mandate, numerous Section 203 compliance problems were reported by monitoring groups. For example, the Asian American Legal Defense and Education Fund (AALDEF) found that ballots had been mistranslated and that some translated materials and signs were either missing, hidden, or otherwise unavailable to voters. They also found that many poll sites had too few interpreters, or that they spoke the wrong language or dialect. Sometimes, nonminority poll workers displayed hostile attitudes toward voters whose English was limited and thwarted those trying to render language assistance by making rude and disparaging remarks. Some even illegally created new voting requirements that applied only to Asians. Many Asian American voters responded to these discriminatory attitudes and behavior by leaving the polling sites and not returning.

Similar voter suppression and harassment issues were reported by key advocacy groups in the Latino and American Indian communities such as the Mexican American Legal Defense and Education Fund (MALDEF), the Puerto Rican Legal Defense and Education Fund (PRLDEF), the National Congress of American Indians (NCAI), and the Voting Rights Division of the American Civil Liberties Union (ACLU).

A 2000 Demographic Profile of the Three Minorities

Today, the challenges to the full suffrage of the three nonwhite groups lie not only in the need to monitor and remove any remaining legal and structural barriers to political participation and representation, but also in the reality of the delayed incorporation of the three nonwhite groups. American Indians have a history of internal colonization, forced removal, and economic exploitation. Asians have faced a lengthened immigration exclusion and citizenship restrictions. And both the Asian American and Latino populations have experienced ongoing rapid growth through post-1965 international migration and natural increase. As illustrated in this section, variations in the growth rate, nativity, citizenship, language ability, socioeconomic status, and geographic distribution of the three populations may present uneven opportunities for each to pursue equal voting rights.

American Indians

The term *American Indian* is used by the U.S. Census Bureau to refer to the American Indian and Alaska Native populations. The 2000 census revealed about 2.5 million (0.9 percent) of

the U.S. population was single-race American Indian and 1.6 million (0.6 percent) was mixed-race American Indian. From 1990 to 2000, the single-race population grew at a rate of 26 percent. The combined single-race and mixed-race population of 4.1 million grew at a rate of 110 percent over the same period.[1] Alaska had the highest share of American Indians in the state's population (19 percent), followed by Oklahoma (11 percent) and New Mexico (10 percent).

Although nationally scanty, American Indians constituted a majority of the population in fourteen counties in the West and twelve counties in the Midwest. Alaska Natives accounted for over 50 percent of the population in nearly all of the boroughs and census areas in northern and western Alaska.

About 5 percent of American Indians were foreign-born; 31 percent were naturalized. The total citizenship rate was 96 percent. Almost three out of every ten American Indians who were five years of age or over spoke a language other than English at home. Of these, 37 percent reported speaking English less than "very well." Overall, one out of every ten American Indians did not speak English "very well."

Latinos

In 2000, 35.3 million members of the U.S. population (12.5 percent) were of Mexican, Puerto Rican, Cuban, South or Central American, or other Spanish origin. Mexicans made up 59 percent of this population, Puerto Ricans 10 percent, and Cubans 3.5 percent. The remaining 28 percent were of other Hispanic origins such as Salvadorans (1.9 percent), Colombians (1.3 percent), and Guatemalans (1.1 percent). From 1990 to 2000, this population increased by 58 percent.

Over three out of four Latinos resided in seven states: Arizona, California, Florida, Illinois, New Jersey, New York, and Texas. California alone accounted for 31 percent of the national Latino population and Texas for 19 percent. States with the highest shares of Latino population were New Mexico (42 percent), California (32.4 percent), Texas (32 percent), and Arizona (25 percent). Latino groups varied widely in terms of residential settlement patterns. Among Mexicans, 55 percent lived in the West, especially in California and Texas. Among Puerto Ricans, 61 percent lived in the Northeast, especially New Jersey and New York. Among Cubans, 74 percent lived in the South, especially Florida.

About 40 percent of Latinos were foreign-born; less than three in ten had become naturalized. The foreign-born rate was highest among Central Americans and South Americans (76 percent and 77 percent, respectively) and lowest among Puerto Ricans (1 percent). About seven out of ten were citizens either by naturalization or birthright. Cubans had the highest share (41 percent) of naturalized citizens, while Central Americans had the highest share (56 percent) of noncitizens. Close to eight in ten Latinos aged five and over spoke a language other than English at home. That rate was over 90 percent among Dominicans and Central Americans. About two in five Latinos spoke English less than "very well," which ranged from 27 percent among Puerto Ricans to 57 percent among Central Americans.

Asian Americans

The term *Asian Americans* refers to people with their origins in the Far East, Southeast Asia, and the Indian subcontinent. In 2000 single-race Asians constituted 10.2 million (3.6 percent) of the U.S. population; mixed-race Asians totaled 1.7 million (0.6 percent). The total U.S. Asian population comprised Chinese, 24 percent; Filipinos, 20 percent; Asian Indians, 16 percent; and Vietnamese, Koreans, and Japanese, about 10 percent each. From 1990 to 2000, the single-race Asian population of 6.9 million grew by 48 percent, and the combined single-race and mixed-race populations of 11.9 million grew by 72 percent. Of the six major groups, Asian Indians topped the growth rate chart with a 133 percent increase, followed by the Vietnamese at 99 percent. The Japanese had the lowest growth rate—35 percent.

In 2000 about half of the Asian American population resided in the West, which had the highest percentage and numbers of multiethnic population. About half of Asian Americans (51 percent) lived in just three states: California, Hawaii, and New York.

About seven in ten Asian Americans were foreign-born; half had acquired citizenship. The foreign-born rate was lowest among the Japanese (40 percent) and highest among Koreans (78 percent). Filipinos had the lowest share of citizenship (26 percent); Asian Indians had the highest (46 percent). Overall, about one in three (35 percent) Asian Americans did not have citizenship. Of the 9.5 million Asian Americans aged five and over, 79 percent spoke a language other than English at home, and about 40 percent spoke English less than "very well." The share of Asian Americans who spoke a language other than English at home ranged from 47 percent among the Japanese to 93 percent among the Vietnamese. As many as 62 percent of Vietnamese spoke English less than "very well"; that percentage was lowest among Filipinos and Asian Indians (24 percent and 23 percent, respectively).

Cross-Racial Comparison of Key Demographics

A cross-racial comparison will reveal that these three nonwhite groups possess differential strengths and constraints in their abilities to pursue equality in voting participation and officeholding. Table 8-1 summarizes the key demographic factors just described for the three groups. It reveals that in 2000 Latinos were the largest nonwhite population that also experienced the highest growth rate among single-race individuals. American Indians and Pacific Islanders reported the highest growth rates when mixed-race individuals were included in the counting. Asian Americans had the highest percentage of foreign-born population, but they were equal to Latinos in terms of the percentages of persons speaking other than English at home and at proficiency levels below "very well." Among all the racial groups, Asian Americans also had one of the highest rates of naturalization, but the lowest rate of citizenship.

As for the resources for political participation, compared with Asian Americans, the Latino and American Indian populations had low family and per capita incomes and high poverty levels (Table 8-1). Although Asian Americans reported higher educational achievement and family income than non-Hispanic whites, they had lower per capita income and a higher poverty level than those whites.

These statistics show that, despite the commonality of sharing a much higher growth rate than the non-Hispanic white and the black populations, the three nonwhite groups differ in their abilities to pursue equality in voting participation and officeholding. Although smallest in population size, American Indians are advantaged by their pocketed settlement patterns and absence of foreign-born noncitizens. These may allow American Indians to make a better claim for proportional representation and voting rights protection through redistricting than Asian Americans or Latinos. Asian Americans, despite being the most affluent of the nonwhite groups, find their political influence discounted by their lack of citizenship and English proficiency as well as by their relatively small overall size and dispersed settlement patterns. Like Asian Americans, Latinos have lower levels of citizenship and English proficiency. Unlike Asian Americans, Latinos are greatly disadvantaged in socioeconomic status when compared with non-Hispanic whites. Nevertheless, because of their relatively concentrated settlement patterns and their continuing efforts in citizenship and voter education and in leadership development, Latinos may be poised to gain from their unparalleled strength in population size and growth rate among the nonwhite groups.

Patterns and Trends in Voting and Officeholding of American Indians, Latinos, and Asian Americans

This section examines data collected by the U.S. government and private individuals or groups on voter registration, voting turnout, and elective officeholding of the three nonwhite communities. When data are available, comparisons to whites and blacks are made. This analysis reveals three significant patterns.

Table 8-1 U.S. Population Characteristics by Race, 2000

	AIAN	Latino	Asian American	NHPI	Black	N-H White
Population (thousands)	2,448	35,238	10,172	379	34,362	194,514
U.S. population share (percent)	0.9	12.5	3.6	0.1	12.3	69.1
Pop. growth since 1990, single race (percent)	26	58	48	9	16	3
Pop. growth since 1990, single and mixed race (percent)	110	58	72	140	22	5
Foreign-born (percent)	5	40	69	20	6	3.5
Naturalized (percent)	31	28	50	40	44	55
Citizen (percent)	96	71	65	88	97	98
Speak other than English at home, aged five and over (percent)	28	79	79	44	7	6
Do not speak English "very well," over age five (percent)	10	41	40	15	3	2
Males/females having college or higher degree, over age twenty-five (percent)	11/12	10/11	48/40	15/13	13/15	29/25
Median family income (in 1999 dollars)	$33,144	$34,397	$59,324	$45,915	$33,255	$54,698
Per capita income (in 1999 dollars)	$12,893	$12,111	$21,823	$15,054	$14,437	$24,819
Have income below poverty level (percent)	26	23	13	18	25	8

Source: U.S. Census Bureau, Summary File 3 (SF 3) 1-in-6 Sample Data, Washington, D.C., 2000. The data reported are for those individuals with a single racial origin, except where noted.

Note: AIAN = American Indian and Alaska Native; NHPI = Native Hawaiian and other Pacific Islander; N-H white = non-Hispanic white.

Voter Registration and
Turnout Rates Remain Static

An obvious and direct approach to assessing the impact of the VRA extensions on American Indians, Latinos, and Asian Americans is to

compare their voter registration and turnout patterns with those of non-Hispanic whites and blacks over the same time frame and electoral context. Table 8-2 presents voter registration rates by race from 1980 to 2002. For presidential elections, the voter registration

Table 8-2 Voter Registration by Race, 1980–2002 (percent)

	Latino		Asian American		American Indian		Black		Non-Hispanic White	
1980	**36**	**(56)**					**60**	**(64)**	**70**	**(74)**
Gap	**34**	**(18)**					**10**	**(10)**	—	
1982	35	(54)					59	(63)	68	(70)
Gap	33	(16)					9	(7)	—	
1984	**40**	**(61)**					**67**	**(72)**	**72**	**(75)**
Gap	**32**	**(14)**					**5**	**(3)**	—	
1986	36	(56)					64	(67)	68	(70)
Gap	32	(14)					4	(3)	—	
1988	**36**	**(59)**					**65**	**(69)**	**71**	**(74)**
Gap	**35**	**(15)**					**6**	**(5)**	—	
1990	32	(55)	20	(40)	52	(55)	59	(64)	67	(70)
Gap	35	(15)	47	(30)	15	(15)	8	(6)	—	
1992	**35**	**(63)**	**27**	**(54)**	**61**	**(63)**	**64**	**(70)**	**74**	**(77)**
Gap	**39**	**(14)**	**47**	**(23)**	**13**	**(14)**	**10**	**(7)**	—	
1994	31	(53)	22	(39)	56	(56)	59	(61)	68	(69)
Gap	37	(16)	46	(30)	12	(13)	9	(8)	—	
1996	**36**	**(59)**	**26**	**(45)**	**61**	**(62)**	**64**	**(67)**	**72**	**(73)**
Gap	**36**	**(14)**	**46**	**(28)**	**11**	**(11)**	**8**	**(6)**	—	
1998	34	(55)	19	(32)	57	(58)	61	(64)	68	(69)
Gap	34	(14)	49	(37)	11	(11)	7	(5)	—	
2000	**35**	**(57)**	**25**	**(43)**	**58**	**(59)**	**64**	**(68)**	**70**	**(72)**
Gap	**35**	**(15)**	**45**	**(29)**	**12**	**(13)**	**6**	**(4)**	—	
2002	33	(53)	19	(31)	n.a.		59	(63)	68	(69)
Gap	35	(16)	49	(38)	n.a.		9	(6)	—	

Source: U.S. Census Bureau, Historical Time Series Tables, Table A-1, Reported Voting and Registration by Race, Hispanic Origin, Sex, and Age Groups: Nov. 1964 to 2002, Current Population Survey Voter Supplement Files, 1990–2000 (ICPSR version), Washington, D.C.

Note: Table shows the percentage of voting-age population registered to vote and, in parentheses the percentage of voting-age citizens registered to vote. Data for Asian Americans and American Indians were not available until 1990. "Gap" refers to the racial gap of voter registration in percentage points between non-Hispanic whites and the respective nonwhite group; n.a. = not available. Entries for the presidential elections are boldfaced.

rates of Latinos among the voting-age population vary little, ranging from 35 percent (in 1992 and 2000) to 40 percent (in 1984). But the racial gaps in voter registration between Latinos and whites are huge, peaking at 39 percentage points in 1992. When racial differences in citizenship rate are taken into account, racial gaps in voter registration shrink to an average of fifteen percentage points over time. Among voting-age citizens, the Latino registration rate was as high as 63 percent in 1992. Nevertheless, from 1980 to 2000 there was only a three percentage point drop in the registration gap between Latino and white citizens of voting age.

The Asian American registration rates among the voting-age population for the three presidential elections reported in Table 8-2 are not higher than the 27 percent posted in 1992, and the racial gaps are no smaller than the forty-five percentage points observed in 2000. Like those for Latinos, the Asian American registration rates among voting-age citizens peaked at 54 percent in 1992. In 2000 that rate dropped to 43 percent, while the racial gaps climbed from twenty-three to twenty-nine percentage points. For American Indians, their registration rate of 61 percent among the voting-age population (and 63 percent among voting-age citizens) in 1992 was the highest of the three nonwhite groups. Their racial gap of eleven percentage points in 1996 was significantly lower than the figures for Asian Americans, but only moderately lower than those for Latinos citizens.

Nevertheless, any one of these racial gaps in voter registration rates is much wider than those found between blacks and whites during the same time period. Black voter registration

was highest, and their racial gap to whites was lowest, in 1984, the year Rev. Jesse Jackson first ran for the presidency. From 1980 to 2000, blacks saw a drop in voter registration gaps from ten to six percentage points among the voting-age population and from ten to four percentage points among voting-age citizens—a trend not shared by Latinos and Asian Americans.

Voter registration patterns in the midterm election series between 1982 and 2002 resembled those observed in the presidential election series. Generally, there was no clear trend in movement among Latinos, but a downward trend was observed among Asians and an upward trend among American Indians, especially among voting-age citizens.

Patterns in voting turnout in the presidential elections between 1980 and 2000 mostly mirrored the reported patterns in voter registration (see Figure 8-1). Among voting-age citizens, voting for all races peaked in the 1992 election, except for black voting rates, which peaked in 1984. The voting rates of Latino citizens were 46 percent in 1980, 52 percent in 1992, and 45 percent in 2000, which represents an average of seventeen percentage points below the white rates, but an average of eighteen percentage points above the Latino rates among voting-age persons. The voting rates of Asian Americans among citizens dropped from 54 percent in 1992 to 43 percent in 2000. Although these rates are an average of twenty-one percentage points above the voting rates for voting-age Asians, they trail the white rates by an average of seventeen percentage points. The voting rate among American Indian citizens was 55 percent in 1992 and 47 percent in 2000. A persistent racial gap of fifteen per-

Figure 8-1 Trends in Voting Rates by Race, 1980–2000

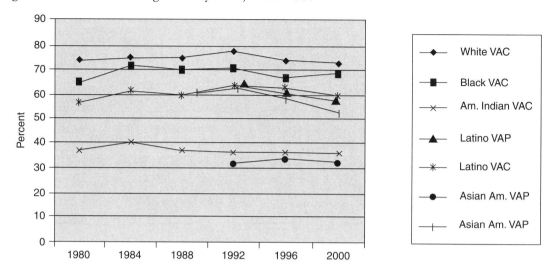

Source: See Table 8-2.
Note: White = non-Hispanic whites; VAC = voting-age citizens; VAP = voting-age population.

centage points below the white rates is evident in the 1992, 1996, and 2000 elections. Compared with the other nonwhite groups, blacks reported much smaller, but still negative, racial gaps in voting among citizens.

When turnout rates are calculated among voting-age citizens who were registered to vote, racial gaps between Asians and whites are rendered insignificant in midterm elections, while reduced to fewer than five percentage points in presidential elections held in the 1990s. Racial gaps remain significant for Latinos and American Indians, but they are reduced to single-digit figures (about eight percentage points) for those elections.[2]

Thus forty years after passage of the VRA of 1965, racial gaps in voting and registration between blacks and whites remain significant, but the sizes of those gaps have been significantly reduced. The story is different for other

nonwhite groups. Despite VRA extensions, contemporary sociodemographic realities appear to have perpetuated the deficit in voter registration and turnout of the other nonwhite groups. As for foreign-born and mostly non-native English-speaking new Americans, their voting rights cannot be protected without ensuring equal access to citizenship and voter registration materials. Special consideration and aggressive enforcement are needed as well to protect the suffrage of native-born U.S. citizens in these minority groups who have limited proficiency in English and are often socioeconomically depressed.

Numbers of Voters and Officeholders Steadily Increase

Although voting participation among non-whites is poor, the number of nonwhite voters and elected officials, especially Latino and

Asian American, has risen steadily over time. This increase can be attributed to the rapid growth of the nonwhite populations, in combination with the coalition-building efforts of community elites and organizations in promoting voting rights, monitoring their enforcement, litigating voting rights violations, and encouraging voluntary assistance. For example, because of the efforts of the Coalition of Asian Pacific Americans for Fair Redistricting (CAPAFR), the 2001 redistricting efforts in California helped to unify many key communities and helped to improve the chances that Asian Americans, as well as Latinos and blacks, would win seats in the state legislature.

The census election data series reported in Table 8-2 reveals that the number of voters in the three nonblack communities is growing at much faster rates than those of non-Hispanic whites and blacks. From 1990 to 2000, the number of Asia American voters grew from less than 1 million to 1.98 million (118 percent). The number of Latino voters grew from 2.89 million to 5.83 million (102 percent) during the same period, as did that of American Indians—from 357,000 to 674,000 (89 percent). By comparison, the growth rate among black voters was 64 percent and among non-Hispanic whites 27 percent. In the general elections of 1990 and 1992, nonwhites made up 15 percent of the electorate. In the election of 2000, the share of nonwhites increased to 19 percent, or about one in five of the American electorate.

Between 1985 and 2004, the number of Latino elected officials rose sharply, especially before 1994 (see Figure 8-2). A similar trend is evident among Asian Americans elected to federal, state, and key local offices; the total number grew from 120 in 1978 to 346 in 2004

Figure 8-2 Latino Elected Officials, 1985–2004

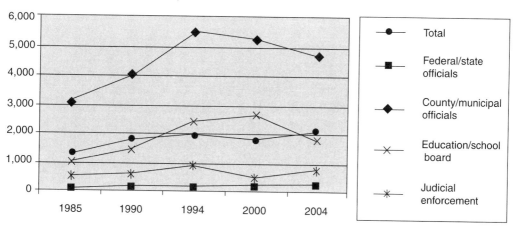

Source: National Association of Latino Elected Officials (NALEO) Education Fund.
Note: The 2004 figures for total and education/school board officials excluded Chicago Local School Council members (LSCs). The number of education/school board officials for 2002, the first year the LSCs were excluded, was 1,603. The 2004 figure of 1,723 represents an increase of 120, despite an apparent decline in the total figure because of the change in methodology after 2000.

(Figure 8-3). This growth rate is particularly sharp at the local level. Reliable statistics for American Indians are available only at the state legislator level. In 1997–1999, twenty-eight American Indian and Alaska Natives served in eight states. In 2003–2004, forty-two served in twelve states.

VRA Coverage Facilitates Representation, but Racial Disparity Persists

Another indicator of the impact of VRA on the political representation of nonblack minorities is the numbers of American Indians, Latinos, and Asian Americans serving in federal, state, and local offices in 2003.[3] Of the 5,049 officials identified nationwide, over 90 percent were elected from jurisdictions covered by the VRA statutes—for example, up to seven in ten Asian American elected officials and about four in ten Latino elected officials were elected from jurisdictions solely covered by Section 203, which mandates foreign-language assistance. As for specific offices, in Congress 100 percent of Latinos and 80 percent of Asian Americans were from VRA-covered jurisdictions; in state legislatures, 60 percent of American Indians, 86 percent of Latinos, and 65 percent of Asian Americans; on city councils, 90 percent of Latinos and 80 percent of Asian Americans; and on school boards, 95 of Latinos and 84 percent of Asian Americans.[4]

These nonwhite elected officials most commonly hold local-level positions as city council members, mayors, and school board members. Among Latinos, 40 percent served on school boards and 38 percent served on city councils. Among Asian Americans, about one-third each served on city councils and on school boards. They also served in states and localities where the ethnic populations are high.

In spite of the persistent gains in minority officeholding, nonwhite communities, especially

Figure 8-3 Asian American Elected Officials, 1978–2004

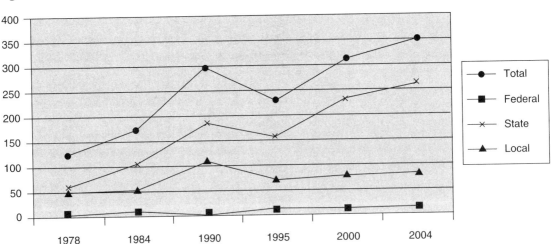

Source: *National Asian Pacific American Political Almanac*, 1st–9th eds. (Los Angeles: UCLA Asian American Studies Center).

American Indians, Latinos, and Asian Americans, still found themselves severely underrepresented in the political leadership structure in 2003. If the parity ratio is calculated as the percentage of a racial group in an elected body compared with its proportion in the population, then each of the nonwhite groups reports a substantial lack of parity in political representation. For example, Latinos constituted 12.5 percent of the national population in 2000, but only 3.5 percent of the membership of the 107th Congress for a parity ratio of 0.28. Similarly, Asian Americans were 3.6 percent in the population, but only 1.1 percent of Congress for a parity ratio of 0.31; and American Indians were 0.9 percent of the population, but were represented by only two members of Congress for a parity ratio of roughly 0.33. By comparison, non-Hispanic whites made up 69 percent of the population, but 88 percent of the membership of Congress for a ratio exceeding the parity of 1.00 by 28 percent. In the nation's state legislatures, 200 Latinos out of a national total of 7,424 members were serving for a parity ratio of 0.22; 97 Asian Americans for a parity ratio of 0.36; and 35 American Indians for a parity ratio of 0.52. As for non-Hispanic whites, again their number of 6,521 put them above parity by 27 percent. An examination of the racial distribution of the nation's key appointed positions at the state level reveals a similar but more equitable pattern of representation.

Conclusion

How did the VRA extensions affect the voting participation and officeholding of the nation's three nonblack minority groups? This chapter argues that the impact on voting and office-

holding for American Indians, Latinos, and Asian Americans has been less dramatic than that on blacks because of the prolonged racial oppression and exclusion from U.S. citizenship and, for Latinos and Asian Americans, the rapid community structural transformation stemming mostly from their large-scale and sustained international migration in contemporary times. In addition, the impact of the VRA may be diluted by continuing implementation and enforcement problems. Although each group has a different combination of strengths and weaknesses in pursuing equal voting rights, these nonblack minorities share a common need to significantly boost voter registration and turnout rates as well as to improve their share of political officeholding.

That said, American Indians, Latinos, and Asian Americans have experienced a steady increase in elective officeholding over the past two decades or so. Moreover, these elective officials at all levels of government come predominantly from VRA-covered jurisdictions, especially those under Section 203 mandating minority language assistance. This tight relationship between the presence of VRA statutes and the election of these minority officials, especially Latinos, along with the equally convincing patterns of minority underparticipation in voting and officeholding, may present the best justification for continuing effective voting rights protection for these rapidly growing segments of the U.S. population and electorate.

Notes

1. Because of the new census practice that allowed persons with mixed ancestry to report one or more racial origin in 2000, researchers best avoid direct, unqualified comparisons of figures generated by the 2000 and earlier censuses.

2. See Lien (2001, 2004) for detailed tables and analysis.
3. Because of the difficulties encountered in collecting data on American Indians in nontribal offices, only those serving in state legislatures and Congress are included in the database.
4. The author thanks the Ford Foundation Gender and Multi-Cultural Leadership Project and the American Civil Liberties Union Southern Regional Office for sharing the initial data for analysis.

References

De la Garza, Rodolfo, and Louis DeSipio. 1997. "Save the Baby, Change the Bathwater, and Scrub the Tub: Latino Electoral Participation after Twenty Years of Voting Rights Act Coverage." In *Pursuing Power: Latinos and the Political System,* edited by F. Chris Garcia. Notre Dame, Ind.: University of Notre Dame Press.

Garcia, John. 1986. "The Voting Rights Act and Hispanic Political Representation in the Southwest." *Publius* 16:49–66.

———. 2003. *Latino Politics in America: Community, Culture, and Interest.* Lanham, Md.: Rowman and Littlefield.

Lien, Pei-te. 2001. *The Making of Asian America through Political Participation.* Pittsburgh: Temple University Press.

———. 2004. "Asian Americans and Voting Participation: Comparing Racial and Ethnic Differences in Recent U.S. Elections." *International Migration Review* 38 (2): 493–517.

Magpantay, Glenn. 2004. "Asian American Access to the Vote: The Language Assistance Provisions (Section 203) of the Voting Rights Act and Beyond." *Asian Law Journal* 11:31–56.

McClain, Paula, and Joseph Stewart Jr. 2002. *"Can We All Get Along?" Racial and Ethnic Minorities in American Politics,* 3d ed. Boulder, Colo.: Westview Press.

McCool, Dan. 1986. "Indian Voting." In *American Indian Policy in the Twentieth Century,* edited by Vine Deloria. Norman: University of Oklahoma Press.

McDonald, Laughlin. 2004/5. "The Voting Rights Act in Indian Country: South Dakota, A Case Study." *American Indian Law Review* 29:43–74.

Nakanishi, Don, and James Lai, eds. 2003. *Asian American Politics: Law, Participation, and Policy.* Lanham, Md.: Rowman and Littlefield.

Paisano, Edna. 1993. *We, the First Americans.* Census 1990 Special Reports Series We-5. Washington, D.C.: U.S. Census Bureau.

Ramirez, Roberto. 2004. *We, the People: Hispanics in the United States.* Census 2000 Special Reports Series CENSR-18. Washington, D.C.: U.S. Census Bureau.

Reeves, Terrance, and Claudette Bennett. 2004. *We, the People: Asians in the United States.* Census 2000 Special Reports Series CENSR-17. Washington, D.C.: U.S. Census Bureau.

Saidel, Judith R. 2005. *Democracy Unrealized: The Underrepresentation of People of Color as Appointed Policy Leaders in State Governments.* Albany: State University of New York, Center for Women in Government and Civil Society.

Schultz, Jeffrey D., Kerry Haynie, Andrew Aoki, and Anne McCulloch, eds. 1999. *Encyclopedia of Minorities in American Politics.* Westport, Conn.: Greenwood Publishing.

Wilkins, David. 2002. *American Indian Politics and the American Political System.* Lanham, Md.: Rowman and Littlefield.

Wolfley, Jeanette. 1991. "Jim Crow, Indian Style: The Disenfranchisement of Native Americans." *American Indian Law Review* 16:167–202.

The Voting Rights Act and Its Discontents

MARK RUSH

In 1982 Congress extended the temporary provision of the Voting Rights Act (VRA) for twenty-five years *(see Documents 25 and 34)*. This extension period was conspicuously longer than the five-year renewal periods Congress had approved in 1965 and 1970 and the seven-year period it had approved in 1975. Thus the extension was a vote of confidence in the act. In effect, Congress was saying that it found it prudent to extend the act's temporary provisions for such a long period. The extension, however, quickly became the subject of sharp debate.

In 1982 Congress also added a new provision, a permanent amendment of the act's Section 2. This amendment statutorily safeguarded minority officeholding. But by adopting the provision, Congress in fact guaranteed a quarter-century of controversy at the very moment it was seeking to signal strong approval for the act.

The policy debate has focused on how best to promote minority officeholding. Implementing Section 2 imposed new constraints on state legislatures that only recently had adjusted to the one-person, one-vote revolution in apportionment. Because of the long-standing debate in American politics about federal regulation of state and local processes, worries about over-regulation of the electoral process occupied a prominent place in the discussion.

The disagreement can be cast in terms of the debate over how to think about rights. The franchise (statutory right to vote) can be considered both a negative and a positive right. Those who have argued that the franchise is essentially a negative right think of it as entitling the voter to access to the polls free of interference from government officials, political associations, and criminal behavior by private citizens—but little more. The negative right approach is by no means an inherently weak, laissez-faire stance. During parts of Reconstruction, the federal government went far in supervising state and local officials and in directly protecting African American voters from violence and intimidation. But in contemporary politics, the negative right view takes on a different cast. Virulent racism has collapsed as a force in American politics. Thus the negative right view looks to a private ordering of race relations once certain basic standards are protected.

By contrast, one can argue that the right to vote must include far more than simple access to voter registration rolls and a voting booth.

Although violence and intimidation of black voters are no longer widespread, subtle forms of racism persist. This positive vision of the franchise imposes an obligation on lawmakers to legally ensure that enfranchised voters cast a meaningful vote—that is, one that will not be rendered pointless by, for example, "gerrymanders" that dilute the influence of minority voters. It is not hard to imagine the bleak possibility that once a disenfranchised people acquires the right to vote, its new formal rights may never actually affect the government and who runs it simply because other electoral rules are depriving them of influence. Under that view, a negative right is no right at all (see Guinier 1994).

The positive right approach calls for government to take affirmative steps to guarantee the right's meaning. Such an approach can mean ensuring that minority voters are actually electing politicians who will effectively represent their interests as they themselves might like them represented. That, in turn, can mean finding a way for minority politicians to get elected and to continue getting elected.

Both conceptualizations of voting rights are reflected in the structure and design of the Voting Rights Act today. The negative aspect of the right appears in Section 4, which suspends the use of literacy tests and other devices, clearing the way for access to the ballot. It also appears in the temporary nature of all of the enforcement provisions and in the procedures that permit jurisdictions covered by Section 4 to "bail out" from coverage.

The positive aspect is visible in Section 5, which requires local and state authorities in covered jurisdictions to seek federal permission for changes to any law dealing with a "stan-

dard, practice, or procedure with respect to voting." It also can be seen in Section 2 (as amended in 1982), which reads:

(a) No voting qualification or prerequisite to voting or standard, practice, or procedure shall be imposed or applied by any State or political subdivision in a manner which results in a denial or abridgement of the right of any citizen of the United States to vote on account of race or color, or in contravention of the guarantees set forth . . . in subsection (b). (b) A violation of subsection (a) is established if, based on the totality of circumstances, it is shown that the political processes leading to nomination or election in the State or political subdivision are not equally open to participation by members of a class of citizens protected by subsection (a) in that its members have less opportunity than other members of the electorate to participate in the political process and to elect representatives of their choice. The extent to which members of a protected class have been elected to office in the State or political subdivision is one circumstance which may be considered: *Provided,*That nothing in this section establishes a right to have members of a protected class elected in numbers equal to their proportion in the population.

The amended Section 2 thus allowed challenges to any voting scheme that had the *effect* of diluting minority voting strength—regardless of whether it had been established with the intent of doing so.

In short, voting rights law contains a tension between the negative and the positive view of the franchise. A novel feature of the Court's struggle to manage this tension is the extent to which it has been influenced by (as demonstrated by the evidence contained in citations and in briefs) legal and political science scholarship. This chapter discusses how the Court's voting rights jurisprudence has developed more or less as a conversation between the Court and its scholarly critics about how best to balance the negative and positive aspects of the franchise while protecting minority voting rights. In this respect, the chapter can be regarded as an "intellectual history" of the Voting Rights Act.

In 1971 Robert G. Dixon Jr. published an article in the journal *PS* entitled "Who Is Listening? Political Science Research in Public Law." In the article, Dixon discussed whether politics research made a difference when courts were confronted with cases involving public policy questions such as redistricting. This chapter demonstrates that the impact of scholarly writing and research on voting rights on the Supreme Court's thinking has been regular and significant since noted scholar Abigail Thernstrom first published *Whose Votes Count? Affirmative Action and Minority Voting Rights* in 1987.

Table 9-1 lists references by the Supreme Court to the cases and authors mentioned in this chapter, but this listing is by no means exhaustive (see the reference list for several important sources that are not cited in this chapter). As the table demonstrates, the Court has indeed stayed in tune with the development and evolution of scholarly thinking about voting rights. In some cases, members of the Court directly cited one of the authors noted (indicated by "C" in the table). In others, an author's work played an important role in the arguments presented in the briefs submitted by the parties to cases (indicated by "B" in the table).

The chapter begins with a discussion of the Court's expansion of the franchise to include a positive right to a meaningful vote for minorities and the academic firestorm this expansion engendered. In addition to addressing the best way to ensure minority representational op-

portunities, the debate over the VRA has focused on the general integrity of the electoral process. The VRA was passed in response to minorities' denial of access to the franchise and the gerrymandering of minorities where they had access to the vote. As the voting rights debate moved into the 1990s, the Court confronted a new conundrum: if it is wrong to gerrymander the political process at the expense of one political group, can we justify manipulating it for their benefit?

While scholars debated this issue, an additional important issue, described in detail in this chapter, was raised by Carol M. Swain (1993): was it possible that creating districts to ensure the election of minority candidates actually harmed minority voters? Although sympathetic to the goal of protecting minority voting rights, scholars such as Swain responded that the creation of U.S House districts drawn to implement Section 2 might actually harm the interests of minority voters, because these districts were created by concentrating minority (that is, heavily Democratic) voting strength into the majority-minority districts. The result of this practice, said Swain, was a corresponding weakening of the Democratic vote elsewhere and a decrease in the number of sympathetic Democratic legislators elected. Swain thus exposed the conflict between seeking effective, partisan representation of the interests of minority voters and ensuring that the House's composition reflected the racial and ethnic diversity of the country. Because of Swain's research, the Court examined and reassessed the assumptions on which it based its analysis of minority voting rights in the 1990s and thereby set off a new round of scholarly debate at the turn of the twenty-first century.

Table 9-1 Impact of Political Science and Legal Literature on the Supreme Court's Voting Rights Decisions

Authors	Shaw v. Reno (1993)	Johnson v. DeGrandy (1994)	Holder v. Hall (1994)	Miller v. Johnson (1995)	Bush v. Vera (1996)	Easley v. Cromartie (2001)	Georgia v. Ashcroft (2003)
Chandler Davidson and Bernard Grofman	C	C	C, B	C, B	C		
Lani Guinier		B	C	B	B		
Pamela S. Karlan			B	B	C		
Richard H. Pildes and Richard G. Niemi					C, B		C
Carol M. Swain		C			B		C
Abigail M. Thernstrom	C	C, B	C	B	B		

Source: Lexis/Nexis.
Note: "B" indicates that the author was cited in at least one brief submitted to the Supreme Court; "C" indicates that a particular author was cited in the case itself.

The chapter concludes with a discussion of the current state of voting rights law. Readers may wonder quite justifiably whether voting rights law can attain equilibrium. Much depends on what Congress does during its consideration of whether to renew the temporary enforcement provisions of the Voting Rights Act—and how the courts and academia respond to Congress.

Signposts in the VRA's Evolution

Like all statutes, the VRA has evolved. The first signpost of that evolutionary process was two decisions that gave rise to the voluminous scholarly debate: *Allen v. State Board of Elections* (1969) and *Thornburg v. Gingles* (1986). *Allen* was an important case, because the Court expanded the scope of the franchise far beyond mere access to the polls *(see Document 28)*. In *Gingles,* almost twenty years later, the Court broadly defined "vote dilution" and set forth three criteria for making a vote dilution challenge under Section 2 of the VRA as amended in 1982. If a plaintiff group could demonstrate that a state failed to draw a district that *could have been drawn* with a majority-black voting population, the state could find itself in violation of the VRA.

In *Allen,* the Supreme Court heard challenges to electoral changes made in several southern states. Despite passage of the VRA, public officials in the South and elsewhere had no intention of docilely conforming to any federal legislation, such as the VRA, designed to alter the political status quo. As Abigail Thernstrom (1987, 4) notes, "By 1969 public officials in Mississippi and elsewhere had made all too plain their readiness to alter the electoral environment by instituting, for instance, county-wide voting, eliminating the single member districts from which some blacks were likely to get elected."

Allen was an aggregation of several cases in which black voters had charged that new laws passed by several southern states required preclearance by the Justice Department. The states argued that because such changes had no impact on black voters' access to the polls, they were not covered by the VRA. The challenged laws included:

- A 1966 Mississippi law that allowed counties to change the manner in which their boards of supervisors were elected (instead of using districts, they could now use at-large elections)
- A 1966 Mississippi law that allowed the boards of education in eleven counties to appoint their superintendents of education (instead of electing the superintendents)
- A 1966 Mississippi law that changed the requirements for independent candidates running in general elections
- A 1966 Virginia law that changed the requirements for casting write-in ballots.

In ruling that Section 5 applied to these kinds of changes to electoral law, the Supreme Court broadened the right to vote. Speaking for the Court, Chief Justice Earl Warren rejected the "narrow construction" of the VRA proffered by the states. Instead, he argued: "The Voting Rights Act was aimed at the subtle, as well as the obvious, state regulations, which have the effect of denying citizens their right to vote because of their race. Moreover, compatible with the decisions of this Court, the Act gives a broad interpretation to the right to vote, recognizing that voting includes 'all action necessary to make a vote effective.' We are convinced that in passing the Voting Rights Act, Congress intended that state enactments such as those involved in the instant cases be subject to the 5 approval requirements" (internal citations omitted). *Allen* thus gave a strong, expansive reading of the practices to which Section 5 of the VRA applied.

A second major signpost in the evolution of the Voting Rights Act came in 1982, when Congress altered Section 2 of the VRA to allow litigants, and the United States via Section 5 (strengthened by *Allen*), to challenge any voting scheme that had the *effect* of diluting minority voting strength. In 1986 in *Thornburg v. Gingles,* the Supreme Court affirmed this view of vote dilution. Speaking for the Court, Justice William J. Brennan Jr. set forth the components of a vote dilution challenge under Section 2:

First, the minority group must be able to demonstrate that it is sufficiently large and geographically compact to constitute a majority in a single-member district. . . . Second, the minority group must be able to show that it is politically cohesive. If the minority group is not politically cohesive, it cannot be said that the selection of a multimember electoral structure thwarts distinctive minority group interests. . . . Third, the minority must be able to demonstrate that the white majority votes sufficiently as a bloc to enable it—in the absence of special circumstances, such as the minority candidate running unopposed . . . —usually to defeat the minority's preferred candidate. (Internal citations omitted.)

Gingles thus placed a great deal of pressure on the states. If the Justice Department or minority plaintiffs could demonstrate that a state had failed to draw a majority-minority district

where one *could* have been drawn, then both Sections 2 and 5 came to bear.

Thernstrom's Misgivings— and the Ensuing Debate

Just after *Gingles,* Abigail Thernstrom published a book—*Whose Votes Count? Affirmative Action and Minority Voting Rights*—that would win wide acclaim in the form of several prestigious awards. On the one hand, she said that *Allen* was "correct and inevitable" (Thernstrom 1987, 30). On the other, she asserted that the ruling in *Allen* (and subsequent cases) set in motion forces that would have unintended and damaging consequences for the integrity of the electoral system and minority voting rights. "Section 5," she argued, "was intended to protect against purposeful discrimination and, beyond that, only against backsliding—attempts to undermine the effectiveness of the enfranchisement that other statutory provisions provided" (p. 236). The new interpretation of Section 2 took "a provision initially inserted [into the VRA] to guard against the manipulation of an electoral system for racist ends" and turned it into "a means to ensure that black votes have value—have the power, that is, to elect blacks" (p. 4).

Thernstrom conceived of the franchise—and therefore the scope of the VRA—in very narrow, negative terms: "The aim of the Voting Rights Act—the *single* aim—was black enfranchisement in the South. Obstacles to registration and voting, that is, were the sole concern of those who framed the statute" (Thernstrom 1987, 3–4). Thernstrom acknowledged that *Allen* was necessary to beat back attempts to buffer the impact of the VRA. But, she said, the Court's expansion of the franchise to include the nature of voting systems and whether a particular office was elective or appointive created incentives for minority voting rights advocates essentially to challenge any electoral arrangement that prevented them from electing a candidate: "By acting to avert such rearguard measures . . . the Court had implicitly enlarged the definition of enfranchisement. Now there were 'meaningful' and 'meaningless' votes—votes that 'counted' and those that did not. And once that distinction had been made, a meaningful vote was almost bound to become an entitlement. It was a subtle but important change: the shift from black ballots safe from deliberate efforts to dilute their impact, on the one hand, to a right to a vote that fully counted, on the other" (Thernstrom 1987, 4). *Allen,* she argued, "began the process by which the Voting Rights Act was reshaped into an instrument for affirmative action in the electoral sphere." The VRA was transformed "from the first truly effective vehicle for the southern black enfranchisement to a means by which political power is redistributed among blacks, whites and (since 1975) Hispanics" (p. 27).

The "affirmative action" policy became manifest in the wake of *Gingles.* As Carol Swain later wrote, the *Gingles* test for vote dilution mandated the creation of a maximum number of majority-minority districts. The result, she argued, was to move the nation one step closer to requiring proportional representation for minorities. To avoid vote dilution suits under the *Gingles* test, states drew "contorted, computer-drawn districts that resembled spiders, masses of bacteria, pitchforks and worse" (Swain 1993, 197; also see Cunningham 2001).

On the one hand, the creation of strangely shaped legislative districts to enhance group representation was unremarkable. Throughout American history, legislative districts had often been drawn to protect or enhance urban, rural, commercial and ethnic interests. And they were drawn to protect incumbents. As Pamela S. Karlan (1996, 301) noted, "In many states, the most observed traditional redistricting principle is the outlandish political gerrymander." So why could bizarre districts not be drawn to protect minority interests?

In this chapter, *gerrymandering* refers to any conscious attempt to manipulate the electoral system in order to achieve a particular result. Accordingly, the term can apply to the pernicious attempts to harm minority voters (frequently associated with bizarrely shaped legislative districts) or the benevolent attempts to engage in "race-conscious redistricting" (that is, a pro-minority gerrymander) that were effected in the wake of the Voting Rights Act. Thus, although gerrymanders had been a tradition in America, they had never been statutorily mandated by a federal policy. If *Gingles* now mandated race-conscious redistricting, it marked an important and controversial shift in voting rights law

Thernstrom's influence was manifested in the 1990s when the Court began to modify the *Gingles* decision. This move by the Court gave rise to a new generation of critics who condemned calls such as Thernstrom's to restrict the scope of the right to vote. Important scholarship underscored Congress's wisdom in establishing an effects standard in Section 2 of the VRA. Studies such as *Quiet Revolution in the South* by Chandler Davidson and Bernard Grofman (1994) indicated that without districts that permitted black voters to elect black officials, there would have been very few black elected officials in the South. As well, a plethora of scholars, perhaps best exemplified by Pamela Karlan and Lani Guinier, broadened the scope of the voting rights discussion, warning the Court that Thernstrom's narrow interpretation of the VRA posed a grave threat to minority voters.

The 1990s: Reconsidering the Scope of the Franchise

In three cases in the 1990s—*Shaw v. Reno* (1993), *Miller v. Johnson* (1995), and *Bush v. Vera* (1996)—the Supreme Court was forced to wrestle with the change in districting law brought about by *Gingles*. In all three cases, the Department of Justice appeared to have forced the state legislatures of North Carolina, Georgia, and Texas, respectively, to maximize the number of majority-minority congressional districts they were drawing. But legislatures also tried to protect House incumbents. The result was the creation of congressional districts with amazingly bizarre shapes.

The Court produced three views of the matter. The controlling camp, led by Justice Sandra Day O'Connor, sought to accommodate concerns about minority representation while constraining the use of race-conscious districting. A second camp, made up of Justices Clarence Thomas and Antonin Scalia, argued that any attention to the racial composition of legislative districts was unconstitutional. The third camp, often led by Justice John Paul Stevens, held that the drawing of legislative districts to help minority voters was constitutional.

The Failed Attempt to Accommodate. Speaking for the Court in *Shaw (Document*

38), Justice O'Connor ruled that a redistricting scheme that was "unexplainable" on grounds other than race would violate the equal protection clause of the Fourteenth Amendment. If the record indicated that racial considerations had played a determining role in the construction of a challenged district *and* if the district's shape indicated that the legislature had forsaken "traditional districting principles" to such an extent that its outline was "highly irregular," "bizarre" and "irrational on its face," then the redistricting plan would run afoul of the equal protection clause.

Shaw, then, rewrote the rules of the districting process. *Gingles* had indicated that if states did not draw districts to enhance minority representational opportunities, they risked a vote dilution challenge under Section 2 of the VRA. According to *Shaw*, if they went too far in drawing majority-minority districts, particularly in states that did not feature large demographic concentrations of African American voters, they risked a Fourteenth Amendment violation. Thus the districting process had to balance new considerations set by the Court.

In the *Shaw* decision, Justice O'Connor wrote that "reapportionment [she should have said *redistricting*] is one area in which appearances do matter." If a districting scheme were so obviously drawn to promote a particular (in this case, minority) group's interests, it would, O'Connor argued, "balkanize" the political process. In this respect, O'Connor's opinion was based on what Richard H. Pildes and Richard G. Niemi (1993, 506–507) called a theory of "expressive harm": "Public policies can violate the Constitution not only because they bring about concrete costs, but also because the very meaning they convey demonstrates inappropriate respect for relevant public values. On this unusual conception of constitutional harm, when a governmental action expresses disrespect for such values, it can violate the Constitution." For Pildes and Niemi, the *Shaw* Court's approach to minority voting rights echoed the approach to affirmative action in the *Regents of the University of California v. Bakke* (1978) decision: it is permissible to promote or protect minority rights, so long as it is done in a manner that is not blatantly based on racial considerations.

The Racial Gerrymandering Camp. In contrast to Justice O'Connor's moderate approach to voting rights, other justices said that racial gerrymandering of any sort was unconstitutional. As Justice Clarence Thomas later stated in *Easley v. Cromartie* (2001): "[R]acial gerrymandering offends the Constitution whether the motivation is malicious or benign." For Justice Thomas, race-conscious redistricting, like affirmative action on the basis of race, was simply "discrimination" (see *Grutter, v. Bollinger* [2003] and *Gratz v. Bollinger* [2003]). Surprisingly, he said that other forms of preferences—such as political patronage hiring and firing—"do not violate any explicit text of the Constitution" (see *Board of County Commissioners, Wabansee County, Kansas v. Umbehr* [1996] in which Scalia and Thomas dissented). Thomas argued simply that the VRA and the Fourteenth Amendment forbade the drawing of legislative districts to promote the interests of racial groups, but did not forbid doing so for any other group or interest. Race was truly a suspect classification in every instance.

Justice Stevens's View of Political Process. Justice Stevens offered a third view: gerryman-

dering on behalf of minority groups was constitutional; gerrymandering at their expense was not. He said in his dissent in *Shaw v. Reno*:

> The difference between constitutional and unconstitutional gerrymanders has nothing to do with whether they are based on assumptions about the groups they affect, but whether their purpose is to enhance the power of the group in control of the districting process at the expense of any minority group, and thereby to strengthen the unequal distribution of electoral power. When an assumption that people in a particular minority group (whether they are defined by the political party, religion, ethnic group, or race to which they belong) will vote in a particular way is used to *benefit* that group, no constitutional violation occurs.

Thus for Stevens gerrymandering on behalf of minorities was no different than any other aspect of interest group politics.

The Unstable Logic of Shaw. *Shaw* was based in significant part on a racial double standard (Raskin 1998) and a logical inconsistency (Polsby and Popper 1993). The racial double standard concerned the appearance of a legislative district and the extent to which it manifested an intent to gerrymander the electoral process: the more bizarre the district, the more likely the Court was to find a constitutional violation—*if* race was involved. As the Court quickly discovered, however, districts could be drawn with bizarre shapes and still pass constitutional muster. Moreover, a district with no bizarre shape that was drawn to help minority candidates could also theoretically pass the *Shaw* test.

The logical inconsistency was identified by Daniel Polsby and Robert Popper (1993). For them, *any* gerrymander was a threat to the integrity of the political process—and the right to cast a meaningful ballot—because it consciously rigged the outcome of an election. Polsby and Popper's reading of *Shaw* indicated that benevolent gerrymanders were oxymoronic: a perversion of the free electoral marketplace was a perversion, period. They argued that gerrymandering (and other methods of political "cheating"), "whether racial or partisan . . . are cut from the same cloth. What makes them objectionable is the notion that the legislature has strayed from its proper domain and played too large a role in constituting itself" (Polsby and Popper 1993, 676). This criticism of redistricting is both powerful and, as yet, unanswered. Polsby and Popper demonstrate that a tainted political process is just that—tainted. The sections that follow will reveal that voting rights jurisprudence and scholarship have yet to address Polsby and Popper's objection in a satisfactory manner.

The Dilution of Shaw. In *Miller v. Johnson* (1995) and *Bush v. Vera* (1996), the Court discovered how poor the *Shaw* standard was and modified its stand against racial gerrymandering. In *Miller,* the Court declared congressional districts in Georgia unconstitutional because the legislative record was replete with evidence that the districting plan (known as the "max-black plan"—see Cunningham 2001) had been drawn with the explicit intent of maximizing the number of majority-minority districts.

Concurring in *Miller,* Justice O'Connor modified her opinion in *Shaw* and addressed the racial double standard that informed it: "The standard [for assessing the constitutionality of districts] would be no different if a legislature had drawn the boundaries to favor some other ethnic group; certainly the standard does not treat efforts to create majority-minority districts *less* favorably than similar efforts on behalf of other groups. . . . Application of the Court's standard does not throw into doubt the vast majority of the Nation's 435 congressional districts, where presumably the States have drawn the boundaries in accordance with their customary districting principles. That is so even though race may well have been considered in the redistricting process." O'Connor thereby acknowledged that race, ethnicity, and other factors are part of the redistricting process. In so doing, she moved away from Thernstrom's point of view and toward that held by Karlan and Justice Stevens. Nonetheless, O'Connor still maintained that the *Shaw* standard at least allowed the Court to police "extreme instances of gerrymandering."

But in his dissent to *Vera,* Justice Stevens challenged the *Miller* majority to explain how it could declare instances of "extreme gerrymandering" to help minorities unconstitutional when equally extreme instances of gerrymandering to protect white incumbents were seemingly beyond constitutional challenge. Writing for the *Vera* majority, Justice O'Connor addressed Stevens's concerns. She explained that "[i]f district lines merely correlate with race because they are drawn on the basis of political affiliation, which correlates with race, there is no racial classification to justify." Texas had asserted that a multitude of factors affected the drafting of the congressional districts. But the Court ruled that the extremely bizarre shapes of the challenged majority-minority districts belied any suggestion that race was *not* a predominant factor in their construction. Still, the weight of Justice Stevens's criticism continued to hamper the Court. If race could be one of many factors in the drafting of district lines, why could it not sometimes predominate—like any other consideration?

Voting Rights in the Twenty-first Century

In 2001 a majority of the Court finally acknowledged the tensions that festered in *Shaw, Miller,* and *Vera.* In *Easley v. Cromartie* (2001), the Court declared North Carolina's congressional districts constitutional, despite their bizarre shapes, because they were the product of a multitude of factors (only one of which was race). In doing so, the Court set forth a standard of proof that made it easier for states to avert a *Shaw* challenge while simultaneously upholding the goals of the VRA. That standard of proof in *Easley* held that so long as states could demonstrate that some factor other than race played an important role in the drafting of legislative district lines, the states could defend a districting scheme by explaining that race did not "predominate." The Court thus drew on O'Connor's statement in *Vera*: "If district lines merely correlate with race because they are drawn on the basis of political affiliation, which correlates with race, there is no racial classification to justify." Thus the Court explained that "the Constitution does not place an *affirmative* obligation upon the legislature to avoid creating districts that turn out to be heavily, even majority, minority. It simply imposes an obligation not to create such districts for predominantly racial, as opposed to political or traditional, districting motivations."

Easley allowed courts to look at a racially remedial gerrymander and declare it nothing more than a partisan or incumbent one. By declaring that race had to be the *predominant* factor in a redistricting plan, the Court enabled

states to defend their plans by offering a plausible partisan alternative explanation for their districting decisions. In this respect, the states could cloak a racial gerrymander in partisan clothing and move on.

In *Easley*, the Court affirmed that the franchise is broader than that called for by Thernstrom. Voters are entitled to have their representation prospects at least acknowledged in the process by which elections are structured. This point, however, does remain controversial. When asked, as Thernstrom did, whose votes should count in the design of electoral districts, advocates of race-conscious districting can offer no principled basis for preferring one type of minority over another.

Thus the evolution of voting rights case law has resulted in reconsideration of the scope of the franchise. The VRA was inspired by a desire to stop the manipulation of the political process at the expense of minorities. As the right to vote was transformed from the negative right that Thernstrom supported into a more positive right, jurists, legal scholars and practitioners all were forced to generalize their thinking about minority rights. A right to have the government ensure that one's vote was meaningful could not be the province of minority voters only. In the 1990s, the Court wrestled with this conundrum and ultimately had to reconcile its jurisprudence with the realities of the American political system and the redistricting process.

As long as districts must be drawn by *someone*, they will be drawn to achieve some purpose—unless they are drawn randomly. In this respect, gerrymandering is inescapable. The result of some twenty years of litigation is that districts may now be drawn to enhance the election prospects of minority candidates in the same way that they may be drawn to enhance the election prospects of any other candidate. Authorities may not discriminate against minority voters. They should take minority representational opportunities into account when drawing legislative and congressional districts, but they may not allow racial factors to predominate. In this regard, the contemporary interpretation of the VRA can be said to grant minority groups the same right to benefit from the manipulation of the political process by gerrymandering that every other group or incumbent shares. This may seem perverse. Yet it could be argued that this is indeed progress.

The Efficacy of Majority-Minority Districts?

The Court's acknowledgment that the franchise had positive and negative components did not end the voting rights debate. Although *Easley* imposed a calm on the debate about the redistricting process, another controversy arose. As the Court and scholars debated the constitutionality of majority-minority districts, Carol Swain asked an important practical question: did such districts actually enhance the representation of minority interests? The *Shaw* debates were based on the assumption that such districts would enhance the representation of minority voters, because they would allow them to elect minority legislators. But Swain noted that majority-minority districts might actually do less to help minority voters than they do to enhance the reelection prospects of incumbent legislators.

In *Black Faces, Black Interests* (1993), Swain suggested that the reelection interests of

minority incumbents might actually be antithetical to the representation interests of minority voters: "Unfortunately, too many voting-rights advocates have failed to make the distinction between descriptive and substantive representation of policy preferences and have failed to acknowledge that what is in the interest of minority politicians is not necessarily in the interest of minority voters. Rather than simply having more minority politicians, voters need more legislators who support their policy preferences" (Swain 1998, 196). Swain argued that the interests of black voters might be better served if they were part of several diverse Democratic constituencies that could send several sympathetic Democratic representatives to a legislature than if they were packed into majority-minority districts, and their votes were used to elect a smaller number of black representatives.

Echoing Abigail Thernstrom (1987 170), Swain noted that this "packing" strategy played into the hands of the Republican Party. By concentrating black (presumably Democratic) voting strength into black-majority districts, state legislatures simply made it easier for Republicans to win in the remaining districts. Black elected legislators would therefore be part of a Democratic legislative caucus that was losing strength to the Republicans.

Swain's research also echoed comments by Lani Guinier. Guinier, too, had expressed concern that majority-minority legislative districts (and single-member districts in general) tend to personalize election campaigning and emphasize the candidate more than the interests of constituents and the issues important to them (Guinier 1994, 82–86). Thus both cast minority voting rights in terms of the representation and potential satisfaction of interests—not necessarily the election of representatives of a particular race.

A Question of Strategy?

Can minority voters still have their interests represented even though they do not comprise a voting majority of a legislative district? Swain argued that they can. If they constitute a sufficient mass of the electorate that they are the *sine qua non* of any electoral majority, their interests will be represented regardless of who is elected. As Guinier (1994, 86–91) noted, however, the creation of such "minority influence" districts would work only under the right circumstances.

The "minority influence" district strategy assumes that black voters can occupy the political middle between or among at least two other groups in a legislative district *and* that the other groups will not coalesce against the black voters' interests. What happens, though, if the other groups form a coalition against the black voters? According to the standard set forth in *Gingles*, this situation would constitute a vote dilution scenario.

In *Georgia v. Ashcroft* (2003), the Supreme Court endorsed Swain's arguments *(see Document 40)*. Speaking for the Court, Justice O'Connor emphasized that

a court should not focus solely on the comparative ability of a minority group to elect a candidate of its choice. While this factor is an important one in the § 5 retrogression inquiry, it cannot be dispositive or exclusive. . . . In order to maximize the electoral success of a minority group, a State may choose to create a certain number of "safe" districts, in which it is highly likely that minority voters will be able to elect the candidate of their choice. Alternatively, a State may choose to create a greater number of [not so safe] districts in which

it is [nonetheless] likely . . . that minority voters will be able to elect candidates of their choice.

She then concluded: "Section 5 gives States the flexibility to choose one theory of effective representation over the other."

Ashcroft provided a defense against claims that minority representational opportunities *depend* on the creation of majority-minority districts. The influence of minority voters would no longer be measured solely in terms of the number of majority-minority districts. Instead, their influence would be assessed in terms of the number of districts in which they played important electoral roles. Thus *Ashcroft*, like *Easley*, diminished the likelihood of a *Shaw* claim. If minority representational opportunities can be achieved with fewer minority voters, redistricters will not need to stretch districts as far as they would in order to create a majority-minority district. As a result, influence districts are less likely to be bizarrely shaped.

Implications: From Minority Voting Rights to Everyone's Voting Rights

It would seem, then, that *Ashcroft* and *Easley* resolved the minority voting rights controversies. *Easley* says a majority-minority district is permissible as long as it is called a partisan or an incumbent gerrymander. *Ashcroft* says one does not even need to draw a majority-minority district to take care of minority voters' interests.

In this respect, the voting rights debate no longer centers on whether the franchise should be regarded in positive or negative terms; in *Easley* and *Ashcroft* the Court managed to establish a balanced middle ground. Instead, the debate now centers on which race-conscious districting policy is best suited to protecting minority representation rights *and* protecting the overall integrity of the electoral process.

Practitioners such as Sam Hirsch (2002) have found the kind of analysis animating *Ashcroft* useful (though note that Hirsch focused on the basis of a case from New Jersey). It gives states options; it avoids a *Shaw* challenge; and it helps to spread minority influence further in the political process. Pamela Karlan (2004), however, has expressed skepticism. Although the *Ashcroft* vision may make sense in theory, in practice it imperils minority representation rights by running the risk that a coalition will form against the minority voters in an influence district.

Even though minority legislators tend to support the creation of influence districts, their support is based on their belief that they can be elected in such districts (see generally *Page v. Bartels* [2001]). As a result, critics such as Karlan question those who equate incumbent reelection prospects with the preservation of minority voters' interests. If the minority incumbent loses, who will speak for the minority voters? In *Ashcroft*, Justice David Souter expressed similar concerns, asking how and whether states could determine in advance that coalitions sympathetic to minority interests would form and endure.

Conclusion: The Evolution and Transformation of the Franchise

The *Ashcroft* debate boils down to an analysis of risk: Do minority voters want to concentrate their power at the expense of the party that represents them? Or should they dilute their own power in hopes that Democrats will

represent them faithfully? Regardless of the answers, the debate is cast in terms of protecting the right of minorities to have as fair a shot at representation as every other group.

As O'Connor noted in *Ashcroft*, one's approach to this risk analysis depends on the theory of representation to which one subscribes. In this respect, voting rights law has indeed advanced quite a long way. When the Court first ventured into the "political thicket" of voting rights law in 1962 in *Baker v. Carr*, Justice Felix Frankfurter protested, warning that there was no clear constitutional basis for assessing different electoral arrangements: "What is actually asked of the Court in this case is to choose among competing bases of representation—ultimately, really, among competing theories of political philosophy." Some forty years later, the Court has come to the realization that there is no constitutional basis on which to make such a choice.

A look back at the intellectual history that began with Thernstrom's criticism reveals that, in many cases, the different scholars were all partly correct and all partly wrong. Thernstrom's fears about manipulation of the electoral process were proven correct in *Shaw*. But her concerns about the "group rights" of minority voters (like Justice Thomas's stand on racial gerrymandering) did not make much sense when viewed within the context of the history of gerrymandering.

Critics such as Karlan got the better of Thernstrom when discussing the scope of the franchise. The narrow, negative conception of the franchise (to register to vote and pull a lever or press a button in the voting booth) would mean little if it were not accompanied by a right to participate in a fair electoral process. Karlan and McCrary (1987–1988, 754) sought to dismiss Thernstrom's assertions that the creation of majority-minority districts played into the hands of incumbents and Republicans. But Thernstrom was vindicated in the 1990s (Thernstrom 1991); cases such as *Page v. Bartels* and *Georgia v. Ashcroft* demonstrated that Republicans were indeed trying to pack minority voters into majority-minority districts. Carol Swain's and Sam Hirsch's analyses also demonstrate that Thernstrom was at least partly right: minority voters can do better in districts in which they do not necessarily comprise a majority. But Swain and Hirsch have no answer to the concerns about minority voters voiced by Karlan, Justice Souter, and Lani Guinier. Does the success of the influence district strategy depend on maintaining "ideal" voting patterns?

In the end, one thing remains clear: the effective exercise of the franchise depends at least in part on carefully policing and, if necessary, manipulating the electoral process. Even though *Easley* and *Ashcroft* diminish the need to create bizarrely shaped districts, the districts created are no less gerrymanders designed to bring about some partisan or ethnic electoral result. In this respect, the analysis and criticism by Polsby and Popper still overshadow the minority voting rights debate.

Ironically, then, the voting rights debate has resulted in the acknowledgment that gerrymandering is inevitable. Someone, somewhere must decide how district lines are drawn. That decision will have clear consequences. The voting rights debate has thus come full circle. In *Allen,* the Court acknowledged that the franchise was rendered less meaningful if it was exercised in a process that had been manipulated. The negative vision of the franchise offered no protection against such manipulation. But paradoxically, the effective exercise of the positive vision of the franchise requires at least some manipulation of or control over the rules of the electoral game. Indeed, a fair electoral system and meaningful vote depend on gerrymandering. To the extent that a vote in a gerrymandered district is somehow diminished, one can take solace in knowing that, thanks to passage of the VRA and the scholarly debates it engendered, under present U.S. law everyone's votes will be diminished equally.

References

Cunningham, Maurice T. 2001. *Maximization, Whatever the Cost: Race, Redistricting, and the Department of Justice.* Westport, Conn.: Praeger.

Davidson, Chandler, and Bernard Grofman, eds. 1994. *Quiet Revolution in the South: The Impact of the Voting Rights Act, 1965–1990.* Princeton N.J.: Princeton University Press.

Dixon, Robert G., Jr. 1971. "Who Is Listening? Political Science Research in Public Law." *PS* 4:19–26.

Guinier, Lani. 1994. *The Tyranny of the Majority: Fundamental Fairness in Representative Democracy.* New York: Free Press.

Hirsch, Sam. 2002. "Unpacking *Page v. Bartels*: A Fresh Redistricting Paradigm Emerges in New Jersey." *Election Law Journal* 1:7–23.

Karlan, Pamela S. 1989. "Maps and Misreadings: The Role of Geographic Compactness in Racial Vote Dilution Litigation." *Harvard Civil Rights– Civil Liberties Law Review* 24:173–248.

———. 1993. "The Rights to Vote: Some Pessimism about Formalism." *Texas Law Review* 71: 1705–1740.

———. 1996. "Still Hazy after All These Years: Voting Rights in the Post-*Shaw* Era." *Cumberland Law Review* 26:287–311.

———. 2004. "*Georgia v. Ashcroft* and the Retrogression of Retrogression." *Election Law Journal* 3:21–36.

Karlan, Pamela S., and Peyton McCrary. 1987–1988. "Without Fear and without Research: Abigail

Thernstrom on the Voting Rights Act." *Journal of Law and Politics* 4:751–777.

Kousser, J. Morgan. 1999. *Colorblind Injustice: Minority Voting Rights and the Undoing of the Second Reconstruction.* Chapel Hill: University of North Carolina Press.

Pildes, Richard H., and Richard G. Niemi. 1993. "Expressive Harms, Bizarre Districts and Voting Rights: Evaluating Election-District Appearances after *Shaw v. Reno.*" *Michigan Law Review* 92 (1993): 483–587.

Polsby, Daniel D., and Robert D. Popper. 1993. "Ugly: An Inquiry into the Problem of Racial Gerrymandering under the Voting Rights Act." *Michigan Law Review* 92 (December): 652–682.

Raskin, Jamin B. 1996. "Bad History, Bad Politics." *American Prospect* (winter): 16.

———. 1998. "The Supreme Court's Racial Double Standard in Redistricting: Bizarre Jurisprudence, Bizarre Scholarship." *Journal of Law and Politics* 14:591–666.

Swain, Carol M. 1993. *Black Faces, Black Interests: The Representation of African Americans in Congress.* Cambridge, Mass.: Harvard University Press.

———. 1998. "An Optimist's View of Minority Representation." In *Redistricting and Minority Representation,* edited by David A. Bositis. Washington, D.C.: Joint Center for Political and Economic Studies.

———. 2004. "Race and Representation: In Our New Multiracial Society, Minorities Need Strategically Effective Coalitions." *American Prospect* (June): A11.

Thernstrom, Abigail M. 1987. *Whose Votes Count? Affirmative Action and Minority Voting Rights.* Cambridge, Mass.: Harvard University Press.

———. 1991. "A Republican Civil Rights Conspiracy: Working Together on Legislative Redistricting." *Washington Post,* September 23, A11.

10 Federal Oversight of Elections and Partisan Realignment

LAUGHLIN MCDONALD

In upholding the constitutionality of the Voting Rights Act (VRA) of 1965, Chief Justice Earl Warren, in *South Carolina v. Katzenbach* (1966), wrote that the fundamental purpose of the act was "to banish the blight of racial discrimination in voting" *(see Document 27)*. The accomplishment of that goal is ongoing, but the act has had at least two other significant consequences. One is greater federal oversight of voting and elections, once thought to be the essential province of the individual states. The other is the acceleration of the defection of southern whites from the Democratic Party, which resulted in a partisan realignment of the South.

This chapter discusses the evolution of the federal regulation of state election procedures after certain Supreme Court decisions in the 1940s and passage of civil rights laws in the 1950s and 1960s, including the Voting Rights Act of 1965, as well as the National Voter Registration Act of 1993 and the Help America Vote Act of 2002. The chapter then traces the defection of southern whites from the Democratic Party beginning in the 1940s in protest over the emerging civil rights movement and the demise of the solid Democratic South and its rebirth as a region largely dominated by the Republican Party.

Federal Oversight of Elections

The Fourteenth and Fifteenth Amendments *(Documents 2 and 3)* were enacted to bestow on former slaves and freedmen all the rights of citizenship, including voting. Yet during the years after Reconstruction, the Supreme Court initially construed the amendments narrowly as neither conferring nor protecting the right to vote, which it deemed to be an incident of state, not federal, citizenship. This view was reinforced by Article I, Section 4, of the Constitution, which provided that "[t]he Times, Places and Manner of holding Elections for Senators and Representatives, shall be prescribed in each State by the Legislature thereof." Thus the basic control over elections was said to reside in the states.

In the 1875 case of *Minor v. Happersett,* the Court dismissed a claim that the state of Missouri's denial of the franchise to women violated the Fourteenth Amendment, saying that it was "unanimously of the opinion that the Constitution of the United States does not confer the right of suffrage upon any one." (Discrimination against women in voting was not prohibited as a matter of federal law until passage of the Nineteenth Amendment in 1920.)

In *Elk v. Wilkins* (1884), the Court also upheld the state of Nebraska's refusal to allow Indians to vote on the grounds that Indians were not citizens and thus, in the absence of being naturalized, were not entitled to the franchise under the Fourteenth and Fifteenth Amendments. (Indians were not naturalized as a matter of general federal law until passage of the Indian Citizenship Act of 1924.)

In *United States v. Reese* (1875) and *James v. Bowman* (1903), the Court declared provisions of the acts passed during Reconstruction to protect newly enfranchised black voters from intimidation either unconstitutional or narrowly construed, because the laws did not prohibit state interference with voting solely on the basis of race or because they reached purely private conduct *(see Document 11)*. In *Williams v. Mississippi* (1898), the Court upheld the constitutionality of literacy tests for registration and payment of poll taxes for voting, despite acknowledging that the purpose of the state requirements was "to disfranchise citizens of the colored race" *(see Document 11)*. In an extraordinarily insensitive opinion, the Court concluded that the laws merely took advantage of "the alleged characteristics of the negro race" and therefore did not violate the Fourteenth Amendment.

The low point in enforcement of the voting rights of racial minorities was plumbed in 1903, when the Supreme Court sidestepped judicial responsibility and dismissed a law suit alleging that five thousand blacks in Montgomery County, Alabama, had been denied registration solely because of their race in violation of the Fourteenth Amendment. The Court held in *Giles v. Harris (Document 11)* that "relief from a great political wrong, if

done, as alleged, by the people of a state and the state itself, must be given by them or by the legislative and political department of the United States."

Some of the Reconstruction Acts survived judicial scrutiny. In *Ex parte Yarbrough (Document 7)*, an 1884 case that involved Section 6 of the Enforcement Act of 1870 *(Document 4)*, the Court upheld a conviction of a group of whites who had beaten a black man for voting in a federal election. But the effect of the post–Reconstruction decisions as a whole was to leave the protection of minority voting rights essentially to the states, which many, particularly those in the South, took to be a green light for disfranchising the very group for whose protection the Fourteenth and Fifteenth Amendments had been enacted.

Although the Court eventually became more receptive to claims of discrimination in voting, the enfranchisement of minorities through litigation proceeded at a snail's pace. The ultimately successful challenge in 1944 to the white primary—the widespread practice in the South of excluding blacks from voting in Democratic primary elections, which were the only elections that really mattered in most southern states—spanned some seventeen years *(see Document 16 for the text of the 1944 case Smith v. Allwright)*.

Despite passage of the Indian Citizenship Act of 1924, American Indians continued to be denied the right to vote (see Chapter 8). Arizona denied Native Americans living on reservations the franchise on the grounds that they were "under guardianship" of the federal government and thus disqualified from voting by the state constitution (this law was finally invalidated in *Harrison v. Laveen* in 1948). Until

1957 Utah denied American Indians living on reservations the right to vote, classifying them as nonresidents under state law. Five states—Idaho, Maine, Mississippi, New Mexico, and Washington—prohibited "Indians not taxed" from voting, although no similar disqualification prevented nontaxpaying whites from casting their ballots (Wolfley 1991, 185). South Dakota also prohibited Native Americans from voting and from holding office.

In an effort to implement more promptly and effectively the guarantees of the Fourteenth and Fifteenth Amendments, Congress passed in 1957 the first civil rights act since 1875. The act created a U.S. Commission on Civil Rights and charged it with collecting information on voting rights violations and denials of equal protection. It also prohibited anyone, whether acting privately or under state law, from interfering with voting in federal elections, and it authorized the United States to bring suit to enforce the new law. In one of the first cases brought under the act, *United States v. Raines* (1959), a federal judge in Georgia ruled that the law was unconstitutional and unenforceable because it reached private conduct. In another suit, *United States v. Alabama* (1960), local election officials delayed the litigation for months by resigning their offices, thereby leaving the government with no proper party to sue. In yet another suit brought against Terrell County, Georgia, the United States won an injunction against the county's discriminatory registration practices, but by 1960 only five blacks had been added to the county's voter rolls. In 1960 the Supreme Court reversed the decision of the Georgia federal court in *United States v. Raines* and upheld the constitutionality of the 1957 act, but liti-

gation proved to be time-consuming and largely ineffective.

Congress was aware of the weaknesses of the 1957 act and attempted to strengthen it by amendments in 1960. Significantly, the amendments authorized the court to "freeze" the qualifications for registration and to appoint referees to supervise the registration process and register qualified voters. The freezing provision was designed to prohibit states from imposing more difficult, ostensibly race-neutral standards on new voters, the effect of which would be to continue the exclusion of unregistered blacks from the franchise. However, the inertia and delay inherent in litigation remained, and plagued implementation of the new voting rights law.

In 1964 Congress again strengthened voting rights with passage of the Omnibus Civil Rights Act. The provisions related to voting required that the same standards for registration be applied to all voters and that any error or omission in registration that was "not material" be disregarded. These new provisions were soon superceded by the Voting Rights Act of 1965.

The inefficiency of the litigation method of enforcing voting rights was apparent from the number of blacks registered after passage of the 1957, 1960, and 1964 acts. In Mississippi, the number of blacks registered to vote increased from 4.4 percent in 1954 to only 6.4 percent in 1964. In Dallas County, Alabama, after four years of litigation by the Department of Justice, only 383 (2.6 percent) out of 15,000 voting-age blacks were registered to vote. As Attorney General Nicholas Katzenbach explained to Congress in 1965 while advocating a different approach, "Litigation on a case-by-case basis simply cannot do the job." Under the existing statutory scheme, he said, progress in minority registration was measured "not in terms of months, but in terms of years." The 1957, 1960, and 1964 acts did, however, reflect a new willingness by Congress to supervise directly the electoral process in the states and a new willingness by the courts to approve this intrusion into what was formerly regarded as the province of the states. The rest of this section describes the operation of the Voting Rights Act of 1965, as well as the National Voter Registration Act (NVRA), designed to facilitate voter registration, and the Help America Vote Act (HAVA) of 2002, enacted in response to the malfunctioning of state electoral processes revealed during the 2000 presidential election and the decision of the Supreme Court in *Bush v. Gore.*

The Voting Rights Act of 1965

Enacted to implement the nondiscrimination provisions of the Fourteenth and Fifteenth Amendments, the Voting Rights Act of 1965 and its subsequent amendments represented the most comprehensive effort by Congress to regulate the state electoral process since Reconstruction *(see Documents 25, 30, 32, and 34).* Not only did the act abolish literacy and other tests used to deny minorities the right to vote, but Section 5 also prohibited "covered" jurisdictions (those that used a discriminatory test or device for voting and in which voter participation was depressed) from implementing new voting procedures without first proving to federal officials that the proposed changes did not have a discriminatory purpose or effect. In *South Carolina v. Katzenbach* (1966), the Supreme Court acknowledged that

Section 5 was an "uncommon exercise of congressional power," but concluded that it was justified by the exceptional history of voting discrimination and the "unremitting and ingenious defiance of the Constitution" in the covered jurisdictions, most of which were in the South *(see Document 27).* Today, sixteen states or parts of states are covered by Section 5, from Florida to Alaska and from New York to California.

Voting practices that deny minority voters the equal opportunity to elect candidates of their choice, such as at-large elections and redistricting plans, but that are not subject to Section 5 review, can be challenged under Section 2 of the act, which was strengthened in 1982 to incorporate a discriminatory "result" standard. Thus voting practices that dilute minority voting strength can be challenged under Section 2 without proving that they were enacted, or are being maintained, with a discriminatory purpose, as would be required for a constitutional challenge.

The 1965 act also provided for the appointment of federal examiners and observers to protect the equal right to vote. The observers, who act as poll watchers, determine whether all eligible persons are allowed to vote and whether ballots are counted properly. Examiners may register or list qualified voters, who are then eligible to vote in all federal, state, and local elections. Through enforcement of the various provisions of the act, minority registration and officeholding have steadily increased in the South and throughout the nation.

In 1975 the protection of the Voting Rights Act was extended to "language minorities," defined as American Indians, Asian Americans,

Alaska Natives, and Latinos *(see Document 34)*. Congress concluded that voting discrimination against language-minority citizens was "pervasive and national in scope." The amendments also expanded the geographic coverage of Section 5 by including in the definition of a "test or device" the use of English-only election materials in jurisdictions where more than 5 percent of the voting-age citizen population was made up of a single language–minority group. As a result of this new definition, the preclearance requirement was extended to counties in California, Florida, Michigan, New Hampshire, New York, and South Dakota, and the states of Alaska, Arizona, and Texas.

Jurisdictions with significant language-minority populations who are limited-English proficient and have high rates of illiteracy are also required to provide voting materials and translation services in languages other than English. Thirty-one states or parts of states, encompassing 466 local jurisdictions, are covered by the bilingual election requirement.

Overall, perhaps the progress in minority registration brought about by the Voting Rights Act is best demonstrated by the 1992 decision of the Voter Education Project, an Atlanta-based organization that historically conducted voter registration throughout the South, to shut down its office.

The National Voter Registration Act of 1993

Building on the congressional supervision of state electoral processes contained in the Voting Rights Act, in 1993 Congress enacted the National Voter Registration Act (NVRA), also known as the Motor Voter Act. The NVRA in large measure superseded the voter registration systems that existed throughout the country.

Congress noted that restrictive registration procedures had been introduced in the United States during the late nineteenth and early twentieth centuries to prevent certain groups from voting—"in the North, the wave of immigrants pouring into the industrial cities; in the South, blacks and the rural poor." The Voting Rights Act had eliminated the more obvious impediments to registration, such as literacy and other tests for voting. The "unfinished business" of registration reform, according to Congress, was to reduce the remaining obstacles to a minimum while maintaining the integrity of the electoral process. Those remaining obstacles, used at various times and in various states, included allowing registration only at the local courthouse, limiting registration to only a few days of the month, denying neighborhood and other voter registration drives, restricting access to voter registration cards, and refusing to designate deputy voter registrars.

The NVRA revolutionized the registration process by requiring states to permit registration by mail, at motor vehicle bureaus, and at all offices in the state that provide public assistance and service to persons with disabilities. Registration forms, which the states are required to accept, may even be retrieved via the Internet.

The Help America Vote Act of 2002

The "Fiasco in Florida," as the disputed 2000 presidential election has been called, was the catalyst for yet another congressional act regulating the electoral process, the Help America Vote Act (HAVA) of 2002. The closest in history, the 2000 presidential election was decided by just a few hundred votes in the state of Florida. Because the vote margin was so narrow, the outcome of the election was thrown into doubt by the disclosure of numerous election irregularities, including the use of the infamous "butterfly ballot" in Palm Beach County (its confusing layout caused a substantial number of voters to miscast their votes), the purging of some fifty thousand alleged felons from the voting rolls (many of the registrants purged were, in fact, eligible to vote under state law), and the use of antiquated punch card voting, which failed to count votes properly, permitted overvoting (casting too many votes for a given office), and provided no notice of errors in voting or an opportunity to correct them.

Al Gore, the Democratic presidential nominee, sought a manual recount of disputed ballots in four counties, but the recount was opposed by Republican George W. Bush, who had been declared the winner. The dispute was ultimately decided by the Supreme Court in *Bush v. Gore* (2000), which enjoined all recounts because the standards for accepting or rejecting contested ballots varied from county to county, and, in its view, "the unequal evaluation of ballots" violated the equal protection clause of the Fourteenth Amendment. The effect of the decision stopping the state's recount was to award the election to Bush. The Court also noted that punch card voting was error-prone and that "it is likely legislative bodies nationwide will examine ways to improve the mechanisms and machinery for voting."

Two years after the decision in *Bush v. Gore.* Congress enacted HAVA. Acting on the Court's finding that the voting technology used in Florida was unreliable, Congress provided for grants to the states that needed to upgrade

or replace their existing voting equipment, thereby ensuring that all voting systems give voters an opportunity to verify the accuracy of their ballots and correct for overvotes. Through HAVA, Congress established the Election Assistance Commission and charged it with establishing and administering voluntary guidelines for elections and maintaining a clearinghouse for information relating to elections, including testing and certifying election equipment. HAVA also requires the following:

- Voting systems used in federal elections must be accessible to persons with disabilities, including persons who are visually impaired.
- States must create a single, uniform, centralized, statewide voter registration list.
- States must permit persons who claim they are registered and eligible, but whose names do not appear on the voter rolls or whose eligibility is challenged, to vote in federal elections by provisional ballot.
- The system used by each state to provide, verify, and count provisional ballots must be uniform throughout the state.
- Voting information must be posted at every polling place on election day, including instructions on how to vote, general information on voting rights under federal and state law, and instructions on how to contact the appropriate official in the event of a violation of those rights.
- States must implement training for poll workers and other elections officials to ensure uniform and nondiscriminatory treatment of all voters.
- States must develop uniform and nondiscriminatory administrative procedures that

allow any person to file a complaint for violations of the act.

As progressive as these features of the act are, several requirements have been criticized as likely to have a negative impact on poor and minority voters. For example, first-time voters who register by mail must provide specified forms of identification at the polls, and registrants must provide a driver's license number or the last four digits of their Social Security number.

More Fallout from Bush v. Gore

Prior to *Bush v. Gore,* the federal courts had generally limited their jurisdiction to hearing and resolving election challenges, because the state courts had procedures for ensuring that the declared winner of an election had actually received the highest number of legally cast votes. The decision of the U.S. Supreme Court to stop the recount in Florida suggested to some observers that the Court had adopted a new "equal evaluation" standard for counting ballots that would subject state electoral practices to even closer judicial scrutiny. Other observers, citing the language of the Court that "[o]ur consideration is limited to the present circumstances," argued that the decision established little except that George W. Bush was president.

Whatever its intended effect, election reform suits challenging the use of punch card voting were filed on the heels of *Bush v. Gore* in California, Florida, Georgia, Illinois, Maryland, and Ohio. Because these states permitted voting by punch cards as well as by other, more reliable technology, the plaintiffs argued that punch cards produced an "unequal evaluation" of bal-lots in violation of the Fourteenth Amendment. All of the suits, with the exception of the one in Ohio, were settled or rendered moot based on agreements by the state to decertify the use of punch cards and adopt more reliable technology. The suit in Ohio is ongoing.

The NVRA, *Bush v. Gore,* and HAVA are evidence of a clear and continuing trend since passage of the Voting Rights Act toward greater supervision of the state electoral process by both the courts and Congress. In the wake of the 2000 election, some elected officials and advocacy groups have even renewed the call for a constitutional amendment establishing the right to vote as a matter of federal law.

One proposed amendment calls for all citizens of voting age to "have the right to vote in any public election held in the jurisdiction in which the citizen resides." The proposal also calls on each state to administer elections "in accordance with election performance standards established by Congress." Such an amendment would in effect nationalize U.S. elections, which historically have been conducted and supervised by officials at the state and county levels. Proponents of the amendment also claim it would allow felons, who are disenfranchised in many states, to vote, and it would permit residents of the District of Columbia to vote for members of Congress (under existing law, residents of the District of Columbia elect a non-voting member to Congress). The adoption of such an amendment would take the nation a long way from the days of the late nineteenth century when the Court was "unanimously of the opinion that the Constitution of the United States does not confer the right of suffrage upon any one."

Partisan Realignment

In addition to its profound effects on the equality of the electoral process, the Voting Rights Act has accelerated a partisan realignment in the United States, particularly in the South. The roots of the defection of conservative whites from the Democratic Party, however, go back to the 1940s and opposition to the national party's support of civil rights laws.

During the 1948 presidential election, southern Democrats, styling themselves "Dixiecrats" and following the leadership of Gov. Strom Thurmond of South Carolina, staged an open revolt against President Harry S. Truman and the national Democratic Party because of their pro–civil rights stance. Truman, in recognition of the injustice of the system of racial segregation, had created the President's Committee on Civil Rights in 1946 to determine ways to strengthen and improve the protection of civil rights. The following year, the committee issued a report, *To Secure These Rights (Document 17)*, and recommended the expansion of the Civil Rights Division of the Department of Justice, the establishment of a permanent Commission on Civil Rights, and the enactment of federal legislation to end discrimination in voting and the administration of justice and to end racial segregation in public schools. On July 26, 1948, by executive order, Truman took the historic step of integrating the country's armed forces.

Gov. Fielding Wright of Mississippi, Thurmond's vice-presidential running mate on the Dixiecrat ticket, officially called the States' Rights Democratic Party, warned that, in calling for the protection of minority rights, Truman and his newly appointed Committee on Civil Rights "aimed to wreck the South and our institutions." Thurmond, for his part, condemned the proposed federal rights initiatives and declared that "there's not enough troops in the army to force the Southern people to break down segregation and admit the negra race into our theaters, into our swimming pools, into our homes, and into our churches." The 1948 platform of the Dixiecrats included the following plank: "We oppose and condemn the action of the Democratic Convention in sponsoring a civil rights program calling for the elimination of segregation, social equality by Federal fiat, regulations of private employment practices, voting and local law enforcement." In the ensuing presidential election, the Thurmond-Wright Dixiecrat ticket polled 1.1 million votes and carried four southern states—Alabama, Louisiana, Mississippi, and South Carolina—marking only the second time since 1876 that the eleven states of the old Confederacy had failed unanimously to support the nominee of the Democratic Party. (The other exception was in 1928 when Catholic candidate Al Smith ran on the Democratic ticket.)

The formal development of the Republican Party in the South began with the 1964 presidential candidacy of Republican senator Barry Goldwater of Arizona, who adopted a "southern strategy" of opposing the Civil Rights Act of 1964. The 1964 act, which prohibited racial discrimination in public and private employment and in public accommodations, was strongly opposed by most southern whites. The Georgia legislature, sparing no invective, called the bill "a grossly unfair, unjust, and diabolical attempt to usurp from the citizens of the United States their God-given and Constitutional freedom to conduct their business and lives in any manner they deem proper."[1] The southern strategy, like the Dixiecrat movement before it, was a calculated effort to attract white Democratic voters who resented the racial changes being imposed on them and being advocated by the national leadership of their own party.

In 1963 Democratic vice president Lyndon B. Johnson accurately predicted the large-scale defection of whites from the Democratic Party in the wake of its efforts in behalf of civil rights. He urged the administration to push for a strong employment and public accommodations bill, because he felt it was the just and moral thing to do. But, he warned, "it might cost us the South" (Bornet 1983, 97). Later, when he succeeded to the presidency after the assassination of President John F. Kennedy, he signed the 1964 Civil Rights Act into law, but as he did so he said to an aide, "I think we just delivered the South to the Republican Party for a long time to come."

Strom Thurmond officially quit the Democratic Party in 1964 in protest of its position on civil rights and joined the ranks of the Republicans. Elsewhere in South Carolina, many Democrats began holding "switching over" parties, at which they publicly denounced the Democratic Party and pledged their new allegiance to the GOP. One of those who did so before the 1964 election was Rep. Floyd Spence of South Carolina. On August 8, 1968, the *Twin-City News* reported that Spence said he was switching over to the Republican Party because of the "undeniable surrender of the Democratic Party to minority, block-voting racial groups" and because of his desire to align himself with a party that has "already undertaken the fight to preserve our way of life."

Two months later, a newspaper in Lexington County, which Spence represented, ran a story on a "switching over" party attended by more than 150 people. Although Goldwater lost his bid for the presidency, his southern strategy helped him to carry, in addition to his home state of Arizona, five states in the former Democratic Solid South: Alabama, Georgia, Louisiana, Mississippi, and South Carolina.

The Voting Rights Act of 1965 was another wedge driven between conservative whites and the national Democratic Party. Paul Rodgers Jr., an assistant attorney general of Georgia, testified before Congress in 1965 that the pending voting rights bill was "a yoke of disgrace" that targeted the South. He also claimed it was an unconstitutional intrusion into the right of states to enact legislation on their own. Carl Sanders, the Democratic governor of the state, wrote directly to President Johnson and urged that the bill be defeated. Comparing it with measures undertaken by Congress during Reconstruction, he said the voting rights bill was designed to punish the South and had been "cut into the grotesque and divisive shreds of provincial application . . . to the shrill discordant counterpoints of a war chant which seeks vengeance."[2]

This and other protests notwithstanding, President Johnson went to the Rotunda of the Capitol on August 6, 1965, almost a hundred years after ratification of the Thirteenth Amendment abolishing slavery, and signed the Voting Rights Act into law. Gazing across the vaulted expanse at a statue of Abraham Lincoln, he called the act "one of the most monumental laws in the entire history of American freedom."

Six southern states—Alabama, Georgia, Louisiana, Mississippi, South Carolina, and

Virginia—in obvious disagreement with the president, promptly challenged the new voting rights law as unconstitutional. The Supreme Court, however, rejected the challenge, concluding that the law was justified by the exceptional history of voting discrimination against racial minorities, particularly in the South.

The presidential candidacy of Democratic governor George C. Wallace of Alabama in 1968 on the American Independent ticket further revealed the deep cleavage between the Democratic Party in the South and its national leadership. At his gubernatorial inauguration in January 1963, Wallace had pledged "segregation now, segregation tomorrow, and segregation forever," and he denounced "the false doctrines of communistic [racial] amalgamation." Six months later, he achieved nationwide notoriety by standing at the entrance of the University of Alabama in defiance of federal authorities in an unsuccessful effort to block desegregation. In his bid for the presidency in 1968 on a third party ticket, Wallace won nearly ten million votes nationwide and carried five southern states, thereby demonstrating how deeply his repeated attacks on the federal government and modern civil rights laws resonated with conservative whites.

Aside from the ongoing dispute over civil and states' rights, the higher levels of black officeholding and participation in party affairs brought about by the Voting Rights Act further incited conservative southern whites to abandon the Democratic Party. Prior to passage of the Voting Rights Act, fewer than two hundred blacks were holding elected office nationwide and fewer than one hundred in the seven southern states covered in their entirety by Sec-

tion 5 of the VRA. By 2001 those numbers had grown to more than 9,000 nationwide and 4,204 in the covered southern states, almost all of whom were elected as Democrats (Joint Center for Political and Economic Studies 1993, xi; U.S. Census Bureau 2005). There is a general consensus that this increase in minority officeholding, which has been described as a "quiet revolution," was a result of the increase in majority-minority electoral districts created through enforcement of the Voting Rights Act (Davidson and Grofman 1994). But as minority officeholding and participation in Democratic Party affairs have increased, so has the defection of conservative whites from the party.

After the landslide reelection of Republican president Richard Nixon in 1972 (who successfully pursued a southern strategy of his own), all eleven states of the old Confederacy, for the first time since Reconstruction, sent at least one Republican to Congress. With Republican president Ronald Reagan's reelection in 1984, Republicans increased their control of southern seats in the U.S. House of Representatives to 37 percent. In the 109th Congress (2005–2007), 77 of the 128 House members from the South and eighteen of the twenty-two U.S. senators from the South were Republicans. In 2005 the GOP also controlled both houses of the legislature in five southern states—Florida, Georgia, South Carolina, Texas, and Virginia—and split control with the Democrats in Tennessee. Finally, seven of the eleven governors of southern states—Alabama, Arkansas, Florida, Georgia, Mississippi, Texas, and South Carolina—were Republicans. Obviously, then, the formerly Democratic Solid South has passed into history.

Some political observers have argued that the decline in fortunes of the Democratic Party can be laid at the doorstep of the increase in majority-black districts, which they claim is a means of "packing" Democratic voters and diminishing their influence. Democrats, however, have lost all but four of the southern seats in the U.S. Senate and seven state governorships, all of which are elected statewide rather than from districts. In addition, voting patterns at the national level reflect the dramatic decline in southern white support of Democratic candidates. In the 2004 presidential election, 71 percent of whites in the South voted for the Republican candidate, George W. Bush. John Kerry, the Democratic candidate, received just 27 percent of the white vote in North Carolina, 23 percent in Georgia, 22 percent in South Carolina, 19 percent in Alabama, and 14 percent in Mississippi. The real reasons for the decline in fortunes of the Democratic Party in the South must therefore be sought elsewhere, including in the dynamic role that race continues to play in the region's politics. But, in any case, the equal right of minorities to elect candidates of their choice cannot morally or legally be denied to ensure the dominance of any particular political party.

'The Party Left Me'

A common mantra of former white Democrats is that they did not leave the Democratic Party but that the party left them. They were simply opposed to big government, federal spending on social programs, and the "liberal" politics of the national Democratic Party, such as support of a woman's right to have an abortion, separation of church and state, and gay rights. In the 1980s, Charles Walker, a white physi-

cian in Charleston County, South Carolina, ran successfully several times for the county council in the 1980s as a Democrat. However, in 1990 he switched parties and ran as a Republican, claiming that "the Democratic Party somehow left the Southern conservatives." But the rise of the predominantly white Republican Party in places like Charleston, while undoubtedly influenced by many factors, is inextricably entwined with the continuing opposition of whites to civil rights and black participation in Democratic Party affairs.

For example, prior to the November 1970 election the Charleston County Democratic Party, in an effort to unify the party and get out the vote, drew up a slate of candidates, which included a black candidate for the county council and another for the house of representatives. In response, the county Republican Party took out a political ad in the local newspaper in which it said that the Democratic Party had "Surrendered Control of your Government to the Bloc-Vote" and to the National Association for the Advancement of Colored People (NAACP). In another ad, the party said that election of the "bloc controlled Democratic slate" would be an open invitation to Ralph Abernathy, the president of the Southern Christian Leadership Conference, which had organized civil rights demonstrations in Charleston, "and his wrecking crew to return to Charleston, more triumphantly and arrogantly."

Not all who remained within the Democratic Party supported the biracial approach in the 1970 election. Some local Democratic phone banks advised voters to "cut the nigger and cut the Jew," referring to Herbert Fielding and Arnold Goodstein, the black and Jewish candidates, respectively, who were campaigning together for the state house.

McKinley Washington, a black candidate who was elected to the state legislature from a majority black district, observed that "the moment some of these precincts got African-American President or African-American Executive Committee men, all of the white folks left the Democratic Party and . . . they went Republican." Whites "did not want to work" with blacks in leadership positions in the Democratic Party. Bernard Fielding, who served a term as county probate judge, agreed that many whites believed "there were too many black people going into the Democratic Party, so they jumped ship and went into the Republican Party." Diane Aghapour, the white chair of the county Democratic Party, said that many whites viewed the Democratic Party as "the black party . . . focused mostly on civil rights issues." Keith Summey, the white mayor of North Charleston, agreed that many whites viewed the Democratic Party as "the party of the blacks." In 1973, when Democrats, including several who were black, won election to office, the local newspaper reported that a "black cloud" had descended over Charleston County.[3]

Kevin Phillips, who was the national Republican Party's main expert on ethnic and racial voting patterns during the 1970s, found that "Negro-Democratic mutual identification" was a prime factor in the growth of the Republican Party in the South. He predicted that with the identification of the Democratic Party as the "Negro party through most of the South," the Republicans would emerge as the majority party in the region and also would attract white working class voters in the North.

During his 1972 presidential campaign, Nixon wrote a memo to his staff ordering them to "use Phillips strategy, don't go for Jews & Blacks" (Carter 1966, 45). The role of race in the partisan realignment, fueled by the Voting Rights Act and increased minority political participation, is apparent.

The Switch in Modern Georgia

With blacks voting for the first time in the state's history, Rufus B. Bullock, a white Republican from Albion, New York, was elected governor of Georgia in 1868 during federal Reconstruction after the Civil War. But once Democrats regained control of the legislature in 1871, Bullock resigned from office and fled the state rather than face certain impeachment. No other Republican was to hold the state's highest office until 2002, when Sonny Perdue was elected governor. Perdue's election, and the Republicans' capture of both houses of the state legislature the next year, completed a process that had its origins in the defection of whites from the Democratic Party, beginning with the Dixiecrats and the southern strategy of the 1960s.

Although some pundits have offered other explanations for Perdue's defeat of Roy Barnes, the seemingly popular Democratic incumbent, perhaps the best explanation for Perdue's upset victory stems from Barnes's successful campaign prior to the 2002 election to remove the Confederate battle flag from its conspicuous place on the state flag. The Confederate battle emblem had been placed on the state flag in 1956 as part of the state's response to the decision in *Brown v. Board of Education* (1954), which struck down racial segregation in the public schools. Georgia's white leadership embraced the philosophy of states' rights, a cornerstone of which was massive resistance to *Brown* and its threat to the southern "way of life" built on white supremacy and segregation. The legislature, with only one dissenting vote, adopted an Interposition Resolution in 1956 declaring the *Brown* decision "null, void and of no force or effect." It pledged to take all measures to defeat "this illegal encroachment upon the rights of [the] people."[4]

The legislature then went on to adopt a new state flag that incorporated the most potent symbol of white defiance of federal authority and the emerging civil right movement: the battle flag of the Confederacy. "[The new flag will] leave no doubt in anyone's mind that Georgia will not forget the teachings of Lee and Stonewall Jackson," said Rep. Denmark Groover, a chief sponsor of the change. "[It] will show that we in Georgia intend to uphold what we stood for, will stand for and will fight for."

Georgia's white leadership lost the battle to nullify the *Brown* decision. But it continued to nurture a states' rights ideology, which frequently bubbled to the surface in the form of opposition to federal civil rights legislation, particularly the Civil Rights Act of 1964 and the Voting Rights Act of 1965. Another manifestation has been the ongoing defection of conservative whites from the Democratic Party. One of those who left the party was Sonny Perdue, who was first elected to the state senate in 1990 as a Democrat, but bolted the party eight years later and was reelected as a Republican.

Prior to the 2002 election, the business and civil rights communities in Georgia began agitating for a change in the state flag. Keeping the old flag, they said, not only was an insult to African Americans, but also would in-

evitably embroil the state in economic boycotts and divisive litigation of the kind that had plagued neighboring Alabama and South Carolina over their flying of the Confederate flag atop their state capitols.

Governor Barnes, bowing to the mounting pressure, pushed through a bill in the general assembly, with virtually no public input or legislative debate, that created a new state flag. The Confederate flag was removed from its central position and was placed inconspicuously at the bottom in a row of other state flags from colonial days to the present. Barnes showed courage and leadership in purging the flag of an admitted and intended symbol of white supremacy, but he also deeply offended many of the state's white voters.

A traveler around the state in the weeks leading up to the November 2002 election could not fail to be struck by the proliferation of pro-flag, anti-Barnes signs and sentiment. In rural Paulding and Polk Counties in the northwest, the Confederate flag was flown in protest in many a front yard. In Dougherty and Worth Counties to the south, signs containing the Confederate flag and the message to "Boot Barnes" were nailed to trees and fence posts along the roads. On the dock of the Kilkenny Marina in coastal Bryan County, the 1956 flag fluttered defiantly in a warming sea breeze blowing in from St. Catherines Sound.

Many things could have cost Barnes votes, including his support of a controversial road project (the Northern Arc) and his policy on education, which teachers complained unfairly held them responsible for poor student performance. But the controversy over the flag was the one most loaded with emotion and symbolism, and probably the costliest for

Barnes. On election night, when Perdue claimed victory, his supporters, almost all of whom were white, crowded around him and triumphantly waved the Confederate flag. And on the day when he took the oath of office in Atlanta, airplanes trailing the Confederate flag circled in the sky overhead.

After the November 2002 election, four white senate Democrats followed Perdue and defected to the Republican Party, giving the GOP a majority (30–26) in the state senate for the first time since Reconstruction. The four defectors were rewarded by being named chairs of important senate committees.

The Confederate flag was the emblem of the mythic and heroic old South, which many whites felt Barnes had dishonored. The flag was also intertwined with a host of other race-related issues, such as white opposition to affirmative action, public spending on social programs that benefited minorities, and redistricting that enhanced African American voting strength. According to one Perdue supporter who undoubtedly spoke for many, Barnes was "too close" to blacks. Whites believed that Sonny Perdue, who said during his campaign that he favored a public referendum on the flag issue, could be counted on to rally around the Confederate flag and all that it represented—if not a return to the pre-*Brown* era, then a refusal to support social programs or capitulate to the demands of the state's black community.

The controversy over the flag continued to simmer during the 2003 session of the state legislature. Perdue backed off of his pledge to hold a referendum on restoring the 1956 flag and accepted a compromise that involved the adoption of yet another state flag—one containing red and white stripes and the state coat of arms in gold on a blue field. After the compromise, signs displaying the Confederate flag and the message "Sonny Lied" appeared around the state.

Georgia has come a long way from the days of white redemption that drove Rufus Bullock from office, as well as from the massive resistance of the 1950s and 1960s. But the recent gubernatorial election shows that race remains divisive in Georgia's political processes and that it continues to drive conservative whites into the ranks of the Republican Party, as it does throughout the South.

Notes

1. *Georgia House Journal*, February 5, 1964, 680; February 10, 1964, 896.
2. This note is in the Lyndon Baines Johnson Library and Museum, LE/HU 2-7, Box 70, 9.
3. All quotes here are taken from the trial transcript of a recent voting rights case in Charleston County, South Carolina, that invalidated the at-large method of electing the county commission because it diluted black voting strength in violation of the VRA. The comments by Kevin Phillips in the next paragraph are taken from the expert report and testimony of Dan Carter, a historian, in the Charleston County case.
4. The quoted language is from the Interposition Resolution, Georgia Laws 1956, 642, as well as contemporaneous Georgia house and senate journals.

References
Bornet, Vaughn Davis. 1983. *The Presidency of Lyndon B. Johnson.* Lawrence: University Press of Kansas.

Bositis, David A., ed. 1998. *Redistricting and Minority Representation.* Lanham, Md.: University Press of America.

Carter, Dan T. 1966. *From George Wallace to Newt Gingrich: Race in the Conservative Counterrevolution, 1963–1994.* Baton Rouge: Louisiana State University Press.

Davidson, Chandler, and Bernard Grofman, eds. 1994. *Quiet Revolution in the South: The Impact of the Voting Rights Act, 1995–1990.* Princeton, N.J.: Princeton University Press.

Dunbar, Leslie W., ed. 1984. *Minority Report: What Has Happened to Blacks, Hispanics, American Indians, and Other Minorities in the Eighties.* New York: Pantheon Books.

Edds, Margaret. 1987. *Free at Last: What Really Happened When Civil Rights Came to Southern Politics.* Bethesda, Md.: Adler and Adler.

Grofman, Bernard, and Chandler Davidson, eds. 1992. *Controversies in Minority Voting: The Voting Rights Act in Perspective.* Washington, D.C.: Brookings.

Joint Center for Political and Economic Studies. 1993. *Black Elected Officials: A National Roster.* Washington, D.C.: Joint Center for Political and Economic Studies.

Kousser, Morgan J. 1974. *The Shaping of Southern Politics: Suffrage Restriction and the Establishment of the One-Party South, 1880–1910.* New Haven, Conn.: Yale University Press.

———. 1999. *Colorblind Injustice: Minority Voting Rights and the Undoing of the Second Reconstruction.* Chapel Hill: University of North Carolina Press.

Lawson, Steven F. 1976. *Black Ballots: Voting Rights in the South, 1944–1969.* New York: Columbia University Press.

Lewinson, Paul. 1932. *Race, Class and Party: A History of Negro Suffrage and White Politics in the South.* Oxford: Oxford University Press.

McDonald, Laughlin. 2003. *A Voting Rights Odyssey: Black Enfranchisement in Georgia.* Cambridge: Cambridge University Press.

Pevar, Stephen L. 1992. *The Rights of Indians and Tribes: The Basic ACLU Guide to Indian and Tribal Rights.* Carbondale: Southern Illinois University Press.

Pildes, Richard H. 1995. "The Politics of Race." *Harvard Law Review* 108:1359.

Swansbrough, Robert H., and David M. Brodsky, eds. 1988. *The South's New Politics: Realignment and Dealignment.* Columbia: University of South Carolina Press.

U.S. Census Bureau. 2005. *Statistical Abstract of the United States: 2004–2005, Black Elected Officials by Office, 1970 to 2001, and State, 2001.* Washington, D.C: U.S. Census Bureau.

Wolfley, Jeanette. 1991. "Jim Crow, Indian Style: The Disenfranchisement of Native Americans." *American Indian Law Review* 16:167.

Woodward, C. Vann. 1960. *The Burden of Southern History.* Baton Rouge: Louisiana State University Press.

Introduction to the Documents

The forty-three documents in this section capture and reflect the main phases of the struggle for minority enfranchisement from the Civil War up to 2005—a year in which the state of Georgia enacted (and the Civil Rights Division of the U.S. Department of Justice explicitly "precleared") voter ID provisions that will disproportionately burden poor and minority voters. In October 2005, an appeals court blocked enforcement of Georgia's new voter ID law, but if the injunction is overturned, critics contend that the law will return minorities in that state to the poll tax era. The documents thus illustrate one of the many meanings of William Faulkner's famous quip "The past is never dead. It's not even past."

The first section of documents, "Defining Voting Rights during Reconstruction," is intended to complement chapter 1. It begins with the 1867 congressional statutes that enfranchised black adult freedmen in the former Confederacy. Only later, in 1870, did the Constitution reflect the change, when the states completed ratification of the Fifteenth Amendment to the Constitution (Document 3). Even so, the Fifteenth Amendment is not self-executing, as the excerpt from one of the ensuing federal elections statutes shows (Document 4). The documents therefore underscore a salient fact about the Fifteenth Amendment: on its own it does nothing; it requires implementing legislation. Indeed, even the laws—such as the Voting Rights Act (VRA)—that do implement the constitutional command depend on strong,

private efforts by minorities to ensure that the statutes change behavior on the ground, and these statutes further require bureaucratic and fiscal resources, the support of officials and of the political parties and the courts of the United States, and massive citizen compliance.

The second section, "Disenfranchising African Americans," underscores these essential truths about the Fifteenth Amendment and the many implementing statutes that have backed up the amendment over time. By the mid-1870s, as Documents 5–6 reveal, the Supreme Court was taking a very equivocal stance toward enforcement of the Fifteenth Amendment. It later reversed itself (Document 7), but by century's end national institutions were occupied by officials who simply backed off from taking the amendment seriously. In the former states of the Confederacy, some devices of democracy, such as the state constitutional convention, were used to push democratic citizens out of the system (Documents 8–10), while judges and presidents essentially shrugged and rationalized the results (Documents 11 and 12). The consequences for the country could not have been more profound—a point emphasized in particular by chapters 2 and 3.

The struggle to, in effect, restore the Constitution is reflected in the documents in the third section, "Restoring Voting Rights" (also see chapter 4). Concerted, patient, and constant political action by African American citizens drove the process (Documents 14, 20, and 23). Also, the Supreme Court began to address the consequences of its earlier acquiescence in the disenfranchisement of black southerners (Documents 13 and 16). The first president to openly recognize the problem of minority disenfranchisement was Harry S. Truman, and Document 17 reflects the influence of his leadership. It was a precursor to the dynamic, eloquent role played by President Lyndon B. Johnson (Document 22).

The statutory progress in restoring the Fifteenth Amendment is also found in this section, including the centerpiece of this volume—the Voting Rights Act (Document 25). The immediate circumstances surrounding the making of the VRA are among the most dramatic in all of American history and are well described in chapter 5. The remarkably helpful role of the Supreme Court in construing the act emerges from Documents 27 and 28. The role of the executive branch—and of activists on the ground—in the aftermath of the statute's passage is on view in Document 26. It provides a fascinating glimpse into the legal defense network that rose out of the intense struggle for voting rights in Mississippi from 1963 through 1966 and that produced many voting rights lawyers who went on to shape the evolution of the VRA. The act's consequences for party politics are foreshadowed in a remarkable, recently discovered postcampaign memo to Sen. Strom Thurmond of South Carolina (Document 29). This document should be read in conjunction with chapter 7.

The final section of documents, "Expanding National Protection and Oversight of Minority Rights," communicates something quite important: the Voting Rights Act, while in many ways the culmination of a long process, itself inaugurated a new phase in American political development. As the history of the Fifteenth Amendment in the nineteenth century reveals, what happens *after* a landmark bill or amendment is passed is just as important as the act of passage itself.

Indeed, the reality of what happened after passage of the VRA is more complex and interesting than its passage. First, the act has required several extensions (see Documents 30–32 and 34 as well as chapter 6). It also has required that within the Justice Department the assistant attorney general for civil rights and the staff of the Voting Section of the Civil Rights Division exercise considerable ability in administering the act's preclearance provision (Document 35). Third, many important effects of the act have only recently emerged, as suggested by Documents 37 and 43. Fourth, the act has been extended to new uses in strengthening the voting rights of nonblack minorities, as suggested by Documents 32, 36, and 42, as well as chapter 8. Finally, although the Supreme Court initially indicated strong support of the Voting Rights Act, a majority of the justices have since become critical of the act's administration, a trend reflected in Documents 33 and 38–40. Even the Justice Department has faltered, as suggested by Document 43.

With very few exceptions, the documents have been edited for both readability and accessibility. The central, instructive passages have been retained in all cases. Full source notes, including URLs for documents available online, are provided for readers who wish to consult the documents in their entirety. Readers are also invited to search further in the vast documentary record that illuminates the events and processes described in this book. This documentary selection is but the tip of a very large iceberg.

I. Defining Voting Rights during Reconstruction

1   Reconstruction Acts, 1867–1868

Anyone reading the Reconstruction Acts will notice in them something quite curious—but also very significant. In these statutes, Congress asks the U.S. Army to do something that armies do not generally do: register hundreds of thousands of new voters and then administer several kinds of special elections. Congress also asks the army, in Section 5 of the First Reconstruction Act and in the residence provisions of the first section of the Fourth Reconstruction Act, to ensure that black adult males vote freely.

Such conscription, so to speak, of this national institution and others to do something they normally do not do has occurred twice over the course of U.S. history, both times when large numbers of African American citizens became new voters: during the First Reconstruction, after the Civil War, and during the Second Reconstruction, at (and after) the height of struggles by the civil rights movement. National officials were thinking so experimentally during the latter period that at one point in late 1964 President Lyndon B. Johnson considered using local U.S. Post Office installations to quickly achieve the federal registration of black southern voters.

In the 1957, 1960, and 1964 Civil Rights Acts (see Document 19), Congress also brought the federal courts to bear on the task of bringing black southern voters into the electorate. These courts were repeatedly pressured by voting rights lawyers in the Justice Department's Civil Rights Division to facilitate the registration of black voters. The lawyers relied on Federal Bureau of Investigation (FBI) agents for help in gathering evidence to present to federal judges in the South. Then, from 1965 to 1968, in the early implementation of the Voting Rights Act, civil servants from the U.S. Census Bureau, under the supervision of the U.S. Office of Personnel Management, worked side by side with local registrars in several Deep South states to process black applications.

Why has the electoral inclusion of black southerners twice—in 1867 and from 1957 to 1968— depended on the emergency conversion of national institutions to unprecedented uses? Much of the answer lies in how the Constitution's assignment of electoral administration has historically advantaged the opponents of black voting rights. Article I, Section 4, places the primary responsibility for the administration of even federal elections with the states: "The Times, Places and Manner of holding Elections for Senators and Representatives, shall be prescribed in each State by the Legislature thereof." A secondary clause does allow Congress to step in—"but the Congress may at any time by Law make or alter such Regulations" (except for the selection of senators). And yet the form of the section and the silence elsewhere in the Constitution about election administration indicate that elections usually should be administered by state and local governments.

Thus, if white coalitions bent on excluding blacks from voting dominated the state and local governments—as they did by early 1867 because of the prior "presidential reconstruction"—the real institutional choices for Congress were very restricted. Either Congress would have to carefully administer federal elections but leave black citizens out of state and local elections (this option was actually considered later, in 1890, in the Federal Elections Bill, often referred to as the Force Bill or the Lodge Bill, after its House sponsor, Henry Cabot Lodge of Massachusetts), or it would have to use a national bureaucracy functioning everywhere in the country. In 1867 only one institution fit that bill: the army.

Another interesting feature of the Reconstruction Acts was the use of loyalty oaths in voter registration. In effect, congressional Republicans were using the registration process to "select in" black voters, who could easily take the prescribed oath, and loyal whites. Thus, initially, many southern white leaders of the former Confederacy were unable to participate in constructing their state governments a second time.

Although it has often been suggested, undoubtedly with some truth, that congressional Republicans were being vindictive, the apparent harshness of this provision also came out of concern for quickly reestablishing basic order. Major white-on-black race riots in some large cities such as Memphis and New Orleans, as well as the ongoing white-on-black homicides in the countryside, often with the apparent connivance of public officials, convinced Congress that it was imperative to quickly establish governments that could be counted on to prevent—or try to prevent and not encourage—massive racial violence. To hammer home the point, the statutes pointedly referred to "rebel States."

Such a perception of the southern situation diverged very sharply from President Andrew Johnson's perception of the matter. For him, the states were no longer "rebel" governments at all; they had been restored to the Union through his unilateral actions between President Abraham Lincoln's assassination and the assembly of the Thirty-eighth Congress in late 1865.

That enormous tension between the congressional and presidential views raises the obvious question: what role did Congress envision in the Reconstruction statutes for the commander in chief? The answer was, a carefully circumscribed role, which becomes apparent if one reads two statutes not reproduced here, the Command of the Army Act and the Tenure of Office Act. By temporarily subordinating the commander in chief to the role of a clerk or agent of Congress, the entire ensemble of statutes effectively set the stage for a constitutional clash of epic proportions. But it is hard to imagine any president sitting still for such a demotion by Congress, no matter how temporary. Even though Johnson could have restrained himself while protesting his situation, he did not. He deliberately violated the Tenure of Office Act by trying to get rid of the secretary of the army, who was trusted by Congress. Because the act prescribed criminal penalties for violation, Johnson thereby made himself a candidate for impeachment and trial.

The logic that required use of a federal bureaucracy—and at that time there was only one capable of carrying out Congress's policy—thus assured a high degree of constitutional tension and conflict in 1867 and 1868. Because Congress had to use the army, it had to contain the president, the commander in chief. That factor has inevitably associated the initial establishment of black voting rights in the United States with constitutional tension. Thus in the mid-1960s, when national officials sought to bypass state and local governments, some of them worried that they were setting the stage for a terrible constitutional crisis. In the end, however, that did not happen. The first time around, however, it did, which is something to keep in mind while reading these statutes. The strengthening of American democracy required pushing at the limits of constitutional forms.

First Reconstruction Act

[*Acts and Resolutions*, 39th Cong., 2d sess., 60. Vetoed by President Andrew Johnson on March 2, 1867, and passed over his veto on the same day.]

WHEREAS no legal State governments or adequate protection for life or property now exists in the rebel States of Virginia, North Carolina, South Carolina, Georgia, Mississippi, Alabama, Louisiana, Florida, Texas, and Arkansas; and whereas it is necessary that peace and good order should be enforced in said States until loyal and republican State governments can be legally established: Therefore

Be it enacted, . . That said rebel States shall be divided into military districts and made subject to the military authority of the United States, as hereinafter prescribed, and for that purpose Virginia shall constitute the first district; North Carolina and South Carolina the second district; Georgia, Alabama and Florida, the third district; Mississippi and Arkansas the fourth district; and Louisiana and Texas the fifth district.

Sec. 2. . . . It shall be the duty of the President to assign to the command of each of said districts an officer of the army, not below the rank of brigadier general, and to detail a sufficient military force to enable such officer to perform his duties and enforce his authority within the district to which he is assigned.

Sec. 3. . . . It shall be the duty of each officer assigned as aforesaid to protect all persons in their rights of person and property, to suppress insurrection, disorder, and violence, and to punish, or cause to be punished, all disturbers of the public peace and criminals, and to this end he may allow local civil tribunals to take jurisdiction of and to try offenders, or, when in his judgment it may be necessary for the trial of offenders, he shall have power to organize military commissions or tribunals for that purpose; and all interference under color of State authority with the exercise of military authority under this act shall be null and void.

Sec. 4. . . All persons put under military arrest by virtue of this act shall be tried without unnecessary delay, and no cruel or unusual punishment shall be inflicted; and no sentence of any military commission or tribunal hereby authorized, affecting the life or liberty of any person, shall be executed until it is approved by the officer in command of the district, and the laws and regulations for the government of the army shall not be affected by this act, except in so far as they conflict with its provisions. . .

Sec. 5. . . When the people of any one of said rebel States shall have formed a constitution of government in conformity with the Constitution of the United States in all respects, framed by a convention of delegates elected by the male citizens of said State, twenty-one years old and upward, of whatever race, color, or previous condition, who have been resident in that State for one year previous to the day of such election, except such as may be disfranchised for participation in the rebellion, or for felony at common law, and when such constitution shall provide that the elective franchise shall be enjoyed by all such persons as have the qualifications herein stated for electors of delegates, and when such constitution shall be ratified by a majority of the persons voting on the question of ratification who are qualified as electors for delegates, and when such constitution shall have been submitted to Congress for examination and approval, and Congress shall have approved the same, and when said State, by a vote of its legislature elected under said constitution, shall have adopted the amendment to the Consti-

tution of the United States, proposed by the thirty-ninth Congress, and known as article fourteen, and when such article shall have become a part of the Constitution of the United States, said State shall be declared entitled to representation in Congress, and senators and representatives shall be admitted therefrom on their taking oaths prescribed by law, and then and thereafter the preceding sections of this act shall be inoperative in said State: Provided, That no person excluded from the privilege of holding office by said proposed amendment to the Constitution of the United States, shall be eligible to election as a member of the convention to frame a constitution for any of said rebel States, nor shall any such person vote for members of such convention.

Sec. 6. . . Until the people of said rebel States shall be by law admitted to representation in the Congress of the United States, any civil governments which may exist therein shall be deemed provisional only, and in all respects subject to the paramount authority of the United States at any time to abolish, modify or control, or supersede the same; and in all elections to any office under such provisional governments all persons shall be entitled to vote, and none others, who are entitled to vote under the provisions of the fifth section of this act; and no person shall be eligible to any office under any provisional governments who would be disqualified from holding office under the provisions of the third article of said constitutional amendment.

Supplementary Reconstruction Act

[*Acts and Resolutions*, 40th Cong., 1st sess., 260. Passed over President Andrew Johnson's veto on March 23, 1867, this act was to hasten the Reconstruction, which would probably have failed under the first act.]

Be it enacted . . That before the first day of September, eighteen hundred and sixty-seven, the commanding general in each district defined by an act entitled "An act to provide for the more efficient government of the rebel States," passed March second, eighteen hundred and sixty-seven, shall cause a registration to be made of the male citizens of the United States, twenty-one years of age and upwards, resident in each county or parish in the State or States included in his district, which registration shall include only those persons who are qualified to vote for delegates by the act as aforesaid, and who shall have taken and subscribed the following oath or affirmation: "I, _____, do solemnly swear (or affirm), in the presence of Almighty God, that I am a citizen of the State of _____; that I have resided in said State for _____ months next preceding this day, and now reside in the county of _____ or the parish of _____, in said State (as the case may be); That I am twenty-one years old; that I have not been disfranchised for participation in any rebellion or civil war against the United States, nor for felony committed against the laws of any State or of the United States; that I have never been a member of any State legislature, nor held any executive or judicial office in any State and afterwards engaged in insurrection or rebellion against the United States, or given aid or comfort to the enemies thereof; and I have never taken an oath as a member of Congress of the United States, or as an officer of the United States, or as a member of any State legislature, or as an executive or judicial officer of any State, to support the Constitution of the United States, and afterwards engaged in insurrection or rebellion against the United States, or given aid or comfort to the enemies thereof; that I will faithfully support the Constitution and obey the laws of the United States, and will, to the best of my ability, encourage others so to do, so help me God;" which oath or affirmation may be administered by any registering officer.

Sec. 2. . . After the completion of the registration hereby provided for in any State, at such time and places therein as the commanding general shall appoint and direct, of which at least thirty days' public notice shall be given, an elec-

tion shall be held of delegates to a convention for the purpose of establishing a constitution and civil government for such State loyal to the Union, said convention in each State, except Virginia, to consist of the same number of members as the most numerous branch of the State legislature of such State in the year eighteen hundred and sixty, to be apportioned among the several districts, counties, or parishes of such State by the commanding general, giving to each representation in the ratio of voters registered as aforesaid, as nearly as may be. The convention in Virginia shall consist of the same number of members as represented the territory now constituting Virginia in the most numerous branch of the legislature of said State in the year eighteen hundred and sixty, to be apportioned as aforesaid.

Sec. 3. . . At said election the registered voters of each State shall vote for or against a convention to form a constitution therefor under this act. Those voting in favor of such a convention shall have written or printed on the ballots by which they vote for delegates, as aforesaid, the words "For a convention," and those voting against such a convention shall have written or printed on such ballots the words "Against a convention." The person appointed to superintend said election, and to make return of the votes given threat, as herein provided, shall count and make return of the votes given for and against a convention; and the commanding general to whom the same shall have been returned shall ascertain and declare the total vote in each State for and against a convention. If a majority of the votes given on that question shall be for a convention, then such convention shall be held as hereinafter provided; but if a majority of said votes shall be against a convention, then no such convention shall be held under this act: Provided, That such convention shall not be held unless a majority of all such registered voters shall have voted on the question of holding such convention.

Sec. 4. . . The commanding general of each district shall appoint as many boards of registration as may be necessary, consisting of three loyal officers or persons, to make and complete the registration, superintend the election, and make return to him of the votes, list of voters, and of the persons elected as delegates by a plurality of the votes cast at said election; and upon receiving said returns he shall open the same, ascertain the persons elected as delegates according to the returns of the officers who conducted said election, and make proclamation thereof; and if a majority of the votes given on the question shall be for a convention, the commanding general, within sixty days from the date of election, shall notify the delegates to assemble in convention, at a time and place to be mentioned in the notification, and said convention, when organized, shall proceed to frame a constitution and civil government according to the provisions of this act and the act to which it is supplementary; and when the same shall have been so framed, said constitution shall be submitted by the convention for ratification to the persons registered under the provisions of this act at an election to be conducted by the officers or persons appointed or to be appointed by the commanding general, as hereinbefore provided, and to be held after the expiration of thirty days from the date of notice thereof, to be given by said convention; and the returns thereof shall be made to the commanding general of the district.

Sec. 5. . . If, according to said returns, the constitution shall be ratified by a majority of the votes of the registered electors qualified as herein specified, cast at said election, at least one half of all the registered voters voting upon the question of such ratification, the president of the convention shall transmit a copy of the same, duly certified, to the President of the United States, who shall forthwith transmit the same to Congress, if then in session, and if not in session, then immediately upon its next assembling; and if it shall, moreover, appear to Congress that the election was one at which all the registered and qualified electors in the State had an opportunity to vote freely and without restraint, fear, or the influence

of fraud, and if the Congress shall be satisfied that such constitution meets the approval of a majority of all the qualified electors in the State, and if the said constitution shall be declared by Congress to be in conformity with the provisions of the act to which this is supplementary, and the other provisions of said act shall have been complied with, and the said constitution shall be approved by Congress, the State shall be declared entitled to representation, and senators and representatives shall be admitted therefrom as therein provided.

Sec. 6. . . All elections in the States mentioned in said "Act to provide for the more efficient government of the rebel States," shall, during the operation of said act, be by ballot; and all officers making the said registration of voters and conducting said elections shall, before entering upon the discharge of their duties, take and subscribe the oath prescribed by the act approved July second, eighteen hundred and sixty-two entitled "An act to prescribe an oath of office:" *Provided,* That if any person knowingly and falsely take and subscribe any oath in this act prescribed, such person so offending and being thereof duly convicted, shall be subject to the pains, penalties, and disabilities which by law are provided for the punishment of the crime of wilful and corrupt perjury.

Sec. 7. . . All expenses incurred by the several commanding generals, or by virtue of any orders issued, or appointments made, by them, under or by virtue of this act, shall be paid out of any moneys in the treasury not otherwise appropriated.

Sec. 8. . . The convention for each State shall prescribe the fees, salary, and compensation to be paid to all delegates and other officers and agents herein authorized or necessary to carry into effect the purposes of this act not herein otherwise provided for, and shall provide for the levy and collection of such taxes on the property in such State as may be necessary to pay the same.

Sec. 9. . . The word article, in the sixth section of the act to which this is supplementary, shall be construed to mean section.

Third Reconstruction Act

[*Statutes at Large,* Vol. 15, 14. Passed over President Andrew Johnson's veto on July 19, 1867. Intended to nullify the interpretation of the Reconstruction Acts by the cabinet and the attorney general.]

Be it enacted . . That it is hereby declared to have been the true intent and meaning of the [acts of March 2, March 23, 1867] that the governments then existing in the rebel States of Virginia, North Carolina, South Carolina, Georgia, Mississippi, Alabama, Louisiana, Florida, Texas, and Arkansas were not legal State governments; and that thereafter said governments, if continued, were to be continued subject in all respects to the military commanders of the respective districts, and to the paramount authority of Congress.

Sec. 2. . . The commander of any district named in said act shall have power, subject to the disapproval of the General of the army of the United States, and to have effect till disapproved, whenever in the opinion of such commander the proper administration of said act shall require it, to suspend or remove from office, or from the performance of official duties and exercise of official powers, any officer or person holding or exercising, or professing to hold or exercise, any civil or military office or duty in such district under any power, election, appointment, or authority derived from, or granted by, or claimed under, any so-called State or the government thereof, or any municipal or other division thereof; and upon such suspension or removal such commander, subject to the disapproval of the General as aforesaid, shall have power to provide from time to time for the performance of the said duties of such officer or person so suspended or removed, by the detail of some competent officer or soldier of the army, or by the appointment of some other person to perform the same, and to fill vacancies occasioned by death, resignation, or otherwise.

Sec. 3. . . The General of the army of the United Sates shall be invested with all the powers of sus-

pension, removal, appointment, and detail granted in the preceding section to district commanders.

Sec. 4. . . The acts of the officers of the army already done in removing in said districts persons exercising the functions of civil officers, and appointing others in their stead, are hereby confirmed: Provided, That any person heretofore or hereafter appointed by any district commander to exercise the functions of any civil office, may be removed, either by the military officer in command of the district, or by the General of the army. And it shall be the duty of such commander to remove from office as aforesaid all persons who are disloyal to the government of the United States, or who use their official influence in any manner to hinder, delay, prevent, or obstruct the due and proper administration of this act and the acts to which it is supplementary.

Sec. 5. . . The boards of registration provided for in the act entitled "An act supplementary to an act . . passed March 23, 1867, shall have power, and it shall be their duty before allowing the registration of any person, to ascertain, upon such facts or information as they can obtain, whether such person is entitled to be registered under said act, and the oath required by said act shall not be conclusive on such question, and no person shall be registered unless such board shall decide that he is entitled thereto; and such board shall also have power to examine under oath, (to be administered by any member of such board,) any one touching the qualification of any person claiming registration; but in every case of refusal by the board to register an applicant, and in every case of striking his name from the list as hereinafter provided, the board shall make a note or memorandum, which shall be returned with the registration list to the commanding general of the district, setting forth the grounds of such refusal or such striking from the list: Provided, That no person shall be disqualified as member of any board of registration by reason of race or color.

Sec. 6. . .The true intent and meaning of the oath prescribed in said supplementary act is, (among other things,) that no person who has been a member of the legislature of any State, or who has held any executive or judicial office in any State, whether he has taken an oath to support the Constitution of the United States or not, and whether he was holding such office at the commencement of the rebellion, or had held it before, and who has afterwards engaged in insurrection or rebellion against the United States, or given aid or comfort to the enemies thereof, is entitled to be registered or to vote; and the words "executive or judicial office in any State" in said oath mentioned shall be construed to include all civil offices created by law for the administration of any general law of a State, or for the administration of justice.

Sec. 7. . . The time for completing the original registration provided for in said act may, in the discretion of the commander of any district, be extended to the 1st day of October, 1867; and the boards of registration shall have power, and it shall be their duty, commencing fourteen days prior to any election under said act, and upon reasonable public notice of the time and place thereof, to revise, for a period of five days, the registration lists, and upon being satisfied that any person not entitled thereto has been registered, to strike the name of such person from the list, and such person shall not be allowed to vote. And such board shall also, during the same period, add to such registry the names of all persons who at that time possess the qualifications required by said act who have not been already registered; and no person shall, at any time, be entitled to be registered or to vote, by reason of any executive pardon or amnesty, for any act or thing which, without such pardon or amnesty, would disqualify him from registration or voting.

Sec. 8. . . Section four of said last-named act shall be construed to authorize the commanding general named therein, whenever he shall deem it needful, to remove any member of a board of registration and to appoint another in his stead, and to fill any vacancy in such board.

Sec. 9. . . All members of said boards of registration and all persons hereafter elected or appointed to office in said military districts, under

any so-called State or municipal authority, or by detail or appointment of the district commanders, shall be required to take and subscribe the ["iron clad" oath].

Sec. 10. . . No district commander or member of the board of registration, or any of the officers or appointees acting under them, shall be bound in his action by any opinion of any civil officer of the United States.

Sec. 11. . . All the provisions of this act and of the acts to which this is supplementary shall be construed liberally, to the end that all intents thereof may be fully and perfectly carried out.

Fourth Reconstruction Act

[*Acts and Resolutions*, 40th Cong., 2d sess., 10. According to the act of March 2, Section 5, and of March 23, Section 5, a majority of registered voters must vote on a state's new constitution, or it would fail. In Alabama, the people had defeated the new constitution by staying away from the polls. This law was to prevent rejection by other states. It became law without the signature of President Andrew Johnson on March 11, 1868.]

Be it enacted . . That hereafter any election authorized by the act passed March 23, 1867 . . shall be decided by a majority of the votes actually cast; and at the election in which the question of the adoption or rejection of any constitution is submitted, any person duly registered in the State may vote in the election district where he offers to vote when he has resided therein for ten days next preceding such election, upon presentation of his certificate of registration, his affidavit, or other satisfactory evidence, under such regulations as the district commanders may prescribe.

Sec. 2. . . The constitutional convention of any of the States mentioned in the acts to which this is amendatory may provide that at the time of voting upon the ratification of the constitution the registered voters may vote also for members of the House of Representatives of the United

States, and for all elective officers provided for by the said constitution; and the same election officers who shall make the return of the votes cast on the ratification or rejection of the constitution, shall enumerate and certify the votes cast for members of Congress.

Source: Walter L. Fleming, comp., *Documentary History of Reconstruction: Political, Military, Social, Religious, Educational, and Industrial, 1865 to 1906* (Cleveland: Clark, 1906).

2   Fourteenth Amendment to the U.S. Constitution, July 9, 1868

The Fourteenth Amendment was reported out to Congress on April 30, 1866, from the Joint Committee on Reconstruction, a special committee formed in late 1865 to hammer out civil rights policy. By mid-June 1866, both houses of Congress had approved the amendment, setting in motion the ratification process by the states. That procedure was completed on July 9, 1868—but only after enormous conflict.

During the 1866 state and national elections, the new constitutional amendment provoked heated arguments. Republicans used the amendment as a campaign platform. They hoped to gain a mandate for a program of reconstruction for the southern states. That the amendment contained a reconstruction program is obvious from reading it, particularly Sections 2–4. It was intended to replace President Andrew Johnson's program of bringing the former Confederate states into the Union while still under former Confederate leadership.

The Republican strategy thus "nationalized" the 1866 midterm elections—that is, in contrast to the local or personality issues that often dominate such elections, these various contests served as a forum of national debate. President Johnson's activism further nationalized the elections. He campaigned vigorously against the Fourteenth Amendment—the first time a president had ever inserted himself so conspicuously into a nonpresidential election cycle. In fact, his energetic involvement presaged the role played today by presidents in elections.

In early 1867, even more conflict erupted between Republicans, on the one hand, and President Johnson and his coalition of very conservative Republicans and Democrats and the so-called "southern conservatives" (in effect, southern Democrats), on the other. Because the 1866 election results produced impressive electoral gains for the Republican Party in Congress, the party appeared to have a mandate for using the Fourteenth Amendment as a program of reconstruction for the still divided nation. But the Republicans' electoral mandate imposed no ratification requirement on the states. Thus Johnson urged the southern states to deny Republicans the ratification they wanted and needed to generate a national consensus on reconstruction and, in the process, generate black voting rights in the South (see Section 2 of the amendment). In the end, only Tennessee approved the amendment in the course of a temporary Republican Party dictatorship in that state, which was ironic because the president was a Tennessean and a former military governor of the state.

Johnson's obstruction of the Fourteenth Amendment drove Republicans to devise "military reconstruction." Their forceful statutory reconstruction of the South—called "congressional reconstruction" as opposed to Johnson's "presidential reconstruction"—paved the way for eventual ratification of the Fourteenth Amendment. Under Congress's new program of military and congressional reconstruction the southern states could not reenter the Union unless they ratified the Fourteenth Amendment.

As for Section 2 of the amendment, it never operated as planned. It was inserted in the amendment to pressure the southern state governments created by Johnson to extend voting rights to African American adult males on their own volition. But Section 2 played no role in Reconstruction. It was easier for the federal government to ignore its command when southern states set about systematically legally disenfranchising African Americans between 1889 and 1907. Some Republican members of Congress urged the application of Section 2 as a response to black disenfranchisement, and they succeeded briefly in putting the idea into the 1904 Republican presidential platform. The great African American scholar, activist, and public commentator W. E. B. DuBois also sought to rally supporters of black civil and voting rights in favor of this plan. But Section 2 was never enforced, in considerable part because President Theodore Roosevelt and his handpicked successor, William Howard Taft, firmly opposed any use of Section 2. Thus this part of the Constitution was extra-constitutionally dropped, even though it remains, without effect, in the Constitution.

By contrast, Section 1 of the Fourteenth Amendment played a very important role in protecting black voting rights in the late twentieth century, especially in the implementation of the Voting Rights Act. Voting rights lawyers, the Department of Justice, the federal courts, and the Supreme Court all relied on Section 1 to prevent efforts motivated by racial animus to undermine the Voting Rights Act. Section 1 has also been used to invalidate measures that predated the Voting Rights Act but that can be shown, through historical research, to have been motivated by racial animus.

Two other things are important to note about the Fourteenth Amendment as it was ratified. Its language "gendered" the Constitution for the first time by explicitly giving rights to men (and by implication denying them to women). This fateful language helped to divide supporters of female and African American suffrage. Later, during the black disenfranchisement years, many female suffrage activists refused to speak out against black disenfranchisement. This tragic stance can be traced to the decision by congressional Republicans to make the Fourteenth Amendment—and later the Fifteenth Amendment—"for men only."

Second, the language of the amendment shows that there was a conscious decision by Republicans to put the Constitution in the way of Native American enfranchisement. The Voting Rights Act today does protect Native Americans, but the struggle for Native American enfranchisement has been very long, and its outcome is still uncertain. The Fourteenth Amendment did much, unfortunately, to delay and diminish electoral influence for Native Americans as well as women.

Amendment XIV

Section 1. All persons born or naturalized in the United States, and subject to the jurisdiction thereof, are citizens of the United States and of the State wherein they reside. No State shall make or enforce any law which shall abridge the privileges or immunities of citizens of the United States; nor shall any State deprive any person of life, liberty, or property, without due process of law; nor deny to any person within its jurisdiction the equal protection of the laws.

Section 2. Representatives shall be apportioned among the several States according to their respective numbers, counting the whole number of persons in each State, excluding Indians not taxed. But when the right to vote at any election for the choice of electors for President and Vice-President of the United States, Representatives in Congress, the Executive and Judicial officers of a State, or the members of the Legislature thereof, is denied to any of the male inhabitants of such State, being twenty-one years of age, and citizens of the United States, or in any way abridged, except for participation in rebellion, or other crime, the basis of representation therein shall be reduced in the proportion which the number of such male citizens shall bear to the whole number of male citizens twenty-one years of age in such State.

Section 3. No person shall be a Senator or Representative in Congress, or elector of President and Vice-President, or hold any office, civil or military, under the United States, or under any State, who, having previously taken an oath, as a member of Congress, or as an officer of the United States, or as a member of any State legislature, or as an executive or judicial officer of any State, to support the Constitution of the United States, shall have engaged in insurrection or rebellion against the same, or given aid or comfort to the enemies thereof. But Congress may by a vote of two-thirds of each House, remove such disability.

Section 4. The validity of the public debt of the United States, authorized by law, including debts incurred for payment of pensions and bounties for services in suppressing insurrection or rebellion, shall not be questioned. But neither the United States nor any State shall assume or pay any debt or obligation incurred in aid of insurrection or rebellion against the United States, or any claim for the loss or emancipation of any slave; but all such debts, obligations and claims shall be held illegal and void.

Section 5. The Congress shall have the power to enforce, by appropriate legislation, the provisions of this article.

3

Fifteenth Amendment to the U.S. Constitution, February 3, 1870

The Fifteenth Amendment is a spare, ambiguous addition to the Constitution, but its essential feature is clear enough. It is, first and foremost, a prohibition of the racial classification of voters in the electoral processes at the three levels of American government—federal, state, and local. The Fifteenth Amendment presumes that almost all electoral administration in the United States properly occurs at the state and local levels. Because the federal government cannot take over that electoral administration, it must instead set a constitutional standard to which such administration must adhere.

On February 26, 1869, when Congress sent the Fifteenth Amendment to the states for ratification, politicians at the national level were completing the restoration of the Union. Reconstituting the states had been, after all, a basic aim of Presidents Abraham Lincoln and Andrew Johnson and indeed of the overwhelming majority of Republicans, Democrats, and "southern conservatives." In the retrospective light of the Fifteenth Amendment, the Reconstruction Acts (Document 1) were apparently meant to do no more than establish a temporary, onetime emergency system of national voter registration and of national electoral administration in the former Confederate states.

Nevertheless, the Fifteenth Amendment's emphasis on prohibiting certain kinds of state and local electoral rules was by no means an inevitable result of the effort to rebuild federalism. Members of Congress debated writing the amendment instead as a positive and explicit grant of a right to vote from the United States. Section 1 of the Fourteenth Amendment did that for civil rights; the Fifteenth could have done so for the right to vote.

Members of Congress also debated explicitly including a right to office for African Americans, something that was then very controversial precisely because African Americans were gaining public office in the reconstructed southern states. For most whites, this change was utterly astonishing. In reconstructed Georgia, in fact, the majority-white legislature ejected its black members on the ground that they had no right to office and were in the legislature illegitimately, requiring a second attempt by Congress to reconstruct that state.

Another element of the debate over the Fifteenth Amendment was whether the amendment should also contain very clear prohibitions of various seemingly non–race-related requirements for voting, such as educational attainment or even holding property. Proponents of this approach wanted to prevent the spread of devious forms of racial exclusion through color-blind devices.

But in the end a simple emphasis on the prohibition of explicitly racial classification informed the language that Congress chose and sent to the states in 1868. Why? What does it mean that this language was chosen over the alternatives?

According to the scholar Xi Wang (author of Chapter 1 in this volume), some Republican members of Congress wished to prevent the amendment from promoting Chinese American suffrage in the

West, and thus preferred the spare wording of the amendment over a national right to vote and over a prohibition of tests and devices. Other Republicans did not want to encourage female suffrage by creating a national right to vote.

Clearly, then, Republicans brought short-run strategic considerations into the framing of the amendment. They sought to fine-tune who came into the electorates of the various states of the Union via the Fifteenth Amendment and who did not. Another strategic element may have been a wish to secure rapid ratification of the amendment. A sparely written amendment would seem more innocuous than an amendment bristling with the kind of specificity that characterized the Fourteenth Amendment. It would therefore pass the state legislatures quickly.

In the end, the southern states were essential to the amendment's ratification. Their readmission to the Union now depended on their ratification not only of the Fourteenth Amendment but also of the Fifteenth Amendment. The Fifteenth Amendment was ratified on February 3, 1870, and formally became part of the Constitution on March 30, 1870.

Ever since, there has been debate about what the drafters of the amendment intended—a debate that perpetuates the choice for ambiguity that seems to have pervaded the drafting and ratification processes. Moderates obviously won out in the congressional forum. That fact and the fairly general nature of the prohibition in the amendment have led some scholars to infer that congressional Republicans were deeply ambivalent about black voting and officeholding. Certainly, the Supreme Court interpreted the amendment very narrowly in the late 1870s. Even as late as 1980 a Supreme Court justice wrote in an opinion for the Court that the Fifteenth Amendment does not confer a nationally derived right to office on African Americans. In short, the text of the amendment might seem to presage the retreat from Reconstruction that eventually occurred, as well as later setbacks to African American voting rights.

Such a pessimistic view is rather hard to rebut. The archival records that would clearly illuminate the congressional deliberation no longer exist. Both the Senate and House floor managers left next to nothing by way of personal documents. Further complicating the search for intent is the eventual repudiation of the Fifteenth Amendment by its Senate floor manager during the struggle over the 1890 federal elections bill. By the same token, it is not so easy to deny the claim that the amendment was meant to be a very strong basis for black voting rights. Within weeks of the amendment's addition to the Constitution, Congress wrote an extraordinarily strong federal statute implementing the amendment (its second section gave Congress that power). This statute was the first of several quite muscular federal elections statutes, which are reproduced in Document 4.

In retrospect, then, in drafting the Fifteenth Amendment Congress did not intend to establish the national election administration that the Reconstruction Acts seemed to foreshadow. The federal elections statutes also reveal that the Fifteenth Amendment in no way presaged a retreat either from Reconstruction or from bold national protection of African American voting rights in those states in which they were subverted by violent resistance and armed conspiracies.

Amendment XV

Section 1. The right of citizens of the United States to vote shall not be denied or abridged by the United States or by any State on account of race, color, or previous condition of servitude.

Section 2. The Congress shall have the power to enforce this article by appropriate legislation.

4   Enforcement Act, May 31, 1870

This statute was repealed by the Democratic-controlled Congress during the second presidential admin-istration (1893–1897) of Democrat Grover Cleveland. But the president, the Justice Department (cre-ated in 1870), the U.S. Marshals Service, and the federal courts enforced it in the first few years after its passage and to some extent thereafter despite resistance from the Supreme Court. The statute was not the only one enacted to enforce voting rights for blacks. There were four others, including a statute di-rected at the white supremacist Ku Klux Klan and another that regulated voting in urban areas and in U.S. House districts in the South, and thus also protected black voting rights.

This excerpt from the statute, which in all has twenty-three sections, repays close reading for the window that it provides into the scope and scale of violent white resistance to black voting rights in the South—and into the strength of the Republican Party's determination to meet and quell that insur-gency. The sections reproduced here show what the majority in Congress thought it could do under the Fifteenth Amendment. It is impossible to read the act and believe that Congress wrote the amendment with the intention of leaving the protection of either civil rights or black voting rights primarily to the states and localities, subject to no more than a prohibition on openly racial statutes and ordinances.

On the contrary, the passage of this statute within a mere two months of ratification of the Fif-teenth Amendment's shows that a majority in Congress believed that, thanks to the ratification of the amendment, the federal government could directly, forcefully, and extensively protect black voting rights. It could do so not only against recalcitrant public officials in the states and localities but also against private individuals engaged in criminal conspiracies (Section 6, for example, refers to conspir-acies of two or more persons traveling "in disguise upon the public highway").

The 1870 statute has a variety of features that, taken together, suggest a powerful and complex program for establishing a new electoral order in the former Confederacy. It establishes criminal penalties—both jail time and fines—for violations of the right to vote. These penalties are applied to public officials who might obstruct the right to vote through corrupt administration of elections and to private individuals. The weight of the sanctions for private individuals is particularly great, because Section 7 permits the United States to simultaneously prosecute and punish any other crimes that occur in conjunction with the electoral violations (note in Section 6 that the present-day value of the $5,000 fine to be collected in 1870 in a region starved for liquidity and capital is about $1.5 million).

Cases brought under the statute were removed immediately to the federal courts, including the cir-cuit courts, which at that time were staffed by very nationalist judges. Law enforcement fell, in the first instance, to federal marshals and commissioners, and they were offered financial incentives for capable enforcement (and threatened with sanctions for dereliction). If all else failed, under Section 13 the president could deploy military force to aid judicial process.

In short, this statute says a great deal about the muscular, nationalist nature of constitutional thought within the Republican Party during the Reconstruction. To be sure, some commentators stress the lim-ited nature of the changes in the Constitution during this period and suggest that the Republican Party never really meant to establish and protect minority rights. But this text plainly suggests otherwise.

Chap. CXIX.—*An Act to enforce the Rights of Citizens of the United States to vote in the several States of this Union, and for other Purposes.*

Be it enacted by the Senate and house of Repre-sentatives of the United States who are or shall be otherwise qualified by law to vote at any election by the people in any State, Territory, district, county, city, parish, township, school district, mu-nicipality, or other territorial subdivision, shall be entitled and allowed to vote at all such elections, without distinction of race, color, or previous condition of servitude; any constitution, law, custom, usage, or regulation of any State or Territory, or by or under its authority, to the contrary notwithstanding.

Sec. 2. And be it further enacted, That if by or under the authority of the constitution or laws of any State, or the laws of any Territory, any act is or shall be required to be done as a prerequisite or qualification for voting, and by such constitution or laws persons or officers are or shall be charged with the performance of duties in furnishing to citizens an opportunity to perform such prerequisite, or to become qualified to vote, it shall be the duty of every such person and officer to give to all citizens of the United States the same and equal opportunity to perform such prerequisite, and to become qualified to vote without distinction of race, color, or previous condition of servitude; and if any such person or officer shall refuse or knowingly omit to give full effect to this section, he shall, for every such offense, forfeit and pay the sum of five hundred dollars to the person aggrieved thereby, to be recovered by an action on the case, with full costs, and such allowance for counsel fees as the court shall deem just, and shall also, for every such offense, be deemed guilty of a misdemeanor, and shall, on conviction thereof, be fined not less than five hundred dollars, or be imprisoned not less than one month and not more than one year, or both, at the discretion of the court.

Sec. 3. And be it further enacted, That whenever, by or under the authority of the constitution or laws of any State, or the laws of any Territory, any act is or shall be required to [be] done by any citizen as a prerequisite to qualify or entitle him to vote, the offer of any such citizen to perform the act required to be done as aforesaid shall, if it fail to be carried into execution by reason of the wrongful act or omission aforesaid of the person or office charged with the duty of receiving or permitting such performance or offer to perform, or acting thereon, be deemed and held as a performance in law of such act; and the person so offering and failing as aforesaid, and being otherwise qualified, shall be entitled to vote in the same manner and to the same extent as if he had

in fact performed such act; and any judge, inspector, or other officer of election whose duty it is or shall be to receive, count, certify, register, report, or give effect to the vote of any such citizen who shall wrongfully refuse or omit to receive, count, certify, register, report, or give effect to the vote of such citizen upon the presentation by him of his affidavit stating such offer and the time and place thereof, and the name of the officer or person whose duty it was to act thereon, and that he was wrongfully prevented by such person or officer from performing such act, shall for every such offense forfeit and pay the sum of five hundred dollars to the person aggrieved thereby, to be recovered by an action on the case, with full costs, and such allowance for counsel fees as the court shall deem just, and on conviction thereof, be fined not less than five hundred dollars, or be imprisoned not less than one month and not more than one year, or both, at the discretion of the court.

Sec. 4. And be it further enacted, That if any person, by force, bribery, threats, intimidation, or other unlawful means, shall hinder, delay, prevent, or obstruct, or shall combine and confederate with others to hinder, delay, prevent, or obstruct, any citizen from doing any act required to be done to qualify him to vote or from voting at any election as aforesaid, such person shall for every such offense forfeit and pay the sum of five hundred dollars to the person aggrieved thereby, to be recovered by an action on the case, with full costs, and such allowance for counsel fees as the court shall deem just, and shall also for every such offense be guilty of a misdemeanor, and shall, on conviction thereof, be fined not less than five hundred dollars, or be imprisoned not less than one month and not more than one year, or both at the discretion of the court.

Sec. 5. And be it further enacted, That if any person shall prevent, hinder, control, or intimidate, or shall attempt to prevent, hinder, control, or intimidate, any person from exercising or in exercising the right of suffrage, to whom the right of suffrage is secured or guaranteed by the fifteenth amendment to the Constitution of the

United States, by means of bribery, threats, or threats of depriving such person of employment or occupation, or of ejecting such person from rented house, lands, or other property, or by threats of refusing to renew leases or contracts for labor, or by threats of violence to himself or family, such person so offending shall be deemed guilty of a misdemeanor, and shall, on conviction thereof, be fined not less than five hundred dollars, or be imprisoned not less than one month and not more than one year, or both, at the discretion of the court.

Sec. 6. And be it further enacted, That if two or more persons shall band or conspire together, or go in disguise upon the public highway, or upon the premises of another, with intent to violate any provision of this act, or to injure, oppress, threaten, or intimidate any citizen with intent to prevent or hinder his free exercise and enjoyment of any right or privilege granted or secured to him by the Constitution or laws of the United States, or because of his having exercised the same, such persons shall be held guilty of felony, and, on conviction thereof, shall be fined or imprisoned, or both, at the discretion of the court,—the fine not to exceed five thousand dollars, and the imprisonment not to exceed ten years,—and shall, moreover, be thereafter ineligible to, and disabled from holding, any office or place of honor, profit, or trust created by the Constitution or laws of the United States.

Sec. 7. And be it further enacted, That if in the act of violating any provision in either of the two preceding sections, any other felony, crime, or misdemeanor shall be committed, the offender, on conviction of such violation of said sections, shall be punished for the same with such punishments as are attached to the said felonies, crimes, and misdemeanors by laws of the State in which the offense may be committed.

Sec. 8. And be it further enacted, That the district courts of the United States, within their respective districts, shall have, exclusively of the courts of several states, cognizance of all crimes and offenses committed against the provisions of this act, and also, concurrently with the circuit

courts of the United States, of all causes, civil and criminal, arising under this act, except as herein otherwise provided, and the jurisdiction hereby conferred shall be exercised in conformity with the laws and practice governing United States courts; and all crimes and offenses committed against the provisions of this act may be prosecuted by the indictment of a grand jury, or, in cases of crimes and offenses not infamous, the prosecution may be either by indictment or information filed by the district attorney in a court having jurisdiction.

Sec. 9. And be it further enacted, That the district attorneys, marshals, and deputy marshals of the United States, the commissioners appointed by the circuit and territorial courts of the United States, with powers of arresting, imprisoning, or bailing offenders against the laws of the United States, and every other officer who may be specially empowered by the President of the United States, shall be, and they are hereby, specially authorized and required, at the expense of the United States, to institute proceedings against all and every person who shall violate the provisions of this act, and cause him or them to be arrested and imprisoned, or bailed, as the case may be, for trial before such court of the United States or territorial court as has cognizance of the offense. And with a view to afford reasonable protection to all persons in their constitutional right to vote without distinction of race, color, or previous condition of servitude, and to the prompt discharge of the duties of this act, it shall be the duty of the circuit courts of the United States, and the superior courts of the Territories of the United States, from time to time, to increase the number of commissioners, so as to afford a speedy and convenient means for the arrest and examination of persons charged with a violation of this act; and such commissioners are hereby authorized and required to exercise and discharge all the powers and the duties conferred on them by this act, and the same duties with regard to offenses created by this act as they are authorized by law to exercise with regard to other offenses against the laws of the United States. . . .

Sec. 12. And be it further enacted, That the commissioners, district attorney, the marshals, their deputies, and the clerks of the said district, circuit, and territorial courts shall be paid for their services the like fees as may be allowed to them for similar services in other cases. The person or persons authorized to execute the process to be issued by such commissioners for the arrest of offenders against the provisions of this act shall be entitled to the usual fees allowed to the marshal for an arrest for each person he or they may arrest and take before any such commissioner as aforesaid, with such other fees as may be deemed reasonable by such commissioner for such other additional services as may be necessarily performed by him or them, such as attending at the examination, keeping the prisoner in custody, and providing him with food and lodging during his detention and until the final determination of such commissioner, and in general for performing such other duties as may be required in the premises; such fees to be made up in conformity with the fees usually charged by the officers of the courts of justice within the proper district or county as near as may be practicable, and paid out of the treasury of the United States on the certificate of the judge of the district within which the arrest is made, and to be recoverable from the defendant as part of the judgment in case of conviction.

Sec. 13. And be it further enacted, That it shall be lawful for the President of the United States to employ such part of the land or naval forces of the United States, or of the militia, as shall be necessary to aid in the execution of judicial process issued under this act. . . .

Source: *Statutes at Large* 16 (1870): 140–46.

II. Disenfranchising African Americans

5   Brief of the United States in *United States v. Cruikshank*, 1875

The first direct Supreme Court test of the Enforcement Act of May 31, 1870, came out of Louisiana. The case tested whether the United States could directly prosecute private individuals who assaulted African Americans for exercising their right to vote. The circumstances of the case are still very astonishing—as is the argument of the United States in the brief. The brief, a set of arguments for why the court should decide for one side over another, was written and argued before the justices in part by U.S. Attorney General George H. Williams, a former Republican senator from Oregon. The federal brief reveals that the administration of Ulysses S. Grant understood federal authority to enforce the right to vote, under the Fifteenth Amendment, in a very broad way.

On April 13, 1873, Easter Sunday, a white militia of three hundred men attacked the municipal building of Colfax, Louisiana, a town named after Grant's first vice president, Schuyler Colfax. The building was held by an armed black militia led by an African American veteran of the Union army. The black militia had—until the white attack—prevented local whites from violently seizing control of the jurisdiction, which they believed would have been a prelude to the informal local disenfranchisement of African Americans. But the white militia came with a cannon. Every member of the black militia, save one, either died in the battle or was later executed by the white militia, and white-on-black attacks erupted in the town and countryside during the ensuing days.

The federal prosecution of several members of the white militia, including William J. Cruikshank, led to the mobilization of a huge legal defense effort in the militia's behalf. In fact, a former associate

Supreme Court justice and a future associate justice participated in defending the white assailants. Participants on all sides understood the importance of the Enforcement Act's first test. The case came to the Court, however, on a highly technical basis that hinged on whether the counts of indictment were properly drafted by the United States. Most of the federal brief treated these matters—but these excerpts reveal much of the constitutional theory—complete with a reference to William Shakespeare—that was presented to the Court by the United States along with the technical argument.

In the Supreme Court of the United States

The United States

vs.

William J. Cruikshank, William D. Irwin, and John P. Hadnot.

No. 609

In Error to the Circuit Court of the United States for the District of Louisiana.

Brief for the United States

. . . The indictment (*returned* June 16, 1873,) is for *conspiracy,* under the sixth section of the Enforcement act of May 30, 1870, which is as follows:

"That if two or more persons shall band or conspire together, or go in disguise upon the public highway, or upon the premises of another, with intent to violate any provisions of this act, or to injure, oppress, threaten, or intimidate any citizen with intent to prevent or hinder his free exercise and enjoyment of any right or privilege granted or secured to him by the Constitution or laws of the United States, or because of his having exercised the same, such persons shall be held guilty of felony, and, on conviction thereof, shall be fined or imprisoned, or both, at the discretion of the court—the fine not to exceed five thousand dollars, and the imprisonment not to exceed ten years; and shall, moreover, be thereafter ineligible to, and disabled from holding, any office or place of honor, profit, or trust created by the Constitution of laws of the United States." (16 Stat., 141.) . . .

[I]nasmuch as the XIVth Amendment to the Constitution establishes the relation of citizenship of the United States independently of any other citizenship, and confers upon Congress the power to enforce that relation by suitable legislation, it seems plain that if such *citizenship* be not merely a *sound,* signifying nothing; if it include (ex. gr.) political and other "rights and privileges" *respecting the Government of the United States,* this amendment empowers and *thus makes it the duty of* Congress to legislate so as to enforce those rights and privileges, whether by protection against criminal assault or otherwise.

Source: U.S. Supreme Court, "Brief for the United States," *The United States v. William J. Cruikshank, William D. Irwin, and John P. Hadnot,* No. 609, undated.

---

6 *United States v. Cruikshank,* Decided March 27, 1876

The opinions in United States v. Cruikshank *(92 U.S. 542) and a companion case,* United States v. Reese *(92 U.S. 214), handed down the same day, March 27, 1876, are usually interpreted as statements of the Supreme Court's hostility to federal enforcement of the Fifteenth Amendment under Section 2 of the amendment. The reality, however, is a bit more complex.*

The decision in Reese *(a case involving Hiram Reese and a fellow Kentucky election official who refused to allow a black man to vote after his poll tax payment had been turned down by another white official) might better be interpreted as an expression of great unease over the future of federalism if the Court accepted the full-blooded assertion of national supremacy embodied in the 1870 Enforcement Act.* Reese *invalidated Sections 3 and 4 of the 1870 Enforcement Act. These sections criminalized racially discriminatory handling of electoral administration by local officials. In saying that these sections went too far, the Court majority sought to contain the implications of the federal government criminally sanctioning local public officials. But the opinion left intact other sections of the enforcement statute that did essentially the same thing. Furthermore, in* Cruikshank *the Court did not say directly that the United States could not prosecute private individuals. Instead, the opinion was essentially a technical ruling about the form of a pleading, as the excerpts of the opinion make clear.*

Nevertheless, at the time the decisions were seen as setbacks to the proposition that the United States could forcefully protect black voting rights, and they revealed that, for justices appointed by Republican presidents, public policy for protecting black voting rights was controversial. Because these opinions emerged about a year before the Compromise of 1877—a congressional bipartisan agreement to go easy on voting and civil rights enforcement that ushered Rutherford B. Hayes into the presidency after a controversial election—these decisions seem in retrospect to foreshadow the contraction of the democratic revolution that was inaugurated with the Fourteenth and Fifteenth Amendments and their enforcement statutes.

UNITED STATES
v.
CRUIKSHANK ET AL.
October Term, 1875

[. . .]

MR. CHIEF JUSTICE WAITE delivered the opinion of the court.

This case comes here with a certificate by the judges of the Circuit Court for the District of Louisiana that they were divided in opinion upon a question which occurred at the hearing. It presents for our consideration an indictment containing sixteen counts, divided into two series of eight counts each, based upon sect. 6 of the Enforcement Act of May 31, 1870. That section is as follows:—

'That if two or more persons shall band or conspire together, or go in disguise upon the public highway, or upon the premises of another, with intent to violate any provision of this act, or to injure, oppress, threaten, or intimidate any citizen, with intent to prevent or hinder his free exercise and enjoyment of any right or privilege granted or secured to him by the constitution or laws of the United States, or because of his hav-

ing exercised the same, such persons shall be held guilty of felony, and, on conviction thereof, shall be fined or imprisoned, or both, at the discretion of the court,—the fine not to exceed $5,000, and the imprisonment not to exceed ten years; and shall, moreover, be thereafter ineligible to, and disabled from holding, any office or place of honor, profit, or trust created by the constitution or laws of the United States.' 16 Stat. 141. . . .

The sixth and fourteenth counts state the intent of the defendants to have been to hinder and prevent the citizens named, being of African descent, and colored, 'in the free exercise and enjoyment of their several and respective right and privilege to vote at any election to be thereafter by law had and held by the people in and of the said State of Louisiana, or by the people of and in the parish of Grant aforesaid.' In Minor v. Happersett, 21 Wall. 178, we decided that the Constitution of the United States has not conferred the right of suffrage upon any one, and that the United States have no voters of their own creation in the States. In United States v. Reese et al., supra, p. 214, we hold that the fifteenth amendment has invested the citizens of the United States with a new constitutional right, which is, exemption from discrimination in the exercise of the elective franchise on account of race, color, or previous condition of servitude. From this it appears that the right of suffrage is not a necessary attribute of national citizenship; but that exemption from discrimination in the exercise of that right on account of race, &c., is. The right to vote in the States comes from the States; but the right of exemption from the prohibited discrimination comes from the United States. The first has not been granted or secured by the Constitution of the United States; but the last has been.

Inasmuch, therefore, as it does not appear in these counts that the intent of the defendants was to prevent these parties from exercising their right to vote on account of their race, &c., it does not appear that it was their intent to interfere with any right granted or secured by the constitution or laws of the United States. We may suspect that race was the cause of the hostility; but it is not so averred. This is material to a description of the substance of the offence, and cannot be supplied by implication. Every thing essential must be charged positively, and not inferentially. The defect here is not in form, but in substance. . . .

The conclusion is irresistible, that these counts are too vague and general. They lack the certainty and precision required by the established rules of criminal pleading. It follows that they are not good and sufficient in law. They are so defective that no judgment of conviction should be pronounced upon them.

The order of the Circuit Court arresting the judgment upon the verdict is, therefore, affirmed; and the cause remanded, with instructions to discharge the defendants. . . .

Source: Findlaw, *United States v. Cruikshank*, 92 U.S. 542 (1876), http://caselaw.lp.findlaw.com/scripts/getcase.pl?navby=case&court=us&vol=92&page=542.

7

Ex parte Yarbrough, Decided March 3, 1884

Scholars and others have often held that the 1876 Court decisions against federal enforcement of the Fifteenth Amendment ended any near-term prospects of federal support for African American voting rights. Yet eight years after Cruikshank and Reese, *the Court unanimously supported such federal enforcement in* Ex parte Yarbrough *(110 U.S. 651) and upheld the conviction of Jasper Yarbrough, who, along with other Ku Klux Klansmen, was charged with beating a black man to prevent him from voting.*

Although he does not overthrow the 1876 precedents, Justice Samuel F. Miller's opinion for the Court nevertheless sharply reduces their weight. The reasons for this judicial about-face are complicated, but they boil down to a belief among all members of the Court that the integrity of U.S. House elections was threatened by white-on-black violence. A close look at the ruling reveals that a vital, inarticulate premise of this decision is the assumption that African American rates of participation in U.S. House elections in the former Confederacy were high. Thus violent assaults by white private individuals on black voters were making a difference to the outcomes of U.S. House elections and to their integrity. The federal government, then, was perfectly justified in directly prosecuting white individuals for criminal conspiracy to obstruct black voters from voting by assault or murder.

THE KU KLUX CASES, 110 U.S. 651 (1884)
Ex parte YARBROUGH and others.
March 3, 1884

[. . .]

MILLER, J.

This case originates in this court by an application for a writ of habeas corpus on the part of

Jasper Yarbrough and seven other persons, who allege that they are confined by the jailer of Fulton county in the custody of the United States marshal for the Northern district of Georgia, and that the trial, conviction, and sentence in the circuit court of the United States for that district, under which they are held, were illegal, null, and void. . . .

If the law which defines the offense and prescribes its punishment is void, the court was without jurisdiction, and the prisoners must be discharged. Though several different sections of the Revised Statutes are brought into the discussion as the foundation of the indictments found in the record, we think only two of them demand our attention here, namely, sections 5508 and 5520. They are in the following language:

'Sec. 5508. If two or more persons conspire to injure, oppress, threaten, or intimidate any citizen in the free exercise or enjoyment of any right or privilege secured to him by the constitution or laws of the United States, or because of his having so exercised the same, or if two or more persons go in disguise on the highway, or on the premises of another, with intent to prevent or hinder his free exercise or enjoyment of any right or privilege so secured, they shall be fined not more than five thousand dollars and imprisoned not more than ten years; and shall, moreover, be thereafter ineligible to any office or place of honor, profit, or trust created by the constitution or laws of the United States.

'Sec. 5520. If two or more persons in any state or territory conspire to prevent, by force, intimidation, or threat, any citizen who is lawfully entitled to vote from giving his support or advocacy, in a legal manner, towards or in favor of the election of any lawfully qualified person as an elector for president or vice-president, or as a member of the congress of the United States, or to injure any citizen in person or property on account of such support or advocacy, each of such persons shall be punished by a fine of not less than five hundred nor more than five thousand dollars, or by imprisonment, with or without hard labor, not

less than six months nor more than six years, or by both such fine and imprisonment.'

The indictments, four in number, on which petitioners were tried, charge in each one all of the defendants with a conspiracy under these sections, directed against a different person in each indictment. On the trial the cases were consolidated, and as each indictment is in the identical language of all the others, except as to the name of the person assaulted and the date of the transaction, the copy which is here presented will answer for all of them:

'We, the grand jurors of the United States, chosen, selected, and sworn in and for the Northern district of Georgia, upon our oaths, present: That heretofore, to-wit, on the twenty-fifth day of July, in the year of our Lord one thousand eight hundred and eighty-three, Jasper Yarbrough, James Yarbrough, Dilmus Yarbrough, Neal Yarbrough, Lovel Streetman, Bold Emory, State Lemmons, Jake Hayes, and E. H. Green, all late of said Northern district of Georgia, did, within the said Northern district of Georgia, and within the jurisdiction of this court, commit the offense of conspiracy, for that the said Jasper Yarbrough, James Yarbrough, Dilmus Yarbrough, Neal Yarbrough, Lovel Streetman, Bold Emory, State Lemmons, Jake Hayes, and E. H. Green did then and there, at the time and place aforesaid, combine, conspire, and confederate together, by force, to injure, oppress, threaten, and intimidate Berry Saunders, a person of color, and a citizen of the United States of America of African descent, on account of his race, color, and previous condition of servitude, in the full exercise and enjoyment of the right and privilege of suffrage in the election of a lawfully qualified person as a member of the congress of the United States of America, and because the said Berry Saunders had so exercised the same, and on account of such exercise, which said right and privilege of suffrage was secured to the said Berry Saunders by the constitution and laws of the United States of America, the said Berry Saunders being then and there lawfully entitled to vote in said election; and, having so then and there conspired, the said Jasper Yarbrough, James Yarbrough, Dilmus Yarbrough, Neal Yarbrough, Lovel Streetman, Bold Emory, State Lemmons, Jake Hayes, and E. H. Green did unlawfully, feloniously, and willfully beat, bruise, wound, and maltreat the said Berry Saunders, contrary to the form of the statute in such case made and provided, and against the peace and dignity of the United States of America. . . .'

Stripped of its technical verbiage, the offense charged in this indictment was that the defendants conspired to intimidate Berry Saunders, a citizen of African descent, in the exercise of his right to vote for a member of the congress of the United States, and in the execution of that conspiracy they beat, bruised, wounded, and otherwise maltreated him; and in the second count that they did this on account of his race, color, and previous condition of servitude, by going in disguise and assaulting him on the public highway and on his own premises. If the question were not concluded in this court, as we have already seen that it is by the decision of the circuit court, we entertain no doubt that the conspiracy here described is one which is embraced within the provisions of the Revised Statutes which we have cited. That a government whose essential character is republican, whose executive head and legislative body are both elective, whose numerous and powerful branch of the legislature is elected by the people directly, has no power by appropriate laws to secure this election from the influence of violence, of corruption, and of fraud, is a proposition so startling as to arrest attention and demand the gravest consideration. If this government is anything more than a mere aggregation of delegated agents of other states and governments, each of which is superior to the general government, it must have the power to protect the elections on which its existence depends, from violence and corruption. If it has not this power, it is left helpless before the two great natural and historical enemies of all republics, open violence and insidious corruption. . . .

Counsel for petitioners, seizing upon the expression found in the opinion of the court in the case of Minor v. Happersett, 21 Wall. 178, that 'the constitution of the United States does not confer the right of suffrage upon any one,' without reference to the connection in which it is used, insists that the voters in this case do not owe their right to vote in any sense to that instrument. But the court was combating the argument that this right was conferred on all citizens, and therefore upon women as well as men. In opposition to that idea, it was said the constitution adopts as the qualification for voters of members of congress that which prevails in the state where the voting is to be done; therefore, said the opinion, the right is not definitely conferred on any person or class of persons by the constitution alone, because you have to look to the law of the state for the description of the class. But the court did not intend to say that when the class or the person is thus ascertained, his right to vote for a member of congress was not fundamentally based upon the constitution, which created the office of member of congress, and declared it should be elective, and pointed to the means of ascertaining who should be electors. The fifteenth amendment of the constitution, by its limitation on the power of the states in the exercise of their right to prescribe the qualifications of voters in their own elections, and by its limitation of the power of the United States over that subject, clearly shows that the right of suffrage was considered to be of supreme importance to the national government, and was not intended to be left within the exclusive control of the states. It is in the following language:

'Section 1. The right of citizens of the United States to vote shall not be denied or abridged by the United States, or by any state, on account of race, color, or previous condition of servitude.

'Sec. 2. The congress shall have power to enforce this article by appropriate legislation.'

While it is quite true, as was said by this court in U.S. v. Reese, 92 U.S. 218, that this article gives no affirmative right to the colored man to vote, and is designed primarily to prevent discrimination against him whenever the right to vote may be granted to others it is easy to see that under some circumstances it may operate as the immediate source of a right to vote. In all cases where the former slave-holding states had not removed from their constitutions the words 'white man' as a qualification for voting, this provision did, in effect, confer on him the right to vote, because, being paramount to the state law, and a part of the state law, it annulled the discriminating word 'white,' and thus left him in the enjoyment of the same right as white persons. And such would be the effect of any future constitutional provision of a state which should give the right of voting exclusively to white people, whether they be men or women. Neal v. Delaware, 103 U.S. 370. In such cases this fifteenth article of amendment does, proprio vigore, substantially confer on the negro the right to vote, and congress has the power to protect and enforce that right.

In the case of U.S. v. Reese, so much relied on by counsel, this court said, in regard to the fif-

teenth amendment, that 'it has invested the citizens of the United States with a new constitutional right which is within the protecting power of congress. That right is an exemption from discrimination in the exercise of the elective franchise on account of race, color, or previous condition of servitude.' This new constitutional right was mainly designed for citizens of African descent. The principle, however, that the protection of the exercise of this right is within the power of congress, is as necessary to the right of other citizens to vote as to the colored citizen, and to the right to vote in general as to the right to be protected against discrimination. The exercise of the right in both instances is guarantied by the constitution, and should be kept free and pure by congressional enactments whenever that is necessary. . . .

The rule to show cause in this case is discharged, and the writ of habeas corpus denied.

Source: Findlaw, *Ex parte Yarbrough*, 110 U.S. 651 (1884), http://caselaw.lp.findlaw.com/scripts/getcase.pl?navby=case&court=us&vol=110&page=651.

8
Speech of Hon. George H. White of North Carolina in the U.S. House of Representatives, January 29, 1901

Disenfranchisement in North Carolina came partly in the form of a violent revolt, organized and led by the North Carolina demagogue Furnifold Simmons against a cross-party alliance of white populists and white and black Republicans. This partisan partnership ran the state between 1893 and 1898—a period known as "fusion government." But by 1899 an avowedly white supremacist Democratic Party had regained control of North Carolina's government. The party had not been afraid to promote violence, such as the white-on-black race riot in Wilmington, North Carolina, in early and mid-November 1898. Democrats' seizure of the state began the process of imitating the disenfranchisement already under way in Florida, Louisiana, Mississippi, South Carolina, and Tennessee.

As a result, the only African American legislator remaining in the U.S. House of Representatives—Republican George H. White of North Carolina—was forced to retire from public life, bleaching the U.S. House for a generation until the election of Republican Oscar De Priest of Illinois in 1929. Fusion government in North Carolina made possible White's two-term career in the U.S. House. He represented the second district of North Carolina, known as the "black second" both for the concentration of black voters in the district and for the succession of African American legislators—four in all—that it sent to Congress between 1874 and 1901.

White's political career had begun with service in the state legislature in the early 1880s and continued with service as a state prosecutor into the early 1890s. Yet despite his deep roots in North Carolina politics, it would have been very difficult for White to campaign openly for a third term. Wilmington was in the second district. With the emergence of political murder in that part of the state, White's life would have been in danger, as would have been the lives of his supporters at campaign events. White therefore made plans to leave North Carolina, and he is buried in Philadelphia, where he had a prosperous legal career until his death in 1918.

About a month before his second and last term in the U.S. House ended, White gave a now famous farewell address. He had been hampered from speaking out against disenfranchisement in the South and in favor of his federal antilynching bill, the first of many such bills proposed in the U.S. House for several decades. When he was finally allowed to speak on January 29, 1901, on a federal program for dispensing seed to farmers, he saw his chance. He talked briefly about the merits of the seed program—and then launched into an address that evidently was received by loud applause from his side of the aisle.

The House being in the Committee of the Whole on the state of the Union, and having under consideration the bill (H.R. 13801) making appropriations for the Department of Agriculture for the fiscal year ending June 30, 1902—

Mr. WHITE said:

. . . Mr. Chairman . . . there are others on this committee and in this House who are far better prepared to enlighten the world with their eloquence as to what the agriculturists of this country need than your humble servant. I therefore resign to more competent minds the discussion of this bill. I shall consume the remainder of my time in reverting to measures and facts that have in them more weighty interests to me and mine than that of agriculture—matters of life and existence.

I want to enter a plea for the colored man, the colored woman, the colored boy, and the colored girl of this country. I would not thus digress from the question at issue and detain the House in a discussion of the interests of this particular people at this time but for the constant and the persistent efforts of certain gentlemen upon this floor to mold and rivet public sentiment against us as a people and to lose no opportunity to hold up the unfortunate few who commit crimes and depredations and lead lives of infamy and shame, as other races do, as fair specimens of representatives of the entire colored race. And at no time, perhaps, during the Fifty-sixth Congress were

these charges and countercharges, containing, as they do, slanderous statements, more persistently magnified and pressed upon the attention of the nation than during the consideration of the recent reapportionment bill, which is now a law. As stated some days ago on this floor by me, I then sought diligently to obtain an opportunity to answer some of the statements made by gentlemen from different States, but the privilege was denied me; and I therefore must embrace this opportunity to say, out of season, perhaps, that which I was not permitted to say in season.

In the catalogue of members of Congress in this House perhaps none have been more persistent in their determination to bring the black man into disrepute and, with a labored effort, to show that he was unworthy of the right of citizenship than my colleague from North Carolina, Mr. KITCHIN. . . .

I might state as a further general fact that the Democrats of North Carolina got possession of the State and local government since my last election in 1898, and that I bid adieu to these historic walls on the 4th day of next March, and that the brother of Mr. KITCHIN will succeed me. Comment is unnecessary. In the town where this young gentleman was born, at the general election last August for the adoption of the constitutional amendment, and the general election for State and county officers, Scotland Neck had a registered white vote of 395, most of whom of course were Democrats, and a registered colored vote of 534, virtually if not all of whom were Republicans, and so voted. When the count was announced, however, there were 831 Democrats to 75 Republicans; but in the town of Halifax, same county, the result was much more pronounced.

In that town the registered Republican vote was 345, and the total registered vote of the township was 539, but when the count was announced it stood 990 Democrats to 41 Republicans, or 492 more Democratic votes counted than were registered votes in the township. Comment here is unnecessary, nor do I think it necessary for anyone to wonder at the peculiar notion my colleague has with reference to the manner of voting and the method of counting those votes, nor is it to be a wonder that he is a member of this Congress, having been brought up and educated in such wonderful notions of dealing out fair-handed justice to his fellow-man. . . .

. . . There never has been, nor ever will be, any negro domination in that State, and no one knows it any better than the Democratic party. It is a convenient howl, however, often resorted to in order to consummate a diabolical purpose by scaring the weak and gullible whites into support of measures and men suitable to the demagogue and the ambitious office seeker, whose crave for office overshadows and puts to flight all other considerations, fair or unfair. . . .

It is an undisputed fact that the negro vote in the State of Alabama, as well as most of the other Southern States, have been effectively suppressed, either one way or the other—in some instances by constitutional amendment and State legislation, in others by cold-blooded fraud and intimidation, but whatever the method pursued, it is not denied, but frankly admitted in the speeches in this House, that the black vote has been eliminated to a large extent. Then, when some of us insist that the plain letter of the Constitution of the United States, which all of us have sworn to support, should be carried out, as expressed in the second section of the fourteenth amendment thereof, to wit:

Representatives shall be apportioned among the several States according to their respective numbers, counting the whole number of persons in each State, excluding Indians not taxed. But when the right to vote at any election for the choice of electors for President and Vice-President of the United States, Representatives in Congress, the executive and judicial officers of a State, or the members of a legislature thereof, is denied to any of the male inhabitants of such State, being twenty-one years of age, and citizens of the United States, or in any way abridged, except for participation in rebellion, or other crime, the basis of representation therein shall be reduced in proportion which the number of such male citizens shall bear to the whole number of male citizens twenty-one years of age in such State.

That section makes the duty of every member of Congress plain, and yet the gentleman from Alabama [Mr. UNDERWOOD] says that the attempt to enforce this section of the organic law is the throwing down of firebrands, and notifies the world that this attempt to execute the highest law of the land will be retaliated by the South, and the inference is that the negro will be even more severely punished than the horrors through which he has already come. . . .

Here's the plain letter of the Constitution, the plain, simple, sworn duty of every member of Congress; yet these gentlemen from the South say "Yes, we have violated your Constitution of the nation; we regarded it as a local necessity; and now, if you undertake to punish us as the Constitution prescribes, we will see to it that our former deeds of disloyalty to that instrument, our former acts of disfranchisement and opposition to the highest law of the land will be repeated many fold." . . .

Individually, and so far as my race is concerned, I care but little about the reduction of Southern representation, except in so far as it becomes my duty to aid in the proper execution of all the laws of the land in whatever sphere in which I may be placed. Such reduction in representation, it is true, would make more secure the installment of the great Republican party in power for many years to come in all of its branches, and at the same time enable that great party to be able to dispense with the further support of the loyal negro vote; and I might here parenthetically state that there are some members of the Republican party to-day—"lily whites," if you please—who, after receiving the unalloyed support of the negro vote for over thirty years, now feel that they have grown a little too good for association with him politically, and are disposed to dump him overboard. I am glad to observe, however, that this class constitutes a very small percentage of those to whom we have always looked for friendship and protection. . . .

Now, Mr. Chairman, before concluding my remarks I want to submit a brief recipe for the solution of the so-called American negro problem. He asks no special favors, but simply demands that he be given the same chance for existence, for earning a livelihood, for raising himself in the scales of manhood and womanhood that are accorded to kindred nationalities. Treat him as a man; go into his home and learn of his social conditions; learn of his cares, his troubles, and his hopes for the future; gain his confidence; open the doors of industry to him; let the word "negro," "colored," and "black" be stricken from all the organizations enumerated in the federation of labor.

Help him to overcome his weaknesses, punish the crime-committing class by the courts of the land, measure the standard of the race by its best material, cease to mold prejudicial and unjust

public sentiment against him, and my word for it, he will learn to support, hold up the hands of, and join in with that political party, that institution, whether secular or religious, in every community where he lives, which is destined to do the greatest good for the greatest number. Obliterate race hatred, party prejudice, and help us to achieve nobler ends, greater results, and become more satisfactory citizens to our brother in white.

This, Mr. Chairman, is perhaps the negroes' temporary farewell to the American Congress; but let me say, Phoenix-like he will rise up some day and come again. These parting words are in behalf of an outraged, heart-broken, bruised, and bleeding, but God-fearing people, faithful, industrious, loyal people—rising people, full of potential force. . . .

The only apology that I have to make for the earnestness with which I have spoken is that I am pleading for the life, the liberty, the future happiness, and manhood suffrage for one-eighth of the entire population of the United States. [Loud applause.]

Source: "Defense of the Negro Race—Charges Answered," Speech of Hon. George H. White of North Carolina in the House of Representatives, January 29, 1901, in "Documenting the American South," University of North Carolina at Chapel Hill, http://docsouth.unc.edu/nc/whitegh/whitegh.html.

---

9 Official Proceedings of the Constitutional Convention of the State of Alabama, May 21–September 3, 1901

The purpose of the 1901 Alabama constitutional convention was announced on the first day that it actually conducted business, May 22. The person who announced it was the just-selected permanent president of the 150-delegate convention, John B. Knox of Calhoun County, who promptly stood up and told the delegates why they were there—as the excerpt shows. The convention made many other changes to the Alabama constitution, but disenfranchisement was its primary goal. Note that Knox refers clearly to President William McKinley's administration's tacit support of disenfranchisement. These are telling details, because they underscore how secure southern Democrats thought they were by 1901 in pushing ahead with disenfranchisement. The fact that these proceedings were printed and widely distributed is also an indication of the confidence that the disenfranchisers now felt.

One should not infer from this document, however, that the disenfranchisers worked only through constitutional conventions. They also used referenda to approve constitutional amendments or passed statutes to achieve their goals. Nor were disenfranchisers completely confident of white support. Much of formal legal disenfranchisement avoided a real test with public opinion and majority rule. Constitutional revisions in Louisiana, Mississippi, and Virginia, for example, were never submitted to a popular vote.

Second Day
MONTGOMERY, ALA.
Wednesday, May 22, 1901. . . .
MR. KNOX - Gentlemen of the
Convention: . . .

Importance of the Issue

In my judgment, the people of Alabama have been called upon to face no more important situation than now confronts us, unless it be when they, in 1861, stirred by the momentous issue of impending conflict between the North and the South, were forced to decide whether they would remain in or withdraw from the Union.

Then, as now, the negro was the prominent factor in the issue.

The Southern people, with this grave problem of the races to deal with, are face to face with a new epoch in Constitution-making, the difficulties of which are great, but which, if solved wisely, may bring rest and peace and happiness. If otherwise, it may leave us and our posterity continuously involved in race conflict, or what may be worse, subjected permanently to the baneful influences of the political conditions now prevailing in the State.

So long as the negro remains in insignificant minority, and votes the Republican ticket, our friends in the North tolerate him with complacency, but there is not a Northern State, and I might go further and say, there is not an intelligent white man in the North, not gangrened by sectional prejudice and hatred of the South who would consent for a single day to submit to negro rule. . . .

And what is it that we want to do? Why it is within the limits imposed by the Federal Constitution, to establish white supremacy in this State.

This is our problem, and we should be permitted to deal with it, unobstructed by outside influences, with a sense of our responsibilities as citizens and our duty to posterity.

Northern Interference

Some of our Northern friends have ever exhibited an unwonted interest in our affairs. It was this interference on their part that provoked the most tremendous conflict of modern times; and there are not a few philanthropists in that section who are still uneasy lest we be permitted to govern ourselves and allowed to live up to the privileges of a free and sovereign people! . . .

. . . [T]he point of their interference is not so much to elevate the black man as it is to humiliate the white man with whom they have been in antagonism.

But we may congratulate ourselves that this sectional feeling which has served to impair the harmony of our common country, and to limit the power and retard the development of the greatest government on earth, is fast yielding to reason.

While we may and do differ from him politically, there is not an enlightened and patriotic Southern man who fails to see that much of this result is due to the honorable and statesman-like policy of the present Chief Executive of these United States, who, by the consideration he has shown our section in many ways, notably in the Spanish-American war, and by refusing to lend his approval to any movement looking to the reduction of our representation in Congress or in the Electoral College, has shown himself capable of being President of the whole country and not merely one section of it and has been enabled to present the spectacle of a re-united country, and contributed much to place our government in the very front rank with the nations of the world.

The Attitude of the Southern Man Towards the Negro

The Southern man knows the negro, and the negro knows him. The only conflict which has, or is ever likely to arise, springs from the effort of ill-advised friends in the North to confer upon him, without previous training or preparation, places of power and responsibility, for which he is wholly unfitted, either by capacity or experience. . . .

White Supremacy by Law

But if we would have white supremacy, we must establish it by law—not by force or fraud. If you teach your boy that it is right to buy a vote, it is an easy step for him to learn to use money to bribe or corrupt officials or trustees of any class. If you teach your boy that it is right to steal votes, it is an easy step for him to believe that it is right to steal whatever he may need or greatly desire. The results of such an influence will enter every branch of society, it will reach your bank cashiers, and affect positions of trust in every department; it will ultimately enter your courts, and affect the administrations of justice.

I submit it to the intelligent judgment of this Convention that there is no higher duty resting upon us, as citizens, and as delegates, than that which requires us to embody in the fundamental law such provisions as will enable us to protect the sanctity of the ballot in every portion of the State.

The justification for whatever manipulation of the ballot that has occurred in this State has been the menace of negro domination. After the war, by force of Federal bayonets, the negro was placed in control of every branch of our Government. Inspired and aided by unscrupulous white men, he wasted money, created debts, increased taxes until it threatened to amount to confiscation of our property. While in power, and within a few years, he increased our State debt from a nominal figure to nearly thirty million dollars. The right of revolution is always left to every people. Being prostrated by the effects of war, and unable to take up arms in their own defense, in some portions of this State, white men, greatly in the minority, it is said . . . used their greater intellect to overcome the greater number of their black opponents. If so such a course might be warranted when considered as the right of revolution, and as an act of necessity for self-preservation. But a people cannot always live in a state of revolution. The time comes, when, if they would be free, happy and contented people, they must return to a Constitutional form of government, where law and order prevail, and where every citizen stands ready to stake his life and his honor to maintain it. . . .

Source: "Official Proceedings of the Constitutional Convention of the State of Alabama," http://www.legislature.state.al.us/misc/history/constitutions/1901/proceedings/1901_proceedings_vol1/1901.html.

10   Alabama Constitution, Ratified November 28, 1901

The legal disenfranchisement of black adult males in the former Confederate states began shortly after the Supreme Court's decision in Ex parte Yarbrough *in 1884 (see Document 7). The process began in Florida in 1889, the result of several years of planning and effort by the leading Democrats in that state. The Mississippi constitutional convention of 1890 then brought the possibility of the legal disenfranchisement of blacks to national attention. In fact, the constitution was mentioned often in congressional debates, as the Republican Party sought to meet the apparently growing threat of black disenfranchisement. Republicans hoped to use the decision in* Yarbrough, *which upheld federal power to punish a private obstruction of the right to vote, as the basis for the federal regulation of House elections in the South, thereby protecting black voting rights. But the Republican effort failed in early 1891. By 1894 the Democratic Party—after regaining control of all branches of the national government for the first time since President James Buchanan's administration—had repealed many of the pieces of the Enforcement Acts of 1870 and 1871. By 1907, all of the former Confederate states were legally restricting black voting rights, either through constitutional change or through statute.*

In general, the panoply of disenfranchising devices consisted of imposing unwieldy personal registration requirements, switching to a printed ballot (itself a kind of literary test), fixing criminal penalties for violating election law, establishing residency requirements, and requiring proof of residency from registrants. The two most famous methods, however, were the poll tax and the literacy test. All of these devices vested enormous discretionary power in local registrars, who functioned as agents of the dominant network of local courthouse notables making up the Democratic Party in any given locale.

Legal disenfranchisement was neutral on its face. Yet, although none of the new state constitutions and relevant statutes was racially explicit, their racial intent was obvious and widely known, and the records of the constitutional conventions (see, for example, Document 9) and legislative debates, as well as the newspaper accounts of these events, fully show racial intent. Nevertheless, the disenfranchisers expected to find some support with the Republican Party, which all along had promoted black voting rights. They also expected that if the language of the new constitutions and statutes was free of any explicit reference to race, they would be able to get away with the change in the federal courts. Finally, they expected that their radical plan could only be met with equally radical measures from the federal government—and that no one opposed to disenfranchisement really had the stomach for that.

The 1901 Alabama constitution usefully illustrates the formal legal aspect of black suffrage restriction. Its drafters intended to shrink the state's electorate as much as possible and to legally create—through a whole new registration of the state's adult males—an electorate that would support one party, white supremacist rule in Alabama. In fact, anyone reading the constitution carefully cannot escape the conclusion that the disenfranchisers were taking aim not only at black voters but also at poor white voters. Third party, populist forces were strong in Alabama in the 1890s. Significantly, they did not believe in restricting black suffrage and instead hoped to keep white supremacists at bay through a cross-racial electoral alliance based on economic protest. The 1901 constitution was designed, then, not only to prevent a reconstruction of Reconstruction, but also to block a resurgence of populism.

In addition to the excerpts from the 1901 Alabama Constitution, comparable provisions from the 1868 and 1875 Alabama constitutions are included here to underscore the extent of the shift against black voting rights by the early twentieth century.

Alabama Constitution of 1901

. . .

ARTICLE VIII. SUFFRAGE AND ELECTIONS

Section 177. Age and citizenship qualifications of electors.

Every male citizen of this State, who is a citizen of the United States, and every male resident of foreign birth, who, before the ratification of this Constitution, shall have legally declared his intention to become a citizen of the United States, twenty-one years old or upward, not laboring under any of the disabilities named in this article, and possessing the qualifications required by it, shall be an elector, and shall be entitled to vote at any election by the people; provided, that all foreigners who have legally declared their intention of becoming citizens of the United States, shall, if they fail to become citizens thereof at the time they are entitled to become such, cease to have the right to vote until they become such citizens.

Section 178. Residency, registration and poll tax requirements for electors.

To entitle a person to vote at any election by the people, he shall have resided in the State at least two years, in the county one year, and in the precinct or ward three months, immediately preceding the election at which he offers to vote, and he shall have been duly registered as an elector, and shall have paid on or before the first day of February next preceding the date of the election at which he offers to vote all poll taxes due from him for the year nineteen hundred and one, and for each subsequent year; provided, that any elector who, within three months next preceding the date of the election at which he offers to vote, has removed from one precinct or ward to another precinct or ward in the same county, incorporated town or city, shall have the right to vote in the precinct or ward from which he has so removed, if he would have been entitled to vote in such precinct or ward but for such removal.

Section 179. Method of voting.

All elections by the people shall be by ballot, and all elections by persons in a representative capacity shall be viva voce.

Section 180. Persons qualified to register as electors Prior to December 20, 1902.

The following male citizens of this State, who are citizens of the United States, and every male resident of foreign birth, who, before the ratification of this Constitution, shall have legally declared his intention to become a citizen of the United States, and who shall not have had an opportunity to perfect his citizenship prior to the twentieth day of December, nineteen hundred and two, twenty-one years old or upwards, who, if their place of residence shall remain unchanged, will have, at the date of the next general election the qualifications as to residents prescribed in Section 178 of this Constitution, and who are not disqualified under Section 182 of this Constitution, shall, upon application be entitled to register as electors prior to the twentieth day of December, nineteen hundred and two, namely: First - All who have honorably served in the land or naval forces of the United States in the war of 1812, or in the war with Mexico, or in any war with the Indians, or in the war between the States, or in the war with Spain, or who honorably served in the land or naval forces of the Confederate States, or of the State of Alabama in the war between the States; or, Second - The lawful descendants of persons who honorably served in the land or naval forces of the United States in the war of the American Revolution, or in the war of 1812, or in the war with Mexico, or in any war with the Indians, or in the war between the States, or in the land or naval forces of the Confederate States, or of the State of Alabama in the war between the States; or, Third - All persons who are of good character and who understand the duties and obligations of citizenship under a republican form of government.

Section 181. Same After January 1, 1903.

After the first day of January, nineteen hundred and three, the following persons, and no others, who, if their place of residence shall remain unchanged, will have, at the date of the next general election, the qualifications as to residence prescribed in Section 178 of this Constitution, shall be qualified to register as electors, provided, they shall not be disqualified under Section 182 of this Constitution. First - Those who can read and write any article of the Constitution of the United States in the English language, and who are physically unable to work; and those who can read and write any article of the Constitution of the United States in the English language, and who have worked or been regularly engaged in some lawful employment, business or occupation, trade or calling for the greater part of the twelve months next preceding the time they offer to register; and those who are unable to read and write, if such inability is due solely to physical disability; or, Second - The owner in good faith, in his own right, or the husband of a woman who is the owner in good faith, in her own right, of forty acres of land situate in this State, upon which they reside; or the owner in good faith, in his own right, or the husband of any woman who is the owner in good faith, in her own right, of real estate, situate in this State, assessed for taxation at the value of three hundred dollars or more, or the owner in good faith, in his own right, or the husband of a woman who is the owner in good faith, in her own right, of personal property in this State assessed for taxation at three hundred dollars or more; provided, that the taxes due upon such real or personal property for the year next preceding the year in which he offers to register shall have been paid, unless the assessment shall have been legally contested and is undetermined.

Section 182. Certain persons disqualified from registering and voting.

The following persons shall be disqualified both from registering and from voting, namely: All idiots and insane persons; those who shall by reason of conviction of crime be disqualified from voting at the time of the ratification of this Constitution; those who shall be convicted of treason, murder, arson, embezzlement, malfeasance in of-

fice, larceny, receiving stolen property, obtaining property or money under false pretenses, perjury, subordination of perjury, robbery, assault with intent to rob, burglary, forgery, bribery, assault and battery on the wife, bigamy, living in adultery, sodomy, incest, rape, miscegenation, crime against nature, or any crime punishable by imprisonment in the penitentiary, or of any infamous crime or crime involving moral turpitude; also any person who shall be convicted as a vagrant or tramp, or of selling or offering to sell his vote or the vote of another, or of making or offering to make false return in any election by the people or in any primary election to procure the nomination or election of any person to any office, or of suborning any witness or registrar to secure the registration of any person as an elector.

Section 183. Qualifications as elector required to participate in primary elections, party conventions, mass meetings or other methods of political party action.

No person shall be qualified to vote or participate in any primary election, party convention, mass meeting or other method of party action of any political party or faction, who shall not possess the qualifications prescribed in this article for an elector, or who shall be disqualified from voting under the provisions of this article.

Section 184. Applicability of article as to elections held after 1902 general election.

No person, not registered and qualified as an elector under the provisions of this article, shall vote at the general election in nineteen hundred and two, or at any subsequent State, county, or municipal election, general, local or special; but the provisions of this article shall not apply to any election held prior to the general election in the year nineteen hundred and two.

Section 185. Oath or affirmation when vote challenged; false oath or affirmation constitutes perjury.

Any elector whose right to vote shall be challenged for any legal cause before an election officer, shall be required to swear or affirm that the matter of the challenge is untrue before his vote shall be received, and any one who willfully swears or affirms falsely thereto shall be guilty of perjury, and upon conviction thereof shall be imprisoned in the penitentiary for not less than one nor more than five years.

Section 186. Legislature to provide for registration procedure after January 1, 1903; procedure for registration prior to January 1, 1903.

The Legislature shall provide by law for the registration, after the first day of January, nineteen hundred and three, of all qualified electors. Until the first day of January, nineteen hundred and three, all electors shall be registered under and in accordance with the requirements of this section, as follows:

First - Registration shall be conducted in each county by a board of three reputable and suitable persons resident in the county, who shall not hold any elective office during their term, to be appointed within sixty days after the ratification of this Constitution, by the Governor, Auditor and Commissioner of Agriculture and Industries, or by a majority of them, acting as a board of appointment. . . .

Third - . . . On Friday and Saturday next preceding the day of election in November, nineteen hundred and two, they shall sit in the court house of each county during such days, and shall register all applicants having the qualifications prescribed by Section 180 of this Constitution, and not disqualified under Section 182, who shall have reached the age of twenty-one years after the first day of August, nineteen hundred and two, or who shall prove to the reasonable satisfaction of the board that, by reason of physical disability or unavoidable absence from the county, they had no opportunity to register prior to the first day of August, nineteen hundred and two, and they shall not on such days register any other persons. When there are two or more court houses in a county, the registrars may sit during such two days at the court house they may select, but shall give ten days' notice, by bills posted at

each of the court houses, designating the court house at which they will sit.

Fourth - The Board of Registrars shall hold sessions at the court house of their respective counties during the entire third week in November, nineteen hundred and two, and for six working days next prior to the twentieth day of December nineteen hundred and two, during which sessions they shall register all persons applying who possess the qualifications prescribed in Section 180 of this Constitution, and who shall not be disqualified under Section 182. In counties where there are more than two court houses the Board of Registrars shall divide the time equally between them. The Board of Registrars shall give notice of the time and place of such sessions by posting notices at each court house in their respective counties, and at each voting place and at three other public places in the county, and by publication once a week for two consecutive weeks in a newspaper, if one be published in the county; such notices to be posted and such publications to be commenced as early as practicable in the first week of November, nineteen hundred and two. Failure on the part of the registrars to conform to the provisions of this article as to the giving of the required notices shall not invalidate any registration made by them.

Fifth - The Board of Registrars shall have power to examine, under oath or affirmation, all applicants for registration, and to take testimony touching the qualifications of such applicants. Each member of such board is authorized to administer the oath to be taken by the applicants and witnesses, which shall be in the following form, and subscribed by the person making it, and preserved by the board, namely: "I solemnly swear (or affirm) that in the matter of the application of _____ _____ for registration as an elector, I will speak the truth, the whole truth, and nothing but the truth, so help me God." Any person who upon such examination makes any wilfully false statement in reference to any material matter touching the qualification of any applicant for registration, shall be guilty of perjury, and upon conviction thereof, shall be imprisoned in the penitentiary for not less than one nor more than five years.

Sixth - The action of the majority of the Board of Registrars shall be the action of the board and a majority of the board shall constitute a quorum for the transaction of all business. Any person to whom registration is denied shall have the right of appeal, without giving security for costs, within thirty days after such denial, by filing a petition in the Circuit Court or court of like jurisdiction held for the county in which he seeks to register, to have his qualifications as an elector determined. Upon the filing of the petition the clerk of the court shall give notice thereof to any Solicitor authorized to represent the State in said county, whose duty it shall be to appear and defend against the petition on behalf of the State. Upon such trial the court shall charge the jury only as to what constitutes the qualifications that entitle the applicant to become an elector at the time he applied for registration, and the jury shall determine the weight and effect of the evidence and return a verdict. From the judgment rendered an appeal will lie to the Supreme Court in favor of the petitioner, to be taken within thirty days. Final judgment in favor of the petitioner shall entitle him to registration as of the date of his application to the registrars. . . .

Section 188. Certain information to be furnished prior to registration.

From and after the first day of January, nineteen hundred and three, any applicant for registration may be required to state under oath, to be administered by the registrar or by any person authorized by law to administer oaths, where he lived during the five years next preceding the time at which he applies to register, and the name or names by which he was known during that period, and the name of his employer or employers, if any, during such period. Any applicant for registration who refuses to state such facts, or any of them, shall not be entitled to register, and any person so offering to register, who wilfully makes a false statement in regard to such matters, or any of

them, shall be guilty of perjury, and upon conviction thereof shall be imprisoned in the penitentiary for not less than one nor more than five years. . . .

Section 194. Poll tax Amount; maximum age for payment; when due and payable; when delinquent; returns of collections to be separate from other collections.

The poll tax mentioned in this article shall be one dollar and fifty cents upon each male inhabitant of the State, over the age of twenty-one years, and under the age of forty-five years, who would not now be exempt by law; but the Legislature is authorized to increase the maximum age fixed in this section to not more than sixty years. Such poll tax shall become due and payable on the first day of October in each year, and become delinquent on the first day of the next succeeding February, but no legal process, nor any fee or commission shall be allowed for the collection thereof. The Tax Collector shall make returns of poll tax collections separate from other collections.

Section 195. Same Payment of tax of another; advance of money for payment in order to influence vote.

Any person who shall pay the poll tax of another, or advance him money for that purpose in order to influence his vote, shall be guilty of bribery and upon conviction therefor shall be imprisoned in the penitentiary for not less than one nor more than five years. . . .

Alabama Constitution of 1868

. . .

ARTICLE VII. ELECTIONS

Section 1. In all elections by the people, the electors shall vote by ballot.

Section 2. Every male person, born in the United States, and every male person who has been naturalized, or who has legally declared his intention to become a citizen of the United States, twenty-one years old or upward, who shall have resided in this State six months next preceding the election, and three months in the county in which he offers to vote, except as hereinafter provided, shall be deemed an elector: Provided, That no soldier, or sailor, or marine in the military or naval service of the United States, shall hereafter acquire a residence by reason of being stationed on duty in this State.

Section 3. It shall be the duty of the General Assembly to provide, from time to time, for the registration of all electors; but the following classes of persons shall not be permitted to register, vote or hold office: 1st, Those, who, during the late rebellion, inflicted, or caused to be inflicted, any cruel or unusual punishment upon any soldier, sailor, marine, employee or citizen of the United States, or who, in any other way, violated the rules of civilized warfare. 2d, Those who may be disqualified from holding office by the proposed amendment to the Constitution of the United States, known as "Article XIV," and those who have been disqualified from registering to vote for delegates to the Convention to frame a Constitution for the State of Alabama, under the act of Congress, "to provide for the more efficient government of the rebel States," passed by Congress March 2, 1867, and the acts supplementary thereto, except such persons as aided in the reconstruction proposed by Congress, and accept the political equality of all men before the law: Provided, That the General Assembly shall have power to remove the disabilities incurred under this clause. 3d, Those who shall have been convicted of treason, embezzlement of public funds, malfeasance in office, crime punishable by law with imprisonment in the penitentiary, or bribery. 4th. Those who are idiots or insane.

Section 4. All persons, before registering, must take and subscribe the following oath: I, _____, do solemnly swear (or affirm) that I will support and maintain the Constitution and laws of the United States, and the Constitution and laws of the State of Alabama; that I am not excluded from registering by any of the clauses in Sec. 3, Article 7, of the Constitution of the State of Alabama; that I will never countenance or aid in the secession of this State from the United States; That I accept the civil and political equality of all men; and agree not to attempt to deprive any person or persons, on account of race, color, or previous condition, of any political or civil right, privilege, or immunity, enjoyed by any other class of men; and furthermore, that I will not in any way injure, or countenance in others any attempt to injure, any person or persons, on account of past or present support of the government of the United States, the laws of the United States, or the principle of the political and civil equality of all men, or for affiliation with any political party. . . .

Alabama Constitution of 1875

. . .

ARTICLE I.
DECLARATION OF RIGHTS

Sec. 38. No educational or property qualification for suffrage or office, nor any restraint upon the same on account of race, color, or previous condition of servitude, shall be made by law. . . .

Source: "Constitution of 1901," http://www.legislature.state.al.us/CodeOfAlabama/Constitution/1901/Constitution1901_toc.htm.

11   Supreme Court Decisions Upholding Disenfranchisement: *Williams v. Mississippi,
Giles v. Harris,* and *James v. Bowman,* 1898–1903

*As southern states began to return to white rule at the turn of the twentieth century, they drafted new
constitutions and passed laws that effectively defeated the purposes of the Fourteenth and Fifteenth
Amendments. The Supreme Court aided these disenfranchising efforts by handing down rulings that
were masterpieces of legal sophistry intended to avoid recognition of the obvious constitutional violation that disenfranchisement represented.*

Williams v. Mississippi, Decided April 25, 1898

*Although the strategy of formal legal black disfranchisement took three forms—constitution making,
constitutional amendment, and ordinary statute—only the first form was tested before the Supreme
Court. The one test of the Mississippi constitution of 1890 was* Williams v. Mississippi *(170 U.S.
213), in which Henry Williams argued that his murder trial was fundamentally unfair because African
Americans could not vote and therefore were ineligible to serve on the jury that tried him (Mississippi
had disenfranchised black voters in 1890 with its constitutional revision that established a heavy poll
tax and complex, burdensome residency requirements). The Supreme Court affirmed Williams's conviction for murder, thereby ensuring his death sentence, by accepting the claim that the 1890 constitution was racially neutral and applied equally to whites and blacks. Thus the "color-blind" language so
carefully crafted for the disenfranchising constitution did what it was supposed to do—give anyone
who wanted to take the language at face value a reason for backing off from federal intervention.*

*A major difficulty the U.S. Supreme Court faced in treating the 1890 constitution as racially neu-
tral, however, was the racist language of the Mississippi Supreme Court in a case that interpreted the
intent of the 1890 constitution. In fact, the Supreme Court of Mississippi plainly stated that the intent
of the 1890 constitution was to end black suffrage—which is precisely what Williams claimed. In effect, then, the Mississippi Supreme Court was a witness for Williams. Justice Joseph McKenna simply
denied the obvious, writing "nothing tangible can be deduced from this"—except, of course, that
Williams would hang.*

WILLIAMS
v.
STATE OF MISSISSIPPI.
No. 531.

April 25, 1898

At June term, 1896, of the circuit court of Washington county, Miss., the plaintiff in error was in-
dicted by a grand jury composed entirely of white
men for the crime of murder. On the 15th day of
June he made a motion to quash the indictment,
which was in substance as follows, omitting rep-
etitions, and retaining the language of the motion
as nearly as possible:

Now comes the defendant in this cause, Henry
Williams by name, and moves the circuit court of
Washington county, Miss., to quash the indictment herein filed, and upon which it is proposed
to try him for the alleged offense of murder: (1)
Because the laws by which the grand jury was selected, organized, summoned, and charged,
which presented the said indictment, are unconstitutional and repugnant to the spirit and letter
of the constitution of the United States of
America, fourteenth amendment thereof, in this:
that the constitution prescribes the qualifications
of electors, and that, to be a juror, one must be an
elector; that the constitution also requires that
those offering to vote shall produce to the elec-

tion officers satisfactory evidence that they have paid their taxes; that the legislature is to provide means for enforcing the constitution, and, in the exercise of this authority, enacted section 3643, also section 3644 of 1892, which respectively provide that the election commissioners shall appoint three election managers, and that the latter shall be judges of the qualifications of electors, and are required 'to examine on oath any person duly registered and offering to vote touching his qualifications as an elector.' And then the motion states that 'the registration roll is not prima facie evidence of an elector's right to vote, but the list of those persons having been passed upon by the various district election managers of the county to compose the registration book of voters as named in section 2358 of said Code of 1892, and that there was no registration books of voters prepared for the guidance of said officers of said county at the time said grand jury was drawn.' It is further alleged that there is no statute of the state providing for the procurement of any registration books of voters of said county, and (it is alleged in detail) the terms of the constitution and the section of the Code mentioned, and the discretion given to the officers, 'is but a scheme on the part of the framers of that constitution to abridge the suffrage of the colored electors in the state of Mississippi on account of the previous condition of servitude by granting a discretion to the said officers as mentioned in the several sections of the constitution of the state and the statute of the state adopted under the said constitution. The use of said discretion can be and has been used in the said Washington county to the end complained of.' After some detail to the same effect, it is further alleged: 'That the constitutional convention was composed of 134 members, only one of whom was a negro. That under prior laws there were 190,000 colored voters and 69,000 white voters. The makers of the new constitution arbitrarily refused to submit it to the voters of the state for approval, but ordered it adopted, and an election to be held immediately under it, which election was held under the election ordinances of the said constitution in No-

vember, 1891, and the legislature assembled in 1892, and enacted the statutes complained of, for the purpose to discriminate aforesaid, and but for that the 'defendant's race would have been represented impartially on the grand jury which presented this indictment,' and hence he is deprived of the equal protection of the laws of the state. It is further alleged that the state has not reduced its representation in congress, and generally for the reasons aforesaid, and because the indictment should have been returned under the constitution of 1869 and statute of 1889, it is null and void. The motion concludes as follows: 'Further, the defendant is a citizen of the United States, and, for the many reasons herein named, asks that the indictment be quashed, and he be recognized to appear at the next term of the court.' . . .

The accused was tried by a jury composed entirely of white men, and convicted. A motion for a new trial was denied, and the accused sentenced to be hanged. An appeal to the supreme court was taken, and the judgment of the court below was affirmed. . . .

Mr. Justice McKENNA, after stating the case, delivered the opinion of the court.

The question presented is, are the provisions of the constitution of the state of Mississippi and the laws enacted to enforce the same repugnant to the fourteenth amendment of the constitution of the United States? That amendment and its effect upon the rights of the colored race have been considered by this court in a number of cases, and it has been uniformly held that the constitution of the United States, as amended, forbids, so far as civil and political rights are concerned, discriminations by the general government or by the states against any citizen because of his race; but it has also been held, in a very recent case, to justify a removal from a state court to a federal court of a cause in which such rights are alleged to be denied, that such denial must be the result of the constitution or laws of the state, not of the administration of them. Nor can the conduct of a criminal trial in a state court be reviewed by this court unless the trial is had under some statute repugnant to the constitution of the United States, or was so conducted as to deprive the accused of some right or immunity secured to him by that instrument. . . . It is not asserted by plaintiff in error that either the constitution of the state or its laws discriminate in terms against the negro race, either as to the elective franchise or the privilege or duty of sitting on juries. These results, if we understand plaintiff in error, are alleged to be effected by the powers vested in certain administrative officers.

Plaintiff in error says:

'Section 241 of the constitution of 1890 prescribes the qualifications for electors; that residence in the state for two years, one year in the precinct of the applicant, must be effected; that he is twenty-one years or over of age, having paid all taxes legally due of him for two years prior to 1st day of February of the year he offers to vote, not having been convicted of theft, arson, rape, receiving money or goods under false pretenses, bigamy, embezzlement.

'Section 242 of the constitution provides the mode of registration; that the legislature shall provide by law for registration of all persons entitled to vote at any election, and that all persons offering to register shall take the oath; that they are not disqualified for voting by reason of any of the crimes named in the constitution of this state; that they will truly answer all questions propounded to them concerning their antecedents so far as they relate to the applicant's right to vote, and also as to their residence before their citizenship in the district in which such application for registration is made. The court readily sees the scheme. If the applicant swears, as he must do, that he is not disqualified by reason of the crimes specified, and that he has effected the required residence, what right has he to answer all questions as to his former residence? Section 244 of the constitution requires that the applicant for registration, after January, 1892, shall be able to read any section of the constitution, or he shall be able to understand the same (being any section of the organic law), or give a reasonable interpretation thereof. Now, we submit that these provisions vest in the administrative officers the full power, under section 242, to ask all sorts of vain, impertinent questions; and it is with that officer to say whether the questions relate to the applicant's right to vote. This officer can reject whomsoever he chooses, and register whomsoever he chooses, for he is vested by the constitution with that power. Under section 244 it is left with the administrative officer to determine whether the applicant reads, understands, or interprets the section of the constitution designated. The officer is the sole judge of the examination of the applicant, and, even though the applicant be qualified, it is left with the officer to so determine; and the said officer can refuse him registration.'

To make the possible dereliction of the officers the dereliction of the constitution and laws, the remarks of the supreme court of the state are quoted by plaintiff in error as to their intent. The constitution provides for the payment of a poll tax, and by a section of the Code its payment cannot be compelled by a seizure and sale of property. We gather from the brief of counsel that its payment is a condition of the right to vote, and, in a case to test whether its payment was or was not optional (Ratcliff v. Beal, 20 South. 865), the supreme court of the state said: 'Within the field of permissible action under the limitations imposed by the federal constitution, the convention swept the field of expedients, to obstruct the exercise of suffrage by the negro race.' And further the court said, speaking of the negro race: 'By reason of its previous condition of servitude and dependencies, this race had acquired or accentuated certain peculiarities of habit, of temperament, and of character, which clearly distinguished it as a race from the whites; a patient, docile people, but careless, landless, migratory within narrow limits, without forethought, and its criminal members given to furtive offenses, rather than the robust crimes of the whites. Restrained by the federal constitution from discriminating against the negro race, the convention discriminates against its characteristics, and the offenses to which its criminal members are prone.' But nothing tangible can be deduced from this. If weakness were to be taken advantage of, it was to be done 'within the field of permissible action under the limitations imposed by the federal constitution,' and the means of it were the alleged characteristics of the negro race, not the administration of the law by officers of the state. Besides, the operation of the constitution and laws is not limited by their language or effects to one race. They reach weak and vicious white men as well as weak and vicious black men, and whatever is sinister in their intention, if anything, can be prevented by both races by the exertion of that duty which voluntarily pays taxes and refrains from crime.

It cannot be said, therefore, that the denial of the equal protection of the laws arises primarily from the constitution and laws of Mississippi; nor is there any sufficient allegation of an evil and discriminating administration of them. The only allegation is ' . . . by granting a discretion to the said officers, as mentioned in the several sections of the constitution of the state, and the statute of the state adopted under the said constitution, the use of which discretion can be and has been used by said officers in the said Washington county to the end here complained of, to wit, the abridgment of the elective franchise of the colored voters of Washington county; that such citizens are denied the right to be selected as jurors to serve in the circuit court of the county; and that this denial to them of the right to equal protection and benefits of the laws of the state of Mississippi on account of their color and race, resulting from the exercise of the discretion partial to the white citizens, is in accordance with the purpose and intent of the framers of the present constitution of said state. . . .'

It will be observed that there is nothing direct and definite in this allegation either as to means or time as affecting the proceedings against the accused. There is no charge against the officers to whom is submitted the selection of grand or petit jurors, or those who procure the lists of the jurors. There is an allegation of the purpose of the convention to disfranchise citizens of the colored race; but with this we have no concern, unless the purpose is executed by the constitution or laws or by those who administer them. If it is done in the latter way, how or by what means should be sworn. We gather from the statements of the motion that certain officers are invested with discretion in making up lists of electors, and that this discretion can be and has been exercised against the colored race, and from these lists jurors are selected. The supreme court of Mississippi, however, decided, in a case presenting the same questions as the one at bar, 'that jurors are not selected from or with reference to any lists furnished by such election officers.' Dixo v. Mississippi (Nov. 9, 1896) 20 South. 839.

We do not think that this case is brought within the ruling in Yick Wo v. Hopkins. . . .

. . . Though the law itself be fair on its face and impartial in appearance, yet, if it is applied and administered by public authority with an evil eye and an unequal hand, so as practically to make unjust and illegal discriminations between persons in similar circumstances, material to their rights, the denial of equal justice is still within the prohibition of the constitution. . . .

This comment is not applicable to the constitution of Mississippi and its statutes. They do not on their face discriminate between the races, and it has not been shown that their actual administration was evil; only that evil was possible under them.

It follows, therefore, that the judgment must be affirmed.

Giles v. Harris, Decided April 27, 1903

Five years after the decision in Williams v. Mississippi, *the last test of the disenfranchising constitutions of the former Confederacy, this one from Alabama, came before the Court. In* Giles v. Harris *(189 U.S. 475), the plaintiff, Jackson W. Giles, sought to have the Court require that the state register him and thousands of other African Africans to vote, claiming that several provisions in the Alabama state constitution* (see Document 10) *combined to prevent them from being able to register.*
The decision for the Court came to hinge on whether the Court had any business providing relief to the plaintiff. In the decision for the Court, Justice Oliver Wendell Holmes said that the Court could not intervene for two reasons. First, if there really was a conspiracy—Holmes had no trouble using the word—to deprive black voters of their votes, then helping one individual would not quell the conspiracy. It would instead make the Court a party to the administration of the conspiracy—something the Court could not do. Yet this was an odd stance: the Court is bound to hear only cases and controversies involving people, and it always rules *for or against a person or persons. All of the other justices ignored this difficulty in Holmes's reasoning. Instead they reframed the issue by pointing out that relief to an individual was proper under circuit court jurisdiction. That stance of course really did not challenge Holmes's claim. The second reason that Holmes announced for denying relief was stronger in a way, but was reminiscent of the rulings of Pontius Pilate. Holmes went on to say that broad racial conspiracies are fundamentally political phenomena and can only be met through executive or legislative action, as if to say, "It's not our job to take care of the Constitution when it is in really deep trouble."*

JACKSON W. GILES, Appt.,
v.
E. JEFF HARRIS, William A. Gunter, Jr., and
Charles B. Teasley, Board of Registrars of
Montgomery County, Alabama.
No. 493.
Submitted February 24, 1903.
Decided April 27, 1903.

Mr. Justice Holmes delivered the opinion of the court:

This is a bill in equity brought by the court: behalf of more than five thousand negroes, citizens of the county of Montgomery, Alabama, similarly situated and circumstanced as himself, against the board of registrars of that county. The prayer of the bill is in substance that the defendants may be required to enroll upon the voting lists the name of the plaintiff and of all other qualified members of his race who applied for registration before August 1, 1902, and were refused, and that certain sections of the Constitution of Alabama, viz., 180, 181, 183, 184, 185, 186, 187, and 188 of article 8, may be declared contrary to the 14th and 15th Amendments of the Constitution of the United States, and void.

The allegations of the bill may be summed up as follows: The plaintiff is subject to none of the disqualifications set forth in the Constitution of Alabama and is entitled to vote, entitled, as the bill plainly means, under the Constitution as it is. He applied in March, 1902, for registration as a voter, and was refused arbitrarily on the ground of his color, together with large numbers of other duly qualified negroes, while all white men were registered. The same thing was done all over the state. Under 187 of article 8 of the Alabama Constitution, persons registered before January 1, 1903, remain electors for life unless they become disqualified by certain crimes, etc., while after that date severer tests come into play which would exclude, perhaps, a large part of the black race. Therefore by the refusal the plaintiff and the other negroes excluded were deprived, not only of their vote at an election which has taken place since the bill was filed, but of the permanent advantage incident to registration before 1903. The white men generally are registered for good under the easy test, and the black men are likely to be kept out in the future as in the past. This refusal to register the blacks was part of a general scheme to disfranchise them, to which the defendants and the state itself, according to the bill, were parties. The defendants accepted their office for the purpose of carrying out the scheme. The part taken by the state, that is, by the white population which framed the Constitution, consisted in shaping that instrument so as to give opportunity and effect to the wholesale fraud which has been practiced. . . .

It seems to us impossible to grant the equitable relief which is asked. . . .

The difficulties which we cannot overcome are two, and the first is this: The plaintiff alleges that the whole registration scheme of the Alabama Constitution is a fraud upon the Constitution of the United States, and asks us to declare it void. But, of course, he could not maintain a bill for a mere declaration in the air. He does not try to do so, but asks to be registered as a party qualified under the void instrument. If, then, we accept the conclusion which it is the chief purpose of the bill to maintain, how can we make the court a party to the unlawful scheme by accepting it and adding another voter to its fraudulent lists? If a white man came here on the same general allegations, admitting his sympathy with the plan, but alleging some special prejudice that had kept him off the list, we hardly should think it necessary to meet him with a reasoned answer. But the relief cannot be varied because we think that in the future the particular plaintiff is likely to try to overthrow the scheme. If we accept the plaintiff's allegations for the purposes of his case, he cannot complain. We must accept or reject them. It is impossible simply to shut our eyes, put the plaintiff on the lists, be they honest or fraudulent, and leave the determination of the fundamental question for the future. If we have an opinion that the bill is right on its face, or if we are undecided, we are not at liberty to assume it to be wrong for the purposes of decision. It seems to us that unless we are prepared to say that it is wrong, that all its principal allegations are immaterial, and that the registration plan of the Alabama Constitution is valid, we cannot order the plaintiff's name to be

registered. It is not an answer to say that if all the blacks who are qualified according to the letter of the instrument were registered, the fraud would be cured. In the first place, there is no probability that any way now is open by which more than a few could be registered; but, if all could be, the difficulty would not be overcome. If the sections of the Constitution concerning registration were illegal in their inception, it would be a new doctrine in constitutional law that the original invalidity could be cured by an administration which defeated their intent. . . .

The other difficulty is of a different sort, and strikingly reinforces the argument that equity cannot undertake now, any more than it has in the past, to enforce political rights, and also the suggestion that state constitutions were not left unmentioned in 1979 by accident. In determining whether a court of equity can take jurisdiction, one of the first questions is what it can do to enforce any order that it may make. This is alleged to be the conspiracy of a state, although the state is not and could not be made a party to the bill. . . . The circuit court has no constitutional power to control its action by any direct means. And if we leave the state out of consideration, the court has as little practical power to deal with the people of the state in a body. The bill imports that the great mass of the white population intends to keep the blacks from voting. To meet such an intent something more than ordering the plaintiff's name to be inscribed upon the lists of 1902 will be needed. If the conspiracy and the intent exist, a name on a piece of paper will not defeat them. Unless we are prepared to supervise the voting in that state by officers of the court, it seems to us that all that the plaintiff could get from equity would be an empty form. Apart from damages to the individual, relief from a great political wrong, if done, as alleged, by the people of a state and the state itself, must be given by them or by the legislative and political department of the government of the United States.

Decree affirmed.

James v. Bowman, Decided May 4, 1903

In the same year that the Court handed down Giles v. Harris, *the Court also handed down* James v. Bowman *(190 U.S. 127), which effectively overturned* Ex parte Yarbrough *(1884). In* Yarbrough, *the Court unanimously ruled that the United States could prosecute and imprison individuals who attacked black voters during an election campaign for the U.S. House or during the election itself* (see Document 7). *The Court also held that Congress had unlimited authority in regulating congressional elections and that such authority included authorizing the United States to directly prosecute individuals under the enforcement statutes of the Fifteenth Amendment. To that extent, in fact, there was a nationally created, and therefore enforceable, right to vote for African Americans.*

In James v. Bowman, *a Kentucky case that involved the use of bribery to intimidate black voters, all of these propositions were simply denied, even though the Court did not directly overrule the precedent in* Ex parte Yarbrough. *Thus the Court declined to do anything about extralegal attempts at disenfranchisement. By 1903, then, both the formal legal and extralegal subversion of the right to vote of African American citizens was not—so far as the Court was concerned—unconstitutional.*

A. D. JAMES, United States Marshal for the Western District of Kentucky, and The United States, Appts.,

v.

HENRY BOWMAN.

No. 213.

Argued March 16, 1903.

Decided May 4, 1903.

In December, 1900, an indictment was found by the United States district court for the district of Kentucky against the appellee, Henry Bowman, and one Harry Weaver, based upon 5507 of the Revised Statutes of the United States (U.S. Comp. Stat. 1901, p. 3712). The indictment charged, in substance, that certain 'men of African descent, colored men, negroes, and not white men,' being citizens of Kentucky and of the United States, were, by means of bribery, unlawfully and feloniously intimidated and prevented from exercising their lawful right of voting at a certain election held in the fifth congressional district of Kentucky on the 8th day of November, 1898, for the election of a representative in the Fifty-sixth Congress of the United States. No allegation is made that the bribery was because of the race, color, or previous condition of servitude of the men bribed. The appellee, Henry Bowman, having been arrested and held in default of

bail, sued out a writ of habeas corpus on the ground of the unconstitutionality of 5507. The district judge granted the writ, following reluctantly the decision of the circuit court of appeals for the sixth circuit, in Lackey v. United States. . . . From that judgment the government has taken this appeal.

Section 5507 is as follows:

'Sec. 5507. *Every person who prevents, hinders, controls, or intimidates another from exercising, or in exercising the right of suffrage, to whom that right is guaranteed by the Fifteenth Amendment to the Constitution of the United States, by means of bribery or threats of depriving such person of employment or occupation, or of ejecting such person from a rented house, lands, or other property, or by threats of refusing to renew leases or contracts for labor, or by threats of violence to himself or family, shall be punished as provided in the preceding section.*'

The 15th Amendment provides:

'Sec. 1. *The right of citizens of the United States to vote shall not be denied or abridged by the United States or by any state on account of race, color, or previous condition of servitude.*

'*Sec. 2. The Congress shall have power to enforce this article by appropriate legislation.*' . . .

Mr. Justice Brewer delivered the opinion of the court:

The single question presented for our consideration is whether 5507 can be upheld as a valid enactment, for, if not, the indictment must also fall, and the defendant was rightfully discharged. On its face the section purports to be an exercise of the power granted to Congress by the 15th Amendment, for it declares a punishment upon anyone who, by means of bribery, prevents another to whom the right of suffrage is guaranteed by such amendment from exercising that right. But that amendment relates solely to action 'by the United States or by any state,' and does not contemplate wrongful individual acts. . . .

. . . In United States v. Reese . . . , we said:

'*The 15th Amendment does not confer the right of suffrage upon anyone. It prevents the states, or the United States, however, from giving preference, in this particular, to one citizen of the United States over another on account of race, color, or previous condition of servitude. Before its adoption this could be done. It was as much within the power of state to exclude citizens of the United States from voting on account of race, etc., as it was on account of age, property, or education. Now it is not. If citizens of one race having certain qualifications are permitted by law to vote, those of another having the same qualifications must be. Previous to this amendment, there was no constitutional guaranty against this discrimination; now there is. It follows that the amendment has invested the citizens of the United States with a new constitutional right which is within the protecting power of Congress. That right is exemption from discrimination in the exercise of the elective franchise on account of race, color, or previous condition of servitude. This, under the express provisions of the 2d section of the Amendment, Congress may enforce by 'appropriate legislation.*"

In passing it may be noticed that this indictment charges no wrong done by the state of Kentucky, or by anyone acting under its authority. The matter complained of was purely as individual act of the defendant. Nor is it charged that the bribery was on account of race, color, or previous condition of servitude. True, the parties who were bribed were alleged to be 'men of African descent, colored men, negroes, and not white men,' and again, that they were 'persons to whom the right of suffrage and the right to vote was then and there guaranteed by the 15th Amendment to the Constitution of the United States.' But this merely describes the parties wronged as within the classes named in the amendment. They were not bribed because they were colored men, but because they were voters. No discrimination on account of race, color, or previous condition of servitude is charged.

. . . [A] statute which purports to punish purely individual action cannot be sustained as an appropriate exercise of the power conferred by the 15th Amendment upon Congress to prevent action by the state through some one or more of its official representatives, and that an indictment which charges no discrimination on account of race, color, or previous condition of servitude is likewise destitute of support by such amendment.

But the contention most earnestly pressed is that Congress has ample power in respect to elections of representative in Congress; that the election which was held, and at which this bribery took place, was such an election; and that therefore under such general power this statute and this indictment can be sustained. The difficulty with this contention is that Congress has not by this section acted in the exercise of such power. It is not legislation in respect to elections of Federal officers, but is leveled at all elections, state or Federal, and it does not purport to punish bribery of any voter, but simply of those named in the 15th Amendment. On its face it is clearly an attempt to exercise power supposed to be conferred by the 15th Amendment in respect to all elections, and not in pursuance of the general control by Congress over particular elections. To change this statute, enacted to punish bribery of persons named in the 15th Amendment at all elections, to a statute punishing bribery of any voter at certain elections would be in effect judicial legislation. It would be wresting the statute from the purpose with which it was enacted and making it serve another purpose. . . .

. . . We are fully sensible of the great wrong which results from bribery at elections, and do not question the power of Congress to punish such offenses when committed in respect to the election of Federal officials. At the same time it is all-important that a criminal statute should define clearly the offense which it purports to punish, and that when so defined it should be within the limits of the power of the legislative body enacting it. Congress has no power to punish

bribery at all elections. The limits of its power are in respect to elections in which the nation is directly interested, or in which some mandate of the national Constitution is disobeyed; and courts are not at liberty to take a criminal statute, broad and comprehensive in its terms and in these terms beyond the power of Congress, and change it to fit some particular transaction which Congress might have legislated for if it had seen fit.

The judgment of the District Court is affirmed.

Sources: Findlaw, *Williams v. Mississippi*, 170 U.S. 213 (1898), http://caselaw.lp.findlaw.com/cgi-bin/getcase.pl?court=us&vol=170&invol=213; *Giles v. Harris*, 189 U.S. 475 (1903), http://caselaw.lp.findlaw.com/scripts/getcase.pl?court=us&vol=189&invol=475; *James v. Bowman*, 190 U.S. 127 (1903), http://caselaw.lp.findlaw.com/scripts/getcase.pl?navby=search&court=US&case=/us/190/127.html.

12   Inaugural Address of President William Howard Taft, March 4, 1909

William Howard Taft's Republican predecessors—William McKinley and Theodore Roosevelt—made it clear that they would do nothing to stop black disenfranchisement and, furthermore, that they would discourage a wing of the Republican Party from fulfilling its commitment to enforcing Section 2 of the Fourteenth Amendment. But Taft differed greatly in that he announced an acceptance of disenfranchisement on a highly formal, public, and constitutional occasion—the inaugural address.

My Fellow-Citizens: . . .

The office of an inaugural address is to give a summary outline of the main policies of the new administration, so far as they can be anticipated. . . .

I look forward with hope to increasing the already good feeling between the South and the other sections of the country. My chief purpose is not to effect a change in the electoral vote of the Southern States. That is a secondary consideration. What I look forward to is an increase in the tolerance of political views of all kinds and their advocacy throughout the South, and the existence

of a respectable political opposition in every State; even more than this, to an increased feeling on the part of all the people in the South that this Government is their Government, and that its officers in their states are their officers.

The consideration of this question can not, however, be complete and full without reference to the negro race, its progress and its present condition. The thirteenth amendment secured them freedom; the fourteenth amendment due process of law, protection of property, and the pursuit of happiness; and the fifteenth amendment attempted to secure the negro against any deprivation of the privilege to vote because he was a negro. The thirteenth and fourteenth amendments have been generally enforced and have secured the objects for which they are intended. While the fifteenth amendment has not been generally observed in the past, it ought to be observed, and the tendency of Southern legislation today is toward the enactment of electoral qualifications which shall square with that amendment. Of course, the mere adoption of a constitutional law is only one step in the right direction. It must be fairly and justly enforced as well. In time both will come. Hence it is clear to all that the domination of an ignorant, irresponsible element can be prevented by constitutional laws which shall exclude from voting both negroes and whites not having education or other qualifications thought to be necessary for a proper electorate. The danger of the control of an ignorant electorate has therefore passed. With this change, the interest which many of the Southern white citizens take in the welfare of the negroes has increased. The colored men must base their hope on the results of their own industry, self-restraint, thrift, and business success, as well as upon the aid and comfort and sympathy which they may receive from their white neighbors of the South.

There was a time when Northerners who sympathized with the negro in his necessary struggle for better conditions sought to give him the suffrage as a protection to enforce its exercise against the prevailing sentiment of the South. The movement proved to be a failure. What remains is the fifteenth amendment to the Constitution and the right to have statutes of States specifying qualifications for electors subjected to the test of compliance with that amendment. This is a great protection to the negro. It never will be repealed, and it never ought to be repealed. If it had not passed, it might be difficult now to adopt it; but with it in our fundamental law, the policy of Southern legislation must and will tend to obey it, and so long as the statutes of the States meet the test of this amendment and are not otherwise in conflict with the Constitution and laws of the United States, it is not the disposition or within the province of the Federal Government to interfere with the regulation by Southern States of their domestic affairs. There is in the South a stronger feeling than ever among the intelligent well-to-do, and influential element in favor of the industrial education of the negro and the encouragement of the race to make themselves useful members of the community. The progress which the negro has made in the last fifty years, from slavery, when its statistics are reviewed, is marvelous, and it furnishes every reason to hope that in the next twenty-five years a still greater improvement in his condition as a productive member of society, on the farm, and in the shop, and in other occupations may come.

The negroes are now Americans. Their ancestors came here years ago against their will, and this is their only country and their only flag. They have shown themselves anxious to live for it and to die for it. Encountering the race feeling against them, subjected at times to cruel injustice growing out of it, they may well have our profound sympathy and aid in the struggle they are making. We are charged with the sacred duty of making their path as smooth and easy as we can. Any recognition of their distinguished men, any appointment to office from among their number, is properly taken as an encouragement and an appreciation of their progress, and this just policy should be pursued when suitable occasion offers.

But it may well admit of doubt whether, in the case of any race, an appointment of one of their number to a local office in a community in which the race feeling is so widespread and acute as to interfere with the ease and facility with which the local government business can be done by the appointee is of sufficient benefit by way of encouragement to the race to outweigh the recurrence and increase of race feeling which such an appointment is likely to engender. Therefore the Executive, in recognizing the negro race by appointments, must exercise a careful discretion not thereby to do it more harm than good. On the other hand, we must be careful not to encourage the mere pretense of race feeling manufactured in the interest of individual political ambition.

Personally, I have not the slightest race prejudice or feeling, and recognition of its existence only awakens in my heart a deeper sympathy for those who have to bear it or suffer from it, and I question the wisdom of a policy which is likely to increase it. Meantime, if nothing is done to prevent it, a better feeling between the negroes and the whites in the South will continue to grow, and more and more of the white people will come to realize that the future of the South is to be much benefited by the industrial and intellectual progress of the negro. The exercise of political franchises by those of this race who are intelligent and well to do will be acquiesced in, and the right to vote will be withheld only from the ignorant and irresponsible of both races. . . .

Source: "Inaugural Address of William Howard Taft," March 4, 1909, Avalon Project at Yale Law School, http://www.yale.edu/lawweb/avalon/presiden/inaug/taft.htm.

III. Restoring Voting Rights

13   *Guinn v. United States,* Decided June 21, 1915

Oklahoma entered the Union in 1907. Article 1, Section 6, of its constitution read: "The State shall never enact any law restricting or abridging the right of suffrage on account of race, color or previous condition of servitude." Apparently, this boilerplate was meant to ease Oklahoma's entry into the Union. Yet advocates of white supremacy soon used the state constitution's initiative and referendum procedures to secure a vote in the August 10, 1910, party primary elections on a literacy test aimed at black voters. To vote against the proposal, a voter had to black out the phrase "for the amendment" printed on the ballot in small lettering. The new amendment contained an escape clause for illiterate and semiliterate white men, known colloquially as a "grandfather clause"—reproduced here in the Supreme Court's opinion in Guinn v. United States *(238 U.S. 347). Essentially, the clause provided a birth date standard that allowed any man to register to vote if he would have been eligible to do so in 1867, a standard that only white men could satisfy.*

The Department of Justice, intervened by criminally prosecuting two local elections officials in Oklahoma for violating the Fifteenth Amendment and two Reconstruction-era enforcement provisions that remained on the books during the administration of general elections in the state in 1910. Those officials acted under authority of the state constitution's "grandfather clause," which restricted the right to vote to whites, thereby openly contradicting the U.S. Constitution. The prosecution was itself a remarkable event. Even more remarkable, the new administration of President Woodrow Wilson concluded the prosecution in good faith, even though Wilson was at that time busy purging senior black federal employees and establishing an elaborate system of workplace racial segregation in federal agencies. Most remarkable, the Supreme Court agreed with the United States in reviewing a certification from the federal trial. In the course of the opinion for the Court in Guinn v. United States, *Chief Justice Edward D. White forcefully rejected the grandfather clause as a transparent ruse that would effectively destroy the Fifteenth Amendment altogether if the United States accepted the states' rights arguments that the lawyers for the elections officials offered.*

At the time, newspapers all over the country pointed out that the decision did not disturb white supremacy. In fact, the decision stated that literacy tests were proper. Just to ensure that there was no effect in Oklahoma, the state legislature passed a statute that automatically registered all voters eligible to vote in the 1914 midterm election. Everyone else had a brief period in which to register in the spring of 1916. Nevertheless, the National Association for the Advancement of Colored People

(NAACP), which participated in the case as amicus curiae (friend of the court) was encouraged by the decision. For an organization just getting off the ground, it was important to have some sort of victory against disenfranchisement, however preliminary.

FRANK GUINN and J. J. Beal
v.
UNITED STATES.
No. 96.
Argued October 17, 1913.
Decided June 21, 1915.

. . .

Mr. Chief Justice White delivered the opinion of the court:

This case is before us on a certificate drawn by the court below as the basis of . . . questions which are submitted for our solution in order to enable the court correctly to decide issues in a case which it has under consideration. Those issues arose from an indictment and conviction of certain election officers of the state of Oklahoma (the plaintiffs in error) of the crime of having conspired unlawfully, wilfully, and fraudulently to deprive certain negro citizens, on account of their race and color, of a right to vote at a general election held in that state in 1910, they being entitled to vote under the state law, and which right was secured to them by the 15th Amendment to the Constitution of the United States. The prosecution was directly concerned with 5508, Revised Statutes, now 19 of the Penal Code [35 Stat. at L. 1092, chap. 321, Comp. Stat. 1913, 10183], which is as follows:

'If two or more persons conspire to injure, oppress, threaten, or intimidate any citizen in the free exercise or enjoyment of any right or privilege secured to him by the Constitution or laws of the United States, or because of his having so exercised the same; or if two or more persons go in disguise on the highway, or on the premises of another, with intent to prevent or hinder his free exercise or enjoyment of any right or privilege so secured, they shall be fined not more than five thousand dollars and imprisoned not more than ten years, and shall, moreover, be thereafter ineligible to any office, or place of honor, profit, or trust created by the Constitution or laws of the United States.' We concentrate and state from the certificate only matters which we deem essential to dispose of the questions asked.

Suffrage in Oklahoma was regulated by 4a, article 3, of the Constitution under which the state was admitted into the Union. Shortly after the admission there was submitted an amendment to the Constitution making a radical change in that article, which was adopted prior to November 8, 1910. At an election for members of Congress which followed the adoption of this amendment, certain election officers, in enforcing its provisions, refused to allow certain negro citizens to vote who were clearly entitled to vote under the provision of the Constitution under which the state was admitted; that is, before the amendment; and who, it is equally clear, were not entitled to vote under the provision of the suffrage amendment if that amendment governed. The persons so excluded based their claim of right to vote upon the original Constitution and upon the assertion that the suffrage amendment was void because in conflict with the prohibitions of the 15th Amendment, and therefore afforded no basis for denying them the right guaranteed and protected by that Amendment. And upon the assumption that this claim was justified and that the election officers had violated the 15th Amendment in denying the right to vote, this prosecution, as we have said, was commenced. At the trial the court instructed that by the 15th Amendment the states were prohibited from discriminating as to suffrage because of race, color, or previous condition of servitude, and that Congress, in pursuance of the authority which was conferred upon it by the very terms of the Amendment, to enforce its provisions had enacted the following (Rev. Stat. 2004, Comp. Stat. 1913, 3966):

'All citizens of the United States who are otherwise qualified by law to vote at any election by the people in any state, territory, district, [. . .] municipality, or other territorial subdivision, shall be entitled and allowed to vote at all such elections without distinction of race, color, or previous condition of servitude; any constitution, law, custom, or usage, or regulation of any state or territory, or by or under its authority, to the contrary notwithstanding.'

. . . [T]he United States . . . says state power to provide for suffrage is not disputed, although, of course, the authority of the 15th Amendment and the limit on that power which it imposes is insisted upon. Hence, no assertion denying the right of a state to exert judgment and discretion in fixing the qualification of suffrage is advanced, and no right to question the motive of the state in establishing a standard as to such subjects under such circumstances, or to review or supervise the same, is relied upon, and no power to destroy an otherwise valid exertion of authority upon the mere ultimate operation of the power exercised is asserted. And applying these principles to the very case in hand, the argument of the government in substance says: No question is raised by the government concerning the validity of the literacy test provided for in the amendment under consideration as an independent standard since the conclusion is plain that that test rests on the exercise of state judgment, and therefore cannot be here assailed either by disregarding the state's power to judge on the subject, or by testing its motive in enacting the provision. The real question involved, so the argument of the government insists, is the repugnancy of the standard which the amendment makes, based upon the conditions existing on January 1st, 1866, because on its face and inherently considering the substance of things, that standard is a mere denial of the restrictions imposed by the prohibitions of the 15th Amendment, and by necessary result re-creates and perpetuates the very conditions which the Amendment was intended to destroy. . . .

. . . Let us consider these subjects under separate headings.

1. The operation and effect of the 15th Amendment. This is its text:

'Section 1. The right of citizens of the United States to vote shall not be denied or abridged by the United States or by any state on account of race, color, or previous condition of servitude.

'Section 2. The Congress shall have power to enforce this article by appropriate legislation.'

(a) Beyond doubt the Amendment does not take away from the state governments in a general sense the power over suffrage which has belonged to those governments from the beginning, and without the possession of which power the whole fabric upon which the division of state and national authority under the Constitution and the organization of both governments rest would be without support, and both the authority of the nation and the state would fall to the ground. In fact, the very command of the Amendment recognizes the possession of the general power by the state, since the Amendment seeks to regulate its exercise as to the particular subject with which it deals.

(b) But it is equally beyond the possibility of question that the Amendment in express terms restricts the power of the United States or the states to abridge or deny the right of a citizen of the United States to vote on account of race, color, or previous condition of servitude. The restriction is coincident with the power and prevents its exertion in disregard to the command of the Amendment. But while this is true, it is true also that the Amendment does not change, modify, or deprive the states of their full power as to suffrage except, of course, as to the subject with which the Amendment deals and to the extent that obedience to its command is necessary. Thus the authority over suffrage which the states possess and the limitation which the Amendment imposes are co-ordinate and one may not destroy the other without bringing about the destruction of both.

(c) While in the true sense, therefore, the Amendment gives no right of suffrage, it was long ago recognized that in operation its prohibition might measurably have that effect; that is to say, that as the command of the Amendment was self-executing and reached without legislative action the conditions of discrimination against which it was aimed, the result might arise that, as a consequence of the striking down of a discrimination clause, a right of suffrage would be enjoyed by reason of the generic character of the provision which would remain after the discrimination was stricken out. Ex parte Yarbrough, . . . A familiar illustration of this doctrine resulted from the effect of the adoption of the Amendment on state Constitutions in which, at the time of the adoption of the Amendment, the right of suffrage was conferred on all white male citizens, since by the inherent power of the Amendment the word 'white' disappeared and therefore all male citizens, without discrimination on account of race, color, or previous condition of servitude, came under the generic grant of suffrage made by the state.

With these principles before us how can there be room for any serious dispute concerning the repugnancy of the standard based upon January 1, 1866 (a date which preceded the adoption of the 15th Amendment), if the suffrage provision fixing that standard is susceptible of the significance which the government attributes to it? Indeed, there seems no escape from the conclusion that to hold that there was even possibility for dispute on the subject would be but to declare that the 15th Amendment not only had not the self-executing power which it has been recognized to have from the beginning, but that its provisions were wholly inoperative. . . .

2. The standard of January 1, 1866, fixed in the suffrage amendment and its significance.

The inquiry, of course, here is, Does the amendment as to the particular standard which this heading embraces involve the mere refusal to comply with the commands of the 15th Amendment as previously stated? This leads us, for the purpose of the analysis, to recur to the text of the suffrage amendment. Its opening sentence fixes the literacy standard which is all inclusive, since it is general in its expression and contains no word of discrimination on account of race or color or any other reason. This, however, is immediately followed by the provisions creating the standard based upon the condition existing on January 1, 1866, and carving out those coming under that standard from the inclusion in the literacy test which would have controlled them but for the exclusion thus expressly provided for. The provision is this:

'But no person who was, on January 1st, 1866, or at any time prior thereto, entitled to vote under any form of government, or who at that time resided in some foreign nation, and no lineal descendant of such person, shall be denied that right to register and vote because of his inability to so read and write sections of such Constitution.'

We have difficulty in finding words to more clearly demonstrate the conviction we entertain that this standard has the characteristics which the government attributes to it than does the mere statement of the text. It is true it contains no express words of an exclusion from the standard which it establishes of any person on account of race, color, or previous condition of servitude, prohibited by the 15th Amendment, but the standard itself inherently brings that result into existence since it is based purely upon a period of time before the enactment of the 15th Amendment, and makes that period the controlling and dominant test of the right of suffrage. In other words, we seek in vain for any ground which would sustain any other interpretation but that the provision, recurring to the conditions existing before the 15th Amendment was adopted and the continuance of which the 15th Amendment prohibited, proposed by in substance and effect lifting those conditions over to a period of time after the Amendment, to make them the basis of the right to suffrage conferred in direct and positive disregard of the 15th Amendment. And the same result, we are of opinion, is demonstrated by considering whether it is possible to discover any basis of reason for the standard thus fixed other than the purpose above stated. We say this because we are unable to discover how, unless the prohibitions of the 15th Amendment were considered, the slightest reason was afforded for basing the classification upon a period of time prior to the 15th Amendment. . . .

Mr. Justice McReynolds took no part in the consideration and decision of this case.

Source: Findlaw, *Guinn v. United States*, 238 U.S. 347 (1915), http://caselaw.lp.findlaw.com/scripts/getcase.pl?court=US&vol=238&invol=347.

14   Responding to the Nineteenth Amendment: "Negro Women in South Hasten to Register Names," *St. Louis Post-Dispatch,* October 10, 1920

Throughout the former Confederacy, ratification of the Nineteenth Amendment was followed by the emergence of black voter registration drives for both men and women in advance of the 1920 general elections. These drives—which have never been studied adequately—appear to have been strongest in southern cities. A particularly forceful drive occurred in Richmond, Virginia, organized and financed in part by Margaret Lena Walker, the owner and president of a prosperous bank that survives to this day. The drives in Virginia appear to have been quite successful; otherwise, it would be hard to understand why Walker ran statewide in 1921 for superintendent of education on the "Lily Black" Republican ticket, accompanied by John Mitchell, a prominent Richmond banker and newspaper publisher, who ran for governor. Elsewhere in the South, the registration drives were often repressed by local officials.

NEGRO WOMEN IN SOUTH HASTEN TO REGISTER NAMES

––––––

Suffrage Ratification Upsets the Democratic Workers and There Is Now Talk of Race Issue Revival

––––––

Whites List Women to Prevent Mishap

––––––

Some Registrars Resign Their Posts Rather Than Enroll Negresses–Conditions Lively in Richmond, Va.

––––––

. . . The argument of Southern partisans against women suffrage to the effect that it would revive the Negro issues at the ballot box is proving to be well founded here. In the city of Richmond prominent Negroes are trying to register 8,500 of their women. It is insisted that these Negresses, many of whom are well educated and property owners, are entitled to the ballot and should not be deprived of it. . . .

Miss Adele Clark, an active member of the Equal Suffrage League of Virginia and head of the Citizenship Committee of that organization, told the *Post-Dispatch* correspondent that the women were being encouraged by Democrats and Republicans alike to register for the November election.

"The Negro women of this city are manifesting deep interest in the suffrage amendment," said Miss Clark.

"About 6,000 women, more than 5,000 of them whites, have qualified by paying the necessary tax, $1.50, and answering satisfactorily the questions of the Registrar. Up to last Saturday night from 700 to 8,000 [sic] colored women were listed. In the last mayoralty primary approximately 13,000 men voted. Estimating from that and the number of women already registered, I would say that the women will match the men in numbers. . . .

"The University of Virginia, William and Mary College, and other educational institutions are helping the women prepare for their new part in politics by conducting classes in citizenship. This work has been going on since early spring.

"Here is the process in Virginia: Each prospective woman voter must be assessed and pay (in advance for 1921) a tax of $1.50 before she can register. When she goes to the Registrar she presents her tax receipt, and is given a blank to fill out in her own hand, without the aid of anyone, giving her name, age, the date and place of her birth, her residence now, and two years proceeding, and stating whether or not she ever voted before. After this is done the Registrar then has a right,at his "discretion" to ask "any question" as to her qualifications as an elector."

Miss Clark did not say so, but the joker for the Negro woman is found in the "discretion" given the Registrar as to her qualifications. The way to the ballot box is rough and rugged if the Registrar is a partisan. He may ask the applicant to read, write and explain a section of the Constitution of the United States.

Source: "Negro Women in South Hasten to Register Names," *St. Louis Post-Dispatch*, October 10, 1920, in National Association for the Advancement of Colored People, *Disfranchisement of Colored Americans in the Presidential Election of 1920* (New York: NAACP, 1920), 18.

15   Letters to the NAACP about Voter Registration, 1936–1939

Although it is a little known fact, during the New Deal black voters in southern cities repeatedly mounted registration drives. They were small, but they laid the foundation for the rapid growth of the National Association for the Advancement of Colored People (NAACP) immediately after World War II in the wake of the Supreme Court case Smith v. Allwright *(see Document 16).*

The three letters that follow (exact transcriptions of the originals) were sent to the NAACP's national headquarters in New York in the 1930s by three African American men—a concerned citizen, a NAACP local branch president, and a representative of a civic club founded to register voters. The letters detail the efforts made and obstacles encountered in registering voters in the three southern states of North Carolina, Virginia, and Georgia.

Ulah, N.C.
Oct. 29, 1936

N.A.A.C.P.
68 Fifth Ave.
New York, N.Y.
Charles H. Houston Special Counsel

Dear Sir:

Just a line to say that we have been having a little trouble over colored people registering, and a few have registered in two town-ships of Randolph Co. N.C. And they are talking of not letting those few vote on election day.

I presented my-self for registration on Saturday Oct. 24 and was refused. The register claimed he did not under stand the Election Laws there fore we would have to go to Herman Cramford chairman of the election Board and get an O.K. slip, and he would be glad to put our names on the books. We objected to that and told him he was subject to enditement if he refused to register qualified people (colored or white) and he only laughed at us and made light of this orginization saying there was enough money on his side to buy the court. He is a very ignorant type of person and didn't know he had to take an oath to be a register. He said he hadn't been sworned in neither had he taken an oath for any thing. The books had been given him and he went to work.

After leaving the register we came back to Herman Cramford's office Chairman of the Election Board (Democratic) of Randolph Co. N.C.

And he after running Roscoe Strickland another colored man who had already registered (The first colored man to register in Randolph County) out of his office and cursing at him as he went he gave me a text and claimed I missed spelled some words and was not qualified to register.

I have been teaching school for 38 years in N.C. and a number of years in this county. But cattaracks are growing over my eyes and I can not see well enough to teach school now. I am getting a friend of mine to write this letter for me.

Another colored man, Oscar Ledwell, was refused after he showed old papers certifying that he was a lineal descendant of a man who registered and voted prior to January 1, 1867. And we are appealing to you for help. And we do hope that it will be possible to make an example out of this register as this is a very tight section of N.C. on colored people voting.

A lot of people are expecting this case to go to court and for that reason I have not been able to get the register's name. However He is "Register of Grant town-ship Randolph Co. N.C."

And Herman Cramford's address is Aheboro [Asheboro], N.C.

Hoping to hear from you at once, I am, Respectfully Yours

A. S. Spinks.

P.S. You will have to register your reply to me, otherwise it will be destroyed before it reaches me.

[Letterhead of the Petersburg, Virginia, branch of the National Association for the Advancement of Colored People]

[Stamped "Apr 26 1937"]

Mr. Thurgood Marshall
Assistant Special Counsel
N.A.A.C.P.
69 Fifth Avenue
New York, N.Y.

Dear Mr. Marshall,

In reply to your letter of April 9, 1937 I wish to give the following information which has been secured through Professor Luther P. Jackson who is a teacher of Government at Virginia State College, Ettrick, Virginia. Mr. Jackson has been very active in the matter of getting the Negroes to vote. He has made several studies of the whole problem.

1. Approximately 7,000 Negroes vote in the general elections in Virginia. Fully 75 per cent of these are urban voters.
2. Negroes participate in Democratic primaries all over the State with the possible exception of a very few counties on the South-Side.
3. Approximately 7,000 vote in the primary and general elections.
4. There is no discrimination whatever on the poll tax since both races are required to pay the tax. Here and there Negroes are discriminated against with respect to registration but this opposition is growing less and less. They have no trouble whatever in any of the cities of Virginia, none in the northern and western counties, and very little in the others. There is no concerted effort to prevent Negroes from registering in any county. For example, the refusal to allow a Negro to register is the stand taken by only one out of four or five registrars in a county. Frequently where there is opposition by a given registrar he can be scared into permitting an applicant to register. The threat of a suit often will bring them around.

The lack of opposition to registration in Virginia grows out of several court decisions on this question, including one important one in 1931. These decisions virtually invalidate the written law on this subject as one reads it in Virginia's constitution.

The hold back in Virginia, then, with respect to voting by Negroes is not the white people so much as it is the lethargy of the Negroes themselves. Some of them are handicapped by the old Republican tradition, others frankly say that "politics is the white folks' business". One of the greatest deterrents for white and black alike is the iron clad poll tax requirement of $1.50 payable six months prior to the general elections, and paid up three years prior to the year one expects to vote. For example in order to vote in 1937 in Virginia the tax must be paid for 1934, 1935, and 1936. Many Negroes lose all interest when they are confronted with $4.50 plus interest and penalty ($5.10) in order to vote six months in advance."

I hope the above information will be some value to the person who is making the survey.

Very truly yours,
[signed]
H. E. Fauntleroy, President
Petersburg Branch
N.A.A.C.P.
901 Wilcox St.
Petersburg, Virginia

[Letterhead of Young Men's Civic Club of Chatham County, Savannah, Georgia]

[Stamped "Mar 18 1939"]

My dear Sirs:

The Young Men Civic Club of this city was organized for the sole purpose of getting more Negroes to become registered voters in this city. There were only 600 registered Negroes out of 45,000 at the time of the club's inception; This was four months ago. Since we have been in operation, we have added some 400 individuals to the list of voters, but now we seemed to have reached a Stone Wall.

Little or no questions were asked of our applicants in the beginning, as we carried them up for registration. But after we had succeeded in placing the first 100 names on the book we found that the book would be closed quite often. Then as we moved in and out about the closed books and were successful in placing 200 more names, the requirement for registration of the applicants became more difficult. They started doubting the age of the applicants, and the registrar demanded such forms as birth certificates, insurance policies, and the old Family Bible. (Birth certificates have only been issued to Negroes about 17 years ago). However we worked through these difficulties until we crossed the 300 mark. Since this could not impede our anxiety, they decided to pull another trick. This was one found in the Georgia Code of Laws, which says who shall vote?

There are five qualifications which will entitle any American citizen residing in the county or state to become a registered voter. This was quite a surprise to us and our applicants had to be prepared to answer thse questions; hence we consulted the law books and familirized ourselves with these five qualifications, as well as drilling them into the minds of our applicants.

As we neared the 400 mark, the situation became more difficult. The qualifications became more exact, they wanted only birth certificates. However we found quite a few with certificates, but these in turn were not accepted, because they could not answer such questions as Who was the president of the U.S. in 1812? at the spur of the moment. Many questions referred back to the nineteenth century.

Our work has come to the point where many are called but few are chose. Please we ask sincerely, to write to us your experiences along these lines; or what has been your experiences in dealing with such matters in the South, especially Georgia. How did you combat such oppositions?

Whatever information you have to give us along these lines would be highly appreciated by this organization. We feel the you have a remedy for the above complaints.

Yours truly,

The Young Men Civic Club.

Source: NAACP Papers, Library of Congress.

16 *Smith v. Allwright*, Decided April 3, 1944

As the National Association for the Advancement of Colored People (NAACP) evolved, its leaders and members challenged the legal and institutional devices that kept black southerners from voting. One strategy was litigation aimed at challenging as racially discriminatory an institution called "the white primary."

The advantage for the NAACP of going after the white primary was its racially explicit nature. The earlier disenfranchising devices, such as the poll tax and the literacy test, targeted black and poor white voters, thereby helping to protect southern Democrats from Republican and third party populist competition. But these devices were not explicitly and textually discriminatory. Later, as levels of education and income rose for all southerners and the poll tax and literacy test became less effective, southern Democrats added one more barrier, the white primary. Because the earlier devices created a one party system in the southern states, this measure was particularly attractive for supporters of white supremacy.

But adding the white primary was a mistake. Like the Oklahoma grandfather clause, the "whites-only" nature of this rule was vulnerable to legal and constitutional challenge. Thus beginning in the early 1920s, the NAACP patiently set about mounting an attack on the white primary in the courts.

Even though victory often seemed unlikely, in the late 1930s and early 1940s a sympathetic Justice Department helped to set the stage for an NAACP victory in the courts by winning a vote fraud case, United States v. Classic (1941), that revolved around a U.S. House primary election in Louisiana. Through that case, the Justice Department established the principle that primary elections for national office could be subject to constitutional and federal regulation.

The NAACP now needed to show that primary elections could not exist without state legal support. If that effort succeeded, then the notion that white primaries were essentially private affairs would fly apart. The Court had accepted this notion in an earlier white primary case from Texas, Grovey v. Townsend (1935). But that was before the victory in Louisiana.

In Smith v. Allwright *(321 U.S. 649), the question before the Court was whether the Democratic Party of Texas and S. S. Allwright, a county official, had violated the Fifteenth Amendment rights of Lonnie Smith, who was denied the right to vote in the state's 1940 Democratic primary. In a bold strategy, the NAACP lawyers, led by Thurgood Marshall, later the Supreme Court's first African American justice, asked the Court to explicitly overrule* Grovey v. Townsend. *A vital element of this strategy—reflected in the opinion for the Court—was proving that the white primary was in no way a private operation. The Court announced that the United States could apply both the Fourteenth and Fifteenth Amendments to white primaries because state governments were officially in the business of running whites-only electoral systems. The lone dissenter in the 8–1 case was Justice Owen Roberts, who wrote the opinion for the Court in* Grovey.

SMITH

v.

ALLWRIGHT, Election Judge, et al.

No. 51.

Reargued Jan. 12, 1944.

Decided April 3, 1944.

. . .

Messrs. Thurgood Marshall, of Baltimore, Md., and William H. Hastie, of Washington, D.C., for petitioner.

Mr. George W. Barcus, of Austin, Tex., for Gerald C. Mann, Attorney General of Texas, as amicus curiae, by special leave of Court.

No. appearance for respondents.

Mr. Justice REED delivered the opinion of the Court.

This writ of certiorari brings here for review a claim for damages in the sum of $5,000 on the part of petitioner, a Negro citizen of the 48th precinct of Harris County, Texas, for the refusal of respondents, election and associate election judges respectively of that precinct, to give petitioner a ballot or to permit him to cast a ballot in the primary election of July 27, 1940, for the nomination of Democratic candidates for the United States Senate and House of Representatives, and Governor and other state officers. The refusal is alleged to have been solely because of the race and color of the proposed voter.

The actions of respondents are said to violate Sections 31 and 43 of Title 81 of the United States Code, 8 U.S.C.A. 31 and 43, in that petitioner was deprived of rights secured by Sections 2 and 4 of Article I2 and the Fourteenth, Fifteenth and Seventeenth Amendments to the United States Constitution. . . .

. . . The Democratic Party of Texas is held by the Supreme Court of that state to be a 'voluntary association,' Bell v. Hill, 123 Tex. 531, 534, 74 S.W.2d 113, protected by Section 27 of the Bill of Rights, Art. 1, Constitution of Texas, from interference by the state except that:

'In the interest of fair methods and a fair expression by their members of their preferences in the selection of their nominees, the State may regulate such elections by proper laws.' . . . That court stated further:

'Since the right to organize and maintain a political party is one guaranteed by the Bill of Rights of this state, it necessarily follows that every privilege essential or reasonably appropriate to the exercise of that right is likewise guaranteed, including, of course, the privilege of determining the policies of the party and its membership. Without the privilege of determining the policy of a political association and its membership, the right to organize such an association would be a mere mockery. We think these rights, that is, the right to determine the membership of a political party and to determine its policies, of necessity are to be exercised by the State Convention of such party, and cannot, under any circumstances, be conferred upon a state or governmental agency.' . . .

. . . The Fourteenth Amendment forbids a state from making or enforcing any law which abridges the privileges or immunities of citizens of the United States and the Fifteenth Amendment specif-

ically interdicts any denial or abridgement by a state of the right of citizens to vote on account of color. Respondents appeared in the District Court and the Circuit Court of Appeals and defended on the ground that the Democratic party of Texas is a voluntary organization with members banded together for the purpose of selecting individuals of the group representing the common political beliefs as candidates in the general election. As such a voluntary organization, it was claimed, the Democratic party is free to select its own membership and limit to whites participation in the party primary. Such action, the answer asserted, does not violate the Fourteenth, Fifteenth or Seventeenth Amendment as officers of government cannot be chosen at primaries and the Amendments are applicable only to general elections where governmental officers are actually elected. Primaries, it is said, are political party affairs, handled by party not governmental officers. . . .

The right of a Negro to vote in the Texas primary has been considered heretofore by this Court. . . .

. . . In Grovey v. Townsend, . . . , this Court had before it another suit for damages for the refusal in a primary of a county clerk, a Texas officer with only public functions to perform, to furnish petitioner, a Negro, an absentee ballot. The refusal was solely on the ground of race. . . . It was decided that the determination by the state convention of the membership of the Democratic party made a significant change from a determination by the Executive Committee. The former was party action, voluntary in character. The latter . . . was action by authority of the State. The managers of the primary election were therefore declared not to be state officials in such sense that their action was state action. A state convention of a party was said not to be an organ of the state. This Court went on to announce that to deny a vote in a primary was a mere refusal of party membership with which 'the state need have no concern,' . . . , while for a state to deny a vote in a general election on the ground of race or color violated the Constitution. Consequently, there was found no ground for holding that the county clerk's refusal of a ballot because of racial ineligibility for party membership denied the petitioner any right under the Fourteenth or Fifteenth Amendments.

Since Grovey v. Townsend and prior to the present suit, no case from Texas involving primary elections has been before this Court. We did decide, however, United States v. Classic. . . . We there held that Section 4 of Article I of the Constitution authorized Congress to regulate primary as well as general elections, . . . , 'where the primary is by law made an integral part of the election machinery.' . . . Consequently, in the Classic case, we upheld the applicability to frauds in a Louisiana primary of 19 and 20 of the Criminal Code, 18 U.S.C.A. 51, 52. Thereby corrupt acts of election officers were subjected to Congressional sanctions because that body had power to protect rights of Federal suffrage secured by the Constitution in primary as in general elections. . . . This decision depended, too, on the determination that under the Louisiana statutes the primary was a part of the procedure for choice of Federal officials. By this decision the doubt as to whether or not such primaries were a part of 'elections' subject to Federal control, which had remained unanswered since Newberry v. United States, . . . , was erased. . . . The fusing by the Classic case of the primary and general elections into a single instrumentality for choice of officers has a definite bearing on the permissibility under the Constitution of excluding Negroes from primaries. This is not to say that the Classic case cuts directly into the rationale of Grovey v. Townsend. This latter case was not mentioned in the opinion. Classic bears upon Grovey v. Townsend not because exclusion of Negroes from primaries is any more or less state action by reason of the unitary character of the electoral process but because the recognition of the place of the primary in the electoral scheme makes clear that state delegation to a party of the power to fix the qualifications of primary elections is delegation of a state function that may make the party's action the action of the

state. When Grovey v. Townsend was written, the Court looked upon the denial of a vote in a primary as a mere refusal by a party of party membership. . . . As the Louisiana statutes for holding primaries are similar to those of Texas, our ruling in Classic as to the unitary character of the electoral process calls for a reexamination as to whether or not the exclusion of Negroes from a Texas party primary was state action.

The statutes of Texas relating to primaries and the resolution of the Democratic party of Texas extending the privileges of membership to white citizens only are the same in substance and effect today as they were when Grovey v. Townsend was decided by a unanimous Court. The question as to whether the exclusionary action of the party was the action of the State persists as the determinative factor. . . .

It may now be taken as a postulate that the right to vote in such a primary for the nomination of candidates without discrimination by the State, like the right to vote in a general election, is a right secured by the Constitution. . . . By the terms of the Fifteenth Amendment that right may not be abridged by any state on account of race. Under our Constitution the great privilege of the ballot may not be denied a man by the State because of his color.

We are thus brought to an examination of the qualifications for Democratic primary electors in Texas, to determine whether state action or private action has excluded Negroes from participation. . . . Texas requires electors in a primary to pay a poll tax. Every person who does so pay and who has the qualifications of age and residence is an acceptable voter for the primary. Art. 2955. . . . Texas requires by the law the election of the county officers of a party. . . . Statutes provide for the election by the voters of precinct delegates to the county convention of a party and the selection of delegates to the district and state conventions by the county convention. . . . Texas thus directs the selection of all party officers.

Primary elections are conducted by the party under state statutory authority. . . .

The state courts are given exclusive original jurisdiction of contested elections and of mandamus proceedings to compel party officers to perform their statutory duties.

We think that this statutory system for the selection of party nominees for inclusion on the general election ballot makes the party which is required to follow these legislative directions an agency of the state in so far as it determines the participants in a primary election. The party takes its character as a state agency from the duties imposed upon it by state statutes; the duties do not become matters of private law because they are performed by a political party. The plan of the Texas primary follows substantially that of Louisiana, with the exception that in Louisiana the state pays the cost of the primary while Texas assesses the cost against candidates. In numerous instances, the Texas statutes fix or limit the fees to be charged. Whether paid directly by the state or through state requirements, it is state action which compels. When primaries become a part of the machinery for choosing officials, state and national, as they have here, the same tests to determine the character of discrimination or abridgement should be applied to the primary as are applied to the general election. If the state requires a certain electoral procedure, prescribes a general election ballot made up of party nominees so chosen and limits the choice of the electorate in general elections for state offices, practically speaking, to those whose names appear on such a ballot, it endorses, adopts and enforces the discrimination against Negroes, practiced by a party entrusted by Texas law with the determination of the qualifications of participants in the primary. This is state action within the meaning of the Fifteenth Amendment. Guinn v. United States. . . .

The United States is a constitutional democracy. Its organic law grants to all citizens a right to participate in the choice of elected officials without restriction by any state because of race. This grant to the people of the opportunity for choice is not to be nullified by a state through casting its electoral process in a form which permits a private organization to practice racial discrimination in the election. Constitutional rights would be of little value if they could be thus indirectly denied. . . .

. . . In reaching this conclusion we are not unmindful of the desirability of continuity of decision in constitutional questions. However, when convinced of former error, this Court has never felt constrained to follow precedent. In constitutional questions, where correction depends upon amendment and not upon legislative action this Court throughout its history has freely exercised its power to reexamine the basis of its constitutional decisions. This has long been accepted practice, and this practice has continued to this day. This is particularly true when the decision believed erroneous is the application of a constitutional principle rather than an interpretation of the Constitution to extract the principle itself. Here we are applying, contrary to the recent decision in Grovey v. Townsend, the well established principle of the Fifteenth Amendment, forbidding the abridgement by a state of a citizen's right to vote. Grovey v. Townsend is overruled.

Source: Findlaw, *Smith v. Allwright,* 321 U.S. 649 (1944), http://caselaw.lp.findlaw.com/scripts/getcase.pl?court=us&vol=321&invol=649.

17   *To Secure These Rights: The Report of the President's Committee on Civil Rights, October 29, 1947*

Soon after the Supreme Court handed down its decision in Smith v. Allwright *in 1944, President Harry S. Truman joined the struggle for civil rights and voting rights, thus securing a place for these issues on the national agenda. Among his actions was the use of an executive order to create a special committee to report to him on the issue. In using the executive order, Truman implicitly followed in the footsteps of President Abraham Lincoln—the Emancipation Proclamation was, after all, an executive order. The committee's 178-page report contained policy proposals that came to fruition in the 1957 and 1960 Civil Rights Acts, during the second administration of President Dwight D. Eisenhower.*

Interestingly, the committee chose to ignore disenfranchisement and instead pictured a steady linear struggle for full democracy when it referred to "steady progress toward the goal of universal suffrage which has marked the years between 1789 and the present." In announcing this claim, which again ignored disenfranchisement, the committee contributed to a view of America's struggles over voting rights that is remarkably widespread and is taught, probably, in most primary and secondary schools.

Executive Order 9808 Establishing the President's Committee on Civil Rights

WHEREAS the preservation of civil rights guaranteed by the Constitution is essential to domestic tranquility, national security, the general welfare, and the continued existence of our free institutions; and

WHEREAS the action of individuals who take the law into their own hands and inflict summary punishment and wreak personal vengeance is subversive of our democratic system of law enforcement and public criminal justice, and gravely threatens our form of government; and

WHEREAS it is essential that all possible steps be taken to safeguard our civil rights:

N[esc]ow, therefore, by virtue of the authority vested in me as the President of the United States by the Constitution and the statutes of the United States, it is hereby ordered as follows:

1. There is hereby created a committee to be known as the President's Committee on Civil Rights, which shall be composed of the following-named members, who shall serve without compensation:

Mr. C. E. Wilson, chairman; Mrs. Sadie T. Alexander, Mr. James B. Carey, Mr. John S. Dickey, Mr. Morris L. Ernst, Rabbi Roland B. Gittelsohn, Dr. Frank P. Graham, The Most Reverend Francis J. Haas, Mr. Charles Luckman, Mr. Francis P. Matthews, Mr. Franklin D. Roosevelt, Jr., The Right Reverend Henry Knox Sherrill, Mr. Boris Shishkin, Mrs. M. E. Tilly, Mr. Channing H. Tobias.

2. The Committee is authorized on behalf of the President to inquire into and to determine whether and in what respect current law-enforcement measures and the authority and means possessed by Federal, State, and local governments may be strengthened and improved to safeguard the civil rights of the people.

3. All executive departments and agencies of the Federal Government are authorized and directed to cooperate with the Committee in its work, and to furnish the Committee such information or the services of such persons as the Committee may require in the performance of its duties.

4. When requested by the Committee to do so, persons employed in any of the executive departments and agencies of the Federal Government shall testify before the Committee and shall make available for the use of the Committee such doc-

uments and other information as the Committee may require.

5. The Committee shall make a report of its studies to the President in writing, and shall in particular make recommendations with respect to the adoption or establishment, by legislation or otherwise, of more adequate and effective means and procedures for the protection of the civil rights of the people of the United States.

6. Upon rendition of its report to the President, the Committee shall cease to exist, unless otherwise determined by further Executive Order.

HARRY S. TRUMAN.

THE WHITE HOUSE, *December 5, 1946.*

The Committee's first task was the interpretation of its assignment. . . .

If our task were to evaluate the level of achievement in our civil rights record, mention would have to be made of many significant developments in our history as a nation. We would want to refer to the steady progress toward the goal of universal suffrage which has marked the years between 1789 and the present. . . .

Until 1944, the white primary, by which participation in the Democratic primary is limited to white citizens, was used in Texas, Alabama, Arkansas, Georgia, Louisiana, and Mississippi as the most effective modern "legal" device for disfranchising Negroes. While some southern Negroes succeeded in spite of various obstacles in voting in general elections, almost none voted in the Democratic primaries. Since the Democratic primary is the only election of any significance, the device of the white primary resulted in exclusion of Negroes from government in these states. Over a period of time, advocates of white supremacy had refined this device to the point where it seemed to be constitutionally foolproof. The command of the Fifteenth Amendment, prohibiting states from abridging suffrage because of race or color, was circumvented by purporting to vest the power to exclude Negroes in the political party rather than in the state.

But in 1944, the United States Supreme Court in the case of *Smith v. Allwright* overruled an earlier decision and held the Texas white primary illegal. It declared that the exclusion rules of the Texas Democratic Party were in effect the rules of the state and were therefore forbidden by the Fifteenth Amendment.

Some states adapted their primary laws to the Supreme Court ruling, others resisted, first, by refusing to open white primaries to Negroes until further litigation made the Texas ruling applicable to them, then, by devising other methods of depriving Negroes of the ballot. Today the effort to preserve the pure white electoral system in these states is continuing. . . .

From the days of the civil rights legislation of the 1860's and 1870's, there remained on the federal statute books scattered provisions of civil rights law. Responsibility for the enforcement of these laws rested with the Department of Justice. From time to time, it took prosecutive action under them but no coordinated program was developed. However, in 1939, to encourage more vigorous use of these laws and to centralize responsibility for their enforcement, Attorney General Frank Murphy established a Civil Rights Section in the Criminal Division of the Department.

This agency has now had eight years of experience. . . .

. . . [O]ne of the most important objectives of this Committee is to strengthen the federal civil rights enforcement machinery. We believe that the achievements of these agencies offer great promise for the future. But only by remedying some of the imperfections in the machinery can this progress be assured. . . .

The Committee's Recommendations

I. *To strengthen the machinery for the protection of civil rights, the President's Committee recommends:*

1. The reorganization of the Civil Rights Section of the Department of Justice to provide for:

The establishment of regional offices:

A substantial increase in its appropriation and staff to enable it to engage in more extensive research and to act more effectively to prevent civil rights violations;

An increase in investigative action in the absence of complaints;

The greater use of civil sanctions;

Its elevation to the status of a full division in the Department of Justice. . . .

4. The establishment of a permanent Commission on Civil Rights in the Executive Office of the President, preferably by Act of Congress;

And the simultaneous creation of a Joint Standing Committee on Civil Rights in Congress. . . .

III. *To strengthen the right to citizenship and its privileges, the President's Committee recommends:*

1. Action by the states or Congress to end poll taxes as a voting prerequisite. . . .

2. The enactment by Congress of a statute protecting the right of qualified persons to participate in federal primaries and elections against interference by public officers and private persons. . . .

3. The enactment by Congress of a statute protecting the right to qualify for, or participate in, federal or state primaries or elections against discriminatory action by state officers based on race or color, or depending on any other unreasonable classification of persons for voting purposes. . . .

4. The enactment by Congress of legislation establishing local self-government for the District of Columbia; and the amendment of the Constitution to extend suffrage in presidential elections, and representation in Congress to District residents. . . .

5. The granting of suffrage by the States of New Mexico and Arizona to their Indian citizens. . . .

Source: *To Secure These Rights: The Report of the President's Committee on Civil Rights* (New York: Simon and Schuster, 1947).

---

18   *The Negro Voter in the South,* **September 1957**

As this excerpt from a 1957 report by the Southern Regional Council reveals, African American voter registration in the South increased dramatically in the 1940s and 1950s. The great majority of black adults in the South of voting age were not registered to vote when this report appeared—about 75 percent—but there is no such thing as 100 percent registration of a voting-age population. If the white voting-age registration in the South at that time—60 percent—indexes the likely maximum for African American registration, then a little over 40 percent of the African American population that one would otherwise expect to be registered was in fact registered by the mid- to late 1950s. The question is: why? Economic growth and increased educational attainment among all southerners account for much of the answer. But another large part of it is the steady, courageous activism evident among black southerners, magnified by the sharp organizational growth in the South of the NAACP.

FOREWORD

It is basic to the American philosophy that a citizen's right to vote is the sovereign remedy for all of his civic grievances. Hence it was only natural that, sooner or later, the school segregation controversy should bring to the fore the question of the Southern Negro's access to the ballot.

For the Southern Regional Council, this question is not a new one. Since 1944, when the courts affirmed the right of Negro citizens to participate in the decisive Democratic primaries, the Council has studied and reported on the growth of Negro suffrage in the region.

By 1956, it was clear that the nature and timing of adjustment to the Supreme Court's school integration decisions would depend in considerable measure on the role of the Negro voter. Yet there had not been a comprehensive survey of Negro suffrage since 1947, when the late Dr. Luther P. Jackson carried out his study for the Southern Regional Council.

To remedy this lack of information, the Council undertook in mid-1956 the most ambitious survey of its kind to date. The aim was to collect, in ten Southern states, county-by-county data on the following:

(1) The number of Negroes registered to vote.
(2) Legal and administrative provisions affecting Negro registration.
(3) The extent and nature of discrimination and intimidation directed at would-be Negro voters.
(4) The prevalence of "apathy" or lack of political consciousness as a cause of Negro disfranchisement.
(5) Actual voting performance by Negroes and its effect on their community status.
(6) The relationship of Negro registration to such social and economic factors as median income, education, type of economy, degree of urbanization, and the like, by counties.

With the aid of a grant from the Fund for the Republic, this appraisal was carried out in each of the ten states during the summer and fall of 1956. . . .

HAROLD C. FLEMING, *Executive Director*
Southern Regional Council
September 1957

Negro Registration: Present and Prospective

During the past decade, Negro registration has climbed steadily, if gradually. Today, there are at least 1,238,000 Negroes on voting rolls in the Southern states.

This figure, based on the estimated number of registrants at the time of the 1956 general election, represents a gain of 229,400 over the 1,008,614 registered in 1952, which in turn was a 413,600 increase over the 595,000 registered in 1947. . . .

Of course, as the number of Negro registrants has been increasing numerically, so has the white. Unless the pace is accelerated, it still will be many years before the registration record of Negroes approaches that of the white South. . . .

The prospect for Negro voting in several of the states as summed up by the field consultants follows:

North Carolina: "Increasing registration by Negroes but not in tremendous numbers . . . .The counties that now restrict Negro registration increasingly will use more legal and sophisticated tactics to neutralize the political effectiveness of the Negro . . . . Regardless of what methods may be used, the Negro is becoming more important politically as direct restrictions on his franchise decline. Many of the registrars who emphasize these restrictive tactics are old and are dying out."

Louisiana: "Unless the Citizens Council enjoys unexpected success in its purgative efforts, it would seem that Negro registration and voting have become a permanent feature of the Louisiana political landscape . . . . In the parishes (counties) where subterfuge is necessary to discourage registration, there is likely to be a registration breakthrough in the not too distant future. In these parishes, where there is a history of suppression, the Negro is quite anxious to obtain the suffrage. . . . In the Mississippi Delta parishes where no Negroes are registered, the prospects are bleak for registration in the immediate future. . . . The urban parishes represent a great untapped reservoir of Negro votes which can be registered with a minimum of difficulty."

South Carolina: "Nothwithstanding the obstacles that are standing in the way of the Negro's complete political freedom, there is evidence that he is on the move politically. This can be attributed to the new kind of leadership found among the Negroes today."

Alabama: While the State Consultant feels that "the future of Negro voting looks brighter," there still are forces at work in Alabama which make a major increase, particularly in the Black Belt, seem unlikely in the immediate future.

Texas: "The Negro is on the way toward becoming a strong political force. . . . The school integration question, although not actually a political issue, is looming large in Texas politics. This gives Negroes a greater sense of political responsibility and the change is beginning to show its effects."

Virginia: "The greatest threat to the increase of the suffrage at present time is the current attack on the NAACP by the state and local governments. . . . On the other hand, there are prospects of increasing Negro participation in politics as revealed by the following facts: . . . A number of counties have centralized registration in the past three or four years. Where there is centralization, there has been a great reduction in the number of discriminatory complaints. . . . Older, often biased registrars . . . are dying out or being replaced by younger persons, better educated and less biased . . . . Political consciousness is growing among Negroes."

Georgia: "The statistical and field studies support the idea that progress of Negro suffrage is made in urbanized and industrialized communities. This is one of the most encouraging factors in terms of the future of Negro suffrage. . . . Georgia is now reaching the break-through point in the distribution of its population toward the urban places of residence. Furthermore, agriculture as a source of income continues to give way to manufacturing and to other sources of income. Thus, the socio-economic trends in the state are in the direction of the kinds of situations in which Negroes are more likely to be registrants and voters."

Florida: "Negro leaders are quite capable of increasing the Negro voting potential. They have been devoting much time and energy to the struggle against Jim Crow-ism, especially as it relates to the public schools and public transportation and have not had much time or energy left to devote to political education and encouragement. . . . They are now launching a determined drive to education the Negro to his suffrage responsibilities."

Table 1—Negro Registration

State	1947	1952	1956
Alabama	6,000	25,224	53,366
Arkansas	47,000	61,413	69,677
Florida	49,000	120,900	148,703
Georgia	125,000	144,835	163,389
Louisiana	10,000	120,000	161,410
Mississippi	5,000	20,000	20,000*
North Carolina	75,000	100,000	135,000
South Carolina	50,000	80,000	99,890
Tennessee	80,000	85,000	90,000
Texas	100,000	181,916	214,000
Virginia	48,000	69,326	82,603
TOTALS	595,000	1,008,614	1,238,038

*Mississippi total is for 1955.

Source: Margaret Price, The Negro Voter in the South (Atlanta: Southern Regional Council, 1957).

19   **Civil Rights Acts of 1957 and 1960**

During the second administration of President Dwight D. Eisenhower, Congress and the president acted in the policy domain of black voting rights for the first time since 1893–1894, when Congress passed legislation that struck most of the Reconstruction-era federal elections statutes from the U.S. Code. The Civil Rights Acts of 1957 and 1960 were intended to facilitate voter registration by black voting-age adults in the former Confederacy. Often the acts are dismissed as trivial in comparison with the Voting Rights Act of 1965, yet in fact they encouraged an enormous voter registration effort among black southerners. In turn, these renewed struggles on the ground focused a great deal of national attention on the barriers to voting rights. The increased conflict between black voters and public officials defending white supremacy set the agenda of the federal government. Indeed, it created considerable pressure to fashion a federal voting rights statute that would fully realize black voting rights.

Civil Rights Act of 1957, September 9, 1957

The Civil Rights Act of 1957 established a national fact-finding commission, the U.S. Commission on Civil Rights, which still exists today. It also created a full division of civil rights within the Department of Justice. These two measures built on the recommendations of the President's Committee on Civil Rights, appointed by President Harry S. Truman. Finally, the 1957 Civil Rights Act empowered the Department of Justice to act in the federal courts on behalf of African American citizens deprived of the right to vote.

AN ACT

To provide means of further securing and protecting the civil rights of persons within the jurisdiction of the United States.

Be it enacted by the Senate and House of Representatives of the United States of America in Congress assembled,

Part I—Establishment of the Commission on Civil Rights
SEC. 101. (a) There is created in the executive branch of the Government a Commission on Civil Rights (hereinafter called the "Commission"). . . .
SEC. 102. (a) The Chairman or one designated by him to act as Chairman at a hearing of the Commission shall announce in an opening statement the subject of the hearing.
(b) A copy of the Commission's rules shall be made available to the witness before the Commission.
(c) Witnesses at the hearings may be accompanied by their own counsel for the purpose of advising them concerning their constitutional rights. . . .

Duties of the Commission
SEC. 104. The Commission shall—
(1) investigate allegations in writing under oath or affirmation that certain citizens of the United States are being deprived of their right to vote and have that vote counted by reason of their color, race, religion, or national origin; which writing, under oath or affirmation, shall set forth the facts upon which such belief or beliefs are based;
(2) study and collect information concerning legal developments constituting a denial of equal protection of the laws under the Constitution; and
(3) appraise the laws and policies of the Federal Government with respect to equal protection of the laws under the Constitution.
(b) The Commission shall submit interim reports to the President and to the Congress at such times as either the Commission or the President shall deem desirable, and shall submit to the President and to the Congress a final and comprehensive report of its activities, findings, and recommendations not later than two years from the date of the enactment of this Act.
(c) Sixty days after the submission of its final report and recommendations the Commission shall cease to exist.

Powers of the Commission
SEC. 105. . . .

(c) The Commission may constitute such advisory committees within States composed of citizens of that State and may consult with governors, attorneys general, and other representatives of State and local governments, and private organizations, as it deems advisable.
(d) Members of the Commission, and members of advisory committees constituted pursuant to subsection (c) of this section, shall be exempt from the operation of sections 281, 283, 284, 434, and 1914 of title 18 of the United States Code, and section 190 of the Revised Statutes (5 U.S.C. 99). . . .

Part II—To Provide for an Additional Assistant Attorney General
SEC. 111. There shall be in the Department of Justice one additional Assistant Attorney General, who shall be appointed by the President, by and with the advice and consent of the Senate, who shall assist the Attorney General in the performance of his duties, and who shall receive compensation at the rate prescribed by law for other Assistant Attorneys General. . . .

Part IV—To Provide Means of Further Securing and Protecting the Right to Vote
SEC. 131. Section 2004 of the Revised Statutes (42 U.S.C. 1971) is amended as follows:
(a) Amend the catch line of said section to read, "Voting rights".

(b) Designate its present text with the subsection symbol "(a)".

(c) Add, immediately following the pres-ent text, four new subsections to read as follows:

"(b) No person, whether acting under color of law or otherwise, shall intimidate, threaten, coerce, or attempt to intimidate, threaten, or coerce any other person for the purpose of interfering with the right of such other person to vote or to vote as he may choose, or of causing such other person to vote for, or not to vote for, any candidate for the office of President, Vice President, presidential elector, Member of the Senate, or Member of the House of Representatives, Delegates or Commissioners from the Territories or possessions, at any general, special, or primary election held solely or in part for the purpose of selecting or electing any such candidate.

"(c) Whenever any person has engaged or there are reasonable grounds to believe that any person is about to engage in any act or practice which would deprive any other person of any right or privilege secured by subsection (a) or (b), the Attorney General may institute for the United States, or in the name of the United States, a civil action or other proper proceeding for preventive relief, including an application for a permanent or temporary injunction, restraining order, or other order. In any proceeding hereunder the United States shall be liable for costs the same as a private person.

"(d) The district courts of the United States shall have jurisdiction of proceedings instituted pursuant to this section and shall exercise the same without regard to whether the party aggrieved shall have exhausted any administrative or other remedies that may be provided by law.

"(e) Any person cited for an alleged contempt under this Act shall be allowed to make his full defense by counsel learned in the law; and the court before which he is cited or tried, or some judge thereof, shall immediately, upon his request, assign to him such counsel, not exceeding two, as he may desire, who shall have free access to him at all reasonable hours. He shall be allowed, in his defense to make any proof that he can produce by lawful witnesses, and shall have the like process of the court to compel his witnesses to appear at his trial or hearing, as is usually granted to compel witnesses to appear on behalf of the prosecution. If such person shall be found by the court to be financially unable to provide for such counsel, it shall be the duty of the court to provide such counsel." . . .

Sec. 161. This Act may be cited as the "Civil Rights Act of 1957".

Approved September 9, 1957.

Civil Rights Act of 1960, May 6, 1960

The Civil Rights Act of 1960 can be read as the federal government's response to deliberate obstruction by local southern elections officials intent on subverting the 1957 Civil Rights Act. The 1960 statute calls for the preservation of elections records and criminalizes willful destruction of such records. It also authorizes the federal courts to take over the registration of black voters. Neither feature of the 1960 law had much effect, but Congress's willingness to devise more forceful measures in response to official obstruction in the South foreshadowed the bold leap that the national government finally took in 1965 with the Voting Rights Act.

AN ACT

To enforce constitutional rights, and for other purposes.

Be it enacted by the Senate and House of Representatives of the United States of America in Congress assembled, That this Act may be cited as the "Civil Rights Act of 1960".

TITLE I
OBSTRUCTION OF COURT ORDERS

SEC. 101. Chapter 73 of title 18, United States Code, is amended by adding at the end thereof a new section as follows:

§ 1509. Obstruction of court orders

Whoever, by threats or force, willfully prevents, obstructs, impedes, or interferes with, or willfully attempts to prevent, obstruct, impede, or interfere with, the due exercise of rights or the performance of duties under any order, judgment, or decree of a court of the United States, shall be fined not more than $1,000 or imprisoned not more than one year, or both. No injunctive or other civil relief against the conduct made criminal by this section shall be denied on the ground that such conduct is a crime. . . .

TITLE III
FEDERAL ELECTION RECORDS

SEC. 301. Every officer of election shall retain and preserve, for a period of twenty-two months from the date of any general, special, or primary election of which candidates for the office of President, Vice President, presidential elector, Member of the Senate, Member of the House of Representatives, or Resident Commissioner from the Commonwealth of Puerto Rico are voted for, all records and papers which come into his possession relating to any application, registration, payment of poll tax, or other act requisite to voting in such election. . . . Any officer of election or custodian who willfully fails to comply with this section shall be fined not more than $1,000 or imprisoned not more than one year, or both.

SEC. 302. Any person, whether or not an officer of election or custodian, who willfully steals, destroys, conceals, mutilates, or alters any record or paper required by section 301 to be retained and preserved shall be fined not more than $1,000 or imprisoned not more than one year, or both.

SEC. 303. Any record or paper required by section 301 to be retained and preserved shall, upon demand in writing by the Attorney General or his representative directed to the person having cus-

tody, possession, or control of such record or paper, be made available for inspection, reproduction, and copying at the principal office of such custodian by the Attorney General or his representative. This demand shall contain a statement of the basis and the purpose therefor. . . .

SEC. 305. The United States district court for the district in which a demand is made pursuant to section 303, or in which a record or paper so demanded is located, shall have jurisdiction by appropriate process to compel the production of such record or paper.

SEC. 306. As used in this title, the term "officer of election" means any person who, under color of any Federal, State, Commonwealth, or local law, statute, ordinance, regulation, authority, custom, or usage, performs or is authorized to perform any function, duty, or task in connection with any application, registration, payment of poll tax, or other act requisite to voting in any general, special, or primary election at which votes are cast for candidates for the office of President, Vice President, presidential elector, Member of the Senate, Member of the House of Representatives, or Resident Commissioner from the Commonwealth of Puerto Rico. . . .

TITLE VI

SEC. 601. That section 2004 of the Revised Statutes (42 U.S.C. 1971), as amended by section 131 of the Civil Rights Act of 1957 (71 Stat. 637), is amended as follows:

(a) Add the following as subsection (e) and designate the present subsection (e) as subsection "(f)":

"In any proceeding instituted pursuant to subsection (c) in the event the court finds that any person has been deprived on account of race or color of any right or privilege secured by subsection (a), the court shall upon request of the Attorney General and after each party has been given notice and the opportunity to be heard make a finding whether such deprivation was or is pursuant to a pattern or practice. If the court finds such pattern or practice, any person of such race or color resident within the affected area shall, for one year and thereafter until the court subsequently finds that such pattern or practice has ceased, be entitled, upon his application therefor, to an order declaring him qualified to vote, upon proof that at any election or elections (1) he is qualified under State law to vote, and (2) he has since such finding by the court been (a) deprived of or denied under color of law the opportunity to register to vote or otherwise to qualify to vote, or (b) found not qualified to vote by any person acting under color of law. Such order shall be effective as to any election held within the longest period for which such applicant could have been registered or otherwise qualified under State law at which the applicant's qualifications would under State law entitle him to vote.

"Notwithstanding any inconsistent provision of State law or the action of any State officer or court, an applicant, so declared qualified to vote, shall be permitted to vote in any such election. The Attorney General shall cause to be transmitted certified copies of such order to the appropriate election officers. The refusal by any such officer with notice of such order to permit any person so declared qualified to vote to vote at an appropriate election shall constitute contempt of court.

"An application for an order pursuant to this subsection shall be heard within ten days, and the execution of any order disposing of such application shall not be stayed if the effect of such stay would be to delay the effectiveness of the order beyond the date of any election at which the applicant would otherwise be enabled to vote.

"The court may appoint one or more persons who are qualified voters in the judicial district, to be known as voting referees, who shall subscribe to the oath of office required by Revised Statutes, Section 1757; (5 U.S.C. 16) to serve for such period as the court shall determine, to receive such applications and to take evidence and report to the court findings as to whether or not at any election or elections (1) any such applicant is qualified under State law to vote, and (2) he has since the finding by the court heretofore specified

been (a) deprived of or denied under color of law the opportunity to register to vote or otherwise to qualify to vote, or (b) found not qualified to vote by any person acting under color of law. In a proceeding before a voting referee, the applicant shall be heard ex parte at such times and places as the court shall direct. His statement under oath shall be prima facie evidence as to his age, residence, and his prior efforts to register or otherwise qualify to vote. Where proof of literacy or an understanding of other subjects is required by valid provisions of State law, the answer of the applicant, if written, shall be included in such reports to the court; if oral, it shall be taken down stenographically and a transcription included in such report to the court.

"Upon receipt of such report, the court shall cause the Attorney General to transmit a copy thereof to the State attorney general and to each party to such proceeding together with an order to show cause within ten days, or such shorter time as the court may fix, why an order of the court should not be entered in accordance with such report. Upon the expiration of such period, such order shall be entered unless prior to that time there has been filed with the court served upon all parties a statement of exceptions to such report. Exceptions as to matters of fact shall be considered only if supported by a duly verified copy of a public record or by a davit of persons having personal knowledge of such facts or by statements or matters contained in such report; those relating to matters of law shall be supported by an appropriate memorandum of law. The issues of fact and law raised by such exceptions shall be determined by the court or, if the due and speedy administration of justice requires, they may be referred to the voting referee to determine in accordance with procedures prescribed by the court. A hearing as to an issue of fact shall be held only in the event that the proof in support of the exception discloses the existence of a genuine issue of material fact. The applicants' literacy and understanding of other subjects shall be determined solely on the basis of answers included in the report of the voting referee.

"The court, or at its direction the voting referee, shall issue to each applicant so declared qualified a certificate identifying the holder thereof as person so qualified.

"Any voting referee appointed by the court pursuant to this subsection shall to the extent not inconsistent herewith have all the powers conferred upon master by rule 53 (c) of the Federal Rules of Civil Procedure. The compensation to be allowed to any persons appointed by the court pursuant to this subsection shall be fixed by the court and shall be payable by the United States.

"Applications pursuant to this subsection shall be determined expeditiously. In the case of any application filed twenty or more days prior to an election which is undetermined by the time of such election, the court shall issue an order authorizing the applicant to vote provisionally. Provided, however, that such applicant shall be qualified to vote under State law. In the case of an application filed within twenty days prior to an election, the court, in its discretion, may make such an order. In either case the order shall make appropriate provision for the impounding of the applicant's ballot pending determination of the application. The court may take any other action, and may authorize such referee or such other person as it may designate to take any other action, appropriate or necessary to carry out the provisions of this subsection and to enforce its decrees. This subsection shall in no way be construed as limitation upon the existing powers of the court.

"When used in the subsection, the word vote includes all action necessary to make a vote effective including, but not limited to, registration or other action required by State law prerequisite to voting, casting a ballot, and having such ballot counted and included in the appropriate totals of votes cast with respect to candidates for public office and propositions for which votes are received in an election; the words affected area shall mean any subdivision of the State in which the laws of the State relating to voting are or have been to any extent administered by a person found in the proceeding to have violated subsection (a); and the words qualified under State law shall mean qualified according to the laws, customs, or usage of the State, and shall not, in any event, imply qualifications more stringent than those used by the persons found in the proceeding to have violated subsection (a) in qualifying persons other than those of the race or color against which the pattern or practice of discrimination was found to exist.

(b) Add the following sentence at the end of subsection

(c) "Whenever, in a proceeding instituted under this subsection, any official of a State or subdivision thereof is alleged to have committed any act or practice constituting a deprivation of any right or privilege secured by subsection (a), the act or practice shall also be deemed that of the State and the State may be joined as a party defendant and, if, prior to the institution of such proceeding, such official has resigned or has been relieved of his office and no successor has assumed such office, the proceeding may be instituted against the State." . . .

Approved May 6, 1960.

Sources: Civil Rights Act of 1957: *Statutes at Large,* 71 (1957), 85th Cong., 1st sess., September 9, 1957; Civil Rights Act of 1960: *U.S. Statutes at Large,* 74 (1960), 86th Cong., 2d sess., May 6, 1960.

20   Testimony of Rev. John Scott before the United States Commission on Civil Rights, September 27, 1960

In establishing the U.S. Civil Rights Commission and empowering it to collect testimony, the Civil Rights Act of 1957 created a federal forum in which local people who had been struggling against white supremacy all of their lives could tell their story. Among these was Rev. John Scott of Lake Providence, Louisiana—a patient, indeed indomitable, activist in the National Association for the Advancement of Colored People (NAACP). Born in 1901, the grandson of an African American veteran of the Union army, Rev. Scott lived until June 1980, long enough to see much of the impact of the Voting Rights Act of 1965. This testimony is from a U.S. Civil Rights Commission hearing in New Orleans on September 27, 1960.

Appendix

. . .

Colonel ROSENFELD. . . .

The first topic on which evidence will be presented is the requirement exacted by certain registrars to produce registered voters of their precinct for the purpose of attesting to the identity of the applicant and the first witness to be called under this topic is the Reverend John Henry Scott, of East Carroll Parish. He will also act as a background witness.

Vice Chairman STOREY. Come around, Mr. Scott. Will you please hold up your right hand and be sworn? Will you hold up your right hand?

. . .

Mr. BERNHARD. If the Commission please, in referring to Reverend Scott's testimony, I would like to point out that Reverend Scott is from East Carroll; that in this particular parish, you will note——

Vice Chairman STOREY. Point out East Carroll.

Mr. BERNHARD. East Carroll is in the northeastern part of the State. You will observe that the nonwhite age 21 and over—that is, the potential Negro voter—constitutes 4,690. The number of colored who are registered is zero; obviously the percent registered over 21 is zero.

At the same time, whites age 21 and over constitute 2,836. Whites registered are 2,826 and the percentage comes out that 99.7 percent of the

white 21 and over are registered in East Carroll Parish.

Vice Chairman STOREY. Thank you, Mr. Bernhard. Now, will you please state your name, your age, and place of residence?

Reverend SCOTT. My name is John Henry Scott. My age is 57.

Vice Chairman STOREY. Where do you live?

Reverend SCOTT. I live in East Carroll Parish.

Vice Chairman STOREY. How long have you lived there?

Reverend SCOTT. I have lived there all my life.

Vice Chairman STOREY. What is your occupation?

Reverend SCOTT. My occupation is minister.

Vice Chairman STOREY. Of what denomination or church?

Reverend SCOTT. Baptist. I am pastoring one of the churches that my great-grandfather organized.

Vice Chairman STOREY. How long have you been pastor of that church?

Reverend SCOTT. I have been pastoring there since 1947. . . .

Vice Chairman STOREY. Are you a registered voter?

Reverend SCOTT. No.

Vice Chairman STOREY. Have you attempted to register?

Reverend SCOTT. Many times.

Vice Chairman STOREY. All right. Now, tell the first time and where, and the circumstances. What happened? Just tell in your own words.

Reverend SCOTT. Well, the first time that I attempted to register, that is back in 1946. Another young man named Rev. Paul Taylor, we decided we would go and try. . . .

. . . Well, we didn't know exactly where the registration office was, so finally we went upstairs, and we go to the door, and I said, "Paul, here is the door," and we went to the door, and the registrar of voters say, "Go to the next door." So we went to look for another door, and when we got back, the door was locked. So we didn't make any attempt to go in. We give up that time.

Vice Chairman STOREY. Where was this? What town and what parish?

Reverend SCOTT. That is East Carroll Parish, Lake Providence, La. . . .

The next time I tried to register must have been about 2 years later, around 1947; the Reverend Mason and I went together. . . .

Went to the same place, the same registrar. She was very nice. She gave us the card to fill. When we filled it she looked at it and said, "Well, we wouldn't know where to find you all," or something, so we went out, and a little later on I decided to go back. I don't know whether I am giving them in the order, but I am truthfully stating it. I believe Brother Atlas and I went—

Vice Chairman STOREY. About how long was that after the second time?

Reverend SCOTT. Well, maybe it would be a year or 6 months before I tried again. . . .

So I decided that probably trying to be a Democrat was making it hard for me to register. . . .

So I decided to put on my next card "Republican." I didn't want to put "Communist" on there, and so when I put "Republican" on, the registrar of voters looked in the office, and she picked out a card, and she looked at it, and she said, "Well, on this card you said you were a Democrat. On this card you are saying you are a Republican." She said, "What are you?"

I said, "Well, I am not anything until you register me."

So she said, "Well, don't you know that you can't change your party that fast?"

So I had to go out.

So, later on, about 1950 . . . Reverend Mason and several others went in, decided to try again, and she gave us all a card, and we filled them out, and she told Reverend Mason that his was perfect, but he would have to get someone to vouch for him or sign, identify him. All of which he was successful, but that didn't work, either. In fact—

Vice Chairman STOREY. Could I ask you how many signed recommendations or vouched for him?

Reverend SCOTT. Well, just one. . . .

But they didn't accept that one. . . .

Vice Chairman STOREY. Did you attempt to register again?

Reverend SCOTT. Yes. Reverend Henderson and I went together, and she told him his was right, and he was fortunate to get a white person to go up there that had not been brought up to the proceedings. And he was turned away, after he had gone down, and they told him what he should do, I guess, and what he shouldn't do. That is my thinking, what he told Reverend Henderson: "I can't fool with that." So he went away. So we were not able to get anyone to come, and if we got them it was to no avail because they had made their mind up not to register anybody. So recently they put a new man or they put a man in office after our present registrar resigned or went on retirement, and we thought we would try him, I believe last September, and several of us went.

Vice Chairman STOREY. How many went along with you? About how many?

Reverend SCOTT. About five. . . . He asked us how long we been living there. Most of us had been living there all of our life, and he said, "Well"—he handed us a form; he said, "You will have to get two qualified electors from your ward and precinct to identify you."

Vice Chairman STOREY. Did you know the registrar personally?

Reverend SCOTT. I didn't know him—— . . . So he didn't register. So the lady that was with me, she said, "I can get two to identify me." I said, "Well, you think you can, but you can't." She said, "But I know I can," she said, "I have some white friends, and we are all Christians." I said, "But Christians and this registration business is different. Nobody's a Christian when it comes down to identifying you."

So she went and tried. She said, "Oh yes; they say they will go with me Monday," and I thought—and she said, "Well, it is just like you said; they told me that they couldn't bother with it."

So we decided to go back, I believe, in July, possibly July 25. . . .

. . . The registrar of voters asked us what did we want. We said we wanted to register. He said, "Do you have anybody to identify you?" I says, "We can identify each other." I said, "We identify folk at the bank and at the post office." I say, "We have come around and got folks out of jail and signed, went on their bond." I said, "We be here long enough to be known."

He said, "No you can't do that. You will have to have two qualified electors from your ward and precinct, and you can't take these forms out for them to sign. You have to bring them to this office." So, he asked us, he said, "Give me your names." One of the men that was with us, he said, "Oh, sure, we will give you our name," and I said, "There is no use in giving you our name. You give us the card to fill out, and we will sign our names to the card."

I said, "But we didn't come to sign up. We came to try to register."

So we could not register. It seemed to be, in my way of thinking—and I'm sorry to have to appear before this Commission; I am sorry to be in New Orleans. I never did think that in America or that a citizen would have to do all of this for an opportunity to vote. . . .

Vice Chairman STOREY. . . . Why do you want to vote?

Reverend SCOTT. Well, I have always felt that was a responsibility that belonged to the citizens, after reading—even Louisiana history and the Constitution of Louisiana and the United States, it says that that belongs to the citizens, and another thing I noticed, it always gives recognition; I noticed the streets where they vote, they were fixed; I noticed the roads where the people lived on where they vote; it was gravel; I noticed the people that vote, the officers of the law respected them and treated them different from the people that didn't vote, and after reading Negro newspapers, traveling quite a bit, I felt like that it was a responsibility, and after my brothers—I didn't go because I was a minister—went to the Army, and back there in World War I, when the President was talking about making the world safe for democracy, and everybody had the right and privilege to participate, it always had been a burning zeal and desire within my heart, and I have never been able to tell my children the reason why that Negroes should be treated in such a way or be cast about. . . .

Commissioner JOHNSON. I wonder if I could ask just one question.

Vice Chairman STOREY. Dean Johnson?

Commissioner JOHNSON. Reverend Scott, as a result of your rather persistent effort to get registered over a considerable amount of time, I was wondering, have you ever been threatened or intimidated because of this kind of activity?

Reverend SCOTT. Well, slightly. I don't like to talk about intimidations. I would rather forget them. I always felt if a fellow thought he was doing you some harm or that he was bluffing you or was upsetting you in your mind, that he would go further, so I just let it go. They have told me not to say anything about it. Well, the officer of the law at that time, sheriff of East Carroll Parish—I can call him name; he is out of office now—Matt Fowler, and we had a meeting. Our—well, at that time the NAACP was having a membership drive and had invited Mr. Daniel E. Byrd to speak for us, and after he go to town, everything was so excited, and they sent for him to come to the courthouse, and they picked me up, and I picked up several other ministers, and we went to the courthouse, and the sheriff told me come to the office, his office, and don't bring anybody. So I went down, and they seated me around a table like that here, and they wanted to know what kind of meeting we were having. He said he had been called up during the day, and someone said that somebody was coming there to teach us how to vote, and I told him no one had to come there to teach us how to vote, that practically all of us knew how to fill out those forms and figure our age correctly and so on. So the collector of court has passed on now to the Great Beyond. He was across the table from me, he said, "If you don't like our way of doing things, why don't you leave here?"

I said, "Well, I was born here, and if I leave here, I might not like the things that go on where I go, but I think I could stay here and try to help correct some of the things." So they wouldn't allow us to have the meeting at the schoolhouse, and we went to a church. When I walked out of the sheriff's office, he said, "You be damned sure and tell him don't say anything about voting." So the next day he picked me up, and he asked me to name some of the leaders and those that understand how to fill out those forms. I say, "Is this

strictly confidential between you and me and nobody else?" And he said, "No; I am not going to promise you that." I said, "I am not going to tell you the names, either." So then he went on to tell me about going to start a riot and so on, like that; he was sheriff, and he had to furnish protection, and he couldn't put up with anything like that. So times moved on.

I just go on, go on because I feel like I am right, and I know where I am going, I know what I am talking about, and I don't care what happens. Whatever happens, I got to go to heaven, and if I go for my people or for the right to vote I would be perfectly satisfied, so that's the way I feel about it.

Commissioner JOHNSON. No further questions.

Vice Chairman STOREY. No further questions. Thank you, Reverend Scott.

Source: *Hearings before the United States Commission on Civil Rights, New Orleans, Louisiana, September 27, 1960, September 28, 1960, May 5, 1960, May 6, 1960* (Washington, D.C.: Government Printing Office, 1961), 15–23.

---

21   Robert Moses's Memoir on the Black Voter Registration Campaign in Mississippi: "Mississippi: 1961–1962"

People often think of the 1960s as a time when protesters were lawless. Such lawlessness certainly characterized a very small but violent leftist student movement in the North. But that much-remarked fact about student protest too easily obscures the constant abuse and intimidation inflicted by local officials and law enforcement officers on civil rights workers trying to give life to constitutional rights in states in the Deep South. This selection from a tape-recorded memoir by the distinguished Student Nonviolent Coordinating Committee leader Robert Moses describes one of the literally countless such incidents that occurred in the first half of the decade in the Deep South, before the nationally riveting incidents in Selma, Alabama.

My name is Robert Moses and I'm field secretary for the Student Nonviolent Coordinating Committee. I first came South July 1960 on a

field trip for SNCC. . . . I returned in the summer of 1961 . . . about the middle of August.

. . . . I accompanied about three people down to Liberty in Amite County to begin our first registration attempt there. One was a very old man, and then two ladies, middle-aged. We left early morning of August 15, it was a Tuesday, we arrived at the courthouse at about 10 o'clock. The registrar came out, I waited by the side for the man or one of the ladies to say something to the registrar. He asked them what did they want, what were they here for in a very rough tone of voice. They didn't say anything, they were literally paralyzed with fear, So, after a while, I spoke up and said that they would like to come to register to vote. So, he asked, "Well, who are you? What do you have to do with them? Are you here to register?" So I told him who I was and that we were conducting a school in McComb and that these people had attended the school and they wanted an opportunity to register. Well, he said that I'd have to wait "cuz there was someone there filling out the form." Well, there was a young white lady there with her husband and she was sitting down completing the registration form. When she finished, then our people started to register one at a time. In the meantime, a procession of people began moving in and out of the registration office. The sheriff, a couple of his deputies, people from the tax office, people who do the drivers' licenses, looking in, staring, moving back out, muttering. A highway patrolman finally came in and sat down in the office. And we stayed that way in sort of uneasy tension all morning. The first person who filled out the form took a long time to do it and it was noontime before he was finished. When we came back, I was not permitted to sit in the office, but was told to sit on the front porch, which I did. We finally finished the whole process at about 4:30; all of the three people had had a chance to register, at least to fill out the form. This was victory, because they had been down a few times before and had not had a chance to even fill out the forms.

On the way home we were followed by the highway patrolman who had spent the day in the registrar's office: Officer Carlyle. He tailed us about ten miles, about twenty-five or thirty feet behind us, all the way back towards McComb. At one point, we pulled off, and he passed us, circled around us and we pulled off as he was passing us in the opposite direction, and then he turned around and followed us again. Finally he flagged us down and I got out of the car to ask him what the trouble was because the people in the car were very, very frightened. He asked me who I was, what my business was, and told me that I was interfering in what he was doing. I said I simply wanted to find out what the problem was and what we were being stopped for. He told me to get back in the car. As I did so, I jotted his name down. He then opened the car door, shoved me in and said, "Get in the car, nigger," slamming the door after me. He then told us to follow him and took us over to McComb where I was told that I was placed under arrest. He called up the prosecuting attorney; he came down, and then he and the highway patrolman sat down and looked through the law books to find a charge. . . .

. . . I was found guilty of this charge of interfering with an officer, and the judge and the county prosecutor went out, consulted, and came back and I was given a suspended sentence, 90 days suspended sentence, and fined $5 for the cost of the court. I refused to pay the $5 cost of the court and argued that I shouldn't be given anything at all and should be set free since I was obviously not guilty. I was taken to jail then, and this was my first introduction to Mississippi jails. I spent a couple of days in jail and was finally bailed out when the bondsman came through, supplied by the NAACP.

Source: Robert Parris Moses, "Mississippi: 1961–1962," in *First Harvest: The Institute for Policy Studies, 1963–1983*, ed. John S. Friedman (New York: Grove Press, 1983). Originally appeared in *Liberation*, January 1970.

22   President Lyndon B. Johnson's Special Message to Congress:
      "The American Promise," March 15, 1965

Both this speech by President Lyndon B. Johnson to a joint session of Congress on March 15, 1965, and the events on the ground in Selma, Alabama, that preceded the speech were truly remarkable.

Selma, a small city on the Alabama River to the west of Alabama's capital, Montgomery, was the site of over a decade of tense, patient struggles by local civil rights leaders, who fought an exceptionally intransigent local white supremacist establishment that was determined to stop all but the slightest level of black voter registration. When that establishment split in two, leading to the election of a mildly reformist mayor (who finally retired from that office in 2000), the local struggle increased in tempo—only to be met by a fierce legal attack from the openly supremacist wing of the establishment, which retained control of the county official machinery of criminal justice.

Local civil rights leaders then reached out to the Student Nonviolent Coordinating Committee (SNCC), the offshoot of local black college student protests held earlier elsewhere in the South, and to the Southern Christian Leadership Conference (SCLC), which had grown out of the National Association for the Advancement of Colored People (NAACP) and now had a regional organization of its own led by Rev. Martin Luther King Jr. Although there is little direct evidence to support the hypothesis, the national civil rights leaders associated with these organizations appear to have seen the invitation as their opportunity to direct a closely watched conflict that would educate the nation and its elected leaders about the need for a new national voting rights statute. Such legislation would supplant the plainly ineffective voting rights measures in the 1957 and 1960 Civil Rights Acts that civil rights leaders had sought, with little success, to implement themselves (with encouragement from the Kennedy administration) in the Deep South. That President Johnson came to understand the educative force of this strategy can be seen in the text of his address to Congress in the passage in which he praises the courage of the protesters.

February and early March 1965 saw the playing out of the critical acts in the drama that civil rights leaders staged before a public fully aware of the unfolding crisis. A brief timeline of the local events telegraphs the extraordinary dynamic that emerged:

Feb. 1—Rev. Martin Luther King Jr. leads a march in Selma and is arrested.
Feb. 6—King emerges from jail and then meets with members of Congress who have traveled to Selma.
Feb. 11—Six hundred people march to the local courthouse.
Feb. 15—Marches are held in Selma and its suburbs (Marion, Camden).
Feb. 18—Local church deacon and farmer Jimmie Lee Jackson is savagely beaten and shot by state police while trying to protect his mother from a beating in the aftermath of a "police riot" in Marion—an action by police that apparently was intended to terrorize civil rights marchers.
Feb. 22—King announces a march from Selma to Montgomery.
Feb. 26—Jimmie Lee Jackson dies in a Selma hospital (still standing today near the former air force base).
March 7—Marchers seeking to march to Montgomery are beaten in a second frenzied police riot on the Edmund Pettus Bridge leading out of Selma—and this time the official violence is captured on national television.
March 9—After a second attempted march, which is called off by King at the last minute, Rev. James Reeb, a white minister from Boston, is beaten by local white thugs and dies en route to a hospital.
March 10—Another attempted march is blocked around Brown's Chapel.
March 15— While the president prepares to address Congress, a courthouse rally is held to honor Reeb.

Observing the events in Selma, the president and his advisers decided to introduce the Voting Rights Act. Indeed, at the outset of 1965 the president knew he wanted to introduce some kind of voting rights statute during his second term in office, but he apparently had no specific timetable. His introduction of the statute thus suggests that LBJ understood that he had been given a political gift by the civil rights movement—a rare opportunity to pass a genuinely strong statute. Recognizing the window of opportunity and seeking to galvanize the legislative process, the president took the unprecedented step of addressing a televised joint session of Congress—the first such speech in American history.

Mr. Speaker, Mr. President, Members of the Congress: . . .

At times history and fate meet at a single time in a single place to shape a turning point in man's unending search for freedom. So it was at Lexington and Concord. So it was a century ago at Appomattox. So it was last week in Selma, Alabama.

There, long-suffering men and women peacefully protested the denial of their rights as Americans. Many were brutally assaulted. One good man, a man of God, was killed. . . .

Many of the issues of civil rights are very complex and most difficult. But about this there can and should be no argument. Every American citizen must have an equal right to vote. There is no reason which can excuse the denial of that right. There is no duty which weighs more heavily on us than the duty we have to ensure that right.

Yet the harsh fact is that in many places in this country men and women are kept from voting simply because they are Negroes.

Every device of which human ingenuity is capable has been used to deny this right. The Negro citizen may go to register only to be told that the day is wrong, or the hour is late, or the official in charge is absent. And if he persists, and if he manages to present himself to the registrar, he may be disqualified because he did not spell out his middle name or because he abbreviated a word on the application.

And if he manages to fill out an application he is given a test. The registrar is the sole judge of whether he passes this test. He may be asked to recite the entire Constitution, or explain the most complex provisions of State law. And even a college degree cannot be used to prove that he can read and write.

For the fact is that the only way to pass these barriers is to show a white skin.

Experience has clearly shown that the existing process of law cannot overcome systematic and ingenious discrimination. No law that we now have on the books—and I have helped to put three of them there—can ensure the right to vote when local officials are determined to deny it.

In such a case our duty must be clear to all of us. The Constitution says that no person shall be kept from voting because of his race or his color. We have all sworn an oath before God to support and to defend that Constitution. We must now act in obedience to that oath.

Wednesday I will send to Congress a law designed to eliminate illegal barriers to the right to vote.

The broad principles of that bill will be in the hands of the Democratic and Republican leaders tomorrow. After they have reviewed it, it will come here formally as a bill. I am grateful for this opportunity to come here tonight at the invitation of the leadership to reason with my friends, to give them my views, and to visit with my former colleagues. . . .

This bill will strike down restrictions to voting in all elections—Federal, State, and local—which have been used to deny Negroes the right to vote.

This bill will establish a simple, uniform standard which cannot be used, however ingenious the effort, to flout our Constitution.

It will provide for citizens to be registered by officials of the United States Government if the State officials refuse to register them.

It will eliminate tedious, unnecessary lawsuits which delay the right to vote.

Finally, this legislation will ensure that properly registered individuals are not prohibited from voting.

I will welcome the suggestions from all of the Members of Congress—I have no doubt that I will get some—on ways and means to strengthen this law and to make it effective. But experience has plainly shown that this is the only path to carry out the command of the Constitution.

To those who seek to avoid action by their National Government in their own communities; who want to and who seek to maintain purely local control over elections, the answer is simple:

Open your polling places to all your people.

Allow men and women to register and vote whatever the color of their skin.

Extend the rights of citizenship to every citizen of this land. . . .

I ask you to join me in working long hours—nights and weekends, if necessary—to pass this bill. And I don't make that request lightly. For from the window where I sit with the problems of our country I recognize that outside this chamber is the outraged conscience of a nation, the grave concern of many nations, and the harsh judgment of history on our acts.

But even if we pass this bill, the battle will not be over. What happened in Selma is part of a far larger movement which reaches into every section and State of America. It is the effort of American Negroes to secure for themselves the full blessings of American life.

Their cause must be our cause too. Because it is not just Negroes, but really it is all of us, who must overcome the crippling legacy of bigotry and injustice.

And we shall overcome.

As a man whose roots go deeply into Southern soil I know how agonizing racial feelings are. I know how difficult it is to reshape the attitudes and the structure of our society.

But a century has passed, more than a hundred years, since the Negro was freed. And he is not fully free tonight.

It was more than a hundred years ago that Abraham Lincoln, a great President of another party, signed the Emancipation Proclamation, but emancipation is a proclamation and not a fact.

A century has passed, more than a hundred years, since equality was promised. And yet the Negro is not equal.

A century has passed since the day of promise. And the promise is unkept.

The time of justice has now come. I tell you that I believe sincerely that no force can hold it back. It is right in the eyes of man and God that it should come. And when it does, I think that day will brighten the lives of every American.

For Negroes are not the only victims. How many white children have gone uneducated, how many white families have lived in stark poverty, how many white lives have been scarred by fear, because we have wasted our energy and our substance to maintain the barriers of hatred and terror?

So I say to all of you here, and to all in the Nation tonight, that those who appeal to you to hold on to the past do so at the cost of denying you your future.

This great, rich, restless country can offer opportunity and education and hope to all: black and white, North and South, sharecropper and city dweller. These are the enemies: poverty, ignorance, disease. They are the enemies and not our fellow man, not our neighbor. And these enemies too, poverty, disease and ignorance, we shall overcome.

Now let none of us in any sections look with prideful righteousness on the troubles in another section, or on the problems of our neighbors. There is really no part of America where the promise of equality has been fully kept. In Buffalo as well as in Birmingham, in Philadelphia as well as in Selma, Americans are struggling for the fruits of freedom.

This is one Nation. What happens in Selma or in Cincinnati is a matter of legitimate concern to every American. But let each of us look within our own hearts and our own communities, and let each of us put our shoulder to the wheel to root out injustice wherever it exists. . . .

The real hero of this struggle is the American Negro. His actions and protests, his courage to risk safety and even to risk his life, have awakened the conscience of this Nation. His demonstrations have been designed to call attention to injustice, designed to provoke change, designed to stir reform.

He has called upon us to make good the promise of America. And who among us can say that we would have made the same progress were it not for his persistent bravery, and his faith in American democracy.

For at the real heart of battle for equality is a deep-seated belief in the democratic process. Equality depends not on the force of arms or tear gas but upon the force of moral right; not on recourse to violence but on respect for law and order. . . .

The bill that I am presenting to you will be known as a civil rights bill. But, in a larger sense, most of the program I am recommending is a civil rights program. Its object is to open the city of hope to all people of all races.

Because all Americans just must have the right to vote. And we are going to give them that right.

All Americans must have the privileges of citizenship regardless of race. And they are going to have those privileges of citizenship regardless of race.

But I would like to caution you and remind you that to exercise these privileges takes much more than just legal right. It requires a trained mind and a healthy body. It requires a decent home, and the chance to find a job, and the opportunity to escape from the clutches of poverty.

Of course, people cannot contribute to the Nation if they are never taught to read or write,

if their bodies are stunted from hunger, if their sickness goes untended, if their life is spent in hopeless poverty just drawing a welfare check.

So we want to open the gates to opportunity. But we are also going to give all our people, black and white, the help that they need to walk through those gates.

My first job after college was as a teacher in Cotulla, Tex., in a small Mexican-American school. Few of them could speak English, and I couldn't speak much Spanish. My students were poor and they often came to class without breakfast, hungry. They knew even in their youth the pain of prejudice. They never seemed to know why people disliked them. But they knew it was so, because I saw it in their eyes. I often walked home late in the afternoon, after the classes were finished, wishing there was more that I could do. But all I knew was to teach them the little that I knew, hoping that it might help them against the hardships that lay ahead.

Somehow you never forget what poverty and hatred can do when you see its scars on the hopeful face of a young child.

I never thought then, in 1928, that I would be standing here in 1965. It never even occurred to me in my fondest dreams that I might have the chance to help the sons and daughters of those students and to help people like them all over this country.

But now I do have that chance—and I'll let you in on a secret—I mean to use it. And I hope that you will use it with me.

This is the richest and most powerful country which ever occupied the globe. The might of past empires is little compared to ours. But I do not want to be the President who built empires, or sought grandeur, or extended dominion.

I want to be the President who educated young children to the wonders of their world. I want to be the President who helped to feed the hungry and to prepare them to be taxpayers instead of taxeaters.

I want to be the President who helped the poor to find their own way and who protected the right of every citizen to vote in every election.

I want to be the President who helped to end hatred among his fellow men and who promoted love among the people of all races and all regions and all parties.

I want to be the President who helped to end war among the brothers of this earth.

And so at the request of your beloved Speaker and the Senator from Montana; the majority leader, the Senator from Illinois; the minority leader, Mr. McCulloch, and other Members of both parties, I came here tonight—not as President Roosevelt came down one time in person to veto a bonus bill, not as President Truman came down one time to urge the passage of a railroad bill—but I came down here to ask you to share this task with me and to share it with the people that we both work for. I want this to be the Congress, Republicans and Democrats alike, which did all these things for all these people.

Beyond this great chamber, out yonder in 50 States, are the people that we serve. Who can tell what deep and unspoken hopes are in their hearts tonight as they sit there and listen. We all can guess, from our own lives, how difficult they often find their own pursuit of happiness, how many problems each little family has. They look most of all to themselves for their futures. But I think that they also look to each of us.

Above the pyramid on the great seal of the United States it says—in Latin—"God has favored our undertaking."

God will not favor everything that we do. It is rather our duty to divine His will. But I cannot help believing that He truly understands and that He really favors the undertaking that we begin here tonight.

Source: *Public Papers of the Presidents of the United States: Lyndon B. Johnson, 1965*, Vol. 1, entry 107 (Washington, D.C.: Government Printing Office, 1966), 281–287.

---

23   **Speech by Rev. Martin Luther King Jr.: "Our God Is Marching On,"**
      March 25, 1965

As Congress and the Justice Department began working on the Voting Rights Act in the days after President Lyndon B. Johnson delivered his historic address to a joint session of Congress (Document 22), the protest in Selma, Alabama, continued to rage. On March 16, protests were held in Selma and in Montgomery, and again in Selma on March 19. At the same time, a less visible struggle had erupted among Alabama officials, the White House, and the federal judiciary over the legal status of the march from Selma to Montgomery. That march had first been proposed as a compromise among divided civil rights leaders over how to react to the death of Selma church deacon and farmer Jimmie Lee Jackson, who was beaten and shot to death by police while trying to protect his mother from them. But the state of Alabama had quickly banned the march. Thus technically the March 7 assault by Alabama state police at the Edmund Pettus Bridge leading out of Selma was an enforcement of the ban (though, of course, it was much more than that).

Federal district judge Frank Johnson agreed to rule on the constitutionality of Alabama's ban. The opponents of voting rights knew that if Judge Johnson did not strike down the ban, they could depict any march to Montgomery as lawless, a violation of federal and state authority, notwithstanding the brutality already shown by the state police. That stigma, in turn, might jeopardize the legislative launch of the new voting rights bill.

But Judge Johnson ruled against Alabama governor George C. Wallace on March 17, thereby removing any legal obstacles to the march. The White House pressured Governor Wallace for a commitment that the state of Alabama would protect the marchers as they trekked from Selma to Mont-

gomery. Wallace, however, refused. President Johnson then called the Alabama National Guard into federal service and deployed U.S. marshals as well. On March 21, the marchers set out, and they arrived in Montgomery on March 25. Today, the National Park Service maintains a Selma-to-Montgomery National Historic Trail, the result of legislation introduced in Congress in the mid-1990s by Democratic representative John Lewis of Georgia, who, in his role as a leader of the Student Non-violent Coordinating Committee (SNCC), walked at the head the of the march on March 7 as it came over the Edmund Pettus Bridge.

Capping off the march, Rev. Martin Luther King Jr. gave an address in Montgomery now known as "Our God Is Marching On." Strikingly, King's luminous speech offered a complete theory of the black disenfranchisement that had occurred at the end of the nineteenth century, one that King took from a work by the great historian C. Vann Woodward, The Strange Career of Jim Crow. *In 1965 the book was already being widely read within the civil rights movement in order to validate the fundamentally hopeful possibility of biracial reconciliation.*

King also referred to the frightful cost of the Selma protest—the deaths of Jimmie Lee Jackson and Rev. James Reeb, a Unitarian minister from Boston. Tragically, neither King nor the thousands who listened to him knew that a third death would occur that very evening—the Ku Klux Klan assassinated one of the march's organizational volunteers, Viola Liuzzo, whose powerful and affecting story is told by Mary Stanton in From Selma to Sorrow: The Life and Death of Viola Liuzzo *(Athens: University of Georgia Press, 1998).*

[Editorial note: In the following speech, audience responses appear in parentheses.]

My dear and abiding friends. . . . Last Sunday, more than eight thousand of us started on a mighty walk from Selma, Alabama. . . .

Now it is not an accident that one of the great marches of American history should terminate in Montgomery, Alabama. (Yes, sir) Just ten years ago, in this very city, a new philosophy was born of the Negro struggle. Montgomery was the first city in the South in which the entire Negro community united and squarely faced its age-old oppressors. (Yes, sir. Well) Out of this struggle, more than bus [de]segregation was won; a new idea, more powerful than guns or clubs was born. Negroes took it and carried it across the South in epic battles (Yes, sir. Speak) that electrified the nation (Well) and the world.

Yet, strangely, the climactic conflicts always were fought and won on Alabama soil. After Montgomery's, heroic confrontations loomed up in Mississippi, Arkansas, Georgia, and elsewhere. But not until the colossus of segregation was challenged in Birmingham did the conscience of America begin to bleed. White America was profoundly aroused by Birmingham because it witnessed the whole community of Negroes facing terror and brutality with majestic scorn and heroic courage. And from the wells of this democratic spirit, the nation finally forced Congress (Well) to write legislation (Yes, sir) in the hope that it would eradicate the stain of Birmingham. The Civil Rights Act of 1964 gave Negroes some part of their rightful dignity, (Speak, sir) but without the vote it was dignity without strength. (Yes, sir)

Once more the method of nonviolent resistance (Yes) was unsheathed from its scabbard, and once again an entire community was mobilized to confront the adversary. (Yes, sir) And again the brutality of a dying order shrieks across the land. Yet, Selma, Alabama, became a shining moment in the conscience of man. If the worst in American life lurked in its dark streets, the best of American instincts arose passionately from across the nation to overcome it. (Yes, sir. Speak) There never was a moment in American history (Yes, sir) more honorable and more inspiring than the pilgrimage of clergymen and laymen of every race and faith pouring into Selma to face danger (Yes) at the side of its embattled Negroes.

The confrontation of good and evil compressed in the tiny community of Selma (Speak,

speak) generated the massive power (Yes, sir. Yes, sir) to turn the whole nation to a new course. A president born in the South (Well) had the sensitivity to feel the will of the country, (Speak, sir) and in an address that will live in history as one of the most passionate pleas for human rights ever made by a president of our nation, he pledged the might of the federal government to cast off the centuries-old blight. President Johnson rightly praised the courage of the Negro for awakening the conscience of the nation. . . .

Our whole campaign in Alabama has been centered around the right to vote. In focusing the attention of the nation and the world today on the flagrant denial of the right to vote, we are exposing the very origin, the root cause, of racial segregation in the Southland. Racial segregation as a way of life did not come about as a natural result of hatred between the races immediately after the Civil War. There were no laws segregating the races then. And as the noted historian, C. Vann Woodward, in his book, *The Strange Career of Jim Crow,* clearly points out, the segregation of the races was really a political stratagem employed by the emerging Bourbon interests in the South to keep the southern masses divided and southern labor the cheapest in the land. You see, it was a simple thing to keep the poor white masses working for near-starvation wages in the years that followed the Civil War. Why, if the poor white plantation or mill worker became dissatisfied with his low wages, the plantation or mill owner would merely threaten to fire him and hire former Negro slaves and pay him even less. Thus, the southern wage level was kept almost unbearably low.

Toward the end of the Reconstruction era, something very significant happened. (Listen to him) That is what was known as the Populist Movement. (Speak, sir) The leaders of this movement began awakening the poor white masses (Yes, sir) and the former Negro slaves to the fact that they were being fleeced by the emerging Bourbon interests. Not only that, but they began uniting the Negro and white masses (Yeah) into a voting bloc that threatened to drive the Bourbon interests from the command posts of political power in the South.

To meet this threat, the southern aristocracy began immediately to engineer this development of a segregated society. (Right) I want you to follow me through here because this is very important to see the roots of racism and the denial of the right to vote. Through their control of mass media, they revised the doctrine of white supremacy. They saturated the thinking of the poor white masses with it, (Yes) thus clouding their minds to the real issue involved in the Populist Movement. They then directed the placement on the books of the South of laws that made it a crime for Negroes and whites to come together as equals at any level. (Yes, sir) And that did it. That crippled and eventually destroyed the Populist Movement of the nineteenth century.

If it may be said of the slavery era that the white man took the world and gave the Negro Jesus, then it may be said of the Reconstruction era that the southern aristocracy took the world and gave the poor white man Jim Crow. (Yes, sir) He gave him Jim Crow. (Uh huh) And when his wrinkled stomach cried out for the food that his empty pockets could not provide, (Yes, sir) he ate Jim Crow, a psychological bird that told him that no matter how bad off he was, at least he was a white man, better than the black man. (Right sir) And he ate Jim Crow. (Uh huh) And when his undernourished children cried out for the necessities that his low wages could not provide, he showed them the Jim Crow signs on the buses and in the stores, on the streets and in the public buildings. (Yes, sir) And his children, too, learned to feed upon Jim Crow, (Speak) their last outpost of psychological oblivion. (Yes, sir)

Thus, the threat of the free exercise of the ballot by the Negro and the white masses alike (Uh huh) resulted in the establishment of a segregated society. They segregated southern money from the poor whites; they segregated southern mores from the rich whites; (Yes, sir) they segregated southern churches from Christianity (Yes, sir);

they segregated southern minds from honest thinking; (Yes, sir) and they segregated the Negro from everything. (Yes, sir) That's what happened when the Negro and white masses of the South threatened to unite and build a great society: a society of justice where none would prey upon the weakness of others; a society of plenty where greed and poverty would be done away; a society of brotherhood where every man would respect the dignity and worth of human personality. (Yes, sir)

We've come a long way since that travesty of justice was perpetrated upon the American mind. James Weldon Johnson put it eloquently. He said:

We have come over a way
That with tears hath been watered. (Yes, sir)
We have come treading our paths
Through the blood of the slaughtered. (Yes, sir)
Out of the gloomy past, (Yes, sir)
Till now we stand at last
Where the white gleam
Of our bright star is cast. (Speak, sir)

Today I want to tell the city of Selma, (Tell them, Doctor) today I want to say to the state of Alabama, (Yes, sir) today I want to say to the people of America and the nations of the world, that we are not about to turn around. (Yes, sir) We are on the move now. (Yes, sir)

Yes, we are on the move and no wave of racism can stop us. (Yes, sir) We are on the move now. The burning of our churches will not deter us. (Yes, sir) The bombing of our homes will not dissuade us. (Yes, sir) We are on the move now. (Yes, sir) The beating and killing of our clergymen and young people will not divert us. We are on the move now. (Yes, sir) The wanton release of their known murderers would not discourage us. We are on the move now. (Yes, sir) Like an idea whose time has come, (Yes, sir) not even the marching of mighty armies can halt us. (Yes, sir) We are moving to the land of freedom. (Yes, sir)

Let us therefore continue our triumphant march (Uh huh) to the realization of the American dream. (Yes, sir) Let us march on segregated housing (Yes, sir) until every ghetto or social and economic depression dissolves, and Negroes and whites live side by side in decent, safe, and sanitary housing. (Yes, sir) Let us march on segregated schools (Let us march, Tell it) until every vestige of segregated and inferior education becomes a thing of the past, and Negroes and whites study side-by-side in the socially-healing context of the classroom.

Let us march on poverty (Let us march) until no American parent has to skip a meal so that their children may eat. (Yes, sir) March on poverty (Let us march) until no starved man walks the streets of our cities and towns (Yes, sir) in search of jobs that do not exist. (Yes, sir) Let us march on poverty (Let us march) until wrinkled stomachs in Mississippi are filled, (That's right) and the idle industries of Appalachia are realized and revitalized, and broken lives in sweltering ghettos are mended and remolded.

Let us march on ballot boxes, (Let's march) march on ballot boxes until race-baiters disappear from the political arena.

Let us march on ballot boxes until the salient misdeeds of bloodthirsty mobs (Yes, sir) will be transformed into the calculated good deeds of orderly citizens. (Speak, Doctor)

Let us march on ballot boxes (Let us march) until the Wallaces of our nation tremble away in silence.

Let us march on ballot boxes (Let us march) until we send to our city councils (Yes, sir), state legislatures, (Yes, sir) and the United States Congress, (Yes, sir) men who will not fear to do justly, love mercy, and walk humbly with thy God.

Let us march on ballot boxes (Let us march. March) until brotherhood becomes more than a meaningless word in an opening prayer, but the order of the day on every legislative agenda.

Let us march on ballot boxes (Yes) until all over Alabama God's children will be able to walk the earth in decency and honor. . . .

In the glow of the lamplight on my desk a few nights ago, I gazed again upon the wondrous sign of our times, full of hope and promise of the future. (Uh huh) And I smiled to see in the newspaper photographs of many a decade ago, the faces so bright, so solemn, of our valiant heroes, the people of Montgomery. To this list may be added the names of all those (Yes) who have fought and, yes, died in the nonviolent army of our day: Medgar Evers, (Speak) three civil rights workers in Mississippi last summer, (Uh huh) William Moore, as has already been mentioned, (Yes, sir) the Reverend James Reeb, (Yes, sir) Jimmie Lee Jackson, (Yes, sir) and four little girls in the church of God in Birmingham on Sunday morning. (Yes, sir) But in spite of this, we must go on and be sure that they did not die in vain. (Yes, sir) The pattern of their feet as they walked through Jim Crow barriers in the great stride toward freedom is the thunder of the marching men of Joshua, (Yes, sir) and the world rocks beneath their tread. (Yes, sir)

My people, my people, listen. (Yes, sir) The battle is in our hands. (Yes, sir). . . .

And so as we go away this afternoon, let us go away more than ever before committed to this struggle and committed to nonviolence. I must admit to you that there are still some difficult days ahead. We are still in for a season of suffering in many of the black belt counties of Alabama, many areas of Mississippi, many areas of Louisiana. I must admit to you that there are still jail cells waiting for us, and dark and difficult moments. But if we will go on with the faith that nonviolence and its power can transform dark yesterdays into bright tomorrows, we will be able to change all of these conditions.

And so I plead with you this afternoon as we go ahead: remain committed to nonviolence. Our aim must never be to defeat or humiliate the white man, but to win his friendship and understanding. We must come to see that the end we seek is a society at peace with itself, a society that can live with its conscience. And that will be a day not of the white man, not of the black man. That will be the day of man as man. (Yes)

I know you are asking today, "How long will it take?" (Speak, sir) Somebody's asking, "How long will prejudice blind the visions of men, darken their understanding, and drive bright-eyed wisdom from her sacred throne?" Somebody's asking, "When will wounded justice, lying prostrate on the streets of Selma and Birmingham and communities all over the South, be lifted from this dust of shame to reign supreme among the children of men?" Somebody's asking, "When will the radiant star of hope be plunged against the nocturnal bosom of this lonely night, (Speak, speak, speak) plucked from weary souls with chains of fear and the manacles of death? How long will justice be crucified, (Speak) and truth bear it?" (Yes, sir)

I come to say to you this afternoon, however difficult the moment, (Yes, sir) however frustrating the hour, it will not be long, (No sir) because "truth crushed to earth will rise again." (Yes, sir)

How long? Not long, (Yes, sir) because "no lie can live forever." (Yes, sir)

How long? Not long, (All right. How long) because "you shall reap what you sow." (Yes, sir)

How long? (How long?) Not long: (Not long)

Truth forever on the scaffold, (Speak)
Wrong forever on the throne, (Yes, sir)
Yet that scaffold sways the future, (Yes, sir)
And, behind the dim unknown,
Standeth God within the shadow,
Keeping watch above his own.

How long? Not long, because the arc of the moral universe is long, but it bends toward justice. (Yes, sir)

How long? Not long, (Not long) because:

Mine eyes have seen the glory of the coming of the
    Lord; (Yes, sir)
He is trampling out the vintage where the grapes of
    wrath are stored; (Yes)
He has loosed the fateful lightning of his terrible swift
    sword; (Yes, sir)
His truth is marching on. (Yes, sir)
He has sounded forth the trumpet that shall never
    call retreat; (Speak, sir)
He is sifting out the hearts of men before His judg-
    ment seat. (That's right)

O, be swift, my soul, to answer Him! Be jubilant my
  feet!
Our God is marching on. (Yeah)
Glory, hallelujah! (Yes, sir) Glory, hallelujah! (All
  right)
Glory, hallelujah! Glory, hallelujah!
His truth is marching on. [Applause]

Source: The Martin Luther King, Jr., Papers Project,
Stanford University, 2002, http://www.stanford.edu/group/
King/publications/speeches/Our_God_is_marching_on.
html.

---

24   Joint Statement of the Senate Judiciary Committee Supporting Adoption of the Voting Rights Act, April 21, 1965

*The Voting Rights Act is widely acknowledged to have been crafted in the executive branch. In this
important way, America's second great legislative effort to protect African American voting rights differed from the first, which was enacted between 1865 and the early 1870s. Then, the initiative lay
with the Republican Party in Congress, and the executive branch did very little. Indeed, there was not
even a Justice Department until 1870, when Congress created it in part to equip the national government to handle the new responsibilities that came with the enforcement of black voting rights.*

*Although the 1965 Voting Rights Act originated in the executive branch, it required enormous ex-
ertion by Congress. The legislative blueprint may have come from outside Congress, but large majorities in both the House and the Senate clearly understood that Congress very much had the power to
enforce the Fifteenth Amendment in the way that the Johnson administration proposed. A particularly
succinct expression of this constitutional claim was revealed in an April 21, 1965, "joint statement"
of twelve members of the Senate Judiciary Committee.*

The proposed legislation implements the explicit
command of the 15th Amendment that the "right
* * * to vote shall not be denied or abridged * * *
by any State on account of race [or] color."

1. *The power of Congress*

Section 2 of the amendment says, with respect
to the 15th article of amendment: "The Congress
shall have power to enforce this article by appropriate legislation" (Amend. XV., § 2). Here, then,
we draw on one of the powers expressly delegated by the people and by the States to the Congress—the power to prevent the denial of
abridgement of the right to vote on account of
race or color.

No statute confined to enforcing the 15th
amendment from racial discrimination in voting
has ever been voided by the Supreme Court. The
criminal laws involved in the cases of *United*
States v. Reese (92 U.S. 214), and *James v. Bowman* (190 U.S. 127), were held bad because they
purported to punish interference with voting on
grounds other than race. Indeed, in *Reese* (92
U.S. at 218), and again in *Bowman* (190 U.S. at
138–139), the Supreme Court expressly recognized the power of Congress to deal with racial
discrimination in voting:

If citizens of one race having certain qualifications are
permitted by law to vote , those of another having the
same qualifications must be. Previous to this amendment, there was no constitutional guarantee against
this discrimination: now there is. It follows that the
amendment has invested the citizens of the United
States with a new constitutional right which is within
the protecting power of Congress. That right is exemption from discrimination in the exercise of the
elective franchise on account of race, color, or previous condition of servitude. This, under the express
provisions of the second section of the amendment,
Congress may enforce by "appropriate legislation."

(See also *United States v. Raines,* 362 U.S. 17 (1957 act); *United States v. Thomas,* 362 U.S. 58 (same); *Hannah v. Larche,* 363 U.S. 420 (Civil Rights Commission rules under 1957 act); *Alabama v. United States,* 371 U.S. 37 (1960 act); *United States v. Mississippi,* No. 73, this term, decided Mar. 8, 1965 (same); *Louisiana v. United States,* No. 67, this term, decided Mar. 6, 1965 (same).)

It remains only to see whether the *means* suggested are appropriate. In the case of *Ex Parte Virginia,* already referred to, still speaking of the three postwar amendments, the Court continues (100 U.S. at 345–346):

Whatever legislation is appropriate, that is, adapted to carry out the objects the amendments have in view,

whatever tends to enforce submission to the prohibitions they contain, and to secure to all persons the enjoyment of perfect equality of civil rights and the equal protection of the laws against State denial or invasion, if not prohibited, is brought within the domain of congressional power. . . .

_____

Source: U.S. Congress, Senate, "Joint Statement of Individual Views by Mr. Dodd, Mr. Hart, Mr. Long of Mississippi, Mr. Kennedy of Massachusetts, Mr. Bayh, Mr. Burdick, Mr. Tydings, Mr. Dirksen, Mr. Hruska, Mr. Fong, Mr. Scott, and Mr. Javits of the Committee of the Judiciary Supporting the Adoption of S. 1564, the Voting Rights Act of 1965," Report 162, Part 3, 89th Cong., 1st sess.

---

25   Voting Rights Act, August 6, 1965

The Voting Rights Act may have been drafted quickly within the Justice Department, but it was drafted well. Attorney General Nicholas de B. Katzenbach apparently did most of the work, but he had some help from Harold H. Greene in the Civil Rights Division and from Solicitor General Archibald Cox. Because no detailed legislative history is available for the Voting Rights Act (a major gap in scholarship on the act), important questions remain unanswered to this day: Did the attorney general consult with the president, and, if so, how much? Did the president play any direct role in the formulation of the act? What roles did the House and Senate play in crafting the statute? Were civil rights leaders and private voting rights lawyers consulted? Most important, how and why were the attorney general and Congress able to draft the statute so well in such a short time (between March and mid-summer of 1965) when there had been no particular plans for such a statute at the beginning of 1965? One day these questions will be answered. When they are, they will likely underscore the central role of Katzenbach's vision, energy, and skill.

AN ACT To enforce the fifteenth amendment to the Constitution of the United States, and for other purposes.

Be it enacted by the Senate and House of Representatives of the United States of America in Congress assembled, That this Act shall be known as the "Voting Rights Act of 1965."

SEC. 2. No voting qualification or prerequisite to voting, or standard, practice, or procedure shall be imposed or applied by any State or political subdivision to deny or abridge the right of any citizen of the United States to vote on account of race or color.

SEC. 3. (a) Whenever the Attorney General institutes a proceeding under any statute to enforce the guarantees of the fifteenth amendment in any State or political subdivision the court shall authorize the appointment of Federal examiners by the United States Civil Service Commission in accordance with section 6 to serve for such period of time and for such political subdivisions as the court shall determine is appropriate to enforce the guarantees of the fifteenth amendment (1) as part of any interlocutory order if the court determines that the appointment of such examiners is necessary to enforce such guarantees or (2) as part of any final judgment if the court finds that violations of the fifteenth amendment justifying equitable relief have occurred in such State or subdivision: Provided, That the court need not authorize the appointment of examiners if any incidents of denial or abridgement of the right to vote on account of race or color (1) have been few in number and have been promptly and effectively corrected by State or local action, (2) the continuing effect of such incidents has been eliminated, and (3) there is no reasonable probability of their recurrence in the future.

(b) If in a proceeding instituted by the Attorney General under any statute to enforce the guarantees of the fifteenth amendment in any State or political subdivision the court finds that a test or device has been used for the purpose or with the effect of denying or abridging the right of any citizen of the United States to vote on account of race or color, it shall suspend the use of tests and devices in such State or political subdivisions as the court shall determine is appropriate and for such period as it deems necessary.

(c) If in any proceeding instituted by the Attorney General under any statute to enforce the guarantees of the fifteenth amendment in any State or political subdivision the court finds that violations of the fifteenth amendment justifying equitable relief have occurred within the territory of such State or political subdivision, the court, in addition to such relief as it may grant, shall retain jurisdiction for such period as it may deem appropriate and during such period no voting qualification or prerequisite to voting, or standard,

practice, or procedure with respect to voting different from that in force or effect at the time the proceeding was commenced shall be enforced unless and until the court finds that such qualification, prerequisite, standard, practice, or procedure does not have the purpose and will not have the effect of denying or abridging the right to vote on account of race or color: Provided, That such qualification, prerequisite, standard, practice, or procedure may be enforced if the qualification, prerequisite, standard, practice, or procedure has been submitted by the chief legal officer or other appropriate official of such State or subdivision to the Attorney General and the Attorney General has not interposed an objection within sixty days after such submission, except that neither the court's finding nor the Attorney General's failure to object shall bar a subsequent action to enjoin enforcement of such qualification, prerequisite, standard, practice, or procedure.

SEC. 4. (a) To assure that the right of citizens of the United States to vote is not denied or abridged on account of race or color, no citizen shall be denied the right to vote in any Federal, State, or local election because of his failure to comply with any test or device in any State with respect to which the determinations have been made under subsection (b) or in any political subdivision with respect to which such determinations have been made as a separate unit, unless the United States District Court for the District of Columbia in an action for a declaratory judgment brought by such State or subdivision against the United States has determined that no such test or device has been used during the five years preceding the filing of the action for the purpose or with the effect of denying or abridging the right to vote on account of race or color: Provided, That no such declaratory judgment shall issue with respect to any plaintiff for a period of five years after the entry of a final judgment of any court of the United States, other than the denial of a declaratory judgment under this section, whether entered prior to or after the enactment of this Act, determining that denials or abridgments of the right to vote on account of race or color through the use of such tests or devices have occurred anywhere in the territory of such plaintiff. An action pursuant to this subsection shall be heard and determined by a court of three judges in accordance with the provisions of section 2284 of title 28 of the United States Code and any appeal shall lie to the Supreme Court. The court shall retain jurisdiction of any action pursuant to this subsection for five years after judgment and shall reopen the action upon motion of the Attorney General alleging that a test or device has been used for the purpose or with the effect of denying or abridging the right to vote on account of race or color.

If the Attorney General determines that he has no reason to believe that any such test or device has been used during the five years preceding the filing of the action for the purpose or with the effect of denying or abridging the right to vote on account of race or color, he shall consent to the entry of such judgment.

(b) The provisions of subsection (a) shall apply in any State or in any political subdivision of a state which (1) the Attorney General determines maintained on November 1, 1964, any test or device, and with respect to which (2) the Director of the Census determines that less than 50 percentum of the persons of voting age residing therein were registered on November 1, 1964, or that less than 50 percentum of such persons voted in the presidential election of November 1964.

A determination or certification of the Attorney General or of the Director of the Census under this section or under section 6 or section 13 shall not be reviewable in any court and shall be effective upon publication in the Federal Register.

(c) The phrase "test or device" shall mean any requirement that a person as a prerequisite for voting or registration for voting (1) demonstrate the ability to read, write, understand, or interpret any matter, (2) demonstrate any educational achievement or his knowledge of any particular subject, (3) possess good moral character, or (4)

prove his qualifications by the voucher of registered voters or members of any other class.

(d) For purposes of this section no State or political subdivision shall be determined to have engaged in the use of tests or devices for the purpose or with the effect of denying or abridging the right to vote on account of race or color if (1) incidents of such use have been few in number and have been promptly and effectively corrected by State or local action, (2) the continuing effect of such incidents has been eliminated, and (3) there is no reasonable probability of their recurrence in the future.

(e)(1) Congress hereby declares that to secure the rights under the fourteenth amendment of persons educated in American-flag schools in which the predominant classroom language was other than English, it is necessary to prohibit the States from conditioning the right to vote of such persons on ability to read, write, understand, or interpret any matter in the English language. (2) No person who demonstrates that he has successfully completed the sixth primary grade in a public school in, or a private school accredited by, any State or territory, the District of Columbia, or the Commonwealth of Puerto Rico in which the predominant classroom language was other than English, shall be denied the right to vote in any Federal, State, or local election because of his inability to read, write, understand, or interpret any matter in the English language, except that, in States in which State law provides that a different level of education is presumptive of literacy, he shall demonstrate that he has successfully completed an equivalent level of education in a public school in, or a private school accredited by, any State or territory, the District of Columbia, or the Commonwealth of Puerto Rico in which the predominant classroom language was other than English.

SEC. 5. Whenever a State or political subdivision with respect to which the prohibitions set forth in section 4(a) are in effect shall enact or seek to administer any voting qualification or prerequisite to voting, or standard, practice, or procedure with respect to voting different from that in force or effect on November 1, 1964, such State or subdivision may institute an action in the United States District Court for the District of Columbia for a declaratory judgment that such qualification, prerequisite, standard, practice, or procedure does not have the purpose and will not have the effect of denying or abridging the right to vote on account of race or color, and unless and until the court enters such judgment no person shall be denied the right to vote for failure to comply with such qualification, prerequisite, standard, practice, or procedure: Provided, That such qualification, prerequisite, standard, practice, or procedure may be enforced without such proceeding if the qualification, prerequisite, standard, practice, or procedure has been submitted by the chief legal officer or other appropriate official of such State or subdivision to the Attorney General and the Attorney General has not interposed an objection within sixty days after such submission, except that neither the Attorney General's failure to object nor a declaratory judgment entered under this section shall bar a subsequent action to enjoin enforcement of such qualification, prerequisite, standard, practice, or procedure. Any action under this section shall be heard and determined by a court of three judges in accordance with the provisions of section 2284 of title 28 of the United States Code and any appeal shall lie to the Supreme Court.

SEC. 6. Whenever (a) a court has authorized the appointment of examiners pursuant to the provisions of section 3(a), or (b) unless a declaratory judgment has been rendered under section 4(a), the Attorney General certifies with respect to any political subdivision named in, or included within the scope of, determinations made under section 4(b) that (1) he has received complaints in writing from twenty or more residents of such political subdivision alleging that they have been denied the right to vote under color of law on account of race or color, and that he believes such complaints to be meritorious, or

(2) that, in his judgment (considering, among other factors, whether the ratio of nonwhite persons to white persons registered to vote within such subdivision appears to him to be reasonably attributable to violations of the fifteenth amendment or whether substantial evidence exists that bona fide efforts are being made within such subdivision to comply with the fifteenth amendment), the appointment of examiners is otherwise necessary to enforce the guarantees of the fifteenth amendment, the Civil Service Commission shall appoint as many examiners for such subdivision as it may deem appropriate to prepare and maintain lists of persons eligible to vote in Federal, State, and local elections. Such examiners, hearing officers provided for in section 9(a), and other persons deemed necessary by the Commission to carry out the provisions and purposes of this Act shall be appointed, compensated, and separated without regard to the provisions of any statute administered by the Civil Service Commission, and service under this Act shall not be considered employment for the purposes of any statute administered by the Civil Service Commission, except the provisions of section 9 of the Act of August 2, 1939, as amended (5 U.S.C. 118i), prohibiting partisan political activity: Provided, That the Commission is authorized, after consulting the head of the appropriate department or agency, to designate suitable persons in the official service of the United States, with their consent, to serve in these positions. Examiners and hearing officers shall have the power to administer oaths.

SEC. 7. (a) The examiners for each political subdivision shall, at such places as the Civil Service Commission shall by regulation designate, examine applicants concerning their qualifications for voting. An application to an examiner shall be in such form as the Commission may require and shall contain allegations that the applicant is not otherwise registered to vote. (b) Any person whom the examiner finds, in accordance with instructions received under section 9(b), to have the qualifications prescribed by State law not inconsistent with the Constitution and laws of the United States shall promptly be placed on a list of eligible voters. A challenge to such listing may be made in accordance with section 9(a) and shall not be the basis for a prosecution under section 12 of this Act. The examiner shall certify and transmit such list, and any supplements as appropriate, at least once a month, to the offices of the appropriate election officials, with copies to the Attorney General and the attorney general of the State, and any such lists and supplements thereto transmitted during the month shall be available for public inspection on the last business day of the month and, in any event, not later than the forty-fifth day prior to any election. The appropriate State or local election official shall place such names on the official voting list. Any person whose name appears on the examiner's list shall be entitled and allowed to vote in the election district of his residence unless and until the appropriate election officials shall have been notified that such person has been removed from such list in accordance with subsection (d): Provided, That no person shall be entitled to vote in any election by virtue of this Act unless his name shall have been certified and transmitted on such a list to the offices of the appropriate election officials at least forty-five days prior to such election.

(c) The examiner shall issue to each person whose name appears on such a list a certificate evidencing his eligibility to vote.

(d) A person whose name appears on such a list shall be removed therefrom by an examiner if (1) such person has been successfully challenged in accordance with the procedure prescribed in section 9, or (2) he has been determined by an examiner to have lost his eligibility to vote under State law not inconsistent with the Constitution and the laws of the United States.

SEC. 8. Whenever an examiner is serving under this Act in any political subdivision, the Civil Service Commission may assign, at the request of the Attorney General, one or more per-

sons, who may be officers of the United States, (1) to enter and attend at any place for holding an election in such subdivision for the purpose of observing whether persons who are entitled to vote are being permitted to vote, and (2) to enter and attend at any place for tabulating the votes cast at any election held in such subdivision for the purpose of observing whether votes cast by persons entitled to vote are being properly tabulated. Such persons so assigned shall report to an examiner appointed for such political subdivision, to the Attorney General, and if the appointment of examiners has been authorized pursuant to section 3(a), to the court.

SEC. 9. (a) Any challenge to a listing on an eligibility list prepared by an examiner shall be heard and determined by a hearing officer appointed by and responsible to the Civil Service Commission and under such rules as the Commission shall by regulation prescribe. Such challenge shall be entertained only if filed at such office within the State as the Civil Service Commission shall by regulation designate, and within ten days after the listing of the challenged person is made available for public inspection, and if supported by (1) the affidavits of at least two persons having personal knowledge of the facts constituting grounds for the challenge, and (2) a certification that a copy of the challenge and affidavits have been served by mail or in person upon the person challenged at his place of residence set out in the application. Such challenge shall be determined within fifteen days after it has been filed. A petition for review of the decision of the hearing officer may be filed in the United States court of appeals for the circuit in which the person challenged resides within fifteen days after service of such decision by mail on the person petitioning for review but no decision of a hearing officer shall be reversed unless clearly erroneous. Any person listed shall be entitled and allowed to vote pending final determination by the hearing officer and by the court.

(b) The times, places, procedures, and form for application and listing pursuant to this Act and removals from the eligibility lists shall be prescribed by regulations promulgated by the Civil Service Commission and the Commission shall, after consultation with the Attorney General, instruct examiners concerning applicable State law not inconsistent with the Constitution and laws of the United States with respect to (1) the qualifications required for listing, and (2) loss of eligibility to vote.

(c) Upon the request of the applicant or the challenger or on its own motion the Civil Service Commission shall have the power to require by subpoena the attendance and testimony of witnesses and the production of documentary evidence relating to any matter pending before it under the authority of this section. In case of contumacy or refusal to obey a subpoena, any district court of the United States or the United States court of any territory or possession, or the District Court of the United States for the District of Columbia, within the jurisdiction of which said person guilty of contumacy or refusal to obey is found or resides or is domiciled or transacts business, or has appointed an agent for receipt of service of process, upon application by the Attorney General of the United States shall have jurisdiction to issue to such person an order requiring such person to appear before the Commission or a hearing officer, there to produce pertinent, relevant, and nonprivileged documentary evidence if so ordered, or there to give testimony touching the matter under investigation, and any failure to obey such order of the court may be punished by said court as a contempt thereof.

SEC. 10. (a) The Congress finds that the requirement of the payment of a poll tax as a precondition to voting (i) precludes persons of limited means from voting or imposes unreasonable financial hardship upon such persons as a precondition to their exercise of the franchise, (ii) does not bear a reasonable relationship to any legitimate State interest in the conduct of elections, and (iii) in some areas has the purpose or effect of denying persons the right to vote because of race or color. Upon the basis of these findings, Congress declares that the constitutional right of citizens to vote is denied or abridged in some areas by the requirement of the payment of a poll tax as a precondition to voting.

(b) In the exercise of the powers of Congress under section 5 of the fourteenth amendment and section 2 of the fifteenth amendment, the Attorney General is authorized and directed to institute forthwith in the name of the United States such actions, including actions against States or political subdivisions, for declaratory judgment or injunctive relief against the enforcement of any requirement of the payment of a poll tax as a precondition to voting, or substitute therefor enacted after November 1, 1964, as will be necessary to implement the declaration of subsection (a) and the purposes of this section.

(c) The district courts of the United States shall have jurisdiction of such actions which shall be heard and determined by a court of three judges in accordance with the provisions of section 2284 of title 28 of the United States Code and any appeal shall lie to the Supreme Court. It shall be the duty of the judges designated to hear the case to assign the case for hearing at the earliest practicable date, to participate in the hearing and determination thereof, and to cause the case to be in every way expedited.

(d) During the pendency of such actions, and thereafter if the courts, notwithstanding this action by the Congress, should declare the requirement of the payment of a poll tax to be constitutional, no citizen of the United States who is a resident of a State or political subdivision with respect to which determinations have been made under subsection 4(b) and a declaratory judgment has not been entered under subsection 4(a), during the first year he becomes otherwise entitled to vote by reason of registration by State or local officials or listing by an examiner, shall be denied the right to vote for failure to pay a poll tax if he tenders payment of such tax for the current year to an examiner or to the appropriate State or local official at least forty-five days prior to election, whether or not such tender would be timely or adequate under State law. An examiner shall have authority to accept such payment from any person authorized by this Act to make an application for listing, and shall issue a receipt for such payment. The examiner shall transmit promptly any such poll tax payment to the office of the State or local official authorized to receive such payment under State law, together with the name and address of the applicant.

SEC. 11. (a) No person acting under color of law shall fail or refuse to permit any person to vote who is entitled to vote under any provision of this Act or is otherwise qualified to vote, or willfully fail or refuse to tabulate, count, and report such person's vote.

(b) No person, whether acting under color of law or otherwise, shall intimidate, threaten, or coerce, or attempt to intimidate, threaten, or coerce any person for voting or attempting to vote, or intimidate, threaten, or coerce, or attempt to intimidate, threaten, or coerce any person for urging or aiding any person to vote or attempt to vote, or intimidate, threaten, or coerce any person for exercising any powers or duties under section 3(a), 6, 8, 9, 10, or 12(e).

(c) Whoever knowingly or willfully gives false information as to his name, address, or period of residence in the voting district for the purpose of establishing his eligibility to register or vote, or conspires with another individual for the purpose of encouraging his false registration to vote or illegal voting, or pays or offers to pay or accepts payment either for registration to vote or for voting shall be fined not more than $10,000 or imprisoned not more than five years, or both: Provided, however, That this provision shall be applicable only to general, special, or primary elections held solely or in part for the purpose of selecting or electing any candidate for the office of President, Vice President, presidential elector, Member of the United States Senate, Member of the United States House of Representatives, or Delegates or Commissioners from the territories

or possessions, or Resident Commissioner of the Commonwealth of Puerto Rico.

(d) Whoever, in any matter within the jurisdiction of an examiner or hearing officer knowingly and willfully falsifies or conceals a material fact, or makes any false, fictitious, or fraudulent statements or representations, or makes or uses any false writing or document knowing the same to contain any false, fictitious, or fraudulent statement or entry, shall be fined not more than $10,000 or imprisoned not more than five years, or both.

SEC. 12. (a) Whoever shall deprive or attempt to deprive any person of any right secured by section 2, 3, 4, 5, 7, or 10 or shall violate section 11(a) or (b), shall be fined not more than $5,000, or imprisoned not more than five years, or both.

(b) Whoever, within a year following an election in a political subdivision in which an examiner has been appointed (1) destroys, defaces, mutilates, or otherwise alters the marking of a paper ballot which has been cast in such election, or (2) alters any official record of voting in such election tabulated from a voting machine or otherwise, shall be fined not more than $5,000, or imprisoned not more than five years, or both .

(c) Whoever conspires to violate the provisions of subsection (a) or (b) of this section, or interferes with any right secured by section 2, 3 4, 5, 7, 10, or 11(a) or (b) shall be fined not more than $5,000, or imprisoned not more than five years, or both.

(d) Whenever any person has engaged or there are reasonable grounds to believe that any person is about to engage in any act or practice prohibited by section 2, 3, 4, 5, 7, 10, 11, or subsection (b) of this section, the Attorney General may institute for the United States, or in the name of the United States, an action for preventive relief, including an application for a temporary or permanent injunction, restraining order, or other order, and including an order directed to the State and State or local election officials to require them (1) to permit persons listed under this Act to vote and (2) to count such votes.

(e) Whenever in any political subdivision in which there are examiners appointed pursuant to this Act any persons allege to such an examiner within forty-eight hours after the closing of the polls that notwithstanding (1) their listing under this Act or registration by an appropriate election official and (2) their eligibility to vote, they have not been permitted to vote in such election, the examiner shall forthwith notify the Attorney General if such allegations in his opinion appear to be well founded. Upon receipt of such notification, the Attorney General may forthwith file with the district court an application for an order providing for the marking, casting, and counting of the ballots of such persons and requiring the inclusion of their votes in the total vote before the results of such election shall be deemed final and any force or effect given thereto. The district court shall hear and determine such matters immediately after the filing of such application. The remedy provided in this subsection shall not preclude any remedy available under State or Federal law.

(f) The district courts of the United States shall have jurisdiction of proceedings instituted pursuant to this section and shall exercise the same without regard to whether a person asserting rights under the provisions of this Act shall have exhausted any administrative or other remedies that may be provided by law

SEC. 13. Listing procedures shall be terminated in any political subdivision of any State (a) with respect to examiners appointed pursuant to clause (b) of section 6 whenever the Attorney General notifies the Civil Service Commission, or whenever the District Court for the District of Columbia determines in an action for declaratory judgment brought by any political subdivision with respect to which the Director of the Census has determined that more than 50 percentum of the nonwhite persons of voting age residing therein are registered to vote, (1) that all persons listed by an examiner for such subdivision have

been placed on the appropriate voting registration roll, and (2) that there is no longer reasonable cause to believe that persons will be deprived of or denied the right to vote on account of race or color in such subdivision, and (b), with respect to examiners appointed pursuant to section 3(a), upon order of the authorizing court. A political subdivision may petition the Attorney General for the termination of listing procedures under clause (a) of this section, and may petition the Attorney General to request the Director of the Census to take such survey or census as may be appropriate for the making of the determination provided for in this section. The District Court for the District of Columbia shall have jurisdiction to require such survey or census to be made by the Director of the Census and it shall require him to do so if it deems the Attorney General's refusal to request such survey or census to be arbitrary or unreasonable.

SEC. 14. (a) All cases of criminal contempt arising under the provisions of this Act shall be governed by section 151 of the Civil Rights Act of 1957 (42 U.S.C.1995).

(b) No court other than the District Court for the District of Columbia or a court of appeals in any proceeding under section 9 shall have jurisdiction to issue any declaratory judgment pursuant to section 4 or section 5 or any restraining order or temporary or permanent injunction against the execution or enforcement of any provision of this Act or any action of any Federal officer or employee pursuant hereto.

(c)(1) The terms "vote" or "voting" shall include all action necessary to make a vote effective in any primary, special, or general election, including, but not limited to, registration, listing pursuant to this Act, or other action required by law prerequisite to voting, casting a ballot, and having such ballot counted properly and included in the appropriate totals of votes cast with respect to candidates for public or party office and propositions for which votes are received in an election. (2) The term "political subdivision" shall mean any county or parish, except that, where registration for voting is not conducted under the supervision of a county or parish, the term shall include any other subdivision of a State which conducts registration for voting.

(d) In any action for a declaratory judgment brought pursuant to section 4 or section 5 of this Act, subpoenas for witnesses who are required to attend the District Court for the District of Columbia may be served in any judicial district of the United States: Provided, That no writ of subpoena shall issue for witnesses without the District of Columbia at a greater distance than one hundred miles from the place of holding court without the permission of the District Court for the District of Columbia being first had upon proper application and cause shown.

SEC. 15. Section 2004 of the Revised Statutes (42 U.S.C.1971), as amended by section 131 of the Civil Rights Act of 1957 (71 Stat. 637), and amended by section 601 of the Civil Rights Act of 1960 (74 Stat. 90), and as further amended by section 101 of the Civil Rights Act of 1964 (78 Stat. 241), is further amended as follows:

(a) Delete the word "Federal" wherever it appears in subsections (a) and (c);

(b) Repeal subsection (f) and designate the present subsections (g) and (h) as (f) and (g), respectively.

SEC. 16. The Attorney General and the Secretary of Defense, jointly, shall make a full and complete study to determine whether, under the laws or practices of any State or States, there are preconditions to voting, which might tend to result in discrimination against citizens serving in the Armed Forces of the United States seeking to vote. Such officials shall, jointly, make a report to the Congress not later than June 30, 1966, containing the results of such study, together with a list of any States in which such preconditions exist, and shall include in such report such recommendations for legislation as they deem advisable to prevent discrimination in voting against citizens serving in the Armed Forces of the United States.

SEC. 17. Nothing in this Act shall be construed to deny, impair, or otherwise adversely affect the right to vote of any person registered to vote under the law of any State or political subdivision.

SEC. 18. There are hereby authorized to be appropriated such sums as are necessary to carry out the provisions of this Act.

SEC 19. If any provision of this Act or the application thereof to any person or circumstances is held invalid, the remainder of the Act and the application of the provision to other persons not similarly situated or to other circumstances shall not be affected thereby.

Approved August 6, 1965.

Source: Voting Rights Act of 1965, Public Law 89-110, 79 Stat. 437, http://www.ourdocuments.gov.

26   Implementation of the Voting Rights Act: Selections from the U.S. Commission on Civil Rights and the Lawyers Constitutional Defense Committee

In Deep South states such as Alabama, Georgia, Louisiana, Mississippi, and South Carolina, large numbers of black voters entered the electorate after passage of the Voting Rights Act of 1965. Passage of the act also placed pressure on state and local officials to continue the expansion of the electorate in other southern states that had begun as early as 1946 in the wake of Smith v. Allwright. *The assertive enforcement of the act by the administration of Lyndon B. Johnson during 1965–1967 was a central factor in the breakthrough to a fully democratic electorate. The federal government set an exceptionally important example by using its new power under the Voting Rights Act to register voters directly. That stance also motivated a wide range of civil rights groups to pursue activities related to voter registration and election observation, often in immediate and close cooperation with federal officials. The following documents detail those efforts.*

U.S. Commission on Civil Rights Report, November 1965

These selections are from a November 1965 typewritten report issued by the U.S. Commission on Civil Rights. Although the excerpts are taken from several different pages, when read in sequence they provide an unusually clear view, from the federal government's perspective, of the ways in which the Voting Rights Act was implemented in its earliest months.

The United States Commission on Civil Rights
Washington, D.C., November, 1965.

The President
The President of the Senate
The Speaker of the House of Representatives

Sirs:

The Commission on Civil Rights presents to you this report pursuant to Public Law 85-315 as amended. . . .

Respectfully yours,

JOHN A. HANNAH, Chairman
EUGENE PATTERSON, Vice Chairman
FRANKIE M. FREEMAN
ERWIN N. GRISWOLD
REV. THEODORE M. HESBURGH, C.S.C.
ROBERT S. RANKIN

* * *

. . .
The Federal examiner provision of the Voting Rights Act of 1965 avoids the need for extensive litigation to compel reluctant State voter registration officials to register persons without discrimination.

When he signed the Act, the President said ". . . if it is clear that State officials still intend to discriminate, then Federal examiners will be sent in to register all eligible voter. . . . When the prospect of discrimination is gone, the examiners will be immediately withdrawn." . . .

Wilson Matthews, Director of the Civil Service Commission's Office of Hearing Examiners, began organizing the examiner program on March 19, the day following the beginning of the legislative hearings. By April 1, an 11-man group had been organized to draft a budget, formulate necessary regulations, define personnel requirements and establish a training course for examiners.

It was decided that the first examiners would be employees of the Civil Service Commission so the Commission could maintain close supervision of the program during the initial months of its operation. . . .

The number of applicants who sought to be listed during the opening weeks of the program far exceeded preliminary estimates. In Dallas County, Alabama, and in Leflore County, Mississippi, examiners and civil rights workers reported that applicants in many cases believed that the Federal examiners would be present in their county for only one day or, at most, a very few days. In these counties, crowds surged into the offices and outer hallways and individuals pushed their way to the examiners' tables as quickly as possible.

In most counties, civil rights workers or community leaders volunteered to keep order in the halls and corridors outside the examiners' offices. In a few counties, the examiners or post office personnel performed this task. In two Alabama counties, civil rights workers suggested the use of nearby churches as assembly points. These workers were permitted to assign priority numbers and accompany applicants to the examiners' offices in small groups so that applicants would not have to stand in the sun and sidewalks outside the offices would not be congested. . . .

COUNTIES WITHOUT FEDERAL EXAMINERS

The law's immediate effect was to terminate complaints of discriminatory administration of literacy tests in Virginia, North Carolina, South Carolina, Louisiana, and Georgia and to permit the registration, in New York, of substantial numbers of citizens educated in American-flag Spanish-speaking schools [*New York Times,* November 3, 1965, 28]. By mid-September, voter registration organizations reported that they knew of no testing procedures being used in these five States. At the time of the Commission's investigation, literacy tests were being used in many Mississippi counties as well as a few counties in Alabama. Delay in registration continued to be a major problem in Alabama, North and South Carolina, and parts of Louisiana. . . .

In counties with examiners, Labor Day marked the beginning of the sharp decrease in the number of applicants who appeared at the examiners' offices. This reflected the exodus of hundreds of civil rights workers from the South to return to their jobs and college and high school studies. The withdrawal of so many civil rights workers brought many voter registration drives to an almost complete halt. In some counties, however, civil rights workers remained and continued their voter education projects. Labor Day also marked the beginning of the harvest season. During this period, workers are occupied in the fields and there is little or no opportunity to attempt to register to vote. Undoubtedly, the departure of civil rights workers and the harvest season also has affected registration in non-examiner counties.

Racial violence related to civil rights activities is another factor which has limited applications in some counties with examiners. The killing of seminarian Jonathan Daniels in Lowndes County, Alabama, on August 20 and the acquittal of his killer on September 30 appear to have been the single most important factor in reducing Negro applications in that county. It is symbolic of conditions there that a pick-up truck with a rifle visibly displayed has been parked daily immediately outside the examiner's office since the opening of the office. Registration workers in the county have reported increasing threats against their lives and continued efforts to intimidate resident Negro leaders. . . .

Answering criticism that he had not authorized enough examiners, the Attorney General told the Rotary Club of Houston, Texas on September 30 that the Department of Justice had "acted quickly and steadily, but we have not acted massively."

"Our aim . . . is not the widespread deployment of an army of Federal examiners," he explained. "The purpose, rather, is to insure that every citizen can vote, and do so according to normal and fair local procedures." The Voting Rights Act, the Attorney General noted, " . . . speaks to local officials as well as the Federal Government. If they don't fulfill their responsibilities under the Act we will fulfill ours." . . .

Selections from the Lawyers Constitutional Defense Committee

These selections are from the Robert W. Lentz Papers in the Swarthmore College Peace Collection. Robert Lentz was a volunteer legal defense lawyer with the Lawyers Constitutional Defense Committee (LCDC) in Mississippi during Freedom Summer 1964 and in 1966 and 1967. The documents reproduced here—a letter from the LCDC to affiliated and interested attorneys, a transcript of one of Lentz's handwritten notes, and an authorization form for Lentz to act as a poll watcher/representative at polling places—illuminate the role that he and other volunteer legal defense lawyers played in helping the Mississippi Freedom Democratic Party to make the Voting Rights Act work "on the ground" in a Deep South state that was renowned for the depth of its racial conflict. Lentz and an African American candidate for local constable found that a local official was refusing to provide lists of voters. The official seemed bent on obstructing the candidate from campaigning and doing so under the cover, it ironically appears, of earlier federal litigation brought under the 1957 and 1960 Civil Rights Acts.

Dear Member of the Bar:

. . .

The Lawyers Constitutional Defense Committee (LCDC) was formed two years ago by the chief of legal officers of the several national civil rights organizations. Its purpose: To provide legal representation to the civil rights movement and the Negro community in the deep South.

In 1964 and 1965 the LCDC sent over 200 volunteer attorneys to Mississippi, Alabama, Louisiana, Florida, Georgia and South Carolina. They defended thousands of civil rights workers on charges ranging from criminal anarchy to speeding, and they filed numerous affirmative law suits designed to assure the enforcement of the Constitution and the various civil rights statutes.

In 1966 the need is no less urgent. The Civil Rights Act of 1964 and the Voting Act of 1965 are not self-enforcing, nor have they much lessened the inclination of Southern law-enforcement officials to resist and to use harassment and brutality to prevent the achievement of a decent society in the South.

WE NEED VOLUNTEER LAWYERS. We need attorneys who will go South for three or four weeks (more, if possible), who will live and work in the Negro community in Sunflower County (Miss.), Plaquemines Parish (La.), or Dorchester County (So. Car.) where there's legal work to be [done] in the J.P. court or the county jail or the sheriff's office. The conditions of work are horrendous, the climate sub-tropical, the courts and law-enforcement agencies hostile, the surrounding environment oppressive, the processes of law a mockery, the risks ever present.

But LCDC volunteer lawyers have gladly given legal service to the people who have made human dignity and equal rights the main item on our country's agenda—and most of them have found this to be the greatest experience of their personal and professional life. . . .

* * *

On November 4, 1967, at 3:15 p.m. . . . Robert W. Lentz, Mr. Johnny Applewhite and [illegible] went to the office of Chancellery Court in Carrollton, Miss. and met with Mrs. Mina Gee. Mr. Lentz asked on behalf of Mr. Applewhite for copies of the voting lists for the 3rd and 4th beats. Mrs. Gee said "I told Mr. Applewhite last week he couldn't have the lists and I told the same thing to a lawyer from Jackson." Lentz: "Are you saying you aren't going to give out any lists for the 3rd & 4th beats?" Mrs. Gee: "Yes, we don't give lists to anyone. Since the federal court case we haven't given out voting lists and then it was with a court order." Lentz: "Before contacting the Atty. Gen. I just want to be clear that you are refusing this candidate a list of registered voters." Mrs. Gee: "Yes."

* * *

AUTHORIZATION FORM

I, JOHNNY APPLEWHITE of BEAT 3 CARROLL COUNTY the undersigned candidate for the office of CONSTABLE, SUPERVISOR, JUSTICE OF PEACE-BEAT 3 in the General Election to be held on the 7th day of November, 1967, certify that ROBERT W. LENTZ is to act as my pollwatcher/representative at any polling place in the area from which I am running for election. The bearer acts under authority of Section 3248 of the Mississippi Code of 1942 as amended and recompiled.

Dated   NOVEMBER 6, 1967
Signed JOHNNY APPLEWHITE

[Witnessed by]
L. C. Smith
James Dixson

Sources: *The Voting Rights Act: The First Months*, a report from the United States Commission on Civil Rights, November 1965, Washington, D.C.; Robert W. Lentz Papers at the Swarthmore College Peace Collection, Swarthmore College, Swarthmore, Pa.

---

27 *South Carolina v. Katzenbach*, Decided March 7, 1966

The Voting Rights Act of 1965 authorized the U.S. attorney general to send federal registrars into any county with a history of practicing racial discrimination in voting. President Lyndon B. Johnson's attorney general, Nicholas de B. Katzenbach, identified such problems in Alabama, Alaska, Georgia, Louisiana, Mississippi, South Carolina, Virginia, thirty-four counties in North Carolina, and a few counties in Arizona, Hawaii, and Idaho. He then acted to suspend local voting regulations. This action resulted in challenges from the states affected.

At least two aspects of the 1966 South Carolina v. Katzenbach *(383 U.S. 301) opinion for the Court by Chief Justice Earl Warren are remarkable. First, it offers a succinct historical sketch of the law and policy of the struggle for African American voting rights. Second, it roundly endorses congressional power to enforce the Fifteenth Amendment. An unusual aspect of* South Carolina v. Katzenbach *is that the Court heard the case under its original jurisdiction, which means it was the first court to hear the case. This very rare use of this jurisdiction heightened the constitutional weight of the opinion for the Court.*

SOUTH CAROLINA v. KATZENBACH, ATTORNEY GENERAL.
ON BILL OF COMPLAINT.
No. 22, Orig.
Argued January 17–18, 1966.
Decided March 7, 1966.

. . .

MR. CHIEF JUSTICE WARREN delivered the opinion of the Court.

By leave of the Court, 382 U.S. 898, South Carolina has filed a bill of complaint, seeking a declaration that selected provisions of the Voting Rights Act of 1965 violate the Federal Constitution, and asking for an injunction against enforcement of these provisions by the Attorney General. Original jurisdiction is founded on the presence of a controversy between a State and a citizen of another State under Art. III, § 2, of the Constitution. See Georgia v. Pennsylvania R. Co.,

324 U.S. 439. Because no issues of fact were raised in the complaint, and because of South Carolina's desire to obtain a ruling prior to its primary elections in June, 1966, we dispensed with appointment of a special master and expedited our hearing of the case.

Recognizing that the questions presented were of urgent concern to the entire country, we invited all of the States to participate in this proceeding as friends of the Court. A majority responded by submitting or joining in briefs on the merits, some supporting South Carolina and others the Attorney General. . . .

The Voting Rights Act was designed by Congress to banish the blight of racial discrimination in voting, which has infected the electoral process in parts of our country for nearly a century. The Act creates stringent new remedies for voting discrimination where it persists on a pervasive scale, and, in addition, the statute strengthens existing remedies for pockets of voting discrimination elsewhere in the country. Congress assumed the power to prescribe these remedies from § 2 of the Fifteenth Amendment, which authorizes the National Legislature to effectuate by "appropriate" measures the constitutional prohibition against racial discrimination in voting. We hold that the sections of the Act which are properly before us, are an appropriate means for carrying out Congress' constitutional responsibilities, and are consonant with all other provisions of the Constitution. We therefore deny South Carolina's request that enforcement of these sections of the Act be enjoined.

I

The constitutional propriety of the Voting Rights Act of 1965 must be judged with reference to the historical experience which it reflects. Before enacting the measure, Congress explored with great care the problem of racial discrimination in voting. The House and Senate Committees on the Judiciary each held hearings for nine days and received testimony from a total of 67 witnesses. More than three full days were consumed discussing the bill on the floor of the House, while the debate in the Senate covered 26 days in all. At the close of these deliberations, the verdict of both chambers was overwhelming. The House approved the bill by a vote of 328–74, and the measure passed the Senate by a margin of 79–18.

Two points emerge vividly from the voluminous legislative history of the Act contained in the committee hearings and floor debates. First: Congress felt itself confronted by an insidious and pervasive evil which had been perpetuated in certain parts of our country through unremitting and ingenious defiance of the Constitution. Second: Congress concluded that the unsuccessful remedies which it had prescribed in the past would have to be replaced by sterner and more elaborate measures in order to satisfy the clear commands of the Fifteenth Amendment. . . .

The Fifteenth Amendment to the Constitution was ratified in 1870. Promptly thereafter, Congress passed the Enforcement Act of 1870, which made it a crime for public officers and private persons to obstruct exercise of the right to vote. The statute was amended in the following year to provide for detailed federal supervision of the electoral process, from registration to the certification of returns. As the years passed and fervor for racial equality waned, enforcement of the laws became spotty and ineffective, and most of their provisions were repealed in 1894. The remnants have had little significance in the recently renewed battle against voting discrimination.

Meanwhile, beginning in 1890, the States of Alabama, Georgia, Louisiana, Mississippi, North Carolina, South Carolina, and Virginia enacted tests still in use which were specifically designed to prevent Negroes from voting. Typically, they made the ability to read and write a registration qualification and also required completion of a registration form. These laws were based on the fact that, as of 1890, in each of the named States, more than two-thirds of the adult Negroes were illiterate, while less than one-quarter of the adult whites were unable to read or write. At the same time, alternate tests were prescribed in all of the named States to assure that white illiterates would not be deprived of the franchise. These included grandfather clauses, property qualifications, "good character" tests, and the requirement that registrants "understand" or "interpret" certain matter.

The course of subsequent Fifteenth Amendment litigation in this Court demonstrates the variety and persistence of these and similar institutions designed to deprive Negroes of the right to vote. Grandfather clauses were invalidated in Guinn v. United States, 238 U.S. 347, and Myers v. Anderson, 238 U.S. 368. Procedural hurdles were struck down in Lane v. Wilson, 307 U.S. 268. The white primary was outlawed in Smith v. Allwright, 321 U.S. 649, and Terry v. Adams, 345 U.S. 461. Improper challenges were nullified in United States v. Thomas, 362 U.S. 58. Racial gerrymandering was forbidden by Gomillion v. Lightfoot, 364 U.S. 339. Finally, discriminatory application of voting tests was condemned in Schnell v. Davis, 336 U.S. 933; Alabama v. United States, 371 U.S. 37, and Louisiana v. United States, 380 U.S. 145.

According to the evidence in recent Justice Department voting suits, the latter stratagem is now the principal method used to bar Negroes from the polls. Discriminatory administration of voting qualifications has been found in all eight Alabama cases, in all nine Louisiana cases, and in all nine Mississippi cases which have gone to final judgment. Moreover, in almost all of these cases, the courts have held that the discrimination was pursuant to a widespread "pattern or practice." White applicants for registration have often been excused altogether from the literacy and understanding tests, or have been given easy versions, have received extensive help from voting officials, and have been registered despite serious errors in their answers. Negroes, on the other hand, have typically been required to pass difficult versions of all the tests, without any outside assistance and without the slightest error. The good-morals requirement is so vague and subjective that it has

constituted an open invitation to abuse at the hands of voting officials. Negroes obliged to obtain vouchers from registered voters have found it virtually impossible to comply in areas where almost no Negroes are on the rolls.

In recent years, Congress has repeatedly tried to cope with the problem by facilitating case-by-case litigation against voting discrimination. The Civil Rights Act of 1957 authorized the Attorney General to seek injunctions against public and private interference with the right to vote on racial grounds. Perfecting amendments in the Civil Rights Act of 1960 permitted the joinder of States as parties defendant, gave the Attorney General access to local voting records, and authorized courts to register voters in areas of systematic discrimination. Title I of the Civil Rights Act of 1964 expedited the hearing of voting cases before three-judge courts and outlawed some of the tactics used to disqualify Negroes from voting in federal elections.

Despite the earnest efforts of the Justice Department and of many federal judges, these new laws have done little to cure the problem of voting discrimination. According to estimates by the Attorney General during hearings on the Act, registration of voting-age Negroes in Alabama rose only from 14.2% to 19.4% between 1958 and 1964; in Louisiana, it barely inched ahead from 31.7% to 31.8% between 1956 and 1965; and in Mississippi it increased only from 4.4% to 6.4% between 1954 and 1964. In each instance, registration of voting-age whites ran roughly 50 percentage points or more ahead of Negro registration.

The previous legislation has proved ineffective for a number of reasons. Voting suits are unusually onerous to prepare, sometimes requiring as many as 6,000 man-hours spent combing through registration records in preparation for trial. Litigation has been exceedingly slow, in part because of the ample opportunities for delay afforded voting officials and others involved in the proceedings. Even when favorable decisions have finally been obtained, some of the States affected have merely switched to discriminatory devices not covered by the federal decrees, or have enacted difficult new tests designed to prolong the existing disparity between white and Negro registration. Alternatively, certain local officials have defied and evaded court orders or have simply closed their registration offices to freeze the voting rolls. The provision of the 1960 law authorizing registration by federal officers has had little impact on local maladministration, because of its procedural complexities. During the hearings and debates on the Act, Selma, Alabama, was repeatedly referred to as the preeminent example of the ineffectiveness of existing legislation. In Dallas County, of which Selma is the seat, there were four years of litigation by the Justice Department and two findings by the federal courts of widespread voting discrimination. Yet, in those four years, Negro registration rose only from 156 to 383, although there are approximately 15,000 Negroes of voting age in the county. Any possibility that these figures were attributable to political apathy was dispelled by the protest demonstrations in Selma in the early months of 1965. . . .

II

The Voting Rights Act of 1965 reflects Congress' firm intention to rid the country of racial discrimination in voting. The heart of the Act is a complex scheme of stringent remedies aimed at areas where voting discrimination has been most flagrant. Section 4(a)–(d) lays down a formula defining the States and political subdivisions to which these new remedies apply. The first of the remedies, contained in § 4(a), is the suspension of literacy tests and similar voting qualifications for a period of five years from the last occurrence of substantial voting discrimination. Section 5 prescribes a second remedy, the suspension of all new voting regulations pending review by federal authorities to determine whether their use would perpetuate voting discrimination. The third remedy,

covered in §§ 6(b), 7, 9, and 13(a), is the assignment of federal examiners on certification by the Attorney General to list qualified applicants who are thereafter entitled to vote in all elections.

Other provisions of the Act prescribe subsidiary cures for persistent voting discrimination. Section 8 authorizes the appointment of federal poll-watchers in places to which federal examiners have already been assigned. Section 10(d) excuses those made eligible to vote in sections of the country covered by § 4(b) of the Act from paying accumulated past poll taxes for state and local elections. Section 12(e) provides for balloting by persons denied access to the polls in areas where federal examiners have been appointed.

The remaining remedial portions of the Act are aimed at voting discrimination in any area of the country where it may occur. Section 2 broadly prohibits the use of voting rules to abridge exercise of the franchise on racial grounds. Sections 3, 6(a), and 13(b) strengthen existing procedures for attacking voting discrimination by means of litigation. Section 4(e) excuses citizens educated in American schools conducted in a foreign language from passing English language literacy tests. Section 10(a)–(c) facilitates constitutional litigation challenging the imposition of all poll taxes for state and local elections. Sections 11 and 12(a)–(d) authorize civil and criminal sanctions against interference with the exercise of rights guaranteed by the Act.

At the outset, we emphasize that only some of the many portions of the Act are properly before us. South Carolina has not challenged §§ 2, 3, 4(e), 6(a), 8, 10, 12(d) and (e), 13(b), and other miscellaneous provisions having nothing to do with this lawsuit. Judicial review of these sections must await subsequent litigation. In addition, we find that South Carolina's attack on §§ 11 and 12(a)–(c) is premature. No person has yet been subjected to, or even threatened with, the criminal sanctions which these sections of the Act authorize. . . . We turn now to a detailed description of these provisions and their present status.

Coverage formula

The remedial sections of the Act assailed by South Carolina automatically apply to any State, or to any separate political subdivision such as a county or parish, for which two findings have been made: (1) the Attorney General has determined that, on November 1, 1964, it maintained a "test or device," and (2) the Director of the Census has determined that less than 50% of its voting-age residents were registered on November 1, 1964, or voted in the presidential election of November 1964. These findings are not reviewable in any court, and are final upon publication in the Federal Register § 4(b). As used throughout the Act, the phrase "test or device" means any requirement that a registrant or voter must "(1) demonstrate the ability to read, write, understand, or interpret any matter, (2) demonstrate any educational achievement or his knowledge of any particular subject, (3) possess good moral character, or (4) prove his qualifications by the voucher of registered voters or members of any other class." § 4(c).

Statutory coverage of a State or political subdivision under 4(b) is terminated if the area obtains a declaratory judgment from the District Court for the District of Columbia determining that tests and devices have not been used during the preceding five years to abridge the franchise on racial grounds. The Attorney General shall consent to entry of the judgment if he has no reason to believe that the facts are otherwise. § 4(a). . . .

South Carolina was brought within the coverage formula of the Act on August 7, 1965, pursuant to appropriate administrative determinations which have not been challenged in this proceeding. On the same day, coverage was also extended to Alabama, Alaska, Georgia, Louisiana, Mississippi, Virginia, 26 counties in North Carolina, and one county in Arizona. Two more counties in Arizona, one county in Hawaii, and one county in Idaho were added to the list on November 19, 1965. Thus far, Alaska, the three Arizona counties, and the single county in Idaho

have asked the District Court for the District of Columbia to grant a declaratory judgment terminating statutory coverage.

Suspension of tests

In a State or political subdivision covered by § 4(b) of the Act, no person may be denied the right to vote in any election because of his failure to comply with a "test or device." § 4(a).

On account of this provision, South Carolina is temporarily barred from enforcing the portion of its voting laws which requires every applicant for registration to show that he:

Can both read and write any section of [the State] Constitution submitted to [him] by the registration officer or can show that he owns, and has paid all taxes collectible during the previous year on property in this State assessed at three hundred dollars or more. S.C.Code Ann. § 262(4) (1965 Supp.).

The Attorney General has determined that the property qualification is inseparable from the literacy test, and South Carolina makes no objection to this finding. Similar tests and devices have been temporarily suspended in the other sections of the country listed above.

Review of new rules

In a State or political subdivision covered by § 4(b) of the Act, no person may be denied the right to vote in any election because of his failure to comply with a voting qualification or procedure different from those in force on November 1, 1964. This suspension of new rules is terminated, however, under either of the following circumstances: (1) if the area has submitted the rules to the Attorney General and he has not interposed an objection within 60 days, or (2) if the area has obtained a declaratory judgment from the District Court for the District of Columbia determining that the rules will not abridge the franchise on racial grounds. . . .

South Carolina altered its voting laws in 1965 to extend the closing hour at polling places from

6 p.m. to 7 p.m. The State has not sought judicial review of this change in the District Court for the District of Columbia, nor has it submitted the new rule to the Attorney General for his scrutiny, although, at our hearing, the Attorney General announced that he does not challenge the amendment. There are indications in the record that other sections of the country listed above have also altered their voting laws since November 1, 1964.

Federal examiners

In any political subdivision covered by § 4(b) of the Act, the Civil Service Commission shall appoint voting examiners whenever the Attorney General certifies either of the following facts: (1) that he has received meritorious written complaints from at least 20 residents alleging that they have been disenfranchised under color of law because of their race, or (2) that the appointment of examiners is otherwise necessary to effectuate the guarantees of the Fifteenth Amendment. In making the latter determination, the Attorney General must consider, among other factors, whether the registration ratio of non-whites to whites seems reasonably attributable to racial discrimination. . . .

The examiners who have been appointed are to test the voting qualifications of applicants according to regulations of the Civil Service Commission prescribing times, places, procedures, and forms. §§ 7(a) and 9(b). Any person who meets the voting requirements of state law, insofar as these have not been suspended by the Act, must promptly be placed on a list of eligible voters. . . .

A person shall be removed from the voting list by an examiner if he has lost his eligibility under valid state law, or if he has been successfully challenged through the procedure prescribed in § 9(a) of the Act. § 7(d). . . .

The listing procedures in a political subdivision are terminated under either of the following circumstances: (1) if the Attorney General informs the Civil Service Commission that all persons listed by examiners have been placed on the official voting rolls, and that there is no longer reasonable cause to fear abridgment of the franchise on racial grounds, or (2) if the political subdivision has obtained a declaratory judgment from the District Court for the District of Columbia, ascertaining the same facts which govern termination by the Attorney General, and the Director of the Census has determined that more than 50% of the non-white residents of voting age are registered to vote. . . .

On October 30, 1965, the Attorney General certified the need for federal examiners in two South Carolina counties, and examiners appointed by the Civil Service Commission have been serving there since November 8, 1965. . . .

III

These provisions of the Voting Rights Act of 1965 are challenged on the fundamental ground that they exceed the powers of Congress and encroach on an area reserved to the States by the Constitution. . . .

. . . Has Congress exercised its powers under the Fifteenth Amendment in an appropriate manner with relation to the States?

The ground rules for resolving this question are clear. The language and purpose of the Fifteenth Amendment, the prior decisions construing its several provisions, and the general doctrines of constitutional interpretation all point to one fundamental principle. As against the reserved powers of the States, Congress may use any rational means to effectuate the constitutional prohibition of racial discrimination in voting. . . .

Section 1 of the Fifteenth Amendment declares that "[t]he right of citizens of the United States to vote shall not be denied or abridged by the United States or by any State on account of race, color, or previous condition of servitude." This declaration has always been treated as self-executing, and has repeatedly been construed, without further legislative specification, to invalidate state voting qualifications or procedures which are discriminatory on their face or in practice. . . . The gist of the matter is that the Fifteenth Amendment supersedes contrary exertions of state power. . . .

South Carolina contends that the cases cited above are precedents only for the authority of the judiciary to strike down state statutes and procedures—that to allow an exercise of this authority by Congress would be to rob the courts of their rightful constitutional role. On the contrary, § 2 of the Fifteenth Amendment expressly declares that "Congress shall have power to enforce this article by appropriate legislation." By adding this authorization, the Framers indicated that Congress was to be chiefly responsible for implementing the rights created in § 1. . . .

Congress has repeatedly exercised these powers in the past, and its enactments have repeatedly been upheld. . . .

The basic test to be applied in a case involving § 2 of the Fifteenth Amendment is the same as in all cases concerning the express powers of Congress with relation to the reserved powers of the States. Chief Justice Marshall laid down the classic formulation, 50 years before the Fifteenth Amendment was ratified:

Let the end be legitimate, let it be within the scope of the constitution, and all means which are appropriate which are plainly adapted to that end, which are not prohibited, but consist with the letter and spirit of the constitution, are constitutional. McCulloch v. Maryland, 4 Wheat. 316, 421. . . .

. . . In the oft-repeated words of Chief Justice Marshall, referring to another specific legislative authorization in the Constitution, "This power, like all others vested in Congress, is complete in itself, may be exercised to its utmost extent, and acknowledges no limitations other than are prescribed in the constitution." Gibbons v. Ogden, 9 Wheat. 1, 196.

IV

Congress exercised its authority under the Fifteenth Amendment in an inventive manner when it enacted the Voting Rights Act of 1965. First: the measure prescribes remedies for voting discrimination which go into effect without any need for prior adjudication. This was clearly a legitimate response to the problem, for which there is ample precedent under other constitutional provisions. . . . Congress had found that case-by-case litigation was inadequate to combat widespread and persistent discrimination in voting, because of the inordinate amount of time and energy required to overcome the obstructionist tactics invariably encountered in these lawsuits. After enduring nearly a century of systematic resistance to the Fifteenth Amendment, Congress might well decide to shift the advantage of time and inertia from the perpetrators of the evil to its victims. The question remains, of course, whether the specific remedies prescribed in the Act were an appropriate means of combating the evil, and to this question we shall presently address ourselves.

Second: the Act intentionally confines these remedies to a small number of States and political subdivisions which, in most instances, were familiar to Congress by name. This, too, was a permissible method of dealing with the problem. Congress had learned that substantial voting discrimination presently occurs in certain sections of the country, and it knew no way of accurately forecasting whether the evil might spread elsewhere in the future. In acceptable legislative fashion, Congress chose to limit its attention to the geographic areas where immediate action seemed necessary. . . .

Coverage formula

We now consider the related question of whether the specific States and political subdivisions within § 4(b) of the Act were an appropriate target for the new remedies. South Carolina contends that the coverage formula is awkwardly designed in a number of respects, and that it disregards various local conditions which have nothing to do with racial discrimination. These arguments, however, are largely beside the point.

Congress began work with reliable evidence of actual voting discrimination in a great majority of the States and political subdivisions affected by the new remedies of the Act. The formula that eventually evolved to describe these areas was relevant to the problem of voting discrimination, and Congress was therefore entitled to infer a significant danger of the evil in the few remaining States and political subdivisions covered by § 4(b) of the Act. No more was required to justify the application to these areas of Congress' express powers under the Fifteenth Amendment. . . .

To be specific, the new remedies of the Act are imposed on three States—Alabama, Louisiana, and Mississippi—in which federal courts have repeatedly found substantial voting discrimination. Section 4(b) of the Act also embraces two other States—Georgia and South Carolina—plus large portions of a third State North Carolina—for which there was more fragmentary evidence of recent voting discrimination mainly adduced by the Justice Department and the Civil Rights Commission. All of these areas were appropriately subjected to the new remedies. In identifying past evils, Congress obviously may avail itself of information from any probative source. . . .

The areas listed above, for which there was evidence of actual voting discrimination, share two characteristics incorporated by Congress into the coverage formula: the use of tests and devices for voter registration, and a voting rate in the 1964 presidential election at least 12 points below the national average. Tests and devices are relevant to voting discrimination because of their long history as a tool for perpetrating the evil; a low voting rate is pertinent for the obvious reason that widespread disenfranchisement must inevitably affect the number of actual voters. Accordingly, the coverage formula is rational in both practice and theory. It was therefore permissible to impose the new remedies on the few remaining States and political subdivisions covered by the formula, at least in the absence of proof that they have been free of substantial voting discrimination in recent years. Congress is clearly not bound by the rules

relating to statutory presumptions in criminal cases when it prescribes civil remedies against other organs of government under § 2 of the Fifteenth Amendment. Compare United States v. Romano, 382 U.S. 136; Tot v. United States, 319 U.S. 463.

It is irrelevant that the coverage formula excludes certain localities which do not employ voting tests and devices but for which there is evidence of voting discrimination by other means. Congress had learned that widespread and persistent discrimination in voting during recent years has typically entailed the misuse of tests and devices, and this was the evil for which the new remedies were specifically designed. . . .

Acknowledging the possibility of overbreadth, the Act provides for termination of special statutory coverage at the behest of States and political subdivisions in which the danger of substantial voting discrimination has not materialized during the preceding five years. . . .

Suspension of tests

We now arrive at consideration of the specific remedies prescribed by the Act for areas included within the coverage formula. South Carolina assails the temporary suspension of existing voting qualifications, reciting the rule laid down by Lassiter v. Northampton County Bd. of Elections, 360 U.S. 45, that literacy tests and related devices are not in themselves contrary to the Fifteenth Amendment. In that very case, however, the Court went on to say, "Of course, a literacy test, fair on its face, may be employed to perpetuate that discrimination which the Fifteenth Amendment was designed to uproot." Id. at 53. The record shows that, in most of the States covered by the Act, including South Carolina, various tests and devices have been instituted with the purpose of disenfranchising Negroes, have been framed in such a way as to facilitate this aim, and have been administered in a discriminatory fashion for many years. Under these circumstances, the Fifteenth Amendment has clearly been violated. See Louisiana v. United States, 380 U.S. 145; Alabama v. United States, 371 U.S. 37; Schnell v. Davis, 336 U.S. 933.

The Act suspends literacy tests and similar devices for a period of five years from the last occurrence of substantial voting discrimination. This was a legitimate response to the problem, for which there is ample precedent in Fifteenth Amendment cases. Ibid. Underlying the response was the feeling that States and political subdivisions which had been allowing white illiterates to vote for years could not sincerely complain about "dilution" of their electorates through the registration of Negro illiterates. Congress knew that continuance of the tests and devices in use at the present time, no matter how fairly administered in the future, would freeze the effect of past discrimination in favor of unqualified white registrants. Congress permissibly rejected the alternative of requiring a complete re-registration of all voters, believing that this would be too harsh on many whites who had enjoyed the franchise for their entire adult lives.

Review of new rules

The Act suspends new voting regulations pending scrutiny by federal authorities to determine whether their use would violate the Fifteenth Amendment. This may have been an uncommon exercise of congressional power, as South Carolina contends, but the Court has recognized that exceptional conditions can justify legislative measures not otherwise appropriate. See Home Bldg. & Loan Assn. v. Blaisdell, 290 U.S. 398; Wilson v. New, 243 U.S. 332. Congress knew that some of the States covered by § 4(b) of the Act had resorted to the extraordinary stratagem of contriving new rules of various kinds for the sole purpose of perpetuating voting discrimination in the face of adverse federal court decrees. Congress had reason to suppose that these States might try similar maneuvers in the future in order to evade the remedies for voting discrimination contained in the Act itself. Under the compulsion

of these unique circumstances, Congress responded in a permissibly decisive manner.

For reasons already stated, there was nothing inappropriate about limiting litigation under this provision to the District Court for the District of Columbia, and in putting the burden of proof on the areas seeking relief. Nor has Congress authorized the District Court to issue advisory opinions, in violation of the principles of Article III invoked by Georgia as amicus curiae. The Act automatically suspends the operation of voting regulations enacted after November 1, 1964, and furnishes mechanisms for enforcing the suspension. A State or political subdivision wishing to make use of a recent amendment to its voting laws therefore has a concrete and immediate "controversy" with the Federal Government. . . . An appropriate remedy is a judicial determination that continued suspension of the new rule is unnecessary to vindicate rights guaranteed by the Fifteenth Amendment.

Federal examiners

The Act authorizes the appointment of federal examiners to list qualified applicants who are thereafter entitled to vote, subject to an expeditious challenge procedure. This was clearly an appropriate response to the problem, closely related to remedies authorized in prior cases. See Alabama v. United States, supra; United States v. Thomas, 362 U.S. 58. In many of the political subdivisions covered by § 4(b) of the Act, voting officials have persistently employed a variety of procedural tactics to deny Negroes the franchise, often in direct defiance or evasion of federal court decrees. Congress realized that merely to suspend voting rules which have been misused or are subject to misuse might leave this localized evil undisturbed. As for the briskness of the challenge procedure, Congress knew that, in some of the areas affected, challenges had been persistently employed to harass registered Negroes. It chose to forestall this abuse, at the same time providing alternative ways for removing persons listed through error or fraud. In addition to the judicial challenge procedure, § 7(d) allows for the removal of names by the examiner himself, and 11(c) makes it a crime to obtain a listing through fraud.

In recognition of the fact that there were political subdivisions covered by § 4(b) of the Act in which the appointment of federal examiners might be unnecessary, Congress assigned the Attorney General the task of determining the localities to which examiners should be sent. There is no warrant for the claim, asserted by Georgia as amicus curiae, that the Attorney General is free to use this power in an arbitrary fashion, without regard to the purposes of the Act. Section 6(b) sets adequate standards to guide the exercise of his discretion, by directing him to calculate the registration ratio of nonwhites to whites, and to weigh evidence of good faith efforts to avoid possible voting discrimination. At the same time, the special termination procedures of § 13(a) provide indirect judicial review for the political subdivisions affected, assuring the withdrawal of federal examiners from areas where they are clearly not needed. . . .

After enduring nearly a century of widespread resistance to the Fifteenth Amendment, Congress has marshalled an array of potent weapons against the evil, with authority in the Attorney General to employ them effectively. Many of the areas directly affected by this development have indicated their willingness to abide by any restraints legitimately imposed upon them. We here hold that the portions of the Voting Rights Act properly before us are a valid means for carrying out the commands of the Fifteenth Amendment. Hopefully, millions of non-white Americans will now be able to participate for the first time on an equal basis in the government under which they live. We may finally look forward to the day when truly [t]he right of citizens of the United States to vote shall not be denied or abridged by the United States or by any State on account of race, color, or previous condition of servitude.

The bill of complaint is
Dismissed.

Source: Findlaw, *South Carolina v. Katzenbach*, 383 U.S. 301 (1966), http://caselaw.lp.findlaw.com/scripts/getcase.pl?navby=case&court=us&vol=383&page=301.

28 *Allen v. State Board of Elections,* Decided March 3, 1969

The Supreme Court's opinion in Allen v. State Board of Elections *(393 U.S. 544) put teeth into Section 5 of the Voting Rights Act. After passage of the Voting Rights Act in 1965, southern states sought to change election rules to undo its effects. In the group of cases under the umbrella of* Allen, *Mississippi's changes to its election code permitting the at-large election of county supervisors (as a substitute for single-member districts), providing only for appointment of superintendents of education (in selected counties), and changing the requirements for independent candidates were challenged in federal court by private citizens.*

Section 5 of the Voting Rights Act required covered jurisdictions to "preclear" any changes to election rules and institutions with the federal government. If the Justice Department, acting on behalf of the federal District Court for the District of Columbia or the district court, blocked the proposed changes, they could not go into effect. Section 5, then, prevented a quiet, massive subversion of the Voting Rights Act, and, overall, its deterrent effect has been incalculable. But realization of Section 5's full impact required voting rights lawyers to bring the Court into the picture. For one thing, the Richard Nixon administration was not inclined to give Section 5 a broad reading. Bowing to its "southern strategy" (described in Chapter 7), the administration ignored the history of voting rights politics and policy. That history taught—and still teaches—that seemingly neutral changes in election rules can disenfranchise minorities. Indeed, the Lyndon B. Johnson administration and Congress had agreed on Section 5 because they had understood that lesson. Thus the Allen *decision was a vital turning point. Had the Court never handed down this opinion, the Voting Rights Act would have had very little impact beyond the direct federal registration that occurred in 1966 and 1967 in selected jurisdictions.*

ALLEN ET AL. v. STATE BOARD OF
ELECTIONS ET AL. APPEAL FROM THE
UNITED STATES DISTRICT COURT FOR
THE EASTERN DISTRICT
OF VIRGINIA. No. 3.
Argued October 15, 1968.
Decided March 3, 1969.

. . .

Pursuant to 4 (b) of the Voting Rights Act of 1965 the provisions of 4 (a), suspending all "tests or devices" for five years, were made applicable to certain States, including Mississippi and Virginia. As a result, those States were prohibited by 5 from enacting or seeking "to administer any voting qualification or prerequisite to voting, or standard, practice, or procedure with respect to voting different from that in force or effect on November 1, 1964," without first submitting the change to the U.S. Attorney General and obtaining his consent or securing a favorable declaratory judgment from the District Court for the District of Columbia. . . .

MR. CHIEF JUSTICE WARREN delivered the opinion of the Court.

These four cases, three from Mississippi and one from Virginia, involve the application of the Voting Rights Act of 1965 to state election laws and regulations. . . .

In South Carolina v. Katzenbach, (1966), we held the provisions of the Act involved in these cases to be constitutional. These cases merely require us to determine whether the various state enactments involved are subject to the requirements of the Act. . . .

. . . Briefly, the Act implemented Congress' firm intention to rid the country of racial discrimination in voting. It provided stringent new remedies against those practices which have most

frequently denied citizens the right to vote on the basis of their race. Thus, in States covered by the Act, literacy tests and similar voting qualifications were suspended for a period of five years from the last occurrence of substantial voting discrimination. However, Congress apparently feared that the mere suspension of existing tests would not completely solve the problem, given the history some States had of simply enacting new and slightly different requirements with the same discriminatory effect. Not underestimating the ingenuity of those bent on preventing Negroes from voting, Congress therefore enacted 5, the focal point of these cases.

Under 5, if a State covered by the Act passes any "voting qualification or prerequisite to voting, or standard, practice, or procedure with respect to voting different from that in force or effect on November 1, 1964," no person can be deprived of his right to vote "for failure to comply with" the new enactment "unless and until" the State seeks and receives a declaratory judgment in the United States District Court for the District of Columbia that the new enactment "does not have the purpose and will not have the effect of denying or abridging the right to vote on account of race or color." . . .

However, 5 does not necessitate that a covered State obtain a declaratory judgment action before it can enforce any change in its election laws. It provides that a State may enforce a new enactment if the State submits the new provision to the Attorney General of the United States and, within 60 days of the submission, the Attorney General does not formally object to the new statute or regulation. The Attorney General does not act as a court in approving or disapproving the state legislation. If the Attorney General objects to the new enactment, the State may still enforce the legislation upon securing a declaratory judgment in the District Court for the District of Columbia. Also, the State is not required to first submit the new enactment to the Attorney General as it may go directly to the District Court for the District of Columbia. The provision for submission to the Attorney General merely gives the covered State a rapid method of rendering a new state election law enforceable. Once the State has successfully complied with the 5 approval requirements, private parties may enjoin the enforcement of the new enactment only in traditional suits attacking its constitutionality; there is no further remedy provided by 5.

In these four cases, the States have passed new laws or issued new regulations. The central issue is whether these provisions fall within the prohibition of 5 that prevents the enforcement of "any voting qualification or prerequisite to voting, or standard, practice, or procedure with respect to voting" unless the State first complies with one of the section's approval procedures. . . .

I.

. . .

The Voting Rights Act does not explicitly grant or deny private parties authorization to seek a declaratory judgment that a State has failed to comply with the provisions of the Act. However, 5 does provide that "no person shall be denied the right to vote for failure to comply with [a new state enactment covered by, but not approved under, 5]." Analysis of this language in light of the major purpose of the Act indicates that appellants may seek a declaratory judgment that a new state enactment is governed by 5. Further, after proving that the State has failed to submit the covered enactment for 5 approval, the private party has standing to obtain an injunction against further enforcement, pending the State's submission of the legislation pursuant to 5. . . . The Attorney General has a limited staff and often might be unable to uncover quickly new

regulations and enactments passed at the varying levels of state government. It is consistent with the broad purpose of the Act to allow the individual citizen standing to insure that his city or county government complies with the 5 approval requirements. . . .

Finding that these cases are properly before us, we turn to a consideration of whether these state enactments are subject to the approval requirements of 5. These requirements apply to "any voting qualification or prerequisite to voting, or standard, practice, or procedure with respect to voting. . . ." The Act further provides that the term "voting" "shall include all action necessary to make a vote effective in any primary, special, or general election, including, but not limited to, registration, listing . . . or other action required by law prerequisite to voting, casting a ballot, and having such ballot counted properly and included in the appropriate totals of votes cast with respect to candidates for public or party office and propositions for which votes are received in an election." . . . Appellees in the Mississippi cases maintain that 5 covers only those state enactments which prescribe who may register to vote. While accepting that the Act is broad enough to insure that the votes of all citizens should be cast, appellees urge that 5 does not cover state rules relating to the qualification of candidates or to state decisions as to which offices shall be elective.

Appellees rely on the legislative history of the Act to support their view, citing the testimony of former Assistant Attorney General Burke Marshall before a subcommittee of the House Committee on the Judiciary:

"Mr. CORMAN. We have not talked at all about whether we have to be concerned with not only who can vote, but who can run for public office and that has been an issue in some areas in the South in 1964. Have you given any consideration to whether or not this bill ought to address itself to the qualifications for running for public office as well as the problem of registration?"

"Mr. MARSHALL. The problem that the bill was aimed at was the problem of registration, Congressman. If there is a problem of another sort, I would like to see it corrected, but that is not what we were trying to deal with in the bill."

Appellees in No. 25 also argue that 5 was not intended to apply to a change from district to at-large voting, because application of 5 would cause a conflict in the administration of reapportionment legislation. They contend that under such a broad reading of 5, enforcement of a reapportionment plan could be enjoined for failure to meet the 5 approval requirements, even though the plan had been approved by a federal court. Appellees urge that Congress could not have intended to force the States to submit a reapportionment plan to two different courts.

We must reject a narrow construction that appellees would give to 5. The Voting Rights Act was aimed at the subtle, as well as the obvious, state regulations which have the effect of denying citizens their right to vote because of their race. Moreover, compatible with the decisions of this Court, the Act gives a broad interpretation to the right to vote, recognizing that voting includes "all action necessary to make a vote effective." . . . We are convinced that in passing the Voting Rights Act, Congress intended that state enactments such as those involved in the instant cases be subject to the 5 approval requirements.

The legislative history on the whole supports the view that Congress intended to reach any state enactment which altered the election law of a covered State in even a minor way. For example, 2 of the Act, as originally drafted, included a prohibition against any "qualification or procedure." During the Senate hearings on the bill, Senator Fong expressed concern that the word "procedure" was not broad enough to cover various practices that might effectively be employed to deny citizens their right to vote. In response, the Attorney General said he had no objection to expanding the language of the section, as the word "procedure" "was intended to be all-inclusive of any kind of practice." Indicative of an intention to give the Act the broadest possible scope, Congress expanded the language

in the final version of 2 to include any "voting qualifications or prerequisite to voting, or standard, practice, or procedure." . . . Similarly, in the House hearings, it was emphasized that 5 was to have a broad scope:

"Mr. KATZENBACH. The justification for [the approval requirements] is simply this: Our experience in the areas that would be covered by this bill has been such as to indicate frequently on the part of State legislatures a desire in a sense to outguess the courts of the United States or even to outguess the Congress of the United States. . . . [A]s the Chairman may recall . . . at the time of the initial school desegregation, . . . the legislature passed I don't know how many laws in the shortest period of time. Every time the judge issued a decree, the legislature . . . passed a law to frustrate that decree.

"If I recollect correctly, the school board was ordered to do something and the legislature immediately took away all authority of the school boards. They withdrew all funds from them to accomplish the purposes of the act." House Hearings 60.

Also, the remarks of both opponents and proponents during the debate over passage of the Act demonstrate that Congress was well aware of another admonition of the Attorney General. He had stated in the House hearings that two or three types of changes in state election law (such as changing from paper ballots to voting machines) could be specifically excluded from 5 without undermining the purpose of the section. He emphasized, however, that there were "precious few" changes that could be excluded "because there are an awful lot of things that could be started for purposes of evading the 15th amendment if there is the desire to do so." House Hearings 95. It is significant that Congress chose not to include even these minor exceptions in 5, thus indicating an intention that all changes, no matter how small, be subjected to 5 scrutiny.

In light of the mass of legislative history to the contrary, especially the Attorney General's clear indication that the section was to have a broad scope and Congress' refusal to engraft even minor exceptions, the single remark of Assistant Attorney General Burke Marshall cannot be given determinative weight. Indeed, in any case where the legislative hearings and debate are so voluminous, no single statement or excerpt of testimony can be conclusive. . . .

The weight of the legislative history and an analysis of the basic purposes of the Act indicate that the enactment in each of these cases constitutes a "voting qualification or prerequisite to voting, or standard, practice, or procedure with respect to voting" within the meaning of 5.

No. 25 involves a change from district to at-large voting for county supervisors. The right to vote can be affected by a dilution of voting power as well as by an absolute prohibition on casting a ballot. . . . Voters who are members of a racial minority might well be in the majority in one district, but in a decided minority in the county as a whole. This type of change could therefore nullify their ability to elect the candidate of their choice just as would prohibiting some of them from voting.

In No. 26 an important county officer in certain counties was made appointive instead of elective. The power of a citizen's vote is affected by this amendment; after the change, he is prohibited from electing an officer formerly subject to the approval of the voters. Such a change could be made either with or without a discriminatory purpose or effect; however, the purpose of 5 was to submit such changes to scrutiny.

The changes in No. 36 appear aimed at increasing the difficulty for an independent candidate to gain a position on the general election ballot. These changes might also undermine the effectiveness of voters who wish to elect independent candidates. . . .

In these cases, as in so many others that come before us, we are called upon to determine the applicability of a statute where the language of the statute does not make crystal clear its intended scope. In all such cases we are compelled to resort to the legislative history to determine whether, in light of the articulated purposes of the legislation, Congress intended that the statute apply to the particular cases in question. We are of the opinion that, with the exception of the statement of

Assistant Attorney General Burke Marshall, the balance of legislative history (including the statements of the Attorney General and congressional action expanding the language) indicates that 5 applies to these cases. In saying this, we of course express no view on the merit of these enactments; we also emphasize that our decision indicates no opinion concerning their constitutionality.

V.

Appellees in the Mississippi cases argue that even if these state enactments are covered by 5, they may now be enforced, since the State submitted them to the Attorney General and he has failed to object. While appellees admit that they have made no "formal" submission to the Attorney General, they argue that no formality is required. They say that once the Attorney General has become aware of the state enactment, the enactment has been "submitted" for purposes of 5. Appellees contend that the Attorney General became aware of the enactments when served with a copy of appellees' briefs in these cases.

We reject this argument. While the Attorney General has not required any formal procedure, we do not think the Act contemplates that a "submission" occurs when the Attorney General merely becomes aware of the legislation, no matter in what manner. Nor do we think the service of the briefs on the Attorney General constituted a "submission." A fair interpretation of the Act requires that the State in some unambiguous and recordable manner submit any legislation or regulation in question directly to the Attorney General with a request for his consideration pursuant to the Act.

VI.

Appellants in the Mississippi cases have asked this Court to set aside the elections conducted pursuant to these enactments and order that new elections be held under the pre-amendment laws. The Solicitor General has also urged us to order new elections if the State does not promptly institute 5 approval proceedings. We decline to take corrective action of such consequence, however. These 5 coverage questions involve complex issues of first impression—issues subject to rational disagreement. The state enactments were not so clearly subject to 5 that the appellees' failure to submit them for approval constituted deliberate defiance of the Act. Moreover, the discriminatory purpose or effect of these statutes, if any, has not been determined by any court. We give only prospective effect to our decision, bearing in mind that our judgment today does not end the matter so far as these States are concerned. They remain subject to the continuing strictures of 5 until they obtain from the United States District Court for the District of Columbia a declaratory judgment that for at least five years they have not used the "tests or devices" prohibited by 4. 42 U.S.C. 1973b (a) (1964 ed., Supp. I). . . .

. . . All four cases are remanded to the District Courts with instructions to issue injunctions restraining the further enforcement of the enactments until such time as the States adequately demonstrate compliance with 5.
It is so ordered. . . .

———————

Source: Findlaw, *Allen v. State Board of Elections*, 393 U.S. 544 (1969), http://caselaw.lp.findlaw.com/scripts/getcase.pl?navby=case&court=us&vol=393&page=544.

---

29   **Memo from Dolly Hamby to Sen. Strom Thurmond, R-S.C., about Appeals to Race in South Carolina Elections, November 6, 1970**

In the fall of 2004, John Monk, an enterprising reporter for The State, *a Columbia, South Carolina, newspaper, revealed the contents of an intriguing postmortem election memo written for Strom Thurmond, then a Republican U.S. senator from the state in which he began his career as a segregationist Democrat. Thurmond received the memo after a key 1970 gubernatorial contest in South Carolina that pitted an openly racist Thurmond protégé, Albert Watson, against a Democrat. The memo candidly emphasized the electoral costs of running a campaign that came across as racist. Shortly after he received this memo, Thurmond began a much noticed shift toward racial moderation.*

The memo is particularly interesting when viewed against the backdrop of the extension of the Voting Rights Act in 1970, which came on the heels of the Supreme Court's decision in Allen v. State Board of Elections *(Document 28). It is not known what role these events played in shaping Thurmond's thinking—and they are not mentioned at all in the memo he received. But the memo could never have been written so candidly unless the writer, the consultant Dolly Hamby, knew that Thurmond was capable of calmly assessing the new political environment and the enormous changes in voting rights that were under way.*

[On letterhead of Bradley, Graham & Hamby Advertising Agency, Inc., Columbia, South Carolina]

November 6, 1970

. . .

Dear Strom:

Below are the factors which combined spelled defeat last Tuesday in my opinion. . . .

8. Serious Mistakes were Made.

In September, a five-minute documentary made by an Atlanta firm hired by the steering committee and over which we had no control, which showed National Guardsmen firing into a group of blacks was shown with Albert doing the commentary. This film was the worst example of raw racism that I have ever seen and was offensive to almost any decent person. No one in

South Carolina equates the blacks here with the types the film showed. The S.C. National Guardsmen were furious. This was the beginning of the loss of the business community and of the moderates who had made up so much of the Nixon vote in 1968. . . .

The "racist" charge REALLY hurt! The survey taken in October showed that the state had moderated considerably on the school situation. No attempt was made to get away from the "racist" label. Strom, South Carolina is much more moderate than many think. This one label cost Albert the metropolitan areas all over the state. . . .

A lot can be learned from this, namely: an appeal to race is no longer a vote-getter. . . .

Best regards.

Cordially,

BRADLEY, GRAHAM & HAMBY
Dolly [signed]
Secretary-Treasurer

Source: Clemson University, Strom Thurmond Collection, Subject: Correspondence Series.

IV. Expanding National Protection and Oversight of Minority Rights

30   Voting Rights Act Extension, June 22, 1970

President Richard Nixon was very conscious of southern white resistance to the Voting Rights Act of 1965, and he tried to satisfy that resentment by pushing for application of the act to the entire country—an entirely symbolic policy idea. Congress resisted him, however, and in the end the president signed the first extension of the Voting Rights Act with good grace. His remarks upon signing the extension precede its text.

Statement on Signing the Voting Rights Act Amendments of 1970
Richard Nixon, June 22nd, 1970

ON WEDNESDAY, Congress completed action on a bill extending and amending the Voting Rights Act of 1965, and sent it to me for signature. As passed, the bill contained a rider which I believe to be unconstitutional: a provision lowering the voting age to 18 in Federal, State, and local elections. Although I strongly favor the 18-year-old vote, I believe—along with most of the Nation's leading constitutional scholars—that Congress has no power to enact it by simple statute, but rather it requires a constitutional amendment.

Despite my misgivings about the constitutionality of this one provision, I have today signed the bill. . . .

. . . Because the basic provisions of this act are of great importance, therefore, I am giving it my approval and leaving the decision on the disputed provision to what I hope will be a swift resolution by the courts.

The Voting Rights Act of 1965 has opened participation in the political process. Although this bill does not include all of the administration's recommendations, it does incorporate improvements which extend its reach still further, suspending literacy tests nationwide and also putting an end to the present welter of State residency requirements for voting for President and

Vice President. Now, for the first time, citizens who move between elections may vote without long residency requirements.

In the 5 years since its enactment, close to 1 million Negroes have been registered to vote for the first time and more than 400 Negro officials have been elected to local and State offices. These are more than election statistics; they are statistics of hope and dramatic evidence that the American system works. They stand as an answer to those who claim that there is no recourse except to the streets. . . .

* * *

Public Law 91-285
AN ACT

To extend the Voting Rights Act of 1965 with respect to the discriminatory use of tests, and for other purposes.

Be it enacted by the Senate and House of Representatives of the United States of America in Congress assembled, That this Act may be cited as the Voting Rights Act Amendments of 1970.

Sec. 2. The Voting Rights Act of 1965 (79 Stat. 437; 42 U.S.C. 1973 et seq.) is amended by inserting therein, immediately after the first section thereof, the following title caption:

"TITLE I—VOTING RIGHTS".

Sec. 3. Section 4(a) of the Voting Rights Act of 1965 (79 Stat. 438; 42 U.S.C. 1973b) is amended by striking out the words "five years" wherever they appear in the first and third paragraphs thereof, and inserting in lieu thereof the words "ten years".

Sec. 4. Section 4(b) of the Voting Rights Act of 1965 (79 Stat. 438; 42 U.S.C. 1973b) is amended by adding at the end of the first paragraph thereof the following new sentence: "On and after August 6, 1970, in addition to any State or political subdivision of a State determined to be subject to subsection (a) pursuant to the previous sentence, the provisions of subsection (a) shall apply in any State or any political subdivision of a State which (i) the Attorney General determines maintained on November 1, 1968, any test or device, and with respect to which (ii) the Director of the Census determines that less than 50 per centum of the persons of voting age residing therein were registered on November 1, 1968, or that less than 50 per centum of such persons voted in the presidential election of November 1968."

Sec 5. Section 5 of the Voting Rights Act of 1965 (79 Stat. 439; 42 U.S.C. 1973c) is amended by (1) inserting after "section 4(a)" the following: "based upon determinations made under the first sentence of section 4(b)", and (2) inserting after "1964," the following: "or whenever a State or political subdivision with respect to which the prohibitions set forth in section 4(a) based upon determinations made under the second sentence of section 4(b) are in effect shall enact or seek to administer any voting qualification or prerequisite to voting, or standard, practice, or procedure with respect to voting different from that in force or effect on November 1, 1968,".

Sec. 6. The Voting Rights Act of 1965 (79 Stat. 437; 42 U.S.C. 1973 et seq.) is amended by adding at the end thereof the following new titles:

"TITLE II—SUPPLEMENTAL PROVISIONS".

"APPLICATION OF PROHIBITION TO OTHER STATES

"**Sec. 201.** (a) Prior to August 6, 1975, no citizen shall be denied because of his failure to comply with any test or device, the right to vote in any Federal, State, or local election conducted in any State or political subdivision of a State as to which the provisions of section 4(a) of this Act are not in effect by reason of determinations made under section 4(b) of this Act.

"(b) As used in this section, the term 'test or device' means any requirement that a person as a prerequisite for voting or registration for voting (1) demonstrate the ability to read, write, understand, or interpret any matter, (2) demonstrate any educational achievement or his knowledge of any particular subject, (3) possess good moral character, or (4) prove his qualifications by the voucher of registered voters or members of any other class.

"RESIDENCE REQUIREMENTS FOR VOTING

"Sec. 202. (a) The Congress hereby finds that the imprisonment and application of the durational residency requirement as a precondition to voting for the offices of President and Vice President, and the lack of sufficient opportunities for absentee registration and absentee balloting in presidential elections—

"(1) denies or abridges the inherent constitutional right of citizens to vote for their president and Vice President;

"(2) denies or abridges the inherent constitutional right of citizens to enjoy their free movement across State lines;

"(3) denies or abridges the privileges and immunities guaranteed to the citizens of each State under article IV, section 2, clause 1, of the Constitution;

"(4) in some instances has the impermissible purpose or effect of denying citizens the right to vote for such officers because of the way they may vote;

"(5) has the effect of denying to citizens the equality of civil rights, and due process and equal protection of the laws that are guaranteed to them under the fourteenth amendment; and

"(6) does not bear a reasonable relationship to any compelling State interest in the conduct of presidential elections.

"(b) Upon the basis of these findings, Congress declares that in order to secure and protect the above-stated rights of citizens under the Constitution, to enable citizens to better obtain the enjoyment of such rights, and to enforce the guarantees of the fourteenth amendment, it is necessary (1) to completely abolish the durational residency requirement as a precondition to voting for President and Vice President, and (2) to establish nationwide, uniform standards relative to absentee registration and absentee balloting in presidential elections.

"(c) No citizen of the United States who is otherwise qualified to vote in any election for President and Vice President shall be denied the right to vote for electors for President and Vice President, or for President and Vice President, in such election because of the failure of such citizen to comply with any durational residency requirement of such State or political subdivision; nor shall any citizen of the United States be denied the right to vote for electors for President and Vice President, or for President and Vice President, in such elections because of failure of such citizen to be physically present in such State or political subdivision at the time of such election, if such citizen shall have complied with the requirements prescribed by the law of such State or political subdivision providing for the casting of absentee ballots in such election.

"(d) For the purpose of this section, each State shall provide by law for the registration of other means of qualifications of duly qualified residents of such State who apply, not later than thirty days immediately prior to any presidential election, for registration or qualification to vote for the choice of electors for President and Vice President or for President and Vice President in such election; and each State shall provide by law for the casting of absentee ballots for the choice of electors for President and Vice President, or for President and Vice President, by all duly qualified residents of such State who may be absent from their election district or unit in such State on the day such election is held and who have applied therefor not later than seven days immediately prior to such election and have returned such ballots to the appropriate election official of such State not later than the time of closing of the polls in such State on the day of such election.

"(e) If any citizen of the United States who is otherwise qualified to vote in any State or political subdivision in any election for President and Vice President has begun residence in such State or political subdivision after the thirtieth day next preceding such election and, for that reason, does not satisfy the registration requirements of such State or political subdivision he shall be allowed to vote for the choice of electors for President and Vice President, or for President and Vice President, in such election, (1) in person in the State or political subdivision in which he resided immediately prior to his removal if he had satisfied, as of the date of his change of residence, the requirements to vote in that State or political subdivision, or (2) by absentee ballot in the State or political subdivision in which he resides immediately prior to his removal if he satisfies, but for his nonresident status and the reason for his absence, the requirements for absentee voting in that State or political subdivision.

"(f) No citizen of the United States who is otherwise qualified to vote by absentee ballot in any State or political subdivision in any election for President and Vice President shall be denied the right to vote for the choice of electors for President and Vice President, or for President and Vice President, in such election because of any requirement of registration that does not include a provision for absentee registration.

"(g) Nothing in this section shall prevent any State or political subdivision from adopting less restrictive voting practices than those that are prescribed herein.

"(h) The term 'State' as used in this section includes each of the several States and the District of Columbia.

"(i) The provisions of section 11(c) shall apply to false registration, and other fraudulent acts and conspiracies, committed under this section.

"JUDICIAL RELIEF

"**Sec. 203.** Whenever the Attorney General has reason to believe that a State or political subdivision (a) has enacted or is seeking to administer any test or device as a prerequisite to voting in violation of the prohibition contained in section 201, or (b) undertakes to deny the right to vote in any election in violation of section 202, he may institute for the United States, or in the name of the United States, an action in a district court of the United States in accordance with sections 1391 through 1393 of title 28, United States Code, for a restraining order, a preliminary or permanent injunction, or such other order as he deems appropriate. An action under this subsection shall be heard and determined by a court of three judges in accordance with the provisions of section 2282 of title 28 of the United States Code and any appeal shall be to the Supreme Court.

"PENALTY

"**Sec. 204.** Whoever shall deprive or attempt to deprive any person of any right secured by section 201 or 202 of this title shall be fined not more than $5,000, or imprisoned not more than five years, or both.

"SEPARABILITY

"**Sec. 205.** If any provision of this Act or the application of any provision thereof to any person or circumstance is judicially determined to be invalid, the remainder of this Act or the application of such provision to other persons or circumstances shall not be affected by such determination.

"**TITLE III—REDUCING VOTING AGE TO EIGHTEEN IN FEDERAL, STATE AND LOCAL ELECTION**

"DECLARATION AND FINDINGS

"**Sec. 301.** (a) The Congress finds and declares that the imposition and application of the requirement that a citizen be twenty-one years of age as a precondition to voting in any primary or in any election—

"(1) denies and abridges the inherent constitutional rights of citizens eighteen years of age but not yet twenty-one years of age to vote—a particularly unfair treatment of such citizens in view of the national defense responsibility imposed upon such citizens;

"(2) has the effect of denying to citizens eighteen years of age but not yet twenty-one years of age the due process and equal protection of the laws that are guaranteed to them under the fourteenth amendment of the Constitution; and

"(3) does not bear a reasonable relationship to any compelling State interest."

(b) In order to secure the constitutional right set forth in subsection (a), the Congress declares that it is necessary to prohibit the denial of the right to vote to citizens of the United States eighteen years of age or over.

"PROHIBITION

Sec. 302. Except as required by the Constitution, no citizen of the United States who is otherwise qualified to vote in any State or political subdivision in any primary or in any election shall be denied the right to vote in any such primary or election on account of age if such citizen is eighteen years of age or older.

"ENFORCEMENT

Sec. 303. (a) (1) In the exercise of the powers of the Congress under the necessary and proper clause of section 8, article I of the Constitution, and section 5 of the fourteenth amendment of the Constitution, the Attorney General is authorized and directed to institute in the name of the United States such actions against states or political subdivisions, including actions for injunctive relief, as he may determine to be necessary to implement the purposes of this title.

"(2) The district courts of the United States shall have jurisdiction of proceedings instituted pursuant to this title, which shall be heard and determined by a court of three judges in accordance with the provisions of section 2284 of title 28 of the United States Code, and any appeal shall lie to the Supreme Court. It shall be the duty of the judges designated to hear the case to assign the case for hearing and determination thereof, and to cause the case to be in every way expedited.

"(b) Whoever shall deny or attempt to deny any person of any right secured by this title shall be fined not more than $5,000 or imprisoned not more than five years, or both.

"DEFINITION

"**Sec. 304.** As used in this title the term 'State' includes the District of Columbia.

"EFFECTIVE DATE

"**Sec. 305.** The provisions of title III shall take effect with respect to any primary or election held on or after January 1, 1971."

Approved June 22, 1970.

Sources: The American Presidency Project, http://www.presidency.ucsb.edu/ws/index.php?pid=2553&st=&st1= (accessed November 1, 2005); "Voting Rights Act Amendments of 1970," Public Law 91-285, July 22, 1970, http://www.southerncouncil.org/pdf/vra1965.pdf (accessed October 3, 2005).

31   Congressional Testimony of Assistant Attorney General for Civil Rights J. Stanley
     Pottinger on the 1975 Extension of the Voting Rights Act, March 5, 1975

These remarks from the U.S. assistant attorney general for civil rights to Congress, offered during the 1975 deliberations over extension of the temporary provisions of the Voting Rights Act, usefully summarize the operation of these provisions up until that point. They also indicate that these provisions will be expanded to cover Latino voters. The act, even in its original conception, took account of discrimination against Puerto Rican voters. But by 1975 Congress and the executive branch had recognized that anti-Latino voting discrimination in the Southwest, California, and New York City was subverting the protections of the Fourteenth and Fifteenth Amendments and that the Voting Rights Act provided remedies for dismantling such discrimination.

TESTIMONY OF J. STANLEY POTTINGER
BEFORE THE SUBCOMMITTEE ON CIVIL
AND CONSTITUTIONAL RIGHTS,
COMMITTEE ON THE JUDICIARY, U.S.
HOUSE OF REPRESENTATIVES
MARCH 5, 1975

I am pleased to appear before the Subcommittee this morning to testify on the extension of those provisions of the Voting Rights Act which are due to expire later this year. . . .

In my testimony I will describe the facts and reasoning which support President Ford's recommended bill, H.R. 2148, which was introduced by Congressmen Hutchinson, McClory, Railsbac[k], Fish and Cohen, and I will also discuss H.R. 939, which Chairman Rodino and Chairman Edwards have introduced. In addition, just last week H.R. 3247 and H.R. 3501 were introduced. These bills propose that additional changes should be made in the Act, primarily to protect further the rights of Mexican-American and Puerto Rican citizens. In my view, as explained in our legal memorandum which has already been placed in the record, the Voting Rights Act, in its various protections against discrimination on account of race or color, does to some extent already cover Mexican-Americans and Puerto Ricans. The possible need for further protection, however deserves careful consideration by the Subcommittee, and I am pleased to see that representatives of these groups and other persons concerned with this question are testifying in these hearings. . . .

The questions before us this morning are whether, in light of present needs, in light of the successes of the Voting Rights Act to date, and in light of the principles of federalism, the Act should be extended. If answered affirmatively, a secondary concern is for how long it should be extended. To properly consider these questions we should examine the workings of the Act. Has it proved workable? Has it promoted nondiscrimination in voting? Does experience under it warrant extending its special coverage provisions to more fully protect the rights of other groups? Has it been so successful that it is no longer needed? How much of a strain of federalism has resulted? I believe that the results of such an examination, together with an examination of the judicial and legislative precedents, strongly support the Administration's proposed five-year extension, H.R. 2148. I will address these questions, first as to the extension of §4(a) of the Act, and second as to §201(a) of the 1970 Amendments; and third as to H.R. 3247 and H.R. 3501.

I. Section 4 is the central provision of the 1965 Act, because that section determines which states shall be subject to the special provisions of the Act relating to the suspension of tests or devices, pre-clearance of changes in voting laws, listing of voters by federal examiners, and the use of federal observers to monitor the conduct of elections. Section 4(b), as amended in 1970, provides for coverage of states and political subdivisions which the Attorney General determines maintained as a prerequisite for voting any test or device on November 1, 1954, or November 1, 1968 and which the Director of the Census certifies had less than 50% voter participation or registration in the Presidential election in 1964 or 1968, respectively. The Supreme Court, in upholding the provision of §4(b) of the 1965 Act that these determinations are not reviewable said: "the findings not subject to review consist of objective statistical determinations by the Census Bureau and a routine analysis of state statutes by the Justice Department." SOUTH CAROLINA v. KATZENBACH, 383 U.S. 301, 333.

Pursuant to these provisions 7 states and 46 political subdivisions were initially determined to come under the 1965 Act. Following extension of the Act in 1970, an additional 62 political subdivisions were covered (including 8 political subdivisions which had been determined to be covered in 1965 but had subsequently "bailed out" under §4(a). . . . While most of the covered jurisdictions are located in the South, some are located in the North and West, particularly in areas with large Native American or Spanish-speaking populations, such as Arizona or New York. . . .

. . . I now want to turn to the other consequences of coverage under §4: . . .

A. PRECLEARANCE

Section 5 of the Act requires preclearance of changes in the voting laws of jurisdictions covered by §4. The jurisdictions must either obtain from the United States District Court for the District of Columbia a declaratory judgment "that such [changed] qualification, prerequisite, standard, practice, or procedure does not have the purpose and will not have the effect of denying or abridging the right to vote on account of race or color" or submit the change to the Attorney General. If the Attorney General does not object to the submission within sixty days, the change may be enforced by the submitting jurisdiction. The Supreme Court, in upholding the constitutionality of §5, said:

Congress knew that some of the States covered by §4(b) of the Act had resorted to the extraordinary stratagem of contriving new rules of various kinds for the sole purpose of perpetuating voting discrimination in the face of adverse federal court decrees. Congress had reason to suppose that these States might try similar maneuvers in the future in order to evade the remedies for discrimination contained in the Act itself. SOUTH CAROLINA v. KATZENBACH, 383 U.S. 301, 335.

The Congressional hearings on the 1970 Amendments to the Voting Rights Act reflect that §5 was little used prior to 1969 and that the Department of Justice questioned its workability. Not until after the Supreme Court, in litigation brought under §5 in 1969 (ALLEN v. STATE BOARD OF ELECTIONS, 393 U.S. 544) did the Department begin to develop standards and procedures for enforcing §5. Congress gave a strong mandate to us to improve the enforcement of §5 by passing the 1970 Amendments. We subsequently promulgated regulations for the enforcement of §5 and directed more resources to §5, so that today enforcement of §5 is the highest priority of our Voting Section. Thus, most of our experience under §5 has occurred within the past five years. Although 4,476 voting changes have been submitted under Section 5 since 1965, between 1965 and 1969 the number of changes submitted was only 323 or 7% of all the Department has received. About 93% of all changes have been submitted since 1970. The year 1971 was the peak year for changes reviewed (1,118) and objections entered (50), a natural occurrence in light of the upcoming elections and redistrictings following the 1970 Census. The past three years, however, have continued to require the Department to review a high number of changes (between 850–1,000 a year). . . .

The following sets forth the states in descending order by numbers of changes submitted. The corresponding numbers of objections entered are also listed.

	Changes	Objections
S. Carolina	941	19
Virginia	891	10
Georgia	809	37
Louisiana	632	37
Mississippi	428	29
Alabama	331	22
N. Carolina	194	6
Arizona	149	2
New York	88	1
California	12	0
Wyoming	1	0
Idaho	0	0
	4,476	163

. . .

A total of 163 objections have been entered since 1965. . . . However, these 163 objections have involved about 300 changes, e.g., one redistricting plan may involve at-large elections, multimember districts, numbered posts and a majority requirement, while another may only involve numbered posts and majority requirement, while another may only involve numbered posts.

The highest number of objections was in 1971 (50), followed by 32, 27, and 30 in the next three years. Thus, it is apparent that the rate of objections has been about the same the past three years, indicating the continuing need for Section 5 review.

Approximately one-third of our objections have been to redistrictings on the state, county and city levels. In contrast, only 9 of our objections have related to annexations, which comprise the highest number of changes submitted.

These statistics tell only part of the story. The substance which lies behind them is even more important. The provisions of Section 5 have proved more complex than was imagined in 1965. It was not until the publication of the Department of Justice regulations in September of 1971 that states and political subdivisions were provided with a number of programs to uncover such changes and to obtain their submission. . . .

Thus, Section 5 has yet to be fully implemented. In some instances voting changes have been implemented even after we notified the state or local authorities of the requirements of Section 5 and even after we had sent objection letters under Section 5. For instance, in Leake County, Mississippi, in 1970 and in Kemper County, Mississippi in 1974 we were forced to file suit in order to prevent these counties from implementing an unsubmitted change to at-large elections for their school board members. And in a number of instances, i.e., the State of Georgia; Jonesboro, Hinesville and Twiggs County, Georgia; and St. James Parish, Louisiana, we had to file suit to prevent intended implementation of a change to which the Attorney General had objected.

Under Section 5, the submitting authority has the burden of showing that the submitted change does not have a racially discriminatory purpose or effect. While some of the Attorney General's objections under Section 5 are based primarily on the submitting authorities' failure to carry this burden, many are based on a conclusion that the change involved is clearly discriminatory. Permit me to cite a few examples.

In recent years we have objected to the change of polling places to an all-white segregated private school (Lafayette Parish, La., July 18, 1971) and to an all-white segregated club (St. Landry Parish, La., Dec. 6, 1972); to a racial gerrymander of voting districts using non-contiguous areas as a part of the district (E. Feliciana Parish, La., Dec. 28, 1971) and a racial gerrymander resulting in "an extraordinarily shaped 19-sided figure that narrows at one point to the width of an intersection, contains portions of three present districts, and suggests a design to consolidate in one district as many black residents as possible" (Orleans Parish, La., August 20, 1971). In several instances covered jurisdictions submitted proposed annexations of white areas, while refusing to annex black areas. . . .

B. EXAMINERS

§6 of the Voting Rights Act, governing the use of Federal examiners, provides for their appointment whenever authorized by a court in a proceeding brought by the Attorney General to enforce the guarantees of the 15th Amendment (§3(a)), or in a covered jurisdiction under §4(b), whenever the Attorney General certifies that he has received meritorious written complaints from 20 or more residents of [a] political subdivision that they have been denied the right to vote under color of law by reason of race or color, or when, in his judgment, "the appointment of examiners is otherwise necessary to enforce the guarantees of the fifteenth amendment". . . . §6(b)(2). In making the latter determination, the Attorney General is required to take into account whether the ratio of nonwhite to white persons registered to vote appears reasonably attributable to violations of the 15th Amendment or whether bona fide efforts are being made to comply. More specifically, the Department considers such factors as how long and how consistently the voter registration office is open, its location in relation to areas where black registration is low and whether offices are set up in outlying areas; whether there has been intimidation of registrants ranging from discourtesy to violence; and whether standards are applied differently to white and black applicants.

Once an area has been designated for federal examiners, at the request of the Attorney General the U.S. Civil Service Commission selects and assigns them. As recognized by the Supreme Court in SOUTH CAROLINA v. KATZENBACH, SUPRA, this section of the Act was necessary because "voting officials have persistently employed a variety of procedural tactics to deny Negroes the franchise, often in direct defiance or evasion of federal court decrees." 383 U.S. at 336. The procedure was designed to cure some of the "localized evil" which might be undisturbed by mere suspension of misused voting rules.

The duty of federal examiners is to list persons who satisfy state voting qualifications which are consistent with federal law and to supply that list monthly to local election officials, who then enter the names on the official voter registry. A procedure for challenging any person listed is provided

in §9. In addition, examiners are available during an election and within forty-eight hours after the closing of the polls to receive complaints that persons otherwise eligible to vote have been denied that right.

Since passage of the Act, approximately 317 examiners have been sent to 73 designated jurisdictions. . . . The majority of designations for examiners occurred from 1965–1967 (61 out of 73); however, 6 additional areas were designated in 1974. The largest number of designations have been made in Alabama (14), Louisiana (11), and Mississippi (38).

Since 1965, 160,358 black persons have been listed by federal examiners. During the period from 1965–1969, a total of 158,384 blacks were listed, and from 1970–1974, the federal examiners listed 1,974 black voters. . . . Estimates based upon data collected by the Voter Education Project in Atlanta, Georgia would indicate that registration of blacks by federal examiners accounted for 34.2% of the total increase in black voter registration in Alabama from 1964–1972. The comparable percentages in other states were 1.9% in Georgia, 13.2% in Louisiana, 27.5% in Mississippi, and 7.4% in South Carolina, with a total overall of 18.9% of black registration being accomplished by federal examiners. . . . In addition, we believe that the overall increase in black registration in the covered southern states from 1.2 million in 1964 to 2.1 million in 1972 has been due, in part, to the knowledge by local registrars that federal examiners will be designated if black persons are not given a meaningful opportunity to register. . . .

C. OBSERVERS

Whenever federal examiners are serving in a particular area, the Attorney General may request that the Civil Service Commission assign one or more persons to observe the conduct of an election to determine whether persons who are entitled to vote are permitted to do so and to observe whether votes cast by eligible voters are being properly counted.

In making the determination that federal observers are needed, the Attorney General considers three basic areas: (1) the extent to which those who will run an election are prepared, so that there are sufficient voting hours and facilities, procedural rules for voting have been adequately publicized, and polling officials, non-discriminately selected, are instructed in election procedures; (2) the confidence of the black community in the electoral process and the individuals conducting the elections, including the extent to which black persons are allowed to be poll officials, and (3) the possibility of forces outside the official election machinery, such as racial violence or threats of violence or a history of discrimination in other areas, such as schools and public accommodations, interfering with the election. Such factors are particularly important in an election where a black candidate or a candidate who has the support of black voters has a good chance of winning the election. Federal observers provide a calming, objective presence in an otherwise charged political atmosphere, and serve to prevent intimidation of black voters at the polls and to assure that illiterate voters are provided with non-coercive assistance in voting. For instance, when the local polling place is located in a white-owned store, the presence of federal observers can alleviate apprehension by black voters that informal voting procedures or other improprieties will be used which will enable the poll officials to know how they voted. . . .

D. OVERALL RESULTS OF VOTING RIGHTS ACT

The overall results of the Voting Rights Act in strengthening the role of black persons in the political process have been significant, but there remains a great deal to be accomplished. Based upon the available data, we estimate that the number of blacks registered to vote has increased from 1.5 to 3.5 million in the eleven-state South and nearly doubled from 1.2 to 2.1 million in the seven Southern states covered by the Voting Rights Act.

The most significant gains in voter registration by blacks have occurred in Mississippi, Louisiana, and Alabama. Prior to the Voting Rights Act, in 1964, less than 10% of the black persons of voting age were registered to vote in Mississippi, although blacks constituted 36% of the voting age population. As of 1971–1972, 62.2% of eligible blacks in Mississippi were registered. Even considering this gain, however black registration is still nearly 10% lower than the rate of white registration in Mississippi. In Louisiana, black registration, expressed as a percentage of voting age population, was 59.17% in 1971–1972 as compared with 32.0% in 1964. However, the rate of black registration in Louisiana is approximately 20% less than that for white persons. A similar pattern exists in Alabama where, although the gain in percentage of black persons registered is 34%, a gap of 23.6% still exists between black and white registration rates. . . .

Another indication of the gains made by black citizens under the Voting Rights Act is the increase in the number of black elected officials. As of April, 1974, there were 2,991 black elected officials in the United States. This includes federal, state, county and municipal governments as well as elected law enforcement and education officials. Approximately 45% of the black elected officials are in municipal government positions including mayors, councilmen, commissioners, and aldermen. . . .

Concentrating on the southern states, the gains from 1965 to 1974 are significant. There were less than 100 black elected officials in the southern states prior to the Voting Rights Act, compared with 565 black elected officials in eleven southern states in 1970, and 1,398 in 1974. . . .

Notwithstanding these gains, out of 101 counties with majority black populations, 38 have no black elected officials in district, county, city or state positions and an additional 11 majority black counties have only one (1) black elected official.

The South's black mayors are, with few exceptions, in small municipalities or in areas in which there is a majority black population. In the seven southern states covered by the Voting Rights Act, only 7% of the seats in the lower houses of state legislatures were held by blacks, while in the upper houses blacks held only 2.5% of the seats. Of the sixteen black United States Representatives, only two are from southern states.

Similarly, although Mississippi ranks second in the nation in the number of black elected officials with 191, black persons hold only 4% of the elective positions despite the fact that over 1/3 of the population in the state is black (36.8%). By pointing to these disparities, I do not mean to suggest that any particular number or percentage of black persons in elective offices is required, but only that the statistics suggest the existence of practices against blacks which have prevented the level of representation that could normally be expected.

The increase in the numbers of blacks registered and voting has also had an incidental effect on the responsiveness of white elected officials to black citizens' needs. We can see this increased responsiveness in recent appointments of blacks to state level positions by the white elected officials.

In summary, there have been significant improvements in the political role of blacks since the passage of the Voting Rights Act, but I have also tried to highlight those areas where more needs to be done. The number of objections which the Attorney General has made to changes in voting laws submitted to him under §5 show that there is still a potential for the passage of legislation which has either as its purpose or effect the exclusion of black voters from their rightful role. This potential could become reality in the absence of some objective control at the federal level.

E. Conclusion

. . .

. . . Congress may wish to consider enacting permanent voting rights legislation, and that would be the appropriate time for considering

whether the suspension of tests or devices should be converted to a permanent ban.

. . . I would like to turn next to the issues raised by H.R. 3247, introduced by Representative Jordan, and H.R. 3501, introduced by Representatives Roybal and Badillo. These bills would amend the Voting Rights Act, so as to provide further protection for the voting rights of Spanish-surnamed Americans. . . . [A]lthough some court decisions already suggest that in order for the right to vote to be effective voters belonging to a substantial minority which speaks a language other than English should be provided election materials in their own language, some states have not reformed their voting laws to comply with those decisions. Accordingly, it would be appropriate for this committee to consider in these hearings whether the definition of the phrase "test or device" as used in the Voting Rights Act should be amended so as to cover English-only elections in areas with large numbers of non-English speaking voters. Such an amendment would, if the Act is extended, require all such areas to provide for bilingual elections. It could be based on the Fifteenth Amendment alone (in which case it should be limited to Asian Americans, Native Americans, Puerto Ricans and Mexican-Americans and other Americans of Latin American origin) or the Fourteenth Amendment. . . .

. . . In conclusion, I believe that the most urgent task of the Committee relating to the Voting Rights Act is to agree promptly on a bill extending §4 and §201 for an additional 5 years. Prompt action is necessary to ensure that the special coverage provision and the nationwide suspension of tests and devices are not allowed to expire. The second task, of equal importance, if not subject to the same constraints, is consideration of the need for additional coverage to protect the rights of Mexican Americans, Puerto Ricans, and Native Americans.

Source: U.S. Department of Justice, Washington, D.C.

32   Voting Rights Act Extension, August 6, 1975

President Gerald R. Ford went through a show of resistance to extension of the Voting Rights Act as part of the Republican Party's strategy of attracting southern white voters. In the end, however, he, as seen in his remarks reproduced here, rather enthusiastically signed the extension.

Remarks Upon Signing a Bill Extending the
Voting Rights Act of 1965
Gerald R. Ford, August 6th, 1975

Mr. Vice President, distinguished Members of the Congress, and other distinguished guests:

I am very pleased to sign today H.R. 6219, which extends as well as broadens the provisions of the Voting Rights Act of 1965.

The right to vote is at the very foundation of our American system, and nothing must interfere with this very precious right. Today is the 10th anniversary of the signing by President Johnson of the Voting Rights Act of 1965, which I supported as a Member of the House of Representatives.

In the past decade, the voting rights of millions and millions of Americans have been protected and our system of government has been strengthened immeasurably. The bill that I will sign today extends the temporary provisions of the act for 7 more years and broadens the provisions to bar discrimination against Spanish-speaking Americans, American Indians, Alaskan natives, and Asian Americans.

Further, this bill will permit private citizens, as well as the Attorney General, to initiate suits to protect the voting rights of citizens in any State where discrimination occurs. There must be no question whatsoever about the right of each eligible American, each eligible citizen to participate in our elective process. The extension of this act will help to ensure that right. I thank the Members of the Congress, I thank their staffs, and I thank all the others who have been helpful in making this signing possible.

* * *

Public Law 94-73

An Act

To amend the Voting Rights Act of 1965 to extend certain provisions for an additional seven years, to make permanent the ban against certain prerequisites to voting, and for other purposes.

Be it enacted by the Senate and House of Representatives of the United States of America in Congress assembled,

TITLE I

Sec. 101. Section 4(a) of the Voting Rights Act of 1965 is amended by striking out "ten" each time it appears and inserting in lieu thereof "seventeen".

Sec. 102. Section 201(a) of the Voting Rights Act of 1965 is amended by—

(1) striking out "Prior to August 6, 1975, no" and inserting "No" in lieu thereof;

and

(2) striking out "as to which the provisions of section 4(a) of this Act are not in effect by reason of determinations made under section 4(b) of this Act." and inserting in lieu thereof a period.

TITLE II

Sec. 201. Section 4(a) of the Voting Rights Act of 1965 is amended by—

(1) inserting immediately after "determinations have been made under" the following: "the first two sentences of";

(2) adding at the end of the first paragraph thereof the following new sentence: "No citizen shall be denied the right to vote in any Federal, State, or local election because of his failure to comply with any test or device in any State with respect to which the determinations have been made under the third sentence of subsection (b) of this section or in any political subdivision with respect to which such determinations have been made as a separate unit, unless the United States District Court for the District of Columbia in an action for a declaratory judgment brought by such State or subdivision against the United States has determined that no such test or device has been used during the ten years preceding the filing of the action for the purpose or with the effect of denying or abridging the right to vote on account of race or color, or in contravention of the guarantees set forth in section 4(f) (2): *Provided*, That no such declaratory judgment shall issue with respect to any plaintiff for a period of ten years after the entry of a final judgment of any court of the United States other than the denial of a declaratory judgment under this section, whether entered prior to or after the enactment of this paragraph, determining that denials or abridgments of the right to vote on account of race or color, or in contravention of the guarantees set forth in section 4(f) (2) through the use of tests or devices have occurred anywhere in the territory of such plaintiff.";

(3) striking out "the action" in the third paragraph thereof, and by inserting in lieu thereof "an action under the first sentence of this subsection"; and

(4) inserting immediately after the third paragraph thereof the following new paragraph: "If the Attorney General determines that he has no reason to believe that any such test or device has been used during the ten years preceding the filing of an action under the second sentence of this subsection for the purpose of with the effect of

denying or abridging the right to vote on account of race or color, or in contravention of the guarantees set forth in section 4(f) (2), he shall consent to the entry of such judgment.".

Sec. 202. Section 4(b) of the Voting Rights Act of 1965 is amended by adding at the end of the first paragraph thereof the following: "On and after August 6, 1975, in addition to any State or political subdivision of a State determined to be subject to subsection (a) pursuant to the previous two sentences, the provisions of subsection (a) shall apply in any State or any political subdivision of a State which (i) the Attorney General determines maintained on November 1, 1972, any test or device, and with respect to which (ii) the Director of the Census determines that less than 50 per centum of the citizens of voting age were registered on November 1, 1972, or that less than 50 per centum of such persons voted in the presidential election of November 1972.".

Sec. 203. Section 4 of the Voting Rights Act of 1965 is amended by adding the following new subsection:

"(f)(1) The Congress finds that voting discrimination against citizens of language minorities is pervasive and national in scope. Such minority citizens are from environments in which the dominant language is other than English. In addition they have been denied equal educational opportunities by State and local governments, resulting in severe disabilities and continuing illiteracy in the English language. The Congress further finds that, where State and local officials conduct elections only in English, language minority citizens are excluded from participating in the electoral process. In many areas of the country, this exclusion is aggravated by acts of physical, economic, and political intimidation. The Congress declares that, in order to enforce the guarantees of the fourteenth and fifteenth amendments to the United States Constitution, it is necessary to eliminate such discrimination by prohibiting English-only elections, and by prescribing other remedial devices.

"(2) No voting qualifications or prerequisite to voting, or standard, practice, or procedure shall be imposed or applied by any State or political subdivision to deny or abridge the right of any citizen of the United States to vote because he is a member of a language minority group.

"(3) In addition to the meaning given the term under section 4(c), the term 'test or device' shall also mean any practice or requirement by which any State or political subdivision provided any registration or voting notices, forms, instructions, assistance, or other materials or information relating to the electoral process, including ballots, only in the English language, where the Director of the Census determines that more than five per centum of the citizens of voting age residing in such State or political subdivision are members of a single language minority. With respect to section 4(b), the term 'test or device', as defined in this subsection, shall be employed only in making the determinations under the third sentence of that subsection.

"(4) Whenever any State or political subdivision subject to the prohibitions of the second sentence of section 4(a) provides any registration or voting notices, forms, instructions, assistance, or other materials or information relating to the electoral process, including ballots, it shall provide them in the language of the applicable language minority group as well as in the English language: *Provided,* That where the language of the applicable minority group is oral or unwritten, the State or political subdivision is only required to furnish oral instructions, assistance, or other information relating to registration and voting.".

Sec. 204. Section 5 of the Voting Rights Act of 1965 is amended by inserting after November 1, 1968," the following: "or whenever a State or political subdivision with respect to which the prohibitions set forth in section 4(a) based upon determination made under the third sentence of section 4(b) are in effect shall enact or seek to ad-

minister any voting qualification or prerequisite to voting, or standard, practice, or procedure with respect to voting different from that in force or effect on November 1, 1972,".

Sec. 205. Sections 3 and 6 of the Voting Rights Act of 1965 are each amended by striking out "fifteenth amendment" each time it appears and inserting in lieu thereof "fourteenth or fifteenth amendment".

Sec. 206. Sections 2, 3, the second paragraph of section 4(a), and sections 4(d), 5, 6, and 13 of the Voting Rights Act of 1965 are each amended by adding immediately after "on account of race or color" each time it appears the following: ", or in contravention of the guarantees set forth in section 4(f) (2)".

Sec. 207. Section 14(c) is amended by adding at the end the following new paragraph:

"(3) The term 'language minorities' or 'language minority group' means persons who are American Indian, Asian American, Alaskan Natives or of Spanish heritage.".

Sec. 208. If any amendments made by this Act or the application of any provision thereof to any person or circumstance is judicially determined to be invalid, the remainder of the Voting Rights Act of 1965, or the application of such provision to other persons or circumstances shall not be affected by such determination.

TITLE III

Sec. 301. The Voting Rights Act of 1965 is amended by inserting the following new section immediately after section 202:

"BILINGUAL ELECTION REQUIREMENTS

"Sec. 203. (a) The Congress finds that, through the use of various practices and procedures, citizens of language minorities have been effectively excluded from participation in the electoral process. Among other factors, the denial of the right to vote of such minority group citizens is ordinarily directly related to the unequal educational opportunities afforded them, resulting in high illiteracy and low voting participation. The Congress declares that, in order to enforce the guarantees of the fourteenth and fifteenth amendments to the United States Constitution, it is necessary to eliminate such discrimination by prohibiting these practices, and by prescribing other remedial devices.

"(b) Prior to August 6, 1985, no State or political subdivision shall provide registration or voting notices, forms, instructions, assistance, or other materials or information relating to the electoral process, including ballots, only in the English language if the Director of the Census determines (i) that more than 5 percent of the citizens of voting age of such State or political subdivision are members of a single language minority and (ii) that the illiteracy rate of such persons as a group is higher than the national illiteracy rate: *Provided,* That the prohibitions of this subsection shall not apply in any political subdivision which has less than five percent voting age citizens of each language minority which comprises over five percent of the statewide population of voting age citizens. For purposes of this subsection, illiteracy means the failure to complete the fifth primary grade. The determinations of the Director of the Census under this subsection shall be effective upon publication in the Federal Register and shall not be subject to review in any court.

"(c) Whenever any State or political subdivision subject to the prohibition of subsection (b) of this section provides any registration or voting notices, forms, instruction, assistance, or other materials or information relating to the electoral process, including ballots, it shall provide them in the language of the applicable minority group as well as in the English language: *Provided,* That where the language of the applicable minority group is oral or unwritten or in the case of

Alaskan natives, if the predominant language is historically unwritten, the State or political subdivision is only required to furnish oral instructions, assistance, or other information relating to registration and voting.

"(d) Any State or political subdivision subject to the prohibition of subsection (b) of this section, which seeks to provided English-only registration or voting materials or information, including ballots, may file an action against the United States in the United States District Court for a declaratory judgment permitting such provision. The court shall grant the requested relief if it determines that the illiteracy rate of the applicable language minority group within the State or political subdivision is equal to or less than the national illiteracy rate.

"(e) For purposes of this section, the term 'language minorities' or 'language minority group' means persons who are American Indian, Asian American, Alaskan Natives, or of Spanish heritage."

Sec. 302. Sections 203, 204, and 205 of the Voting Rights Act of 1965, are redesigned as 204, 205, and 206, respectively.

Sec. 303. Section 203 of the Voting Rights Act of 1965, as redesignated section 204 by section 302 of this Act, is amended by inserting immediately after "in violation of section 202," the following: "or 203,".

Sec. 304. Section 204 of the Voting Rights Act of 1965, as redesignated section 205 by section 302 of this Act, is amended by striking out "or 202" and inserting in lieu thereof ", 202, or 203".

TITLE IV

Sec. 401. Section 3 of the Voting Rights Act of 1965 is amended by striking out "Attorney General" the first three times it appears and inserting in lieu thereof the following "Attorney General or an aggrieved person".

Sec. 402. Section 14 of the Voting Rights Act of 1965 is amended by adding at the end thereof the following new subsection:

"(e) In any action or proceeding to enforce the voting guarantees of the fourteenth or fifteenth amendment, the court, in its discretion, may allow the prevailing party, other than the United States, a reasonable attorney's fee as part of the cost.".

Sec. 403. Title II of the Voting Rights Act of 1965 is amended by adding at the end thereof the following new section:

"Sec. 207. (a) Congress hereby directs the Director of the Census forthwith to conduct a survey to compile registration and voting statistics: (i) in every State or political subdivision with respect to which the prohibitions of section 4(a) of the Voting Rights Act of 1965 are in effect, for every statewide general election for Members of the United States House of Representative after January 1, 1974; and (ii) in every State or political subdivision for any election designated by the United States Commission on Civil Rights. Such survey shall only include a count of citizens of voting age, race or color, and national origin, and a determination of the extent to which such persons are registered to vote and have in the elections surveyed.

"(b) In any survey under subsection (a) of this section no person shall be compelled to disclose his race, color, national origin, political party affiliation, or how he voted (or the reasons therefor), nor shall any penalty be imposed for his failure or refusal to make such disclosures. Every person interrogated orally, by written survey or questionnaire, or by any other mean with respect to such information shall be fully advised of his right to fail or refuse to furnish such information.

"(c) The Director of the Census shall, at the earliest practicable time, report to the Congress the results of every survey conducted pursuant to the provisions of subsection (a) of this section."

"(d) The provisions of section 9 and chapter 7 of title 13 of the United States Code shall apply to any survey, collection, or compilation of registration and voting statistics carried out under subsection (a) of this section,"

Sec. 404. Section 11(c) of the Voting Rights Act of 1965 is amended by inserting after "Columbia," the following words: "Guam, or the Virgin Islands,".

Sec. 405. Section 5 of the Voting Rights Act of 1965 is amended—

(1) by striking out "except that neither" and inserting in lieu thereof the following: "or upon good cause shown, to facilitate an expedited approval within sixty days after such submission, the Attorney General has affirmatively indicated that such objection will not be made. Neither an affirmative indication by the Attorney General that no objection will be made, not";

(2) by placing after the word "failure to object" a comma; and

(3) by inserting immediately before the final sentence thereof the following: "In the event the Attorney General affirmatively indicates that no objection will be made within the sixty-day period following receipt of a submission if additional information comes to his attention during the remainder of the sixty-day period which would otherwise require objection in accordance with this section.".

Sec. 406. Section 203 of the Voting Rights Act of 1965, as redesignated 204 by section 302 of this Act, is amended by striking out "section 2282 of title 28" and inserting "section 2284 of title 28" in lieu thereof.

Sec. 407. Title III of the Voting Rights Act of 1965 is amended to read as follows:

"TITLE III—EIGHTEEN-YEAR-OLD VOTING AGE

"ENFORCEMENT OF TWENTY-SIXTH AMENDMENT

"Sec. 301. (a) (1) The Attorney General is directed to institute, in the name of the United States, such actions against States or political subdivisions, including actions for injunctive relief, as he may determine to be necessary to implement the twenty-six article of amendment to the Constitution of the United States.

"(2) The district courts of the United States shall have jurisdiction of proceedings instituted under this title, which shall be heard and determined by a court of three judges in accordance with section 2284 of title 28 of the United States Code, and any appeal shall lie to the Supreme Court. It shall be the duty of the judges designated to hear the case to assign the case for hearing and determinations thereof, and to cause the case to be in every way expedited.

"(b) Whoever shall deny or attempt to deny any person of any right secured by the twenty-sixth article of amendment to the Constitution of the United States shall be fined not more than $5,000 or imprisoned not more than five years, or both.

"DEFINITION

"Sec. 302. As used in this title, the term 'State' includes the District of Columbia.".

Sec. 408. Section 10 of the Voting Rights Act of 1965 is amended—

(1) by striking out subsection (d);
(2) in subsection (b), by inserting "and section 2 of the twenty-fourth amendment" immediately after "fifteenth amendment"; and

(3) by striking out "and" the first time it appears in subsection (b), and inserting in lieu thereof a comma.

Sec. 409. Section 11 of the Voting Rights Act of 1965 is amended by adding at the end the following new subsection:

"(e) (1) Whoever votes more than once in an election referred to in paragraph (2) shall be fined not more than $10,000 or imprisoned not more than five years, or both.

"(2) The prohibition of this subsection applies with respect to any general, special, or primary election held solely or in part for the purpose of selecting or electing any candidate for the office of President, Vice President, presidential elector, Member of the United States Senate, Member of the United States House of Representatives, Delegate from the District of Columbia, Guam, or the Virgin Islands, or Resident Commissioner of the Commonwealth of Puerto Rico.

"(3) As used in this subsection, the term 'votes more than once' does not include the casting of an additional ballot if all prior ballots of that voter were invalidated, not does it include the voting in two jurisdictions under section 202 of this Act, to extent two ballots are not cast for an election to the same candidacy or office."

Sec. 410. Section 3 of the Voting Rights Act of 1965 is amended by inserting immediately before "guarantees" each time it appears the following "voting".

Approved August 6, 1975.

Sources: The American Presidency Project, http://www.presidency.ucsb.edu/ws/index.php?pid=5157&st=&st1= (accessed November 3, 2005); "Voting Rights Act Amendments of 1975," Public Law 94-73, August 6, 1975, http://www.southerncouncil.org/pdf/vra1965.pdf (accessed October 3, 2005).

33   *Beer v. United States,* Decided March 30, 1976

In Beer v. United States *(425 U.S. 130), which involved redistricting in New Orleans, the Supreme Court majority lined up behind the values of using a concept called "retrogression" as a way to regulate the preclearance process. By retrogression, the majority meant any election plan that made black voters worse off than they were before in terms of either access to the ballot or effective representation. The Court ruled that retrogressive plans could not be precleared. A minority of the Court feared, however, that the concept of retrogression took away as much as it gave. Plans that did relatively little to improve black electoral influence, even if they did* something, *could be precleared—or so they worried. The dissenting justices claimed that the Court was limiting the use of Section 5 of the Voting Rights Act and doing so in a way that Congress did not intend. Congress did not mean a minimalist approach to fulfillment of the Fourteenth and Fifteenth Amendments; it meant instead to overcome decades of constitutional subversion as fully as possible. In the end,* Beer's *proposal of the retrogression concept probably caused little harm and did provide some sort of useful benchmark. The opinion for the Court also clearly stated that intentionally discriminatory plans of any kind could not be precleared.*

BEER ET AL. v. UNITED STATES ET AL.
APPEAL FROM THE UNITED STATES
DISTRICT COURT FOR
THE DISTRICT OF COLUMBIA.
No. 73-1869.
Argued March 26, 1975. Reargued November 12, 1975.
Decided March 30, 1976.

. . .

MR. JUSTICE STEWART delivered the opinion of the Court.

Section 5 of the Voting Rights Act of 1965 prohibits a State or political subdivision subject to 4 of the Act from enforcing "any voting qualification or prerequisite to voting, or standard, practice, or procedure with respect to voting different from that in force or effect on November 1, 1964," unless it has obtained a declaratory judgment from the District Court for the District of Columbia that such change "does not have the purpose and will not have the effect of denying or abridging the right to vote on account of race or color" or has submitted the proposed change to the Attorney General and the Attorney General has not objected to it. The constitutionality of this procedure was upheld in South Carolina v. Katzenbach, 383 U.S. 301, and it is now well established that 5 is applicable when a State or political subdivision adopts a legislative reapportionment plan. Allen v. State Board of Elections, 393 U.S. 544; Georgia v. United States, 411 U.S. 526.

The city of New Orleans brought this suit under 5 seeking a judgment declaring that a reapportionment of New Orleans' councilmanic districts did not have the purpose or effect of denying or abridging the right to vote on account of race or color. The District Court entered a judgment of dismissal, holding that the new reapportionment plan would have the effect of abridging the voting rights of New Orleans' Negro citizens. 374 F. Supp. 363. The city appealed the judgment to this Court, claiming that the District Court used an incorrect standard in assessing the effect of the reapportionment in this 5 unit. We noted probable jurisdiction of the appeal. 419 U.S. 822.

I

New Orleans is a city of almost 600,000 people. Some 55% of that population is white and the remaining 45% is Negro. Some 65% of the registered voters are white, and the remaining 35% are Negro. In 1954, New Orleans adopted a mayor-council form of government. Since that time the municipal charter has provided that the city council is to consist of seven members, one to be elected from each of five councilmanic districts, and two to be elected by the voters of the city at large. The 1954 charter also requires an adjustment of the boundaries of the five single-member councilmanic districts following each decennial census to reflect population shifts among the districts.

In 1961, the city council redistricted the city based on the 1960 census figures. That reapportionment plan established four districts that stretched from the edge of Lake Pontchartrain on the north side of the city to the Mississippi River on the city's south side. The fifth district was wedge shaped and encompassed the city's downtown area. In one of these councilmanic districts, Negroes constituted a majority of the population, but only about half of the registered voters. In the other four districts white voters clearly outnumbered Negro voters. No Negro was elected to the New Orleans City Council during the decade from 1960 to 1970.

After receipt of the 1970 census figures the city council adopted a reapportionment plan (Plan I) that continued the basic north-to-south pattern of councilmanic districts combined with a wedge-shaped, downtown district. Under Plan I Negroes constituted a majority of the population in two districts, but they did not make up a majority of registered voters in any district. The largest percentage of Negro voters in a single district under Plan I was 45.2%. When the city submitted Plan I to the Attorney General pursuant to 5, he objected to it, stating that it appeared to "dilute black voting strength by combining a number of black voters with a larger number of white voters in each of the five districts." He also expressed the view that "the district lines [were not] drawn as they [were] because of any compelling governmental need" and that the district lines did "not reflect numeric population configurations or considerations of district compactness or regularity of shape."

Even before the Attorney General objected to Plan I, the city authorities had commenced work on a second plan—Plan II. That plan followed the general north-to-south districting pattern common to the 1961 apportionment and Plan I. It produced Negro population majorities in two districts and a Negro voter majority (52.6%) in one district. When Plan II was submitted to the Attorney General, he posed the same objections to it that he had raised to Plan I. In addition, he noted that "the predominantly black neighborhoods in the city are located generally in an east to west progression," and pointed out that the use of north-to-south districts in such a situation almost inevitably would have the effect of diluting the maximum potential impact of the Negro vote. Following the rejection by the Attorney General of Plan II, the city brought this declaratory judgment action in the United States District Court for the District of Columbia.

The District Court concluded that Plan II would have the effect of abridging the right to vote on account of race or color. It calculated that if Negroes could elect city councilmen in proportion to their share of the city's registered voters, they would be able to choose 2.42 of the city's seven councilmen, and, if in proportion to their share of the city's population, to choose 3.15 councilmen. But under Plan II the District Court concluded that, since New Orleans' elections had been marked by bloc voting along racial lines, Negroes would probably be able to elect only one councilman—the candidate from the one councilmanic district in which a majority of the voters were Negroes. This difference between mathematical potential and predicted reality was such that "the burden in the case at bar was at least to demonstrate that nothing but the redistricting proposed by Plan II was feasible." 374 F. Supp., at 393. The court concluded that "[t]he City has not made that sort of demonstration; indeed, it was conceded at trial that neither that plan nor any of its variations was the City's sole available alternative." Ibid.

As a separate and independent ground for rejecting Plan II, the District Court held that the failure of the plan to alter the city charter provision establishing two at-large seats had the effect in itself of "abridging the right to vote . . . on account of race or color." As the court put it: "[T]he City has not supported the choice of at-large elections by any consideration which would satisfy the standard of compelling governmental interest, or the need to demonstrate the improbability of its realization through the use of single-member districts. These evaluations compel the conclusion that the feature of the city's electoral scheme by which two councilmen are selected at large has the effect of impermissibly minimizing the vote of its black citizens; and the further conclusion that for this additional reason the city's redistricting plan does not pass muster." Id., at 402.

The District Court therefore refused to allow Plan II to go into effect. As a result there have been no councilmanic elections in New Orleans since 1970, and the councilmen elected at that time (or their appointed successors) have remained in office ever since.

II
A

The appellants urge, and the United States on reargument of this case has conceded, that the District Court was mistaken in holding that Plan II could be rejected under 5 solely because it did not eliminate the two at-large councilmanic seats that had existed since 1954. The appellants and the United States are correct in their interpretation of the statute in this regard.

The language of 5 clearly provides that it applies only to proposed changes in voting procedures. "[D]iscriminatory practices . . . instituted prior to November 1964 . . . are not subject to the requirement of preclearance [under 5]." U.S. Commission on Civil Rights, The Voting Rights Act: Ten Years After, p. 347. The ordinance that adopted Plan II made no reference to the at-large councilmanic seats. Indeed, since those seats had been established in 1954 by the city charter, an ordinance could not have altered them; any change in the charter would have required approval by the city's voters. The at-large seats, having existed without change since 1954, were not subject to review in this proceeding under 5.

B

The principal argument made by the appellants in this Court is that the District Court erred in concluding that the makeup of the five geographic councilmanic districts under Plan II would have the effect of abridging voting rights on account of race or color. In evaluating this claim it is important to note at the outset that the question is not one of constitutional law, but of statutory construction. A determination of when a legislative reapportionment has "the effect of denying or abridging the right to vote on account of race or color," must depend, therefore, upon the intent of Congress in enacting the Voting Rights Act and specifically 5.

The legislative history reveals that the basic purpose of Congress in enacting the Voting Rights Act was "to rid the country of racial discrimination in voting." South Carolina v. Katzenbach, 383 U.S. at 315. Section 5 was intended to play an important role in achieving that goal:

"Section 5 was a response to a common practice in some jurisdictions of staying one step ahead of the federal courts by passing new discriminatory voting laws as soon as the old ones had been struck down. That practice had been possible because each new law remained in effect until the Justice Department or private plaintiffs were able to sustain the burden of proving that the new law, too, was discriminatory. . . . Congress therefore decided, as the Supreme Court held it could, 'to shift the advantage of time and inertia from the perpetrators of the evil to its victim,' by 'freezing election procedures in the covered areas unless the changes can be shown to be nondiscriminatory.'" H. R. Rep. No. 94-196, pp. 57–58. . . .

By prohibiting the enforcement of a voting-procedure change until it has been demonstrated to the United States Department of Justice or to a three-judge federal court that the change does not have a discriminatory effect, Congress desired to prevent States from "undo[ing] or defeat[ing] the rights recently won" by Negroes. H. R. Rep. No. 91-397, p. 8. Section 5 was intended "to insure that [the gains thus far achieved in minority political participation] shall not be destroyed through new [discriminatory] procedures and techniques." S. Rep. No. 94-295, p. 19.

When it adopted a 7-year extension of the Voting Rights Act in 1975, Congress explicitly stated that "the standard [under 5] can only be fully satisfied by determining on the basis of the facts found by the Attorney General [or the District Court] to be true whether the ability of minority groups to participate in the political process and to elect their choices to office is augmented, diminished, or not affected by the change affecting voting. . . ." H.R. Rep. No. 94-196, p. 60 (emphasis added). In other words the purpose of 5 has always been to insure that no voting-procedure changes would be made that would lead to a retrogression in the position of racial minorities with respect to their effective exercise of the electoral franchise.

It is thus apparent that a legislative reapportionment that enhances the position of racial minorities with respect to their effective exercise of the electoral franchise can hardly have the "effect" of diluting or abridging the right to vote on account of race within the meaning of 5. We conclude, therefore, that such an ameliorative new legislative apportionment cannot violate 5 unless the new apportionment itself so discriminates on the basis of race or color as to violate the Constitution.

The application of this standard to the facts of the present case is straightforward. Under the apportionment of 1961 none of the five councilmanic districts had a clear Negro majority of registered voters, and no Negro has been elected to the New Orleans City Council while that apportionment system has been in effect. Under Plan II, by contrast, Negroes will constitute a majority of the population in two of the five districts and a clear majority of the registered voters in one of them. Thus, there is every reason to predict, upon the District Court's hypothesis of bloc voting, that at least one and perhaps two Negroes may well be elected to the council under Plan II. It was therefore error for the District Court to conclude that Plan II "will . . . have the effect of denying or

abridging the right to vote on account of race or color" within the meaning of 5 of the Voting Rights Act.

Accordingly, the judgment of the District Court is vacated, and the case is remanded to that court for further proceedings consistent with this opinion.

It is so ordered.

MR. JUSTICE STEVENS took no part in the consideration or decision of this case. . . .

MR. JUSTICE WHITE, dissenting.

With MR. JUSTICE MARSHALL, I cannot agree that 5 of the Voting Rights Act of 1965 reaches only those changes in election procedures that are more burdensome to the complaining minority than pre-existing procedures. As I understand 5, the validity of any procedural change otherwise within the reach of the section must be determined under the statutory standard—whether the proposed legislation has the purpose or effect of abridging or denying the right to vote based on race or color.

This statutory standard is to be applied here in light of the District Court's findings, which are supported by the evidence and are not now questioned by the Court. The findings were that the nominating process in New Orleans' councilmanic elections is subject to majority vote and "anti-single-shot" rules and that there is a history of bloc racial voting in New Orleans, the predictable result being that no Negro candidate will win in any district in which his race is in the minority. In my view, where these facts exist, combined with a segregated residential pattern, 5 is not satisfied unless, to the extent practicable, the new electoral districts afford the Negro minority the opportunity to achieve legislative representation roughly proportional to the Negro population in the community. Here, with a seven-member city council, the black minority constituting approximately 45% of the population of New Orleans, would be entitled under 5, as I construe it, to the opportunity of electing at least three city councilmen—more than provided by the plan at issue here.

Bloc racial voting is an unfortunate phenomenon, but we are repeatedly faced with the findings of knowledgeable district courts that it is a fact of life. Where it exists, most often the result is that neither white nor black can be elected from a district in which his race is in the minority. As I see it, Congress has the power to minimize the effects of racial voting, particularly where it occurs in the context of other electoral rules operating to muffle the political potential of the minority. I am also satisfied that 5 was aimed at this end, among others, and should be so construed and applied. See City of Richmond v. United States, 422 U.S. 358, 370–372 (1975).

Minimizing the exclusionary effects of racial voting is possible here because whites and blacks are not scattered evenly throughout the city; to a great extent, each race is concentrated in identifiable areas of New Orleans. But like bloc voting by race, this too is a fact of life, well known to those responsible for drawing electoral district lines. These lawmakers are quite aware that the districts they create will have a white or a black majority; and with each new district comes the unavoidable choice as to the racial composition of the district. It is here that 5 intervenes to control these choices to the extent necessary to afford the minority the opportunity of achieving fair representation in the legislative body in question.

Applying 5 in this way would at times require the drawing of district lines based on race; but Congress has this power where deliberate discrimination at the polls and the relevant electoral laws and customs have effectively foreclosed Negroes from enjoying a modicum of fair representation in the city council or other legislative body.

Since Plan II at issue in this case falls short of satisfying 5 and since I agree with MR. JUSTICE MARSHALL that the city has failed to present sufficiently substantial justifications for its proposal, I respectfully dissent and would affirm the judgment of the District Court. . . .

Source: Findlaw, *Beer v. United States,* 425 U.S. 130 (1976), http://caselaw.lp.findlaw.com/scripts/getcase.pl?court=US&vol=425&invol=130.

34   Voting Rights Act Extension, June 29, 1982

President Ronald Reagan began his 1980 campaign for the presidency with a speech in the Mississippi county where civil rights workers James Chaney, Michael Schwerner, and Andrew Goodman were murdered in 1964—and he never mentioned their deaths. Many observers saw this omission as evidence of Reagan's indifference to civil and voting rights. Indeed, initially his administration opposed extension of the Voting Rights Act. But he cheerfully signed a strengthening of the act, engineered in large part by Republican senator Robert J. Dole of Kansas. Indeed, during Reagan's presidency the assistant attorney general for civil rights, William Bradford Reynolds, very conscientiously and effectively enforced the Voting Rights Act. Reagan's remarks precede the text of the 1982 Voting Rights Act extension.

Remarks on Signing the Voting Rights Act Amendments of 1982
Ronald Reagan, June 29th, 1982

Well, I am pleased today to sign the legislation extending the Voting Rights Act of 1965.

Citizens must have complete confidence in the sanctity of their right to vote, and that's what this legislation is all about. It provides confidence that constitutional guarantees are being upheld and that no vote counts more than another. To so many of our people—our Americans of Mexican descent, our black Americans—this measure is as important symbolically as it is practically. It says to every individual, "Your vote is equal; your vote is meaningful; your vote is your constitutional right."

I've pledged that as long as I'm in a position to uphold the Constitution, no barrier will come between our citizens and the voting booth. And this bill is a vital part of fulfilling that pledge.

This act ensures equal access to the political process for all our citizens. It securely protects the right to vote while strengthening the safeguards against representation by forced quota. The legislation also extends those special provisions applicable to certain States and localities, while at the same time providing an opportunity for the jurisdictions to bail out from the special provisions when appropriate. In addition, the bill extends for 10 years the protections for language minorities.

President Eisenhower said, "The future of the Republic is in the hands of the American voter." Well, with this law, we make sure the vote stays in the hands of every American.

Let me say how grateful I am to these gentlemen up here, the Members of the House and Senate from both sides of the aisle, and particularly those on the Senate Judiciary Committee, for getting this bipartisan legislation to my desk.

Yes, there are differences over how to attain the equality we seek for all our people. And sometimes amidst all the overblown rhetoric, the differences tend to seem bigger than they are. But actions speak louder than words. This legislation proves our unbending commitment to voting rights. It also proves that differences can be settled in a spirit of good will and good faith.

In this connection, let me also thank all the other organizations and individuals—many who are here today—who worked for this bill. As I've said before, the right to vote is the crown jewel of American liberties, and we will not see its luster diminished.

The legislation that I'm signing is the longest extension of the act since its enactment and demonstrates America's commitment to preserving this essential right. I'm proud of the Congress for passing this legislation. I'm proud to be able to sign it.

And without saying anything further, I'm going to do that right now.

* * *

Public Law 97-205
97th Congress

An Act

To amend the Voting Rights Act of 1965 to extend the effect of certain provisions, and for other purposes.

Be it enacted by the Senate and House of Representatives of the United States of America in Congress assembled, That this Act may be cited as the "Voting Rights Act Amendments of 1982".

Sec. 2. (a) Subsection (a) of section 4 of the Voting Rights Act of 1965 is amended by striking out "seventeen years" each place it appears and inserting in lieu thereof "nineteen years".

(b) Effective on and after August 5, 1984, subsection (a) of section 4 of the Voting Rights Act of 1965 is amended—

(1) by inserting "(1)" after "(a)";

2) by inserting "or in any political subdivision of such State (as such subdivision existed on the date such determinations were made with respect to such State), though such determinations were not made with respect to such subdivision as a separate unit," before "or in any political subdivision with respect to which" each place it appears;

(3) by striking out "in an action for a declaratory judgement" the first place it appears and all that follows through "color through the use of such tests or devices have occurred anywhere in the territory of such plaintiff.", and inserting in lieu thereof "issues a declaratory judgement under this section.";

(4) by striking out "in an action for a declaratory judgment" the second place it appears and all that follow through "section 4(f)(2) through the use of tests or devices have occurred anywhere in the territory of such plaintiff.", and inserting in lieu thereof the following:

"issues a declaratory judgment under this section. A declaratory judgment under this section shall issue only if such court determines that during the ten years preceding the filing of the action, and during the pendency of such action—

"(A) no such test or device has been used within such State or political subdivision for the purpose or with the effect of denying or abridging the right to vote on account of race or color or (in the case of a State or subdivision seeking a declaratory judgement under the second sentence of this subsection) in contravention of the guarantees of subsection (f)(2);

"(B) no final judgment of any court of the United States, other than the denial of declaratory judgment under this section, has determined that denial or abridgements of the right to vote on account of race or color have occurred anywhere in the territory of such State or political subdivision or (in the case of a State or subdivision seeking a declaratory judgment under the second sentence of this subsection) that denials or abridgments of the right to vote in contravention of the guarantees of subsection (f)(2) have occurred anywhere in the territory of such or subdivision and no consent decree, settlement, or agreement has been entered into resulting in any abandonment of a voting practice challenged on such grounds; and no declaratory judgment under this section shall be entered during the pendency of an action commenced before the filing of an action under this section and alleging such denial or abridgments of the right to vote;

"(C) no Federal examiners under this Act have been assigned to such State or political subdivision;

"(D) such State or political subdivision and all governmental units within its territory have complied with section 5 of this Act, including com-

pliance with the requirement that no change covered by section 5 has been enforced without preclearance under section 5, and have repealed all changes covered by section 5 to which the Attorney General has successfully objected or as to which the United States District Court for the District of Columbia has denied a declaratory judgment;

"(E) the Attorney General has not interposed any objection (that has not been overturned by a final judgment of a court) and no declaratory judgment has been denied under section 5, with respect to any submission by or on behalf of the plaintiff or any governmental unit within its territory under section 5, and no such submissions or declaratory judgment actions are pending; and

(F) such State or political subdivision and all governmental units within its territory—

"(i) have eliminated voting procedures and methods of election which inhibit or dilute equal access to the electoral process;

"(ii) have engaged in constructive efforts to eliminate intimidation and harassment of persons exercising rights protected under this Act; and

"(iii) have engaged in other constructive efforts, such as expanded opportunity for convenient registration and voting for every person of voting age and the appointment of minority persons as election officials throughout the jurisdiction and at all stages of the election and registration process.

"(2) To assist the court in determining whether to issue a declaratory judgment under this subsection, the plaintiff shall present evidence of minority participation, including evidence of the levels of minority group registration and voting, changes in such levels over time, and disparities between minority-groups and non-minority-group participation.

"(3) No declaratory judgment shall issue under this subsection with respect to such State or political subdivision is such plaintiff and governmental units within its territory have, during the period beginning ten years before the date the judgment is issued, engaged in violations of any provision of the Constitution or laws of the United States or any State or political subdivision with respect to discrimination in voting on account of race or color or (in the case of a State or subdivision seeking a declaratory judgment under the second sentence of this subsection) in contravention of the guarantees of subsection (f)(2) unless the plaintiff establishes that any such violations were trivial, were promptly corrected, and were not repeated.

"(4) The State or political subdivision bringing such action shall publicize the intended commencement and any proposed settlement of such action in the media serving such State or political subdivision and in appropriate United States post offices. Any aggrieved party may as of right intervene at any stage in such action.";

(5) in the second paragraph—

(A) by inserting "(5)" before "An action"; and

(B) by striking out "five" and all that follows through "section 4(f)(2).", and inserting in lieu thereof "ten years after judgment and shall reopen the action upon motion of the Attorney General or any aggrieved person alleging that conduct has occurred which, had that conduct has occurred which, had that conduct occurred during the ten-year periods referred to in this subsection, would have precluded the issuance of a declaratory judgment under this subsection. The court, upon such reopening, shall vacate the declaratory judgment issued under this section if, after the issuance of such declaratory judgment was issued, a final judgment against the State of subdivision with respect to which such declaratory judgment was issued, or against any governmental unit within that State or subdivision, determines that denials or abridgments of the right to vote on account of race or color have occurred anywhere in the territory of such State or political subdivision or (in the case of a State or subdivision which sought a declaratory judgment under the second sentence of this subsection) that denials or abridgments of the right to vote in contravention of the guarantees of subsection (f)(2)

have occurred anywhere in the territory of such State or subdivision, or if, after the issuance of such declaratory judgment, a consent decree, settlement, or agreement has been entered into resulting in any abandonment of a voting practice challenged on such grounds."; and

(6) by striking out "If the Attorney General" the first place it appears and all that follows through the end of such subsection and inserting in lieu thereof the following:

"(6) If, after two years from the date of the filing of a declaratory judgment under this subsection, no date has been set for a hearing in such action, and that delay has not been the result of an avoidable delay on the part of counsel for any party, the chief judge of the United States District Court for the District of Columbia may request the Judicial Council for the Circuit Court of the District of Columbia to provide the necessary judicial resources to expedite any action filed under this section. If such resources are unavailable within the circuit, the chief judge shall file a certificate of necessity in accordance with section 292(d) of title 28 of the United States Code.

"(7) The Congress shall reconsider the provisions of this section at the end of the fifteen-year period following the effective date of the amendments made by the Voting Rights Act Amendments of 1982.

"(8) The provisions of this section shall expire at the end of the twenty-five-year period following the effective date of the amendments made by the Voting Rights Act Amendments of 1982.

"(9) Nothing in this section shall prohibit the Attorney General from consenting to an entry of judgment if based upon a showing of objective and compelling evidence by the plaintiff, and upon investigation, he is satisfied that the State or political subdivision has complied with the requirements of section 4(a)(1). Any aggrieved party may as of right intervene at any stage in such action.".

(c) Section 4(f)(4) of the Voting Rights Act of 1965 is amended by inserting after "unwritten" in the proviso the following: "or in the case of

Alaskan Natives and American Indians, if the predominate language is historically unwritten".

(d) Section 203 (c) of such Act is amended by inserting after "Natives" in the proviso the following: "and American Indians".

Sec. 3. Section 2 of the Voting Rights Act of 1965 is amended to read as follows:

"Sec. 2. (a) No voting qualification or prerequisite to voting or standard, practice, or procedure shall be imposed or applied by any State or political subdivision in a manner which results in a denial or abridgment of the right of any citizen of the United States to vote on account of race or color, or in contravention of the guarantees set forth in section 4(f)(2), as provided in subsection (b).

(b) A violation of subsection (a) is established if, based on the totality of circumstances, it is shown that the political processes leading to nomination or election in the State or political subdivision are not equally open to participation by members of a class of citizens protected by subsection (a) in that its members have less opportunity than other members of the electorate to participate in the political process and to elect representatives of their choice. The extent to which members of a protected class have been elected to office in the State or political subdivision is one circumstance which may be considered: *Provided,* That nothing in this section establishes a right to have members of a protected class elected in numbers equal to their proportion in the population.".

Sec. 4. Section 203(b) of the Voting Rights Act of 1965 is amended by striking out "August 6, 1985" and inserting in lieu thereof "August 6, 1992", and the extension made by this section shall apply only to determinations made by the Director of the Census under clause (i) of section 203(b) for members of a single language minority who do not speak or understand English adequately enough to participate in the electoral process when such a determination can be made by the Director of the Census based on the 1980 and subsequent census data.

Sec. 5. Effective January 1, 1984, title II of the Voting Rights Act of 1965 is amended by adding at the end the following section:

"VOTING ASSISTANCE

"Sec. 208. Any voter who requires assistance to vote by reason of blindness, disability, or inability to read or write may be given assistance by a person of the voter's choice, other than the voter's employer or agent of the employer or office or agent of the voter's union.".

Sec. 6. Except as otherwise provided in this Act, the amendments made by this Act shall take effect on the date of the enactment of this Act.

Approved June 29, 1982.

Sources: The American Presidency Project, http://www. presidency.ucsb.edu/ws/index.php?pid=42688&st=&st1= (accessed November 3, 2005); "Voting Rights Act Amendments of 1982," Public Law 97-205, June 29, 1982, http:www.southerncouncil.org/pdf/vra1965.pdf (accessed October 3, 2005).

35   U.S. Department of Justice Letters Objecting to Changes in North Carolina Election Laws, 1986–1994

North Carolina is often considered a racially progressive southern state. The following letters sent by the Civil Rights Division of the U.S. Department of Justice to three different North Carolina jurisdictions object to proposed voting changes and suggest that black voters' influence over local government in that state was still being contested, albeit subtly, into the 1990s.

[Letterhead] U.S. Department of Justice
Civil Rights Division

Office of the Assistant Attorney General
Washington, D.C. 20530

[stamped "MAY 5 1986"]

William C. Brewer, Jr.
Speight, Watson and Brewer
P. O. Drawer 99
Greenville, North Carolina 27835-0099

Dear Mr. Brewer:

This refers to . . . various board of education matters in Pitt County, North Carolina. . . .

Under Section 5 of the Voting Rights Act, the submitting authority has the burden of showing that a submitted change has no discriminatory purpose or effect. . . . Our analysis of the submitted voting changes has been complicated by the fact that, prior to this submission, the Pitt County Board of Education had failed to submit for Section 5 review any of the changes affecting the method of electing board members effectuated since the enactment of the Voting Rights Act of 1965. In this regard, we note that, as of November 1, 1964, the operative date of the Voting Rights Act, county board members were appointed by the legislature following a primary election held for the purpose of determining candidates to be submitted to the legislature for its consideration. Candidate residency districts were added to the primary election structure in 1965

at the same time that the board was increased in size.

The origins of the at-large structure presently used to elect the county board remain confused. We are aware that certain state-wide legislation . . . mandated at-large elections for the Pitt County Board of Education but we have been advised that such legislation was not implemented fully in Pitt County. It is clear, however, that at-large elections were required by Chapter 360, H.B. 769 (1971), and that that legislation constitutes a part of your current submission.

Our analysis reveals that patterns of racial bloc voting prevailing in Pitt County make it virtually impossible for black voters in the county to participate meaningfully in the school board elections under the unprecleared at-large structure that has been used since 1971. The county school board has failed to provide a satisfactory nonracial explanation for establishing the election system currently being implemented. . . . I must, on behalf of the Attorney General, interpose a Section 5 objection to the at-large voting procedures being used for the election of members of the existing county school board.

Our review of the proposed merger legislation (Chapter 2, H.B. No. 29 (1985), and Chapter 495, N.B. No. 1397 (1985)) proceeds from our analysis of the present method of electing the county board, which method is incorporated to a significant extent in the merger legislation. In this connection, we note that as opposed to the existing county board, the existing city school board is elected pursuant to voting procedures that have satisfied the preclearance requirements of Section 5 and have afforded black citizens an opportunity for effective political participation. The proposed merger plan provides that eight positions on the board for the merged school districts will be filled from the current eight county residency districts and that the Greenville Township area will constitute a four-member residency district; all positions will be elected on an at-large basis.

The submission reveals a recognition by the county that the merger legislation will not afford black citizens an equal opportunity for effective political participation. It was recognized that black citizens had been unable to elect candidates of their choice to the county board, and that the four-member city residency district would reduce the opportunity for effective single-shot voting, a device that has been utilized by blacks in the city school board district to their benefit in past elections. In an apparent effort to cure the disparate racial impact of the election method in the merger legislation, the supplemental provisions of Chapter 495 were enacted allowing for the appointment of three identified black citizens to serve on the merged district board until 1992 at which time a new, and at this time undefined, election plan is promised to be implemented.

The totality of facts here indicate that the merger legislation will result in a retrogression from the present position of city voters to elect candidates of their choice to the board. The submission reveals also that the method of election chosen was recognized by the county to have a discriminatory impact on black voters. The Voting Rights Act does not envision that the discriminatory impact of election procedures will be overcome by racial based appointments. . . . Accordingly, on behalf of the Attorney General, I must object to the voting changes to be occasioned by the merger legislation. . . .

[Signature:]
William Bradford Reynolds
Asst. AG for Civil Rights

* * *

[Letterhead] U.S. Department of Justice
Civil Rights Division

Voting Section
P.O. Box 66128
Washington, D.C. 20035-6128

[Stamped "JUN 28 1990"]

Aubrey S. Tomlinson, Jr., Esq.
Davis, Sturges & Tomlinson
P.O. Drawer 708
Louisburg, North Carolina 27549

Dear Mr. Tomlinson:

This refers to Chapter 306, H.B. No. 555 (1967), which provides for a change from a plurality to a majority-vote requirement in primary elections for the board of commissioners in Franklin County, North Carolina, submitted to the Attorney General pursuant to Section 5 of the Voting Rights Act of 1965, as amended, 42 U.S.C. 1973c. We received your initial submission on March 21 and 22, and May 3, 1990.

We have carefully considered the information you have provided as well as information from the Census and other interested parties. We note at the outset that while the population of Franklin County is 41% black, no black has ever been elected to the Franklin County Commission, although in May of this year for the first time ever a black has received his party's nomination for a seat on the commission. The five commission members are elected at large by residency districts in partisan elections. Prior to the adoption of Chapter 306, a plurality of the vote was sufficient to obtain nomination for a position on the commission. Since 1968, however, because Chapter 306 was enforced despite the absence of Section 5 preclearance, nomination has required a majority vote in the primary, and this was interpreted as authorizing runoff elections in cases where no candidate received a majority. In 1978 the enforcement of this change denied the Democratic Party nomination to a black candidate who received a plurality of the vote in the primary but who was subsequently defeated in a runoff.

In jurisdictions where elections are characterized by racial bloc voting a majority-vote requirement has been recognized as having the potential to dilute minority voting strength by producing head-to-head contests in which the victor is determined by the white voting majority. . . . Our review of Franklin County election returns indicates that while blacks have achieved some success in contests for county positions, racial bloc voting remains present to a significant degree. Thus the change from a plurality-win system to a majority-vote requirement appears to effect a retrogression in the position of minority voters in Franklin County, especially since, in school board elections where the plurality-win system continues in effect, black voters have enjoyed a fair degree of success.

Under Section 5 of the Voting Rights Act, the submitting authority has the burden of showing that a submitted change has no discriminatory purpose or effect. . . . In light of the considerations discussed above, I cannot conclude, as I must under the Voting Rights Act, that the burden has been sustained in this instance. Therefore, on behalf of the Attorney General, I must object to the adoption of a majority-vote requirement in primary elections for the Franklin County Commission. . . .

Sincerely,

John R. Dunne
Assistant Attorney General
Civil Rights Division

* * *

[Letterhead] U.S. Department of Justice
Civil Rights Division

Office of the Assistant Attorney General
Washington, D.C. 20530

September 13, 1994

William Sam Byassee, Esq.
Smith, Helms, Mulliss & Moore
P. O. Box 21927
Greensboro, North Carolina 27420

Dear Mr. Byassee:

This refers to the increase in number of commissioners from five to six, the change in method of election from at large to four single-member districts and two at large (with no numbered positions), and the districting plan for the Town of Mt. Olive in Wayne County, North Carolina, submitted to the Attorney General pursuant to Section 5 of the Voting Rights Act of 1965, as amended, 42 U.S.C. 1973c. . . .

. . . According to the 1990 Census, the population of Mt. Olive (including several post-1990 annexations) is approximately 4,700, of whom about 53 percent are black. About 49 percent of the town's voting age population is black and currently blacks constitute 45 percent of the town's registered voters. The town is governed by a mayor and a five-member board of commissioners elected at large, by plurality vote, to two-year concurrent terms. . . .

Despite the town's substantial minority population and numerous black candidates, there has never been more than one black elected to the board of commissioners at any one time. . . . This election history led representatives of the black community to file suit in May 1993 under Section 2 of the Voting Rights Act, 42 U.S.C. 1973, challenging the at-large method of election. . . .

The filing of the Section 2 suit impelled the town to adopt a new method of election, however, the town chose to adopt the system now submitted for Section 5 review over the strenuous opposition of the Section 2 plaintiffs and the black community in general. Particular concern was raised regarding the opportunity of black voters to elect their preferred candidate to either of the at-large seats (as well as concerning the unnecessary "packing" of black population in a 97 percent black district). Our analysis suggests that given the presence of polarized voting and the limited success that black voters have enjoyed when five at-large seats are elected, there is considerable doubt as to whether black voters would have a significant opportunity to elect any at-large member under the proposed election method.

The board of commissioners proposed the instant election plan in September 1993, after the Section 2 plaintiffs agreed in July 1993 to the board's proposal to settle the lawsuit by adopting a plan of four single-member districts and one at-large seat. The change in the board's position followed an August public hearing in which black residents unanimously supported the adoption of a district method of election while several white leaders opposed altering the at-large system. Subsequently, in November 1993, when one of the black plaintiffs was elected to the board (as its only black member), the board petitioned the Section 2 court to prohibit her from participating in board discussions or voting on the method of election issues raised by the Section 2 litigation. . . .

Under Section 5 of the Voting Rights Act, the town has the burden of showing that the submitted changes have neither a discriminatory purpose nor a discriminatory effect. . . . In light of the considerations discussed above, I cannot conclude, as I must under the Voting Rights Act, that the town's burden has been sustained in this instance with regard to the proposed method of election. . . .

We note that under Section 5 the town of Mt. Olive has the right to seek a declaratory judgment from the United States District Court for the District of Columbia that the objected-to changes have neither the purpose nor will have the effect of denying or abridging the right to vote on account of race or color. In addition, the town may request that the Attorney General reconsider the objection. However, until the objection is withdrawn or a judgment from the District of Columbia court is obtained, the objected-to changes continue to be legally unenforceable. . . .

Sincerely,

Deval L. Patrick
Assistant Attorney General
Civil Rights Division

Source: U.S. Department of Justice.

---

36 Voting Rights Language Assistance Act and Its Enforcement, 1992–2004

The three documents that follow—a 1992 extension of the Voting Rights Act to include minority language assistance, a description by a legal expert of the recent U.S. Census Bureau determination of the jurisdictions covered under the extension, and an Arizona preclearance submission under Section 5 of the act—illustrate that the Voting Rights Act also regulates how nonblack minorities experience the act of voting. They reveal that Congress has asked state and local elections officials to help voters who do not speak English easily. The last document also shows, however, that a majority of Arizona voters worry that the increasingly bilingual population in Arizona is a threat to the integrity of the electoral process. In short, helping non–English-speaking voters to vote is a controversial matter.

Since 1975 Congress has required bilingual ballots in areas of the country where 5 percent of the voters both constitute a language minority and have rates of English illiteracy higher than the national rate. This feature of the Voting Rights Act differs from but also complements the extension of pre-clearance provisions to southwestern states and to California in order to promote the voting rights of Hispanic Americans. The schedule for the review of these language assistance provisions—the Section 203 measures—and their amendments changed in 1982, requiring Congress to revisit them in 1992.

Because the 1992 Language Assistance Act extended Section 203 for fifteen years, Section 203 ex-pires when the other temporary enforcement provisions of the Voting Rights Act expire in 2007. Sec-tion 203 has inspired a few jurisdictions to provide bilingual ballots in Spanish and Korean on their own, without a legal requirement.

The actual implementation of the language assistance provisions of the Voting Rights Act is the re-sponsibility of the director of the U.S. Census Bureau, who must use the mathematical and demo-graphic criteria specified in the act. The director publishes the list of covered jurisdictions after the census, which last happened in 2002. But the list requires further clarification. The public service "news alert" published by a Phoenix law firm and reproduced here illustrates how the director's desig-nations require explanation.

Whether Section 203 actually promotes voting among its target constituencies is not clear. Politi-cal scientist S. Karthick Ramakrishnan reports in his book Democracy in Immigrant America: Changing Demographics and Political Participation *(Stanford University Press, 2005) that, on their own, they do not. Political scientist Michael Jones-Correa reports in unpublished work that these provisions do appear to have an impact, net of other relevant factors, that would promote registra-tion and voting by language minorities.*

Consequently, whether Arizona's Proposition 200 (precleared by the Justice Department under Sec-tion 5) actually threatens the goals of Section 203 (or of Section 5) is not clear. Ramakrishnan shows in his book that threats to the political status of first-generation immigrants spurs them to become more involved politically. Proposition 200 may have just that effect, because many first-generation im-migrants in Arizona view it as stigmatizing them.

An Act
To amend the Voting Rights Act of 1965 with re-spect to bilingual election requirements.

Be it enacted by the Senate and House of Rep-resentatives of the United States of America in Congress assembled,

SECTION 1. SHORT TITLE.

This Act may be cited as the 'Voting Rights Language Assistance Act of 1992'.

SEC. 2. EXTENSION OF LANGUAGE MINORITY PROVISIONS.

Subsection (b) of section 203 of the Voting Rights Act of 1965 (42 U.S.C. 1973aa-1a(b)) is amended to read as follows:

'(b) BILINGUAL VOTING MATERIALS RE-
QUIREMENT—

'(1) GENERALLY- Before August 6, 2007, no covered State or political subdivi-sion shall provide voting materials only in the English language.

'(2) COVERED STATES AND POLITI-CAL SUBDIVISIONS—

'(A) GENERALLY- A State or political subdivision is a covered State or political subdivision for the pur-poses of this subsection if the Di-rector of the Census determines, based on census data, that—

'(i)(I) more than 5 percent of the citizens of voting age of such State or political subdivision are members of a single lan-guage minority and are lim-ited-English proficient;

'(II) more than 10,000 of the citizens of voting age of such political subdivision are members of a single language minority and are limited-English proficient; or

'(III) in the case of a political subdivision that contains all or any part of an Indian reservation, more than 5 percent of the American Indian or Alaska Native citizens of voting age within the Indian reservation are members of a single language minority and are limited-English proficient; and

"(ii) the illiteracy rate of the citizens in the language minority as a group is higher than the national illiteracy rate.

'(B) EXCEPTION- The prohibitions of this subsection do not apply in any political subdivision that has less than 5 percent voting age limited-English proficient citizens of each language minority which comprises over 5 percent of the statewide limited-English proficient population of voting age citizens, unless the political subdivision is a covered political subdivision independently from its State.

(3) DEFINITIONS- As used in this section—

'(A) the term 'voting materials' means registration or voting notices, forms, instructions, assistance, or other materials or information relating to the electoral process, including ballots;

'(B) the term 'limited-English proficient' means unable to speak or understand English adequately enough to participate in the electoral process;

'(C) the term 'Indian reservation' means any area that is an American Indian or Alaska Native area, as defined by the Census Bureau for the purposes of the 1990 decennial census;

'(D) the term 'citizens' means citizens of the United States; and

'(E) the term 'illiteracy' means the failure to complete the 5th primary grade.

(4) SPECIAL RULE- The determinations of the Director of the Census under this subsection shall be effective upon publication in the Federal Register and shall not be subject to review in any court.'.

Speaker of the House of Representatives.
Vice President of the United States and
President of the Senate.

Source: Voting Rights Language Assistance Act of 1992, 102d Cong., 2d sess., H.R. 4312, January 3, 1992, http://thomas.loc.gov/cgi-bin/query/D?c102:1:./temp/~c102ylxF0t::.

* * *

Director of the Census Bureau Makes Determinations of Jurisdictions Subject to the Minority Language Assistance Provisions of the Voting Rights Act

. . .

How the Minority Language Assistance Determinations Were Made

The language minority provisions of the Voting Rights Act apply to four language groups: "persons who are American Indian, Asian American, Alaskan Natives, or of Spanish heritage." 42 U.S.C. § 19731(c)(3). Congress intended that the census definition for each of these language groups be applied to determine which languages have to be offered in covered jurisdictions. The four language groups were selected for coverage based upon the following evidence: members of the groups had suffered from voting or other forms of discrimination that limited their access to the political process; members of each language group faced severe language barriers and illiteracy; and each of the four groups had depressed voter registration and turnout. Other language groups were not included because there was no evidence that they experienced similar difficulties in voting.

Under Section 203(c) of the Voting Rights Act, a State or political subdivision is covered by the minority language assistance provisions if it has a sufficient number of "limited-English proficient" single-language minority citizens who experience a higher illiteracy rate than the national average. "Limited English proficient" is defined as the inability "to speak or understand English adequately enough to participate in the electoral process." 42 U.S.C. § 1973aa-1a(b)(3)(B). The requisite number of minority language citizens reside in a State or political subdivision if the Director of the Census determines any one of the following: more than five percent of the voting-age citizens (persons 18 years and older) are members of a single language minority and are limited-English proficient; more than 10,000 voting-age citizens are members of a single language minority and are limited-English proficient; or in a political subdivision containing any part of an Indian reservation, more than five percent of the American Indian or Alaska Native voting-age citizens are members of a single language minority and are limited-English proficient. See 42 U.S.C. § 1973aa-1a(b)(2)(A).

Jurisdictions also are covered by the minority language assistance provisions if they meet the three requirements of section 4(f)(4) of the Voting Rights Act: over five percent of the voting-age citizens on November 1, 1972 were members of a single language minority group; the United States Attorney General finds that election materials were provided in English only on November 1, 1972; and the Director of the Census determines that fewer than fifty percent of voting-age

citizens were registered to vote on November 1, 1972 or that fewer than fifty percent voted in the November 1972 Presidential election. See 42 U.S.C. § 1973b(b). States or political subdivisions covered under Section 4(f)(4) have to comply with Section 203 of the Voting Rights Act and also are subject to all of the special provisions of the Voting Rights Act, including obtaining administrative approval from the Attorney General or the United States District Court for the District of Columbia before implementing any voting changes ("administrative preclearance" under Section 5 of the Voting Rights Act), the use of federal examiners to enroll and list eligible voters, and election coverage by federal observers.

The Section 203 determinations made by the Director of the Census on July 26, 2002 replace the previous Section 203 determinations. No further determinations were made under Section 4(f)(4) of the Voting Rights Act, and existing 4(f)(4) determinations remain in effect and are unaffected by the new Section 203 determinations.

The Number of Covered Jurisdictions
Currently, Section 4(f)(4) covers language minority groups in three States in their entirety (Alaska, Arizona and Texas), and a total of nineteen counties or townships in six other States. See 28 C.F.R. pt. 55.

As a result of the new determinations made by the Director of the Census, the number of States covered in whole or in part by Section 203 has increased from twenty-seven States to thirty. Three States now are covered in their entirety by Section 203 (California, New Mexico, and Texas for Hispanic groups), in addition to the two other States covered Statewide under Section 203 because of previous Section 4(f)(4) determinations (Alaska for Alaskan Native groups and Arizona for Hispanic groups). Two States that previously were covered in part by Section 203, Iowa and Wisconsin, no longer are covered. Section 203 coverage has been extended to political subdivisions of five States not previously covered: Kansas, Maryland, Montana, Nebraska, and Washington.

Demographic changes have led to 27 political subdivisions losing their coverage under Section 203 and the addition of 73 new political subdivisions. A total of 295 political subdivisions nationwide now are covered. Forty-eight of the covered political subdivisions have to provide assistance in more than one language: 31 in two languages; 14 in three languages; two in four languages; and one, Los Angeles County, California, in six languages (Spanish, Chinese, Filipino, Japanese, Korean, and Vietnamese).

Federal regulations provide that "[w]here a political subdivision (e.g., a county) is determined to be subject to" the minority language assistance provisions of the Voting Rights Act, "all political units that hold elections within that political subdivision (e.g., cities, school districts) are subject to the same requirements as the political subdivision." 28 C.F.R. § 55.9.

The Number of Covered Languages

The number of States and political subdivisions that have to provide assistance in various languages breaks down as follows:

- Spanish language assistance must be provided Statewide in Arizona, California, New Mexico, Texas, and a total of 224 political subdivisions in 20 States. . . ;
- Alaskan Native language assistance must be provided Statewide in Alaska and 13 political subdivisions of Alaska;
- American Indian language assistance must be provided in a total of 75 political subdivisions in 18 States;
- Chinese language assistance must be provided in a total of 6 counties in California, Honolulu County, Hawaii, Cook County, Illinois, 3 counties in New York, and Kings County, Washington;
- Filipino language assistance must be provided in the Kodiak Island Borough of Alaska, three counties in California, and two counties in Hawaii;

- Vietnamese language assistance must be provided in three counties in California and in Harris County, Texas;
- Korean language assistance must be provided in two counties in California and in Queens County, New York; and
- Japanese must be provided in Los Angeles County, California and Honolulu County, Hawaii.

South Dakota had the largest number of political subdivisions added under American Indian coverage, more than doubling from 8 under the previous determinations up to 18 under the new determinations. Two States that previously did not have to provide language assistance to any American Indian groups, Montana and Nebraska, now are covered under Section 203 as a result of the new determinations. The breadth of coverage for jurisdictions required to provide assistance in Alaskan Native and American Indian languages is especially striking under the new determinations, with assistance required for 21 different language groups identified by the Census Bureau.

[Tables in original document have been omitted.]

Language assistance actually has to be provided in more than the 21 Alaskan Native and American Indian languages because many of the language groups . . . include several different languages or dialects. For example, the Pueblo American Indian group includes the Havasupai, Hopi, Keres, Tiwa, and Towa Indian languages. The Sioux American Indian group includes the Dakota, Lakota, and Nakota languages. Many of the descriptions for language minority groups changed as a result of new Census Bureau definitions.

Language Requirements for Covered States and Political Subdivisions

Congress enacted Section 203 to remove obstacles posed by illiteracy and lack of adequate bilingual language assistance for members of language minority groups. The minority language assistance provisions initially were adopted in 1975 for a period of ten years, were extended for an additional ten years in 1982, and another fifteen years in 1992. The provisions expire on August 6, 2007, unless Congress extends them further.

Once a jurisdiction is covered by Section 203, all "voting materials" it provides in English generally must be provided in the language of all groups or sub-groups that triggered coverage. Voting materials include the following:

• Voter registration materials
• Voting notices (including information about opportunities to register, registration deadlines, time/places/locations of polling places, and absentee voting)
• All election forms
• Polling place activities and materials
• Instructions
• Publicity
• Ballots
• Other materials or information relating to the electoral process
• Assistance

See 42 U.S.C. § 1973aa-1a(c); 28 C.F.R. §§ 55.15, 55.18. Written materials generally do not have to be provided to members of Alaskan Native and American Indian groups whose languages historically are unwritten. Instead, oral instructions, assistance, or other information in the covered language must be available for members of those groups at every stage of the electoral process. See 42 U.S.C. § 1973aa-1a(c).

The minority language assistance provisions apply to all stages of the electoral process for "any type of election, whether it is a primary, general or special election." It includes not only elections of officers, but elections on such matters as bond issues, constitutional amendments and referendums. Federal, State, and local elections are covered, as well as special district elections,

such as school districts and water districts. 28 C.F.R. § 55.10.

The costs of compliance can be greatly minimized by the selective use of "targeting." Targeting allows a jurisdiction to comply with Section 203 by providing bilingual materials and assistance only to the language minority citizens and not to every voter in the jurisdiction. The availability of oral language assistance requires compliance with an "effectiveness" standard, in which the number of persons available to provide assistance may be determined by the actual demands for assistance. See 28 C.F.R. § 55.20(c). Ultimately, it is the covered jurisdiction's responsibility for determining what is necessary for compliance with the minority language assistance provisions. See 28 C.F.R. § 55.2(c).

The United States Department of Justice Continues to Aggressively Enforce the Minority Language Assistance Provisions

The Bush Administration has made enforcement of the minority language assistance provisions of the Voting Rights Act one of their highest civil rights priorities. . . .

The Justice Department has been very successful in securing federal consent decrees from jurisdictions that fail to comply with the minority language provisions of the Voting Rights Act. The costs of noncompliance can be tremendous, both in terms of litigation expenses, bad publicity, and the prospect of federal oversight including, but not limited to, consent orders and the use of federal observers on election day. For example, in September 2000, Passaic County, New Jersey became the first jurisdiction in the country to have its election system taken over by an Elections Monitor, who was appointed by a three-judge federal court. As a result of Passaic County's violations of Section 203, the County ultimately incurred hundreds of thousands of dollars in additional legal fees and expenses, as well as immeasurable losses in terms of bad press for obstructing and impairing the fundamental right to vote.

Source: Bryan Cave LLP Public Elections Compliance News Alert, "Director of the Census Bureau Makes Determinations of Jurisdictions Subject to the Minority Language Assistance Provisions of the Voting Rights Act," September 2002, http://www.bryancave.com/FILES/tbl_s7 Publications/Details33/606/PXLaborAlert-September 2002.pdf (accessed September 30, 2005).

* * *

Office of the Attorney General

State of Arizona

TERRY GODDARD
ATTORNEY GENERAL

Jessica G. Funkhouser

[end of letterhead]

December 9, 2004

VOTING RIGHTS ACT SUBMISSION

VIA FEDERAL EXPRESS/OVERNIGHT DELIVERY TO:

Mr. Joseph Rich
Chief, Voting Section
Civil Rights Division
Room 7254—NWB
U.S. Department of Justice
1800 G Street, N.W.
Washington, D.C. 20006

Re: Submission under Section 5 of the Voting Rights Act
Proposition 200, Initiative Measure, Sections 3, 4, and 5.

Dear Mr. Rich:

Expedited consideration of this submission is requested under 28 C.F.R. § 51.34. At the general election on November 2, 2004, a majority of Arizona voters approved Proposition 200. The submitted law, Proposition 200, Sections 3, 4, and 5, amends Title 16 of the Arizona statutes to require applicants registering to vote to provide evidence of United States citizenship with the application and voters to present identification at the polling place to obtain a ballot. Sections 1, 2, 6 and 7 do not contain procedures affecting voting, and therefore are not submitted for preclearance.

Expedited consideration is required because local jurisdictions will be holding elections on March 8, 2005 and will need time to preclear their local procedures affecting the conduct of their elections before early voting begins on February 3, 2005.

This submission is made under Section 5 of the Voting Rights Act of 1965, as amended. For your convenience, the following information is set forth as prescribed by 28 C.F.R. § 51.27:

A. <u>COPY OF ENACTMENT:</u>

A copy of Proposition 200 is attached. . . .

B. <u>COPY OF EXISTING STATUTE:</u>

A copy of the existing Title 16 statutes amended by Proposition 200 is attached. . . .

C. <u>EXPLANATION OF CHANGES:</u>

The essential changes were summarized by the Arizona Legislative Council pursuant to A.R.S. § 19-124 and published in the publicity pamphlet printed by the Arizona Secretary of State pursuant to A.R.S. § 19-123. The entire portion of the publicity pamphlet pertaining to Proposition 200 is attached. . . .

The impartial analysis by the Arizona Legislative Council relating to changes to Title 16 in Proposition 200 is as follows:

ANALYSIS BY LEGISLATIVE COUNCIL

Proposition 200 would require that evidence of United States citizenship be presented by every person to register to vote, that proof of identification be presented by every voter at the polling place prior to voting, that state and local government verify the identity of all applicants for certain public benefits and that government employees report United States immigration law violations by applicants for public benefits.

Proposition 200 provides that for purposes of registering to vote, satisfactory evidence of United States citizenship includes:

- an Arizona driver or nonoperating identification license issued after October 1, 1996.
- a driver or nonoperating identification license issued by another state if the license indicates that the person has provided proof of United States citizenship.
- a copy of the applicant's birth certificate.
- a United States passport, or a copy of the pertinent pages of the passport.
- United States naturalization documents or a verified certificate of naturalization number.
- a Bureau of Indian Affairs card number, tribal treaty card number or tribal enrollment number.
- other documents or methods of proof that may be established by the federal government for the purpose of verifying employment eligibility.

The county recorder shall indicate this information in the person's permanent voter file for at least two years. A voter registration card from another county or state does not constitute satisfactory evidence of United States citizenship. A person who is registered to vote on the date that Proposition 200 becomes effective is not required to submit evidence of citizenship unless the person moves to a different county. Once a person has submitted evidence of citizenship, the person is not required to resubmit the evidence when making changes to voter registration information in the county where

the evidence has been submitted.

Proposition 200 requires that prior to receiving a ballot at a polling place, a voter must present either one form of identification that contains the name, address and photograph of the person or two different forms of identification that contain the name and address of the person. . . .

G. PARTY RESPONSIBLE FOR CHANGE:

These changes are the result of a ballot proposition approved by the majority of Arizona voters in the 2004 General Election.

H. AUTHORITY FOR MAKING CHANGE:

The people of Arizona are vested with the power to adopt initiative measures amending the Arizona Statutes independently of the legislature pursuant to Ariz. Const. art. IV, pt. 1, § 1(1), (2). . . .

K. ENFORCEMENT OF CHANGE:

As far as the State is aware, the changes contained in Sections 3, 4, and 5 of Proposition 200 have not yet been enforced or administered.

L. SCOPE OF CHANGE:

The changes contained in Proposition 200 affect the entire jurisdiction.

M. REASONS FOR THE CHANGE:

The reasons for the change are described in Proposition 200 and the arguments in support of the measure included in the publicity pamphlet distributed to voters. . . .

N. ANTICIPATED EFFECT ON MEMBERS OF RACIAL OR LANGUAGE MINORITY GROUPS:

According to the Chair of the Protect Arizona Now Committee, which circulated the initiative petitions and supported the passage of Proposition 200, the changes contained in Proposition 200 were made without discriminatory intent and will have no discriminatory effect on members of racial or language minority groups. . . .

To assist the Civil Rights Division in assessing whether Proposition 200 was made with discriminatory intent or whether the measure has a discriminatory effect on members of racial or language minority groups, and because this was a controversial measure, the submission includes the following supplemental information suggested by 28 C.F.R. § 51.28(f):

1. The breakdown of votes cast in each county in favor of or against Proposition 200. . . .
2. Information from exit polls regarding the vote on Proposition 200. . . .
3. The list of Town Hall meetings held by the Arizona Secretary of State to discuss the pros and cons of all the ballot measures prior to the election. . . .
4. Articles, press releases and other public information published about the proposition before and after the election. . . .

O. PAST OR PENDING LITIGATION:

1. Two unsuccessful challenges attempting to remove Proposition 200 from the ballot were brought before the election. . . .
2. A suit seeking a declaration relating to the definition of "state and local public benefits" contained in Section 6 of the Proposition, which is not submitted for preclearance, was filed. . . .

3. A suit challenging both the public benefits and voting-related provisions of Proposition 200 was filed in the Federal District Court for the District of Arizona. . . . The Suit alleges that voting-related provisions of Proposition 200 are inconsistent with the NVRA, violate the Twenty-Fourth Amendment, deny Equal Protection, and violate Section 2 of the Voting Rights Act. . . . The Court entered a temporary restraining order on November 30, 2004, temporarily enjoining the state from implementing Proposition 200. . . .
4. The Arizona Secretary of State has also requested an Attorney General Opinion relating to acceptable forms of identification for voting. . . .

If you have any questions regarding this submission or if you require any additional information, please contact me as soon as possible.

[Tab for closing]
Very truly yours,

Terry Goddard
Arizona Attorney General
Mary O'Grady
Solicitor General

Jessica Funkhouser
Special Counsel

Source: Office of the Attorney General, State of Arizona.

37   "Seizing a Voice in Democracy: The Mississippi Redistricting Campaign,"
March 2001

This excerpt from a private, foundation-sponsored study shows that in key respects the Voting Rights Act did not really begin to change Mississippi politics until the 1990s. Mississippi is, of course, a state with an exceptional history of race relations. But the fact that Mississippi politics took nearly thirty years to respond fairly fully to the Voting Rights Act does raise questions about what would happen— both in Mississippi and elsewhere—if the enforcement process ended in 2007.

MISSISSIPPI'S VOTING-RIGHTS PROGRESS
AND POTENTIAL

Despite enactment of the Voting Rights Act in 1965, Mississippi fought African-American political participation every step of the way, with hostile courts, official defiance, and widespread violence and intimidation. . . . There was virtually no black representation in the Mississippi Legislature (or in other offices) until breakthrough victories in the 1979 elections—5 years after the Voting Rights Act. That year the U.S. Supreme Court finally forced a hostile local three-judge district court to adopt a legislative redistricting plan with black-majority districts. There was no black congressional representation in Mississippi until 1986. Again, the creation of the first black-majority district came about only after the Supreme Court invalidated the Legislature's 1980 redistricting plan. . . .

REDISTRICTING IN THE 1990s

. . . [I]n 1990, a coalition of attorneys who had been active in redistricting work in the past formed the Mississippi Redistricting Coalition (MRC) as a vehicle "to change the way redistricting work was done" in Mississippi. . . . [T]he MRC involved communities in the redistricting process, mobilizing hundreds of concerned citizens to attend meetings of the Legislature's Joint Committee on Legislative Reapportionment beginning in the fall of 1990. The momentum continued in 1991 with a series of 12 workshops, covering 25 counties. . . .

AFRICAN-AMERICANS ENGAGED IN THE
REDISTRICTING PROCESS

In workshops throughout the state, community residents learned about the politics and history of redistricting, as well as the tactics that have been used to prevent African-Americans from obtaining real representation. They also gained practical skills like data analysis and how to draw district lines. Considerable attention was paid to understanding legal standards and requirements of the Voting Rights Act. Their lawyers helped prepare the training materials and participated in the workshops. Traditionally, the redistricting process had been considered the domain of the county supervisors, state legislators and the lawyers who did battle with them. Now, African-American communities at the grassroots level were getting involved, learning the laws and regulations and beginning to participate in the redistricting process.

REDISTRICTING THE STATE LEGISLATURE

. . . Because of Mississippi's history of discrimination against African-American political participation, the state was required to obtain approval (preclearance) of its plan by the U.S. Department of Justice (DOJ). . . . DOJ denied preclearance, finding that the 1991 Plan had been adopted with a discriminatory purpose.

. . . [E]fforts to convince the Legislature to adopt a plan that complied with the Voting Rights Act continued into 1992. When a heated battle over the selection of the speaker of the House arose in 1992, the Legislative Black Caucus held the balance of power between two Democratic contenders. . . . [T]he vote for speaker eventually led in 1992 to passage of a districting plan that created even *more* majority-black districts than a court would have ordered. The court subsequently upheld the plan, and it was used for the first time in court-ordered 1992 special elections. . . .

REDISTRICTING ON THE LOCAL LEVEL

With political power in Mississippi highly concentrated at the local level, it was critical to create districts in which accountable African-Americans could be elected to county boards, city councils and school boards. . . .

The experience in Tallahatchie County typifies the local redistricting process that occurred in communities across the Delta in the early 1990s. . . .

. . . [T]he Tallahatchie County Redistricting Committee, along with demographers from the Southern Regional Council in Atlanta . . . developed several plans and submitted them to the County Board of Supervisors. In the face of considerable community pressure, the Board quickly abandoned its recalcitrant position and began drawing its own plan for redistricting. After a six-month campaign in which African-Americans packed the Board meetings and kept the community pressure on, the Board of Supervisors agreed to negotiate with the Tallahatchie Redistricting Committee over new district lines. This was unprecedented—the first time the all-white Board ever agreed to negotiate with an African-American organization. . . .

. . . Over a four-month period in the spring of 1991, the Tallahatchie County Redistricting Committee participated in more than a dozen publicly held negotiating sessions with the Tallahatchie Board of Supervisors. A large contingent of community members were at each meeting, demonstrating the resolve of the black community. Initially, the supervisors would not even speak to the African-American representatives, leaving the verbal sparring to their lawyer and de-

mographer. Gradually, however, the supervisors came to respect the expertise and outright persistence of the Tallahatchie County Redistricting Committee members. The supervisors "were blown away" by seemingly small things, such as the fact that the community had notebooks and access to the same information about the process that the supervisors had. . . .

The community and the all-white Board eventually agreed on a plan that would create three majority-black districts out of five. But this hard-won victory unraveled when white farmers who had boycotted the negotiations demanded that the supervisors withdraw from the plan. The supervisors caved in . . . and adopted a plan that was essentially the same as the existing one, under which no African-American had ever been elected.

As with the state Legislative districts, the U.S. Department of Justice refused to preclear the Tallahatchie Board's redistricting plan. . . . For more than a year, the battle languished in the courts. . . .

. . . [T]he federal court finally ordered a new interim plan for Tallahatchie Supervisor districts and scheduled a special election for November 1992. The plan created three majority-black districts. . . . In the election, African-American candidates ended up winning two of the five supervisor seats. The third African-American candidate lost by only 19 votes. Candidates strongly supported by the African-American community also won a majority of seats on the County Election Commission and one of two County Justice Court seats.

RESULTS FROM THE REDISTRICTING CAMPAIGN

The 1992 elections were a watershed. . . . The number of African-American members of the state Legislature doubled from 21 to 42, giving African-Americans a substantial voting bloc in the state Senate and House. . . .

The 1995 elections brought another three African-American members to the state Legislature, raising the total to 45. . . . The 1995 elections resulted in African-Americans representing 30 percent of the county supervisors statewide. A statewide referendum followed, which proposed to reduce the number of supervisors per county from five to three. Such a move would have forced the creation of larger districts, making it more difficult to create electable black districts. The referendum was defeated with a strong education and mobilization effort in the black community. . . .

Once African-American representatives obtained seats on governing bodies, they were able to create alliances with white officials. In Tallahatchie County, for example, . . . the two African-American supervisors discovered an ally in a white supervisor who represented a large number of fixed income, elderly constituents. With the white supervisor as the third vote, the Board adopted a resolution establishing an ambulance service which the previous, all-white Board had rejected. The white supervisor realized that forming an alliance with the newly elected African-Americans could save lives in his district. . . .

The enlarged contingent of African-Americans in the state Legislature also has made it possible to form coalitions with members of the white majority on certain issues. In 1997, they were able to obtain a $650 million appropriation for education spending over five years. This huge increase in the education budget was the direct result of efforts by the bigger and more powerful Legislative Black Caucus. When legislation was vetoed by the governor, many white legislators wanted to compromise and bring the appropriation down to $380 million. The Legislative Black Caucus took the lead and demanded no compromise and attempted to override the veto. It succeeded. The veto was overridden in the Senate by one vote and in the House by three votes. That was not the only success: in 1995, 130 years after the Civil War, the Mississippi Legislature finally ratified the 13th Amendment to the Constitution, which prohibits slavery.

Source: Penda D. Hair, "Seizing a Voice in Democracy: The Mississippi Redistricting Campaign," in Louder Than Words: Lawyers, Communities and the Struggle for Justice: A Report to the Rockefeller Foundation, New York, March 2001, http://www.rockfound.org/OnlineLibrary/Announcement/32.

38   *Shaw v. Reno,* Decided June 28, 1993

In 1982 Congress amended Section 2 of the Voting Rights Act to promote minority officeholding. In doing so, it partially remedied a key weakness of the Fifteenth Amendment—its textual silence on whether minorities have a right to office. The opinion for the Court in the 1993 case of Shaw v. Reno (509 U.S. 630) sketches, however, several constitutional and political perils that might emerge as by-products of official efforts to promote black officeholding. In essence, the majority opinion holds that overcoming the legacies of disenfranchisement is too serious a matter to be done sloppily or badly, which is why the case is remanded.

When it was handed down, the per curiam opinion created consternation and outrage among many supporters of the Voting Rights Act. They believed that it delegitimated the goal of minority officeholding by suggesting so strongly that realizing that goal might risk offending the Constitution. Those who liked the opinion thought that Justice Sandra Day O'Connor, who wrote the opinion, was taking a stand against so-called electoral affirmative action. In retrospect, it appears that neither reaction captures O'Connor's sincere interest in ensuring that the statute and the Constitution are in harmony as much as possible.

RUTH O. SHAW, ET AL.,
APPELLANTS v. JANET RENO, ATTORNEY
GENERAL ET AL.
APPEAL FROM THE UNITED STATES
DISTRICT COURT FOR THE EASTERN
DISTRICT OF NORTH CAROLINA
No. 92-357
Argued April 20, 1993
Decided June 28, 1993

. . .

Justice O'Connor delivered the opinion of the Court. . . .

Forty of North Carolina's one hundred counties are covered by 5 of the Voting Rights Act of 1965, 42 U.S.C. 1973c, which prohibits a jurisdiction subject to its provisions from implementing changes in a "standard, practice, or procedure with respect to voting" without federal authorization. . . . Because the General Assembly's reapportionment plan affected the covered counties, the parties agree that 5 applied. The State chose to submit its plan to the Attorney General for preclearance.

The Attorney General, acting through the Assistant Attorney General for the Civil Rights Division, interposed a formal objection to the General Assembly's plan. . . . In the Attorney General's view, the General Assembly could have created a second majority-minority district "to give effect to black and Native American voting strength in this area" by using boundary lines "no more irregular than [those] found elsewhere in the proposed plan," but failed to do so for "pretextual reasons." . . .

. . . [T]he General Assembly enacted a revised redistricting plan . . . that included a second majority-black district. The General Assembly located the second district not in the south-central to southeastern part of the State, but in the north-central region along Interstate 85.

The first of the two majority-black districts contained in the revised plan, District 1, is somewhat hook shaped. . . .

The second majority-black district, District 12, is even more unusually shaped. It is approximately 160 miles long and, for much of its length, no wider than the I-85 corridor. It winds in snake like fashion through tobacco country, financial centers, and manufacturing areas "until it gobbles in enough enclaves of black neighborhoods." . . .

[A]ppellants instituted the present action in the United States District Court for the Eastern District of North Carolina. Appellants alleged not that the revised plan constituted a political gerrymander, nor that it violated the "one person, one vote" principle, but that the State had created an unconstitutional racial gerrymander. Appellants are five residents of Durham County, North Carolina, all registered to vote in that county. . . .

[A]ppellants contended that the General Assembly's revised reapportionment plan violated several provisions of the United States Constitution, including the Fourteenth Amendment. They alleged that the General Assembly deliberately "create[d] two Congressional Districts in which a majority of black voters was concentrated arbitrarily—without regard to any other considerations, such as compactness, contiguousness, geographical boundaries, or political subdivisions" with the purpose "to create Congressional Districts along racial lines" and to assure the election of two black representatives to Congress. . . .

The three-judge District Court granted the federal appellees' motion to dismiss. The court agreed unanimously that it lacked subject matter jurisdiction by reason of 14(b) of the Voting Rights Act, 42 U.S.C. 1973l(b), which vests the District Court for the District of Columbia with exclusive jurisdiction to issue injunctions against the execution of the Act and to enjoin actions taken by federal officers pursuant thereto. . . .

By a 2-to-1 vote, the District Court also dismissed the complaint against the state appellees. The majority found no support for appellants' contentions that race-based districting is prohibited by Article I, 4, or Article I, 2, of the Constitution, or by the Privileges and Immunities Clause of the Fourteenth Amendment. It deemed appellants' claim under the Fifteenth Amendment essentially subsumed within their related claim under the Equal Protection Clause. That claim, the majority concluded, was barred by United Jewish Organizations of Williamsburgh, Inc. v. Carey, 430 U.S. 144 (1977). . . .

We noted probable jurisdiction. "The right to vote freely for the candidate of one's choice is of the essence of a democratic society. . . ." For much of our Nation's history, that right sadly has been denied to many because of race. The Fifteenth Amendment, ratified in 1870 after a bloody Civil War, promised unequivocally that "[t]he right of citizens of the United States to vote" no longer would be "denied or abridged by any State on account of race, color, or previous condition of servitude."

But "[a] number of states . . . refused to take no for an answer and continued to circumvent the fifteenth amendment's prohibition through the use of both subtle and blunt instruments, perpetuating ugly patterns of pervasive racial discrimination." Blumstein, Defining and Proving Race Discrimination: Perspectives on the Purpose vs. Results Approach from the Voting Rights Act. Ostensibly race-neutral devices such as literacy tests with "grandfather" clauses and "good character" provisos were devised to deprive black voters of the franchise. Another of the weapons in the States' arsenal was the racial gerrymander—"the deliberate and arbitrary distortion of district boundaries . . . . for [racial] purposes." In the 1870's, for example, opponents of Reconstruction in Mississippi "concentrated the bulk of the black population in a 'shoestring' Congressional district running the length of the Mississippi River, leaving five others with white majorities." E. Foner, Reconstruction: America's Unfinished Revolution, 1863-1877, p. 590 (1988). Some 90 years later, Alabama redefined the boundaries of the city of Tuskegee "from a square to an uncouth twenty-eight-sided figure" in a manner that was alleged to exclude black voters, and only black voters, from the city limits.

Alabama's exercise in geometry was but one example of the racial discrimination in voting that persisted in parts of this country nearly a century after ratification of the Fifteenth Amendment. In some States, registration of eligible black voters ran 50% behind that of whites. Congress enacted the Voting Rights Act of 1965 as a dramatic and severe response to the situation. The Act proved immediately successful in ensuring racial minorities access to the voting booth; by the early 1970's, the spread between black and white registration in several of the targeted Southern States had fallen to well below 10%.

But it soon became apparent that guaranteeing equal access to the polls would not suffice to root out other racially discriminatory voting practices. Drawing on the "one person, one vote" principle, this Court recognized that "[t]he right to vote can be affected by a dilution of voting power as well as by an absolute prohibition on casting a ballot." Where members of a racial minority group vote as a cohesive unit, practices such as multimember or at-large electoral systems can reduce or nullify minority voters' ability, as a group, "to elect the candidate of their choice." Accordingly, the Court held that such schemes violate the Fourteenth Amendment when they are adopted with a discriminatory purpose and have the effect of diluting minority voting strength. Congress, too, responded to the problem of vote dilution. In 1982, it amended 2 of the Voting Rights Act to prohibit legislation that results in the dilution of a minority group's voting strength, regardless of the legislature's intent.

It is against this background that we confront the questions presented here. In our view, the District Court properly dismissed appellants' claims against the federal appellees. Our focus is on appellants' claim that the State engaged in unconstitutional racial gerrymandering. That argument strikes a powerful historical chord: it is unsettling how closely the North Carolina plan resembles the most egregious racial gerrymanders of the past.

An understanding of the nature of appellants' claim is critical to our resolution of the case. In their complaint, appellants did not claim that the General Assembly's reapportionment plan unconstitutionally "diluted" white voting strength. They did not even claim to be white. Rather, appellants' complaint alleged that the deliberate segregation of voters into separate districts on the basis of race violated their constitutional right to participate in a "color-blind" electoral process.

. . . That concession is wise: this Court never has held that race-conscious state decisionmaking is impermissible in all circumstances. What appellants object to is redistricting legislation that is so extremely irregular on its face that it rationally can be viewed only as an effort to segregate the races for purposes of voting, without regard for traditional districting principles and without sufficiently compelling justification. For the reasons that follow, we conclude that appellants have stated a claim upon which relief can be granted under the Equal Protection Clause. . . .

Appellants contend that redistricting legislation that is so bizarre on its face that it is "unexplainable on grounds other than race," Arlington Heights, supra, at 266, demands the same close scrutiny that we give other state laws that classify citizens by race. Our voting rights precedents support that conclusion. . . .

Put differently, we believe that reapportionment is one area in which appearances do matter. A reapportionment plan that includes in one district individuals who belong to the same race, but who are otherwise widely separated by geographical and political boundaries, and who may have little in common with one another but the color of their skin, bears an uncomfortable resemblance to political apartheid. It reinforces the perception that members of the same racial group—regardless of their age, education, economic status, or the community in which they live—think alike, share the same political interests, and will prefer the same candidates at the polls. We have rejected such perceptions elsewhere as impermissible racial stereotypes. . . . By perpetuating such notions, a racial gerrymander may exacerbate the very patterns of racial bloc voting that majority-minority districting is sometimes said to counteract.

The message that such districting sends to elected representatives is equally pernicious. When a district obviously is created solely to effectuate the perceived common interests of one racial group, elected officials are more likely to believe that their primary obligation is to represent only the members of that group, rather than their constituency as a whole. This is altogether antithetical to our system of representative democracy. . . .

For these reasons, we conclude that a plaintiff challenging a reapportionment statute under the Equal Protection Clause may state a claim by alleging that the legislation, though race neutral on its face, rationally cannot be understood as anything other than an effort to separate voters into different districts on the basis of race, and that the separation lacks sufficient justification. It is unnecessary for us to decide whether or how a reapportionment plan that, on its face, can be explained in nonracial terms successfully could be challenged. Thus, we express no view as to whether "the intentional creation of majority-minority districts, without more," always gives rise to an equal protection claim. We hold only that, on the facts of this case, appellants have stated a claim sufficient to defeat the state appellees' motion to dismiss. . . .

Racial classifications of any sort pose the risk of lasting harm to our society. They reinforce the belief, held by too many for too much of our history, that individuals should be judged by the color of their skin. Racial classifications with respect to voting carry particular dangers. Racial gerrymandering, even for remedial purposes, may balkanize us into competing racial factions; it threatens to carry us further from the goal of a political system in which race no longer matters—a goal that the Fourteenth and Fifteenth Amendments embody, and to which the Nation continues to aspire. It is for these reasons that race-based districting by our state legislatures demands close judicial scrutiny.

In this case, the Attorney General suggested that North Carolina could have created a reasonably compact second majority-minority district in the south-central to southeastern part of the State. We express no view as to whether appellants successfully could have challenged such a district under the Fourteenth Amendment. We also do not decide whether appellants' complaint stated a claim under constitutional provisions other than the Fourteenth Amendment. Today we hold only that appellants have stated a claim under the Equal Protection Clause by alleging that the North Carolina General Assembly adopted a reapportionment scheme so irrational on its face that it can be understood only as an effort to segregate voters into separate voting districts because of their race, and that the separa-

tion lacks sufficient justification. If the allegation of racial gerrymandering remains uncontradicted, the District Court further must determine whether the North Carolina plan is narrowly tailored to further a compelling governmental interest. Accordingly, we reverse the judgment of the District Court and remand the case for further proceedings consistent with this opinion.

It is so ordered.

Source: Findlaw, *Shaw v. Reno*, 509 U.S. 630 (1993), http://caselaw.lp.findlaw.com/scripts/getcase.pl?court=us&vol=509&invol=.

39   *Reno v. Bossier Parish School Board,* Decided January 24, 2000

When a majority of the Supreme Court takes a civil or voting rights case and someone on the Court wants to do something that makes minorities worse off, the result can often (though not always) be a per curiam *opinion riddled with confusing formalism that somehow attracts a majority. Does* Reno v. Bossier Parish School Board *(520 U.S. 47) fit that generalization?*

In his per curiam *opinion, Justice Antonin Scalia announces that purposely discriminatory plans to change electoral procedure—which do not also have the effect of making minorities worse off than they were before—can be precleared under Section 5 of the Voting Rights Act. It is very doubtful that Congress ever intended such a use of Section 5—and, interestingly, Scalia completely ignores congressional intent and fastens on definitional and linguistic issues to arrive at his conclusion. Furthermore, for about a quarter of a century it was widely understood among voting rights lawyers, federal judges, and the Supreme Court itself that the Court's decision in* Beer v. United States *(Document 33) expressly preserved the power to deny preclearance to intentionally discriminatory schemes of any kind. Scalia dismisses this feature of the* per curiam *opinion in* Beer *as "dictum," however. He notes, to be sure, that genuinely offensive and unconstitutional schemes can be taken to court. But the whole purpose of preclearance was to shift the burden of realizing the Fifteenth Amendment's purposes away from the United States or from private plaintiffs and onto state and local governments.*

If Congress renews Section 5 by 2007 it may decide to rewrite Section 5 in order to address the destructive impact of this decision. If it does not do so, then it is likely that preclearance will be much weaker in the future.

JANET RENO, ATTORNEY GENERAL,
APPELLANT
98-405   *v.*
BOSSIER PARISH SCHOOL BOARD
GEORGE PRICE, *et al.,* APPELLANTS
98-406   *v.*
BOSSIER PARISH SCHOOL BOARD
On Appeals from the United States District
Court for
the District of Columbia
[January 24, 2000]

JUSTICE SCALIA delivered the opinion of the Court. These cases present the question whether §5 of the Voting Rights Act of 1965, 79 Stat. 439, as amended, 42 U. S. C. §1973c, prohibits preclearance of a redistricting plan enacted with a discriminatory but nonretrogressive purpose. . . .

Bossier Parish is governed by a 12-member Police Jury elected from single-member districts for 4-year terms. In the early 1990s, the Police Jury set out to redraw its electoral districts in order to account for demographic changes reflected in the decennial census. In 1991, it adopted a redistricting plan which, like the plan then in effect, contained no majority-black districts, although blacks made up approximately 20% of the parish's population. On May 28, 1991, the Police Jury submitted its new districting plan to the Attorney General; two months later, the Attorney General granted preclearance.

The Bossier Parish School Board (Board) is constituted in the same fashion as the Police Jury, and it too undertook to redraw its districts after the 1990 census. During the course of that redistricting, appellant-intervenor George Price, president of the local chapter of the National Association for the Advancement of Colored People (NAACP), proposed that the Board adopt a plan with majority-black districts. In the fall of 1992, amid some controversy, the Board rejected Price's suggestion and adopted the Police Jury's 1991 redistricting plan as its own.

On January 4, 1993, the Board submitted its redistricting plan to the Attorney General for pre-

clearance. Although the Attorney General had precleared the identical plan when submitted by the Police Jury, she interposed a formal objection to the Board's plan, asserting that "new information"—specifically, the NAACP plan proposed by appellant-intervenor Price—demonstrated that "black residents are sufficiently numerous and geographically compact so as to constitute a majority in two single-member districts." The Attorney General disclaimed any attempt to compel the Board to "adopt any particular plan," but maintained that the Board was "not free to adopt a plan that unnecessarily limits the opportunity for minority voters to elect their candidates of choice." . . .

After the Attorney General denied the Board's request for reconsideration, the Board filed the present action for judicial preclearance of the 1992 plan in the United States District Court for the District of Columbia. Section 5 of the Voting Rights Act authorizes preclearance of a proposed voting change that "does not have the purpose and will not have the effect of denying or abridging the right to vote on account of race or color." Before the District Court, appellants conceded that the Board's plan did not have a prohibited "effect" under §5, since it did not worsen the position of minority voters. (In *Beer v. United States,* 425 U. S. 130 (1976), we held that a plan has a prohibited "effect" only if it is retrogressive.) Instead, appellants made two distinct claims. First, they argued that preclearance should be denied because the Board's plan, by not creating as many majority-black districts as it should create, violated §2 of the Voting Rights Act, which bars discriminatory voting practices. Second, they contended that, although the Board's plan would have no retrogressive effect, it nonetheless violated §5 because it was enacted for a discriminatory "purpose."

The District Court granted preclearance. . . . [T]he District Court . . . concluded . . . that allegations of dilutive effect and of discriminatory animus were insufficient to establish retrogressive intent. . . .

In their jurisdictional statements in this Court, appellants contended, first, that the District Court's conclusion that there was no evidence of discriminatory but nonretrogressive purpose was clearly erroneous, and second, that §5 of the Voting Rights Act prohibits preclearance of a redistricting plan enacted with a discriminatory but nonretrogressive purpose. Appellants did not challenge the District Court's determination that there was no evidence of retrogressive intent. . . .

Appellants press the two claims initially raised in their jurisdictional statements: first, that the District Court's factual conclusion that there was no evidence of discriminatory but nonretrogressive intent was clearly erroneous, and second, that §5 of the Voting Rights Act prohibits preclearance of a redistricting plan enacted with a discriminatory but nonretrogressive purpose. . . .

. . . [I]n order to obtain preclearance under §5, a covered jurisdiction must demonstrate that the proposed change "does not have the purpose and will not have the effect of denying or abridging the right to vote on account of race or color." . . . A covered jurisdiction, therefore, must make two distinct showings: first, that the proposed change "does not have the purpose . . . of denying or abridging the right to vote on account of race or color," and second, that the proposed change "will not have the effect of denying or abridging the right to vote on account of race or color." The covered jurisdiction bears the burden of persuasion on both points. . . .

Appellants contend that in qualifying the term "purpose," the very same phrase does *not* impose a limitation to retrogression—*i.e.,* that the phrase "abridging the right to vote on account of race or color" means retrogression when it modifies "effect," but means discrimination more generally when it modifies "purpose." We think this is simply an untenable construction of the text, in effect recasting the phrase "does not have the purpose and will not have the effect of *x*" to read "does not have the purpose of *y* and will not have the effect of *x*." . . .

Appellants point out that we did give the purpose prong of §5 a broader meaning than the effect prong in *Richmond v. United States,* 422 U. S. 358 (1975). . . .

It must be acknowledged that *Richmond* created a discontinuity between the effect and purpose prongs of §5. We regard that, however, as nothing more than an *ex necessitate* limitation upon the effect prong in the particular context of annexation. . . . We found it necessary to make an exception to normal retrogressive-*effect* principles, but not to normal retrogressive-*purpose* principles, in order to permit routine annexation. That sheds little light upon the issue before us here.

Appellants' only textual justification for giving the purpose and effect prongs different meanings is that to do otherwise "would reduce the purpose prong of Section 5 to a trivial matter," . . .

. . . [They] . . . contend that . . . it would be "untenable" to conclude . . . that the phrase "abridging the right to vote on account of race or color" refers only to retrogression in §5 . . . in light of the fact that virtually identical language elsewhere in the Voting Rights Act—and indeed, in the Fifteenth Amendment—has never been read to refer only to retrogression. See §2(a) of the Voting Rights Act, 42 U. S. C. §1973(a) ("No voting [practice] shall be imposed or applied by any State or political subdivision in a manner which results in a denial or abridgement of the right of any citizen of the United States to vote on account of race or color . . ."); U.S. Const., Amdt. 15, §1 ("The right of citizens of the United States to vote shall not be denied or abridged by the United States or by any State on account of race, color, or previous condition of servitude"). The term "abridge," however—whose core meaning is "shorten," see Webster's New International Dictionary 7 (2d ed. 1950); American Heritage Dictionary 6 (3d ed. 1992)—necessarily entails a comparison. It makes no sense to suggest that a voting practice "abridges" the right to vote without some baseline with which to compare the practice. In §5 preclearance proceedings—which uniquely deal only and specifically with *changes* in voting procedures—the baseline is the status quo that is proposed to be changed: If the change "abridges the right to vote" relative to the status quo, preclearance is denied, and the status quo (however discriminatory *it* may be) remains in effect. In §2 or Fifteenth Amendment proceedings, by contrast, which involve not only changes but (much more commonly) the status quo itself, the comparison must be made with an hypothetical alternative: If the *status quo* "results in [an] abridgement of the right to vote" or "abridge[s] [the right to vote]" relative to what the right to vote *ought to be,* the status quo itself must be changed. Our reading of "abridging" as referring only to retrogression in §5, but to discrimination more generally in §2 and the Fifteenth Amendment, is faithful to the differing contexts in which the term is used. . . .

. . . [A]s we have repeatedly noted, in vote-dilution cases §5 prevents nothing but backsliding, and preclearance under §5 affirms nothing but the absence of backsliding. . . . This explains why the sole consequence of failing to obtain preclearance is continuation of the status quo. To deny preclearance to a plan that is *not* retrogressive—*no matter how unconstitutional it may be*—would risk leaving in effect a status quo that is even worse. For example, in the case of a voting change with a discriminatory but nonretrogressive purpose and a discriminatory but ameliorative effect, the result of denying preclearance would be to preserve a status quo with more discriminatory effect than the proposed change. . . .

. . . [A]ppellants note that, in *Beer,* this Court stated that "an ameliorative new legislative apportionment cannot violate §5 unless the apportionment itself so discriminates on the basis of race or color as to violate the Constitution." 425 U.S., at 141. Appellants contend that this suggests that, at least in some cases in which the covered jurisdiction acts with a discriminatory but nonretrogressive dilutive purpose, the covered ju-

risdiction should be denied preclearance because it is acting unconstitutionally.

We think that a most implausible interpretation. . . . If the statement in *Beer* had meant what appellants suggest, it would . . . have been gutting *Beer*'s holding (since a showing of discriminatory but nonretrogressive effect *would* have been a constitutional violation and *would,* despite the holding of *Beer,* have sufficed to deny preclearance). A much more plausible explanation of the statement is that it referred to a constitutional violation *other than* vote dilution—and, more specifically, a violation consisting of a "denial" of the right to vote, rather than an "abridgement." Although in the context of denial claims, no less than in the context of abridgement claims, the antibacksliding rationale for §5 (and its effect of avoiding preservation of an even worse status quo) suggests that retrogression should again be the criterion, arguably in that context the word "deny" (unlike the word "abridge") does not import a comparison with the status quo.

In any event, it is entirely clear that the statement in *Beer* was pure dictum: The Government had made no contention that the proposed reapportionment at issue was unconstitutional. . . . And though we have quoted the dictum in subsequent cases, we have never actually applied it to deny preclearance. . . . We have made clear, on the other hand, what we reaffirm today: that proceedings to preclear apportionment schemes and proceedings to consider the constitutionality of apportionment schemes are entirely distinct. . . .

. . . §5 explicitly states that neither administrative nor judicial preclearance " 'shall bar a subsequent action to enjoin enforcement' of [a change in voting practice]." 509 U. S., at 654 (quoting 42 U. S. C. §1973c). That fully available remedy leaves us untroubled by the possibility that §5 could produce preclearance of an unconstitutionally dilutive redistricting plan. . . .

In light of the language of §5 and our prior holding in *Beer,* we hold that §5 does not prohibit preclearance of a redistricting plan enacted with a discriminatory but nonretrogressive purpose. Accordingly, the judgment of the District Court is affirmed.

It is so ordered.

Source: Findlaw, *Reno v. Bossier Parish School Board,* 520 U.S. 47 (2000), http://caselaw.lp.findlaw.com/cgi-bin/getcase.pl?court=US&navby=case&vol=000&invol=98-405.

---

40   *Georgia v. Ashcroft,* Decided June 26, 2003

In Georgia v. Ashcroft (539 U.S. 461) Justice Sandra Day O'Connor proposes the idea that "influence districts" may work just as well as majority-minority districts in helping a state to comply with the goals of the Voting Rights Act. An influence district has enough minority voters to force whoever is elected from the district to pay attention to what black voters want; a majority-minority district has enough minority voters to assure a minority politician of a legislative career, which means that the number of minority voters in a majority-minority district is larger than that in an influence district.

Again, evident in the opinion is O'Connor's self-consciously pragmatic approach to making the Voting Rights Act work in a way that protects it from criticism that it is just about electoral affirmative action, so to speak. O'Connor also relies very heavily in her opinion on evidence of pragmatism among black politicians and legislators in Georgia in the redistricting process. But, again, her opinion can also be read as proof of the Court's reluctance to forcefully promote black officeholding—a reluctance that can be traced all the way back to Justice Potter Stewart's decision in Beer v. United States *(Document 33). The textual silence of the Fifteenth Amendment on the right to office haunts this case, as it does many others since passage of the Voting Rights Act.*

GEORGIA v. ASHCROFT, ATTORNEY GENERAL, et al.
Appeal from the United States District Court for the District of Columbia
No. 02-182. Argued April 29, 2003—Decided June 26, 2003

. . .

Justice O'Connor delivered the opinion of the Court.

In this case, we decide whether Georgia's State Senate redistricting plan should have been precleared under §5 of the Voting Rights Act of 1965, 79 Stat. 439, as renumbered and amended, 42 U.S.C. §1973c. Section 5 requires that before a covered jurisdiction's new voting "standard,

practice, or procedure" goes into effect, it must be precleared by either the Attorney General of the United States or a federal court to ensure that the change "does not have the purpose and will not have the effect of denying or abridging the right to vote on account of race or color." 42 U.S.C. §1973c. Whether a voting procedure change should be precleared depends on whether the change "would lead to a retrogression in the position of racial minorities with respect to their effective exercise of the electoral franchise." We therefore must decide whether Georgia's State Senate redistricting plan is retrogressive as compared to its previous, benchmark districting plan. . . .

After the 2000 census, the Georgia General Assembly began the process of redistricting the Senate once again. No party contests that a substantial majority of black voters in Georgia vote Democratic, or that all elected black representatives in the General Assembly are Democrats. The goal of the Democratic leadership—black and white—was to maintain the number of majority-minority districts and also increase the number of Democratic Senate seats. For example, the Director of Georgia's Legislative Redistricting Office, Linda Meggers, testified that the Senate Black Caucus "'wanted to maintain'" the existing majority-minority districts and at the same time "'not waste'" votes.

The Vice Chairman of the Senate Reapportionment Committee, Senator Robert Brown, also testified about the goals of the redistricting effort. Senator Brown, who is black, chaired the subcommittee that developed the Senate plan at issue here. Senator Brown believed when he designed the Senate plan that as the black voting age population in a district increased beyond what was necessary, it would "pus[h] the whole thing more towards [the] Republican[s]." And "correspondingly," Senator Brown stated, "the more you diminish the power of African-Americans overall." Senator Charles Walker was the majority leader of the Senate. Senator Walker testified that it was important to attempt to maintain a Democratic majority in the Senate because "we [African-Americans] have a better chance to participate in the political process under the Democratic majority than we would have under a Republican majority." At least 7 of the 11 black members of the Senate could chair committees.

The plan as designed by Senator Brown's committee kept true to the dual goals of maintaining at least as many majority-minority districts while also attempting to increase Democratic strength in the Senate. Part of the Democrats' strategy was not only to maintain the number of majority-minority districts, but to increase the number of so-called "influence" districts, where black voters would be able to exert a significant—if not decisive—force in the election process. As the ma-

jority leader testified, "in the past, you know, what we would end up doing was packing. You put all blacks in one district and all whites in one district, so what you end up with is [a] black Democratic district and [a] white Republican district. That's not a good strategy. That does not bring the people together, it divides the population. But if you put people together on voting precincts it brings people together."

The plan as designed by the Senate "unpacked" the most heavily concentrated majority-minority districts in the benchmark plan, and created a number of new influence districts. The new plan drew 13 districts with a majority-black voting age population, 13 additional districts with a black voting age population of between 30% and 50%, and 4 other districts with a black voting age population of between 25% and 30%. According to the 2000 census, as compared to the benchmark plan, the new plan reduced by five the number of districts with a black voting age population in excess of 60%. Yet it increased the number of majority-black voting age population districts by one, and it increased the number of districts with a black voting age population of between 25% and 50% by four. As compared to the benchmark plan enacted in 1997, the difference is even larger. Under the old census figures, Georgia had 10 Senate districts with a majority-black voting age population, and 8 Senate districts with a black voting age population of between 30% and 50%. The new plan thus increased the number of districts with a majority black voting age population by three, and increased the number of districts with a black voting age population of between 30% and 50% by another five.

The Senate adopted its new districting plan on August 10, 2001, by a vote of 29 to 26. Ten of the eleven black Senators voted for the plan. The Georgia House of Representatives passed the Senate plan by a vote of 101 to 71. Thirty-three of the thirty-four black Representatives voted for the plan. No Republican in either the House or the Senate voted for the plan, making the votes of the black legislators necessary for passage. The Governor signed the Senate plan into law on August 24, 2001, and Georgia subsequently sought to obtain preclearance. . . .

The United States, through the Attorney General, argued in District Court that Georgia's 2001 Senate redistricting plan should not be precleared. It argued that the plan's changes to the boundaries of Districts 2, 12, and 26 unlawfully reduced the ability of black voters to elect candidates of their choice. The United States noted that in District 2, the black voting age population dropped from 60.58% to 50.31%; in District 12, the black voting age population dropped from 55.43% to 50.66%; and in District 26, the black voting age population dropped from 62.45% to 50.80%. Moreover, in all three of these districts, the percentage of black registered voters dropped to just under 50%. The United States also submitted expert evidence that voting is racially polarized in Senate Districts 2, 12, and 26. . . .

A three-judge panel of the District Court held that Georgia's State Senate apportionment violated §5, and was therefore not entitled to preclearance. Judge Sullivan, joined by Judge Edwards, concluded that Georgia had "not demonstrated by a preponderance of the evidence that the State Senate redistricting plan would not have a retrogressive effect on African American voters'" effective exercise of the electoral franchise. . . .

Judge Oberdorfer dissented. He would have given "greater credence to the political expertise and motivation of Georgia's African-American political leaders and reasonable inferences drawn from their testimony and the voting data and statistics." He noted that this Court has not answered "whether a redistricting plan that preserves or increases the number of districts statewide in which minorities have a fair or reasonable opportunity to elect candidates of choice is entitled to preclearance, or whether every district must remain at or improve on the benchmark probability of victory, even if doing so

maintains a minority super-majority far in excess of the level needed for effective exercise of [the] electoral franchise."

After the District Court refused to preclear the plan, Georgia enacted another plan, largely similar to the one at issue here, except that it added black voters to Districts 2, 12, and 26. The District Court precleared this plan. No party has contested the propriety of the District Court's preclearance of the Senate plan as amended. Georgia asserts that it will use the plan as originally enacted if it receives preclearance.

We noted probable jurisdiction to consider whether the District Court should have precleared the plan as originally enacted by Georgia in 2001, 537 U.S. 1151, and now vacate the judgment below. . . .

Georgia argues that even if compliance with §2 does not automatically result in preclearance under §5, its State Senate plan should be precleared because it does not lead to "a retrogression in the position of racial minorities with respect to their effective exercise of the electoral franchise."

While we have never determined the meaning of "effective exercise of the electoral franchise," this case requires us to do so in some detail. First, the United States and the District Court correctly acknowledge that in examining whether the new plan is retrogressive, the inquiry must encompass the entire statewide plan as a whole. Thus, while the diminution of a minority group's effective exercise of the electoral franchise in one or two districts may be sufficient to show a violation of §5, it is only sufficient if the covered jurisdiction cannot show that the gains in the plan as a whole offset the loss in a particular district.

Second, any assessment of the retrogression of a minority group's effective exercise of the electoral franchise depends on an examination of all the relevant circumstances, such as the ability of minority voters to elect their candidate of choice, the extent of the minority group's opportunity to participate in the political process, and the feasibility of creating a nonretrogressive plan. . . . "No single statistic provides courts with a shortcut to determine whether" a voting change retrogresses from the benchmark.

In assessing the totality of the circumstances, a court should not focus solely on the comparative ability of a minority group to elect a candidate of its choice. While this factor is an important one in the §5 retrogression inquiry, it cannot be dispositive or exclusive. The standard in §5 is simple—whether the new plan "would lead to a retrogression in the position of racial minorities with respect to their effective exercise of the electoral franchise."

The ability of minority voters to elect a candidate of their choice is important but often complex in practice to determine. In order to maximize the electoral success of a minority group, a State may choose to create a certain number of "safe" districts, in which it is highly likely that minority voters will be able to elect the candidate of their choice. Alternatively, a State may choose to create a greater number of districts in which it is likely—although perhaps not quite as likely as under the benchmark plan—that minority voters will be able to elect candidates of their choice.

Section 5 does not dictate that a State must pick one of these methods of redistricting over another. Either option "will present the minority group with its own array of electoral risks and benefits," and presents "hard choices about what would truly 'maximize' minority electoral success." On one hand, a smaller number of safe majority-minority districts may virtually guarantee the election of a minority group's preferred candidate in those districts. Yet even if this concentration of minority voters in a few districts does not constitute the unlawful packing of minority voters, such a plan risks isolating minority voters from the rest of the state, and risks narrowing political influence to only a fraction of political districts. And while such districts may result in more "descriptive representation" because the representatives of choice are more likely to mirror

the race of the majority of voters in that district, the representation may be limited to fewer areas.

On the other hand, spreading out minority voters over a greater number of districts creates more districts in which minority voters may have the opportunity to elect a candidate of their choice. Such a strategy has the potential to increase "substantive representation" in more districts, by creating coalitions of voters who together will help to achieve the electoral aspirations of the minority group. It also, however, creates the risk that the minority group's preferred candidate may lose. Yet as we stated in *Johnson v. De Grandy, supra,* at 1020:

"[T]here are communities in which minority citizens are able to form coalitions with voters from other racial and ethnic groups, having no need to be a majority within a single district in order to elect candidates of their choice. Those candidates may not represent perfection to every minority voter, but minority voters are not immune from the obligation to pull, haul, and trade to find common political ground, the virtue of which is not to be slighted in applying a statute meant to hasten the waning of racism in American politics."

Section 5 gives States the flexibility to choose one theory of effective representation over the other.

In addition to the comparative ability of a minority group to elect a candidate of its choice, the other highly relevant factor in a retrogression inquiry is the extent to which a new plan changes the minority group's opportunity to participate in the political process. " '[T]he power to influence the political process is not limited to winning elections.' "

Thus, a court must examine whether a new plan adds or subtracts "influence districts"—where minority voters may not be able to elect a candidate of choice but can play a substantial, if not decisive, role in the electoral process. In assessing the comparative weight of these influence districts, it is important to consider "the likelihood that candidates elected without decisive minority support would be willing to take the minority's interests into account." In fact, various studies have suggested that the most effective way to maximize minority voting strength may be to create more influence or coalitional districts.

Section 5 leaves room for States to use these types of influence and coalitional districts. Indeed, the State's choice ultimately may rest on a political choice of whether substantive or descriptive representation is preferable. The State may choose, consistent with §5, that it is better to risk having fewer minority representatives in order to achieve greater overall representation of a minority group by increasing the number of representatives sympathetic to the interests of minority voters.

In addition to influence districts, one other method of assessing the minority group's opportunity to participate in the political process is to examine the comparative position of legislative leadership, influence, and power for representatives of the benchmark majority-minority districts. A legislator, no less than a voter, is "not immune from the obligation to pull, haul, and trade to find common political ground." Indeed, in a representative democracy, the very purpose of voting is to delegate to chosen representatives the power to make and pass laws. The ability to exert more control over that process is at the core of exercising political power. A lawmaker with more legislative influence has more potential to set the agenda, to participate in closed-door meetings, to negotiate from a stronger position, and to shake hands on a deal. Maintaining or increasing legislative positions of power for minority voters' representatives of choice, while not dispositive by itself, can show the lack of retrogressive effect under §5.

And it is also significant, though not dispositive, whether the representatives elected from the very districts created and protected by the Voting Rights Act support the new districting plan. . . . The representatives of districts created to ensure continued minority participation in the political process have some knowledge about how "voters will probably act" and whether the proposed change will decrease minority voters' effective exercise of the electoral franchise. . . .

Given the evidence submitted in this case, we find that Georgia likely met its burden of showing nonretrogression. . . .

The dissent's analysis presumes that we are deciding that Georgia's Senate plan is not retrogressive. To the contrary, we hold only that the District Court did not engage in the correct retrogression analysis because it focused too heavily on the ability of the minority group to elect a candidate of its choice in the majority-minority districts. While the District Court engaged in a thorough analysis of the issue, we must remand the case for the District Court to examine the facts using the standard that we announce today. We leave it for the District Court to determine whether Georgia has indeed met its burden of proof. The dissent justifies its conclusion here on the ground that the District Court did not clearly err in its factual determination. But the dissent does not appear to dispute that if the District Court's legal standard was incorrect, the decision below should be vacated.

The purpose of the Voting Rights Act is to prevent discrimination in the exercise of the electoral franchise and to foster our transformation to a society that is no longer fixated on race. As Congressman Lewis stated: "I think that's what the [civil rights] struggle was all about, to create what I like to call a truly interracial democracy in the South. In the movement, we would call it creating the beloved community, an all-inclusive community, where we would be able to forget about race and color and see people as people, as human beings, just as citizens." While courts and the Department of Justice should be vigilant in ensuring that States neither reduce the effective exercise of the electoral franchise nor discriminate against minority voters, the Voting Rights Act, as properly interpreted, should encourage the transition to a society where race no longer matters: a society where integration and color-blindness are not just qualities to be proud of, but are simple facts of life.

IV

The District Court is in a better position to reweigh all the facts in the record in the first instance in light of our explication of retrogression. The judgment of the District Court for the District of Columbia, accordingly, is vacated, and the case is remanded for further proceedings consistent with this opinion.

It is so ordered.

Source: Findlaw, *Georgia v. Ashcroft* 539 U.S. 461 (2003), http://caselaw.lp.findlaw.com/scripts/getcase.pl?court=US&vol=000&invol=02-182.

41   *United States v. Charleston County, South Carolina*, Decided April 29, 2004

This decision by the Fourth Circuit affirming the decision of the district court that the electoral structure of Charleston County, South Carolina, violated the Voting Rights Act is full of lessons about what an appellate court does in reviewing a lower court. The circuit court says, in effect, that nothing that the district court did was "clearly erroneous" and that therefore the circuit court cannot overturn the district court's finding. But the decision also underscores the circuit court's deference to the reasonableness of the district court's decision in light of the difficulty facing any judge who must assess all of the relevant evidence, much of which is ambiguous or disputable unless it is seen in the context of other relevant evidence. Finally, it is remarkable that Charleston County was in violation of the Voting Rights Act from 1969 until the circuit court's affirmation of the district court. This fact is a reminder that statutes are not self-enacting. That the Charleston County electoral scheme was precleared in error, for all intents and purposes, in 1969 also shows the long-lasting influence of the Nixon administration's "southern strategy" on the implementation of the Voting Rights Act.

UNITED STATES COURT OF APPEALS FOR THE FOURTH CIRCUIT
United States v. Charleston County, South Carolina

. . .

Appeals from the United States District Court for the District of South Carolina, at Charleston. . . .

Affirmed by published opinion. Judge Wilkinson wrote the opinion, in which Judge Niemeyer and Judge Duncan joined. . . .

OPINION
WILKINSON, Circuit Judge:

Since 1969, Charleston County, South Carolina has been governed by a County Council composed of nine members elected in countywide, partisan elections. Despite the County's substantial minority population, few minority-preferred candidates, and very few minority candidates, have ever been elected to the Council. The United States brought this suit, alleging that the County's at-large election of its Council diluted minority voting strength in violation of Section 2 of the Voting Rights Act of 1965. The district court agreed, finding that the County's severe voting polarization, its particular electoral structure, and its sheer size combined to deny minority voters an equal opportunity to elect their preferred representatives. Because the district court's finding is not clearly erroneous, we affirm.

I.

Located in the southeastern corner of South Carolina, where the Ashley and Cooper Rivers converge on the Atlantic, Charleston County covers over nine hundred square miles. It includes tiny municipalities like Awendaw and McClellanville; islands like Kiawah and Seabrook; and of course cities like Charleston, the state's second largest. The County is ethnically as well as geographically diverse. The third most populous of the state's forty-six counties, it has the second highest total number of black residents. . . .

. . . As of November 2000, 177,279 people were registered to vote in Charleston County, 122,557 (69.1%) of whom were white and 54,722 (30.9%) of whom were nonwhite. . . .

The County Council oversees local governance on issues ranging from economic development to public safety, and it is composed of nine members elected to staggered terms in at-large, partisan elections. Candidates for the Council run from four residency districts: three Council seats are reserved for residents of the City of Charleston, three for residents of North Charleston, two for residents of West Ashley, and one for a resident of East Cooper. . . .

The County's modified at-large system, in which all of the County's residents may vote for candidates residing in specific areas of the County, was created in 1969, and it was precleared by the Attorney General under Section 5 of the Voting Rights Act. . . . In 1989, the County's residents narrowly rejected a referendum to switch from the at-large electoral system to a single-member district system. Both the County and the United States agree that voting on the referendum was extremely polarized: at least 98% of minority voters approved the switch to single-member districts, while at least 75% of white voters wanted to retain at-large elections.

Since 1970, 41 people have been elected to the County Council, only three of whom are minorities. . . .

II.

. . .

Section 2(a) of the Voting Rights Act prohibits a State or its political subdivision from imposing any voting practice that "results in a denial or abridgement of the right of any citizen of the United States to vote on account of race color. . . ." 42 U.S.C. § 1973(a). Section 2(b), as amended in 1982, further provides that a violation of § 2(a) occurs

if, based on the totality of the circumstances, it is shown that the political processes leading to nomination or election in the State or political subdivision are not equally open to participation by members of a class of citizens protected by [§ 2(a)] in that its members have less opportunity than other members of the electorate to participate in the political process and to elect representatives of their choice.

Id. § 1973(b). The 1982 amendment made clear that Section 2 condemns not only voting practices borne of a discriminatory intent, but also voting practices that "operate, designedly or otherwise," to deny "equal access to any phase of the electoral process for minority group members." S. Rep. No. 97-417, at 28, 30 (1982), *reprinted in* 1982 U.S.C.C.A.N. 177, 205, 207 (hereinafter "Senate Report"); *see also Chisom v. Roemer,* 501 U.S. 380, 393-95 & nn.20-21 (1991).

In *Thornburg v. Gingles,* 478 U.S. 30 (1986), the Supreme Court established the framework for claims that an at-large voting system dilutes minority voting strength in violation of § 2 of the Voting Rights Act. According to the Court, three preconditions are necessary to a finding of vote dilution:

First, the minority group must be able to demonstrate that it is sufficiently large and geographically compact to constitute a majority in a single member district. . . .

Second, the minority group must be able to show that it is politically cohesive. . . .

Third, the minority must be able to demonstrate that the white majority votes sufficiently as a bloc to enable it . . . usually to defeat the minority's preferred candidate.

Gingles, 478 U.S. at 50-51. . . . If these three preconditions are satisfied, then the trier of fact must determine whether, based on the totality of the circumstances, there has been a violation of Section 2. *Johnson v. DeGrandy*, 512 U.S. 997, 1011–12 (1994); *Cane v. Worcester County*, 35 F.3d 921, 925 (4th Cir. 1994).

In determining which circumstances courts should take care to consider, the Supreme Court has turned for guidance to the Senate Report that accompanied Congress's 1982 amendments to the Voting Rights Act. . . . According to Congress and the Court, the most important factors in the inquiry into the totality of the circumstances are the "extent to which minority group members have been elected to public office in the jurisdiction," and "the extent to which voting in the elections of the state or political subdivision is racially polarized." . . . If these factors are present, other considerations "are supportive of, but *not essential to*" a § 2 claim: the history of voting-related discrimination in the State or political subdivision; the extent to which the State or political subdivision has used voting practices that enhance the opportunity for discrimination against the minority group, such as unusually large election districts or anti-single shot provisions; the exclusion of minorities from the candidate slating process; the use of racial appeals in political campaigns; and the degree to which past discrimination in such areas as education, employment and health has hindered the ability of minorities to participate effectively in the political process. *Id.* . . .

On July 10, 2002, the United States District Court for the District of South Carolina . . . granted summary judgment to the United States and the private plaintiffs as to the three *Gingles* preconditions. The district court then held a trial on the remaining issue: whether, based on the totality of the circumstances, the County's at-large electoral method violated § 2. On March 6, 2003, the district court agreed with the United States that the County's at-large system diluted minority voting strength, depriving minority voters of an equal opportunity to participate in the political process and elect representatives of their choice. However, the district court rejected the private plaintiffs' claim that the County's at-large system was adopted with the intent to discriminate against minority voters.

Charleston County now appeals the district court's decision. The County does not challenge the district court's finding that the United States had established the first two *Gingles* preconditions: the County concedes not only that its minority voters are sufficiently numerous and geographically compact to constitute a majority in a single-member district, but also that they are politically cohesive. The County, however, does contend that the district court erred in granting summary judgment to the plaintiffs on the third *Gingles* precondition—the presence of white racial bloc voting. The County also contends that, even if the three *Gingles* preconditions were satisfied, the district court clearly erred in determining that the at-large voting scheme diluted minority voting strength in violation of § 2. . . .

III.

The crux of the County's argument, from the outset of this litigation, has been that voting in Charleston County is polarized as a result of partisanship rather than race. . . .

. . . According to the County, the district court improperly discounted substantial evidence that party affiliation, not racial animus, drives voting in the County, which has an increasingly strong Republican base. . . .

. . . [M]inorities can win election to the Council, so long as they share the political philosophy that prevails among the majority of Charleston County's residents. . . .

We need not inquire whether we would have been persuaded by the County's evidence in the first instance, for our function is not to reweigh the evidence presented to the district court.

Claims of vote dilution require trial courts to immerse themselves in the facts of each case, and to engage in "an intensely local appraisal of the design and impact of the contested electoral mechanisms." . . . ("[R]esolution of the question of vote dilution is a fact intensive enterprise to be undertaken by the district court."). The Supreme Court has been explicit that in order to "preserve[ ] the benefit of the trial court's particular familiarity with the indigenous political reality," we may set aside a trial court's finding of vote dilution only if it is clearly erroneous. . . .

. . . [T]he County repeatedly asserts that the district court mistakenly considered only *minority* candidates' success, rather than *minority-preferred* candidates' success, as part of the totality of the circumstances. . . .

Yet the district court did not treat the lack of minority electoral success as conclusive proof of vote dilution. Rather, pursuant to the clear command of Congress and the Supreme Court, the district court treated minimal minority electoral success as but one factor in the totality of the circumstances inquiry. . . . The district court recognized that the number of minorities elected to office, while relevant to vote dilution, was not dispositive, and it went on to analyze a host of other factors that weighed in its decision. The court was aware that the ultimate question remained whether minority voters were able to elect their preferred candidates, whatever the candidates' race. . . .

. . . The County cannot credibly claim that the district court's focus was too narrow, or its analysis too slipshod. . . .

. . . [A]lthough the County argued that partisanship rather than race drives the County's racially polarized voting patterns, there was no systematic proof to support its claim. . . . Even assuming that the effects of partisanship and race on voting could have been isolated and measured, no such evidence was before the district court. As both parties' experts testified, and as the district court explained, party registration information and survey research are the primary data relied on by political scientists in determining the effect of political partisanship on electoral outcomes. Neither datum is available for Charleston County Council elections, because the County does not require that voters register by party for general elections and neither the County nor the United States has conducted any survey research. . . .

The County's evidence of partisanship in this case was also far from persuasive on its own terms. . . . [L]ooking at County Council elections since the early 1990s, white Democrats have at least occasionally won, while minority Democrats have invariably lost. Although minority voters give more cohesive support to minority Democratic candidates than to white Democratic candidates, the opposite is true among white voters. This is consistent with the parties' evidence that white and minority voters are more often racially polarized in Council general elections involving at least one minority candidate. Thus even controlling for partisanship in Council elections, race still appears to play a role in the voting patterns of white and minority voters in Charleston County. Or at least it was not clearly erroneous for the district court to so conclude.

V.

The result here is required by the framework Congress established for vote-dilution claims in § 2; the proof scheme the Supreme Court set forth for such actions in *Gingles*; and, most significantly, by the findings of fact the district court made in this case, findings that were not clearly erroneous.

We need not decide whether any of the factors on which the district court relied—the County's severe voting polarization and minimal minority electoral success, its hybrid electoral structure, or its sheer size—would have been enough in isolation to prove a violation of § 2. . . . *See Gingles*, 478 U.S. at 45 ("[T]here is no requirement that any particular number of factors be proved, or that a majority of them point one way or the other.") (quoting Senate Report at 29). Taken in combination, these factors were sufficient to prove a § 2 violation. Indeed, the County's own expert appeared to support, rather than undermine, the district court's conclusions. Based on evidence submitted by all parties, the district court conducted a "searching practical evaluation" of local electoral conditions in the County, and its conclusion that Charleston County's at-large system violated § 2 of the Voting Rights Act is not clearly erroneous. *Id.* (quoting Senate Re-

port at 30). The judgment of the district court is therefore

AFFIRMED.

———

Source: *United States v. Charleston County, South Carolina* United States Court of Appeals for the Fourth Circuit, No. 03-2112, http://pacer.ca4.uscourts.gov/opinion.pdf/032111.P.pdf.

---

42   Table on Geographic Expansion of the Voting Rights Act, 2004

One indication of the greater success of the "Second Reconstruction" is the geographic extension of the Voting Rights Act beyond the states of the former Confederacy. The act has an original historical "core" intended to combat racial discrimination, but it now serves to help with electorally incorporating Latino, Native American, and Asian American voters. In an important sense, it is now a national system of electoral regulation.

Table 9.6 The Extended Voting Rights Act in 2004

Section 5 Preclearance	Section 4(f)(4) Language Assistance	Section 203 Balloting Assistance, by Number of Geographic Subdivisions and Languages
Alabama	Alaska (statewide)	Alaska (26): Eskimo, Aleut, American Indian and Native, Filipino, Athabascan
Alaska	Arizona (statewide)	Arizona (22): Apache, Navajo, Pueblo, Tohono O'Odham, Yaqui, Yuman, Spanish
Arizona	Texas (statewide)	
California (4)	California (3)	
Florida (5)	Florida (5)	California* (17): Non-US Indigenous, Chinese, Filipino, Japanese, Korean, Vietnamese, Yuman
Georgia	Michigan (2)	
Louisiana	North Carolina (1)	
Michigan (2) †	New York (2)	Colorado (10): Navajo, Ute, Spanish
Mississippi	South Dakota (2)	Connecticut (7): Spanish
New Hampshire (17) †		Florida (10): Seminole, Spanish
New York (3)		Hawaii (2): Chinese, Filipino, Japanese
North Carolina (40)		Idaho (5): American Indian
South Carolina		Kansas (6): Spanish
South Dakota (2)		Louisiana (1): American Indian
Virginia ‡		Maryland (1): Spanish
Texas		Massachusetts (6): Spanish
		Michigan (1) Spanish

Table 9.6 continued

Section 5 Preclearance	Section 4(f)(4) Language Assistance	Section 203 Balloting Assistance, by Number of Geographic Subdivisions and Languages
		Mississippi (9): Choctaw
		Montana (2): Cheyenne
		Nebraska (2): Sioux, Spanish
		Nevada (6): Paiute, Shoshone, Other tribe; Spanish
		New Jersey (7): Spanish
		New Mexico (11): Navajo, Pueblo
		New York (7): Chinese, Korean, Spanish
		North Dakota (2): Sioux
		Oregon (1): Spanish
		Pennsylvania (1): Spanish
		Rhode Island (2): Spanish
		South Dakota (18): Cheyenne, Sioux
		Texas* (3): Pueblo, Other tribe, Vietnamese
		Utah (2): Navajo, Ute
		Washington (4): Chinese, Spanish

Sources: For Section 5 coverage: http://www.usdoj.gov:80/crt/voting/sec_5/covered.htm; for section 4 (f)(4) and section 203 coverage: Bryan Cave LLP Public Elections Compliance News Alert, "Director of the Census Bureau Makes Determination of Jurisdictions Subject to the Minority Language Assistance Provisions of The Voting Rights Act," September 2002, at www.bryancave.com/pubs; Daniel Levitas, ACLU Voting Rights Project, "Reauthorizing the Voting Rights Act of 1965: Assessing the Geographic and Political Terrain" (ACLU Civil Liberties Union Foundation, Southern Regional Office: n.d. [2004?]); 67 Fed. Reg. 48,871 (July 26, 2002).

Note: In the section 5 column, numbers in parentheses refer to number of counties under coverage. Where there is a dagger (†), the number in parentheses refers to towns or townships, not counties. If no number is noted parenthetically, then the entire state is under coverage. The double dagger (‡) refers to three political subdivisions in Virginia that have bailed out from section 5 coverage via section 4 procedures: Fairfax County, Frederick County, and Shenandoah County. In the section 4 (f)(4) and section 203 columns, numbers in parentheses refer to local jurisdictions under coverage, e.g., counties and towns. Both sections mandate language assistance, e.g., bilingual ballots. Section 4 (f)(4) jurisdictions comply not only with section 203 but also with section 5 preclearance. When section 203 applies to an entire state (denoted by an asterisk, *), it applies only to state election officials.

Source: Richard M. Valelly, *The Two Reconstructions: The Struggle for Black Enfranchisement* (Chicago: University of Chicago Press, 2004), Table 9.6.

43   Complaint against the Georgia Photo ID Amendment, September 19, 2005

The voter identification statute described in this complaint—a petition for injunctive relief against the statute—was submitted to the U.S. Justice Department under Section 5 of the Voting Rights Act of 1965. Quite remarkably, the Justice Department "precleared" the statute, leading those alarmed by the statute and by the possibilities it raises to turn to the courts. Why the Justice Department precleared the statute is a mystery that has not yet been cleared up.

IN THE UNITED STATES DISTRICT COURT
FOR THE NORTHERN DISTRICT OF
GEORGIA
ROME DIVISION

COMMOM CAUSE/GEORGIA;
LEAGUE OF WOMEN VOTERS
OF GEORGIA, INC.; THE
CENTRAL PRESBYTERIAN
OUTREACH AND ADVOCACY
CENTER, INC.; GEORGIA
ASSOCIATION OF BLACK ELECTED
OFFICIALS, INC., THE NATIONAL
ASSOCIATION FOR THE ADVANCEMENT
OF COLORED PEOPLE (NAACP), INC.,
through its Georgia State Conference of
Branches; GEORGIA LEGISLATIVE BLACK
CAUCUS; CONCERNED BLACK
CLERGY OF METRPOLITAN
ATLANTA, INC., the following
qualified and registered voters
under Georgia law:
MR. TONY WATKINS
MRS. CLARA WILLIAMS

Plaintiffs,

v.

MS. EVON BILLUPS, Superintendent of
Elections for the Board of Elections and
Voter Registration for Floyd County and the
City of Rome, Georgia: MS. TRACY

BROWN, Superintendent of Elections of
Bartow County, Georgia; MR. GARY
PETTY, MS. MICHELE HUDSON,
MS. AMANDA SPENCER, MR. RON
McKELVEY, AND MS. NINA
CRAWFORD, members of the Board of
Elections and Registration of Catoosa
County, Georgia; JUDGE JOHN PAYNE,
Superintendent of Elections of Chattooga
County, Georgia; MS. SHEA HICKS,
Superintendent of Elections for Gordon
County, Georgia; MS. JENNIFER A.
JOHNSON, Superintendent of Elections
for Polk County, Georgia; MR. SAM
LITTLE, Superintendent of Elections for
Whitfield County, Georgia; individually
and in their respective official capacities as
superintendents or members of the
elections boards in their individual
counties, and as CLASS
REPRESENTATIVES under Fed.R. Civ.P.
23 (b)(1) and (b)(2) of a class consisting of
all superintendents and members of city
and county boards of elections
throughout the State of Georgia; and

HON. CATHY COX, individually and in
her official capacities as Secretary of State
of Georgia and Chair of the Georgia
Elections Board.

Defendants.

COMPLAINT FOR DECLARATORY AND INJUNCTIVE RELIEF

This is an action to have the Photo ID requirement in the 2005 amendment to O.C.G.A. § 21-2-417 (Act No. 53), declared unconstitutional both on its face and as applied, and to enjoin its enforcement on the ground that it imposes an unauthorized, unnecessary and undue burden on the fundamental right to vote of hundreds of thousands of registered Georgia voters in violation of Art. II, § I, ¶ II of the Georgia Constitution, the Fourteenth and Twenty-Fourth Amendments to the United States Constitution, the Civil Rights Act of 1964 (42 U.S.C. § 1971 (a)(2)(A) and (a)(2)(B)), Section 2 of the Voting Rights Act of 1965 (42 U.S.C. § 1973 (a)) and 42 U.S.C. §§ 1983 and 1988.

1.

The Plaintiffs are: . . .

(i) **Mr. Tony Watkins**, an African-American citizen and duly qualified and registered voter residing in the City of Rome and Floyd County, Georgia, who does not possess a Georgia driver's license, passport or other form of government-issued photo identity, and cannot readily obtain a Photo ID card from the State Department of Driver Services; and

(ii) **Mrs. Clara Williams**, an African-American citizen and duly qualified and registered voter residing in the City of Atlanta and Fulton County, Georgia, who does not possess a Georgia driver's license, passport or other form of government-issued photo identity, and cannot readily obtain a Photo ID card from the State Department of Driver Services. . . .

Pre-Existing Georgia Law

8.

Prior to the 1998 elections, voters in Georgia, like registered voters in a majority of other states, were not required to present any form of identification as a condition of voting.

9.

As a result of the adoption by the General Assembly of O.C.G.A. § 21-2-417 in 1997, registered voters in Georgia were required for the first time to identify themselves by presenting one of seventeen forms of identification to election officials as a condition of being admitted to, and allowed to vote at the polls. Former O.C.G.A. § 21-2-417.

10.

Under O.C.G.A. § 21-2-417 as it existed prior to its amendment by Act 53 in 2005, registered voters were permitted, but were not required, to present a Georgia driver's license or other form of official photographic identification as a method of identification as a condition of voting. Voters were free, however, to use any of eight other methods of identification, including such commonly available documents as a birth certificate, a social security card, a copy of a current utility bill, a government check, a payroll check, or a bank statement that showed the name and address of the voter. Former O.C.G.A. § 21-2-417(1)(10), (11), (14), (15), (16).

11.

In addition, registered voters who did not have or were unable to find one of the seventeen forms of photographic or non-photographic identification specified in O.C.G.A. § 21-2-417(a) were entitled under Georgia law, as it existed prior to the enactment of Act 53, to be admitted to the polls, issued a ballot and allowed to vote simply by signing a statement under oath swearing or affirming that he or she is the person identified on the elector's certificate. O.C.G.A. § 21-2-417(b).

The New Photo ID Requirement

12.

In 2005, the General Assembly of Georgia adopted Act 53, which amended O.C.G.A. § 21-

2-417, to require all registered voters in Georgia who vote *in person* in all primary, special or general elections for state, national, and local offices held on or after July 1, 2005, to present a government-issued photographic identification card ("Photo ID") to election officials as a condition of being admitted to the polls and before being issued a ballot and allowed to vote ("The new Photo ID requirement").

13.

The Secretary of State, as the Chief Election Officer in Georgia, informed the General Assembly before the passage of Act 53 in a letter . . . , and also informed the Governor in a letter . . . before he signed the bill into law, that there had been no documented cases of fraudulent voting by persons who obtained ballots unlawfully by misrepresenting their identities as registered voters to poll workers reported to her office during her nine years as Secretary of State.

14.

Only 1 of 43 African-American legislators in both houses of the General Assembly voted in favor of the bill.

15.

Act 53 was signed by Georgia's Governor, Sonny Perdue, on April 22, 2005, and the Photo ID requirements in the bill became effective on July 1, 2005, subject to pre-clearance by the United States Department of Justice, which was granted on August 26, 2005.

16.

At the same time that it voted to require the presentation of a Photo ID, the General Assembly also voted to amend O.C.G.A. § 40-5-103(a), **by doubling the minimum fee for a Photo ID** from $10 to $20 for a 5-year Photo ID, and also authorizing a new 10-year Photo ID for a fee of $35. Ga. Laws 2005, p. 334 (Act No. 68) § 17-24(a).

17.

As a result of the adoption of Act 53, Georgia became one of only two (2) states that requires registered voters to present a photo identification as an absolute condition of being admitted to the polls and allowed to cast a ballot in federal, state and local elections. A majority of thirty (30) states do not require registered voters to present any form of identification as a condition of admission to polls or casting a ballot, while a minority of twenty (20) states require voters to present some form of identification at the polls, but of these, only two states (Georgia and Indiana) require that voters present a Photo ID as the sole method of identification required as a condition of voting.

18.

The press release prepared by the Communications Office of Georgia Act 53 states that only the following forms of Photo ID will be acceptable after the effective date of the Act:

Acceptable Forms of ID

- Georgia Driver's License
- State Identity Card
- Passport
- Government Employee ID Card
- Military ID Card
- Tribal ID Card.

19.

According to the same press release from the House Communications Office, the following forms of voter identification that had been acceptable prior to the enactment of Act 53 will no longer be accepted by election officials as valid forms of voter identification after the effective date of the Act:

Forms of ID No Longer Valid

- Birth Certificate
- Social Security Card

- Certified Naturalization Document
- Current Utility Bill
- Bank Statement
- Government Check or Paycheck
- Other Government Documents

The New Photo ID Requirement Applies Only to Voters Who Vote In Person And Does Not Apply to People Who Vote By Mail

20.

The new Photo ID requirement in Act 53 applies only to registered voters who vote *in person*. The General Assembly imposed no similar Photo ID requirement on absentee voters, except those who are voting for the first time.

21.

Although the Secretary of State had informed the members of the General Assembly and the Governor prior to the enactment of Act 53, that her office had received many complaints of voter fraud involving absentee ballots and no documented complaints of fraud that involve ballots that were cast in person at the polls, the General Assembly ignored this information and arbitrarily chose instead to require only those registered voters who vote in person to present a Photo ID as a condition of voting, but deliberately refused to impose the same requirement on absentee voters (other than first time voters). O.C.G.A. § 21-2-417.

The Photo ID Requirement Imposes An Undue Burden On The Right To Vote

22.

The new Photo ID requirement became effective on August 26, 2005, and imposes an unnecessary and undue burden on the exercise of the fundamental right to vote of hundreds of thousands of citizens of Georgia who are fully eligible, registered and qualified to vote, but who do not have Georgia driver's licenses, passports, or government employer ID cards or other forms of official photographic identification issued by the state or federal government.

23.

Compliance with the new Photo ID requirement will present an especially high obstacle for registered voters who are (a) poor and do not own a car or truck and do not have passports because they cannot afford to travel on a passport outside the United States; (b) elderly and no longer drive (or have a passport which allows them to travel outside the United States); (c) visually impaired and are unable to drive (or travel on a passport outside the United States); (d) physically impaired and are unable to drive (or travel on a passport outside the United States); (e) residents of retirement or nursing homes who, by choice or necessity, do not have driver's licenses or passports; and (f) students without automobiles or passports who have Photo ID's issued by private colleges and universities (*e.g.*, Emory, Morehouse, Mercer), but who cannot vote in Georgia without first acquiring a Photo ID issued by the state or federal government.

24.

AARP and the League have estimated that 152,000 of those who voted in the general election in Georgia in 2004 were over 60 years of age and did not have Georgia driver's licenses.

25.

The Department of Driver Services ("DDS") is the only state agency in Georgia from which a registered voter may obtain an official Photo ID.

26.

To obtain a Photo ID card from the DDS, a registered voter must (a) travel to a DDS office, (b) present an original or certified copy of a birth certificate or other "verifiable evidence" stating the applicant's name and birth date (O.C.G.A. § 40-5-1020; and (c) pay a fee of $20 for a 5-year Photo ID or $35 for a 10-year Photo ID.

27.

There are currently only 56 DDS locations throughout the entire State of Georgia from which an official state Photo ID may be obtained (*see* Department of Driver Services website at www.dds.ga.gov). These offices are only open from 9:00 a.m. to 5:00 p.m. Tuesday through Saturday, but are closed on Sundays and Mondays and evenings, times when voters might be able to obtain a Photo ID without having to take time off from work.

28.

There is not a single DDS office located within the City of Atlanta, Georgia's largest city, or in the city of Rome, which means that registered voters who are residents of those cities are required to travel outside the limits to obtain the required Photo ID.

29.

There are currently only 56 DDS offices in the entire State of Georgia, which means that tens of thousands of registered voters who live in 103 of Georgia's 159 counties must travel outside their home counties to a DDS office located in another county to obtain a Photo ID.

30.

To make matters worse, the DDS offices in urban areas typically have long lines and it is often necessary for a person to stand in line 3 or 4 hours to renew a Georgia driver's license or obtain a Photo ID. . . .

The $20 Fee For A Photo ID Is A Poll Tax On The Right To Vote

32.

The $20 fee for a 5-year Photo ID and the $35 fee for a 10-year Photo ID are a poll tax on the right to vote. . . .

33.

Act 53 imposes an undue burden on the right to vote of voters who will be required to expend time and money to acquire the underlying documents needed to be issued a Photo ID card and to travel to state offices to be issued a Photo ID.

34.

The $20 (or $35) fees are also discriminatory because they are not required to be paid by all voters as a condition of voting. Voters who have a Georgia driver's license, a passport, or a government-issued Photo ID are not required to pay a $20 (or $35) fee for a Photo ID. Absentee voters who do not have driver's licenses, passports or other Photo ID (other than first-time voters) are also not required to present a Photo ID as a condition of receiving an absentee ballot, and, therefore, are not required to pay $20 (or $35) for the privilege of voting, while other similarly situated voters who vote in person and do not have driver's licenses or passports and are not government employees are required to pay a $20 (or $35) fee for a Photo ID as a condition of being admitted to the polls.

35.

Moreover, payment of the $20 (or $35) fee is not a one-time expense (nor is the time, inconvenience and expense and lost wages involved to travel to a DDS office). Unlike voter registration cards which are issued free of charge and never expire, a $20 Photo ID card is valid for only *five years*. . . .

The Waiver Of The Fee Is Ineffective

36.

Section 66 of Act 53 amended O.C.G.A. § 40-5-103 to allow the DDS to issue a Photo ID to a registered voter "who swears under oath that he or she is *indigent and cannot pay* the fee for the identification card, that he or she desires an identification card in order to vote in a primary or election in Georgia and that he or she does not have any other form of identification that is acceptable at the polls under Code Section 21-2-417 for identification at the polls in order to vote."

37.

If the statute is read literally, even a registered voter who is "indigent" (a term that is undefined in the Act and vague in its general usage) cannot qualify for the waiver of the $20 fee under the first requirement of the statute if he or she has at least $20, because he or she cannot truthfully swear that he or she *cannot pay the fee* as required by the plain wording of the statute.

38.

A voter may not be able to qualify for the waiver under the second requirement of the statute because the tern "indigent" in the 2005 amendment to O.C.G.A. § 40-5-103 is not defined and is so vague that a person of ordinary intelligence can only guess at the meaning of the term "indigent" in this context. Moreover, the Act leaves clerical personnel in each of the 56 DDS offices (and local district attorneys) free to apply their own subjective interpretations of the term "indigent" in determining whether a particular individual is eligible for a waiver of the $20 fee. . . .

40.

Finally, the waiver of the $20 fee for registered voters who are "indigent" and "cannot pay the fee," does not relieve a registered voter who does not have a valid Georgia driver's license, a passport, or other form of official photo ID of the burden and expense of having to travel by bus or taxi to a DDS office that may be located in another city or county, miles from their homes or places of work to obtain a Photo ID in order to vote. . . .

The New Photo ID Requirement Will Have A Disparate Impact On African American Voters

41.

The new Photo ID requirement will also have a disparate impact on the right to vote of registered voters who are African Americans, as compared to voters who are white, because African-American voters in Georgia, as a group, are (a) less affluent than whites, and (b) are three times less likely to own or have access to a motor vehicle than are whites, according to recent data published by the U.S. Census Bureau. Census Survey File 3 (SF3) HCT33B.

It Is Impossible For Some Voters To Obtain A Photo ID

42.

The Georgia Department of Driver Services requires an applicant to present an *"original or a certified copy"* of a birth certificate issued by an official state agency as a condition of obtaining a Photo ID, and has also stated that "Hospital birth certificates are not acceptable." . . .

43.

A registered voter who was born in Georgia and does not have the original or a certified copy of his or her original birth certificate, must apply to the Georgia Division of Public Health and pay a search fee of $10 and an additional fee of $10 for a certified copy of his or her birth certificate. . . .

44.

It is impossible for a registered voter who does not have a Photo ID to obtain a certified copy of his or her birth certificate from the Georgia Division of Public Health because the Georgia Division of Public Health demands the following:

Required Information

The person requesting a certified copy of a birth record must provide . . . a signed request form, and a photocopy of your valid photo ID, such as a driver's license, state-issued ID card, or employer issued photo ID. . . .

45.

Moreover, it is impossible for registered voters who were born in Georgia before 1919 to obtain a certified copy of their birth certificates because the Georgia Division of Public Health does not maintain a record of births prior to 1919. *Id.*

46.

Finally, many older and less affluent registered voters cannot obtain a Photo ID because they do not have birth certificates on file with the Department of Vital Statistics in Georgia or other states for a variety of reasons: (a) because they were born before such records were recorded and maintained, (b) because they were informally adopted and have lived for years under the name of their adoptive parents, rather than the name under which they were born, among other reasons. . . .

———

Source: U.S. District Court for the Northern District of Georgia, Rome Division.

Reauthorization of the 1965 Voting Rights Act: What Expires and What Does Not

The Voting Rights Act was never meant to be a quick fix. Recognizing that many states and local governments have continued to erect barriers to minority political participation, no fewer than five presidents—Lyndon B. Johnson, Richard Nixon, Gerald R. Ford, Ronald Reagan, and George Bush—have supported the enactment or reauthorization of key parts of the law.

Notably, each time the law has been renewed by Congress, a Republican president has ratified the bill. On signing the 1982 extension, which passed Congress by a vote of 389–24, President Reagan called the right to vote the "crown jewel" of American liberties.

In 2007 three crucial sections of the Voting Rights Act will expire unless Congress votes to renew them. These include:

- A requirement that states and local jurisdictions with a documented history of discriminatory voting practices submit planned changes in their election laws or procedures to the U.S. Department of Justice or the U.S. District Court for the District of Columbia for preclearance. A bipartisan congressional report in 1982 warned that without this provision discrimination would reappear "overnight."

- Requirements that new citizens and other Americans who are limited in their ability to speak English can receive assistance when voting.
- The authority to send federal examiners and observers to monitor elections.

These provisions are explained in greater detail, below.

The Voting Rights Act of 1965: What Does Expire

1. Section 4 Coverage Formula, 42 U.S.C. § 1973b

Section 4(b) of the act, 42 U.S.C. § 1973b(b), contains a formula defining jurisdictions subject to, or "covered" by, special remedial provisions of the act. The special provisions are discussed below. Jurisdictions are covered if they used a "test or device" for voting and less than half of voting-age residents were registered or voted in the 1964, 1968, or 1972 presidential elections. Coverage is determined by the attorney general and the director of the census, and is not judicially reviewable. Coverage, and with it the application of the special provisions, is set to expire in August 2007.

2. Section 5 Preclearance, 42 U.S.C. § 1973c

Section 5, 42 U.S.C. § 1973c, known as the "preclearance" requirement, is one of the special provisions of the act whose application is triggered by the coverage formula in Section 4(b). Section 5 requires covered jurisdictions to get approval, or preclearance, from federal authorities (either the attorney general or the federal court for the District of Columbia) prior to implementing any changes in their voting laws or procedures. The jurisdiction has the burden of proving that a proposed change does not have the purpose and would not have the effect of denying or abridging the right to vote on account of race or color or membership in a language minority. Jurisdictions covered by Section 5 are Alabama, Alaska, Arizona, California (five counties), Florida (five counties), Georgia, Louisiana, Michigan (two towns), Mississippi, New Hampshire (ten towns), New York (three counties), North Carolina (forty counties), South Carolina, South Dakota (two counties), Texas, and Virginia (U.S. Department of Justice, Section 5 Covered Jurisdictions [January 28, 2002]). Section 5, unless extended, will expire in August 2007.

3. Assignment of Federal Examiners and Poll Watchers by the Attorney General, 42 U.S.C. §§ 1973d, e, f & k

The attorney general can assign federal examiners to covered jurisdictions pursuant to Sections 6(b), 7, 9, and 13(a) of the act, 42 U.S.C. §§ 1973d, e, and k, to list qualified applicants who are thereafter entitled to vote in all elections. The attorney general is also authorized by Section 8 of the act, 42 U.S.C. § 1973f, to appoint federal poll watchers in places to which federal examiners have been assigned. These provisions are set to expire in August 2007.

4. Bilingual Voting Materials Requirement, 42 U.S.C. § 1973aa-1a

Certain states and political subdivisions are required by 42 U.S.C. § 1973aa-1a to provide voting materials in languages other than English. While there are several tests for "coverage," the requirement is imposed upon jurisdictions with significant language minority populations who are limited-English proficient and where the illiteracy rate of the language minority is higher than the national rate. Covered jurisdictions are required to furnish voting materials in the language of the applicable minority group as well as in English. Jurisdictions required to provide bilingual election procedures for one or more language minorities include the entire states of California, New Mexico, and Texas, and several hundred counties and townships in Alaska, Arizona, Colorado, Connecticut, Florida, Hawaii, Idaho, Illinois, Kansas, Louisiana, Maryland, Massachusetts, Michigan, Mississippi, Montana, Nebraska, Nevada, New Jersey, New Mexico, New York, North Dakota, Oklahoma, Oregon, Pennsylvania, Rhode Island, South Dakota, Utah, and Washington (67 Fed. Reg. 48872 [July 26, 2002]). The bilingual voting materials requirement is scheduled to expire in August 2007.

The Voting Rights Act of 1965: What Does Not Expire

1. The Ban on 'Tests or Devices,' 42 U.S.C. § 1973aa

The Voting Rights Act, 42 U.S.C. § 1973aa, bans the use of any "test or device" for registering or voting in any federal, state, or local election. A "test or device" includes literacy, understanding, or interpretation tests; educational or knowledge requirements; good character tests; proof of qualifications by "vouchers" from third parties; or registration procedures or elections conducted solely in English where a single language minority comprises more than 5 percent of the voting-age population of the jurisdiction (42 U.S.C. § 1973b[c] and [f][3]). "Language minorities" are defined as American Indians, Asian Americans, Alaska Natives, and those of Spanish heritage (42 U.S.C. § 1973aa-1a[e]). The ban on tests or devices is nationwide and permanent.

2. The 'Results' Standard of Section 2, 42 U.S.C. § 1973

Section 2 of the Voting Rights Act, 42 U.S.C. § 1973, prohibits the use of any voting procedure or practice that "results" in a denial or abridgement of the right to vote on account of race or color or membership in a language minority. Section 2 applies nationwide and is permanent.

3. Voter Assistance, 42 U.S.C. § 1973aa-6

By amendment in 1982, the Voting Rights Act, 42 U.S.C. § 1973aa-6, provides that any voter who requires assistance to vote by reason of blindness, disability, or inability to read or write may be given assistance by a person of the voter's choice, other than the voter's employer or union. The voter assistance provision is nationwide and permanent.

4. Court Appointment of Federal Examiners, 42 U.S.C. § 1973a

In any action to enforce the voting guarantees of the Fourteenth or Fifteenth Amendments a court may, pursuant to Section 3(a) of the act, 42 U.S.C. § 1973a, appoint federal examiners

to register voters. The federal examiner provision is nationwide and permanent, although it is rarely, if ever, used today.

5. Civil and Criminal Penalties, 42 U.S.C. §§ 1973i and 1973j

Sections 11 and 12 of the act, 42 U.S.C. §§ 1973i and 1973j, authorize the imposition of civil and criminal sanctions on those who interfere with the right to vote, fail to comply with the act, or commit voter fraud. These provisions are permanent and nationwide.

6. Pocket Trigger, 42 U.S.C. § 1973a(c)

Section 3(c) of the act, 42 U.S.C. § 1973a(c), the so-called "pocket trigger," requires a court that has found a violation of voting rights protected by the Fourteenth or Fifteenth Amendments as part of any equitable relief to require a jurisdiction for an "appropriate" period of time to preclear its proposed new voting practices or procedures. The preclearance process provided for in § 1973a(c) is similar to that described in the discussion below of Section 5 of the act, 42 U.S.C. § 1973c. There is no expiration date for the pocket trigger.

7. Presidential Elections, 42 U.S.C. § 1973aa-1

By amendments in 1970, Section 202, 42 U.S.C. § 1973aa-1, the act abolished durational residency requirements and established uniform standards for absentee voting in presidential elections. These provisions are permanent and nationwide.

Index

Page numbers in italics indicate illustrations. References to the appendix materials also include document numbers.